CLIMB TAFRAOUT

Holiday Sun Rock in Morocco's Anti-Atlas

1ST EDITION | 2017

An Oxford Alpine Club Guide

by Steve Broadbent

CLIMB TAFRAOUT
Holiday Sun Rock in Morocco's Anti-Atlas

1st Edition, 2017
by Steve Broadbent

Published in the EU by the Oxford Alpine Club
www.oxfordalpineclub.co.uk

ISBN for this volume 978-0-9935486-2-8

All uncredited images and design by Steve Broadbent ©2017

GeoGraphics Cartography by GeoGraphics

ANTI-ATLAS ANCHOR FUND

Proceeds from the sale of this guidebook support the safe replacement of abseil anchors in the Anti-Atlas.

There are an estimated 100 to 150 abseil anchors in-situ in the Anti-Atlas, mostly 'tat' left behind by climbers at the end of a route. Increasing amounts of Nylon tat on popular rappel routes are not only unsightly, but are rapidly weakened in the Moroccan sunshine, creating potentially unsafe anchors.

Since 2012, Climb-Tafraout have been replacing soft anchors on the most popular descent routes with galvanised steel slings. These slings do not damage the rock, require no bolting, and have a massive life-span compared with nylon or kevlar alternatives.

We hope to improve safety on the main abseil routes whilst maintaining a traditional no-bolting ethic. If you would like to help support this expensive work then please make a donation online at www.climb-tafraout.com/anti-atlas-anchor-fund

Thank you.

PLEASE READ THIS!

Rock climbing is an inherently dangerous activity, and users of this guidebook should have a full understanding of the risks involved. The Anti-Atlas is not a suitable destination for novice climbers, and routes described in this guide require relevant experience, skills, and careful judgement. This guidebook is a selection of routes described in the Tafraout-area 'Livre d'Escalade' kept in the Hotel Les Amandiers – many of these remain unchecked and descriptions are those provided by the first ascensionists. Information in this book may therefore be inaccurate, and users should not treat it as a substitute for good 'mountain-sense'.

Front Cover Photograph: James Lam on *Wall Street* (E1 5b) at Tizi Gzaouine Crag on the Eastern Escarpment of Jebel el Kest (page 148).

Area Map
Crag Selector
Intro
The Climbing
How to Use
Suggested Climbs
Tafraout Granite
Anergui
Ameln Valley
Tarakatine Pass
Sidi M'Zal
Jebel Taskra
Idaougnidif
Afantinzar
Samazar
Aouguenz
Tagzene
Tagmout
History
Index

CONTENTS

ACKNOWLEDGEMENTS

The mountains around Tafraout are a magical place, and over the last ten years they have provided us with some of the most incredible experiences and friendships that a climber could wish for. This guidebook represents a personal obsession with the rock climbs of the Anti-Atlas, and a project in which I have relied on the help of dozens of individuals. Firstly, of course, I must thank my wife, Katja, with whom I have enjoyed countless adventures on these crags, and an equal number of frustrating days looking for routes, taking photographs and drawing maps. She has also, once again, proved herself as proof-reader extraordinaire!

For this latest edition I must also thank the newest members of the 'Climb-Tafraout' team... Dave and Lina Arthur have played a huge role in the realisation of this guide, accompanying us on research trips, belaying, photographing, bouncing ideas around, and once again giving up their time to proof-read the initial text.

It was Sven Letourneau and Jude Waller who first opened our eyes to the climbing potential of Tafraout, and to them we are both eternally grateful. Sally Fitton helped get the ball rolling on our first guidebook to the north side, and has continued to provide assistance and motivation with the publishing.

Claude Davies, who wrote the first guidebook to the region back in 2004, not only showed us all the way in the first place, but has provided invaluable assistance with the south-side material, including many of the historical photographs. Les Brown, Mike Mortimer, Jim Fotheringham, and the late Derek Walker also provided lots of fantastic material about their early climbs. Graham 'Egg' Everitt and James Strongman have checked many lines on the south-side – between them they probably have more knowledge about Ameln climbing than anyone else around. Graham Little has provided numerous topos and photographs, and the ever-enthusiastic Ron Buckley has cajoled his team, including Chris Clarke, Ian Dugdale and Jim Nuttall, up dozens of new routes in the valley, keeping me busy, just when I thought I'd got it all...

Martin Bennett and Alan Blackburn, and their team from the Fylde MC, have been equally busy and equally helpful in recording and reporting routes, as well as providing numerous photographs for the book. Likewise my thanks go to the unstoppable Ron Kenyon, who's been one of the key personalities in the development of the climbing here. Thanks also to Guy Robertson, Paul Ross, Charlie Boscoe, Will Sheaff, Richard Rogers and Jon Roberts for their contributions to the south-side material.

On the north side, the late Ben Wintringham, along with Pete Johnson and Mike Mortimer provided invaluable material for our first edition, which is also included in this latest guide. Topher Dagg provided many detailed descriptions for routes in Samazar; and Tom Stedall, Steve Cayzer and Andy Morris have also made significant contributions. Alberto Rampini and Silvia Mazzani have made my life so much easier by providing superb topos and photographs of their additions to the north side of the range.

Of course, I would also like to thank the huge group of Oxford-based climbers that have shared adventures with me, and also taken photographs and checked lines. They include: Arnaud Viel, Emmanuel Freudenthal, Caroline Culwick, Sally Fitton, Sesh Nadathur, Elie Dekoninck, Rachel Mellor, Matt Mellor, Iza Pstrucha, Pete Cawley, Will Benfold, Ania Piotrowski, Sarah Pemberton, Tom Codrington, Cameron Hall, Patrick Timoney, Chris Bull, Jenny Burrow, Aileen Robertson, Niall Hedderley, Zoe Bouras, and Daniyal & Cecilie Mueenuddin.

It would also be remiss of me not to mention the work of previous guidebook writers, who have shared the daunting task of making sense of the new-route books: Claude Davies, Emma Alsford, Paul Donnithorne, and Palan Martin, who first documented the sport climbs on the granite around Tafraout.

In Tafraout, I must give special thanks to Mohammed and Lahcen, of Maison Troc, and all of the staff of the Hotel les Amandiers – particularly Hassan and Mohammed for keeping us in beer. Thanks also to the staff of Restaurant La Kasbah, and all of the locals who have provided us with information and fascinating stories about Tafraout and its history.

Finally, of course, I must apologise to anyone who I've missed. With such a huge team of people contributing over such a long timescale there are bound to be omissions, for which I'm sorry!

Area Map
Crag Selector
Intro
The Climbing
How to Use
Suggested Climbs
Tafraout Granite
Anergui
Ameln Valley
Tarakatine Pass
Sidi M'Zal
Jebel Taskra
Idaougnidif
Afantinzar
Samazar
Aouguenz
Tagzene
Tagmout
History
Index

Area Maps:

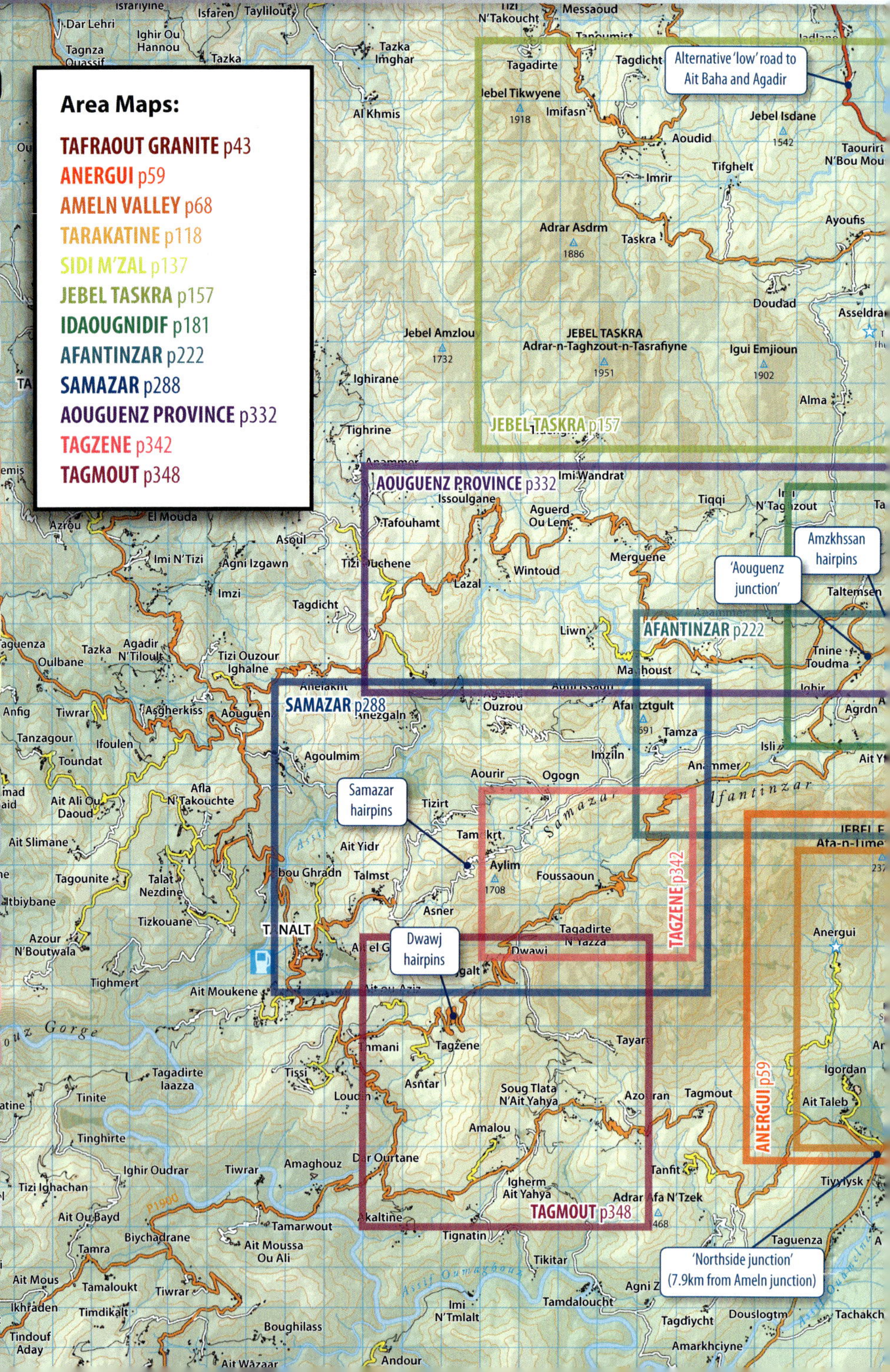

IN CASE OF EMERGENCY

Tafraout Police +212 (0)528 800061

Tafraout Ambulance +212 (0)528 862993

British Consulate +212 (0)528 841219

British Embassy +212 (0)537 633333

Area Map
Crag Selector
Intro
The Climbing
How to Use
Suggested Climbs
Tafraout Granite
Anergui
Ameln Valley
Tarakatine Pass
Sidi M'Zal
Jebel Taskra
Idaougnidif
Afantinzar
Samazar
Aouguenz
Tagzene
Tagmout
History
Index

Area Map Page 4

Area Map
Crag Selector
Intro
The Climbing
How to Use
Suggested Climbs
Tafraout Granite
Anergui
Ameln Valley
Tarakatine Pass
Sidi M'Zal
Jebel Taskra
Idaougnidif
Afantinzar
Samazar
Aouguenz
Tagzene
Tagmout
History
Index

CRAG SELECTOR

Area	Crag	Pitches	Page	Sunshine	Shade available	Suitable for kids	Access by hitching	Roadside	Bolt protected	Traditional gear	Drive from Tafraout	Walk-in time	Routes D – HS	Routes MVS – HVS	Routes E1 – E3	Routes E4 +	★1	★2	★3
Tafraout Granite – Map p43	A. Yelmo Carpantonico	1	44	✓		✓	✓	✓	✓		0:05	0:10	0	0	2	4	5	0	0
	B. Tazka's 2nd Dome	3	45	✓		✓	✓	✓	✓	✓	0:05	0:10	1	1	1	0	2	1	0
	C. Flake Quake	4	46	✓			✓	✓		✓	0:05	0:10	0	1	0	0	0	1	0
	D. Black Wall	1	46		✓	✓	✓		✓	✓	0:05	0:20	0	6	6	1	6	0	2
	E. High Sierra	4	48	✓			✓	✓		✓	0:10	0:10	1	1	0	0	0	0	1
	F. Amalu Wall	1	50		✓	✓	✓		✓		0:15	0:15	0	0	0	3	0	3	0
	G. Painted Rocks	1	50	✓		✓	✓	✓		✓	0:15	0:02	0	1	0	0	1	0	0
	H. Eflodne	3	51		✓	✓	✓	✓	✓	✓	0:10	0:05	1	2	2	0	0	1	0
Anergui – Map p59	A. Anergui Playground	1	59	✓		✓		✓		✓	0:40	0:02	4	5	0	0	6	2	0
	B. Anergui Lower	6-8	61	✓				✓		✓	0:40	0:15	1	8	1	0	4	3	0
	C. Anergui Upper	4-6	63	✓						✓	0:40	0:40	0	8	3	0	1	7	1
	D. Jebel el Kest	Many	66	✓						✓	0:40	0:10	3	0	0	0	0	1	1
The Ameln Valley – Map p68	A. Blue Spring Crag	1	72	✓		✓		✓		✓	0:15	0:10	5	7	3	0	2	4	0
	B. Black Crag (Tazult)	1	74		✓	✓				✓	0:10	0:30	2	9	2	0	5	1	1
	C. Lion's Face	Many	76	✓						✓	0:10	1:00+	2	7	0	0	0	5	0
	D. Crag K (Asgaour Gorge)	2-3	79	✓						✓	0:10	0:40	0	4	11	3	4	6	4
	E. Mosque Valley Slabs	1	84	✓			✓			✓	0:10	0:50	2	3	7	0	3	2	1
	F. Palm Tree Gorge	1	86	✓	✓	✓	✓			✓	0:10	0:15	5	11	13	4	22	9	0
	G. Tizgut Gorge	1-4	91	✓	✓					✓	0:20	0:30	4	28	8	1	21	7	4
	H. Prophet Peak	Many	99	✓	✓		✓			✓	0:15	1:30	2	0	0	0	1	0	1
	I. The White Tower	6	103	✓			✓			✓	0:15	1:30	0	6	2	0	0	1	3
	J. Point 1937	2	108	✓			✓			✓	0:15	1:45	0	0	1	0	0	0	1
	K. Hidden Wall	3-4	110	✓	✓		✓			✓	0:15	1:40	0	2	3	0	2	1	1
	L. Profanisaurus Pinnacle	1	111	✓	✓		✓			✓	0:15	1:40	0	2	1	0	3	0	0
	M. Tifghalt Lower	6-8	112	✓			✓			✓	0:15	1:00	1	8	0	0	2	3	0
	N. Tifghalt Upper	5	114	✓			✓			✓	0:15	1:20	0	4	0	0	0	4	0
	O. Crag W	5-6	115	✓			✓			✓	0:15	1:05	1	6	5	0	1	3	1
p118	A. Tarakatine Pass	1	118	✓	✓	✓	✓	✓		✓	0:20	0:10	125	18	2	0	71	8	0
	B. Adrar Idekel	-	135	✓			✓	✓		✓	0:20	0:15	1	0	0	0	1	0	0

CRAG SELECTOR

Area	Crag	Pitches	Page	Sunshine	Shade available	Suitable for kids	Access by hitching	Roadside	Bolt protected	Traditional gear	Drive from Tafraout	Walk-in time	Routes D – HS	Routes MVS – HVS	Routes E1 – E3	Routes E4 +	★1	★2	★3
Sidi M'Zal Area – Map p137	A. Fylde Crag	3-4	137	✓	✓		✓			✓	0:30	0:30	1	4	2	0	2	1	1
	B. Greek Buttress	6-7	139	✓	✓		✓			✓	0:35	0:50	0	5	5	0	3	1	4
	C. Arch Wall	5-6	142	✓	✓		✓			✓	0:35	1:00	1	2	4	0	3	1	2
	D. Dinosaur Wall	2-4	144		✓		✓			✓	0:35	0:30	0	0	11	1	3	2	2
	E. Tizi Gzaouine Crag	1	146	✓	✓	✓		✓		✓	0:40	0:05	19	11	4	1	14	5	4
	F. Tizi Gzaouine Gorge	1	151	✓	✓	✓		✓		✓	0:40	0:05	13	3	0	0	7	0	0
	G. Boar Walls	1-3	154		✓					✓	0:50	0:40	2	3	2	2	2	0	3
Jebel Taskra – Map p157	A. Tramline Slabs	2-4	158	✓	✓					✓	1:00	0:45	6	20	14	0	16	12	6
	B. Asseldrar Thumb	8-10	164	✓	✓					✓	1:00	0:30	0	3	6	1	2	4	4
	C. Tifghelt Buttress	1-2	168	✓	✓					✓	1:10	0:40	2	3	9	1	3	5	5
	D. Echo Wall	2	171	✓	✓					✓	1:10	0:20	0	1	4	1	2	1	3
	E. Snowman's Bluff	1-2	172		✓					✓	1:15	0:20	0	1	7	0	2	4	1
	F. Taskra East Pillars	5-6	174	✓	✓			✓		✓	1:15	0:15	1	5	1	0	3	2	2
	G. Imrir Crags	1-2	176	✓	✓					✓	1:15	0:40	0	5	14	2	6	9	4
Idaougnidif Area – Map p181	A. Amzkhssan Wall	3-4	182	✓		✓		✓		✓	1:00	0:02	8	1	0	0	5	0	0
	B. Tassila Bastion	1	184	✓		✓		✓		✓	1:00	0:10	6	6	1	0	4	3	0
	C. Adrar Iffran	2-5	187	✓	✓					✓	1:00	0:30	2	11	9	3	6	11	3
	D. Arrow Rock	1	193		✓					✓	1:00	0:40	1	5	3	0	2	1	2
	E. Adrar Asmit	4-7	194	✓	✓					✓	1:00	1:00	3	2	2	1	4	3	1
	F. Shepherd's Crag	1	198	✓	✓					✓	1:00	0:20	7	7	0	0	9	0	0
	G. Adrar Umlil	2-5	200	✓	✓					✓	1:00	1:00	22	20	29	3	20	28	15
	H. Col Crags	1-2	218	✓				✓		✓	1:00	0:10	12	12	6	0	13	5	1
Afantinzar – Map p222	A. Ighir Crags	5-7	223	✓						✓	1:15	0:30	3	9	2	0	1	7	3
	B. Akida	2-3	226	✓						✓	1:15	0:35	4	1	0	0	0	5	0
	C. Harram Peak	5-7	228	✓						✓	1:15	1:00	0	2	0	0	1	1	0
	D. The Sanctuary	6-7	229		✓					✓	1:15	0:20	0	2	8	0	1	3	1
	E. Lower Eagle Crag	6-9	233	✓	✓					✓	1:15	0:20	1	2	5	0	1	4	3
	F. Upper Eagle Crag	4-7	236		✓					✓	1:15	0:35	0	1	16	2	2	10	3
	G. Griffin Rock	1	242	✓	✓	✓		✓		✓	1:15	0:10	4	12	26	4	17	13	2
	H. Anammer Crags	1	248	✓		✓		✓		✓	1:15	0:05	67	38	13	0	43	23	8
	I. Ksar Rock	1-4	268	✓	✓			✓		✓	1:15	0:10	13	38	28	1	16	34	20

Area Map
Crag Selector
Intro
The Climbing
How to Use
Suggested Climbs
Tafraout Granite
Anergui
Ameln Valley
Tarakatine Pass
Sidi M'Zal
Jebel Taskra
Idaougnidif
Afantinzar
Samazar
Aouguenz
Tagzene
Tagmout
History
Index

Area Map
Crag Selector
Intro
The Climbing
How to Use
Suggested Climbs
Tafraout Granite
Anergui
Ameln Valley
Tarakatine Pass
Sidi M'Zal
Jebel Taskra
Idaougnidif
Afantinzar
Samazar
Aouguenz
Tagzene
Tagmout
History
Index

CRAG SELECTOR

Area	Crag	Pitches	Page	Sunshine	Shade available	Suitable for kids	Access by hitching	Roadside	Bolt protected	Traditional gear	Drive from Tafraout	Walk-in time	Routes D – HS	Routes MVS – HVS	Routes E1 – E3	Routes E4 +	★1	★2	★3
Samazar – Map p288	A. Agouti & Igiliz	4+	290	✓				✓		✓	1:30	0:05	3	3	0	0	4	1	0
	B. Aylim	Many	294	✓	✓			✓		✓	1:40	0:20	6	11	3	0	8	2	6
	C. Waterfall Walls	Many	305		✓					✓	1:40	0:25	0	5	5	1	4	5	0
	D. Dragon Rock	1-6	308	✓	✓					✓	1:40	0:25	3	23	25	2	15	18	16
	E. Safinah	10	322	✓						✓	1:45	0:25	0	2	1	0	1	1	1
	F. Aguerd Cioch	3-4	324	✓				✓		✓	1:40	0:10	1	5	1	0	4	3	0
	G. Icebox Canyon	2	326		✓					✓	1:30	0:20	0	3	8	1	2	4	2
	H. Afantztgult	Many	328	✓						✓	1:30	0:15	1	3	0	0	2	2	0
Aouguenz – Map p332	A. Temple Slabs	1-3	332		✓			✓		✓	1:10	0:05	4	1	1	0	4	0	1
	B. Hairpin Slabs	4	334		✓			✓		✓	1:15	0:10	1	1	0	0	1	0	1
	C. Azumer Crag	1	336		✓	✓		✓		✓	1:15	0:50	12	9	2	0	5	6	1
	D. Kakaa Wall	3-4	338	✓	✓					✓	1:45	0:30	0	0	2	0	0	0	2
	E. Faulty Towers	1-3	339	✓	✓					✓	1:45	0:30	0	7	9	1	5	4	8
p342	A. Tagzene Gorge	1	342	✓	✓	✓		✓		✓	1:15	0:10	19	5	0	0	15	4	1
	B. Babouche Buttress	5	347	✓				✓		✓	1:15	0:15	0	1	0	0	0	0	1
Tagmout – p348	A. Adrar Imtwan	3	349	✓						✓	1:00	0:40	2	1	0	0	2	0	0
	B. Akaltine Edge	1	350	✓	✓	✓		✓		✓	0:40	0:02	13	12	2	0	13	2	1
	C. Robin Hood Rocks	1-2	354	✓				✓		✓	0:40	0:10	15	34	25	5	16	29	18
	D. Maid Marion Rocks	1	372	✓	✓	✓		✓		✓	0:20	0:50	19	5	1	0	11	2	1

For more recommendations for where to go in different conditions, see the suggested climbs section on page 38.

Katja Broadbent on *The Scoop* (VS 4c) at Akaltine Edge. ➲
Photo: Steve Broadbent

CLIMB TAFRAOUT

INTRODUCTION

Welcome to Tafraout – a magical climbing oasis on the doorstep of Europe: a place where you can enjoy winter sun, good quality rock, and adventurous traditional climbs amidst the stunning sub-Saharan scenery. This is a place with a little bit of everything, from roadside cragging, bouldering, and even the odd sport route, to epic mountain adventures. It's a paradise of enchanting pink granite and endless orange quartzite; a place immersed in an exotic culture and a relaxed attitude to life, where only the most adventurous tourists have ventured. For climbers who live and breathe traditional, ground-up climbing it's hard to imagine a more suitable and convenient winter destination. Those who thrive on solitude, adventure, and a closeness to nature, need look no further.

As a climbing destination, Tafraout has rocketed into public awareness in recent years, but despite constant attention from European climbers since 1991, the vast area of Jebel el Kest and the Anti-Atlas mountains easily absorbs the influx of visitors. Climbing here is rather like stepping back in time to a period when unclimbed lines still littered our hillsides. Here you will find no polish on the rock, and with the exception of some chalk on the most popular routes, you will see little evidence of those who have passed before. A keen eye for route-finding will, therefore, make the difference between a pleasant ascent of a classic route, and a 'brilliant' off-route adventure.

Tafraout, however, is more than just another winter-sun climbing destination: it is a fascinating cultural journey, brimming with character, overflowing with adventure, and under-written by a bizarre colonialism. Climbers motivated solely by grades and technical difficulty will perhaps miss out on Tafraout's greatest pleasures. Those who climb for the experience, the adventure, and arrive with a healthy sense of humour, on the other hand, are about to discover something very special indeed...

ABOUT THIS GUIDEBOOK

Climbing guidebooks to Tafraout and the Anti-Atlas have progressed at a staggering rate since Claude Davies' landmark Cicerone guide first described the Ameln Valley in 2004. Since then, no less than 7 different books have been published, as climbers have explored ever more corners of the Anti-Atlas range, recording new routes at the rate of about two hundred per winter. That rate of development has begun to slow down in recent years, and whilst in the past the majority of climbers were coming to look for new routes, today most visiting climbers arrive in Tafraout to savour some of the 2000 or so existing climbs, many of which have achieved classic status.

This guidebook is the first of a kind, describing more than 1400 high quality climbs across the entire range, providing a 'one-stop-shop' not only for first-time visitors, but also those people making multiple repeat visits. Although it is a selective guide, instead of choosing the best climbs we have merely omitted the 'poorer' quality crags, thus providing almost definitive coverage of most of the worthwhile climbing that Tafraout has to offer, from 800m adventures to technical roadside cragging, and even sport climbing and bouldering on the granite tors round Aguerd Oudad.

OTHER GUIDEBOOKS

Tafraout: Rock Climbing in Morocco's Anti-Atlas

Published by the OAC in 2013, the definitive guidebook series is now out of print. Online updates are available from the Climb-Tafraout website.

Tafraout Pocket Guides

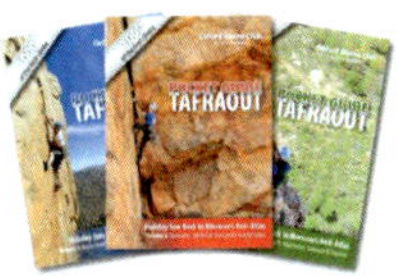

Published in 2014, these handy and popular pocket-sized guidebooks are still a valuable resource for climbers wanting to carry a guidebook up multi-pitch routes. They cover the entire range in three volumes.

Morocco Rock

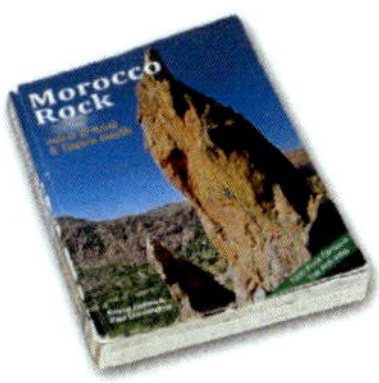

Published in 2012, this was a definitive guide to climbs on the north side of Jebel el Kest. Still widely available.

ONLINE RESOURCES

Before you visit Tafraout, make sure you visit our website for latest updates, free stuff, and discounts:

CLIMB TAFRAOUT **www.climb-tafraout.com**

- Online trip planner, with flight, car hire and accommodation advice.
- Exclusive discounts on Tafraout hotels.
- Packing lists, maps, and other useful resources for your trip.
- Free downloads, including topos and maps.
- Guidebook updates and new-route information.

MAPS

Until recently the Anti-Atlas region was poorly mapped and finding your way around was notoriously difficult. Today, however, the area is covered by three series of *GeoGraphics* maps, all of which will be of interest to the climber:

Tourist Explorer Map 1

This double-sided map features a 1:750000 road map of southern Morocco, as well as a 1:150000 'piste map' of the Anti-Atlas region from Ait Baha to Tafraout, perfect for exploring the area by car or on bike.

Outdoor Activity Maps 1-5

The whole area is covered at 1:50000 scale by this series of handy A2 MiniMaps, great for finding your way to the crag in the car and on foot. Also useful for exploring the range on rest-days and bad weather days.

Adventure Map 2

For hikers and trekkers wishing to explore the Jebel el Kest escarpment on foot, this 1:25000, double-sided A1 MiniMap represents the most detailed mapping of the Anti-Atlas region currently available.

Excerpts from all of these maps have been used throughout this guidebook, but to get the most out of your Tafraout adventure, sheet maps can be purchased in our online store at

CLIMB TAFRAOUT **www.climb-tafraout.com**

Town Plan Page 23

Tafraout, baking under Saharan sunshine in October. Blue, cloudless skies are common during early and late season, although it can still get cold at night.

Tafraout, following a flash flood in December. Major weather events are rare, but dramatic!

WHEN TO VISIT

Throughout the winter months the Anti-Atlas have an almost perfect climate for climbing. The long winter season, which runs from late September right through to the end of April, is one of the biggest attractions for trad climbers looking to escape the wet European weather.

Although Tafraout can see rain at any time throughout the winter, it is rare and unlikely to spoil a climbing trip. Likewise, an unusually cool airmass can sink down from Europe at any time, bringing surprisingly chilly temperatures to the higher mountain crags. Climbers visiting the area between November and March are, therefore, advised to bring lightweight waterproofs, whilst thermal shirts or fleeces will almost certainly be required throughout the season. Of course, during the heat of the day, temperatures in the high twenties will necessitate cool, loose clothing when climbing.

Typical conditions are as follows:

September - October

As the summer heat begins to subside in late September, conditions are usually hot and dry. Thunderstorms are possible, though rare, and prolonged rain is very unlikely. North-facing, high-altitude crags come into their own, whilst the lower, south-facing crags of the Ameln Valley can be unbearably hot. Daytime temperatures vary between 20 and 30 degrees.

November - December

Traditionally this is the wet season, but don't let that put you off as rain is rarely prolonged enough to put a stop to climbing. Temperatures can get quite chilly, particularly in the shade or during the evenings, and thermal clothing will be required. Cloud cover can make the higher crags rather unpleasant, so head for low-lying, south-facing routes.

January - February

The early Spring can be unpredictable – if the Autumn was wet then January and February are usually dry, with pleasant temperatures around 15 to 20 degrees and long periods of clear skies and perfect climbing conditions. If, however, the Autumn was very dry then rain frequently falls in the early Spring.

March - April

Spring usually gives excellent climbing conditions, with hot daytime temperatures (between 15 and 25 degrees) and long periods of sunshine. Exceptionally, winter rain can persist right through to the end of March, though this is unlikely. The land is usually green, with almond blossom and wild flowers creating a particularly spectacular landscape.

GETTING TO TAFRAOUT

The oasis town of Tafraout (alternatively Tafraoute or Tafrawt) is located in the Anti-Atlas mountains, in the southwest of Morocco. It is most easily reached by car from **Agadir** (a 2½ hour drive) or **Marrakech** (a 5½ hour drive).

Flights

A number of UK airlines operate services to **Agadir Al Massira**, with return flights typically costing between £180 and £300 per person. Ryanair, British Airways, easyJet, Thomas Cook and Thomson services operate from a variety of UK airports, though flights are limited and can be expensive at short notice.

Flying to **Marrakech Menara** is usually a cheaper alternative, and most major airlines run daily flights from a wide variety of European airports. Return flights from the UK typically cost between £130 and £250.

Public Transport

Hiring a car is strongly recommended, as it makes it much easier to visit the majority of crags in this book. That said, it is not uncommon for people to find themselves without private transport, and the following notes will hopefully be of use.

Tafraout is served by a variety of inter-city bus services and taxis (of the *grande* and *petit* varieties), which make a trip by public transport perfectly feasible, if a little adventurous.

Agadir and Marrakech both serve as bases for an overland adventure to Tafraout, and direct bus services run from both cities. The best service, routing from Marrakech to Tafraout via Agadir, Inezgane, Ait Melloul, Tiznit, Idaousmlal and Ait Wafka is operated by **CTM**, and tickets can be booked at **www.ctm.ma**. Seats on the outbound journey often fill up several days in advance and so prior booking is advised. For the return journey it is usually possibly to book seats at the CTM office in Tafraout the evening before travel. The bus leaves Tafraout every day at 8am, taking about 9 hours to reach Marrakech.

From Agadir it is also possible to reach Tafraout by Grande Taxi. The airport is located out of town, so travellers wishing to benefit from down-town rental rates or take public transport to Tafraout will need to go by taxi into the city (about 150 Dirhams). The onward journey from Agadir bus station is usually made via Tiznit, for which it is advisable to negotiate a price before travel (30 Dirham is normal). The Grande Taxis will wait until they are full before departing, and this can take up to an hour. At Tiznit you will often be dropped off at the south-eastern side of the town walls, from where you will need to walk round the outside of the walls to *Ave du 20 Aout*, which runs out of the wall at *Bab Mechouar*, on the south-western side. The Grande Taxi lot is at the end of *Ave du 20 Aout*, where it is easy to get a seat to Tafraout for about 30 Dirhams.

Climbers' Airport and Crag Transfers

Although not the cheapest option, private transfers are available through Tafraout-based **Maison Troc**, who offer airport pick-ups, as well as lifts to and from crags. This service can also be useful for hikers wishing to leave their car at one end of a walk. Contact Lahcen on **+212 67303909** to arrange.

Hiring a Car

Most climbers visiting Tafraout will want to hire a car for the duration of their stay, and it is advisable to book online before your trip. All major rental agencies have desks at both Agadir and Marrakech airports, and good deals have been found through brokers such as **Holiday Autos** and **Rhino Car Hire**.

Although many of the Anti-Atlas crags are accessed via unsurfaced tracks (known as *pistes*), 4WD is not necessary provided care is taken. A standard car typically costs between £150 and £200 per week at Agadir or Marrakech airports. The quality of cars has been found to be generally poor, with bald tires, unserviceable equipment and missing jacks frequently reported.

Area Map
Crag Selector
Intro
The Climbing
How to Use
Suggested Climbs
Tafraout Granite
Anergui
Ameln Valley
Tarakatine Pass
Sidi M'Zal
Jebel Taskra
Idaougnidif
Afantinzar
Samazar
Aouguenz
Tagzene
Tagmout
History
Index

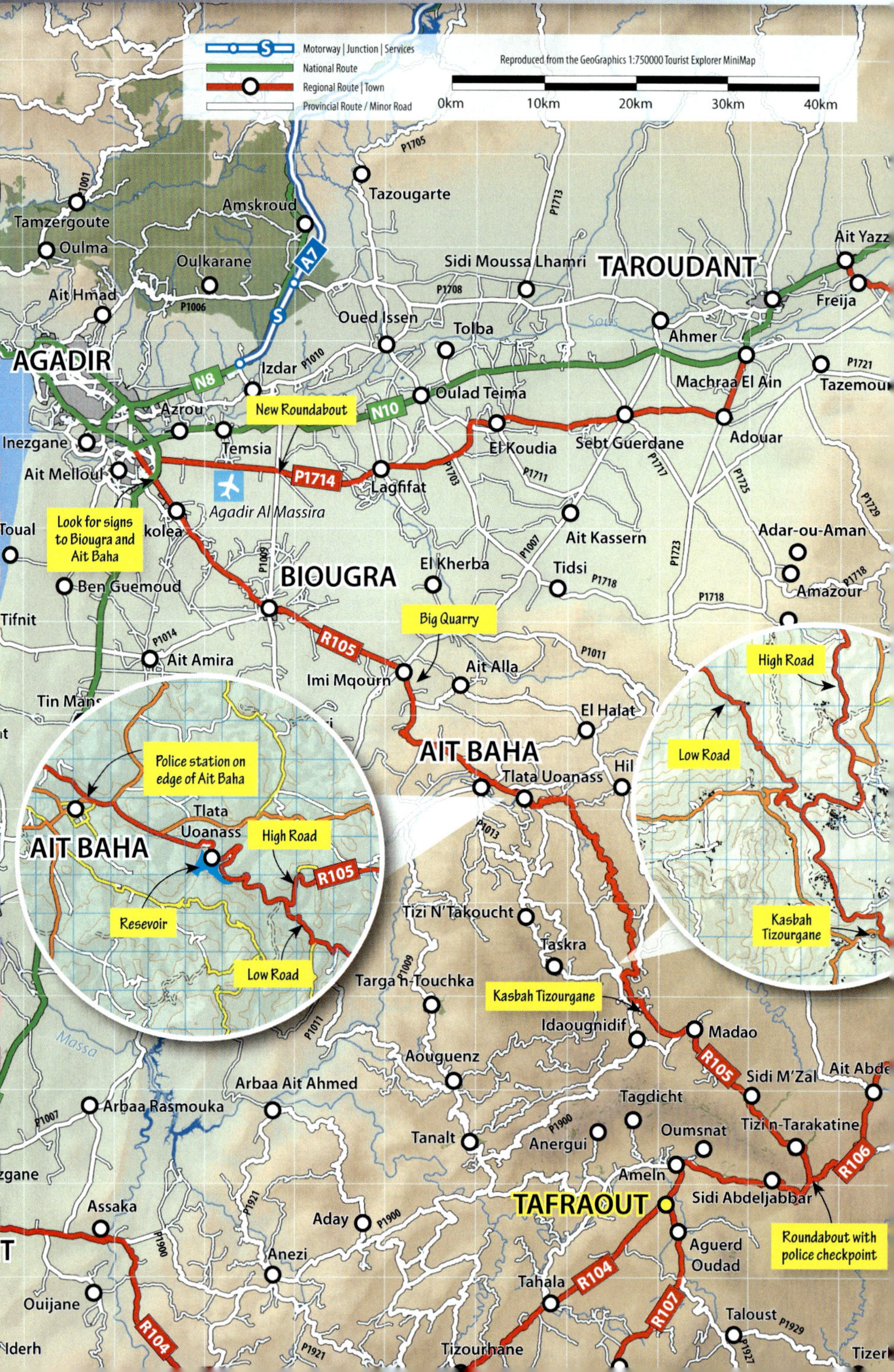
Motorway | Junction | Services
National Route
Regional Route | Town
Provincial Route / Minor Road
Reproduced from the GeoGraphics 1:750000 Tourist Explorer MiniMap
0km
10km
20km
30km
40km
AGADIR
TAROUDANT
BIOUGRA
AIT BAHA
TAFRAOUT
TIZNIT
Tamzergoute
Oulma
Amskroud
Tazougarte
Oulkarane
Ait Hmad
Sidi Moussa Lhamri
Ait Yazza
Freija
Oued Issen
Tolba
Ahmer
Izdar
Azrou
Inezgane
Temsia
Oulad Teima
Machraa El Ain
Tazemour
Ait Melloul
El Koudia
Sebt Guerdane
Adouar
Lagfifat
Agadir Al Massira
New Roundabout
Look for signs to Biougra and Ait Baha
Toual
Ait Kassern
Adar-ou-Aman
El Kherba
Tidsi
Amazour
Ben Guemoud
Tifnit
Big Quarry
Ait Amira
Imi Mqourn
Ait Alla
El Halat
Tin Mans
Tlata Uoanass
Hil
Police station on edge of Ait Baha
Tlata Uoanass
High Road
Resevoir
Low Road
Kasbah Tizourgane
Tizi N'Takoucht
Taskra
Targa n-Touchka
Idaougnidif
Madao
Aouguenz
Sidi M'Zal
Ait Abde
Arbaa Ait Ahmed
Arbaa Rasmouka
Tagdicht
Tanalt
Anergui
Oumsnat
Tizi n-Tarakatine
Ameln
Sidi Abdeljabbar
Imerzgane
Assaka
Aday
Aguerd Oudad
Roundabout with police checkpoint
Anezi
Tahala
Ouijane
Talous
Iderh
Tizourhane
Tizer
Massa
A7
N8
N10
N1
R105
R104
R106
R107
P1714
P1705
P1001
P1006
P1708
P1713
P1010
P1703
P1711
P1717
P1725
P1729
P1721
P1723
P1007
P1009
P1718
P1014
P1011
P1013
P1900
P1921
P1929
P1927

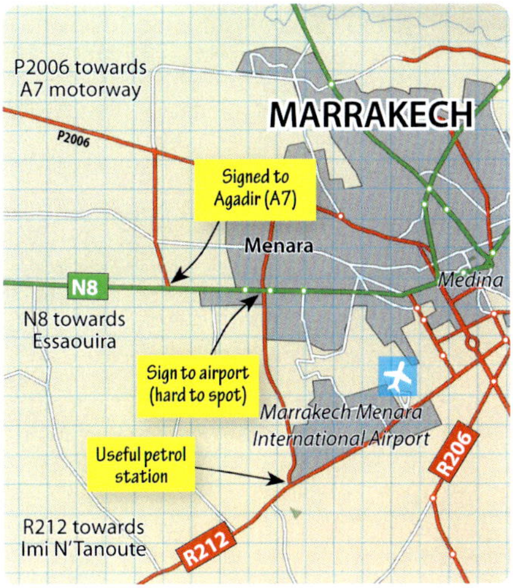

Escaping Marrakech

Although Agadir provides the simplest access to Tafraout and the Anti-Atlas, many people will choose to travel via Marrakech as part of a wider tour of Morocco, or perhaps to take in the excellent sport-climbing of the Todra Gorge.

Marrakech itself is a superb city and well-worth a visit in its own right. Countless hotels are available to suit all budgets, and the city boasts many excellent restaurants that reflect its modern and cosmopolitan image, as well as more traditional tastes. The central square, **Place Jma el Fna**, comes alive every evening with a fascinating variety of street artists, snake charmers, and vendors serving a baffling array of dishes, the likes of which you're unlikely to find anywhere outside of Africa. Surrounding the square is one of the best examples of a Moroccan *Souq* (market) that you'll ever see, and getting lost amongst its maze of narrow streets is a brilliant way of working up an appetite for a meal of sheep brain or eyeballs back in the square – assuming you can find your way back, that is.

For car drivers, however, the centre of Marrakech is best avoided. Frequent buses run from the airport terminal to the centre of town, so it's usually easier to leave your rental car at the airport and explore the city on foot.

At some point, of course, you're going to want to drive from Marrakech to Tafraout (for some, this happens sooner rather than later). Exit the airport and turn right at the roundabout onto the R212. Continue for approximately 4.2km to a right turn at the edge of the built up area. There is a useful petrol station here for filling up on your return to the airport. Continue north for 5.8km, then turn left on the N8 – this junction is usefully signposted to the airport on your return journey. The N8 can either be followed through Oudaya to the motorway, or take the signposted route via the P2006.

The journey along the A7 motorway leads to the Agadir/Inezgane/Ait Melloul ring road, takes about 2 hours, and costs approximately 80Dh in tolls.

The Drive from Agadir

Agadir Al Massira airport is located conveniently east of the city, so there's no need to drive into Agadir itself. From the airport, turn right and follow the P1714 for 5km to the first major roundabout. Turn right here and continue to Biougra.

This large market town can be very busy during rush hour or on market day, when pedestrians, donkeys, lorries, oblivious locals, and out-of-their depth westerners all share the road into town. At night it is worth paying particular attention to cyclists, who rarely have lights and frequently cycle on the wrong side of the road.

The road comes to an end at a major T-junction. Turn left here, following the R105 out of town and on towards Ait Baha. A large quarry is passed on the left, just before the road begins its climb into the hills, and Ait Baha is reached in approximately 45 minutes. Keep going straight on, passing the town on the right (there is a police station on the left).

Beyond Ait Baha bear right at the junction (i.e. follow the main road) and continue until the road snakes past a large reservoir. Just after this there is a fork, at which you can choose between the high road (more mountainous, with more traffic) and the low road (more rural, and probably the safer option). Both of these roads come back together again just before the famous Kasbah Tizourgane. Here the north side of Jebel el Kest provides a magnificent backdrop to one of the best examples of a Moroccan Kasbah, and for climbers the sense of excitement grows, as vast quartzite crags begin to drift in and out of view to the southwest.

Almost immediately before the walled village itself there is a turning to the right that is sometimes incorrectly sign-posted to Tafraout (this road actually leads to the market town of Idaougnidif, and on to the superb climbing valleys of Afantinzar and Samazar). Instead, keep on the main road, following it past Madao (Madaw), Sidi M'Zal, Tizi N'Tarakatine, and then to a roundabout on a high col (police checkpoint here). Turn right, climbing up towards the crest of the Tarakatine Pass, from where the full

The adventure begins... Ron Buckley asking for directions on the drive down to Tafraout.
Photo: Jim Nuttal

extent of the Ameln Valley and the south face of Jebel el Kest come magnificently into view.

Descending into the Ameln Valley, the high Tifghalt crags are passed on the right, before Tizgut Ridge blocks the view into the Tizgut Gorge, where Joe Brown's legendary Tizgut Crack lurks. On past Oumsnat, to the famous Lion's Face (you won't recognise it from this angle), and the main junction in Ameln – reference point for most of the driving directions in this book. Follow the road round to the left, and Tafraout is just around the corner...

MONEY

Many travellers to Morocco experience some difficulties with obtaining and using money, so the following notes will hopefully be of use to those visiting the area for the first time. The local currency is the **Moroccan Dirham** (DH or MAD), and in 2016 the exchange rate was approximately 12DH = £1, or 10DH = 1 Euro. The Dirham is a controlled currency, but can be obtained in the UK before your journey from *Bureaux de Change* beyond passport control. A much better exchange rate, however, will be available from the bank in Tafraout, so it's only worth changing as much as you will need for the journey, or for your hire-car and petrol if it's not pre-paid. Note that a maximum of 1000DH can be exported from the country, and officials in Marrakech airport have been seen searching wallets of passengers going through security.

Taking plenty of cash with you from the UK will prevent any time-consuming difficulties with ATMs and banks. Outside of the big cities it is safest to assume you will require Dirhams to obtain petrol, food, and accommodation. A tank of petrol will cost between 300DH and 600DH (depending on where you get the fuel). In Tafraout there are three cash machines, and whilst they have proved more reliable than the one at Marrakech airport they have still been known to eat credit cards. If this happens, you can just go into the bank and retrieve your card from inside (as long as they're open).

Most hotels will require payment in cash. This includes the Hotel Les Amandiers, who will accept cash-only payment in Dirhams, Euros, Sterling, or any combination thereof. There is no extra charge for this, and the exchange rate is generally perfectly acceptable. Many visitors have, therefore, found it convenient to take a reserve supply of Sterling in order to settle the hotel bill at the end of the trip. This allows you to efficiently use up all of your Dirhams before your flight home, without complicated calculations of how much cash to get.

Finally, it is worth noting that smaller shops and businesses will be unable to accept large notes (e.g. 200DH) for small transactions, as they generally don't have enough change. Larger notes are always accepted in petrol stations or the supermarket, and residents of Les Amandiers can exchange them at the hotel reception.

PROVISIONS

Large supermarkets are available in Marrakech and Agadir, and these may prove useful for those intending to wild-camp, or those looking to purchase their own alcohol.

Once in Tafraout, provisions are limited but perfectly adequate for a climbing trip when staying in one of the hotels in town. The excellent Berber round-bread (*pain ronde*) is a staple diet, and is available from many of the small shops in town, along with bottled water, fizzy drinks, processed cheese, crisps, pastries, and other snacks. Sweets and chocolate bars (including Mars and Snickers) are available in some of the shops, and on hot days a small supermarket opposite the school even provides a welcome source of ice-cream. A large variety of fruit and vegetables is available from market stalls throughout the town, at very low prices.

For climbers staying at the Kasbah Tizourgane or the Anammer guesthouse on the north side of the range, limited supplies are available from the market in Idaougnidif, and packed lunches are available from the Kasbah itself. A visit to Tafraout or Ait Baha will

The world's smallest banana? We're not sure...
Photo: Elie Dekoninck

often be called for to restock on climbing snacks during the trip.

PETROL & CAR MAINTENANCE

There are several petrol stations in Tafraout, and these will be obvious on a first visit. They all sell unleaded (*sans plomb* or *super*) as well as diesel (*diesel* or *gasoil*) at very reasonable prices. Expect to pay about 400DH to fill up your tank.

In case of car difficulties the first point of contact should be your rental agency, but for things like new tyres there are a number of mechanics in town who provide a good service. If in any doubt, you can always ask advice from the Amandiers hotel reception.

For those staying on the north side of the range it is important to keep an eye on your fuel situation. There is petrol available in Idaougnidif, but finding it is not simple, and it's very easy to find yourself stuck a long way from assistance. There is also a small petrol station on the road running north out of Tanalt.

HEALTH, SAFETY & TRAVEL ADVICE

Morocco, and particularly the Tafraout area, is generally a safe place for travellers, and there are no restrictions on travel. To date, no problems have been reported by climbers visiting Tafraout.

Immigration

British, European and American nationals do not require entry visas to Morocco for visits lasting less than 3 months. Passports must be valid for a minimum period of 6 months from the date of entry in the country.

Road Safety

Morocco has a very poor road safety record, and all visitors are advised to exercise caution on the roads. In order to address the problem the government have introduced draconian fines for traffic offences, and numerous police check-points may be encountered on the roads around Tafraout. If you do have an encounter with local traffic police then it is important to bear in mind that they might not all be as regulated as you might expect back home. They are, however, likely to hold significant authority to stop, search, detain and fine people on the spot. Cash fines for offences are more expensive and more spontaneous than they are in the UK, and are entirely legal. You should, however, always ensure that you will be provided with an official receipt before you hand over any money.

Vaccinations & Disease

Morocco is not a particularly high-risk destination, though some diseases which are not common in the UK are prevalent in the country. For climbers visiting Tafraout for short trips (up to 4 weeks) and staying in a hotel, no vaccinations are required. Rabies still exists in the area, and numerous water-borne diseases, including Schistosomiasis, mean that it's worth avoiding the temptation to take a cooling dip in mountain pools. Tetanus is common, and travellers are advised to make sure that boosters are up to date before their visit.

For visitors staying for longer than 4 weeks, or those wild-camping for extended periods, vaccinations may be advisable, and a visit to your GP is recommended. Hepatitis A, Hepatitis B, TB and Typhoid are all prevalent in the country and vaccinations may be recommended dependent on the nature of your trip.

Finally, it is worth mentioning that any injury that requires medical treatment during your stay should be referred to medical professionals on your return to the UK – even relatively small wounds have been known to become seriously infected, and gangrene has been reported following medical treatment in Tafraout.

Medical Facilities

There are no organised rescue services in the Anti-Atlas, and all visitors must take responsibility for their own well-being in the area. A pharmacy in Tafraout provides a range of first-aid equipment, and a small medical centre will treat minor ailments. More serious conditions will be referred to the nearest hospital in Ait Baha or Agadir. Emergency numbers can be found on page 5.

ACCOMMODATION

The oasis town of Tafraout is at the heart of the Anti-Atlas climbing community, and has been the traditional base for climbers since the likes of Joe Brown, Chris Bonington, Derek Walker and Les Brown began their exploration of the quartzite crags on the south face of Jebel el Kest in the early 1990s. Here, for almost twenty years, they frequented the famous Hotel les Amandiers, lapping up 'four-star' colonial luxury, overlooked by the mighty crags of Jebel el Kest. It's a romantic image that takes one back to the golden age of rock-climbing on the high crags of the Lake District and Snowdonia. Thankfully, here, very little has changed.

Accommodation in Tafraout

Tafraout provides the widest range of facilities for visiting climbers, including numerous places to eat, plenty of shops, petrol, hammams, banks, ATMs, a pharmacy, and a small medical centre. It is situated to the south of Jebel el Kest, in full view of all of the south-side crags, which can be reached in between 10 and 30 minutes from the town. The north-side crags are somewhat further, taking between 40 and 90 minutes by car. Buses, taxis, bike, and even car rental, are available in the town. Recommended hotels are as follows:

HOTEL **LES AMANDIERS**

This large hotel sits on a hillside overlooking the town, and has become the centre of the Tafraout climbing community. Its well-stocked bar usually has at least a handful of British climbers established in it, and the ever-growing new-routes book (*Livre d'Escalade*) is kept closely guarded behind the hotel reception.

The hotel is immaculately clean, with safe chlorinated tap water, and a large restaurant serving a mixture of simple Moroccan and International dishes. The staff are extremely friendly, and speak good French, English and German. Double, twin, and triple rooms are available, and all are en-suite with either a bath or a shower. There is an outdoor swimming pool for hotel guests, where enjoying a cold beer on the terrace, lit by alpenglow on Jebel el Kest, is a thoroughly recommended experience.

Free wi-fi is available to all guests, and the centre of Tafraout is easily reached in five minutes on foot.

Email: hotellesamandierstafraoute@gmail.com
Website: http://www.hotel-lesamandiers.com
Tel: +212 (0)528 800008
Rooms: ~~350Dh~~ or 300Dh* (single) | ~~450Dh~~ or 330Dh* (Double) | ~~500Dh~~ or 430Dh* (Triple).
(*reduced prices if booked through www.climb-tafraout.com)

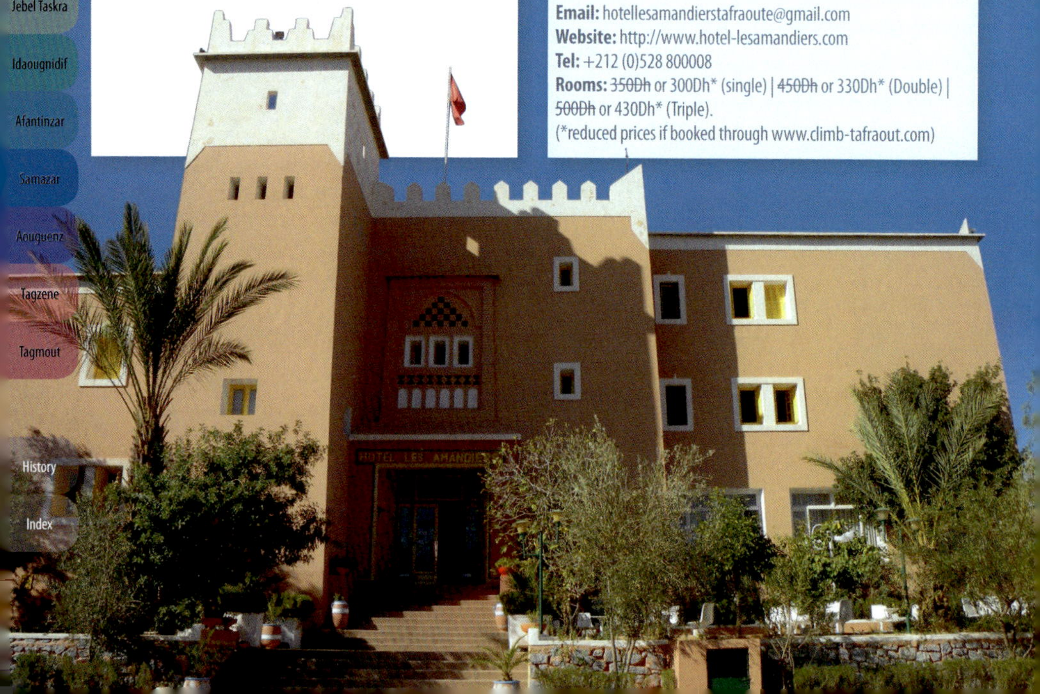

HOTEL **SALAMA**

2 AIR CON

This recently renovated hotel sits right in the centre of Tafraout, and is a popular option for climbers thanks to its attractive prices. The hotel is full of character, furnished throughout in traditional Moroccan style.

Website: http://www.hotelsalama.com
Tel: +212 (0)528 800026
Rooms: 180Dh (single) | 260Dh (double) | 320Dh (triple)

AUBERGE **L'ESCALADE**

1

Self-catering apartments, providing good value accommodation right next to the excellent *Restaurant La Kasbah*. Facilities include air-con, fridges, washing machines and hot showers. Double, triple and family apartments available.

Email: Mohamed_tafraout@yahoo.com
Tel: +212 (0)691 850401 / +212 (0)660 954269
Rooms: 200Dh (double) | 300Dh (triple) | 500Dh (room for 5)

HOTEL **ARGANA**

1

A very pleasant family run guest-house that offers budget accommodation in the centre of town. The family who run this hotel also own *Restaurant La Kasbah*, just across the road, which does some of the best tagines in town.

Website: http://www.argana-tafraout.com
Tel: +212 (0)528 801496
Rooms: 150Dh (basic) | 250Dh (en-suite) | 300Dh (family)

HOTEL **LES AMIS**

1

For travellers on a very tight budget, this excellent little auberge is highly recommended. It has nine basic rooms with shared bathrooms, and offers good value accommodation right in the centre of Tafraout.

Email: auberge.lesamis@yahoo.fr
Tel: +212 (0)623 826488
Rooms: 150Dh (double or twin)

The bridge in the centre of Tafraout on a rainy day.

Accommodation in the Ameln Valley

A number of small guest-houses and hotels provide accommodation in the Ameln Valley, with the advantage of being very close to some of the south-side crags. It's worth bearing in mind, however, that there are very limited facilites here, and trips into Tafraout are likely to be required for supplies, or any variety of food. For those with a car, the average driving times to the crags are similar to those when staying in Tafraout, although climbers travelling on foot will benefit from the proximity to a limited number of crags.

HOTEL CHEZ AMALIYA

2 | BAR | AIR CON

This very pleasant, European-owned hotel is located close to the main junction in Ameln. It offers very attractive, authentically decorated and family-friendly rooms in an superb setting beneath the Lion's Face. A very picturesque swimming pool and terrace are particularly appreciated on hot days.

Email: info@chezamaliya.com
Website: http://www.chezamaliya.com
Tel: +212 (0)528 800065
Rooms: 330Dh (single) | 500Dh (Double) | 1000Dh (Suite)

HOTEL TÊTE DU LION

2 | BAR

Also located close to Ameln, this hotel is a good option for those wishing to explore the Ameln valley who don't mind being away from the amenities of Tafraout. The rooms are basic, but clean, and excellent home-cooked food is available in the evenings. Alcohol is also available.

Email: latetedulion@yahoo.fr | tetedulion@tafraout.info
Tel: +212 (0)528 801165
Rooms: 250Dh (single) | 300Dh (Double) | 350Dh (Triple)

AUBERGE TILILA

1

Basic accommodation in the village of Asgaour, close to the Lion's Face and within walking distance of several good crags.

Email: abraz70@hotmail.fr
Rooms: Prices on request.

The Ameln Valley, with greenery flourishing following the winter rains.

Accommodation on the North Side

Accommodation on the north side of Jebel el Kest is very limited, and the lack of provisions and facilities mean that most teams will feel the need to visit Tafraout to re-stock at some point during their trip. Access to the north-side crags is obviously much quicker, and the following guest houses can provide an excellent base for a few days exploring the northern part of the range.

KASBAH TIZOURGANE ★2

The magnificent walled Kasbah at Tizourgane is one of the most impressive pieces of Moroccan architecture in the region, and staying at the small family-run guest house in the heart of the fortified village is a great way to see a little bit of genuine Berber culture. The Kasbah is ideally situated for climbing on the north side of the range, and has become correspondingly popular amongst climbers in recent years, particularly those who aren't keen on long drives! Home-cooked food is available in the evenings, but the variety can be rather limited and no alcohol is available. The owners are very welcoming, and speak good English. Rooms can be quite cold in winter months, so warm clothing is advised...

Email: info@tizourgane-kasbah.com
Website: http://www.tizourgane-kasbah.com
Tel: +212 (0)661 941350
Rooms: 360Dh (Double) | 540Dh (Triple)

KSAR ROCK GUESTHOUSE

Located in Anammer village, underneath the south face of Ksar Rock, this small guest house provides unique accommodation for climbers, within easy walking distance of some of the best climbing in the range. The accommodation is basic, but the young owners, Mahfoud and Fatima, speak good English and French, and their kind hospitality will add a fascinating cultural experience to any climbing trip to the area.

One double bedroom is available, and beds can also be made up in a large sitting room with balcony, which affords stunning views across to the Grand Wall of Lower Eagle Crag.

Accommodation is provided on a full-board basis, including dinner, bed, and breakfast. A fridge is available for guests' use, so if you can manage a supermarket visit in Agadir then you can enjoy a cold beer at the end of the day!

The guesthouse is located on the left, as you walk up through Anammer, just before the end of the village. It is shown on the photo on page 268.

Email: mahfoudabdoun@gmail.com
Tel: +212 (0)671 897796 | +212 (0)648 475447
Rooms: Approx 300Dh (two people, full board)

MADAO GUESTHOUSE

A small cafe / guesthouse in Madao provides accommodation that might be useful for climbers on a budget.
Rooms: 220Dh (room with breakfast)

The Kasbah Tizourgane, with the north side of Jebel el Kest behind.

Town Plan Page 23

CAMPING

Few climbers choose to camp in the Anti-Atlas, perhaps due to the limitations on airline baggage, the lack of surface drinking water, and the presence of snakes and scorpions throughout the range. That said, there are options available for those who prefer to sleep under canvas.

The **'3 Palms'** campsite in Tafraout provides clean showers and washing facilities, and is usually busy with European motor-homes. Tents are welcome, but there is no grass. The site is rumoured to be chemically treated so as to be 'snake free', though this has not been confirmed!

Wild camping options are very limited, and there have been several incidences of climbers being asked to move on by the local population. Remember that all of the land here is privately owned, and often provides a source of food for the Berbers, even when this is far from obvious to western eyes. Short-term bivouacs are possible at the base of higher crags, well away from villages, though great care should be taken to leave no trace of your visit. It goes without saying that all water requirements will have to be met with bottled water.

The schoolhouse junction in Samazar provides the only feasible roadside bivi spot, though tents must not be left up here during the day, and all trace of your stay must be removed on a daily basis.

PLACES TO EAT IN TAFRAOUT

The local food tends to be simple, cheap, and of limited variety. **Tagine** (slow-cooked stew) is the most popular dish and is available in most restaurants and cafes, along with **couscous** and **brochettes** (meat kebabs). There are a number of eateries in Tafraout, and in general the hygiene of these establishments has not come under question. However, standards are not comparable to those seen in the UK, and a lack of safe water, soap, and clean toilets, coupled with the presence of animal waste, pests and flies around town does not inspire confidence. As a general rule, the dangers are small and certainly not as substantial as those in India and the Himalaya, or other parts of Africa. Avoid drinking non-chlorinated tap water and eating ice cream, but salads, vegetables, fruit, rice, and meat seem to be safe.

Climbers staying in Tafraout have a huge choice of restaurants and cafes available to them, and exploring these is part of the 'Tafraout experience'. It is, therefore, not within the scope of this guide to describe them in detail, other than the following recommendation:

RESTAURANT **LA KASBAH**

This excellent family-owned restaurant is located on the Aguerd Oudad road, opposite the **Maison Troc** carpet shop, and is a favourite lunchtime venue for the more affluent locals, who often congregate here to share a tagine and seemingly endless games of cards. This fact is a good advert for the quality of the food here, and indeed the Kasbah is known for some of the best tagines in town – particularly the local **Khalia**. Unlike some of the more tourist-focussed eateries in town, the Kasbah is all about home-cooked, quality food, and the friendly staff are happy to accommodate a variety of dietary needs. Indeed, the vegetarian tagines are the best in the area.

The ambience is one of traditional Moroccan affluence, and the low tables and sofas provide a peaceful and comfortable place to hang out and drink mint tea. Since it is both owned and frequented by the more 'nomadic' demographic, it is also a good place to procure illicit alcohol (there's a reason the nomads are there to play cards). Wine and beer is often available even if not on the menu, but please use some discretion as there are religious sensitivities.

Full menu: 90 – 120 Dh

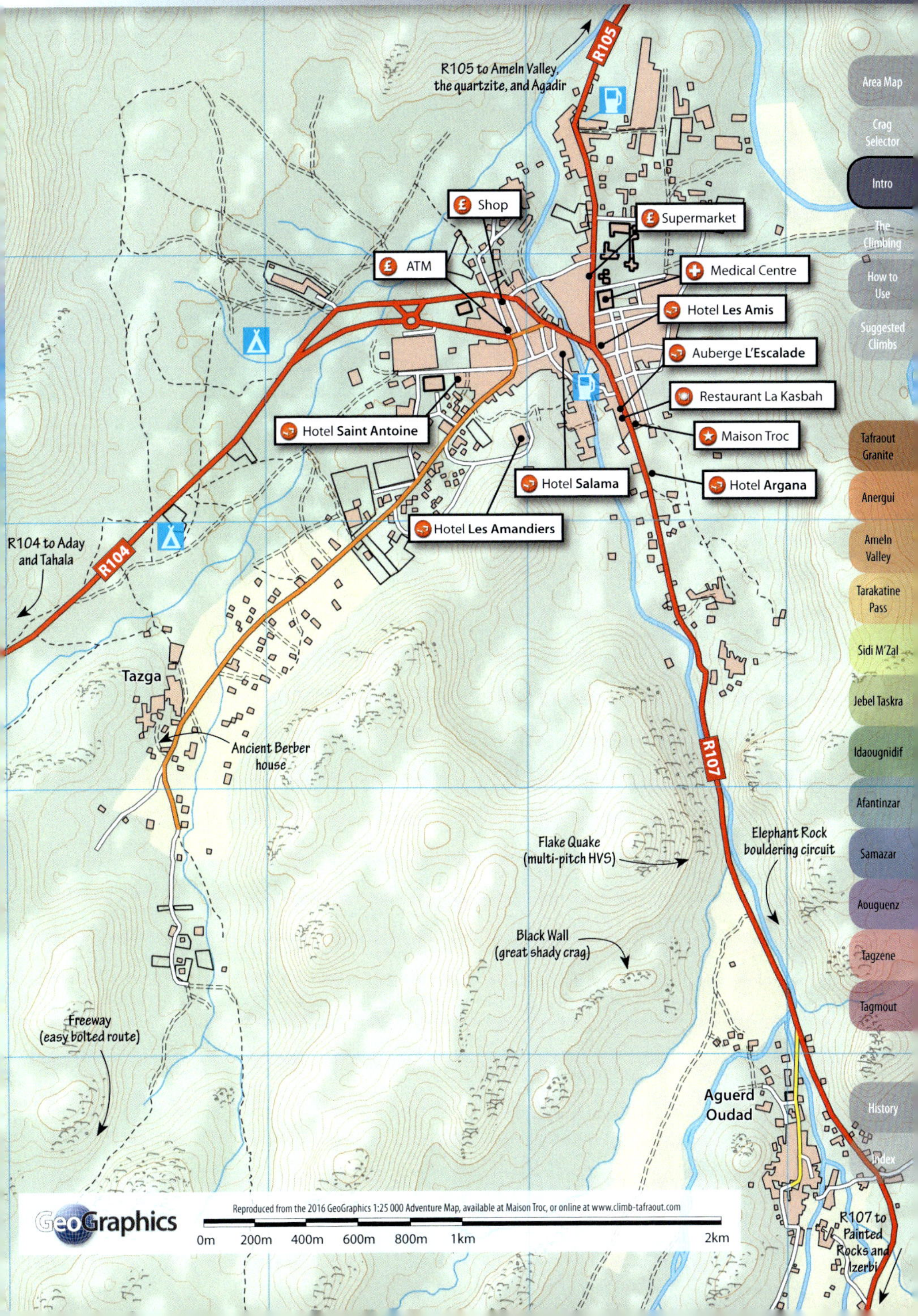
R105 to Ameln Valley, the quartzite, and Agadir
R105
Shop
Supermarket
ATM
Medical Centre
Hotel Les Amis
Auberge L'Escalade
Restaurant La Kasbah
Maison Troc
Hotel Saint Antoine
Hotel Salama
Hotel Argana
Hotel Les Amandiers
R104 to Aday and Tahala
R104
Tazga
Ancient Berber house
R107
Flake Quake (multi-pitch HVS)
Elephant Rock bouldering circuit
Black Wall (great shady crag)
Freeway (easy bolted route)
Aguerd Oudad
R107 to Painted Rocks and Izerbi
GeoGraphics
Reproduced from the 2016 GeoGraphics 1:25 000 Adventure Map, available at Maison Troc, or online at www.climb-tafraout.com
0m 200m 400m 600m 800m 1km 2km

Town Plan Page 23

The Amandiers bar in Tafraout, popularised by the original Ameln pioneers, is still a popular haunt for visiting climbers.

ALCOHOL

Morocco is a Muslim country and the religion does not allow the consumption of alcohol. Throughout the countryside, and in smaller towns and villages, therefore, you are unlikely to find any alcohol at all. In Tafraout, however, many of the nomadic people and Touareg tribes do not follow the same religious guidelines and will sometimes be seen consuming alcohol in public.

During French rule in the first part of the 20th Century the country's favourable climate was exploited in the production of wine, and although exports are not what they once were, the authorities are certainly not averse to selling wine to Westerners. Today, most large tourist hotels are likely to serve a reasonable selection of wine, beer and spirits.

For a cold beer in Tafraout, the **Hotel les Amandiers** is really the only place to consider, with its dimly lit but well-stocked bar, large Moroccan lounge, and pool-side terrace. The local **Flag** beer will cost you about 25Dh for a bottle, and spirits are also available, though rather over-priced. Wine is only available during meal times when the staff have access to the cellar. The bar has long been a popular hang-out for carpet-sellers, motorcyclists and European climbers, so the atmosphere is usually a convivial one.

PEOPLE & CULTURE

The Berber people of the Anti-Atlas follow many of the traditions of the Arabic world, and their hospitality is equally well renowned. The locals in and around Tafraout are genuine and friendly people, who are usually pleased to host European travellers in their town. Having said that, their culture is very different to that of Western Europe, and tourists should ensure these differences are properly respected during their visits.

RELIGION

Most Berbers follow Islamic beliefs, and whilst the people are not as devout as in some parts of the world they are still a relatively religious race – a fact borne out by the frequent calls to prayer that echo around the remote valleys and across Tafraout. The Muslim Berbers are forbidden to consume alcohol, and it is not generally available for purchase. Morocco does, however, produce its own beer and wine for sale to foreign tourists, and they do not take offence at Europeans drinking provided that a modicum of discretion is exercised.

STANDARDS FOR TRAVELLERS

European travellers should remember that taking photographs can cause great offence to Muslims. As a general rule, always ask people before taking a photograph of them, and never attempt to take photos of women, or any government buildings.

All public displays of affection, including men and women holding hands should be avoided. In Arabic countries it is common to see men holding hands – this is an accepted sign of friendship, but affection between the sexes is not expected in public.

Finally, travellers should adhere to accepted standards of dress – remember that in the Berber culture people are simply not accustomed to many European practices, and inappropriate clothing can easily and innocently cause offence, particularly to the elderly. Knees should always be covered when out in public, so long trousers or long skirts should be worn rather than shorts. Likewise, shoulders should remain covered, so avoid wearing sleeveless T-shirts or strappy tops unless on high crags well away from shepherds, farmers, and villagers.

Berber lady in traditional dress, extracting oil from the ubiquitous argan nuts.

As the number of western climbers visiting the region continues to grow, please help us to maintain a good relationship with the local population – if you see people climbing topless, or sporting the kind of clothing that might be well-suited to a hot Spanish sport crag then please do not copy them. Keep shoulders covered, and dress with consideration.

LANGUAGE

The local language is Berber, but almost everyone understands Arabic. The better educated, including most waiters, mechanics, police, shopkeepers and so on will also have a basic understanding of French. Only very few people speak any English, apart from some hotel staff and the incredibly successful carpet-sellers. A few useful words in Arabic are *Salamalaykum* (hello, or good day), *Shokran* (thank you), and *Marsalama* (goodbye).

BEING A GUEST

It is not uncommon to be invited into someone's house for tea, or to be offered food. Be aware that when offered tea, you will most likely be given food, and it is ungracious to leave without accepting. If offered food it is polite to refuse once, but then accept the offer when they persist! Once you have accepted food, remember the following:

- Eat with the right hand only.
- Do not stop eating until other people do so, but keep nibbling slowly to show you are nearly full. If you do stop eating, the hosts will be obliged to stop as well.
- If you empty your plate, the host will assume they did not feed you sufficiently, and will certainly produce more food. Try to eat well, but leave a small amount.

BUYING SOUVENIRS

In the Souqs throughout Morocco, customers are expected to negotiate the price of non-food goods, and in some places even accommodation. Be prepared for this and, whatever your strategy, make sure the coins and notes in your wallet match what you're saying to the vendor. It is not unreasonable to offer as low as half the asking price for most gift items in Souqs, and then expect to pay about three-quarters.

STANDARD OF LIVING

Outside of town, in the small villages throughout Afantinzar and Samazar, the impression of poverty is generally a false one. Many of the people are relatively wealthy, and having earned money in the cities have chosen a living in the countryside. Encouraging young children into begging is not to be recommended, so it's best not to give in to kids pestering tourists for sweets.

Local children in Tafraout.

Town Plan Page 23

Ben Lister on *Skyline* (E1) at Robin Hood Rocks (page 361).
Photo: Steve Broadbent

CARPETS

Carpet selling is big business in Tafraout, and the ubiquitous carpet sellers of Maisons Troc and Touareg are never far from the action in town. Unlike some of those in larger cities, the staff of both of these shops are friendly, trustworthy people who are sympathetic to the priorities and budgets of climbers. In fact, the carpet sellers of Maison Troc are strong supporters of the Tafraout climbing community, and have been influential in representing the needs of climbers and protection of the natural environment through lobbying of local government.

Even so, most climbers have a natural resistance to the insistence of the carpet sellers – but a visit to the carpet shop in your own time is a highly recommended way to spend a rest day. **Maison Troc**, on the Aguerd Oudad road not only offers a superb glimpse into the country's culture, but also a chance to marvel at some true works of art. Its proprietors show impeccable hospitality and will be able to find a Moroccan souvenir to suit any budget.

The exquisite hand-made carpets here start from around £35 for a small rug, with larger ones costing several hundred pounds. Because Tafraout is somewhat off the beaten track the tourist mark-up is not unreasonably high compared with that in cities such as Marrakech, and although bartering is expected, the salesmen here are proud of their reputation and will not risk exaggerating prices just for a quick profit.

Mohammed and Lahcen, of Maison Troc, who have been supporting climbers in the town for as long as climbers have been coming here. Of course, they can also sell you a perfect souvenir of your trip!

A little bit about **TAFRAOUT...**

Like most of the settlements in the Anti-Atlas, Tafraout, meaning a bowl or water channel, falls out of translation with several spellings. Strictly speaking, *Tafraout* is probably the most correct, following the Berber convention of starting and ending all place names with the letter 'T'. Western climbers have, however, been using the alternative *Tafraoute* for many years now, which seems to have been widely adopted from the French. Visitors may also see the name *Tafrawt* on some signs and milestones.

The town itself is an ancient trading post, where the Touareg people from the Sahara have settled happily alongside the indigenous Berbers from the Anti-Atlas. It's always been something of an 'alternative' kind of place, successfully retaining its Berber roots despite the enforced spread of Arabic through Morocco. It's a place full of mystery and a stronghold of occultism – superstition here runs deeper than the usual reliance on nature and the seasons: inexplicable artefacts await the exploratory climber, and tales of eldritch encounters lurk not too deep in society. Desert spirits tease the unwary, and mythical goat-eating dragons roam the hills, whilst elderly gentlemen use inexplicable techniques to cure people of all sorts of ills. Stay here for long enough, and you'll almost start to believe...

To the casual tourist, of course, Tafraout's spiritual undertones are well-hidden beneath its unquestionable natural beauty: a feature that draws people here by the coach-load throughout the year. Generally, the tourists who pass through here stay for just one or two days, taking in a visit to Aguerd Oudad and the famous Painted Rocks and going *en-masse* to the carpet shop. A few arrive in motorhomes, and some stay longer, exploring the gorges, seeking out ancient rock engravings, or perhaps making an ascent of Afa-n-Tmezgadiwine, the highest point of Jebel el Kest.

Town Plan Page 23

Area Map
Crag Selector
Intro
The Climbing
How to Use
Suggested Climbs
Tafraout Granite
Anergui
Ameln Valley
Tarakatine Pass
Sidi M'Zal
Jebel Taskra
Idaougnidif
Afantinzar
Samazar
Aouguenz
Tagzene
Tagmout
History
Index

VEGETATION

As you might expect, most of the vegetation in the Anti-Atlas is of the prickly variety and is present on many of the climbs. Three plants of particular note are described below.

Prickly Pear

This is the common 'cactus'-like plant that is seen throughout the region. It and its spines are not particularly tough, but if brushed against, the spines will embed in skin and clothing and be particularly inconvenient. The plant was traditionally used by the local people to create boundaries to keep out wild boar, and although it and its fruit are edible, they don't seem to be a particularly popular food-source.

Euphorbia

This small cactus rarely grows more than 6 or 7 inches in height, and plants tend to be found in relative isolation. Whilst it is common on the south-facing crags of the Ameln Valley, it is fortunately a rare sight in Afantinzar and Samazar. When disturbed in any way, the Euphorbia releases a white milk which is a powerful irritant that can remain on ropes and clothing for some considerable time. Whilst it is not dangerous externally, the effect on skin is similar to a bad nettle sting. It can be neutralised with climbing chalk.

Argan

The endemic argan tree has been at the heart of the local economy for hundreds of years, producing wood for burning, food for the goats, cosmetics, nuts, and of course the extremely valuable argan oil, which is the region's most important export. The oil is still produced, by hand, by women in the local villages, and the numerous argan-oil products available in Tafraout make excellent souvenirs and gifts. At the crags, of course, the argan tree provides welcome shade, but its resilient and prickly branches provide yet more scratches to exploring climbers...

WILDLIFE

As well as common lizards, ground squirrels, hares, wild dogs, and domestic cats, the Anti-Atlas is home to a few more hazardous creatures. Fortunately they are all very timid, and encounters are rare.

Snakes

Three types of venomous snake have been reported in Morocco, but sightings are rare between November and March. Anyone venturing into the backcountry during the warmer months (including April and October) should take particular care.

The **Horned Viper** is a short, broad snake with a speckled pattern, found mostly in desert regions and rock outcrops. It is usually nocturnal and hides in rodent holes or underneath rocks, but it can be quick to strike if disturbed. Its highly toxic venom attacks red blood cells, and is usually fatal if anti-venom is not given rapidly following a bite.

The longer, slender **Rock Viper** is a more frequent sight around Tafraout but fortunately very timid. The snake often hides in small shrubs and will usually make its presence well known in order to give an approaching threat chance to back away. If this chance is not taken then the Viper will attack in self-defence. If a bite does occur, reassure the casualty, gently wash the wound, and evacuate to medical aid as soon as possible. Do not attempt to suck out venom, apply pressure, or tourniquet.

The Anti-Atlas mountains are also home to the **Egyptian Black Cobra**, and attacks by this highly dangerous and distinctive snake are usually fatal. Fortunately the Cobra is a very rare snake, and only one encounter by a climber has been reported. Rapid evacuation to medical aid is required in the case of a bite.

Scorpions

Worldwide deaths from scorpion stings outnumber those due to snake bites by ten to one, and at least six main species of scorpion can be found in the mountains around Tafraout. Fortunately, the most common scorpions (brown or pale-coloured) do not usually pose a serious threat to humans, but the deadly **Androctonus**, or fat-tailed scorpion, has been frequently sighted in the region and is responsible for a significant number of human deaths, with over 60% of encounters occurring during hot summer afternoons.

Scorpions are nocturnal, preferring to hide under rocks or in burrows during daytime hours. They are not aggressive creatures, but have been known to crawl into unprotected packs or boots during bivouacs, where they can easily become trapped and defensive. Due to the difficulties in identifying the different species, climbers are advised to treat all scorpions as potentially dangerous, cover boots at night, and avoid walking round crags bare-footed.

Spiders

Fortunately Morocco does not have the range of poisonous spiders that one might expect, and indeed there are no spiders that will cause problems for climbers in the region.

Wild Boar

The elusive wild boar are prevalent across the Anti-Atlas, and evidence of their activities is frequently seen at crags. Although not inherently aggressive, these animals could attack if startled, particularly if young are present. Avoid encounters by making plenty of noise when approaching undergrowth and dens.

Big Cats

Any historical big cat population has probably now died out, although a suspected leopard skull has been found high on Jebel Taskra.

Varan

If legend is to be believed, then the mighty Varan is by far the most dangerous of creatures to inhabit the landscape around Tafraout, though encounters are mercifully rare. The Varan was somewhat exaggerated by Japanese science fiction (weighing 60,000 tonnes with the ability to fly at mach 1.5), but surprisingly this carnivorous reptile is very real, and numerous sightings have been reported in the hills around Tafraout. Evidence of its activities (in the form of mutilated goats) has also been reported by locals.

Joking aside, the real-life Varan is a type of monitor lizard which grows to a remarkable 1.5m in length. Its ability to fly at mach 1.5 is unconfirmed but climbers are nevertheless advised to stay away from deep caves in remote places (if only because Godzilla is described as one of its allies)...

THE CLIMBING

One of the appealing things about the climbing here is the tremendous variety on offer, and with bouldering, cragging, multi-pitch, and long mountain routes all within easy reach, every day of a Tafraout climbing holiday can be different.

Fundamentally, the region is split into two areas, with adventurous, traditionally protected quartzite to the north, and interesting roadside granite to the south.

Quartzite

(North of the Ameln Valley, including the Ameln Crags, Jebel el Kest, Afantinzar, Samazar, Idaougnidif, Tanalt, and Jebel Taskra).

Quartzite is a unique climbing medium, producing extremely satisfying low- to mid-grade routes with excellent holds, good protection, large stances and steep pitches. Many of the buttresses appear either difficult or unattractive from the road but on closer inspection reveal solid rock with some surprisingly easy routes. Having said that, the Anti-Atlas is not a suitable place for large groups of novice climbers.

Most of the routes here do not require a high level of skill, strength, or fitness – instead they advocate careful movement, thoughtful protection, and plenty of big-route experience. This is adventure trad-climbing at its very best, where skilful route-finding, prudence, yet a confident approach, will be rewarded with some incredible climbing.

Less experienced parties are advised to choose their initial routes with care, as the comfortable atmosphere of quartzite climbing can often mask the seriousness of many of the longer routes. The quality of the quartzite varies from immaculate to dangerous, and unless care is taken it is possible to stray quickly onto worryingly unstable ground. On the majority of faces, however, the rock is amazingly sound and almost always better than it looks from below. In general, it is only the very pale orange rock that crumbles, but care should always be taken with large blocks which could be loose in any situation. Much of the climbing is up steep pitches on excellent positive jugs – how they remain attached is a mystery, but the quartzite always seems to be stronger and more solid than you'd expect.

Steve Broadbent on *Soul and Romance* (E4) – immaculate quartzite in Corners Gully at Dragon Rock, Samazar (page 321).
Photo: Lina Arthur

BEWARE OF LOOSE ROCK

The Anti-Atlas are known for the superb quality of the quartzite, but do not be misled – this is still an adventurous destination, and routes here have seen very little traffic. Loose blocks and flakes still lie in wait, even on the more popular routes, and climbers should adopt a cautious approach.

A number of serious accidents have occurred here when climbers have pulled off large loose blocks, and a worrying number of teams have had their ropes cut by falling rock.

- **Treat all blocks with suspicion, testing them before pulling up.**
- **Beware of flat 'flake edges' that are often poorly attached.**
- **Always wear a helmet at the crag, even when you're not climbing.**
- **Think about where you belay, and where rocks are going to fall if your leader pulls something off.**

Granite

(South of the Ameln Valley, including Tafraout, Tazka, Aguerd Oudad and the Painted Rocks).

Tafraout itself sits in a bowl of granite tors which provide an eclectic mix of bouldering, sport, and esoteric trad. The molten rock which made this spectacular landscape cooled slowly, creating large abrasive crystals that aren't always well attached, and this, combined with a lack of weathering, has created the rather crumbly rock that is a feature of Tafraout granite climbing. Intense heating during the summer further worsens the problem, creating an abundance of exfoliating flakes of all sizes.

In amongst the acres of poor rock, however, are isolated pockets of excellent climbing on good quality granite. Indeed, no trip to Tafraout is complete without at least one day exploring this remarkable landscape, in which you'll find some of the best slab climbs and best off-width cracks that the Anti-Atlas have to offer.

Oops! A classic Anti-Atlas benightment. The Saharan sun goes down very quickly, leaving behind a long, cold night for which shorts and T-shirts are entirely inappropriate...

STRATEGY

Routes vary from friendly single-pitch outings to long full-day mountain adventures. Whilst walk-ins are generally quite short, descents can be long and involved, and almost impossible to locate in the dark. Overnight temperatures at 2000m drop nearly to freezing, and all parties setting off on long routes should carry spare clothing, food, head torches, and a survival blanket at the very least. Unplanned bivouacs are neither pleasant, nor uncommon.

Some mobile phone coverage is evident, so it's always worth carrying a phone in your pack in case medical assistance is required, though no organised mountain rescue service exists. A selection of useful numbers can be found on page 5.

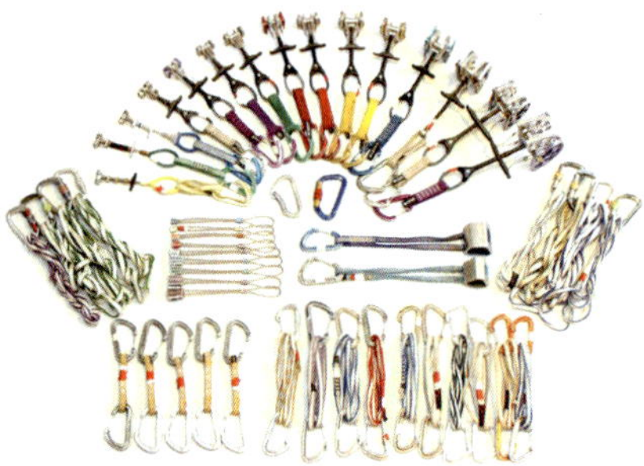

EQUIPMENT

Protection is generally good, and pitches can be quite long, so a comprehensive rack is advisable. In general, the rock is well suited to camming devices, and a full set, with some doubles, will be required on longer routes. A set of nuts and a few hexes will complete a typical Anti-Atlas rack, along with extra slings and a good range of extenders and quickdraws.

ETHICS

Despite it being 20 years since the first British pioneers began to open up the quartzite crags of the Anti-Atlas, Jebel el Kest is still a 'developing' destination. Today, a huge variety of climbing styles, ever-increasing visitor numbers, and the proximity to Tafraout's granite sport crags create the potential for conflicting ethics in the region, particularly given the lack of historical foundation. Quartzite provides an ideal medium for adventurous traditional climbing, with a combination of solid natural protection and challenging un-protectable walls which will provide obvious temptation to bolters.

In recent years a number of bolted lines have appeared on quartzite crags, and although these have predominantly been single pitch cragging venues, alarming reports of a bolted line up the Lion's Face itself hint at a potential conflict in the future. To date, these isolated bolted routes have been established with an apparent disregard for – or lack of knowledge of – the 'local' ethic: in some cases accidentally retro-bolting existing traditional climbs.

Although it is impossible to dictate how people enjoy the natural environment, climbers are strongly encouraged to help maintain the adventure trad ethic in the Anti-Atlas and preserve its unique appeal.

Please do not place bolts on the quartzite of Jebel el Kest or Jebel Taskra, either for protection or anchors.

On the granite tors around Tafraout and Aguerd Oudad, on the other hand, bolting has been the norm since the earliest days of climbing in the region. Climbers placing bolts on the granite are encouraged to bolt responsibly, using modern stainless steel bolts. Power drills are currently acceptable in the area, so there should be no excuse for tiny holes and unsafe bolts. Likewise, if you are going to bolt a route then please bring enough hangers – there has been a trend for stealing hardware from neighbouring routes: a practice that spoils the enjoyment of this area for future visitors.

FIXED ANCHORS

On popular crags a number of shared rappel routes have been equipped with steel cables or chains in order to avoid ever-increasing amounts of nylon 'tat' which is unsightly and does not fare well over the summer in the Saharan Sun. This work has been funded and supported by Climb-Tafraout and the local population.

THE ENVIRONMENT

It goes without saying that all visitors to the Anti-Atlas have a responsibility to preserve the natural landscape, as this magnificent and fragile climbing environment will not last long if we do not respect and look after it. Morocco is a relatively poor, developing Arabic country, and those unfamiliar with such cultures are urged to take heed of advice given in the introductory chapters of this guide. By doing so we will help to preserve the unique appeal of Tafraout's climbing, its stunning landscape, and important relations with the native Berber people for whom these hills have provided an existence for the best part of 3000 years.

- **Respect the customs and religion of the local people.**
- **Do not drop litter, even though there may already be 'local' rubbish lying on the ground.**
- **Please don't leave toilet paper at the foot of the crag. This has become a particular problem at Ksar Rock.**
- **Try not to damage ancient terraces or walk across cultivated land.**
- **Keep noise to a minimum and adopt a 'low-impact' approach at all times.**

ACCESS

Many of the crags described in this guidebook lie within, or are approached via land that is used by the rural Berbers for agriculture. As well as this, several crags overlook settlements and make use of private tracks for access. At the time of publication the local people are very friendly towards climbers, and no access problems have been reported. In order that this remains the case, all climbers are asked to adopt a low-impact approach when climbing near habitation.

NEW ROUTING

There is still scope for new-routing in the mountains around Tafraout, and for those with the relevant skills and experience this can be one of the most enjoyable aspects of a trip to Tafraout. Be warned, however – the quartzite is dangerously loose in places, and there's no one to rescue you if it all goes wrong. Climb within your capabilities, take care out there... And please, no bolts on the quartzite!

If you do climb a new route in the region, please record it in the *Livre d'Escalade* which is kept behind reception in the Hotel Les Amandiers. This fascinating document is the definitive source of route information and makes an interesting read on a rest day in Tafraout. For climbers staying on the north side who do not get a chance to visit Tafraout, a smaller 'book of climbs' has been started at the Kasbah Tizourgane.

Details of routes should also be entered online at www.climb-tafraout.com, or emailed to new-routes@oxfordalpineclub.co.uk for inclusion in future editions of this guidebook.

CLIMB TAFRAOUT **www.climb-tafraout.com**

Area Map
Crag Selector
Intro
The Climbing
How to Use
Suggested Climbs
Tafraout Granite
Anergui
Ameln Valley
Tarakatine Pass
Sidi M'Zal
Jebel Taskra
Idaougnidif
Afantinzar
Samazar
Aouguenz
Tagzene
Tagmout
History
Index

PACKING LIST

Anti-Atlas climbing trips do not require large amounts of gear, and the baggage restrictions of budget airlines are not usually a problem. The following list outlines some things to consider packing…

- ☐ Rack (include spare rap tat)
- ☐ Double ropes (60m recommended)
- ☐ Chalk bag & extra chalk
- ☐ Harness, nut key & belay device
- ☐ Rock shoes
- ☐ Knife
- ☐ Helmet
- ☐ Lightweight climbing pack
- ☐ Emergency bivi
- ☐ 1st Aid Kit, compass & survival blanket
- ☐ Headtorch
- ☐ Sunglasses, sunblock & lip balm
- ☐ Sun hat & bandana
- ☐ Camera & batteries
- ☐ Wash kit
- ☐ Approach shoes
- ☐ Light, tough climbing trousers
- ☐ Spare trousers
- ☐ Socks & underwear
- ☐ Short-sleeved T-shirts
- ☐ Long-sleeved T-shirt
- ☐ Thermal leggings
- ☐ Mid-weight fleece top
- ☐ Softshell / outer fleece
- ☐ Lightweight windproof
- ☐ Light waterproofs
- ☐ Swimming kit (for the aprés-climb...)
- ☐ Beanie & thin gloves
- ☐ Passport & flight details
- ☐ Car hire details / car park details
- ☐ Credit cards (and bank numbers)
- ☐ Cash (Sterling / Euros / Dirham)
- ☐ This guidebook
- ☐ Free downloads from climb-tafraout.com
- ☐ Mobile phone & charger

HOW TO USE THIS GUIDEBOOK

This guidebook covers a large and complicated region, as well as a huge variety of climbing styles and route lengths. As a result, applying a consistent approach to the descriptions has been challenging. The following notes should help you find your way around...

Layout, Maps and Geography.

The climbing has been broken down into 12 distinct chapters corresponding to geographic areas. They are listed in coloured thumb-tabs down the side of each page.

On the first page of each chapter is a 1:50 000 scale approach map, showing the location of the crags in that area. In the header bar at the top of every page is a reference back to the area map page.

A whole-area overview map is included on page 4, showing the relative locations of all of the chapter area maps.

Crag Information Box

Each crag description starts with an information box giving background information and approach details. The following symbols are used to give an overview of the style of crag:

- Sunshine available.
- Shade — Shade available.
- Families — This crag is suitable for families with small children.
- Hitch — This crag can be reached without a car, either by walking, hitching, or cycling.
- Roadside — A roadside crag.

Route Descriptions

The following symbols are used to highlight the character of individual routes:

- WIDE — This route requires big gear (typically size 5 or 6 camming devices).
- CRACK — This route requires crack-climbing techniques such as jamming.
- THIN — This route relies on small wires for protection.
- STEEP — A steep or pumpy climb for its grade, requiring big biceps!
- SLAB — A delicate slab route with some balancy friction moves.
- GEAR — This climb is well-protected and therefore reasonably safe for its grade.

BOLD A bold climb with poor protection or long run-outs... requires a cool head.

CARE! There's danger here, so watch out! This could be due to sharp, rope-cutting edges, unsafe blocks, or big groundfall potential.

ADVENTURE A long adventurous outing for which a sense of humour is advised.

UNCHECKED This route has not been checked or details were unavailable. The line on the topo may be wrong.

PRICKLY Some spiky vegetation might be encountered on this climb.

MOSSY This route can be rather lichenous or mossy and is not advised in wet weather.

LOOSE Friable rock - This will not usually detract from the route for teams with some experience of adventure climbing.

ABSEIL This climb requires an abseil descent, for which equipment may not be in-situ.

On crags where there is a mix of traditionally protected and bolted routes, the following additional symbols are used:

TRAD A traditionally protected climb (only indicated on granite crags).

SPORT A bolt-protected route. This does not always mean that hangers are in place, or that a route is totally safe.

MIXED This route is protected by a mix of bolts and traditional gear.

Topo Symbols

The following symbols are shown on topos:

5m A typical time to approach this sector from the nearest car-parking (in minutes).

This sector usually gets sunshine throughout the day.

AM This sector gets sunshine during the morning / afternoon as indicated.

SHADE This sector is usually in the shade.

Grades

The grading of climbs is always a highly subjective matter, particularly in a region such as the Anti-Atlas where routes have seen so few ascents. Users of this book should therefore treat all of the grades with caution, particularly on the longer mountain routes for which details are often rather vague. In many cases the grades given in this book are those suggested by the first ascent party, who had the added difficulty of uncertainty.

The UK adjectival grading system has been widely adopted in the Anti-Atlas, and a comparison with other systems is shown below.

French sport grades have historically been used on Tafraout's granite crags, and this tradition has been maintained in this edition where appropriate. In more recent years, the American (Yosemite Decimal) system has been used to describe granite routes protected by a mixture of bolts and traditional gear.

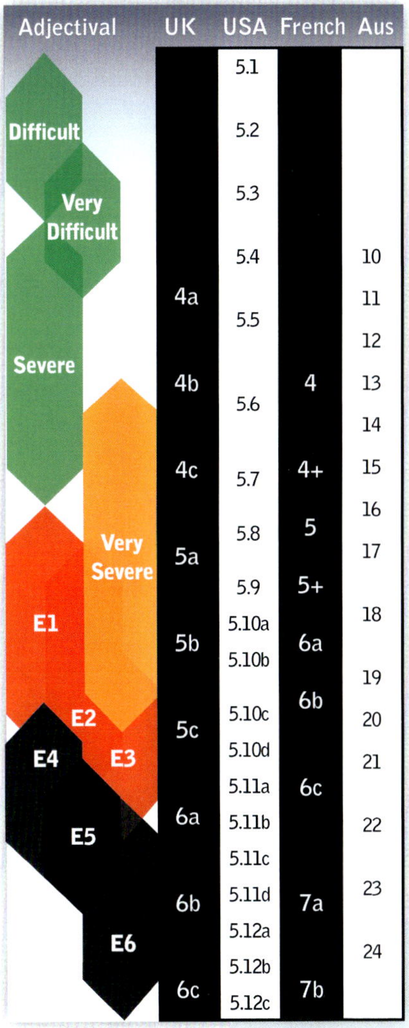

Area Map
Crag Selector
Intro
The Climbing
How to Use
Suggested Climbs
Tafraout Granite
Anergui
Ameln Valley
Tarakatine Pass
Sidi M'Zal
Jebel Taskra
Idaougnidif
Afantinzar
Samazar
Aouguenz
Tagzene
Tagmout
History
Index

Area Map
Crag Selector
Intro
The Climbing
How to Use
Suggested Climbs
Tafraout Granite
Anergui
Ameln Valley
Tarakatine Pass
Sidi M'Zal
Jebel Taskra
Idaougnidif
Afantinzar
Samazar
Aouguenz
Tagzene
Tagmout
History
Index

RECOMMENDED ROUTES

The following lists outline some of the region's best routes, and although it is by no means exhaustive this selection should give first-time visitors a few ideas of where to start:

CLASSIC SINGLE PITCH ROUTES

Route	Grade	Walk-in	Page
Life and Fate	E5 6a	25 min.	171
Magic Carpet Ride	E5 6a	15 min.	371
The Asgaour Crack	E4 6a	40 min.	79
Hello Picasso	E4 6a	5 min.	367
Soul and Romance	E4 5c	25 min.	321
Crackerjack	E3 5c	10 min.	243
Cristal	E3 5b	25 min.	355
Park End	E3 5b	5 min.	255
Honker	E2 5b	30 min.	170
Skyline	E1 5b	30 min.	361
Gritstone Fugitive	E1 5b	5 min.	264
Leaving Las Vegas	E1 5b	60 min.	207
Wall Street	E1 5b	5 min.	148
Cobra Crack	HVS 5b	40 min.	295
Kingpin	HVS 5a	5 min.	273
Black Wall Crack	F5+	15 min.	46
Cirque du Soleil	VS 4c	5 min.	150
Paladin	VS 4b	10 min.	280
Sahara	MVS 4b	5 min.	275
Imhotep	Severe	5 min.	373

SPORT CLIMBS

Route	Grade	Walk-in	Page
El Tocho	F8a+/b	20 min.	53
Morocco Airlines	F7c	15 min.	50
Fender Stratocaster	F6c	10 min.	44
Black Wall	F6b	15 min.	46

ROUTES FOR REST DAYS

Route	Grade	Walk-in	Page
Flake Quake	HVS 4c	10 min.	46
High Sierra	5.7	10 min.	48
Eflodne NW Buttress	5.6	5 min.	51
Freeway	5.4	10 min.	45
SE Ridge Adrar Idekel	–	15 min.	135

MULTI-PITCH CLASSICS

Route	Grade	Walk-in	Page
The Flying Scotsmen	E6 6b	45 min.	160
Adventures Beyond...	E5 6b	25 min.	165
The Orgasmatron	E3 5c	25 min.	165
Voyager	E2 5b	30 min.	191
Firesword	E2 5b	15 min.	314
Great Corner	E1 5b	60 min.	143
Tizgut Crack	E1 5b	35 min.	95
The Golden Compass	E1 5b	60 min.	208
Delirium	E1 5b	20 min.	298
Central Buttress	E1 5b	15 min.	300
The Lion King	HVS 5b	60 min.	206
Crazy Mushrooms...	HVS 5b	15 min.	347
Jungle Book	HVS 5b	25 min.	321
White Tower Direct	HVS 5a	90 min.	107
White Tower Original	HVS 5a	90 min.	106
Spacewalk	HVS 5a	70 min.	277
Multiple Pillars of...	HVS 5a	15 min.	175
Eagle's Beak	HVS 4c	40 min.	64
Labyrinth Ridge	VS 5a	5 min.	301
Scimitar Ridge	VS 5a	20 min.	323
Central Buttress	VS 4c	15 min.	300
Guillotine Direct	VS 4c	30 min.	191
Pink Lady	VS 4c	20 min.	235
Tower Ridge	VS 4b	30 min.	329
Auld Lang Syne	HS 4c	80 min.	213
Apollo	HS 4b	15 min.	310
Pan's Labyrinth	HS 4b	15 min.	174
Noah's Ark	HS 4b	10 min.	281
Sun Ribbon Arête	HS 4b	10 min.	362
Snakehike	HS 4a	10 min.	334
Pinnacle Ridge	Severe	90 min.	100
Dragon Ridge	Severe	15 min.	310
Igiliz/Agouti Traverse	Severe	5 min.	290
Wild Country	V.Diff	60 min.	196
The Angel's Crest	Difficult	10 min.	66

Katja Broadbent on *Honker* (E2), one of Tafraout's best wide crack pitches, on the Upper West Walls at Tifghelt (page 170). ➲
Photo: Steve Broadbent

Area Map
Crag Selector
Intro
The Climbing
How to Use
Suggested Climbs
Tafraout Granite
Anergui
Ameln Valley
Tarakatine Pass
Sidi M'Zal
Jebel Taskra
Idaougnidif
Afantinzar
Samazar
Aouguenz
Tagzene
Tagmout
History
Index

SUGGESTED CRAGS

A full comparison table of crags is given on page 6, but the following suggestions may be helpful for those looking to plan cragging based on various criteria:

ESCAPE FROM THE HEAT

When it's getting too hot, head for higher crags, or shady north-facing walls. **Azumer Crag** (page 336) is good for some low-grade single pitch, whilst **Icebox Canyon** (page 326), **Dinosaur Wall** (page 144) and the **Sanctuary** (page 229) have some harder offerings. **Tramline Slabs** (page 158) are another good choice, as are many of the crags of the Takoucht Escarpment of Jebel Taskra. For easy multi-pitch, don't miss **Hairpin Slabs** (page 334), whilst **Griffin Rock** (page 242) is a good bet for harder single pitch routes.

Although it's fairly low-lying, **Akaltine Crag** (page 350) stays in the shade for most of the day, and is a good option for short steep routes. On the south side, **Black Crag** (page 74) tends to stay shady, and the short routes on the **Tarakatine Pass** (page 118) are usually manageable. Also, don't miss the 3-pitch roadside *NW Buttress* of **Eflodne** (page 51).

IN POOR WEATHER

Believe it or not, it can sometimes be cold or wet in the Anti-Atlas, and at these times you'll want to look for low-lying, south-facing crags. **Robin Hood Rocks** (page 354) and **Maid Marion Rocks** (page 372) are famously warm venues that tend to get better weather than most places.

In the Ameln Valley, **Blue Spring Crag** (page 72) and **Palm Tree Gorge** (page 86) are good options, whilst the eastern edges of **Tizi Gzaouine Crag** (page 146) and **Tizi Gzaouine Gorge** (page 151) have saved many a wet day.

Granite bouldering is also a viable option, and numerous easy circuits are described in the granite chapter of this guide.

MULTI-PITCH CRAGGING

For roadside routes, don't miss **Ksar Rock** (page 268) in Afantinzar, and **Dragon Rock** (page 308) in Samazar. For some more remote climbing, head to **Adrar Umlil** (page 200).

Negotiating the crux overlap on *The Asgaour Crack* (E4) – Steve Broadbent climbing. (page 79).

Photo: Katja Broadbent

SINGLE PITCH VENUES

For easily-accessible single pitch venues, check out **Anammer Crags** (page 248), or for something a little harder then **Griffin Rock** (page 242) is a good option. **Robin Hood** (page 354) is home to some of the area's best single and short multi-pitch lines, whilst **Tizi Gzaouine** (page 146) and **Palm Tree Gorge** (page 86) are other popular venues.

LONGER ADVENTURES

The Anti-Atlas are home to numerous classic mountain adventures, of which the following are particularly recommended: Jebel el Kest via the *Angel's Crest* (Difficult / Severe, page 66), *Pinnacle Ridge* on Prophet Peak (Severe, page 100), *Sun Ribbon Arête* (HS, page 362), *Tower Ridge* on Afantztgult (VS, page 328), *Scimitar Ridge* on Safinah (VS, page 323), *Labyrinth Ridge* on Aylim (VS, page 301), and *Central Buttress* on Aylim (VS or E1, page 300).

CRAGS FOR FAMILIES

Tafraout is a brilliant place to take the kids, and there are some excellent child-friendly venues that are particularly suitable for picnics and little ones...

Crag	Page
Aguerd Slabs	54
Elephant Rock Bouldering	55
2nd Tor Bouldering	56
3rd Tor Bouldering	57
Anergui Playground	59
Palm Tree Gorge	86
Tizi Gzaouine Crag	146
Tizi Gzaouine Gorge	151
Tassila Bastion	184
Griffin Rock	242
Anammer Crags	248
Azumer Crag	336
Tagzene Gorge	342
Akaltine Edge	350
Maid Marion Rocks	372

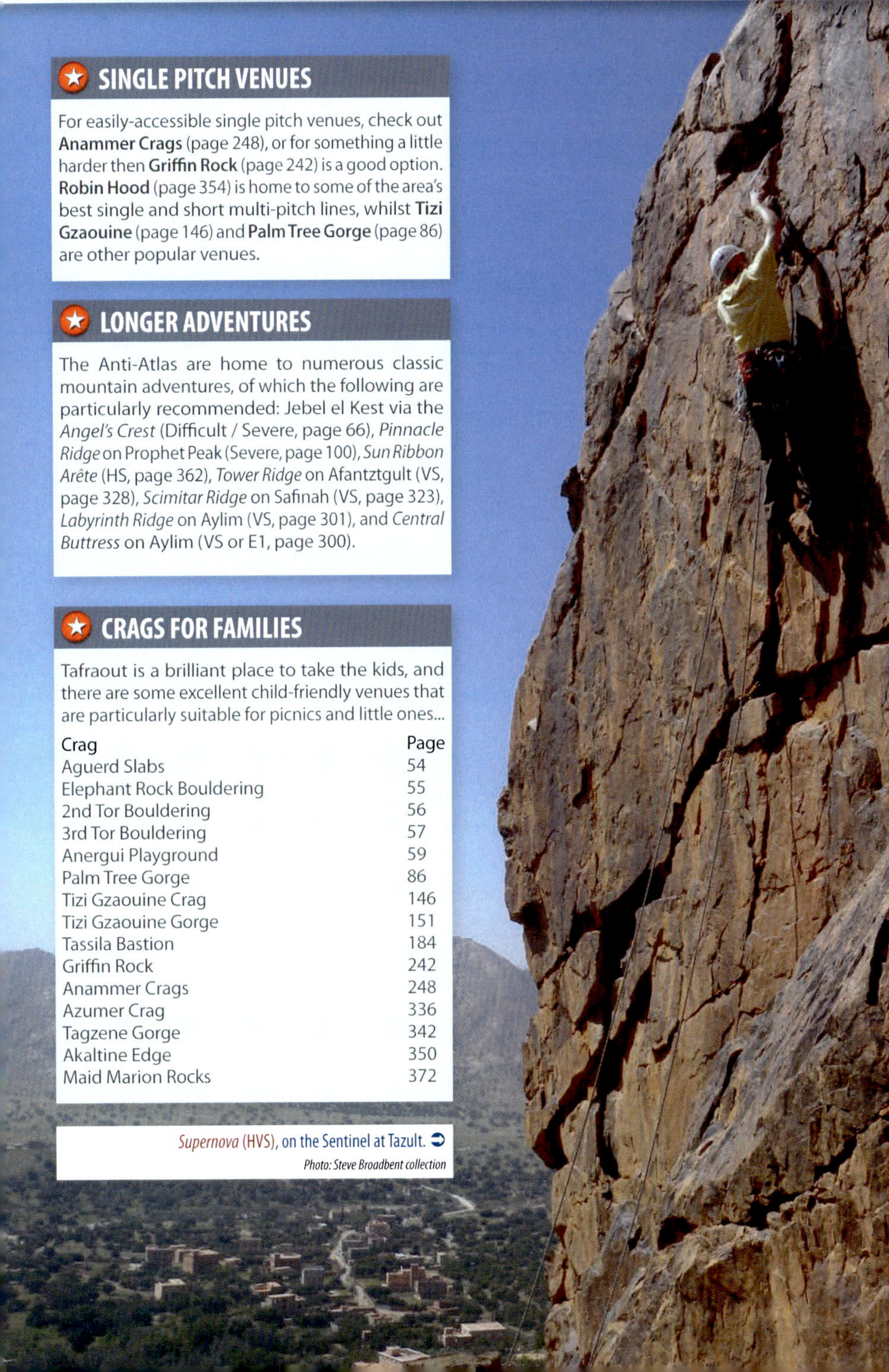

Supernova (HVS), on the Sentinel at Tazult. ➲

Photo: Steve Broadbent collection

Area Map
Crag Selector
Intro
The Climbing
How to Use
Suggested Climbs
Tafraout Granite
Anergui
Ameln Valley
Tarakatine Pass
Sidi M'Zal
Jebel Taskra
Idaougnidif
Afantinzar
Samazar
Aouguenz
Tagzene
Tagmout
History
Index

OTHER THINGS TO DO

When it's too wet to climb, or you fancy a break from climbing then why not...

Go for a walk or scramble

There is endless potential for hiking in the Anti-Atlas, and although the description of specific walks is beyond the scope of this guide, the following are recommended:

1) **Adrar Idekel** – described on page 135, the ascent of Adrar Idekel is an excellent way to spend a wet day, featuring some fun scrambling on good rock.

2) **The Tizgut Ridge** – the rocky crest above Tizgut provides a good scramble. See map on page 70.

3) **Adrar Afa N'Tzek** – there is a nice scramble up the north (Tanfit) ridge, shown on the OAC Jebel el Kest Adventure Map (grid 2615).

4) **Jebel el Kest** – an ascent of this 2375m summit is highly recommended, affording excellent panoramic views. Ascents from Tagdicht and Anergui are covered by the OAC Jebel el Kest Adventure Map, available online or at Maison Troc in Tafraout.

Visit the Painted Rocks

The Painted Rocks are perhaps the most famous element of Tafraout's granite landscape. They were coloured in 1984 by Belgian artisit Jean Verame with the help of the Tafraout fire brigade and 18 tonnes of blue, pink, red, and black paint. This peculiar and controversial work of art is still both marvelled at, questioned, and deplored today despite significant weathering over time. A project was undertaken in 2012 to re-paint the rocks and restore them to their former glory. The rocks are located about 7km south of Tafraout, and can be reached either by car via the R107, or on foot or bike via Blue Rocks Valley from Aguerd Oudad. See map on page 42.

Visit some traditional Berber villages

There is a wealth of fascinating culture around Tafraout and the Ameln Valley. Traditional Berber homes are open to visitors in the villages of Oumsnat (Ameln Valley, map page 68) and Tazga (map page 42).

Stroll around the Souq

The busy market (*souq*) is the very heart of Tafraout, selling everything from traditional Berber slippers (*Babouche*) to a wide range of herbs and spices. There are many bargains to be had amongst the dozens of shops, so it's a perfect place to head if you're looking for gifts to take home. It's also a great stop-off if you're in the business of Voodoo dolls...

Buy a carpet

Pay a visit to Maison Troc on the Aguerd Oudad road and learn all about the Berbers' most famous export.

Hire a bike

There is a cycle hire shop on the Aguerd Oudad road, opposite Restaurant La Kasbah. The semi-desert backcountry to the south of Tafraout is an excellent landscape to explore on two-wheels, whilst more determined cyclists may wish to visit the impressive Ait Mansour Gorge, some 25km south of town. Maps are available from www.climb-tafraout.com or Maison Troc in Tafraout.

Go bouldering

Four bouldering circuits are included in the granite chapter of this guide, providing some fun bouldering within easy reach of Tafraout.

OTHER PLACES TO CLIMB

There are several other excellent climbing venues in Morocco, which can be combined with a visit to Tafraout:

Todra

This historically popular limestone gorge features a good variety of single- and multi-pitch sport routes in a very impressive setting. It is located on the south side of the Atlas Mountains near Tinghir, approximately 8 hours drive from Tafraout. More information online at www.climb-todra.com, or in the OAC Todra Topo, available for purchase on the OAC website: www.oxfordalpineclub.co.uk

Taghia

Morocco's premier limestone big-wall venue, with routes reaching 600-800m in height, mostly in the upper grades. See www.christian-ravier.com/sites/taghia_topo.html for more information.

The High Atlas

Many superb mountaineering opportunities exist in the Atlas Mountains, from easy walks through to winter mountaineering routes and technical ice climbs. The Toubkal Massif is the main centre, shown on the OAC Toubkal & Oukaimeden Adventure map. See www.toubkalmap.com

Johnny Dawes on *Rumpus* (E4), at the 2nd Tor in Aguerd Oudad's Blue Rock's Valley. ➲

Photo: Steve Broadbent

Map Page 43

Area Map
Crag Selector
Intro
The Climbing
How to Use
Suggested Climbs
Tafraout Granite
Anergui
Ameln Valley
Tarakatine Pass
Sidi M'Zal
Jebel Taskra
Idaougnidif
Afantinzar
Samazar
Aouguenz
Tagzene
Tagmout
History
Index

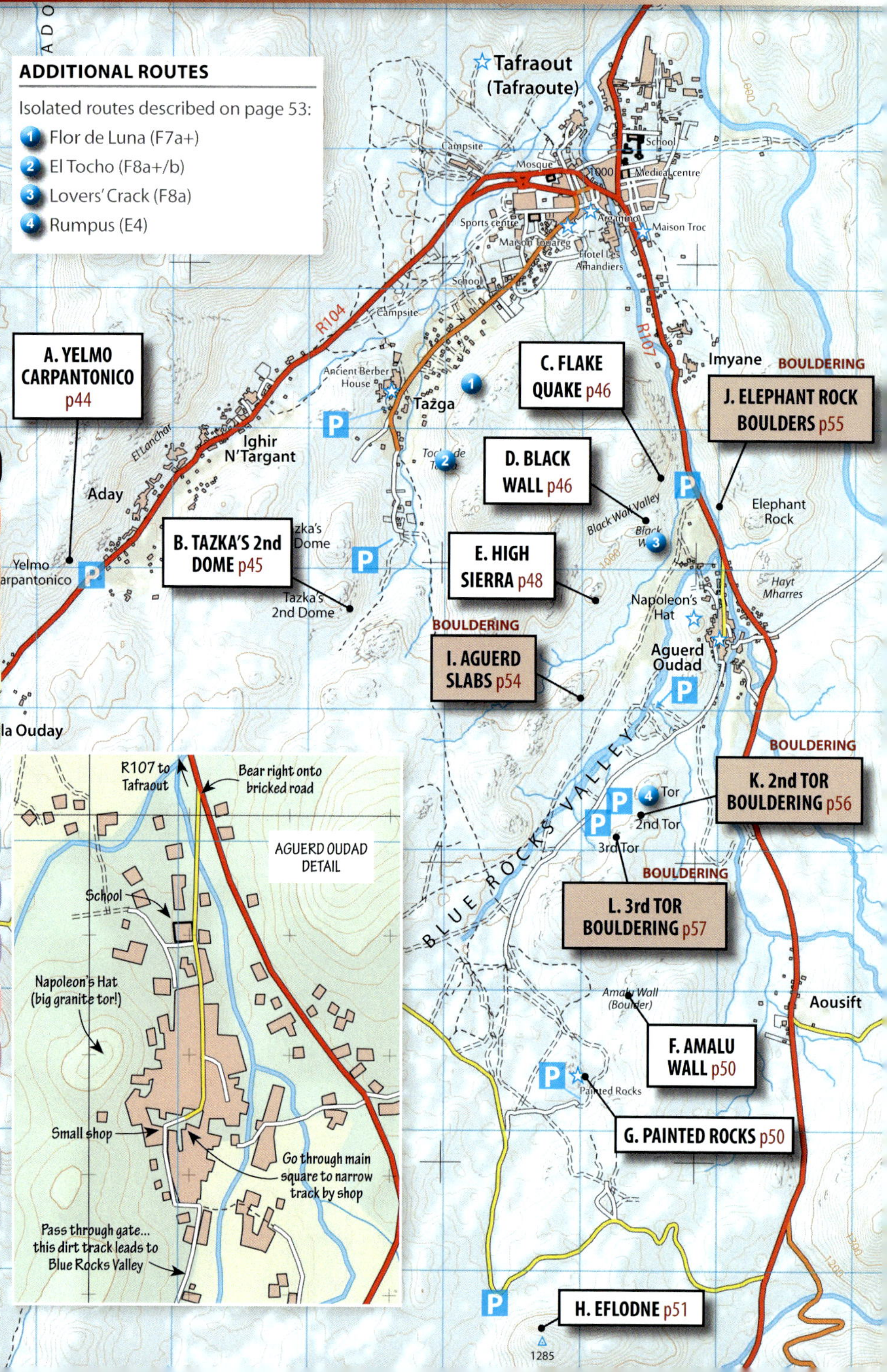

GRANITE

The stunning granite landscape around Tafraout came under the scrutiny of climbers as early as 1962 and has seen sporadic development ever since. In 1987, Dennis Gray's comparison of Tafraout to Joshua Tree or Hampi fired the oasis into the limelight, sparking new interest from European sport-climbers, and almost certainly planting the seeds for the development of the quartzite in the early nineties.

Whilst British teams concentrated their efforts on the mountain crags of Jebel el Kest, climbers from Spain, France and Italy were enjoying an altogether more 'relaxed' adventure on the spectacular tors closer to town, creating an eclectic mix of sport routes, esoteric trad climbs, and crumbly-death horror shows, as well as some excellent top-grade climbing.

In more recent times, a number of excellent low-grade multi-pitch granite adventures have been established, and routes such as *Freeway*, *Flake Quake* and *High Sierra* now provide fun, low-commitment 'rest day' activities that will suit even the most ardent quartzite and trad fanatics. Likewise, a handful of easy bouldering circuits provide worthwhile sport for an evening or short day.

Unfortunately, the granite here is extremely coarse-grained, sees little weathering, and suffers from relentless exfoliation in the searing summer heat. This has, in some places, created loose, crumbly rock that most climbers will not enjoy. As such, Tafraout granite climbing did develop something of a bad reputation, but whilst it is true that there are some very crumbly routes here, isolated pockets of good rock present the opportunity for some brilliant climbing, and the pitches included in this chapter are all worth seeking out. In fact, it is fair to say that those who pass through Tafraout and *don't* climb on the granite, at least once, are missing out on one of the town's 'experiences'!

All of the granite climbing and bouldering can be reached easily by car or on foot from Tafraout, and is generally located very close to the road.

TO BOLT OR NOT TO BOLT?

Patchy attempts to develop Tafraout as a sport climbing destination have left the granite tors around town with a bewildering smattering of bolted lines amongst perfectly protectable crack climbs. This is in part due to the crumbly nature of the granite here, as whilst individual routes can be of very high quality, it is rare to find a whole crag worth developing. In this guide we have attempted to pick out a representative selection of what is available.

Today, the local ethic is that bolts are acceptable on the granite in order to create worthwhile routes. With so much high quality 'adventure climbing' available on the quartzite, the granite experience is all about accessibility, and whether it's on hard single pitch test-pieces, or easy multi-pitch romps, bolts can add a lot to that experience.

In order to give a better idea of the style of routes, the following symbols are used throughout this chapter to indicate the required protection:

SPORT The route is predominantly bolted. That said, this is not a sport climbing destination, so please treat with caution!

TRAD The route requires a traditional rack of nuts and cams for protection and belays.

MIXED The route has bolted sections but will require traditional protection to supplement.

Area Map
Crag Selector
Intro
The Climbing
How to Use
Suggested Climbs
Tafraout Granite
Anergui
Ameln Valley
Tarakatine Pass
Sidi M'Zal
Jebel Taskra
Idaougnidif
Afantinzar
Samazar
Aouguenz
Tagzene
Tagmout
History
Index

A YELMO CARPANTONICO

Shade · Families · Hitch · Roadside

Drive from Tafraout: **5 minutes**
Walk-in: **10 minutes**

An impressive slab, just to the south of Aday, offering some of the best and most popular sport routes in Tafraout. The slab faces southeast and gets lots of sunshine during the morning, when it can feel rather scorching. Approach easily in about 10 minutes from roadside parking at the south end of the village.

1. Condemor F5+
CRACK · TRAD

The diagonal crack at the left side of the short wall.
Miguel Ángel Lozano & Juan Luis Monge, 1996.

2. Kie-13 F6c+ ★
SLAB · SPORT

Very nice climbing up the wall to the right of the diagonal crack.
Miguel Ángel Lozano & Juan Luis Monge, 1996.

3. Salan Pradery F7a ★
SLAB · SPORT

Tricky slab climbing on excellent rock.
Miguel Ángel Lozano & Juan Luis Monge, 1997.

4. Detrás del Chador F6b+ ★
SLAB · MIXED

Two pitches up the slab, starting just right of the palm tree and gradually easing towards the top.
Miguel Ángel Lozano & Juan Luis Monge, 1996.

James Kniffen on the popular slab of *Fender Stratocaster* (6c).
Photo: Jeremy Jones

5. La Pestañi me Enniqueló F6c+ ★
SPORT

A challenging little pitch up sandy crimps.
Miguel Ángel Lozano & Juan Luis Monge, 1997.

6. Fender Stratocaster F6c ★
SLAB · SPORT

The right-hand line is a very worthwhile and frequently attempted climb on good crimps.
Miguel Ángel Lozano & Juan Luis Monge, 1997.

Yelmo Carpantónico
AM · 10m

Photo: Marco Marrosu

B TAZKA'S 2nd DOME

Shade Families Hitch Roadside Drive from Tafraout: **5 minutes** Walk-in: **10 minutes**

Tazka's Second Dome is a magnificent little viewpoint, worth a visit on a short day. The parking area is reached in five minutes from Tafraout, and the walk-in and descent are similarly short.

Take the left fork in Tazga village and continue as the track deteriorates. Soon it makes a sharp left turn just after a large compound on the left. Ample parking is available on the right. From the parking, follow a rough track in a southwesterly direction, crossing on to the south side of the stream bed. The crag is located on the right-hand side a short distance beyond.

DESCENT: Head up right over the fine little summit, then descend the northeast ridge a short way until it is possible to scramble down on the left (north) side of the ridge. From easy slopes below, a path bears right back towards the parking area. Since the descent comes out close to the parking, it is advisable not to leave anything at the base of the route.

1. Freeway 5.4 ★2 SLAB SPORT

125m. Enjoyable easy padding up the left side of the south face, with fine views from the summit, particularly at sunset. Too easy to be called a sport route, *Freeway* is best described as an easy multi-pitch route with bolts: great for rest days, kids and bimbles! The route and belays are fully equipped, requiring 10 quickdraws.
1) 40m (5.4) Start close to the arête at the left side of the dome. A few tricky slab moves gain easier ground, then an easy traverse leads up rightward to a belay.
2) 45m (5.4) Runout padding up bobbly granite. Belay at the right side of a cave.
3) 30m (5.3) Walk up right then mantel up the steep left wall. Walk up, then to the right, to finish up the final bolted slab. Descend by continuing up over the summit and down the northeast ridge.
Steve Broadbent & Anna Piotrowski, October 2013

2. Shardana E2 5b ★1 SLAB TRAD

110m. Good climbing up the tempting seams right of *Freeway*.
1) 30m (5b) Climb up and traverse right with difficulty to gain the obvious crack.
2) 50m (5a) Follow the diagonal crack to gain the easy slab beneath the roof. Follow this to belay under the roof.
3) 30m (4c) Avoid the roof on the right-hand side then continue up the shallow corner above to the summit.
Marco Marrosu & Francesco Ruiu, April 2015

3. Bees Attack VS 4c ★1 SLAB TRAD

130m. Follows more broken ground to the right of the main slabs, providing a good adventure at this grade.
1) 45m (4c) Climb slabs to gain a belay just left of a large jutting block overhang.
2) 35m (4b) Move up right behind the block and climb up left of the corner to a belay by a bush.
3) 50m (4c) Continue up slabs to gain a final corner, which leads to the summit ridge.
Marco Marrosu & Francesco Ruiu, April 2015

Area Map
Crag Selector
Intro
The Climbing
How to Use
Suggested Climbs
Tafraout Granite
Anergui
Ameln Valley
Tarakatine Pass
Sidi M'Zal
Jebel Taskra
Idaougnidif
Afantinzar
Samazar
Aouguenz
Tagzene
Tagmout
History
Index

C FLAKE QUAKE

Shade Families Hitch Roadside
Drive from Tafraout: **5 minutes**
Walk-in: **10 minutes**

Driving south from Tafraout the narrow valley opens out just before reaching the village of Aguerd Oudad. The following route climbs a prominent series of curved flakes on the south-facing hillside on the right (west) side of the road at this point. It is approached easily from roadside parking in approximately 10 minutes.

1. Flake Quake HVS 4c ★2

BOLD WIDE

95m. The two tempting flake corners provide a fun wide-crack adventure up the south-facing slabs, walkable from Tafraout and highly recommended. Some hollow rock requires care but does not detract from this very popular climb. Big cams helpful.

1) 30m (4b) The lower flake crack is a good warm-up for antics higher up. Exit left to a good ledge.

2) 10m (4b) Scramble up to beneath the wide corner crack, which gives an excellent pitch. Walk up 50m, then scramble up to the base of the imposing right-facing corner.

3) 25m (4c) Layback the corner with increasing difficulty. Pull left into the groove at the top and bridge up to a wobbly belay on the chockstone above the sandy crevasse!

4) 30m (4c) Continue left and make a tricky move into the continuation groove. This is easier than it looks, and leads to a fine finish.

Steve Broadbent & Sarah Pemberton, November 2012

D BLACK WALL

Shade Families Hitch Roadside
Drive from Tafraout: **5 minutes**
Walk-in: **15 minutes**

The Black Wall has long been Tafraout's most popular sport climbing venue, thanks to a selection of good mid-grade routes and the fact that it stays in the shade for much of the day. Abseil anchors have recently been re-equipped with 10mm stainless anchors, making this a much less serious venue than in the past.

Two approaches are possible, both starting from roadside parking on the Aguerd Oudad road beneath *Flake Quake*. Walk southwest along a dry riverbed beneath Flake Quake, then turn right up a boulder-choked valley (awkward) to reach the crag on the left. A longer but technically simpler approach can be made by continuing along the dry river bed beneath a rock wall on the right (*Lover's Crack*), then cutting back up rightwards to gain the shoulder on the east side of the crag.

THE BLACK WALL

1. Luces del Desierto F6b — UNCHECKED CRACK TRAD

A short hand to finger crack on the southeast face.

2. Black Wall Arête F5 — ABSEIL MIXED

35m. Start around the corner on the left, then follow the left-most bolted line on the northwest face.

3. Unnamed F5 ★1 — ABSEIL MIXED

35m. Good climbing up the crack and bolted wall above.

4. The Black Wall F6b ★3 — ABSEIL SPORT

35m. The centre of the black wall is a local classic, and one of Tafraout's must-do routes, weighing in at about E2 5c. The direct start has now been bolted, and the climb is equipped for a convenient abseil descent.

5. Black Wall Crack F5+ ★3 — ABSEIL CRACK MIXED

35m. The prominent hand-to-fist crack gives a first class pitch, and one of the best granite cracks in the region. Start with difficulty, following the crack to vegetation. Step left here onto the exposed face for a fluttery, bolted finale. Tricky HVS 5b for the discerning trad climber.

6. Unnamed F6a+ ★1 — ABSEIL SPORT

35m. A good but intimidating climb, with some dirt and the odd run-out. The crux is at the third bolt.

7. Unnamed F5 — ABSEIL MOSSY CRACK TRAD

35m. The cracks to the right are rather traditional.

8. Danza Kuduro F5 ★

ABSEIL SPORT

35m. A good, varied climb that is fully protected with modern 10mm bolts. Start left of the argan trees and go up to a huge flake. Climb up the left side of this, then step right to a bold slabby finish.

Steve & Katja Broadbent, December 2016.

9. Unnamed F6a

ABSEIL MIXED

35m. Start up a crack between the two argan trees, then follow the somewhat scary line of bolts on the left.

10. Unnamed F6a ★

ABSEIL MIXED

35m. The right-hand crack behind the argan tree leads to a bolted slab.

11. Unnamed F6b+ ★

ABSEIL SPORT

35m. A delicate and crimpy start right of the flake leads to a horizontal break. Easier climbing above to finish as for the previous two routes.

12. Unnamed F5

ABSEIL MIXED

This short route is located on the northwest face, up a layback crack (one bolt) to a lower-off.

TRANSAHARANIA

This is a huge boulder with an ancient shelter at its base, located on the opposite side of Black Wall Valley. It holds a single, excellent route:

13. Transaharania E4 6a ★

ABSEIL CRACK TRAD

A beautiful hands and layback crack, accessed via a tricky overhanging start.

Palan Martin, 2003.

Area Map
Crag Selector
Intro
The Climbing
How to Use
Suggested Climbs
Tafraout Granite
Anergui
Ameln Valley
Tarakatine Pass
Sidi M'Zal
Jebel Taskra
Idaougnidif
Afantinzar
Samazar
Aouguenz
Tagzene
Tagmout
History
Index

Area Map
Crag Selector
Intro
The Climbing
How to Use
Suggested Climbs
Tafraout Granite
Anergui
Ameln Valley
Tarakatine Pass
Sidi M'Zal
Jebel Taskra
Idaougnidif
Afantinzar
Samazar
Aouguenz
Tagzene
History
Index

E HIGH SIERRA

Shade · Families · Hitch · Roadside

Drive from Tafraout: **10 minutes**
Walk-in: **10 minutes**

This slabby granite tor is located due west of Napoleon's hat, midway between the Black Wall and the Aguerd Slabs. It is possible to scramble up to the summit plateau round the back left side, or more directly from the front right, although the summit block itself can only be reached by climbing.

The shortest approach is from parking as for the Aguerd Slabs. Turn off the R107 into Aguerd Oudad, following the brick road through the centre of the village and leaving the main square via the small track next to the shop, as shown on the map on page 42. Follow this track out of the village, passing a gate and on into Blue Rocks Valley. Just before the first wadi crossing a smaller track turns off on the right. Follow this and park at its end, next to a large sandy wadi. The tor is visible approximately 1km to the northwest.

1. Southwest Corner Moderate SLAB TRAD

120m. This straightforward climb follows blocks and then a slabby corner/groove up the southwest front of the tor.

2. High Sierra 5.7 ★3 SLAB MIXED

120m. The obvious line up the huge flake gives a fun climb with great variety and is a classic of its type. The route is partially bolted, but requires a set of medium to large cams for pitch 2. Start by scrambling in from the left side to gain a gearing up area beneath a large block right of a prominent pinnacle.

1) 30m (5.7) Climb a short blocky groove on the right to gain a left-slanting ramp along the top of the large block. Follow this up left to the arête, where a difficult move (crux) gains the slab above. Follow this more easily to a belay.

2) 30m (5.6) Move left and climb the excellent rising undercut flake, protected by medium to large cams. Belay on natural gear at a block.

3) 45m (5.4) Climb the slab past a single bolt to regain the monster flake. Follow this to where it bends horizontally right, then step up left (bolt) and trend up left to a belay.

4) 15m (5.6) Walk up round the left side of the summit block to climb a bolted pitch up its northwest side.

Andi Turner making the most of *Transaharania* (E4 6a) as storm clouds threaten the quartzite of Jebel el Kest. ➲
Photo: Pete Wilson

DESCENT: *High Sierra* is equipped for a 3-pitch abseil descent from bolted anchors. Alternatively it is possible to walk off the back left side.

Catherine Kenyon on the irresistible *Azules de Vergara* (HVS 5a) at the Painted Rocks.
Photo: Ron Kenyon

F AMALU WALL

Drive from Tafraout: **15 minutes**
Walk-in: **15 minutes**

This irresistible shady wall is reached in about 15 minutes from the Painted Rocks, and is home to a trio of desperate routes on tiny crimps and nonexistent rugosities...

1. Living Like Shadows F7a ★2 SPORT

15m. The left-hand line gives some tremendous climbing, avoiding the arête until near the top.
Palan & Talo Martin, Kathi Urch, 2007

2. Ninja Berber F7b ★2 SPORT

15m. Desperate crimping up the 'slab', with a high crux.
Talo & Palan Martin, Kathi Urch, 2007

3. Morocco Airlines F7c ★2 SPORT

15m. One of Tafraout's best sport climbs, taking a thin line of invisible crimps to a shared lower-off.
Palan & Talo Martin, Kathi Urch, 2007

G PAINTED ROCKS

Drive from Tafraout: **15 minutes**
Walk-in: **2 minutes**

Painted in 1984 by Belgian artist Jean Veramme, Tafraout's painted rocks have always been a popular bohemian hang-out and continue to attract all sorts of visitors, who mostly wander around wondering why Veramme painted them in the first place. Today's paint scheme is not the original one, but is just as intriguing, and just as slippery to climb on.

A single climb is worthy of attention, but the rocks are a very popular and worthwhile 'rest-day' venue, with almost no walk-in.

1. Azules de Vergara HVS 5a ★1 CRACK TRAD

25m. The striking crack up the main blue 'boulder' is a local classic. Once bolted, it now provides a very slippery but well-protected trad climb that sees many ascents.

H EFLODNE

Drive from Tafraout: **10 minutes**
Walk-in: **5 minutes**

The super little summit of Eflodne (marked as spot height 1285m on the MiniMap series) is located approximately 2km south of the Painted Rocks. Comprised of the best granite in the region, its north face stays in the shade for most of the day and is approached easily in a matter of minutes from the road to the Painted Rocks. The summit itself gives one of the best viewpoints Tafraout has to offer, and an ascent is highly recommended – as well as the climbs on the north face there is an easy walk up the left (east) side, and an attractive scramble up to the right of NW Buttress.

DESCENT: It is possible to descend easily on foot down the east flank (climber's left), or by scrambling down the west side. Alternatively, a 3-pitch abseil down the line of NW Buttress is fully equipped.

1. Unnamed F5

60m. A line of bolts up the attractive shady slab to gain the mid-height tree belay.

2. Road 96 F5

130m. Follow bolts leftwards up the slab to gain a groove to the tree. Continue up the upper slab to the summit.
Oliver Guenay, 2007

3. Unnamed F6a+

60m. The slab, gaining the tree from the right side.
Oliver Guenay, 2007

4. Pai Mu Tan F6a

60m. Start up a shallow groove, then continue boldly up the slab to steep moves up to the tree belay.
Oliver Guenay, 2007

5. Northwest Buttress 5.6 ★★

115m. An excellent little climb on some of the best rock in the area. The climbing is mostly very straightforward and the route is fully bolted. At the right side of the north face is a short, steep wall. Start in a bay immediately right of this.
1) 33m (5.6) Climb easily leftwards to a weakness in the overhang. Pull through this on large flakes to gain the slab above. Friction up this to a spacious belay ledge.
2) 35m (5.4) Walk left along the ledge, then go up easy ground to a short steep section to a belay at the right side of another large ledge.
3) 47m (5.6) Step right and pad easily up leftwards to a tricky section of friction climbing left of a tiny groove. Continue over easy ground above and climb a broken groove before moving leftwards to a hidden belay in another groove.
Steve Broadbent, Daniyal Mueenuddin & Zoe Bouras, December 2016.

Area Map
Crag Selector
Intro
The Climbing
How to Use
Suggested Climbs
Tafraout Granite
Anergui
Ameln Valley
Tarakatine Pass
Sidi M'Zal
Jebel Taskra
Idaougnidif
Afantinzar
Samazar
Aouguenz
Tagzene
Tagmout
History
Index

The Black Wall (F6b) near Aguerd Oudad is one of Tafraout's best and most popular bolted routes, giving a long technical pitch on perfect granite. Andi Turner, belayed by Bob Thomas.
Photo: Pete Wilson

ADDITIONAL ROUTES

Shade Families Hitch Roadside Drive from Tafraout: **5 to 10 mins.** Walk-in: **5 to 20 minutes**

The following climbs don't really belong to any crag as such, but are isolated gems, scattered around the Tafraout back-country and well worth seeking out. Locations are shown on the map on page 43.

FLOR DE LUNA

This overhanging wall is clearly seen on the hillside above the road before reaching the village of Tazka.

1. Flor de Luna F7a+ ★3 CRACK TRAD

Big fists and pumpy laybacking up the perfect right-facing dihedral, giving one of the best climbs of its type in Tafraout.

TOCHO DE TAZKA

This super little pinnacle is located on the top of the ridge above Tazga.

2. El Balcón de Tazka F7b+ ★3 SPORT

Terrific climbing up the well-positioned steep arête. Superb!

Francisco Blanco, Carlos Ruiz 'Snoopy' & Celso Martínez 'Finuco', 1997.

3. El Tocho F8a+/b ★3 STEEP SPORT

Dani Andrada's masterpiece gives some incredible, steep and pumpy climbing up the shady north-facing wall.

Daniel Andrada, Pedro Pons, Ruth Planells & Nuria Martín, 1999.

LOVERS' CRACK

This infamous test-piece is located on the right, just beyond the entrance to Black Wall Valley.

4. Lovers' Crack F8a ★3 CRACK MIXED

The crack up the centre of the wall is one of Tafraout's best and hardest granite cracks. Powerful crux moves over the roof lead to slightly easier climbing up the right-hand crack above.

RUMPUS

Located on the small tor just opposite the 2nd Tor bouldering circuit (see page 56).

5. Rumpus E4 5c ★3 WIDE TRAD

12m. The slanting off-width crack in the blocks at the top of the slab gives a tremendous full-body experience, and one of the best E4s in Tafraout.

Johnny Dawes & Steve Broadbent, March 2012.

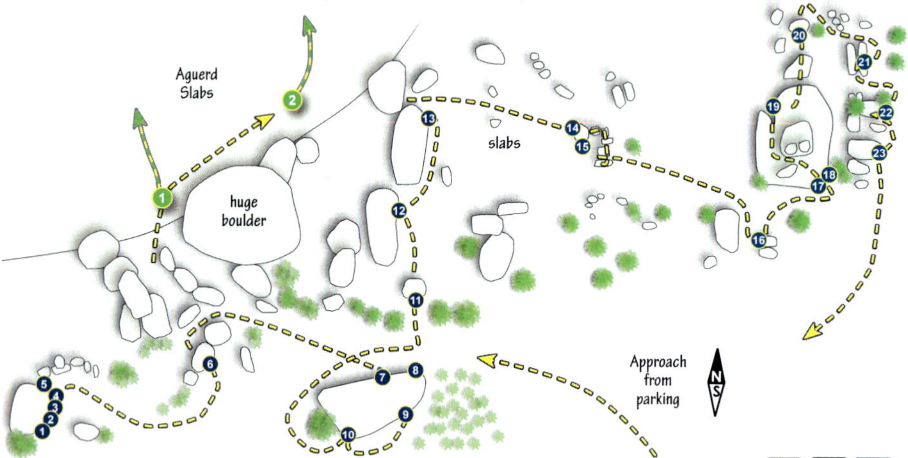

AGUERD SLABS BOULDERING

Shade · Families · Hitch · Roadside

Drive from Tafraout: **10 minutes**
Walk-in: **10 minutes**

A nice family-friendly circuit with mostly easy problems and a couple of tough cruxes. There are also a handful of very easy routes on the slabs above, suitable for kids. From Tafraout take the road south towards Aguerd Oudad, turning off into the village along a narrow bricked road. Pass through the village square and take a narrow track leaving the 'far left-hand' corner of the square. This track soon makes a sharp right-hand bend and leaves the village at a gate. Take the first small track on the right, just before the main track crosses a small wadi. Park at the end of the drivable track, then walk in a westerly direction towards obvious slabs (about 10 minutes walk)

23 problems between Font 3 and Font 5+.

DESCENT: Descent from the routes can be made by scrambling down either side, or by abseil.

1. Kwazi F3+

SLAB · BOLD · SPORT

60m. Climb the white streak, with a steepening at half height. The top section is very easy indeed.

Steve, Katja & Lydia Broadbent, January 2016.

2. Captain Barnacles F3

SLAB · BOLD · MIXED

85m. A pleasant easy climb up the central corner system. A couple of medium-sized cams may be useful to supplement the spaced bolts.

1) 40m. Follow the corner / flakes to a belay above large perched flakes.

2) 45m. Go up leftwards on very easy ground to the tip of the small overlap above. Surmount this on its left side (cam runner useful) and finish up the slab above.

Steve, Katja & Lydia Broadbent, December 2015.

3. Zuma F3+

SLAB · BOLD · SPORT

63m. The white streak up the centre of the main slab is a fun route for the kids.

1) 31m. Bold but easy climbing up to a belay in a depression.

2) 32m. Continue up the white streak to a single bolt protecting a steeper move up past a hollow flake.

Steve, Katja, Ben & Lydia Broadbent, January 2016.

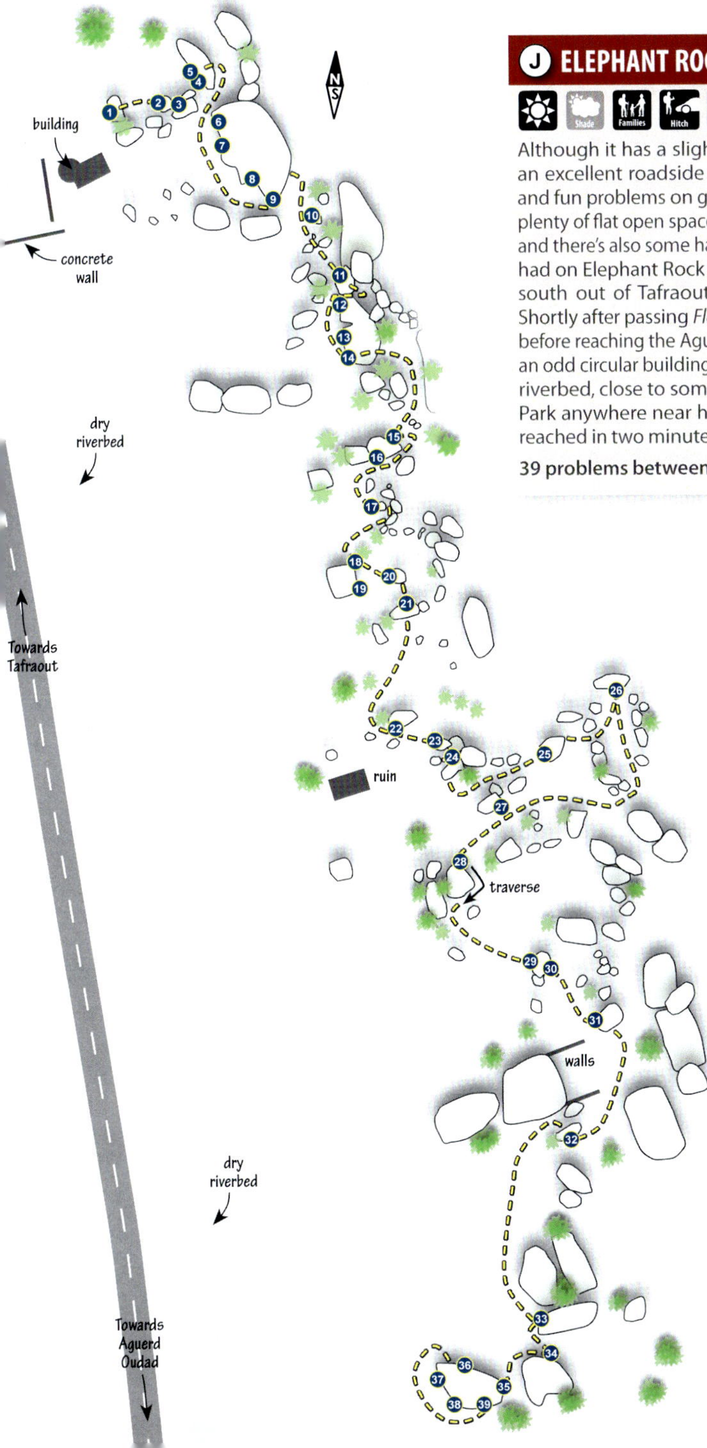

J ELEPHANT ROCK BOULDERING

Shade · Families · Hitch · Roadside

Drive from Tafraout: **10 minutes**
Walk-in: **2 minutes**

Although it has a slightly 'urban' feel to it, this is an excellent roadside circuit, with lots of varied and fun problems on good quality granite. There's plenty of flat open space, making it suitable for kids, and there's also some hard(ish) sport climbing to be had on Elephant Rock itself. Approach by driving south out of Tafraout towards Aguerd Oudad. Shortly after passing *Flake Quake* on the right, and before reaching the Aguerd Oudad turn-off, look for an odd circular building on the opposite side of the riverbed, close to some concrete flood defences. Park anywhere near here, and the problems are reached in two minutes.

39 problems between Font 3 and Font 5+.

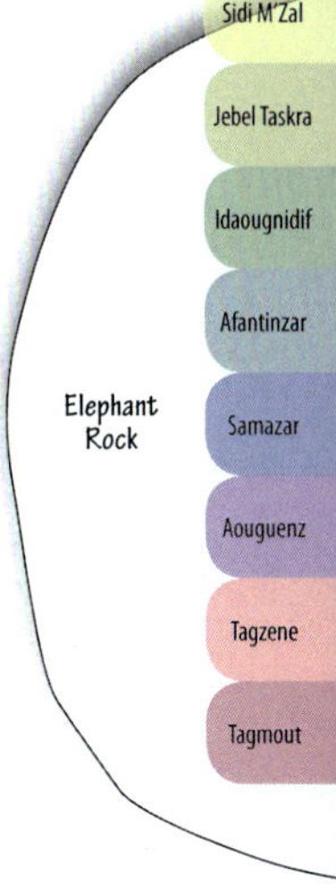

Area Map
Crag Selector
Intro
The Climbing
How to Use
Suggested Climbs
Tafraout Granite
Anergui
Ameln Valley
Tarakatine Pass
Sidi M'Zal
Jebel Taskra
Idaougnidif
Afantinzar
Samazar
Aouguenz
Tagzene
Tagmout
History
Index

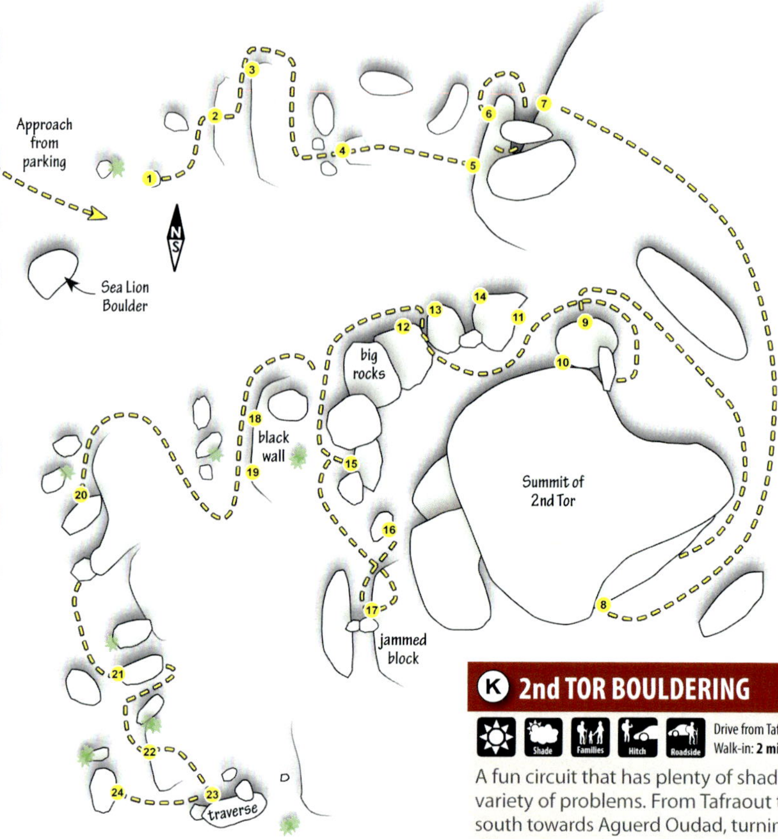

K 2nd TOR BOULDERING

Shade Families Hitch Roadside

Drive from Tafraout: **10 minutes**
Walk-in: **2 minutes**

A fun circuit that has plenty of shade and a good variety of problems. From Tafraout take the road south towards Aguerd Oudad, turning off into the village along a narrow bricked road. Pass through the village square and take a narrow track leaving the 'far left-hand' corner of the square. This track soon makes a sharp right-hand bend and leaves the village at a gate. Continue along Blue Rocks Valley, passing the 1st Tor on the left until a small parking area appears on the left just after the tor.

24 problems between Font 3 and Font 5.

View looking south across Blue Rocks Valley

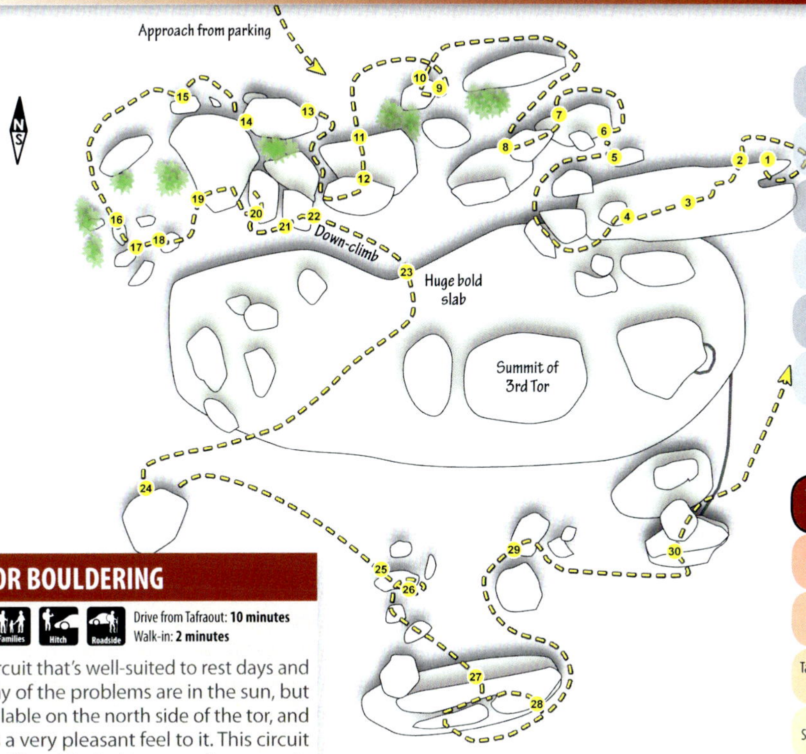

L 3rd TOR BOULDERING

Shade | Families | Hitch | Roadside

Drive from Tafraout: **10 minutes**
Walk-in: **2 minutes**

A popular circuit that's well-suited to rest days and picnics. Many of the problems are in the sun, but shade is available on the north side of the tor, and the area has a very pleasant feel to it. This circuit features lots of fun slab climbing, as well as a couple of very bold highballs.

From Tafraout take the road south towards Aguerd Oudad, turning off into the village along a narrow bricked road. Pass through the village square and take a narrow track leaving the 'far left-hand' corner of the square. This track soon makes a sharp right-hand bend and leaves the village at a gate. Continue along Blue Rocks Valley, passing the 1st Tor on the left until the 2nd and 3rd Tors come into sight. Park anywhere on the left.

30 problems between Font 3 and Font 5.

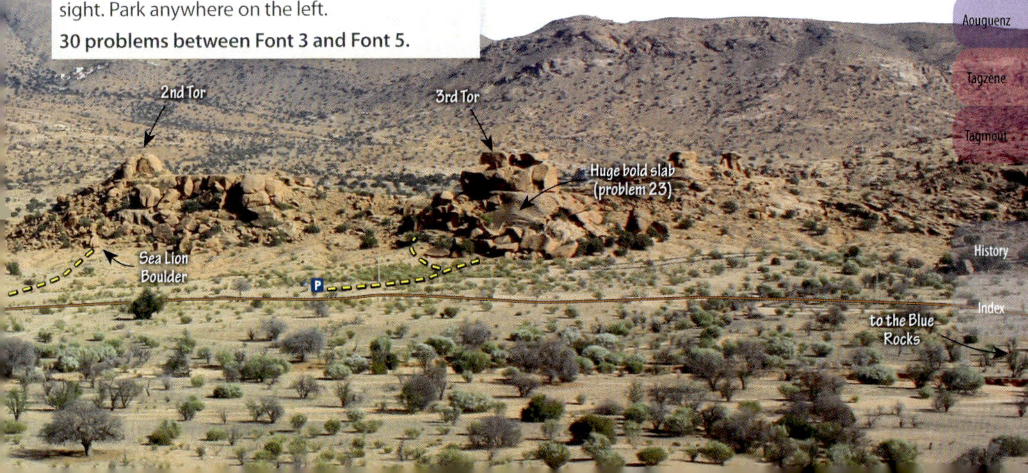

Area Map
Crag Selector
Intro
The Climbing
How to Use
Suggested Climbs
Tafraout Granite
Anergui
Ameln Valley
Tarakatine Pass
Sidi M'Zal
Jebel Taskra
Idaougnidif
Afantinzar
Samazar
Aouguenz
Tagzene
Tagmout
History
Index

Map Page 59

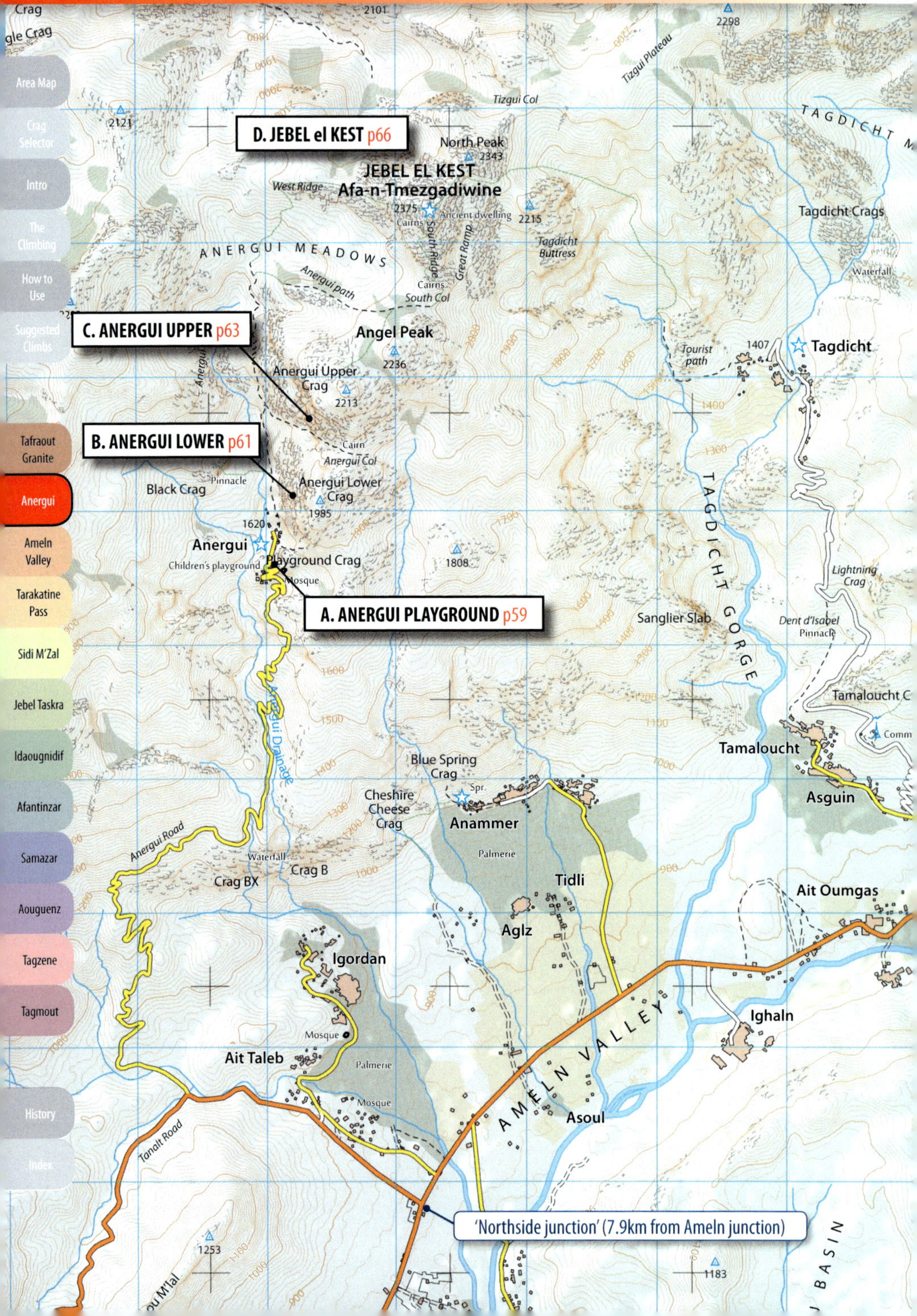
D. JEBEL el KEST p66
C. ANERGUI UPPER p63
B. ANERGUI LOWER p61
A. ANERGUI PLAYGROUND p59
'Northside junction' (7.9km from Ameln junction)
JEBEL EL KEST
Afa-n-Tmezgadiwine
North Peak
2343
West Ridge
2375
Ancient dwelling
2215
Cairns
South Ridge
Great Ramp
Tagdicht Buttress
South Col
Tizgui Col
Tizgui Plateau
2298
2101
2121
ANERGUI MEADOWS
Anergui path
Angel Peak
2236
Anergui Upper Crag
2213
Cairn
Anergui Col
Anergui Lower Crag
1985
Pinnacle
Black Crag
1620
Anergui
Children's playground
Playground Crag
Mosque
1808
Anergui Drainage
Blue Spring Crag
Spr.
Cheshire Cheese Crag
Anammer
Palmerie
Tidli
Aglz
Anergui Road
Waterfall
Crag BX
Crag B
Igordan
Mosque
Ait Taleb
Palmerie
Mosque
Tanalt Road
1253
AMELN VALLEY
Asoul
Ighaln
Ait Oumgas
Tamaloucht
Asguin
Tamaloucht C
Comm
TAGDICHT GORGE
Sanglier Slab
Dent d'Isabel Pinnacle
Lightning Crag
Tagdicht
1407
Tourist path
Tagdicht Crags
Waterfall
TAGDICHT M
1183
BASIN
Crag
gle Crag
Area Map
Crag Selector
Intro
The Climbing
How to Use
Suggested Climbs
Tafraout Granite
Anergui
Ameln Valley
Tarakatine Pass
Sidi M'Zal
Jebel Taskra
Idaougnidif
Afantinzar
Samazar
Aouguenz
Tagzene
Tagmout
History
Index

ANERGUI

This isolated high basin, situated just below the 2375m summit of Jebel el Kest, is historically one of the main climbing centres of the Anti-Atlas, and as soon as you round the final hairpin into the village you'll see why. Indeed, in this one small valley there is an almost daunting amount of rock, including some of the biggest crags and longest mid-grade routes the range has to offer. As such, this is a destination that should be considered a high priority for parties climbing on the south side of the range.

The Berber name 'Anergui' literally means *'the angels from above'* – an appropriate name for this unique place, nestled high in the mountains and only recently accessible by road. The locals, who are incredibly welcoming despite the remote setting of their village, have been keen to promote Anergui as a rock-climbing destination, though their efforts have unfortunately placed the village at the forefront of a recent bolting controversy.

Access is via a recently-concreted road that snakes its way up the hillside above Igordan, at the west end of the Ameln Valley. The steep, single-track road has few passing places, big drops and sharp bends, and is something of a worthwhile experience in its own right. Nervous passengers are advised to stay away... or at least close their eyes!

From a spacious parking and turning area at the very end of the road, a seemingly endless expanse of rock is visible – ample variety from single-pitch roadside amusements to intimidating long adventures. Most of the climbs here receive lots of sunshine, but due to the high altitude it is often still possible to climb here on warm days.

For those more interested in some spectacular hill-walking, Anergui is one of the popular starting points for an ascent of Jebel el Kest, and an exploration of the trails up to and beyond the upper crag will reveal some memorable views across Tafraout and the Ameln Valley.

A ANERGUI PLAYGROUND

Shade | Families | Hitch | Roadside

Drive from Tafraout: **40 minutes**
Walk-in: **2 minutes**

This fun little wall sits right above the sports pitch, next to the road just before the car park at the top of the village. It holds a handful of nice single-pitch climbs, and although they heat up quickly in the afternoon sun, shade (along with various playground amusements) is available on the opposite side of the road. The crag is particularly family friendly, as young ones can entertain themselves in the playground while the grown-ups climb...

DESCENT: Either scramble easily leftwards or set up a 40m abseil down the line of *Acca Dacca*.

1. Playground Arête VS 4c ★2 STEEP

50m. The prow up the left side of the wall gives the first of several brilliant pitches hereabouts. Start from bushes behind the shelter, at the foot of the descent gully, and climb the technical wall with considerable interest. There is a possible belay on a large terrace above, from where the route finishes magnificently through overhangs in the narrow buttress left of the gully.
Steve Broadbent & Anna Piotrowski, October 2013

2. Playground Groove MVS 4b

50m. This route starts up a prominent black streak to gain the easier groove above. Finish up the rather loose gully beyond, or more interestingly up the face to the left.
Steve Broadbent & Adam Jorna, October 2013

➲ "Ever on up..." Anergui was a new playground in 1998, and, as ever, Joe Brown was on hand to have some fun.
Claude Davies collection

Map Page 59

3. Tapestry of Nations HVS 4c ★1 STEEP

50m. Good, varied climbing, giving one of the most absorbing roadside routes at Anergui, despite a rather contrived line. Best climbed as two pitches with a belay on the mid-height terrace.

1) 30m (4b) The technical wall to the right of the black streak is bold to start, and leads with increasing satisfaction to the terrace.

2) 20m (4c) Move up left into the bottom of the upper gully of *Playground Groove*. From here, pull up rightwards and make a scintillating traverse amongst the overhangs... keep going as far as you can, and don't look down!

Steve Broadbent & Tim Culwick, October 2013

4. Angry Nature HS 4a ★1

40m. The slabby wall has some very nice climbing.

Steve Broadbent & Victoria Nockles, October 2013

5. Acca Dacca Severe ★1

40m. After a rather rattly start (bold and unprotected), this pleasant climb has some excellent moves through the small overlap, before finishing up the buttress to the left of a wide crack.

Cameron Hall & Steve Broadbent, October 2011

6. Urban Rock HS 4b ★1

40m. Another nice climb, this time starting from the wall at the edge of the sports pitch. Climb a crack in the lower slab to gain a niche, then exit up the right-hand corner crack.

Steve Broadbent & Cameron Hall, October 2011

7. Art Attack HVS 5a ★2 STEEP

40m. Brilliant climbing up the steep cracked-prow to the right, giving an excellent little pitch. Climb the blankest part of the lower slab to gain steep cracks up the overhanging prow. This is overcome via a sequence of superb athletic moves which you'll wish went on a little longer.

Steve Broadbent & Cameron Hall, October 2011

8. The Ocker Rocker HS 4b ★1

40m. The corner to the right has a surprisingly awkward move to escape left from under the overhangs, and is no push-over at this grade. High feet, odd rock-overs, or other weirdness may be required...

Cameron Hall & Steve Broadbent, October 2011

9. Live Wire VS 4b ★1

40m. The prow up the right side of the wall is an excellent climb that gets more difficult and altogether more emotional towards the top. It finishes at an electric cable. Bzzzzp.

Steve Broadbent & Cameron Hall, October 2011

B ANERGUI LOWER

Shade · Families · Hitch · Roadside

Drive from Tafraout: **40 minutes**
Walk-in: **15 minutes**

The enormous Lower Crag dominates the village of Anergui, towering a thousand feet straight up from the houses. Not surprisingly, this was the first crag hereabouts to see attention from climbers in the late 1990s, being an irresistible objective when seen from the village.

In reality, the routes here tend to involve some rather rambling climbing and do not necessarily follow strong natural lines, but if you're looking for adventure then you've come to the right place.

DESCENT: Continue over the summit of the Lower Crag, heading north to the col between the Lower and Upper crags (Anergui Col). Turn left here, descending below the Upper Crag, staying close to the steep walls on the right. Do not try and follow a broad gully leftwards, but instead follow the path over a small shoulder/col. Just after this, turn left to descend hairpins down to the main path which leads back south to the village.

Lower Crag Left

PM · 15m

1. Artful Dodger VS 4c ★1

ADVENTURE

300m. A good climb up the Central Buttress. Start in the bay to the right, climbing up leftwards to gain the crest of the buttress. The original way finishes up the left side of the buttress, but a more direct finish, *Fagin's Variation*, was recorded in 2005.

Joe Brown & Pete Turnbull, 2002.

2. Polish Direct HVS 4c

ADVENTURE

250m. The steep pillar up the back wall of the main bay has an adventurous reputation. Several parties have reported difficult climbing on suspect rock, though the route remains a popular objective.

Jacek Skrzyoczynski & Andrzej Łoś, December 2004.

3. Talk Armada VS 4b ★2

ADVENTURE

280m. The right wall of the main bay provides some excellent climbing on good rock, and remains in the shade a little longer than most routes hereabouts. It features a low crux, with large amounts of easy climbing up the fine upper wall, and is one of the best routes of its grade at Anergui. Start below a groove leading up and right.

1) 30m (4c) Climb up to a flake crack, step right, then move up into a hanging groove. Continue past a ledge and up a steep wall to belay below a corner.

2) 25m (4a) Climb the corner for 8m, then pull up left and follow a subsidiary groove to another belay.

3) 25m (4b) Follow the chimney to a chockstone, then move left and climb the rib until it is possible to step back right into the groove, which leads to a belay on the left.
4) 25m (4a) Make an awkward pull over a polished step, followed by easy scrambling to a col.
5) 40m (-) A steep wall leads to a slab, then steps and corners to a tree belay.
6) 10m (-) Scramble up to a higher belay.
7) 30m (-) Follow a left-slanting groove, then pull right around a nose and go up a ramp to a belay.
8) 50m (-) Climb the easy stepped wall above to a big ledge.
9) 45m (-) Finish up the wall above, trending left to a notch on the skyline. Approximately 100m of scrambling remains to the top of the crag.
Geoff Hornby & Susie Sammut, March 2005

4. Final Demand HVS 4c

ADVENTURE

250m. Start up a prominent groove, then escape left onto ledges on the left side. An early route, *Middle Way (VS 4b)* joins here. The route up the face above is rather vague.
David Jones & Joe Brown, 2003.

Directly above the village, in the centre of the Main Wall, is a large couloir system. The next three routes all start up this couloir, with easy climbing in the lower section.

5. First Impression E1 5b

ADVENTURE

300m. An early foray onto the cliff, giving adventurous climbing up the buttress left of the couloir.
Joe Brown & Derek Walker, 1998.

6. Grandads' Groove HVS 5a ★1

ADVENTURE LOOSE

250m. The big groove above the couloir is a strong natural line and gives a challenging but worthwhile climb with some good positions. Dubious rock in places.
Derek Walker, Chris Bonington & Les Brown, 2002.
This route was originally named "Grandads' Gruesome Groove" on account of the dubious rock. All three of the first ascensionists had recently become grandfathers prior to the first ascent.

7. Naseby HVS 5a ★2

ADVENTURE LOOSE

250m. The wall to the right is the most famous route at Anergui, and although there are better routes elsewhere in the range this climb sees frequent ascents. The initial pitches up the couloir are straightforward and are often soloed, before 4 or 5 more difficult pitches up a major crack-system in the right wall. The crux roof is somewhat loose and care is required.
Derek Walker & Chris Bonington, 2001.
At the start of the climb, Bonington checked the altimeter – it read 1645, the year of the Battle of Naseby which ended the Civil War.

8. Delectation VS 4c ★1

UNCHECKED

300m. Few details are known about this early attempt at the wall to the right of the couloir, which appears to share significant ground with the following climb...
Les Brown & Pete Turnbull, March 1998.

9. Physical Graffiti MVS 4b ★1

310m. Following "the obvious groove system between *Delectation* and the *SW Ridge*", this climb provides a more direct solution to the wall right of the central couloir.

1) 50m (-) Easy cracks and grooves lead to a belay below a vegetated groove.

2) 40m (4b) Move right and climb a crack, passing a bulge on the right.

3) 10m (-) Easy climbing to a big ledge.

4) 35m (-) Go up an attractive clean slab to gain a groove, then move left to a belay on the arête.

5) 45m (-) Step back right and follow the easy groove to a ledge beneath a fragile wall, which is climbed with some trepidation.

6) 40m (-) Go up the easy wall above to a right-facing corner, which leads to a large block. Turn the block on the left to reach a belay.

7) 30m (-) Easy climbing up to a big ledge beneath overhangs.

8) 10m (4b) Pull through the overhang on the left.

9) 50m (-) A groove system leads easily to the top.

Paul Seabrook & Geoff Hornby, March 2007.

10. Southwest Ridge Severe ★2

300m. With an easy approach and stunning views, the vague ridge-line up the right side of the lower crag is a very pleasant amble, despite a rather arduous descent down the southern slopes of the crag. More usually, however, this route forms the first stage of one of Tafraout's best easy mountain days – *The Angel's Crest* (see page 66). The first pitches are the most difficult, but can easily be avoided by scrambling further up gullies to the right.

Claude Davies & Pete Turnbull, 2003.

C ANERGUI UPPER

Shade Families Hitch Roadside

Drive from Tafraout: **40 minutes**
Walk-in: **40 minutes**

The upper crag at Anergui is a magical place to climb. Situated up and left from the main crag and topping out at almost 7000ft above sea level, it is the highest developed crag in the whole range, and the views from the upper tier are accordingly spectacular. The whole crag forms an enormous pale-coloured dome high above Anergui, with its southwestern side carved away to create the steep wall on which most of the routes are located. Above this the rock is more easily angled, and provides endless opportunities for scrambling.

The approach is reasonably long, but on a good path throughout. Head north from the village, passing beneath the full length of the lower crag and underneath the next minor buttress. Beyond this a path zigzags up rightwards, turning back to the southeast and climbing up a terrace along the base of the upper crag. See overview photo below.

DESCENT: Most routes finish on a terrace halfway up the face. Walk rightwards along the terrace, from where a few steps of scrambling gain the cairned Anergui Col. From here, follow the good path back down beneath the crag.

For routes that finish on the summit, descent is made by walking easily northwards, then swinging left to join the Jebel el Kest path (see map on page 67).

Area Map
Crag Selector
Intro
The Climbing
How to Use
Suggested Climbs
Tafraout Granite
Anergui
Ameln Valley
Tarakatine Pass
Sidi M'Zal
Jebel Taskra
Idaougnidif
Afantinzar
Samazar
Aouguenz
Tagzene
Tagmout
History
Index

Area Map
Crag Selector
Intro
The Climbing
How to Use
Suggested Climbs
Tafraout Granite
Anergui
Ameln Valley
Tarakatine Pass
Sidi M'Zal
Jebel Taskra
Idaougnidif
Afantinzar
Samazar
Aouguenz
Tagzene
Tagmout
History
Index

1. Stairway to Heaven HVS 4c ★2 ADVENTURE

~350m. Whilst theoretically straightforward, *Stairway to Heaven* is a long, traditional route that epitomises Anti-Atlas adventure-climbing. The climb picks its way up the left side of the southwest face and continues all the way to the summit on immaculate rock, with interesting climbing and superb positions throughout. Exact details of the line are not clear (then again, how could they be with a route of this nature?) so subsequent ascensionists are advised to approach with a sense of humour and keen eye for adventure.

Chris Bonington, Mike Mortimer, Joe Smith & Derek Walker, March 2005

2. Riding the Wild Wind HVS 4c ★2 ADVENTURE

~340m. A direct venture up the intimidating overhangs, giving brilliant climbing on good rock, and providing an arduous day out. Start as for the left-hand start to *Eagle's Beak*.

1) 60m (4c) A long pitch, which some people prefer to split. Climb straight up to the triangular overhang – the original way turned this on the left, though either side is possible.

2) 55m (4c) Climb a slab to a short black groove. Follow this, exiting rightwards at the overhang. Continue to a stance above.

3) 55m (4c) Go up to the impressive groove and follow it to easier ground.

4-7) 170m. Easy climbing to the top.

Mike Mortimer & Simon Brown, March 2013

3. Eagle's Beak HVS 4c ★3 ADVENTURE

~320m. The original way up the Upper Crag is a tremendous classic climb that ranks amongst the best mid-grade mountain routes in the region, providing a perfect example of quartzite adventure climbing. The lower part of the route gains and follows a prominent leftwards traverse across a hanging slab, above which climbers are left to follow their instincts to the summit. Those with poorly-developed instincts, however, may instead meander aimlessly to benightment. A variety of starts have been recorded and it is possible that ground is shared with other long routes hereabouts.

Chris Bonington & Derek Walker, 2003.

4. Tranquility Grooves E1 5a ★2

130m. The groove line immediately left of *White Noise* gives excellent climbing, but with some poor rock on pitch 4.
1) 30m (4c) Climb the crack and groove above, stepping right to a stance below overhangs.
2) 20m (5a) Follow the twin cracks on the left to a fine move out right under the overhang. Continue more easily to a ledge.
3) 40m (4c) Go left to the rib, move up, then back right into a steep groove. This leads to another good ledge below overhangs.
4) 18m (5a) Move right to a sentry box, then pull strenuously leftwards on suspect rock. Move up, then traverse rightwards to the arête. Finish steeply up left to a stance.
5) 22m (-) Easy climbing rightwards to the top.

5. White Noise HVS 4c ★1 STEEP

150m. A strong and unlikely-looking line up some steep and intimidating ground, giving a fine climb that is low in the grade. Start in a bay just left of *Eagle's Perch*.
1) 25m (4c) Climb a steep crack in the right wall of the bay to blocks. Traverse to a large ledge.
2) 20m (4a) Ascend the chimney until it's possible to move right onto the front of the buttress. Continue to a stance beneath a roof.
3) 25m (4c) Move back into the chimney and climb the left wall to a fine traverse left with difficult moves to a stance.
4) 25m (4c) Climb the steep groove above and continue to a stance just right of the continuation corner.
5) 15m (4c) Go up the corner to another comfortable stance.
6) 35m (4a) An easier pitch up rightwards to the terrace.
Dave Absolom, Chris Bonington, Mike Mortimer & Derek Walker, 2007.

6. Skywalker E2 5b ★2 STEEP

150m. The continuation of the *Eagle's Perch* groove gives a very fine pitch. Start up the initial groove as for that route.
1) 45m. Climb the deceptively steep groove to a stance just before things get difficult...
2) 30m. A tremendous pitch. Go up the groove, then hand-traverse out left to an exposed semi-rest on the edge. Move left again to gain easier ground that leads up to a stance at the top of the groove.
3) 75m. Easy climbing above to gain the terrace.
Jim Fotheringham & Mike Mortimer, March 2007.

7. The Eagle's Perch HVS 5a ★2 STEEP

140m. Another impressive climb that takes a commanding line up the front of the buttress. Start at a square-cut groove opposite stacked flat-topped blocks.
1) 20m (5a) The fine groove is steeper than it looks!
2) 25m (4c) Continue up the groove until it is possible to move right easily along a ledge. Climb up diagonally right across a slab to an exposed stance.
3) 35m (4c) Good climbing up steps and cracks.
4) 55m (4a) A steep start then easy slabs lead to the terrace.
Chris Bonington & Mike Mortimer, March 2005.

8. White Mischief HVS 5a ★2 STEEP

135m. A varied climb that starts beneath the upper part of *Eagle's Perch*, directly below a prominent triangular roof at 45m.
1) 15m (4a) Climb a short groove to a large ledge, then move right and go up easily to a belay below a jammed block.
2) 30m (4c) Step left and climb the steep groove on the left to a belay below the triangular roof.
3) 25m (5a) Go up the corner above, then traverse right under the roof and step up to a ledge. Continue up the wall above to a belay on the right.
4) 40m (4c) The fine upper wall has well-spaced protection. Trend left at the top to a good stance.
5) 25m (-) Easy climbing up to the terrace.
Mike & Marjorie Mortimer, March 2007.

9. Where Eagles Dare HVS 5a ? UNCHECKED STEEP

130m. The centre of the steep wall has been climbed via the shallow left-facing corner, though few details are known.

10. Red Brick Cruisers HVS 5a ? UNCHECKED STEEP

130m. The wall immediately left of the large chimney is likely to be harder than the grade suggests.
Mike & Marjorie Mortimer, April 2009.

11. Eagle's Nest E1 5b ★1

150m. The huge corner up the right side of the wall will either attract or deter... 5 good 30m pitches gain the terrace, moving left through the huge roof near the top.
Paul Donnithorne & Emma Alsford, March 2007.

D JEBEL EL KEST SUMMIT

Shade Families Hitch Roadside

Drive from Tafraout: **40 minutes**
Walk-in: **various**

At 2375m above sea level, the summit of Jebel el Kest is the highest point on the escarpment, and a very special place indeed. The mountain dominates the Anti-Atlas, defining its geography, shaping its landscape, and influencing its people. It is the provider of water to the hundreds of settlements that outline its periphery and, not surprisingly, is one of Tafraout's most important tourist attractions.

Dozens of tourists ascend the mountain each season, many of them with a local guide and overnight stop in the village of Tagdicht. For climbers, the best line of ascent is from Anergui via the *Angel's Crest* – a stunning mountain scramble that should be a high priority for those in search of a big mountain day.

1-3. Jebel el Kest via The Angel's Crest
Difficult / Severe 3 ADVENTURE

~3.5km. A superb link-up, providing a magnificent mountaineering day out to the highest point in the range. The route is mostly walking, with three long sections of climbing on which the grade can be varied as required. The first (avoidable) pitches are the hardest, followed by unavoidable sections up to 'Difficult' in the upper sections. The route starts right from the village, and is usually completed in 6 to 10 hours from car to car. See map opposite.

A) ***1 – The SW Ridge (300m, Severe / Difficult)*** – The right-hand skyline of the lower crag has a couple of pitches of Severe climbing at the start, which can be avoided (sometimes accidentally) by traversing in from a gully on the right. Above a large ledge the climbing becomes steadily easier, eventually petering out into scrambling.

B) From the summit of the Lower Crag the Upper Crag is clearly visible. Walk to a col at the foot of the Upper Crag (Anergui Col), from where a grassy terrace leads leftwards across the face. The next pitch of climbing starts from the left end of this terrace.

C) ***2 – The Angel's Crest (160m, Difficult)*** – Climb straight upwards from the end of the terrace on steep, sometimes poorly protected terrain with large holds. Approximately 4 pitches to easier ground.

D) Scramble up over the summit of the Upper Crag, then traverse the western slopes of Angel Peak. Bear right, ascending gradually to the South Col of Jebel el Kest.

E) ***3 – The South Ridge (500m, Easy)*** – Start from the col at the foot of the south ridge, scrambling up and traversing left to a gully. Go up this to a cairned weakness in the left wall. Climb the wall, trending up left into a groove system. Follow this to easier ground and walk across the face to another gully on the right. The way ahead looks uninviting, but a narrow ledge traverses the left wall close to the top of the gully. There is a tricky exposed step at the end, which can be hard to spot in descent. From here, easier ground leads up rightwards back towards the ridge and up to the summit.

Claude Davies & Pete Turnbull, 2003 (SW Ridge.)
Steve & Katja Broadbent, 2013 (Angel's Crest and South Ridge).

4. Southwest Face Difficult / Severe

~300m. The southwest face of the summit pyramid can be climbed by a variety of vague lines that have not been recorded in detail. Short walls up to about Severe may be encountered amongst large amounts of easier climbing.

Martin Jones, 2013.

5. West Ridge Easy 2

~500m. The obvious western ridge of the summit pyramid gives a very fine scramble in ascent, or a fitting descent from the popular *Angel's Crest* route.

Jonathan Williams, 2014.

DESCENT: The best descent from the summit is to scramble down the West Ridge to the West Col. From here, turn left (south) and descend into Anergui Meadows. From the western end of the meadows, numerous cairns (hard to spot) mark the path, descending via devious ramps and ledges before contouring round to the top of a grassy col which marks the western extremity of Anergui's Upper Crag. From here a very good trail zigzags down towards the village. This descent requires care with route-finding, and is notoriously difficult to follow in the dark.

Area Map
Crag Selector
Intro
The Climbing
How to Use
Suggested Climbs
Tafraout Granite
Anergui
Ameln Valley
Tarakatine Pass
Sidi M'Zal
Jebel Taskra
Idaougnidif
Afantinzar
Samazar
Aouguenz
Tagzene
Tagmout
History
Index

Area Map
Crag Selector
Intro
The Climbing
How to Use
Suggested Climbs
Tafraout Granite
Anergui
Ameln Valley
Tarakatine Pass
Sidi M'Zal
Jebel Taskra
Idaougnidif
Afantinzar
Samazar
Aouguenz
Tagzene
Tagmout
History
Index

THE AMELN VALLEY

The awesome southern front of Jebel el Kest stretches for some 35 kilometres from Tagmout at the western end to the Tarakatine Pass in the east, rising to 2375m at its highest point – the summit pyramid of Afa-n-Tmezgadiwine. Running parallel to the escarpment is the fertile Ameln Valley, providing the last reliable water supplies before the arid granite landscape leads off southwards towards the semi-desert and Saharan fringes. The valley floor is scattered with isolated settlements, built up around the outflows of mountain streams which provide a year-round water source. In contrast to the high pastures and rugged mountain scenery of the north side, Ameln is a place of beautiful oases, palmeries, and fascinating ancient architecture.

Indeed, the many varied villages around which the crags are located provide a superb cultural experience that is very different and perhaps even more rewarding than that to be found further north.

It is here that Tafraout climbing first took off in 1991, at the hands of the 'Ameln pioneers', who based themselves in Tafraout's Amandiers Hotel for an annual climbing pilgrimage to the area. From the comfortable terrace of the hotel, a bewildering array of crags presents itself, and it is to these crags that the pioneers headed throughout the 1990s. Traditionally, and in contrast to the north side of the range, these crags were characterised by short drives and punishing walk-ins, although in recent years a number of very accessible single-pitch cragging venues have been developed just outside several of the villages. Beyond, distant high crags, seemingly endless in extent, tower high above the valley, many of them far out of reach of all but the most dedicated teams.

As a result, there's a tremendous variety of climbing here, from long multi-pitch adventures on the high

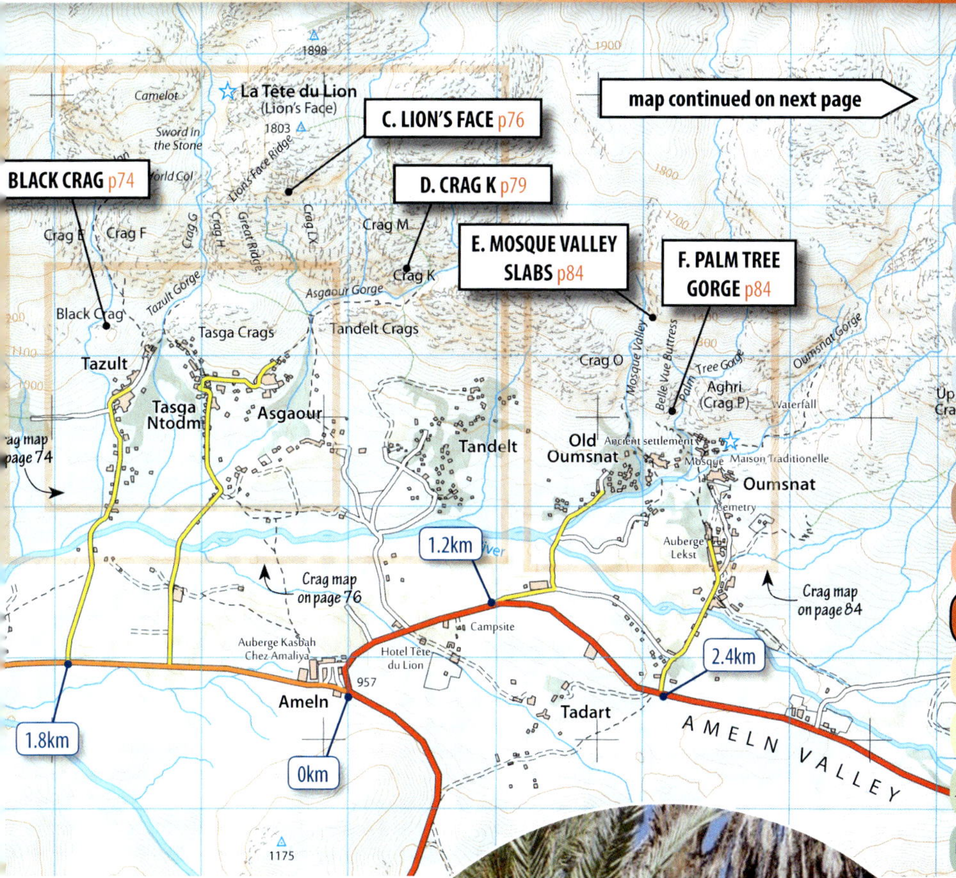

crags, to relaxed single-pitch cragging on the lowest and warmest venues the Anti-Atlas has to offer. In general, most of the crags face south and are best visited during mid-season when temperatures are not so high. At this time of year they provide superb cragging when some of the crags on the north side can be uncomfortably cool.

➲ The original team of Ameln Valley pioneers exploring the valley in 1992, when they made the first dedicated climbing trip to the Ameln Valley. Left to right: Pete Turnbull, Joe Brown, Trevor Jones, Les Brown, Claude Davies.
Claude Davies collection

Area Map
Crag Selector
Intro
The Climbing
How to Use
Suggested Climbs
Tafraout Granite
Anergui
Ameln Valley
Tarakatine Pass
Sidi M'Zal
Jebel Taskra
Idaougnidif
Afantinzar
Samazar
Aouguenz
Tagzene
Tagmout
History
Index

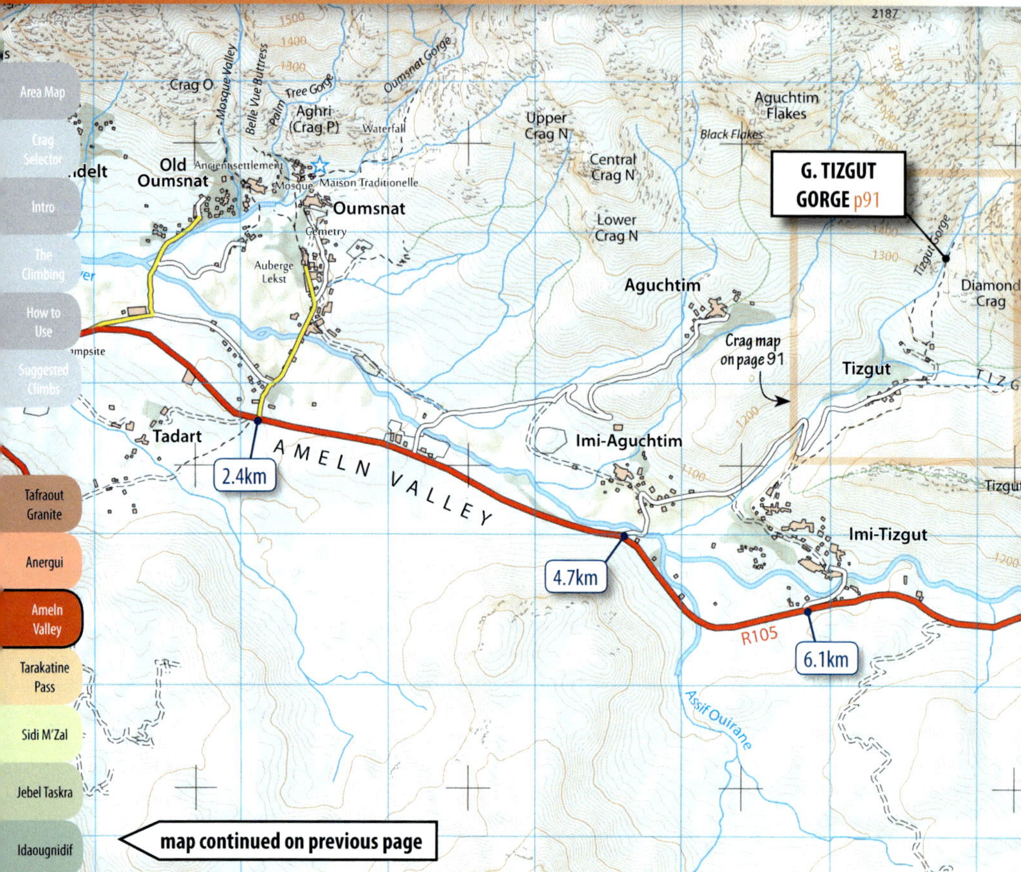

All of the Ameln crags are reached in less than 20 minutes by car from Tafraout, and many are suitable venues for those without their own transport – it is often possible to hitchhike to the bigger villages such as Oumsnat or Tifghalt.

Crags are described in this chapter from west to east along the valley. Distances shown on the map are referenced from the main Y-shaped junction in Ameln. More detailed approach maps are shown on the relevant crag pages.

SITES OF INTEREST IN AMELN

Numerous sites of interest are found throughout the famous 26 villages of the Ameln Valley, and many of the walk-ins described in this chapter pass through some fascinating and historic cultural spots...

In Oumsnat, check out the Maison Traditionelle, where residents give an interesting tour, explaining ingenious domestic equipment, animals' quarters and summer terrace. The village is also famous for its traditional Berber architecture, which sees new houses built on top of old ones when they became too small or run-down.

From here it is possible to walk west to Tandelt, where an old cemetery is all that remains of a former Jewish community in the village – a place known for its silverware, much of which bears Jewish symbols.

Continuing west beneath the Lion's Face, and the impressive Tagdicht Gorge is the affluent village of Anammer (or Anameur), which translates as "place of water" or "spring". Sure enough, at the end of the village is one of the valley's most reliable and sacred freshwater springs, providing welcome refreshment on hot days.

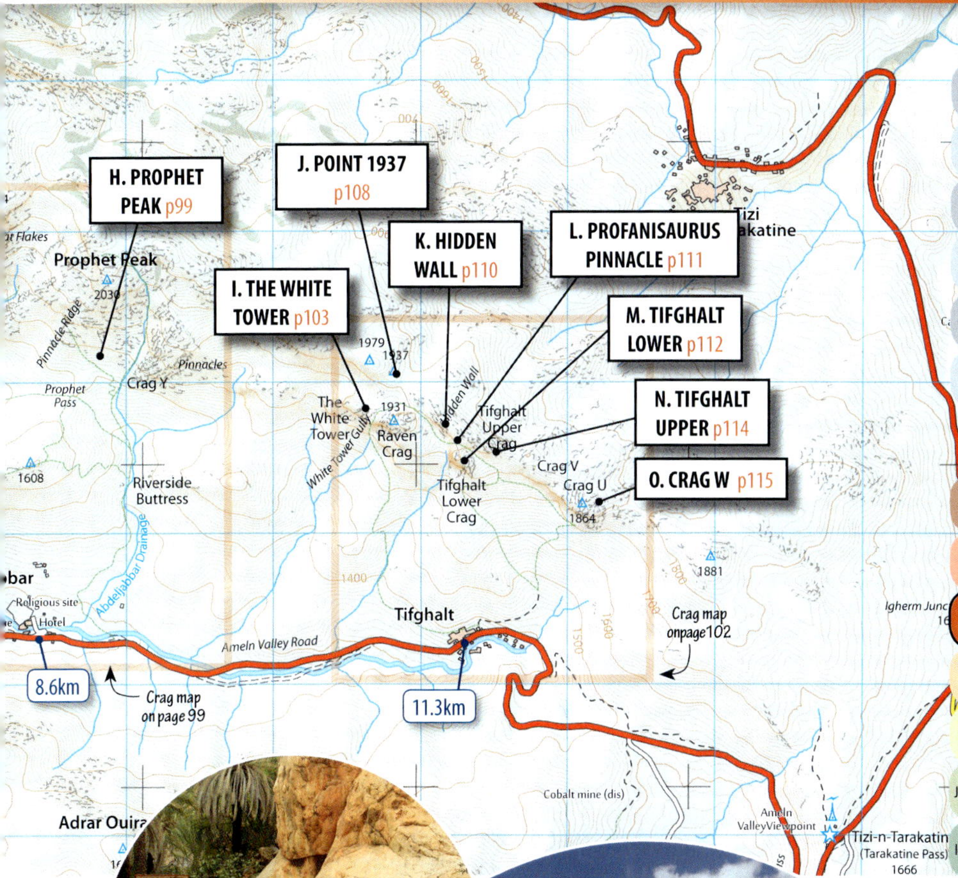

The *Source Bleu* at Anammer.

The Lion's Face towers above the fertile Ameln Valley at Asgaour. These crags were the first to attract the attention of British climbers in the early 1990s.

Area Map
Crag Selector
Intro
The Climbing
How to Use
Suggested Climbs
Tafraout Granite
Anergui
Ameln Valley
Tarakatine Pass
Sidi M'Zal
Jebel Taskra
Idaougnidif
Afantinzar
Samazar
Aouguenz
Tagzene
Tagmout
History
Index

Map Page 68

Area Map
Crag Selector
Intro
The Climbing
How to Use
Suggested Climbs
Tafraout Granite
Anergui
Ameln Valley
Tarakatine Pass
Sidi M'Zal
Jebel Taskra
Idaougnidif
Afantinzar
Samazar
Aouguenz
Tagzene
Tagmout
History
Index

A BLUE SPRING CRAG

Shade Families Hitch Roadside

Drive from Tafraout: **15 minutes**
Walk-in: **10 minutes**

This fun little crag is located on the hillside just above the west end of Anammer Village. Although most of the outcrops here are unattractive for climbing, the following routes are on very good rock and provide a low-commitment amusement for an evening, or when bad weather threatens the rest of the range. The crag is particularly suitable for top-ropes and groups.

A small parking area is located in the middle of Anammer village, from where the concreted road continues beneath a large water tank to the end of the houses, where Anammer's famous blue spring provides a year-round water supply. Follow a small path uphill from the spring until the crag comes into view on the right-hand side in a couple of minutes.

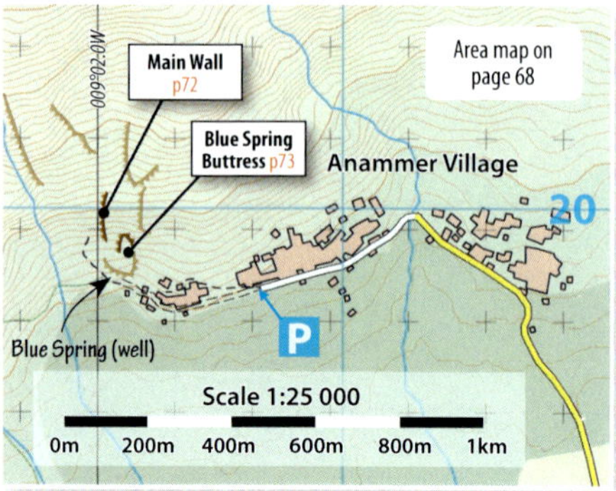

THE MAIN WALL

A very friendly west-facing wall of solid quartzite, about 15 to 20 metres in height.

DESCENT: An easy scramble down the back side. Climbers wishing to climb multiple routes may wish to set up an abseil, for which many anchors exist.

1. Aloe Aloe VS 4c ★2 GEAR STEEP

15m. A good, steep pitch over the small overlap at the left side of the wall.
Steve Broadbent & Anna Piotrowski, October 2013.

2. Call to Pimms VS 4a

15m. Difficult climbing through the overlap in the left-hand groove. Place high gear in the overlap of *Aloe Aloe*, then pull up rightwards into the thin groove. Finish easily up the left-hand groove above.
Steve Broadbent & Anna Piotrowski, October 2013.

3. The Twits VS 4c ★1

15m. An amusing grovel up the very obvious wide groove, finishing direct up the central crack.
Steve Broadbent & Anna Piotrowski, October 2013.

4. Who is Chris Waddle and What is the Fast Show? HVS 4c

15m. A worthwhile climb through the overlap in the centre of the wall, where some poor holds hinder progress. Step left above to finish more easily.
Steve Broadbent & Anna Piotrowski, October 2013.

5. Fear of Shakespear E1 5a

15m. The sandy groove has some technical moves through the overlap, with little in the way of gear.
Steve Broadbent & Anna Piotrowski, October 2013.

6. Securicat HS ★1

15m. A very nice climb, with good steep moves. Start up the crack to gain the overlap, which is surmounted directly on excellent holds. Finish up the short wall above.
Steve Broadbent & Anna Piotrowski, October 2013.

7. Meteorologicos Mit Paula V.Diff

15m. Climb the wall via a vague crack, passing a small euphorbia to gain the large ledge. Finish up left via a steep move as for *Buttonwood*.
Steve Broadbent & Anna Piotrowski, October 2013.

8. Buttonwood Difficult

15m. The obvious groove to a ledge. Finish steeply up left.
Steve Broadbent & Anna Piotrowski, October 2013.

BLUE SPRING BUTTRESS

This small outcrop is located slightly downhill and behind the main wall, and is most easily seen from the descent from the previous routes.

9. Travel Bug E1 5c ★2 GEAR STEEP

15m. A superb, steep pitch starting at the base of the arête. Climb up right via a steep ramp, then step left around the arête onto the overhanging face. Power up this on big holds with plenty of protection. *Vanessa Wills & David Gray, February 2014.*

10. Bee Sahara Severe ★2

15m. The undercut wall to the left of the obvious crack gives a brilliant little pitch, with perfectly formed holds and bags of exposure.
Steve Broadbent & Anna Piotrowski, October 2013.

11. Blue Spring Crack MVS 4a ★2 WIDE

15m. The obvious corner crack is as good as it looks. A couple of size 4 cams make things easier.
Steve Broadbent & Anna Piotrowski, October 2013.

12. Edison's Revenge VS 5b CRACK

15m. The right-hand crack is accessed with extreme difficulty. A bold layback might work, but may land you in the cactus below. Perhaps it's a strenous hand jam instead?
Steve Broadbent & Anna Piotrowski, October 2013.

13. Hop E1 5a BOLD

15m. The arête to the right is a bold undertaking, on which small wires provide psychological protection only.
David Gray & Vanessa Wills, February 2014.

14. Skip HVS 5a BOLD

15m. The centre of the slab has a bouldery crux through the initial bulge.
David Gray & Vanessa Wills, February 2014.

15. Jump Severe BOLD

15m. A fun solo up the right-hand side of the slab.
David Gray & Vanessa Wills, February 2014.

Blue Spring Buttress
PM 10m

B BLACK CRAG, TAZULT

Shade · Families · Hitch · Roadside

Drive from Tafraout: **10 minutes**
Walk-in: **30 minutes**

This shady little crag lies hidden from view behind a subsidiary ridge-line above Tazult. Although it has not been extensively developed, there are enough routes here to pass a short day, and whilst the rock here is not as good as that on much of the massif, there are a handful of very worthwhile climbs. The crag remains in shade for much of the day, and is therefore an excellent choice during spells of hot weather, when the thought of spending another long day in the sun does not appeal.

The approach is fairly straightforward from a parking area in Tazult. Continue to the end of the road, then follow a path a short way until it passes between two houses. Turn left here to follow water-pipes up the hill past ancient buildings. After about 15 minutes this path reaches a small rocky tower at the top of the initial hill – this is The Sentinel, and holds a handful of good climbs. Continue beyond The Sentinel a short way to small fields on the next flat level, from where an easy walk leftwards across the hillside gains Black Crag itself.

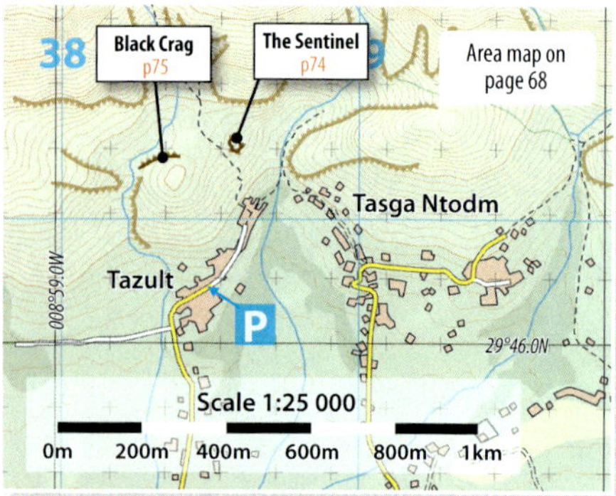

THE SENTINEL

This fine little tower of rock lies right by the side of the path above Tazult and is passed on the walk-in to Black Crag. Shade is available for much of the day, and the pleasant setting makes a suitable spot for families and picnics.

1. Sentinel Crack HVS 5a ★2 GEAR CRACK

20m. The tempting crack that cleaves the south face above the path gives an excellent pitch.
Caroline Culwick & Steve Broadbent, March 2011.

2. Wishing for an Abseil V.Diff ★1 GEAR

15m. The easiest way up (and sadly down) the tower is via the northwest corner, which provides a surprisingly good climb with plentiful protection.
Caroline Culwick & Steve Broadbent, March 2011.

DESCENT: Descent from the summit is awkward, as abseil anchors are difficult to arrange. A tricky downclimb (VD) is the usual solution.

3. Super Nova HVS 5a ★1 STEEP GEAR CRACK

15m. The obvious crack up the centre of the east face is steep, strenuous and very photogenic.
Steve Broadbent & Caroline Culwick, March 2011. Photo page 39.

Sentinel South Face
20m

BLACK CRAG

4. Black Velvet HVS 5a

15m. Starts just to the left of *Route 2*, moving diagonally up left to tiptoe through a scoop.
Ian Dugdale & Jim Nuttall, March 2013.

5. Route 2 Very Difficult

15m. Follows the left edge of the pedestal, then the continuation corner above.
Ewan Withey & Paul Winder, March 2007.

6. Original Route HVS 5a

15m. Rather lichenous climbing up the crack just to the right of the pedestal.
Paul Winder & Ewan Withey, March 2007.

Further right is a large detached pinnacle, and right again is a steep wall. The next route climbs the arête to the right of the pinnacle.

7. Block Rockin Beat VS 4b ★1

20m. A nice line up the arête to the right of the gully, just right of the pinnacle. Start in the gully, quickly moving up right onto the arête and face to a steep finish.
Ian Dugdale, March 2013.

8. Ebony and Ivory E2 5c (BOLD)

20m. Hard climbing, starting 5m to the right of the previous route by a white tree. Climb small edges to gain the faint crack, which provides marginal protection in the form of small wires. A few more hard moves remain before things ease off.
Jim Nuttall & Ian Dugdale, March 2013.

9. Intergalactic Social Blunder HVS 5a ★1

20m. The overhang-capped gully used to provide an excellent route, though recent rockfall may have now left it rather unstable. Start up the left wall of the gully, following a flake system to below the overlap. Pull through this with good protection to an easier finish.
Caroline Culwick & Steve Broadbent, March 2011.

10. Bohemia HVS 5b ★3

20m. A very fine and varied climb up the rib and slab just right of the overhang-capped gully, representing the top of its grade. Start just right of the arête and make some difficult moves on small holds to reach jugs through steeper ground. This leads to a sumptuous finale up the upper wall.
Steve Broadbent & Caroline Culwick, March 2011.

11. Bukovina HVS 5a

20m. The face right of *Bohemia*. Start at a vague rib and trend up left towards *Bohemia*. Cross a small overlap, then follow a right-slanting crack to a finish up the flake.
Andy Nisbet, Geoff Cohen & Gerry Rooney, March 2014.

12. Sihad E2 5c (BOLD)

15m. A rather bold outing up the obvious rising traverse at the right side of the wall. The start is poorly protected, and hard, but things ease considerably above.
Ewan Withey & Paul Winder, March 2007.

13. Our Cousin The Starfish MVS 4b ★1

20m. A pleasant climb. Start below a broken gully and make bold moves off the ground to gain the gully. Move left above, to finish up the excellent face and weakness in the capping overhangs.
Steve Broadbent & Caroline Culwick, March 2011.

Area Map
Crag Selector
Intro
The Climbing
How to Use
Suggested Climbs
Tafraout Granite
Anergui
Ameln Valley
Tarakatine Pass
Sidi M'Zal
Jebel Taskra
Idaougnidif
Afantinzar
Samazar
Aouguenz
Tagzene
Tagmout
History
Index

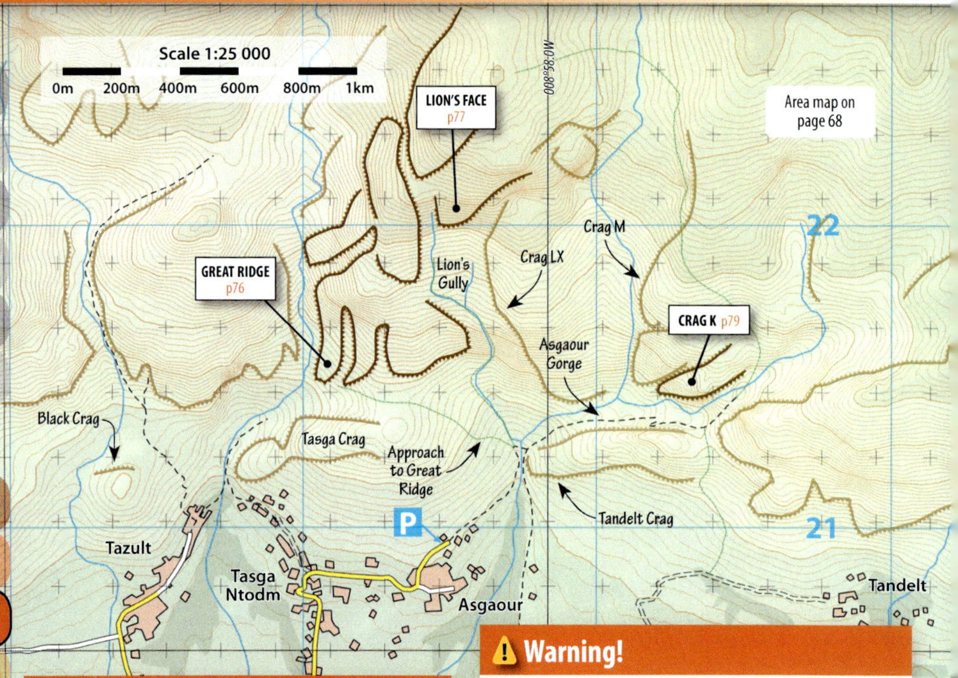

Area Map
Crag Selector
Intro
The Climbing
How to Use
Suggested Climbs
Tafraout Granite
Anergui
Ameln Valley
Tarakatine Pass
Sidi M'Zal
Jebel Taskra
Idaougnidif
Afantinzar
Samazar
Aouguenz
Tagzene
Tagmout
History
Index

C THE LION'S FACE

Shade Families Hitch Roadside

Drive from Tafraout: **10 minutes**
Walk-in: **40 minutes to 3 hours**

Towering above the main junction at Ameln, the mighty Lion's Face is probably the most famous feature of the escarpment. Below the face itself, the Asgaour Gorge cuts through a lower line of crags then swings sharply eastward, running behind the sunny Tandelt Crag and on to the ever-popular Crag K (page 79).

The easiest access into the gorge is from Asgaour: take the first turning on the right when heading west from Ameln, then follow the track through Tasga Ntodm where it swings through 90 degrees to the right. Shortly after entering the village a narrow concrete road turns off left up the hill – follow this and park at its end. A good path then heads eastward into the gorge.

The Lion's Face and two associated ridge-lines provide some of the biggest days out that Tafraout has to offer, and despite some questionable rock and vegetation in places, the climbs here are curiously irresistible. Fast and competent teams will enjoy some memorable adventures for which early starts, efficiency and determination are advised. Many people, however, underestimate the scale of this formidable piece of rock and cold nights out on the mountainside are not uncommon.

⚠ Warning!

Routes on the Lion's Face are adventurous undertakings that will not suit everyone! Only approximate descriptions are given here, and teams are advised to adopt an 'exploratory' approach.

DESCENT: The walk down from the summit is a long and spectacular, best (but rarely) done in the daylight. From the summit there is a simple scramble down onto the plateau, from where the route heads east across the top of a slabby couloir. A path then cuts rightward across the top of Crag M before descending into the gully beyond Crag K. Some cairns are evident, though care is required.

THE GREAT RIDGE

Running up the left side of this complex area of crags and walls is the magnificent *Great Ridge*, which is one of the valley's most infamous climbs. From the entrance to the Asgaour Gorge walk leftwards up easy slopes to gain an attractive col behind the top of Tasga Crag. The first two routes are reached from this col.

1. The Great Ridge VS 5a ★2 ADVENTURE

800m. The big one! Some 800m of height gain and approximately one kilometre of involved ridge climbing make for a long trip. Isolated sections of excellent climbing are interspersed with extensive broken, vegetated ground which demand a certain sense of adventure and motivation to succeed. Several towers are encountered along the way, involving downclimbs or time-consuming abseils, and although many teams attempt the route in a day, success is extremely rare and bivouac equipment should be carried. Escape rightwards is possible after the first summit or from the notch after the Great Tower (both routes require abseils). Two possible starts lead to the first summit, both giving excellent climbing.

1-West Start) The more difficult and classic *Western Ridge* is gained at a notch and features some fine ridge climbing, staying mostly on the crest. There is an excellent 4c crack near the top, before an intricate descent to a narrow notch. An unpleasant vegetated groove then gains the first summit.

1-East Start) The *Eastern Ridge* gives steady climbing up a fine ridge, but is slightly less classic than the western start.

2) From the first summit there is an involved down-climb to a notch through which a vague path passes. The route above the first notch is rather unattractive, starting up a steep (4c) corner directly above the notch. Continue along a fine ridge to the summit of the Great Tower.

3) Traverse the summit ridge of the Great Tower then abseil into the second notch (70m or 20m, depending on which way you locate!) From here, descend rightwards to below an easy couloir, and climb this until a traverse right gains the final ridge. This gives delectable climbing to the summit.

Les Brown & Trevor Jones, 1994 (Western Ridge).
Les Brown, Pete Turnbull & Roy Warner (as far as the First Tower).
Les Brown & Trevor Jones (upper ridge from a scramble approach).
Les Brown & Pete Turnbull, 1998 (complete ascent via Western Ridge & Great Tower).

2. The Armchair Mountaineer HS 4b ★2

The big left-facing dihedral gives a fine 3-pitch climb on good rock, leading to the first summit of the *Great Ridge*. Approach by scrambling up the gully right of the *Western Ridge* and start up slabs on the right to gain the base of the corner. Go up this, finishing out left on a varnished face.

Kendra Kurihara & Rob Dillon, March 2012.

THE LION'S FACE

Climbs on the Lion's Face itself are major undertakings, not to be underestimated. The approach up Lion's Gully is long and frustrating, and the cairned way up the true left bank involves some difficult and dangerous scrambling that may require a rope. It is also possible to scramble up the continuation of Lion's Gully to reach the left side of the face, though this route is also a challenging experience... Allow at least 2 hours and plenty of optimism to reach the foot of the climbs.

3. Lion's Face Ridge VS 4c ★2 (ADVENTURE)

400m. The ridge up the left side of the Lion's Face is another major undertaking involving approximately 12 pitches of excellent climbing.

Les Brown, Claude Davies, Derek Walker & Pete Turnbull, 1997.

4. Are We There Yet? Severe (ADVENTURE)

180m. A variation start to the previous route. Start by bushes at the base of a left-slanting roof/groove, stepping up right over boulders to gain the face. This leads up to the *Lions Face Ridge* in three long pitches.

Danny Woodward & Tiffany Caprarella, December 2008.

5. The Sallee Rovers VS 4c (ADVENTURE)

400m. This major variation climbs the wall between the *Lion's Face Ridge* and the *Lion's Face*, joining that route below the huge roof. The first ascent team were forced to endure a freezing night on the face during one of Tafraout's biggest storms in recent times.

Bruce Kerry & Jane Johnson, March 2005.

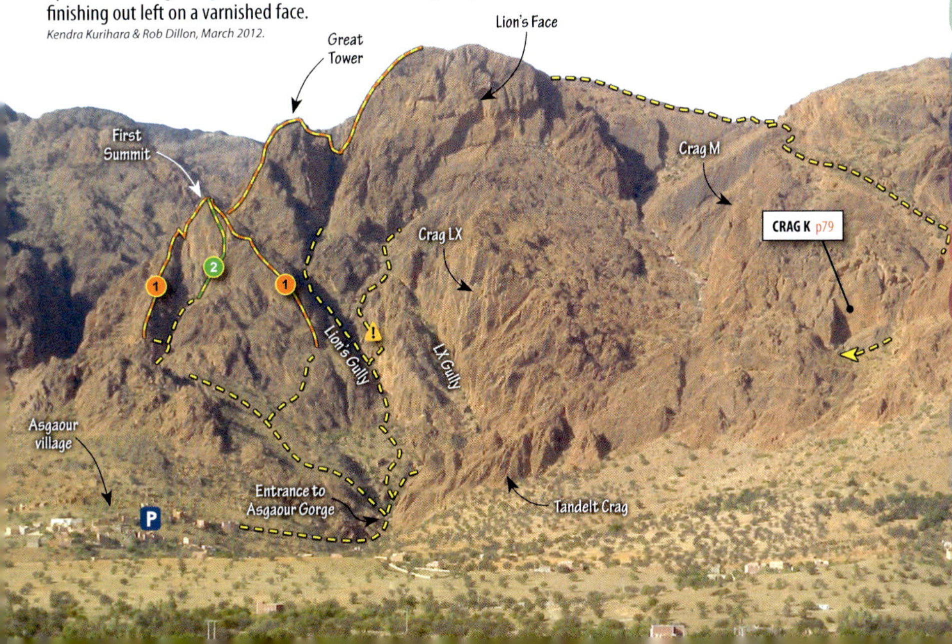

Map Page 68

Area Map
Crag Selector
Intro
The Climbing
How to Use
Suggested Climbs
Tafraout Granite
Anergui
Ameln Valley
Tarakatine Pass
Sidi M'Zal
Jebel Taskra
Idaougnidif
Afantinzar
Samazar
Aouguenz
Tagzene
Tagmout
History
Index

6. The Lion's Face Original HVS 5a ★2 (ADVENTURE)

300m. The original way up the Lion's Face is a historic climb, taking the left side of the face and passing to the right of the 'eye'. A long approach and epic descent make for a memorable day out... There is some confusion about the line of the initial pitches, and many teams gain the upper section via *L'Occhio*, which provides a more logical start.

Paul Ross & Les Brown, 1995.

This was one of the most significant Anti-Atlas ascents of the nineties, and was recorded in the new-route book as follows... "Climb the grey buttress leading to the chin of the lion. Go up the wall to the west of the mouth until it is possible to traverse right and ascend directly to its nose on the west side. Climb to the eye and cross onto the bridge of the nose, then take the vertical furrow in its brow. 9 pitches, 300m+, grade 5+."

7. L'Occhio HVS 5a ★2 (ADVENTURE)

300m. A modern classic, though like many routes hereabouts this adventurous route was first climbed in error, when the first-ascent team failed to locate the line of the *Original Route*. The climb starts on a flat belay under a yellow dihedral crack.

1) 45m. Climb the dihedral, move right then climb straight up to a rocky ledge.

2) 55m. Move right up a red wall, then back left and climb up the steep red pillar.

3) 60m. Climb steep walls, then a red slab on the right.

4) 45m. Easier climbing up to the left side of the 'eyebrow'.

5) 40m. Follow the pillar straight up, then a ramp leading rightwards to an exposed belay at the left end of the 'eyebrow'.

6) 40m. Climb up corners and walls to gain the ridge.

7-10) Continue up the *Lion's Face Ridge*.

Alberto Rampini & Silvia Mazzani, October 2010.

8. Polish Route VS 4c (UNCHECKED)

300m. The first big chimney to the right of the overhangs. Few details are known about this remote and adventurous climb.

Jacek Skrzypczynski & Andrej Łoś, December 2004.

9. Lion's Garden VS 4c (UNCHECKED)

165m. This route climbs a corner-system up the right side of the face, but details of the line are vague. Start up left of a plated wall, then climb a 30m pitch via a chimney through steep ground to gain the corner. Follow this to the ridge, from where 200m of scrambling gains the summit.

O.Guenay, H.Heuser & D.Kuch, December 2007.

D CRAG K, ASGAOUR

Shade Families Hitch Roadside

Drive from Tafraout: **10 minutes**
Walk-in: **40 minutes**

The North Wall of the Asgaour Gorge is one of the most important cragging venues in the Ameln Valley, being home to some of the region's hardest crag climbs. The wall, usually referred to as Crag K, lies in the upper section of the gorge, behind the back side of Tandelt Crag.

The climbing here, whilst often vegetated, is in a magnificent setting, and despite the relatively easy approach, has a pleasantly remote feel to it.

From parking in Asgaour village follow a small track alongside water pipes, heading eastwards to the entrance of the gorge. The path cuts across slabs at the entrance to the gorge before turning right and crossing over the stream. From here, ascend zigzags on the south side (true left bank) of the stream before passing beneath the shady South Wall, where some of the valley's hardest test-pieces lurk. The prominent blade of rock that forms Crag K is then clearly visible ahead on the opposite side of the gorge, with the narrow gully that forms 'the back side' separating it from the main hillside on the left. See approach map on page 76.

THE BACK SIDE

The back side of Crag K is an immense and intimidating vertical wall of impressive proportions, and home to one of the valley's most infamous wide cracks. It also provides an exhilarating abseil descent from routes on the front face.

Access is via the narrow gully which separates Crag K from the main hillside. Scramble up into the gully and continue beyond the unclimbable(?) wall until the obvious, stunning feature comes into sight on the right-hand side:

1. The Asgaour Crack E4 6a ★3 WIDE ABSEIL

55m. Welcome to the gates of Hell... Asgaour's answer to Tizgut's eponymous crack is an even more daunting endeavour, in which wide-crack connoisseurs will savour unrivalled masochistic pleasures. Speleological escapes may be tempting, but vary from easy and dirty, to perilous horror-show squeezes. E4 with plenty of very big gear, or HVS for old-school cragsmen...

1) 40m (6a) Climb up to a chockstone, then squirm strenuously to very hard moves out under the overhang, where any illusions of security well and truly evaporate. Continue more easily above to a belay on slabs out left.

2) 15m (4b) Finish up easy slabs to an abseil descent from blocks.

Steve & Katja Broadbent, March 2014.

Photo page 39.

Looking up towards Crag K from the entrance to the Asgaour Gorge

Map Page 68 & 76

THE MAIN CRAG

The first two routes on the main crag climb the west-facing wall at the foot of the narrow gully behind the crag.

DESCENT: There are two options for descent – either make one long, free-hanging abseil from a notch in the summit ridge into the gully behind the crag (hidden chain anchor under the upper chockstone), or traverse rightwards along the summit ridge to scramble down the east (right) end.

2. Valentine Day E4

ABSEIL

100m. A hard eliminate up the west-facing wall at the left end of the crag, sharing the initial chimney with *Anti-Climax*.
1) (5c) Start up a wide chimney to a ramp, then climb a hard crack leading to a belay in a left-facing corner.
2) (6a) Go up a slab, moving right to a tree. Climb the crack behind the tree to a ledge beneath a steep final crack. Follow this to the top.
Graham Everitt, Tom Leppert & Ian Wilson, February 2010.

3. Anti-Climax VS 5a

ABSEIL

125m. An adventurous ramble up the west-facing wall overlooking the descent gully.
1) Climb a chimney, then move right along a ledge to gain a fine hand-crack. Follow this to a belay below vegetation.
2) Go left up a slab, then climb a crack in the wall behind a tree. Traverse right to a corner crack, then belay on a ramp.
3) Traverse up right to reach the notch and abseil descent.

4. The Traverse VS 4c

150m. A good, long excursion across the upper part of the wall. Start at the bottom left, close to the foot of the descent gully, and climb ramps up rightwards to gain the upper face. Keep traversing right to finish at the top right side of the crag.
Les Brown & Pete Turnbull, 1992.

5. Left Ramp VS 4c ★

ABSEIL PRICKLY GEAR

200m. A popular outing, the narrow ramp system crossing the face would be a three-star route were it not for the vegetation on pitch 2. Follow the ramp with tremendous exposure for two pitches to a prominent left-slanting corner. Climb this, then meander vaguely rightwards towards the notch (abseil point).
Les Brown, Pete Turnbull, Roy & Hazel Warner, 2000. Photo next page.

6. Right Ramp VS 4c ★

ABSEIL PRICKLY

125m. The lower ramp, this time traversing beneath the blank wall to a finish straight up to the notch.
Les Brown, Pete Turnbull & Roy Warner, 2000.

7. Crawl to Prayer E3 5c

ABSEIL

90m. Difficult climbing up the pillar left of the notch, with a mildly ridiculous 2nd pitch!
1) Start up cracks to the left of *Great Schism* to gain a belay on *Right Ramp*.
2) Crawl along the ledge to gain a standing position, then move up right to gain a crack system that leads to a belay on *Left Ramp*.
3) Climb through the overhang above to finish up a further system of cracks.
Ian Wilson & Tom Leppert, February 2010.

8. Way of the Infidel E1 5b ★

ABSEIL PRICKLY

90m. A reasonable climb, with bonus bushwhack.
1) 45m (5b) Climb a chunky-looking crack beneath the right-hand of two V-overhangs. Step right at the overhang and traverse to a blocky roof, then continue up right to the top of the corner, belaying on the slab as for *Right Ramp*.
2) 30m (-) Climb a crack then traverse right and fight through a tree (unpleasant) to belay on the ramp.
3) 15m (-) Finish up a pleasant chimney to easy ground.
Rob Dillon & Kendra Kurihara, March 2007.

9. Storm in a Tea Cup E1 5b ★

90m. A good, varied climb. Start beneath orange overlaps, at a slabby arête.
1) 50m (5a) Climb the arête and a slabby buttress above to a ledge beneath the headwall.
2) 40m (5b) Take a right-slanting diagonal groove in the wall, with increasing difficulty, to reach easier ground.
Graham Everitt, Tom Leppert & N.Redfern, February 2010.

10. Great Schism E2 5b ★2 ABSEIL WIDE

100m. The big left-facing corner in the centre of the face gives a popular climb up a good direct line. The Schism itself can be avoided via an easier crack to the left.
Joe Brown & Claude Davies, 1999.

11. One Love E2 5b ★2 ABSEIL

100m. Another difficult climb, this time taking the wall to the right of *Great Schism* and meeting that route at the big corner.
1) 50m (5b) Climb a series of thin cracks to gain the corner.
2) 40m (5b) Climb the crack to the left of the corner.
Graham Everitt, Tom Leppert & Ian Wilson, February 2010.

12. Call to Prayers E2 5b ★2 CRACK

90m. Two long crack pitches up the pillar at the right side of the face, providing some excellent climbing.
1) 45m (5a) Start up short corners, trending leftwards to gain a fine crack. Climb this, then move right to belay below a chimney-crack.
2) 45m (5b) Squirm up the chimney-crack then finish up the continuation crack above.
Chris King, Ron Kenyon & Shaun Brown, 2003.

13. Special K E3 5c ★3

90m. The fine wall left of *Waiting for the Barbarians*.
1) 45m (5b) Climb the centre of the wall to an overhang. Move right here to the apex, then on through the upper wall, trending left to belay as for *Call to Prayers*.
2) 45m (5c) Step right to gain a crack on the front face. Follow this to its end, then step right again to finish directly up the steep headwall.
Graham Everitt, Tom Leppert, James Strongman & Ian Wilson, February 2010.

14. Waiting for the Barbarians E3 6a ★2 CRACK

75m. The impressive wall up the right side of the front face gives a technically demanding climb of great quality.
1) 35m (5c) Climb up to gain a rightward-rising crackline which is followed with interest to a stance.
2) 40m (6a) Climb more easily up to where the wall steepens. Place a high runner, then move 2m left to difficult moves up to a ledge (crux). Move up, then rightwards along a diagonal fault line before finishing back left to the top.
Chris King, Ron Kenyon & Shaun Brown, 2003.

15. Onionskin Crack E2 5b ★2 ABSEIL CRACK

25m. The obvious diagonal splitter crack at the right side of the face is an excellent 'little' challenge, with a fiendish boulder-problem start and unexpected difficulties higher up. Descend by abseil from the bush.
Ian Wilson & Esther Bott, 2006.

Area Map
Crag Selector
Intro
The Climbing
How to Use
Suggested Climbs
Tafraout Granite
Anergui
Ameln Valley
Tarakatine Pass
Sidi M'Zal
Jebel Taskra
Idaougnidif
Afantinzar
Samazar
Aouguenz
Tagzene
Taoumout
History
Index

Area Map
Crag Selector
Intro
The Climbing
How to Use
Suggested Climbs
Tafraout Granite
Anergui
Ameln Valley
Tarakatine Pass
Sidi M'Zal
Jebel Taskra
Idaougnidif
Afantinzar
Samazar
Aouguenz
Tagzene
Tagmout
History
Index

Just to the right of the main part of the crag is a smooth orange wall that is home to three excellent test-pieces...

16. Tis Good Craic E2 5c ★2 (CRACK)

65m. The superb big corner up the left side of the orange wall has some loose rock low down, but improves quickly with height.

1) 30m (5b) Start up the overhanging crack in the corner until it is possible to step right onto a slab. Follow the left-hand crack through more steep ground above to a belay.

2) 35m (5c) A tremendous pitch up the clean corner-crack, moving right at the overhang.

H.Hennessy, M.Walsh & J.Gallway, December 2007.

17. The Flying Scotsmen E6 6b ★3

110m. For some time this was Tafraout's hardest quartzite climb – a brilliantly varied route that epitomises hard adventure climbing in the valley. A small RP provides the last runner before a monster run-out which has seen its fair share of scary air-time. Cracking stuff!

1) 40m (6b) The thin diagonal crack left of *Hospitality Attack* provides a well-protected but desperately strenuous start. Step right at a small ledge and continue up a further crack to a belay ledge.

2) 10m (-) Walk left to the base of another thin crack.

3) 40m (6a) A serious pitch that may still contain some friable rock. Follow the crack past two small ramps to gain a third ramp veering slightly left. Climb up rightwards along the third ramp with increasing trepidation and continue to a crack. Go up this to a hanging belay at the base of a prominent flake.

4) 30m (5c) Go up the flake and finish up a fine wide crack.

Trevor Woods & Guy Robertson, October 2003.

18. Hospitality Attack E3 5c ★3 (CRACK)

110m. The original way up the desperate orange wall is an infamous classic that should be high on any tick-list. Its original grade of 5b did little to adequately describe the difficulties of what is a major adventure-climb in a remote environment and stunning setting.

1) 15m. Start on top of blocks and climb a system of cracks up left to a ledge.

2) 45m. Step left and climb a short crack to another ledge, then move left again to gain the obvious right-slanting diagonal crack. Follow this up to blocks until it is possible to bridge into the white hanging groove and belay in a niche.

3) 50m. Tiptoe out left below the roof and pull up to gain the big left-slanting crack. Race along this into a final vertical crack that proves surprisingly awkward.

Neil Dyer & Jude Spancken, 2001.

Ben Lister on pitch 3 of *Left Ramp* (VS 4c) on Asgaour's Crag K (previous page).

Photo: Steve Broadbent

Map Page 68

E MOSQUE VALLEY SLABS

Shade · Families · Hitch · Roadside

Drive from Tafraout: **10 minutes**
Walk-in: **50 minutes**

This attractive wall is clearly visible from the Ameln Valley, sitting on the right (true left) bank of Mosque Valley above Old Oumsnat. The wall faces south, gets all the sun there is going, and with a sheltered position can become something of a heat-trap in hot weather.

The approach up Mosque Valley is best made from Old Oumsnat. Take the first of the Oumsnat turnings from the Ameln Valley road, then follow a right fork after crossing the first major riverbed. This leads to ample parking amongst some isolated houses in between New and Old Oumsnat. From here, take a reasonable path towards the hillside, descending to cross a major riverbed and then climbing steeply to the highest of the ancient buildings. From this point a good path traverses left into the gorge – follow it to the stream and continue for about 75m until a vague trail cuts back up right alongside a concrete water-leat. This leads up the left (true right) side of the gorge, passing Crag O on the left, from where the slabs are clearly visible about 10 minutes further up the gorge.

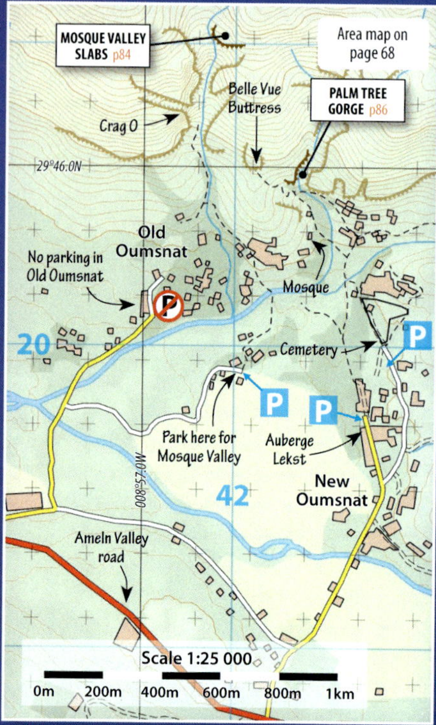

1. Left Roof E1 5b

35m. This route climbs the left-hand weakness though the prominent roofs at the left side of the wall. Below the fault in the roof are twin V-cracks – start up the right-hand of the two cracks, left of a black streak. Climb to a terrace, then go diagonally left to the fault in the roof. Climb through this and continue to the top.

Brian Davison & Paul Wood, December 2014.

2. Zoo Station HVS 4c

50m. Pleasant climbing up the side of the black streak to break through the mid-height overlap.

James Strongman, B.Wagner, Graham & Ruth Everitt, February 2008.

3. The Real Thing E2 5b

50m. Super climbing above the prickly bushes, heading up to the right side of the overlaps.
James Strongman, B.Wagner, Graham & Ruth Everitt, February 2008.

4. Even Better than the Real Thing E2 5b

50m. Another excellent climb. Start from a prickly pear and follow the left-slanting break before launching straight up the wall above.
James Strongman, B.Wagner, Graham & Ruth Everitt, February 2008.

5. One Tree Hill E2 5b

50m. The centre of the wall is gained via a small tree and followed with interest.
James Strongman, B.Wagner, Graham & Ruth Everitt, February 2008.

6. Bullet in the Blue Sky E3 5b

50m. Difficult and rather bold climbing up the wall immediately right of the small tree.
James Strongman, B.Wagner, Graham & Ruth Everitt, February 2008.

7. Wild Horses E2 5c

50m. Good climbing, directly up the centre of the face from a shallow left-facing corner.
James Strongman, B.Wagner, Graham & Ruth Everitt, February 2008.

8. Helter Skelter HVS 5a

50m. A slightly more amenable proposition up the wall to the right. Start up a rightwards-curving undercut to gain the mid-height ledge system.
James Strongman, B.Wagner, Graham & Ruth Everitt, February 2008.

9. Mysterious Ways HVS 5a

50m. Another worthwhile climb, taking the vague groove right of the mid-height ledges.
James Strongman, B.Wagner, Graham & Ruth Everitt, February 2008.

10. Achtung Baby E1 5a

50m. Climb up to the right side of a small overhang at the right end of the wall. Finish straight up the wall above.
James Strongman, B.Wagner, Graham & Ruth Everitt, February 2008.

11. Black Spot HS

30m. At the right side the angle of the wall eases and the slab contains a prominent black spot near its centre. Start right of a tree and climb through the black spot to the top.
Brian Davison & Paul Wood, December 2014.

12. Zigzag Very Difficult

30m. A weaving line up the right side of the wall, where it merges with the col, provides the easiest way up the crag. It can also be used as a descent by the competent...
Brian Davison & Paul Wood, December 2014.

James Strongman on *Wild Horses* (E2 5c), Mosque Valley Slabs ➲
Photo: Graham Everitt

Area Map
Crag Selector
Intro
The Climbing
How to Use
Suggested Climbs
Tafraout Granite
Anergui
Ameln Valley
Tarakatine Pass
Sidi M'Zal
Jebel Taskra
Idaougnidif
Afantinzar
Samazar
Aouguenz
Tagzene
Tagmout
History
Index

F PALM TREE GORGE

Shade · Families · Hitch · Roadside

Drive from Tafraout: **10 minutes**
Walk-in: **15 minutes**

A superb little climbing ground, with plenty of easily-accessible routes, good rock, and a lovely setting right on the edge of Oumsnat village. Palm Tree Gorge is the narrow gorge that cuts into the hillside directly above the old village, and for climbers looking for a break from the longer routes of Jebel el Kest it is an excellent and relaxing venue with routes to suit most abilities.

The gorge continues high into the mountains, but the climbing is focused around the short buttresses of clean solid rock which form the entrance to the ravine, where magnificent date palms provide an attractive backdrop and welcome shade.

Oumsnat is a notoriously complicated village to navigate through. Thankfully, however, most paths will get you to the right place eventually, so a detailed description of the approach is of limited value. The closest parking is in the centre of New Oumsnat, at the Auberge Lekst (see map on page 84). Take the narrowing track between the final houses and into trees beyond, from where a myriad of small paths then wind their way towards the extensive ruins of Old Oumsnat. The outflow from Palm Tree Gorge passes beneath a prominent white mosque, and a couple of good paths run alongside it, converging on the left (true right) bank of the stream just below the entrance to the gorge. At this point the path begins zigzagging steeply up the slope to the left towards Belle Vue Buttress, but a small path leads off to the right into the narrow gorge entrance. Entrance Wall is clearly visible on the left at the point where this small path enters the gorge.

DESCENT: From most of the routes it is possible to descend easily to the left, passing above Entrance Wall to reach a short down-climb just left of the first routes. For a number of climbs, including those on the opposite side of the gorge, the quickest descent is by abseil – a fact that is usually obvious on a first visit.

ENTRANCE WALL

This short but excellent south-facing slab lies just outside the entrance to the gorge on the left (true right) bank, overlooking the path up to Belle Vue Buttress.

1. Bahrain Difficult ★1 BOLD

20m. Pleasant but unprotected climbing up the cracked-rib at the left side of the slabby wall.
Steve Broadbent (solo), February 2012.

2. Rum Keg Very Difficult ★1

20m. The broken rib immediately left of the black slab has some nice moves on big holds.
Steve Broadbent (solo), February 2012.

3. Rockin' Zebra VS 4b ★1 SLAB

25m. An attractive climb up the hairline 'non-crack' in the centre of the black slab. Climb the slab then move up left until it is possible to traverse out right across the steep sidewall with plentiful gear and exposure.
Steve Broadbent & Will Benfold, February 2012.

4. Fact or Friction VS 4c ★1

25m. Superb climbing up the vague groove in the right side of the slab leads to some bold moves beneath the roof. Traverse left here, avoiding the flake ledge beneath for as long as you can!
Will Benfold & Steve Broadbent, February 2012.

5. Tumbleweed HS 4b ★

25m. The obvious groove to the right of the slab has a fun chimneying finish.

Will Benfold & Steve Broadbent, February 2012.

6. Trader Vics Severe ★

25m. Another worthwhile climb that is better than it looks. Take cracks just right of the right-hand rib, accessed from a low start to the right.

Steve Broadbent & Will Benfold, February 2012.

7. To Close to Zero E4 6b ★ THIN

30m. The thin seam up the smooth, steep wall takes an assortment of tiny gear, and leads with difficulty to easier climbing above.

Vanessa Wills & David Gray, February 2014.

8. TNT E5 6b ★

30m. The next seam to the right is a notch harder. Continue up over a bulge to finish more easily up the ramp to the right.

David Gray & Vanessa Wills, February 2014.

9. Terry Le Fronde E2 5b ★

30m. Start 2m left of *Salif Kieta*, where crossed palms touch the wall. Go up to a left-facing overhanging flake, stepping left at its top to avoid cactus. Climb up onto a slab, finishing rightwards up the groove to a belay.

Vanessa Wills & David Gray, February 2014.

Area Map
Crag Selector
Intro
The Climbing
How to Use
Suggested Climbs
Tafraout Granite
Anergui
Ameln Valley
Tarakatine Pass
Sidi M'Zal
Jebel Taskra
Idaougnidif
Afantinzar
Samazar
Aouguenz
Tagzene
Tagmout
History
Index

TOUAREG TOWER

Immediately right of Entrance Wall is the entrance to the gorge itself. Touareg Tower stands above a pleasant shady clearing which provides an ideal 'racking up' or lunch spot...

10. Salif Keita E2 5b

PRICKLY

25m. The euphorbia-capped groove and wall to the left of *Scimitar*.

Graham & Ruth Everitt, February 2008.

11. Scimitar E3 6a ★1

THIN

25m. Start at the slanting undercut and move left into a thin crack. Climb up this before finishing up the wall to the right.

Chris King & Barry Clarke, October 2004.

12. Baba Maal E2 5c ★2

30m. Starts just right of *Scimitar*, below a short stepped groove in the overhang. Climb directly up the wall to the groove, which leads with difficulty to the wall above. Move slightly left and go up the wall to finish left of the flake crack of *Farouk's Fundaments*. A short crack and final bulging block round off an excellent climb.

Graham & Ruth Everitt, February 2008.

13. Farouk's Fundaments VS 4b ★2

25m. The wide crack to the left of the pinnacle is a justifiably popular climb. Move left just below a bush and finish up a flake crack on the front face.

Ron Kenyon & Geoff Somers, October 2004.

14. Surgical Reverso E1 5a ★1

BOLD

25m. Swarm up the right-hand side of the pinnacle before attacking the blank wall above. Finish up the groove as for *Jarrad*.

John Lunch & Ed Luke, January 2014.

15. Crocodile Dundee VS 4c ★2

BOLD

30m. A great little climb. Start just left of the pool and traverse up right with a difficult move to gain the crack up the right side of the pinnacle. Move right onto the excellent bold rib to join *Jarrad* for a steep finish.

Steve Broadbent & Will Benfold, February 2012.

16. Jerad HVS 5a ★2

35m. An excellent direct line starting just above the pool. Climb directly up the crack system to cross the corner system of *Jarrad* below bulging flakes. Climb up the flakes, then step right and pull up onto the final arête of *Original Route*.

Jordan & John Phethean, February 2014.

17. Jarrad MVS 4b ★2

30m. Super climbing up the fine corner above the pool. Follow the slabby corner to a challenging finish up the steep crack above.

Geoff Somers & Ron Kenyon, October 2004.

To the right are double V-cracks above a small pool.

18. Original Route VS 4c ★1

30m. An intimidating climb, taking the arete left of the 'V' notch.

Chris King & Barry Clarke, October 2004.

19. Howzat VS 4c ★1

30m. Gain the left-hand 'V' as for the *Original Route*. From here take the crack on the right before finishing up the crack on the left.

Geoff Somers & Ron Kenyon, October 2004.

20. Lizard Lunch HVS 5a

30m. The groove right of *Howzat*.

Paul Donnithorne & Don Sargeant, April 2016.

21. Hideous Kinky E2 5c ★1

30m. The crackline in the wall right of *Howzat* leads to some steep, poor rock. Move right here, around the arête, and cross a slab to finish up a corner.

Egg & Ruth Everitt, March 2014.

RED WALL

Up and right of the double V-cracks is a high wall of S-shaped cracks. This is known as Red Wall and is home to a number of harder wall climbs.

22. Berber Buttress HVS 5a ★1

40m. The prominent arête to a ledge at 2/3 height. Move slightly right from here and finish up the wall above.
Ron Kenyon & Geoff Somers, October 2004.

23. Cabaret E2 5b ★1

40m. The corner to the right leads to a belay on the ledge. From here go up another corner then traverse 5m rightwards to the base of a crack. Climb this over a bulge and finish up the wall above.
Chris King & Barry Clarke, October 2004.

24. Spagetti Western HVS 5b ★1 STEEP

30m. An audacious outing up the centre of the Red Wall. Start by scrambling up through a V-notch to gain a prominent ledge. *This initial section is not visible on the topo.* The ledge can also be reached by climbing the first pitch of *Moulin Rouge*. Start just left of a prickly pear and climb the central crack with a short corner to finish.

25. Moulin Rouge E2 5b ★1

50m. A good, challenging climb that takes a left-facing corner at the right side of the Red Wall. Start at a fig tree in the bed of the gorge, 20m right of *Berber Buttress*.
1) 20m (4c) Step off the fig tree and climb the wall and bulging groove to the belay ledge. *This pitch is not visible on the topo.*
2) 30m (5b) Climb awkwardly rightwards into the groove and follow it to finish up the wall above.
Chris King & Barry Clarke, October 2004.

26. Pasties and Scones E3 5c ★1 WIDE STEEP

35m. The daunting wide crack above the right-hand end of the ledge should be reserved for those who think overhanging off-width cracks are a good thing. Start from the V-notch and battle your way to a hiding place under the overhang. It is usual to spend some time here, summoning courage for the fine off-width finale.
James Strongman, Ian Wilson & Tom Leppert, February 2010.

27. Scooby Doo E1 5b 2

60m. An atmospheric route, starting up *Pasties and Scones*. Gain the initial ledge at 10 metres, then climb a few moves up that route until it is possible to move right into the right-facing groove. Pass a bulge, then traverse 3 metres further right to climb the main groove.

Paul Donnithorne & Don Sargeant, April 2016.

EAST BANK

On the east (true left) side of the gorge entrance, opposite Touareg Tower lies an eye-catching arête. The rock here is steeper and rather more sandy than that on the west bank, but this does not detract from the quality of the following superb climbs...

28. Aspen Rap E2 5b 1

50m. Climbs the groove 8 metres left of *Tresonga*.

1) 20m (5b) Start just left of a large boulder and follow the groove to a cave belay.

2) 30m (5b) Trend up right to climb a fine corner and wide crack.

Paul Donnithorne & Don Sargeant, April 2016.

29. Tresonga E2 5c 2

30m. The dark, overhanging crack 8m left of the arête at the entrance to the gorge will jump out at some folk, and be dismissed as desperate by many. Jam your way up the initial wide crack to a sloping ledge, then move right into a thin crack, before a final traverse right on sloping footholds gives access to yet another crack. Finish up this with relief.

James Strongman, Ian Wilson & Tom Leppert, February 2010.

30. Feet of Clay E3 6a 2

30m. Start just right of the large boulder and climb dusty, overhung rock into the finger crack above. This eventually widens to narrow hands, and leads to a shared finish with the previous route.

David Gray & Vanessa Wills, February 2014.

31. Casino Royale E4 5c 2

30m. A mega-testpiece up the striking arête at the entrance to the gorge, providing one of Oumsnat's big ticks. A strong hand is needed for a brutal pull past the obvious jam before better holds give access to the mesmerising shallow groove above, in which one's resolve will be well and truly tested...

James Strongman, Ian Wilson & Tom Leppert, February 2010.

32. Sentry Duty E5 6b 1

30m. Start just right of *Casino Royale*, at a sentry box. Climb a crack, then follow a diagonal seam leftwards through a small bulge. Continue up into the hanging corner, then pull right via a crack onto the headwall beyond.

Vanessa Wills & David Gray, February 2014.

33. Ca Va Severe 1

30m. The easiest way up to the top of the pillar is somewhat vegetated initially, but features some very nice climbing on the final wall.

David Gray & Vanessa Wills, February 2014.

DESCENT: All of the routes on the East Bank require abseil descents, and climbers are therefore advised to carry replacement anchors.

G TIZGUT GORGE

Shade Families Hitch Roadside Drive from Tafraout: **20 minutes** Walk-in: **30 minutes**

The prominent gorge above Tizgut is a major centre of Tafraout cragging, and has remained one of the most popular destinations for western climbers since Joe Brown's ascent of the peerless *Tizgut Crack* in 1993. In the years since then the gorge has seen extensive new-route activity and now boasts the largest collection of high-quality, mid-length multi-pitch climbs on this side of the massif.

The rock is generally high quality, although some lines have become more vegetated in recent years. Whilst the gorge is generally a warm, sunny place, there is usually plenty of shade to be found, making it a worthwhile choice in most conditions.

The approach from the village of Tizgut is relatively straightforward, despite the myriad of small paths. Park in the village immediately before the road turns steeply downhill to the river. Walk down this hill, cross the river, then take a small path on the right at an electricity pylon by the first pink house. Follow this path up the hill, heading for a lone house up and right, from where a good path traverses leftwards to the entrance of the gorge. The first buttress, Castle Mound, is located outside of the gorge on the west side but is easily reached by traversing left from here. To reach the routes in the main gorge follow an ancient path up the right (true left) side of the stream bed.

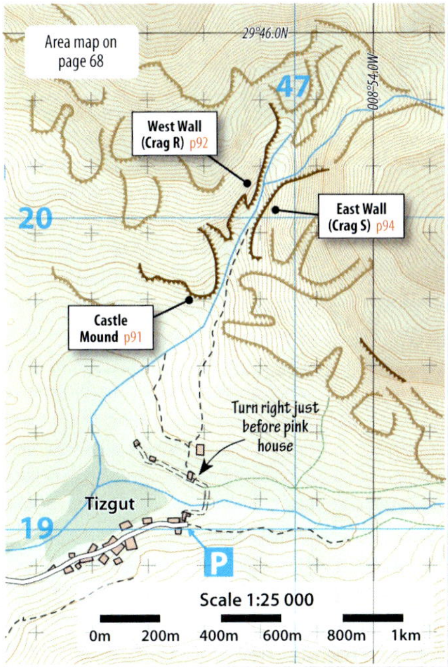

CASTLE MOUND

This smaller buttress is located on the left side of the gorge entrance as viewed from the approach. It holds a number of pleasant pitches with simple walk-off descents.

1. Magical Mystery Tour VS 4b PRICKLY

25m. The centre of the black face has become vegetated in recent years. Bold climbing, avoiding the crack on the right.

2. You For Beer HVS 5a ★

32m. Climb the steep wall and arête boldly to a break at 10 metres, from where cracks lead up to a ledge.

3. Fire Below HS 4a ★ GEAR

32m. The first major corner system left of the front face is well-protected.

4. Hole in the Leg MVS 4b ★

32m. A pleasant climb up the crack system on the left side of the steep south-facing wall.

Area Map
Crag Selector
Intro
The Climbing
How to Use
Suggested Climbs
Tafraout Granite
Anergui
Ameln Valley
Tarakatine Pass
Sidi M'Zal
Jebel Taskra
Idaougnidif
Afantinzar
Samazar
Aouguenz
Tagzene
Tagmout
History
Index

THE WEST WALL (CRAG R)

Originally known as Crag R, the left side of the main gorge (true right bank) is rather more broken and easily angled than its opposite number. It holds a selection of mid-grade, multi-pitch climbs that catch the sun throughout the morning. Routes are described from left to right (i.e. working up the gorge in the direction of approach).

The first three routes are located in a vague bay low down in the gorge.

5. Eblis VS 4c

150m. Takes slabby ground at the left end of the wall.

Dave Jones, Joe Brown, Pete Turnbull & Claude Davies, 2003.

6. Riblah VS 4c ★1

75m. The rib to the right of the slabs is worthwhile.

Dave Jones, Joe Brown & Claude Davies, 2003.

7. Tapered Rib VS 4c

75m. The next rib to the right.

Derek Walker & Chris Bonington, 2003.

8. Lost Pillar HVS 5a

120m. This route climbs up to the left of a prominent triple roof behind the tower climbed by *Egg's Reward*.

1) 40m (4c) Climb the centre of the wall to belay below the triple roof, level with a tree to the right.

2) 40m (5a) Climb the groove and crack left of the overhangs.

3) 40m (-) Scramble up to the top of the cleft and cross it. An abseil sling can be reached by down -limbing on the right side of the cleft and abseiling to the tree mentioned in pitch 1.

Brian Davison & Paul Wood, December 2014.

The next feature upstream is an attractive tower with a wide crack up its front face.

9. Egg's Reward E1 5b ★3 ABSEIL

50m. Brilliant climbing vaguely following the left arête of the tower.

Graham Everitt & Ian Wilson, March 2011.

10. Day of the Tentacle HVS 5b ★2 ABSEIL

60m. An excellent, challenging climb that requires a bold and powerful approach.

1) 25m (4c) The lower crack gives some nice climbing to a vegetated belay ledge.

2) 35m (5b) The wide right-hand crack above has a very difficult move to get established. Descend by abseil from a variety of in-situ gear.

Caroline Culiwck & Steve Broadbent, March 2011.

11. Black Streak HVS 5a

150m. One of the more difficult propositions on the face, this route gains and climbs the vague black streak above the cracked tower.

Joe Brown & Claude Davies, 1996.

12. Appian Way VS 4b ★1 GEAR

150m. Pleasant climbing up the centre of the face. Climb up to an early crux up a steep crack, from where easy climbing leads to the big upper crack.

Joe Brown & Claude Davies, 1998.

13. Golden Pillar MVS 4a ★1

150m. The attractive narrow buttress runs the full height of the cliff and provides some worthwhile climbing.
Claude Davies & Pete Turnbull, 1993.

14. Superi HS 4a ★1 STEEP

150m. A long and popular climb tackling the steep buttress towards the right side of the wall. The impending wall at half-height provides some challenging climbing that can be avoided on the left.
Claude Davies & Trevor Jones, 1993.

15. Anything Goes MVS 4a ★1

150m. The crag's original line.
Joe Brown & Pete Turnbull, 1992.

16. Right Again MVS 4a ★1 ? UNCHECKED

150m. This route takes a long ridge-line at the far right end of the wall, although few details are known.
Claude Davies & Roger Salisbury, 1998.

The next route is located on the small buttress in the centre of the gorge, a few yards up from *Salus* and *Right Again*.

17. Tangerine Dream VS 5a ★2

A good outcrop-style route taking the groove in the centre of the buttress, well protected with medium cams.
Mark Anstiss & Ben Lister, October 2014.

West Wall (central)
AM 35m

Area Map
Crag Selector
Intro
The Climbing
How to Use
Suggested Climbs
Tafraout Granite
Anergui
Ameln Valley
Tarakatine Pass
Sidi M'Zal
Jebel Taskra
Idaougnidif
Afantinzar
Samazar
Aouguenz
Tagzene
Tagmout
History
Index

Map Page 70

Area Map
Crag Selector
Intro
The Climbing
How to Use
Suggested Climbs
Tafraout Granite
Anergui
Ameln Valley
Tarakatine Pass
Sidi M'Zal
Jebel Taskra
Idaougnidif
Afantinzar
Samazar
Aouguenz
Tagzene
Tagmout
History
Index

THE EAST WALL (CRAG S)

The steeper, right (true left) wall of the Tizgut Gorge is home to some of Tafraout's most infamous test-pieces. Routes are described from left to right, working down the gorge from the upper left end.

18. Trivial Pursuit Severe ★1

50m. The slabby ground at the top of the main gorge gives one of the crag's few good easy climbs.

Joe Brown & Pete Turnbull, 1996.

19. Yer Tiz HVS 5a ★1

70m. Pleasant climbing, starting 3 metres left of *Salus*.

1) 40m (4b) Climb the crack, then a right-trending flake to belay on *Salus*.

2) 30m (5a) Pull up right into a slim groove / ramp above and right of *Salus*. Continue to easier ground.

Joe Brown & Pete Turnbull, 2000.

20. Salus VS 4c ★2

CRACK

80m. This obvious corner, tucked away at the left side of the main face is a much bigger climb than first appearances suggest, and one of the best VS climbs in the gorge.

Joe Brown & Pete Turnbull, 2000.

21. Tizgut Rib VS 4c ★1

80m. The rib just to the right is one of the crag's classic 'ticks' and well worth a visit.

Joe Brown, Pete Turnbull & Roy Warner, 2000.

22. Ahmed VS 4c

100m. A meandering line up the slabby walls.

Joe Brown, Pete Turnbull & Roy Warner, 2000.

23. Tizgud Crack E2 5b ★2

120m. Not to be confused with the rather more famous *Tizgut Crack*, this challenging climb starts some 10m left of *Tagine*, below the left-hand of two twin cracks.

1) 45m (5b) Climb the crack with considerable difficulty up an 'Amen Corner' to a groove. Follow this before stepping left to a belay on *Ahmed*.

2) 45m (5a) Move back right around the rib to the bottom of the upper crack. Climb this, with a short excursion onto the right wall and a superbly positioned finish.

3) 30m (4c) The wall above eventually eases.

Ron Kenyon & Chris King, 2004.

DESCENT: All routes finish on a broad slanting terrace, from where it is possible to descend either left (down-climb required) or right (walking.)

24. Tizgut Diagonal E2 5c

120m. A big route up the left side of the central buttress. **1)** Start up *Tagine* to gain an obvious left-trending diagonal crack. This leads to a belay below a crack in the upper arête. **2)** Climb the crack on the right side of the arête, step right and finish up a bold slab.

Ian Wilson & Tom Leppert, February 2011.

25. Tagine E2 5c

125m. A brilliant crack climb, providing a fine and uncompromising alternative to *Tizgut Crack*. Start up the finger-hand crack and climb for two pitches (5b, 5c) to a belay on top of a pillar. Finish up a groove as for *Tizgut Buttress*.

Sean Paling & Val Gillet, 1999.

26. Wagha Wagha Wagha E3 6a

110m. Another audacious climb up the intimidating steep wall left of *Tizgut Crack*. Climb up a thin crack between *Tagine* and *Tizgut Crack*, to reach good gear in the overlap. Move down to traverse a line of footholds into the centre of the wall, then climb a hanging flake onto the upper wall.

Graham Everitt & W.Szymanovicz, Feb 2011.

27. Tizgut Crack E1 5b

100m. Joe Brown's unmissable quartzite masterpiece is one of Tafraout's most infamous climbs; and rightly so. This epic corner-crack is everything you'd expect, and then a little bit more, providing a full-on, world-class wide crack experience. E1 with plenty of big cams...
1) 35m (5b) Sustained climbing up the unrelenting crack, which gets wider, harder, and altogether more emotional as height is gained. Step right to a sloping stance by a huge flake.
2) 40m (5b) A couple of tricky moves on suspect rock gain easier ground, from where one final well-protected move in a steep corner marks the end of the difficulties.
3) 20m (-) Easy climbing to the top.

Joe Brown, Claude Davies & Trevor Jones, 1993.

28. Tizgut Buttress HVS 5a

150m. An intricate buttress climb that wends its way up the highest part of the crag. Climb the lower buttress to the right of *Tizgut Crack*, to belay as for that route at the huge flake. From here climb through some steep suspect rock (as for the *Crack*) before moving leftwards to finish up the left-hand buttress.

Les Brown & Pete Turnbull, 1997.

29. Flying Grandfathers E4 6b

125m. Details of this recent addition are not exactly clear, but this technically challenging climb appears to start up the corner immediately right of *Tizgut Crack*. From a good belay ledge it takes suspect-looking rock (some ground probably shared with *Tizgut Buttress*) to a difficult crack in the steep ground above. Step left above this to an easier finish up a corner crack.

W.Szymanovicz, Tom Leppert, Ian Wilson & Graham Everitt, February 2011.

Map Page 70

30. Tizgut Direct E1 5a UNCHECKED

125m. A direct eliminate up the front of the buttress between *Tizgut Buttress* and *Tizgut Arête*, although details of the first ascent are uncertain.

31. Tizgut Arête E1 5a ★2 BOLD

125m. Another superb climb, with magnificent positions. Climb the right side of the buttress until it gets steeper – the original way went right from here, onto a ramp across the south-facing wall. The excellent direct finish (E2 5b) makes for an even better line.

Joe Brown & Derek Walker, 1998 (right-hand finish).
Steve Burns & Valerie Partington, March 2012 (direct finish).

32. Tizgut Corner HVS 5a ★2 PRICKLY GEAR CRACK

100m. The corner to the right has some vegetation these days, but provides an excellent route with some well-protected crack climbing in its upper section.

Joe Brown & Claude Davies, 1998.

33. Cactus Corner VS 4c PRICKLY

100m. The next corner is slightly easier but also features some vegetation.

Paul Ross & Trevor Jones, 1995.

34. Tizgut Slab Recess VS 4c ★1 LOOSE BOLD

110m. A good but rather bold climb, with a tremendous first pitch. Afterwards, imagination is required to find a satisfactory finish, the corner above being marred somewhat by loose rock.

Claude Davies & Pete Turnbull, 1995.

35. Right Recess VS 4b ★1

125m. The shady recess to the right.

Joe Brown & Pete Turnbull, 2000.

36. Aladdin VS 4c ★1

100m. Stepped orange walls to an upper slab.

Joe Brown & Claude Davies, 1999.

37. Springbok VS 4c ★1

100m. Climb ledges trending up left until a traverse right breaks through steeper ground above. Either step round the arête into a groove, or climb a steep crack above the traverse to gain easier ground.

Les Brown, Pete Turnbull & Roy Warner, 1999.

38. Great Chimney Very Difficult PRICKLY

80m. The deep chasm has little to recommend it, but is included here for completeness.

Andrew Wielochowski & John Temple, March 2008.

39. Casablanca HVS 5a

LOOSE BOLD

80m. A varied climb with a poor start, but nice positions above. Start at the left toe of the buttress, below the *Great Chimney*.

1) 30m (4b) Go up steps on the left side of the buttress until it is possible to head up rightwards on good holds to a flake runner in the centre of the face. From here, further bold moves lead up right to the right side of the buttress, where a swing right gains a ledge. This pitch is poorly protected and features some loose rock.

2) 15m (4c) Bridge up, then swing left to a narrow ledge. Move left to regain ledges on the front of the buttress. Climb the centre of the face, moving right on underclings then back left to belay below steep cracks.

3) 15m (5a) Go right over blocks to the right edge of the buttress. After a slight bulge things ease, with straightforward climbing over blocks to various belays.

4) 20m (-) Follow the pleasant slabby ridge to the top of the buttress.

Andrew Wielochowski & John Temple, March 2008.

40. Sam's Shadow VS 4b ★1

85m. Some nice climbing, though rather disjointed. The route remains in the shade for much of the day, and is therefore a good choice during hot weather.

1) 10m (-) Scramble easily up to a tree in the wide vegetated chimney.

2) 30m (4b) Climb the slabby corner beneath the impending left wall of *Play It Again Sam*. At a slight bulge make a delicate traverse left, then step down to a crevasse stance.

3) 20m (-) Go easily leftwards to a cave / corner below the *Casablanca* buttress.

4) 25m (-) Climb a steep crack 4m left of the cave to gain a ledge. Move right along this, into the corner to finish up a final chimney.

Andrew Wielochowski & Noel Williams, March 2008.

41. Play it Again Sam Severe ★1

70m. A very pleasant climb, with a superb final pitch. This route follows the long, narrow rib at the far right end of the main crag, just upstream from where the descent path rejoins the path along the bed of the gorge. Start on a big ledge at the base of the rib.

1) 20m. Climb the front of the rib, then move right to a ledge. Follow this for 2m until it is possible to climb up to a spike belay on the crest of the ridge.

2) 30m. Climb a smooth slab and continue up the rib until it steepens. Move right here and go up a right-facing corner to a fine stance beneath a large rectangular roof.

3) 20m. Move up and swing left on good holds to regain the rib. A final wall and crack complete a fine outing.

Andrew Wielochowski & John Temple, March 2008.

42. Again and Again MVS 4b ★1

70m. Good quality, well-protected climbing starting in a slabby corner immediately right of the rib of *Play It Again Sam*.

1) 45m (4b) Climb corners until it is possible to traverse up right across slabs to a slight bulge. Surmount this, then follow easier ground passing a tree and moving up left into a corner. Belay on a good stance.

2) 25m (4a) Continue up the easy corner and go up to gain the notch below the summit of the *Play It Again Sam* rib. Steep cracks then lead easily to the summit.

John Temple & Andrew Wielochowski, March 2008.

Map Page 70

SIDI ABDELJABBAR

The tiny hamlet of Sidi Abdeljabbar lies on the main road just to the west of Tifghalt, recognisable by a large hotel right on the roadside. The settlement is one of the holiest places in Morocco, as it is believed to be the burial site of one of the family members of the Prophet Mohammed – a fact that draws hundreds of Moroccans here on an annual pilgrimage (the word 'Sidi' in the name referring to a holy place). During the pilgrimage the car park, roadside, and village itself, become an enormous marketplace, bustling with street traders selling everything from kettles to crafts, cashing in on the influx of visitors. Climbers, on the other hand, are strongly advised to stay away – the alternative approach from Tizgut being a much more sensible option at these times.

Stories about the magical nature of this location abound, but whatever your beliefs, doubts or scepticisms about the healing properties of Sidi Abdeljabbar, there can be no doubt about the magic of its landscape. Exploring the marvellous high cirque above the Abdeljabbar Drainage is a privilege for the adventurous trad-climber, who will discover a teasing complexity of unclimbed ridges, walls and summits, where the quality of the adventure will more than make up for the fact that picking out a line can seem almost impossible. By the end of the day, when thighs are burning from the long approach and descent, and the rock glows in the golden sunset, it's hard not to feel a spiritual connection with the place – maybe there is something in those stories after all...

Sidi Abdeljabbar is reached in approximately 15 minutes from Tafraout, following the main road eastward out of Ameln towards the Tarakatine Pass. The Sidi Abdeljabbar Hotel, built for the annual influx of pilgrims, is a prominent landmark by the roadside. A large parking area is located on the left some 400m beyond the hotel.

From here the Abdeljabbar Drainage, with its high cirque of peaks beyond, is clearly visible, and the approach route needs little description. An alternative approach can be made from the village of Tizgut, following a vague path on the south side of the river towards a prominent high col below Prophet Peak.

Due to the holy status of this settlement, and to maintain a good relationship between climbers and the local community, it is important that all climbers respect Muslim standards of dress and behaviour: shoulders and knees should be covered, and public displays of affection should be avoided at all times.During the pilgrimage climbers should approach the cirque from Tizgut.

H PROPHET PEAK

Drive from Tafraout: **15 minutes**
Walk-in: **1 hour 30 minutes**

The left-most summit in the magnificent cirque above the Sidi Abdeljabbar drainage tops 2000m in altitude and is home to a couple of excellent long climbs. Prophet Peak, however, is a reclusive mountain, hiding behind the Tizgut Ridge and very much keeping itself to itself. When driving down the Ameln road we are afforded the merest glimpse up the Abdeljabbar drainage: a view that can only hint at the alpine nature of this superb summit. Climb a route here, however, and Prophet Peak will, all of a sudden, stand out from every viewpoint in the valley – a unique and prominent jagged peak, and one of the most identifiable on the escarpment.

Despite the distinctly mountainous and adventurous nature of the climbs here, the rock is generally excellent, and vegetation on routes is minimal. This makes the two long ridges here amongst the finest routes of their kind in the region, and parties looking for low-grade, alpine scrambles will not be disappointed.

Both routes are long mountain endeavours that require a speedy approach, particularly during the winter months. Competence in route finding and moving together over easy ground will be of benefit, although the possibility of escape after the third pinnacle reduces the overall seriousness.

Two approaches are possible. The first is from the parking area at Sidi Abdeljabbar, as described on the previous page. Allow approximately 1hr30 to reach the base of the peak. *Pinnacle Ridge* is then gained by walking up a diagonal terrace leading to a notch on the left skyline (see topo). The second approach, useful during the annual Sidi Abdeljabbar pilgrimage, is to park at Tizgut and follow a vague trail up the south side of the valley towards a prominent col between Prophet Peak and the Tizgut Ridge.

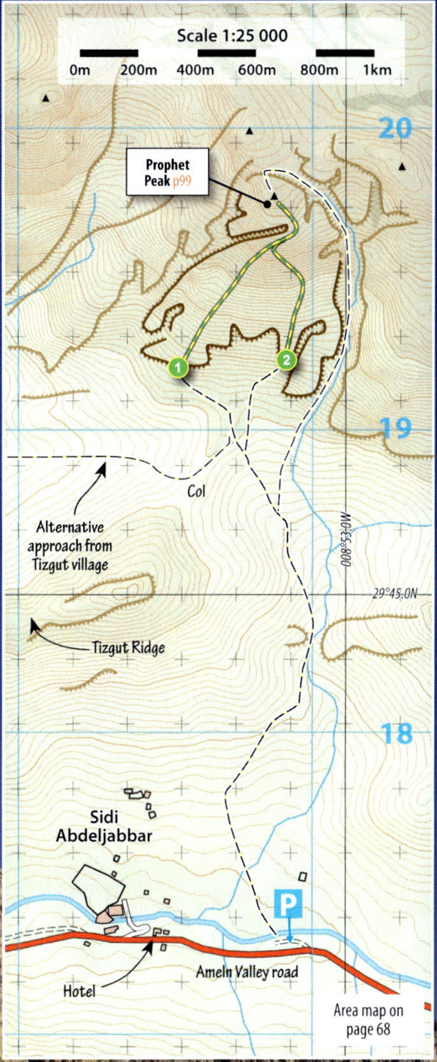

DESCENT: Descent from the main summit is via the major gully system to the east of the peak. From the summit, cairns lead in a northerly direction to a short down-climb. This gains a devious system of ramps which can be followed to the hillside below. Turn southeast, descending into the gully to the east of the summit, soon arriving at a steep constriction. The ancient Berber trail to the summit of Prophet Peak makes use of a chockstone-bridge and wobbly balanced steps to overcome this section, but climbers encountering this in descent for the first time will almost certainly use a rope, either to protect the worrying downclimb or to abseil past it. Below the constriction ropes can be put away, and the gully followed with relative ease down to the cirque.

The first half of this descent, as far as the chockstone bridge, can be very difficult in the dark.

Map Page 70

1. Pinnacle Ridge Severe ★3

600m. The left-hand skyline gives a tremendous mountain day out, every bit as good as its Scottish namesake, providing one of the valley's best long 'easy' routes. The climb starts from a small notch in the ridge, accessed via a rising vegetated terrace.

A) From the notch climb easy ground trending up left and then along the easy ridge to the first pinnacle (This pinnacle is clearly visible from the approach).

B) Large amounts of scrambling over big ledges and easy-angled ground to gain another notch. Move left here on a small ledge and climb a corner system up the left side of the ridge. Continue along the ridge until a steep tower blocks the way. Turn the tower on the right and climb a steep chimney on its right side. This has a difficult exit to the summit ridge of the second pinnacle (junction with *Mountaineer's Route*).

C) Downclimb the ridge on its right side to gain the notch between the second and third pinnacles. Straightforward climbing then leads to the third pinnacle.

D) Climb along the crest of the ridge right to its end, where a short downclimb on the left-hand side leads to a chockstone in the notch between the third pinnacle and main summit.

E) From the chockstone climb straight up onto an airy finger, from where an exposed and somewhat traumatic move regains the main face (crux). Move up right to a good ledge, then continue up rightwards heading for the right-hand of two black chimneys. Climb the right-hand black chimney, then a short steep wall to reach the summit.

Steve & Katja Broadbent, January 2013.

2. The Mountaineer's Route Severe ★1

600m. A worthwhile adventure up the right side of the face. The lower section involves numerous tricky walls interspersed with easier climbing, making efficient rope-work difficult. Higher up, excellent easy ridges necessitate a speedy approach, before the route joins *Pinnacle Ridge* for a superb alpine finale.

A) Start on the left side of the toe of the buttress and climb the ridge to a large cracked wall. A shorter wall then gains a notch and chockstone.

B) Climb up to gain a traverse on the right side of the ridge, then go up a groove to belay below a wall with a large bush above. Climb this, initially rightwards, then back left to exit past the left side of the bush.

C) Gradually easier climbing as far as the large flat top of Asterisk Summit.

D) The ridge swings left and narrows, providing excellent airy scrambling to the top of the second pinnacle on *Pinnacle Ridge*. Continue from section (C) in above route description.

Pete Cawley & Aeron Buchanan, January 2013 (as far as Asterisk Summit).
Steve & Katja Broadbent, January 2013 (complete ascent).

Pete Cawley & Aeron Buchanan on the shared crux pitch of *Pinnacle Ridge* (Severe) and *Mountaineer's Route* (Severe), above the third pinnacle of Prophet Peak ➲

Photo: Steve Broadbent

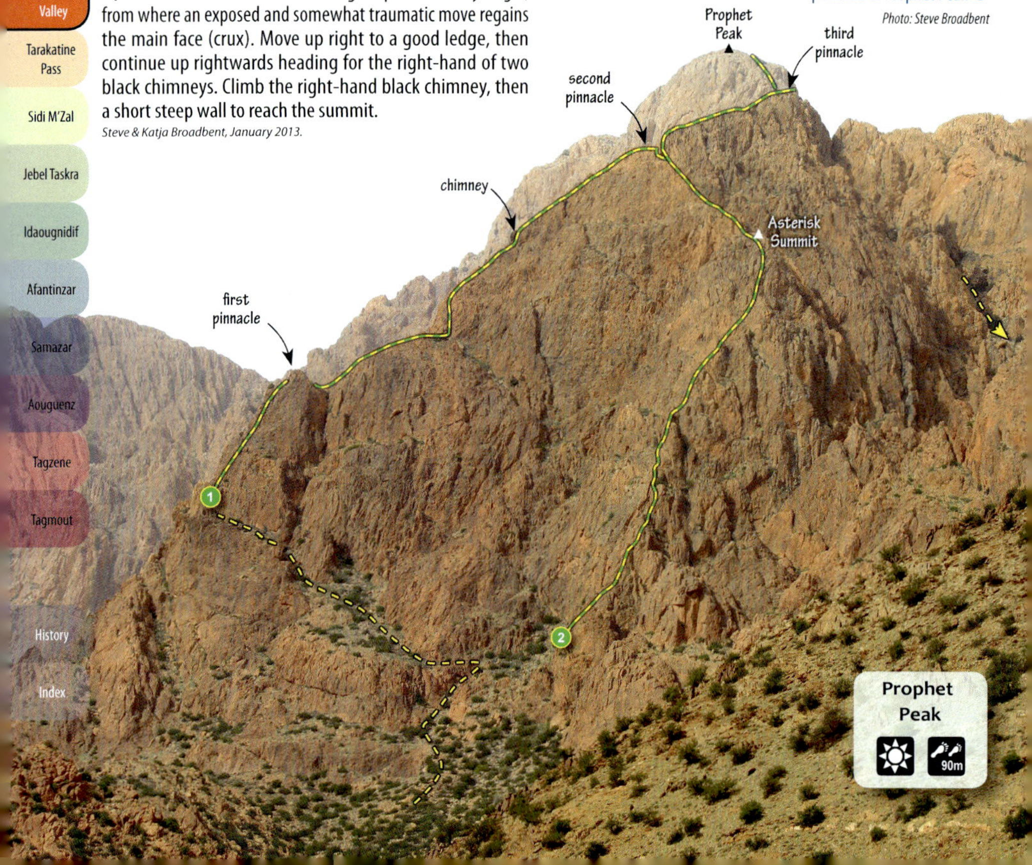

TIFGHALT AREA

No climber passing over the Tarakatine Pass en-route to Tafraout will fail to notice the impressive buttresses above Tifghalt, forming the eastern end of the enormous line of crags which make up the Jebel el Kest Massif. Not surprisingly, these were the first crags to see attention from climbers during the relatively recent development of Anti-Atlas quartzite.

These are big crags that epitomise the Anti-Atlas adventure climbing of the early 1990s, and despite their obvious appeal and prominent location above the main road, they have remained untamed and relatively under-developed ever since.

There is, of course, a good reason for this. The Tifghalt crags form an incredibly complex and extensive maze of climbable rock. Descriptions of the routes have always been famously vague, and after an excruciating morning walking-in, teams have been known to spend the best part of a day just finding the climb they set out to do. Often, therefore, people don't return, and new-route activity has been correspondingly limited.

Almost all of the routes here are multi-pitch climbs in fine situations high above the Ameln Valley. Long walk-ins are rewarded with magnificent views, but most of the routes here turn into full-day outings.

Tifghalt is easily reached in about 15 minutes by car from Tafraout. Turn right at the main junction in Ameln and follow the Ameln Valley road towards the Tarakatine Pass. There is a large hotel at Sidi Abdeljabbar at the east end of the Tizgut Ridge, from where the Abdeljabbar crags are visible at the head of a major valley. Tifghalt, the final village before the road climbs up to the pass, is located approximately 2km further along the main road.

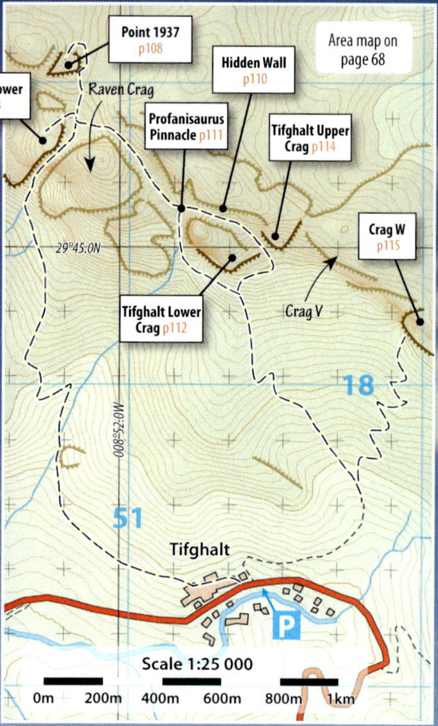

Because all the walk-ins here start from roadside parking on the Ameln Valley road, these crags are good options for hitch-hikers; most traffic leaving Tafraout will either be heading west to Tahala and Tiznit (the wrong way!) or north to Sidi M'Zal, Ait Baha and Biougra (the right way!) Likewise, for the return journey, almost all traffic descending from the pass will be bound for Tafraout at the end of the day.

I THE WHITE TOWER

Drive from Tafraout: **15 minutes**
Walk-in: **1 hour 30 minutes**

This magnificent crag, 'tucked away somewhere behind Crag U', is home to Tafraout's most famous rock climb. Indeed, the endless slog across demoralising hillsides, interspersed with painful thrashes through aggressive vegetation has been a worthwhile pilgrimage for more visiting climbers than any other approach of similar length. Thankfully there aren't many of similar length.

The crag was prosaically described as 'Crag U Left-Hand' in the valley's original guidebook – one of 4 unrelated buttresses gathered together under the Crag U title, continuing a long tradition of ambiguity in the history of Tafraout's most popular mountain crag.

Originally referred to as the 'Buttress west of E Buttress', Crag U Left-Hand (the crag, that is) was to briefly adopt the name 'Bonatti Pillar' – the subtitle given to the original 1998 route. Meanwhile *Bonatti Pillar* (the 1998 Original Route) was confusingly labelled '*Heaven's Gate*' in a later volume of the Tafraout new-route book. The route (probably the only climb in the range that you can get away with calling 'the route') eventually settled down to the rather catchy *White Tower* on Crag U Left Hand. Then, shortly after the publication of an already confusing guidebook, along came another route next door, called... *The Bonatti Pillar*.

Such confusion did little to promote development of these cliffs, but much to promote the route (call it what you will), for pretty much everyone who survived the walk-in found themselves drawn to one climb (no matter what they thought they were heading for, or what it may or may not have been called). In a futile attempt to make sense of it all, the route up the White Tower (sometimes called *The White Tower*) is referred to in this guide as *The Original Route*. The *Bonatti Pillar* (2005) is referred to as the *Bonatti Pillar*, and people who point out the fact that this continuation of route-name confusion is likely to be escalated by the repeated route-name *Original Route* on Crag W will not be referred to at all.

By now, the approach to the White Tower needs little introduction, other than a reassurance that it most definitely is worth it. Two options exist, and whichever one you take you'll wish it had been the other. The first is to park about 1km west of Tifghalt and follow a dry stream bed to the northeast. Eventually it is necessary to gain height on the left (true right) bank and cross a broad spur from where the crag is visible. A more popular and less steep approach starts from parking in the village itself, as shown on the map opposite. Gain a small track behind the houses on the north (left, when going up towards the pass) side of the road. Follow this, traversing west then north across the hillside to eventually gain a stream-valley that runs up from the road (route of the first approach). Head up this valley a short way, but eventually leave it to climb up the left (true right) bank onto a broad spur, from where the crag is visible. Continue traversing left from here to gain the narrow gully underneath the White Tower itself.

Map Page 70 & 102

Area Map
Crag Selector
Intro
The Climbing
How to Use
Suggested Climbs
Tafraout Granite
Anergui
Ameln Valley
Tarakatine Pass
Sidi M'Zal
Jebel Taskra
Idaougnidif
Afantinzar
Samazar
Aouguenz
Tagzene
Tagmout
History
Index

DESCENT: The summit of the tower is surprisingly 'summit-like' and a short down-climb is required on the north side to regain the main hillside. From here an easy walk leads rightwards to the top of the White Tower Gully which can be followed back to the base of the routes. An alternate descent to Tifghalt village can be made by continuing the traverse beneath the Hidden Wall to descend via the Tifghalt Lower approach.

The White Tower itself is a narrow pillar of clean rock, rising from White Tower Gully. The first routes climb the buttress to the left of the White Tower itself...

1. Keswick Lads' Outing HVS 5a

ADVENTURE

~250m. This route starts at the toe of the buttress, down and left of the main tower and the narrow approach gully. In the words of the first ascensionists... "Climb 2½ pitches to the terrace, then follow easy rock to a crevasse". Another pitch then leads up to below two overhanging off-widths beneath the prominent large corner. These are thankfully easier than they look, giving access to the big corner above. Follow this, then move right and up to another terrace. Go along the terrace to pinnacles, get involved in a crevasse, then somehow find your way to the summit in a final long pitch...

P.Ross & W.Freelands, 1998.

2. Central Pillar of the Friends E1 5a

3

280m. A good climb up the attractive rib and pillar, starting low down in White Tower Gully.

1) 40m (5a) Climb up to a prominent crack, which is followed to a ledge.

2) 50m (4b) Follow the pillar to belay on a big ledge.

3) 25m (4a) Climb the wall, starting from the right and moving up diagonally left to reach the edge of the pillar. Follow this to a belay beneath an attractive dihedral.

4) 40m (4c) Follow the dihedral and pillar above to a ledge.

5) 40m (-) Walk to a huge boulder, then squeeze through a big crack inside the boulder to reach the gap between the boulder and main face.

6) 40m (5a) Climb a ramp from right to left to gain a thin finger crack. Follow this for a few metres, then use another crack on the right until it is possible to move 5 metres right to the edge of the pillar. Climb the edge of the pillar to a spike belay beneath a crack.

7) 40m (4c) Do not climb the crack, but instead move left on the other side and climb a steep slab to easier ground to a big ledge.

8) 45m (4b) climb black rock, then a thin pillar to easier ground to the summit.

Jean Males & Simon Destombes, February 2016.

3. Elizur HVS 5a

UNCHECKED

200m. At the left side of the main tower is a long corner (taken by *Etam*). This climb meanders up the wall immediately left of this corner, although details of the exact line are not clear.

Joe Brown, Claude Davies & Pete Turnbull, March 1999.

4. Etam HVS 5a

200m. The long corner immediately left of the main tower, escaping leftwards when things get steep. At the top join *Keswick Lads' Outing* and finish up right to the summit of the tower.

Joe Brown & Pete Turnbull, 2000.

The White Tower

PM 90m

5. The Bonatti Pillar E1 5b ★2

200m. A major undertaking up the impressive arête at the left side of the front face of the White Tower; bold, intimidating, but easier than it looks. Worrying rock adds to the seriousness of what is already a big outing up one of the region's great faces. Start 10m right of *Etam*.

1) 15m (5a) Climb a crack, passing a prickly pear then move right into a groove. Climb this to a good ledge on the right.

2) 5m (5a) Climb the groove above, then swing right to another ledge.

3) 30m (5b) Go up the wall and groove to the big overhang. Move left under this and pull onto a ledge on the left. Climb another groove, passing a bulge before moving left via a horizontal crack to a ledge.

4) 30m (5b) Another groove, moving left at the top, then stepping back right to belay.

5) 5m (4c) Climb diagonally right to easier ground and a ledge beneath a crack (junction with *Original Route*).

6-7) 75m (4a) Follow cracks up left as for the *Original Route*.

Ben & Marion Wintringham, November 2004

Area Map
Crag Selector
Intro
The Climbing
How to Use
Suggested Climbs
Tafraout Granite
Anergui
Ameln Valley
Tarakatine Pass
Sidi M'Zal
Jebel Taskra
Idaougnidif
Afantinzar
Samazar
Aouguenz
Tagzene
Tagmout
History
Index

6. White Tower Original Route HVS 5a ★3

165m. The most famous and popular route of its type in Morocco is steady at the grade and only slightly over-hyped. Described by its first ascensionists as "the only weakness in the pillar", the *White Tower Original* climbs the attractive south face of the main tower, rising from the claustrophobic depths of White Tower Gully. It is a line of undeniable quality for which a description is almost unnecessary. For climbers operating at the VS grade, this is one of the best and most obvious 'big ticks' of Tafraout. Many variations have been reported in the upper section, with little effect on the overall grade.

1) 40m (5a) Climb the obvious crack in the right-facing corner, stepping right at the first steep section. Continue up left to a poor belay at the top of the corner.

2) 35m (5a) Climb up, then make difficult exposed moves leftwards to gain the left edge of the first flake. Follow this more easily to reach a superb steep crack up the second flake, which provides sensational climbing in a fine position. Continue up a weakness to a small ledge. (A poorer alternative to this pitch follows the corner above the belay at 5b.)

3) 35m (4b) Trend up left and follow a shallow right-facing corner above. It is also possible to work rightwards from the belay to join the final pitches of the *Direct Route* above the black ledge.

4) 35m (4c) Continue up, following the easiest line trending generally leftwards to ledges on the left side of the tower.

5) 20m (-) Easy ground gains the summit.

Joe Brown, Les Brown & Derek Walker, 1998.

Walker recalls this route being so obvious from the road that he was "surprised that the team had not been there before". The first pitch was deemed to be "typically Joe", so that pitch went to him. Les got the steep slabs above, with Walker finishing the route to the summit. The group referred to the climb for many years as The Bonatti Pillar, but this name was vetoed by one of the group at some point, simply becoming The White Tower instead.

Many consider this to be one of the finest climbs in the range, put up by a formidable team whose names are synonymous with the very best of Anti-Atlas adventure climbing. It is fitting that Walker's recollections of this route were his final contribution to Tafraout climbing before he sadly passed away in January 2013.

Alan Blackburn on the second pitch of Tafraout's most popular climb: Joe Brown's celebrated *White Tower Original* (HVS 5a)

Photo: Martin Bennett

Joe 'Morty' Smith in the early days on Tifghalt's *White Tower Original* (HVS 5a) .

Photo: Claude Davies

7. White Tower Direct (Slot Machine) HVS 5a ★3 BOLD

170m. A magnificent climb at the top end of its grade. Although less historically popular than its neighbour, the *Direct Route* is every bit as good, giving a more difficult, more bold, and altogether more sustained climb of exceptional quality. Isolated areas of poor rock do not detract from what is one of Tafraout's best multi-pitch HVS routes.

1) 30m (4c) The wide crack is merely an appetizer for things to come, and leads to an uncomfortable belay beneath the obvious, intimidating slot.

2) 25m (5a) Well-protected climbing up the slot until the left-hand crack closes down. From here bold moves lead out left to the arête, where an assortment of poor gear does little to calm the nerves. Climb the front face with trepidation to another poor stance in the groove.

3) 25m (4a) A remarkable pitch, both for its position and its simplicity. Pull up left on jugs to gain the brilliant front face of the tower, then climb a vague right-facing corner to a good ledge.

4) 30m (4c) Go up the fine wall above to a small ledge (possible belay). Tricky undercut moves up a left-slanting crack lead to another sublime wall. Belay on a comfortable black ledge.

5) 40m (5a) Good climbing straight up the twin cracks, getting progressively steeper to a rather worrying finish.

6) 20m (4a) Move up left, relishing perfect rock, stunning views, and easy moves to the top of a memorable climb.

Steve Broadbent & Cameron Hall, October 2011.

8. Gibbethon VS 4c PRICKLY

160m. The big groove at the right side of the main tower is a slightly easier proposition, passing some vegetation en-route.

Joe Brown & Pete Turnbull, 2001.

Area Map
Crag Selector
Intro
The Climbing
How to Use
Suggested Climbs
Tafraout Granite
Anergui
Ameln Valley
Tarakatine Pass
Sidi M'Zal
Jebel Taskra
Idaougnidif
Afantinzar
Samazar
Aouguenz
Tagzene
Tagmout
History
Index

Area Map
Crag Selector
Intro
The Climbing
How to Use
Suggested Climbs
Tafraout Granite
Anergui
Ameln Valley
Tarakatine Pass
Sidi M'Zal
Jebel Taskra
Idaougnidif
Afantinzar
Samazar
Aouguenz
Tagzene
Tagmout
History
Index

J POINT 1937

Drive from Tafraout: **15 minutes**
Walk-in: **1 hour 45 minutes**

Situated above and behind the White Tower, Pt 1937 is certainly not the easiest crag to access, but its position on the crest of the escarpment makes for stunning views, not only along the full length of the Ameln Valley, but also to the east across Tizi N'Tarakatine and the rolling landscape beyond.

The crag has a steep and friable-looking west face, with more gently angled slabby ground on the southeast side. A single route has been recorded to date, but many more are no doubt awaiting a first ascent.

There are two possible approaches: either follow the White Tower approach and scramble right to the top of White Tower Gully, from where the crag is clearly visible, or approach via Tifghalt Lower Crag, continuing over the col behind Raven Crag to reach the top of White Tower Gully.

Both approaches are long and steep, and as a result a better option is to complete a route on the White Tower or Tifghalt Lower on the way to Point 1973.

DESCENT: To descend from the summit scramble down the east side, swinging north to gain a small col. From here turn right and descend in an easterly direction through vegetation (not as bad as it looks). Do not be tempted to head west from the col, as this ends in steep drops.

1. Bollinger E2 5c ★★★ GEAR

75m. A marvellous, technical pitch with well-protected, thought-provoking climbing in a fine position.
1) 50m (-) The easy first pitch is little more than a means of accessing the delights to be had above... Start up a black groove from the toe of the buttress, then follow easy scrambling to where the ground steepens. Move left here to belay on a small ledge on the extreme left side of the buttress, about 3m below an enormous boulder.
2) 25m (5c) Go up past the left side of the enormous boulder and make a superb flake- traverse left to gain the tempting hanging corner. This gives technical climbing with plenty of protection and ample exposure.
Steve Broadbent & Pete Cawley, 2012.

Teams climbing side by side on *White Tower Original* (HVS), left, and *White Tower Direct* (HVS), right. These two classic climbs are amongst the best multi-pitch crag routes in the Anti-Atlas. ➲
Photo: Steve Broadbent

Area Map
Crag Selector
Intro
The Climbing
How to Use
Suggested Climbs
Tafraout Granite
Anergui
Ameln Valley
Tarakatine Pass
Sidi M'Zal
Jebel Taskra
Idaougnidif
Afantinzar
Samazar
Aouguenz
Tagzene
Tagmout
History
Index

K HIDDEN WALL

Shade · Families · Hitch · Roadside

Drive from Tafraout: **15 minutes**
Walk-in: **1 hour 40 minutes**

This attractive orange wall lurks out of sight above and behind the main Tifghalt Lower crag. Given the length and complexity of the approach it is hardly surprising that only a handful of routes have been recorded here, although scope certainly exists for more.

The wall is best approached as for Tifghalt Lower. Skirt rightwards underneath Tifghalt Lower Crag and go up the gully between the Lower and Upper crags. This leads over a small col – Hidden wall is the wall on the right-hand side as you descend the other side of this col. A prominent pinnacle can be seen on the slopes below the wall (Profanisaurus Pinnacle).

DESCENT: It is possible to descend by scrambling down to the right, although for routes finishing close to the arete an abseil from the top of *Throw Us A Bone* is an easier option.

1. Highway HVS 5a ★1 (Unchecked)

120m. This good but seldom-climbed route takes a fault line up the steep wall leading to an overhang and corner system. The exact line is uncertain, and the topo below should be used with caution!

1) 35m. Climb the wall via an indefinite crack / groove system. This leads to a corner below an overhang.
2) 20m. Climb the overhang and belay in corner.
3) 35m. Follow the corner to a large ledge.
4) 30m. Finish up the cracked wall above.

Les Brown & Roy Warner. March 1999.

2. Gotta Argan Accumulator E3 6a (Unchecked)

80m. The centre of the wall gives a difficult climb in a fine setting. Descend by scrambling down to the right.

3. Traverse of the Infidels E2 5c ★2 (Abseil)

80m. Brilliant climbing up the wall left of the arête.

1) 25m (5b) Start up a crack left of the arête, and follow it to a belay in a sentry box.
2) 20m (5b) Follow a rising traverse to a horizontal break. Go left along this to belay in a large chimney.
3) 35m (5c) A splendid pitch. Move back right and ascend steep grooves with difficulty. Traverse rightwards along the

higher break to a gap in the roofs, pulling through this before moving up right to the abseil at the top of the next route.

4. Throw Us a Bone E1 5b ★3 ABSEIL

80m. The arête to the right is a hidden gem, with three magnificent pitches starting from the top of the col at the right side of the Hidden Wall. Descent is by two abseils (from a tree and then the belay at the top of pitch 2).

1) (5b) Climb the arête direct, moving onto the right side at 15 metres before continuing direct to a large ledge. The wall above is technical but protection can found. Climb it to another large ledge and a belay.

2) (5b) Step left and climb the wall then regain the arête and follow it direct to a large ledge with a good spike belay.

3) (4c) Climb the arête directly – bold but straightforward. On reaching flat ground, traverse right to a tree belay in the gully.

Peter Riley & Charlie Boscoe, November 2011.

5. Saif Crack VS 5a ★1 ABSEIL

60m. Very pleasant climbing up the crack in the wall a few metres right of the arête. Climb the curving crack up leftwards to join the arête, then follow it to an abseil descent from the top of *Throw Us a Bone*.

L PROFANISAURUS PINNACLE

Shade | Families | Hitch | Roadside — Drive from Tafraout: **15 minutes** Walk-in: **1 hour 40 minutes**

This striking arrowhead pinnacle is located below the Hidden Wall, behind Tifghalt Lower crag. The shapely summit has no easy means of access, and descent, un-surprisingly, is by abseil. Like most of the routes hereabouts, the pinnacle has seen few ascents and parties are **strongly advised to replace the abseil anchor before descent.**

There are two possible approaches, but both are rather tiresome. The first option is to ascend the gully to the left of Tifghalt Lower (passing to the right of Raven Crag). The pinnacle is located at the point where the broad gully forks behind the lower crag. An alternative option is to approach from Tifghalt Upper crag, passing over the col behind Tifghalt Lower and descending beneath Hidden Wall.

6. Colonel's Crack VS 4c ★1 ABSEIL

25m. The original line of ascent follows the prominent wide crack on the uphill face to a direct finish.

Scott Malina-Derben & John Evans, October 2009.

7. Bumble Bee Pants HVS 5a ★1 ABSEIL

25m. Excellent climbing up the NE arête of the pinnacle, starting up a thin, slightly overhanging crack just right of a wide corner crack. Follow the arête to the summit, turning any difficulties on the right.

Charlie Boscoe & Peter Riley, November 2011.

8. Tired Dog Crack E2 5b ★1 BOLD ABSEIL

25m. Climb the left-hand of the 2 wide cracks on the north face to a bold and technical wall (crux). Climb this direct, finishing on the NE arête.

Peter Riley & Charlie Boscoe, November 2011.

M TIFGHALT LOWER CRAG

Shade · Families · Hitch · Roadside

Drive from Tafraout: **15 minutes**
Walk-in: **1 hour**

The 'main' crag at Tifghalt sits slightly in front of the long line of high crags that includes Tifghalt Upper, and Crags V and W. From the road, the Lower crag appears as an attractive series of ridges and gullies, and with the shortest approach of any of the Tifghalt crags it has seen the most development.

All routes here are adventurous, multi-pitch outings and the crag has seen numerous benightments.

Park at the top end of Tifghalt village, where a small path heads back left behind the houses. Follow this initially, but go up right before (i.e. east of) the houses to reach a better path which traverses the hillside rightwards about 50 yards above the level of the road. This path contours around the hillside before swinging left into a basin beneath crags V and W (see map on page 102). Eventually the path becomes vague, and it is necessary to pick a way easily up the stony hillside.

DESCENT: From the top of the crag it is possible to scramble down the back side and descend into the gap between the Lower and Upper crags.

WEST BUTTRESS

The left-hand summit is the highest of three buttresses which make up the lower crag. It can be identified by a prominent black groove running down the centre of the face, clearly visible from the approach.

1. Harbinger HS 4a ★2 ADVENTURE

~270m. The left side of the buttress is a popular adventure that is frequently underestimated. 7 long pitches provide a full complement of 'adventure-trad' challenges. Start to the left of a black corner and follow 'the obvious line of weakness' up a series of corners and cracks... or get lost like most folk do...

Derek Walker, Les Brown & Pete Turnbull, 1997

A variation start involving 2 pitches of VS 4c has been climbed to the left of this line.

2. Ciao Lucio VS 5a

270m. A fine adventure up the attractive buttress. The first belay is at an olive tree, which is worth identifying on the approach.

1) 60m (-) Climb up to the olive tree.
2) 30m (-) Go up a wide-angled corner to a belay on the left side.
3) 20m (-) Continue up the dihedral to a huge block on a large terrace.
4) 55m (5a) Climb a prominent crack to the right of the large block, leading to a roof. Traverse right here to reach a small palm.
5) 15m (-) Easy climbing to a belay up and right.
6) 50m (4b) Go up an easy ramp on the right, then straight up the ridge.
7) Scramble up slabs to reach *Harbinger*.
8) Easy climbing to the top.

Giorgio Mallucci & Elisabetta Galli, October 2011.

3. Freelander VS 4c

~270m. Another worthwhile route that follows corners and cracks towards the massive roof high on the face. After threading a way through this (intricate) follow more grooves and ramps to the top. Difficult route-finding will no doubt be compounded by this rather vague description.

Bill Freelands & Paul Ross, 1997.

4. Direct Route HVS 5a

270m. The wall to the left of the black groove is a challenging proposition that finds its way through some intimidating and overhanging ground.

Les Brown & Derek Walker, 2001.

5. The Black Groove HVS 5a

250m. The obvious, terrifying chasm gives a tremendous classic climb, and, for those who like that kind of thing, one of the best routes hereabouts. Follow the groove with considerable interest to its top, then finish up a difficult corner crack. Approximately 5 pitches from base to summit. Eek!

Les Brown & Derek Walker, 2001.

6. The Great Escape HVS 5a

250m. A route of some notoriety taking the pillar to the right of the *Black Groove*. The climb is a serious undertaking, featuring some difficult and bold climbing in a fine but intimidating position.

Joe Brown & Pete Turnbull, 2000.

EAST BUTTRESS

This is the central of the three 'summits', separated from the West Buttress by a deep gully.

7. Vulture HVS 5a

180m. Climb the front of the buttress to slabby ground at two-thirds height. The steep final walls are then avoided by an escape leftwards.

Les Brown & Pete Turnbull, 1999.

8. Barbary Falcon VS 4c

180m. Start from the right-hand side of the buttress, trending easily up left to the foot of a steep rib. Go up this to gain a slab beneath large overhangs, which are avoided on the right. Climb up to the right of a loose red corner-crack, then follow a rib to a chimney. Finish up this and a short wall to the summit.

Les Brown & M.Howlett, March 2005.

RIGHT-HAND BUTTRESS

This much smaller buttress lies at the right side of the crag, underneath the steep wall of Tifghalt Upper.

9. Circle Seat VS 4c

100m. The obvious line of ramps skirting round the right side of the buttress.

Claude Davies & Trevor Jones, 1996.

N TIFGHALT UPPER CRAG

Shade · Families · Hitch · Roadside

Drive from Tafraout: **15 minutes**
Walk-in: **1 hour 20 minutes**

This tall, slender buttress is located on the right-hand side and slightly above the Lower Crag when viewed from the standard approach. It is a high mountain crag in a remote environment, with tremendous views across the Ameln Valley and Adrar Mqorn. A series of prominent grooves and cracks provide obvious natural lines but, as with most of the Tifghalt crags, a lengthy walk-in has ensured minimal development in the 20 years since the first climbs were made here.

The crag is accessed via Tifghalt Lower (see previous page for description). From the lower crag a straightforward walk (about 15-20 minutes) gains the foot of the routes here.

1. Afternoon Wall VS 4c ★2

130m. The parallel crack system up the left side of the main face is a very worthwhile climb in a superb setting. It is climbed in 3 or 4 pitches to the summit.

Les Brown & Paul Ross, 1996.

2. The Baron's Largesse HVS 5a ★2 STEEP

135m. Another good route, this time tackling the centre of the wall with lots of exposure.

1) 25m (5a) Start up the obvious curving groove (steep), then move right past a big block to a comfortable stance.

2) 25m (5a) Climb up a groove, avoiding euphorbia on the right. An awkward step left then gains a steep rib which is followed to an exposed stance.

3) 40m (4c) Continue up the rib until forced left into a niche. Move up to a stance on the left by a pinnacle.

4) 35m (4c) A steep groove to easier ground.

5) 20m (4a) A few interesting moves then easier climbing to the top.

Chris Bonington & Mike Mortimer, March 2005.

3. Central Chimney VS 4c ★2

140m. The central chimney is an impressive line at this grade.

Joe Brown & Derek Walker, 1998.

4. Black Cracks HVS 5a ★2

140m. This once-popular route takes the black chimney-cracks up the right side of the face, and is a traditional quartzite adventure in a magnificent setting. Don't be put off by the ferns...

Joe Brown & Pete Turnbull, 1996.

CRAG W

Shade Families Hitch Roadside Drive from Tafraout: **15 minutes** Walk-in: **1 hour 5 minutes**

This massive barrel-shaped crag marks the eastern end of the Jebel el Kest escarpment, towering above the main road as it descends into the Ameln Valley from the Tarakatine Pass. It is one of the most prominent and impressive crags on the south side of the range – highly visible to climbers on their journey to Tafraout from Agadir. Not surprisingly, therefore, it was the first quartzite to be explored by the Ameln pioneers in the early nineties, when Les Brown and Trevor Jones put up their *Original Route* on the southwestern front.

From parking at the top end of Tifghalt village, locate a reasonable path running east, some 30 yards above the level of the road. This can either be gained straight up the hillside, or by following a vague path that heads initially westward behind the houses. Turn off this almost immediately and follow a narrow path uphill through prickly pears to gain the start of the main path running east. The main path contours around the hillside before swinging left into a broad basin with the Tifghalt crags towering above. Crag W, at the right-hand end of the escarpment, is easily seen above, and is reached by a long ascent up the hillside.

1. Adullam VS 4c

UNCHECKED

250m. The buttress at the left side of the west face gives one of the easier climbs hereabouts.
Claude Davies & Pete Turnbull, 1997.

2. Old Friends E1 5b

UNCHECKED

250m. The attractive tower just left of a major double gully-system in the west face. Climb the buttress until it steepens, then move right across the gully wall. Eventually it is possible to regain the front of the buttress and follow it to the summit.
Joe Brown, Claude Davies, Les Brown, Trevor Jones & Pete Turnbull, 1993.
Climbed as a rope of five by the original team of Anti-Atlas pioneers, with Joe Brown leading all of the way. During the ascent one of the seconds (who wishes to remain anonymous!) dropped a cam, giving rise to a barrage of adverse comments from the leader. Further such comments were once more forthcoming when it began to snow – an unusual event for which the team were not prepared.
The dropped cam was retrieved 8 years later during the first ascent of Kestrel.

3. Kestrel VS 4c

UNCHECKED

250m. This intimidating climb starts up the narrow pillar within the double gully-system, following it to a steepening. Work rightwards here onto the main buttress and climb up the wall on the left side of the great flake.
Les Brown, Derek Walker & Chris Bonington, 2001.

4. The Great Flake E1 5b

ADVENTURE STEEP

300m. A climb of considerable difficulty. Start at the lowest point of the west face and climb up to a tree-covered ledge. Traverse right to a pinnacle, then move up left to gain slabs which lead up to a terrace to the right of the overhanging flake. Climb the overhang to the top of the pinnacle and finish more easily.
Joe Brown, Les Brown, Derek Walker & Pete Turnbull, 1998.

5. Middle Ground E1 5b

ADVENTURE CRACK

300m. A big outing up the right side of the west face. Climb the main corner until it steepens, then move out right to gain a vertical off-width corner-crack. Go up this to gain easier ground to the top.
Joe Brown & Claude Davies, 1992.

Crag W SW Face

PM 1hr05

Area Map
Crag Selector
Intro
The Climbing
How to Use
Suggested Climbs
Tafraout Granite
Anergui
Ameln Valley
Tarakatine Pass
Sidi M'Zal
Jebel Taskra
Idaougnidif
Afantinzar
Samazar
Aouguenz
Tagzene
Tagmout
History
Index

6. Spacewalk HVS 5a ★3

300m. The classic of the crag is one of Tafraout's better-known climbs, with some excellent but committing situations. Retreat from the upper section would be extremely troublesome. Start up a flake crack at the foot of the prow between the west and south faces, then traverse left for 2 pitches onto a vague ramp-system that trends up left onto the west face. Continue up this, following the easiest line to the top.

Joe Brown, Derek Walker & Chris Bonington, 2001.

7. Original Route HVS 5a ★2

275m. This good mountaineering route was the first quartzite climb recorded in the valley. Start up a corner just left of the prow between the west and south faces. Move right around a rib on pitch 2 to avoid a loose corner. This gains the ridge, then a steep wall to final grooves. Approximately 7 pitches to the top.

Les Brown & Trevor Jones, 1991.

8. Opening Bid HVS 5a ★2

275m. Another fine climb, although some confusion exists about the exact line. Initial pitches appear to be up similar ground to *Spacewalk* and *Original Route*, though this climb breaks out right onto the south face somewhat earlier than the original.

Joe Brown & Claude Davies, 1992.

9. Red Wall HVS 5a ★2

250m. A big classic climb up the attractive south face. Start just left of a short gully, then traverse a weakness up right. Climb a steep vertical corner to reach easier ground, then trend left to join the *Original Route*.

Derek Walker & Les Brown, 1997.

The wall to the right has been climbed a number of times, but accurate lines were not recorded. It is believed that the following climb shares most of its ground with a route recorded in 2010 as *Some Like It Hot*.

10. Barbary Toast E2 5c

~180m. Difficult climbing up the wall to the right of *Red Wall*.

1) Start up a right-facing corner to a ledge, then follow a cracked wall to crux moves through a roof. Belay on a ramp above and to the left.

2) Step left and go up flakes to a roof. Move left then up to another ramp, which is followed up left to a tree belay.

3) Go up the rib to the right of the tree, then climb a chimney behind a flake. Move up left to another tree belay.

4) Move up right and follow easy rock to the top.

John Lyall & Jon Preston, November 2004.

11. Shoe Ladies E2 5b

180m. This bold climb starts in a recess beyond a pillar to the right of *Barbary Toast*.

1) Climb a crack in the slab on the right, then pull through the overlap on the left. Move right across a broken wall to a left-facing corner crack and follow this to a ledge.

2) Step right and climb up to a ramp. Go up this, then move left onto a belay.

3) Finish rightwards up the ramp.

Ian Wilson, James Strongman & Tom Leppert, February 2010.

12. Sticky Arête Very Difficult ★1

The second ridge-line to the right of the main buttress provides a pleasant beginner's climb on excellent quartzite.

Tom Pitcairn & Andy Hedgecock, January 2004.

Spacewalk (HVS) was one of the original classic climbs of the Ameln Valley. Malcolm Phelps climbing.
Photo: Jim Unwin

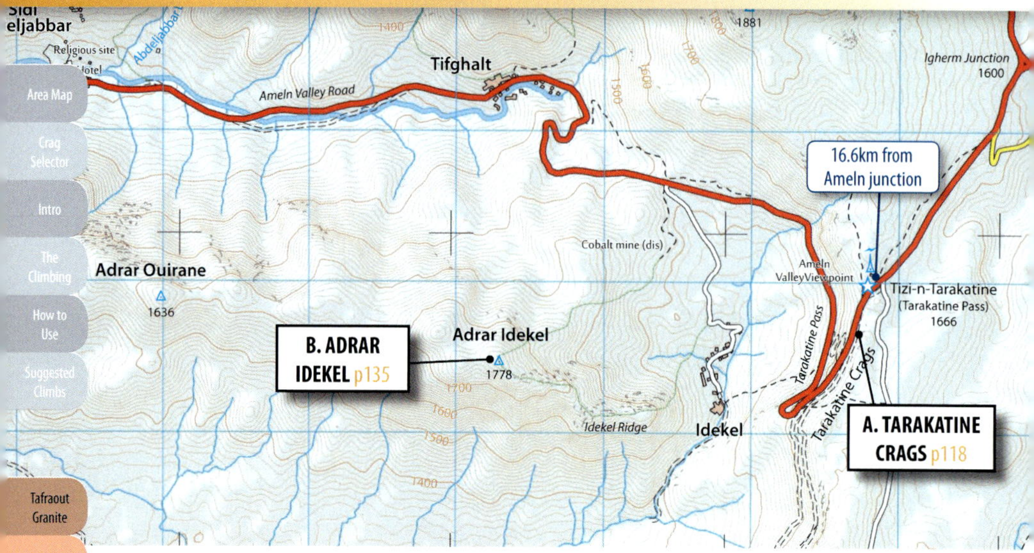

Area Map
Crag Selector
Intro
The Climbing
How to Use
Suggested Climbs
Tafraout Granite
Anergui
Ameln Valley
Tarakatine Pass
Sidi M'Zal
Jebel Taskra
Idaougnidif
Afantinzar
Samazar
Aouguenz
Tagzene
Tagmout
History
Index

(A) TARAKATINE CRAGS

Shade | Families | Hitch | Roadside

Drive from Tafraout: **20 minutes**
Walk-in: **2 to 20 minutes**

The small but extensive craglets of the Tarakatine Pass are usually overlooked by climbers passing along the main road out of the Ameln Valley – Perhaps no surprise given the scale of Crags U, V, and W, which tower above the terraced hillside above the road. Closer inspection, however, reveals plenty of worthwhile climbing, and indeed this crag comes into its own when low cloud precludes grander things or you've only got a couple of hours to spare.

There are lots of short, friendly, low-grade climbs here in a magnificent setting with fine views across Adrar Idekel and the Ameln Valley, and it's a great spot for a few evening solos on the way back to Tafraout. Be warned, however, there is nothing taller than 12m, so if you're looking for long routes you'd better go elsewhere.

The rock is a slightly unusual conglomerate, and whilst it is not generally as solid as Jebel el Kest quartzite, it does provide some interesting climbing on good positive holds. There is some friable rock, particularly towards the northern end of the crag, but the quality improves significantly around the main buttresses.

Access from Tafraout couldn't be easier – indeed the short drive and almost nonexistent walk-in are two of the crag's greatest features.

A good but unsurfaced track leaves the main road just to the east of the summit of the Tarakatine Pass, heading south across high, featureless ground. Take this track and park after 100m or so, from where an easy but pathless stroll up gentle slopes to the west gains the top of the crags. An alternative approach follows the old road beneath the crags, starting just where the unsurfaced track leaves the main road. Most of the climbing is located just minutes from the car.

The routes here are between 4m and 12m in length, and for many people a rack and rope is often unnecessary. Some of the higher or harder routes may require a short rope and the odd gear placement to protect them.

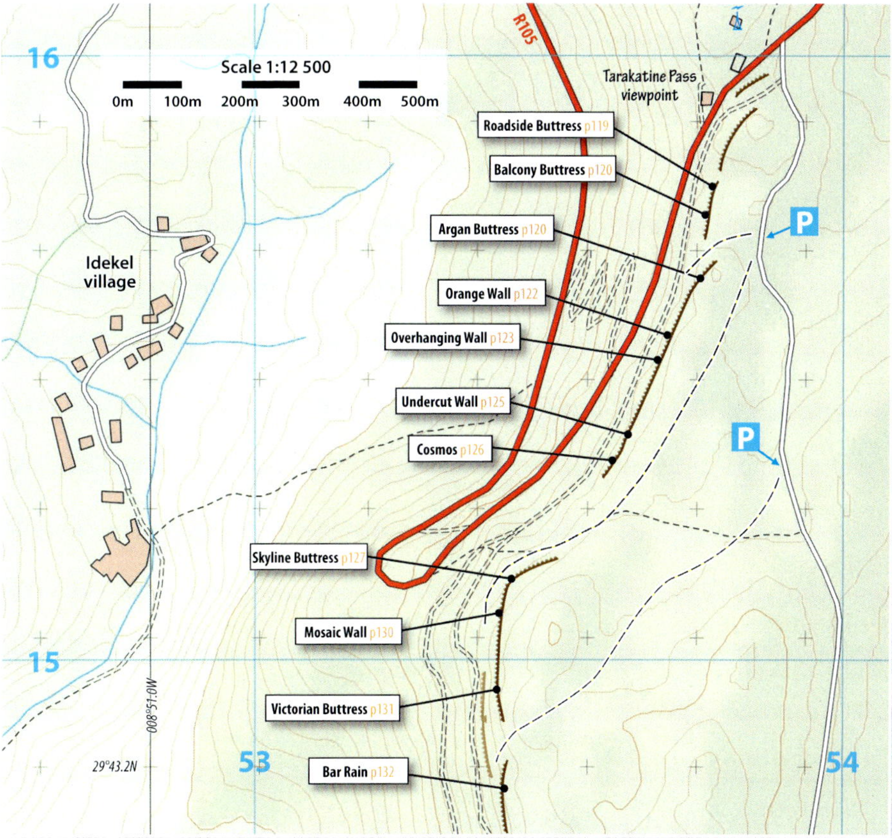

Area Map
Crag Selector
Intro
The Climbing
How to Use
Suggested Climbs
Tafraout Granite
Anergui
Ameln Valley
Tarakatine Pass
Sidi M'Zal
Jebel Taskra
Idaougnidif
Afantinzar
Samazar
Aouguenz
Tagzene
Tagmout
History
Index

ROADSIDE BUTTRESS

The first buttress just above large boulders by the old road has a couple of short amusements, though the rock here is considerably less solid than on the main crag.

1. Fandango HS 4c

5m. The left-slanting crack on the left wall.

Steve Broadbent (solo), April 2010.

2. New Way Severe

5m. Broken blocks to the left of the arête.

Steve Broadbent (solo), April 2010.

To the right is a descent gully, then an area of rotten rock before a large steep wall. The next climb lies in the corner to the right of this wall.

3. Gingerbread Difficult 1

6m. Climb steps up the right wall of the corner to gain the top of the pillar.

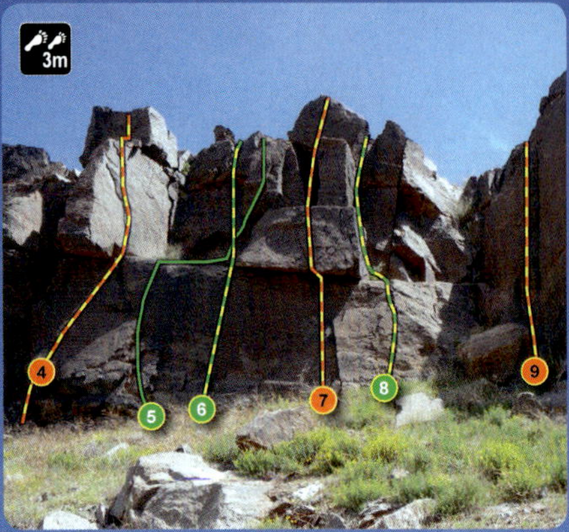

BALCONY BUTTRESS

The next worthwhile buttress to the right has a prominent square balcony at half-height, with a handful of tempting crack lines leading up to it.

4. Sidewalk VS 4c

8m. Climb the lower slab to the left side of the balcony with some difficulty. From here, head up the left wall to the top.
Hamish Legge (solo), April 2012.

5. Balcony Indirect HS 4b

10m. Climb leftwards up broken ledges to a tricky move right to gain the balcony. Either finish up the back corner (severe) or step out up the small prow to the right (4b).
Steve Broadbent (solo), April 2010.

6. Balcony Crack Severe ★1

8m. The excellent little crack, finishing up the back corner above the balcony.
Steve Broadbent (solo), April 2010.

7. Bal-Can-He VS 4c

8m. Classic gritstone crack climbing through the overhang.
Fruit & Lorna Fewtrell, November 2013.

8. Rib and Chimney Difficult

8m. Straightforward climbing up the rib and chimney.
Steve Broadbent (solo), April 2010.

9. Wall Climb MVS 4b

6m. The steep wall up the left side of the impressive arête is a tricky solo.
Hamish Legge (solo), April 2012.

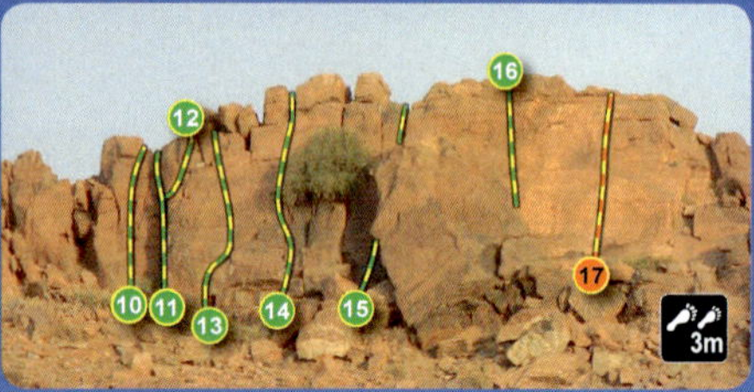

ARGAN BUTTRESS

This cracking little buttress forms the left end of the crag's upper tier, and holds some of the best climbs hereabouts. It can be identified by a large leaning pinnacle and a tree at half height.

10. Hazy Days Difficult

5m. The cracked wall left of the corner.
Steve Broadbent (solo), April 2010.

11. Steve's Layback Very Difficult ★1 CRACK

5m. The short corner is a little gem.
Steve Broadbent (solo), April 2010.

12. Cowboy Variation Hard Difficult ★1

6m. Escaping right underneath the curving overlap is slightly easier, but just as much fun.
Peter Hill (solo), October 2010.

13. False Start HS 4c ★1

7m. The left side of the front wall has a very taxing start, but eases considerably above.
Steve Broadbent (solo), April 2010.

14. Argan Crack Severe ★1 CRACK

7m. The obvious crack-line just left of the tree is a nice climb with a cheeky top-out...
Steve Broadbent (solo), April 2010.

15. Katie's Bush Severe CRACK

6m. The crack tucked away to the right of the tree.
Peter Hill (solo), October 2010.

16. Shame About the Tiger HVD ★1 STEEP

7m. This pleasant problem starts directly behind the large pinnacle and climbs up some impressively steep ground.
Steve Broadbent (solo), October 2010.

17. To Hell in a Hyundai MVS 5a ★1

7m. The thin vegetated crack to the right of the pinnacle.
Peter Hill (solo), October 2010.

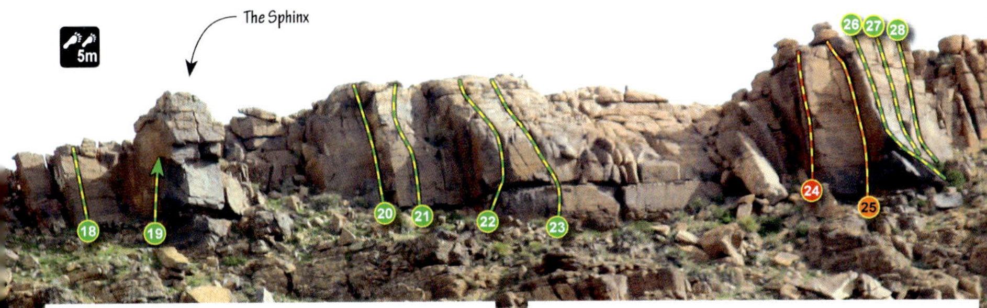

THE SPHINX

To the right of Argan Buttress is a prominent Sphinx-like rock. Two routes have been climbed here...

18. Amateur Dentistry HVD

5m. The simple crack up the short wall left of the Sphinx.
Cameron Hall (solo), October 2010.

19. Lizard Radar Severe

5m. Thin cracks up the left side of the Sphinx.
Peter Hill (solo), October 2010.

SECOND BUTTRESS

Further right is an attractive buttress with a desperately blank and curiously unclimbed corner...

20. Jenga Severe

LOOSE

7m. The stacked blocks provide a rather loose ascent.
Peter Hill (solo), October 2010.

21. Sugar High HS 4c ★1

7m. A highly technical route up the hairline cracks in the wall left of the blank corner.
Steve Broadbent (solo), October 2010.

22. Razor Blade Fandango HS 4c ★1

CRACK

8m. The tempting hanging crack up the front of the buttress is a nice climb with some good protection and painful hand-jams. You might want a rope for this one.
Steve Broadbent & Cameron Hall, October 2010.

23. Amnesia Difficult

7m. Easy steps lead to a high notch in the front face.
Steve Broadbent (solo), April 2010.

QUINTUS

The next buttress to the right is identifiable by a long off-width corner that gives one of the crag's finest climbs.

24. Caecilius Shot the Sheriff E1 5a ★1

BOLD

8m. The overhanging square rib to the left of the corner is a challenging proposition, with steep, high moves above half-height gear. Notoriously easy to top-rope, but mentally trying on lead. An escape (or cheat) leftwards into the gully is often frustratingly possible.
Steve Broadbent & Peter Hill, October 2010.

25. Quintus MVS 4b ★2

8m. The tempting wide corner crack is one of the best climbs on the crag, and would hold its own amongst many Peak District classics. Small pro is available, and despite appearances the route doesn't really require off-width technique. Big cams, however, turn it into a delightful romp that is sure to bring a smile to your face...
Steve Broadbent, Cameron Hall & Peter Hill, October 2010.

The next three routes climb the front wall to the right of the big corner...

26. Trigger Happy MS ★1

BOLD

9m. The fine arête is gained via the slab on the right and followed to a final loose flake. It provides good, photogenic climbing.
Steve Broadbent (solo), April 2010.

27. Tiger Crack MS ★1

GEAR CRACK

8m. The crack straight up the front face is a worthwhile route, and even has protection.
Steve Broadbent (solo), April 2010.

28. Grumio Coquus Est MS ★1

8m. Excellent climbing up the right side of the front face.
Steve Broadbent (solo), October 2010.

Area Map
Crag Selector
Intro
The Climbing
How to Use
Suggested Climbs
Tafraout Granite
Anergui
Ameln Valley
Tarakatine Pass
Sidi M'Zal
Jebel Taskra
Idaougnidif
Afantinzar
Samazar
Aouguenz
Tagzene
Tagmout
History
Index

THE ORANGE WALL

Further right still is a clean orange wall with an attractive layback corner at its right side. Immediately right of this corner is another wall, cleaved by a handful of good easy cracks.

29. Messerschmitt Crack Very Difficult — CRACK

6m. The rather average crack at the far left side of the wall.
Peter Hill (solo), October 2010.

30. Blitzkrieg HS 4b ★ — CRACK

6m. The crack in the left side of the main orange wall used to have a rickety flake that now lies shattered on the ground.
Steve Broadbent (solo), October 2010.

31. Achtung Spitfire! Severe ★ — CRACK

6m. The obvious corner is a masterful little climb that is easier than it looks thanks to good holds on the arête.
Peter Hill (solo), October 2010.

32. Telic Very Difficult ★ — CRACK

6m. The left-hand crack is a steep pitch with excellent holds and a tricky top-out.
Steve Broadbent (solo), April 2010.

33. Herrick Very Difficult ★

6m. The right-hand 'crack' is actually a superb little face climb.
Steve Broadbent (solo), October 2010.

34. Beaver Dam Severe ★

6m. Blocky sidepulls up the right side of the wall.
Steve Broadbent (solo), October 2010.

DINGOVILLE BUTTRESS

In between the Orange Wall and a prominent pinnacle (the Egg Timer) is some more broken rock, featuring a short overhanging wall above a high sloping ledge. This gives...

35. Dingoville VS 4c ★ — BOLD, STEEP

8m. A bold proposition up the overhanging wall. Gain the sloping ledge easily before some very steep and stretchy moves up rightwards gain the top. The route has a bad landing and no protection, but is a worthwhile frightener!
Peter Hill (solo) October 2010.

36. Rubber Duck MVS 4b

8m. Very pleasant climbing up the initial wall to gain the hanging arête. Getting up this usually involves some naughty use of the groove to the right.
Steve Broadbent (solo), October 2010.

37. The Beard of a Welshman HS 4a

6m. The wall to the left of the prominent pinnacle.
Peter Hill (solo) October 2010.

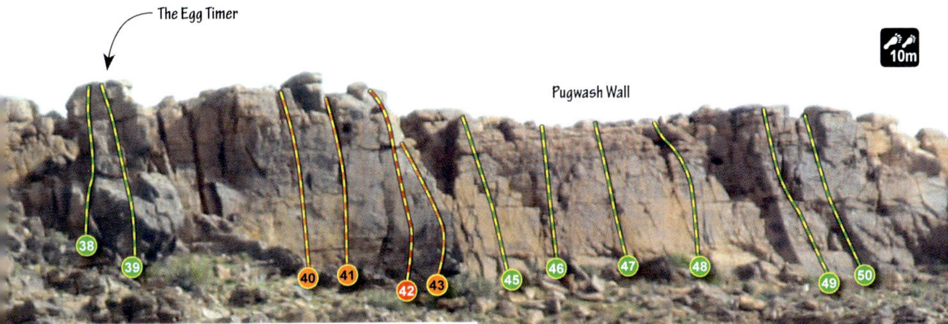

THE EGG TIMER

A single climb has been recorded up the front of the odd-shaped pinnacle just to the right...

38. Eggy Soldier Mild Severe ★

5m. Start up the left arête of the Eggtimer to gain a ledge. Pull over the overlap above and finish up the pinnacle.
Lina & Dave Arthur, September 2013.

39. The Egg Timer HVD ★

5m. The front of the pinnacle has a very tricky undercut start with easier climbing above.
Steve Broadbent (solo), April 2010.

OVERHANGING WALL

Immediately right of the Egg Timer is a deceptively steep wall.

40. Badger Man MVS 4a ★ STEEP

6m. Twin cracks up the left side of the steep wall.
Steve Broadbent (solo), April 2011.

41. The Mongoose VS 4b ★ STEEP

6m. Climb the tempting crack-line to a round hole near the top. A significantly steeper proposition than first appearances would suggest, and one of the more difficult solos of the crag.
Steve Broadbent (solo), April 2010.

42. Adaptations of Base E1 5c ★ THIN

6m. The thin seam gives a very worthwhile climb. Strong fingers and a handful of RPs will make things seem altogether more reasonable.
Caroline Culwick & Steve Broadbent, March 2011.

43. Really? VS 4b ★

6m. Difficult climbing just left of the arête.
Hamish Legge (solo), April 2012.

44. Black Slab Severe

6m. The black slabby wall at the right hand side is something of an eliminate, with no bridging allowed at this grade. Finish direct with a long reach.
Steve Broadbent (solo), April 2010.

PUGWASH WALL

The rather diminutive cracked wall immediately to the right holds a number of short climbs that are worth a quick solo.

45. Needle Wall HVD ★

4m. The left side of the wall, up an arrowhead pinnacle.
Steve Broadbent (solo), October 2010.

46. Munter Mule Moderate

4m. The wall just to the right of the arrowhead pinnacle.
Cameron Hall (solo), October 2010.

47. Seaman Staines Difficult

4m. The crack above the boulder.
Cameron Hall (solo), October 2010.

48. Captain Pugwash Severe

4m. The wall to the left of the small gully.
Peter Hill (solo), October 2010.

49. Master Bates Very Difficult

5m. The broken wall immediately right of the small gully.
Cameron Hall (solo), October 2010.

50. Roger the Cabin Boy Severe

5m. The thin seam to the right.
Cameron Hall (solo), October 2010.

51. Directissimo Severe

6m. Straight up the wall to the right of *Roger the Cabin Boy*.
Joe Gallacher (solo), November 2014

52. SWMC Woz Ere Difficult

6m. Easy climbing up the right-hand side of this short wall.
Matthew Moore (solo), November 2014

DESERT FROG AREA

The next major buttress to the right has a leaning black corner.

53. Monsieur Antelope Severe ★1

6m. Pleasant climbing up the short jagged arête.
Peter Hill (solo), October 2010.

54. La Vie en Mauve Severe

6m. Something of an eliminate line, gaining the arête from the right side.
Peter Hill (solo), October 2010.

55. La Vie en Mauve Direct Severe

6m. Straight up above the start of *La Vie en Mauve*.
Joe Gallacher (solo), November 2014.

56. New Route Fever Difficult

6m. The obvious groove to the right of *La Vie en Mauve*.
Matthew Moore (solo), November 2014.

57. Stairway to Devon Difficult ★1

6m. The stepped wall just left of the corner is a pleasant route with good holds.
Steve Broadbent (solo), October 2010.

58. Desert Frog VS 4c ★2

7m. A superb little micro-route that has gear, but is best soloed anyway. Climb the corner until a daunting traverse rightwards on small incuts gains the high triangular groove. Pull into this in a very exposed position, then stretch for the top. Great stuff.
Peter Hill (solo), October 2010

59. Wensleydale Difficult

6m. The short groove and wall just right of the arête.
Peter Hill (solo), October 2010

60. Pig Pen Difficult

6m. Straightforward climbing up the right side of the right-hand wall.
Steve Broadbent (solo), October 2010

TWIN BUSHES

This imaginatively named buttress is identified by... you guessed it... two bushes half-way up the rock.

Just to the left of the buttress itself is a very short layback corner, which provides a worthwhile boulder problem. The main routes are on the front of the buttress to the right of the bushes - a handful of very pleasant and technical low-grade amusements...

61. Waider Widda Difficult ★1

8m. Nice climbing up cracks in the buttress right of the two bushes.
Steve Broadbent (solo), October 2010

62. Groove Route Mild Severe

8m. A worthwhile climb with an interesting start up the leaning groove (hard for the short). Continue more easily above.
Steve Broadbent (solo), October 2010

63. Wadder Wadda Very Difficult ★1

8m. The front of the right-hand buttress is another pleasant climb, finishing up a short groove on the right side.
Steve Broadbent (solo), October 2010

THE BROWN SLABS

Immediately right of the Twin Bushes Buttress is an area of attractive, easy-angled brown rock.

64. Dirty Dancing Very Difficult ★

8m. The left-hand cracked buttress.
Steve Broadbent (solo), October 2010.

65. H Twenty Very Difficult

8m. The left-slanting line on the main slab.
Steve Broadbent (solo), October 2010.

66. Brown Slab Direct Severe

8m. Climb straight up the bold wall above the leaning block, with little in the way of protection.
Steve Broadbent (solo), October 2010.

67. Brown Slabs Crack HVD

8m. The tempting crackline running up right from the leaning block.
Steve Broadbent (solo), October 2010.

68. Brown Slabs Groove HS 4a

8m. The wall just left of the dark groove.
Hamish Legge (solo), April 2012.

69. Flickba Very Difficult ★

8m. Good climbing up the flat arête just right of a small groove. Finish to the left of the final steepening.
Steve Broadbent (solo), October 2010.

70. Bear in the Air Severe ★

8m. A curiously technical climb with some good moves. Start as for the previous route then step right, making a difficult move off a peculiar pocket to gain a left-slanting groove. Follow this with interest to the top.
Steve Broadbent (solo), October 2010

UNDERCUT WALL

The next buttress is a tall black wall with an undercut base.

71. Sillysally Hard Severe

9m. Pleasant climbing up the left side of the wall, via a thin crack. This leads to a steep and bold finish up slightly overhanging rock...
Steve Broadbent (solo), October 2010

72. Direct Route HS 4b ★

9m. Audacious climbing up the steep wall.

73. Huygen's Groove Severe ★

9m. The obvious right-slanting groove.
Steve Broadbent (solo), March 2011

74. The Holland Arena Severe ★

9m. Climb steps to gain the steep crack on the front face. This leads to a flowery ledge and finish as for the previous climb.
Steve Broadbent (solo), March 2011

75. Boris The Spider Severe ★

9m. A steep, airy climb on good holds. Climb a right-trending corner before finishing left up the slot.
Caroline Culwick, March 2011

76. Fuzzy Thinking HVD

9m. The right side of the buttress, using an odd hole.
Steve Broadbent (solo), March 2011

77. Resorting to Buff Very Difficult ★

9m. This route climbs an initial low tower before finishing up the wall above.
Caroline Culwick, March 2011

78. 633 Squadron HS 4b ★

9m. Good steep climbing up the narrow pillar to the right, with a prominent short roof. Escaping leftwards is all too easy, but the direct approach is more fun.
Steve Broadbent (solo), March 2011

Area Map
Crag Selector
Intro
The Climbing
How to Use
Suggested Climbs
Tafraout Granite
Anergui
Ameln Valley
Tarakatine Pass
Sidi M'Zal
Jebel Taskra
Idaougnidif
Afantinzar
Samazar
Aouguenz
Tagzene
Tagmout
History
Index

COSMOS

This is the last main buttress before a section of lower rocks leads to the taller Skyline Buttress.

79. Rib Tickler Severe ★1

7m. The rounded rib is accessed from the left side, and provides a pleasant, if rather indirect climb.
Steve Broadbent (solo), March 2011.

80. Cosmos HS 4b ★2

7m. The fine crack up the front face is one of the better pitches hereabouts, gained from a steep start.
Steve Broadbent (solo), March 2011.

81. Adequate Pink HS 4a ★1

7m. The central groove is a slightly easier proposition than its neighbour, but still has some difficult moves to get established.
Caroline Culwick (solo), March 2011.

82. The Pale Blue Dot Very Difficult ★1

7m. The short face to the right, accessed via a steep V-groove in the lower black.
Steve Broadbent (solo), March 2011.

83. Shark Bait VS 5b

7m. A sit-start boulder problem up the fin, finishing up the wall above.
Hamish Legge, April 2012.

84. Adrian Von Trip Stamp Donk V.Diff ★1

7m. The groove and hairline crack to the right gives another pleasant pitch.
Steve Broadbent (solo), March 2011.

85. George is a Chav HS 4a ★1

7m. Some nice moves up the next crack to the right, although it's something of an eliminate.
Caroline Culwick, March 2011.

86. Colin The Caterpillar Severe ★1

7m. Tricky moves up the short wall gain a large ledge, from where bobbly twin cracks lead easily to the top.
Caroline Culwick, March 2011

SKYLINE BUTTRESS LEFT

To the west of the main section of the upper tier there is a substantial gap in the crags, where a number of ancient paths climb up to the plateau above (numerous cairns). The crag starts again at the Skyline Buttress, shortly before swinging round southwards. Skyline Buttress itself appears to be a tall, impressive buttress, but closer inspection reveals some poor quality rock.

A small number of lines have been climbed, with the first of them being located on a slabby brown buttress to the left of the main buttress.

87. Tile Terror Severe

7m. The left-hand of two cracks on the left side of the wall.
Steve Broadbent (solo), April 2011.

88. Onion Terror Difficult

7m. The slabby chimney is almost fun, but doesn't require much chimneying.
Steve Broadbent (solo), April 2011.

89. High in Pork Gelatine Very Difficult

7m. The slabby wall has a couple of tricky steps low down.
Caroline Culwick (solo), April 2011.

SKYLINE BUTTRESS

The main Skyline Buttress immediately to the right features a tall undercut rib and steep overhung corners, but has some poor-quality rock.

90. Bôite Diabolique HS 4b ★1 STEEP

8m. Steep moves through the overhang are not immediately obvious, and might provide soloists with something to think about. Leaders, on the other hand, will find good gear throughout.
Steve Broadbent (solo), April 2011.

BROWN GIRL

To the right of Skyline Buttress is an attractive slab and steep corner. Unfortunately the rock here is poor, and the main features are not attractive for climbing. The following pair of routes tackle the blocky wall just to the left.

91. Fried Fish Difficult

8m. The blocky wall is nothing special.
Steve Broadbent (solo), April 2011.

92. Johnny Cakes Difficult

8m. The crack and upper flake.
Caroline Culwick (solo), April 2011.

93. Khal Kalash HS 4b

8m. The wall to the right of *Johnny Cakes* has a bold start to mid-height gear, then an easier finish up the obvious crack.
John Stevenson & Tom Frost, April 2014

LITTLE BUTTRESS

This minor buttress has a prominent hole on the right wall of a short descent gully.

94. Crushed Witch Very Difficult ★ SLAB

6m. Very pleasant friction climbing up the slab to the left of the short descent gully.
Steve Broadbent (solo), April 2011.

95. Something's Munching My Hole Very Difficult ★

6m. Go past the obvious hole to reach the crack.
Caroline Culwick (solo), April 2011.

Right of this is an unclimbed vegetated corner, before the next climb...

96. Gin Haze Severe ★ STEEP

6m. The face to the right has a surprisingly steep finish.
Caroline Culwick (solo), April 2011.

97. Sleepy Haze Mild Severe ★ STEEP

6m. The easy-looking rib to the right is another good climb with a steep finish.
Steve Broadbent (solo), April 2011.

The short routes on the Tarakatine Pass provide ideal solos, or a good rest-day activity. Caroline Culwick on *Something's Munching my Hole* (VD).
Photo: Steve Broadbent

BOOGIE BUTTRESS

Continuing to the right there is an area of lower rocks and a cairn. The next buttress is identifiable by a prominent finger of rock, and is home to another concentration of good short climbs.

98. Funky Town Mild Severe ★1

5m. A tempting amusement up the left-hand rib, with an intriguing fun move off the ground.
Steve Broadbent (solo), April 2011.

99. Friendly Black Lizard Severe

6m. The left side-wall is pleasant enough.
Caroline Culwick (solo), April 2011.

100. Flatland HVD ★1

6m. The shallow groove leads to a steep finish.
Steve Broadbent (solo), April 2011.

101. Grisly Spider Very Difficult ★1

6m. Prickly cracks up the front face lead to a ledge and easier finish.
Caroline Culwick (solo), April 2011.

102. Blame it on the Boogie HVD ★2 STEEP

6m. An unlikely climb, and one of the best routes of this grade on the crag. Climb the blank-looking wall to an overhanging finish. Superb!
Steve Broadbent (solo), April 2011.

103. Hypercube Severe ★1

6m. A tricky little number up the steep groove to the right. The upper moves are awkward, particularly without the reassurance of a rope...
Steve Broadbent (solo), April 2011.

104. Pink Trousers Difficult

6m. The rib on the right side of the buttress is easy enough, accessed via a short crack next to a curious hole.
Caroline Culwick (solo), April 2011.

105. Teenie Tiny Difficult

4m. The tiny broken wall just around the corner to the right is almost too small to mention.
Caroline Culwick (solo), April 2011.

INSPECTOR GADGET

At this point the face swings round to the south, stretching off into the distance as far as the eye can see. The first two buttresses hold some excellent climbs...

106. Inspector Gadget MVS 4b

STEEP

6m. The flake crack is steep, off-balance, and provides one of the best solos on the crag, thankfully not as hard as you think it's going to be...

Steve Broadbent (solo), April 2011.

107. Lie-Ins and Tigers HS 4b

8m. The steep, tricky corner to the right.

Steve Broadbent (solo), April 2011.

108. Lions are Good HS 4c

8m. A brilliant climb, heading leftwards up the black wall towards the notch.

Steve Broadbent (solo), April 2011.

To the right of *Lions Are Good* is an attractive clean-cut arête that remains unclimbed at the time of going to press, although for those who could resist the temptation to escape right it might provide a superb, technical problem.

The next route takes an obvious crack in the wall to the right of this arête.

109. Place of Space Severe

8m. The crack in the side-wall gives some pleasant climbing. It also provides a bridging escape for those who chicken out of the arête to the left!

Caroline Culwick (solo), April 2011.

110. Shame About the Tiger Severe

8m. The brown rib to the right has a tricky steep finish that is usually avoided on the right.

Steve Broadbent (solo), April 2011.

MOSAIC WALL

This is the first buttress after the face swings round to the south. It holds one of the crag's best easy climbs

111. Scene of Sun Severe

6m. The small wall left of a prominent v-groove.

Caroline Culwick (solo), April 2011.

112. Sand and Sangria Very Difficult

6m. The rib to the right of the v-groove.

Steve Broadbent (solo), April 2011.

113. Mosaic Wall Difficult

10m. A superb little climb, and one of the best routes at this grade on the pass. The blocky wall to the right leads to ledges. Move right and finish up a short groove.

Steve Broadbent (solo), April 2011.

114. Too Much Sun HS 4a

8m. Converging cracks past the bush lead to a difficult finish.

Caroline Culwick (solo), April 2011.

BLACK BUTTRESS

To the right of Mosaic Wall the crag becomes rather insignificant for approximately 70 yards, after which there is a tall black buttress with a twin slab immediately left of it. This holds:

115. Mafipulation HS 4b

8m. The left-hand side of the slab.
Steve Broadbent (solo), March 2012.

116. Jane Grey Severe 4a

8m. The right-hand side of the slab.
Will Benfold (solo), March 2012.

117. Layback for the Win VS 5a ★★

12m. The tempting right-facing corner, just left of the cave, succumbs to a confident layback.
Steve & Katja Broadbent, January 2013.

CAVE BUTTRESS

The next buttress can be identified by a prominent cave at its base.

118. Vanillin MVS 4b ★

8m. A surprisingly good climb, despite the 'escape' rightwards. Start just left of the cave and climb a black wall before skulking off to the right.
Steve Broadbent (solo), March 2012.

The next two routes are on the short sidewall to the right...

119. Left Crack Severe

6m. The left-hand crack and arête.

120. Right Crack Severe

6m. Make use of both the right-hand cracks.

VICTORIAN BUTTRESS

121. Victorian Cronies HS 4b

7m. Pleasant climbing up the crack to the left of the prominent off-width crack.
Pete Cawley & Aeron Buchanan, January 2013.

122. Spring Sprout Mushroom Lollipop Person HS 4a

7m. The wide crack above the huge open-book corner feels exposed right from the word go. If you're soloing, then you'd better not fall...
Steve & Katja Broadbent, January 2013.

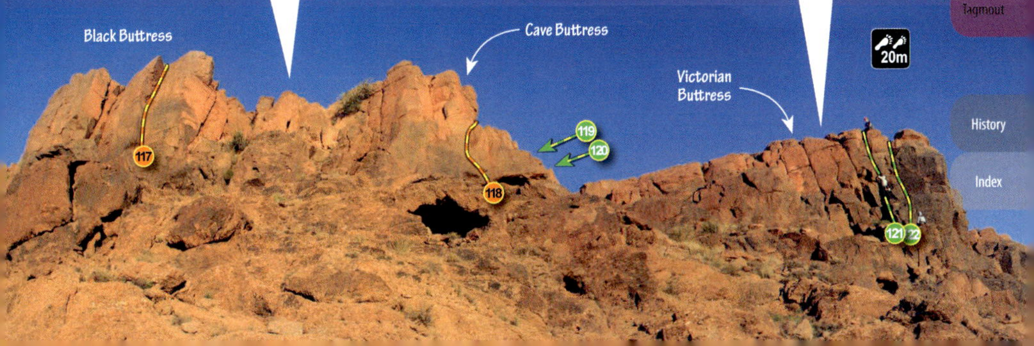

Area Map
Crag Selector
Intro
The Climbing
How to Use
Suggested Climbs
Tafraout Granite
Anergui
Ameln Valley
Tarakatine Pass
Sidi M'Zal
Jebel Taskra
Idaougnidif
Afantinzar
Samazar
Aouguenz
Tagzene
Tagmout
History
Index

BAR RAIN

South of Victorian Buttress there is a gap in the crags, where a vague path descends from a prominent col. This point is most easily reached by walking southwest up a shallow valley as shown on the map on page 118.

The following climbs are located just south of the col:

123. Purple Monkey Dishwasher Severe 4a

6m. The narrow slab with a white right-wall.
Will Benfold (solo), March 2012.

124. Takeshi's Castle Severe 4a ★

7m. Good climbing up the blocky recessed wall.
Steve Broadbent (solo), March 2012.

125. American Beige Severe ★

7m. The flat pillar to the right of the groove.
Steve Broadbent (solo), October 2015.

126. Gateau de Chien Very Difficult

6m. The short wall above a boulder.
Mark Condon (solo), October 2015.

127. Bar Rain Severe

6m. The thin crack up the wall left of the central scoop.
Steve Broadbent (solo), March 2012.

128. Bubble Trouble Difficult

6m. The central scoop in the front of the slab.
Steve Broadbent (solo), March 2012.

129. Adam's Arête Hard Severe ★

7m. The fin to the right of the rounded groove.
Caroline Culwick (solo), October 2015.

130. Fernet Branca Severe 4a

7m. The slab to the right of the fin.
Will Benfold (solo), March 2012.

The next route is on the sidewall, just to the right...

131. Mandatory Trousers Severe

7m. The crack up the side-wall of the buttress.
Mark Condon (solo), October 2015.

132. Bodies in the Boot Difficult

6m. Climbs a short arête right of the descent gully.
Mark Condon (solo), October 2015

133. Dick Dastardly Hard Severe

7m. The little roof gives a pleasant problem.
Mark Condon (solo), October 2015

134. Penelope Pitstop Difficult

7m. The narrowing groove to the left of the prominent buttress.
Steve Broadbent (solo), October 2015

135. Banana Split Severe

7m. The scary stacked pillar hopefully won't fall down...
Mark Condon (solo), October 2015

136. Ant Orgy Severe

7m. The v-corner a short way to the right of the prominent stacked pillar.
Caroline Culwick (solo), October 2015

137. Cutty Snark Very Difficult

7m. The small slab to the right of a bush.
Mark Condon (solo), October 2015

138. Bicycle Storm Severe

7m. Good climbing up the narrow crack just right of the arête. Step right at the top to finish up the front of the buttress.
Steve Broadbent (solo), October 2015

Area Map
Crag Selector
Intro
The Climbing
How to Use
Suggested Climbs
Tafraout Granite
Anergui
Ameln Valley
Tarakatine Pass
Sidi M'Zal
Jebel Taskra
Idaougnidif
Afantinzar
Samazar
Aouguenz
Tagzene
Tagmout
History
Index

VICTORY BUTTRESS

Right of the slabs of *Bar Rain*, the crag swings round the corner and there is another scramble descent gully. Beyond this is a fine tall buttress that gives some of the best climbs on the crag, though you're probably going to want a rope here...

139. Cold Feet Mild Severe

15m. The shady groove up the left side of the buttress gives a worthwhile climb, but watch out for the hollow flake...
Steve Broadbent (solo), March 2012.

140. Havana Buttress Severe ★1 GEAR

15m. An excellent climb on good rock. The flat-faced buttress is gained from the right-hand side and followed on excellent holds.
Steve & Katja Broadbent, January 2017.

141. Breakfast means Breakfast MVS 4b ★1

15m. Climb the tricky wall to a high groove on the left. Rock up rightwards onto an excellent slabby finale.
Steve & Katja Broadbent, January 2017.

142. Battle Royale VS 4b ★2

15m. The front of the prominent pillar is an excellent climb on good rock.
Will Benfold (solo), March 2012.

143. Victory Groove Severe ★1

15m. The v-groove to the right gives one of the best routes of its grade hereabouts. Climb the fine initial groove, then step left into the upper groove.
Steve Broadbent (solo), March 2012.

144. Celestial HS 4b ★1 GEAR

15m. Good climbing up the tempting quartz corner, with good protection throughout.
Steve & Katja Broadbent, Daniyal Mueenuddin, January 2017.

145. Victory Crack HVS 5b ★2

15m. The photogenic wide crack up the right-hand side of the buttress is one of the best routes at the crag. It can be easily tamed with a large cam, but without it provides some thought-provoking moves.
Steve Broadbent, January 2017.

Steve and Katja Broadbent on *Victory Crack* (HVS).
Photo: Zoe Bouras

B ADRAR IDEKEL

Shade Families Hitch Roadside

Drive from Tafraout: **20 minutes**
Walk-in: **15 minutes**

Adrar Idekel (1894m) is the attractive peak sitting at the eastern end of the Ameln Valley, clearly seen from the Tarakatine Pass, from where a tempting ridge stretches out above the village of Idekel (or Idikel) (meaning *palm of the hand*). Although not really a climb, the following route is included as a good wet weather activity. Park at a junction on the main road where a small track is signposted to Idikel.

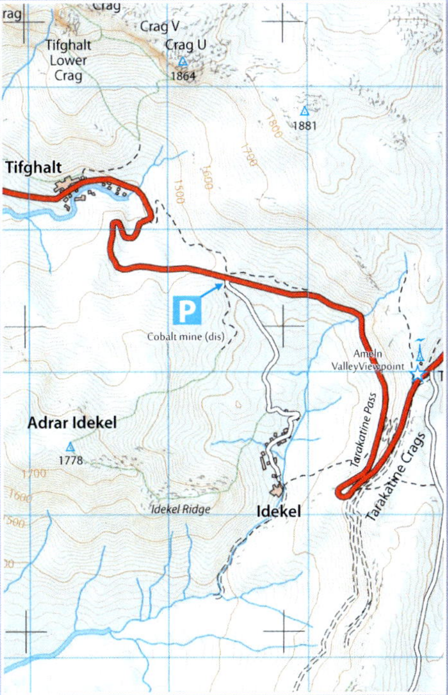

1. Southeast Ridge Grade I (scramble) ★1

The attractive ridge line gives a very pleasant scramble on which the difficulty can be varied to suit most tastes. Approach along the track to Idekel, but strike off across the hillside before reaching the village. Scramble up to the left end of the ridge, and follow it over a series of interesting towers to the fine little summit. Interesting, avoidable scrambling and tremendous views to Adrar Mqorn and the Jebel el Kest escarpment make for a fun little outing that can be completed in any weather. Descend easy slopes to the north, where an ancient cobalt mine adds some speleological interest to the day. The round trip takes about 2 to 3 hours.

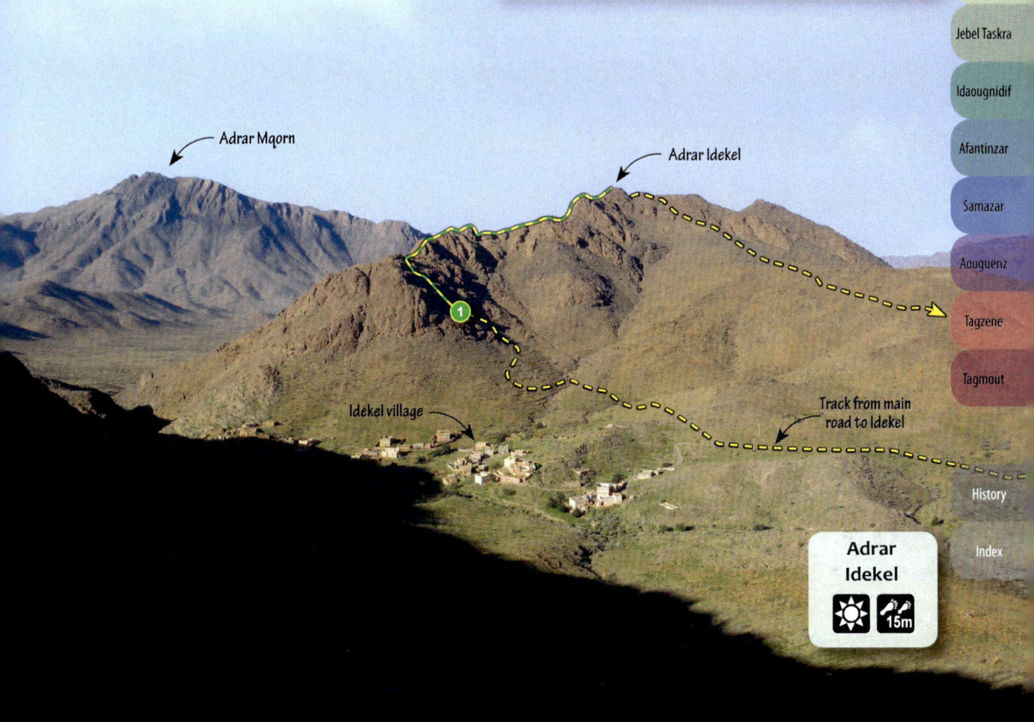

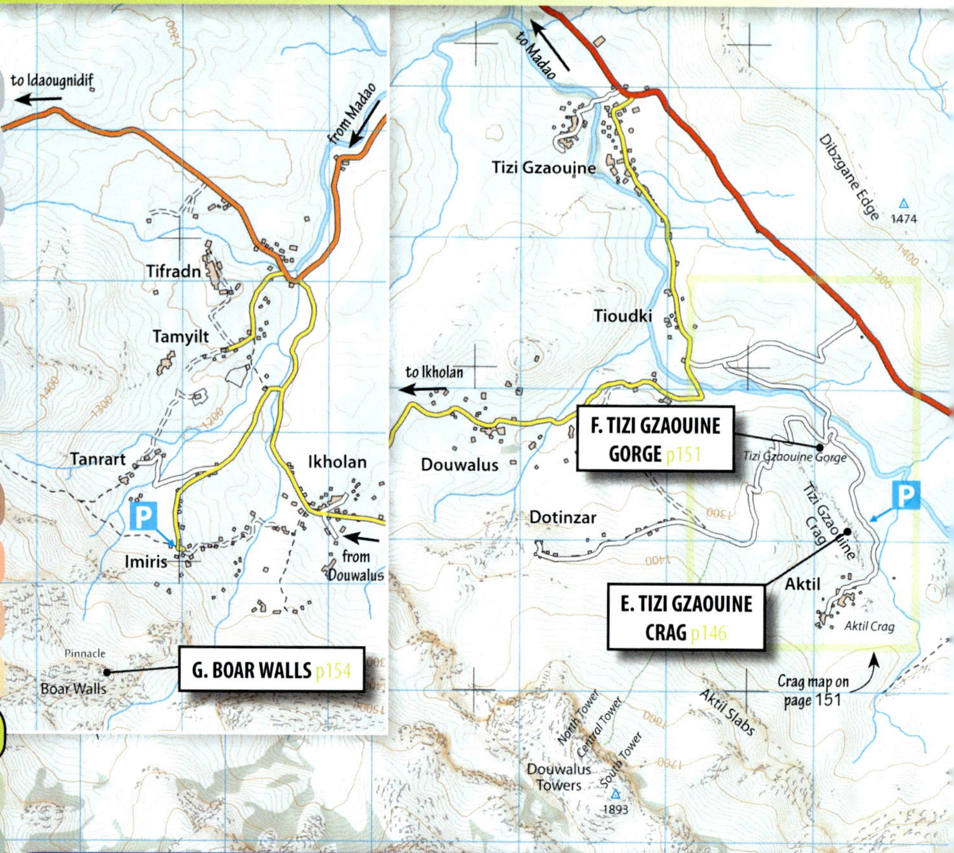
to Idaougnidif
from Madao
Tifradn
Tamyilt
1551
Tanrart
Ikholan
Imiris
from Douwalus
Pinnacle
Boar Walls
G. BOAR WALLS p154
to Madao
Tizi Gzaoujne
Dibzgane Edge
1474
Tioudki
to Ikholan
Douwalus
F. TIZI GZAOUINE GORGE p151
Tizi Gzaouine Gorge
Dotinzar
Tizi Gzaouine Crag
Aktil
E. TIZI GZAOUINE CRAG p146
Aktil Crag
Crag map on page 151
Aktil Slabs
North Tower
Central Tower
South Tower
Douwalus Towers
1893
Avalon
Lost World Col

Fylde Crags
SHADE
20m
Approach Walls
Main Wall
Cut back left up gully to Main Wall
Approach up valley from Taourirt Wazal

SIDI M'ZAL

The Eastern end of the Jebel el Kest massif forms an impressive escarpment above the villages of Sidi M'Zal, Tizi Gzaouine and Madao, and whilst the rock here is not as reliable as that in other areas, there is some very worthwhile climbing on a good variety of crags. The bigger cliffs are concentrated around the settlement of Sidi M'Zal, where the magnificent Arch Wall dominates the view – this is usually the first big line to catch the climber's eye during the drive from Agadir to Tafraout.

Further north, the delightful Tizi Gzaouine Crag sits low in the valley, and is often a dry venue when winter rain puts the higher crags out of bounds.

It also provides an ideal opportunity for a few short routes on the drive between Tafraout and the airport.

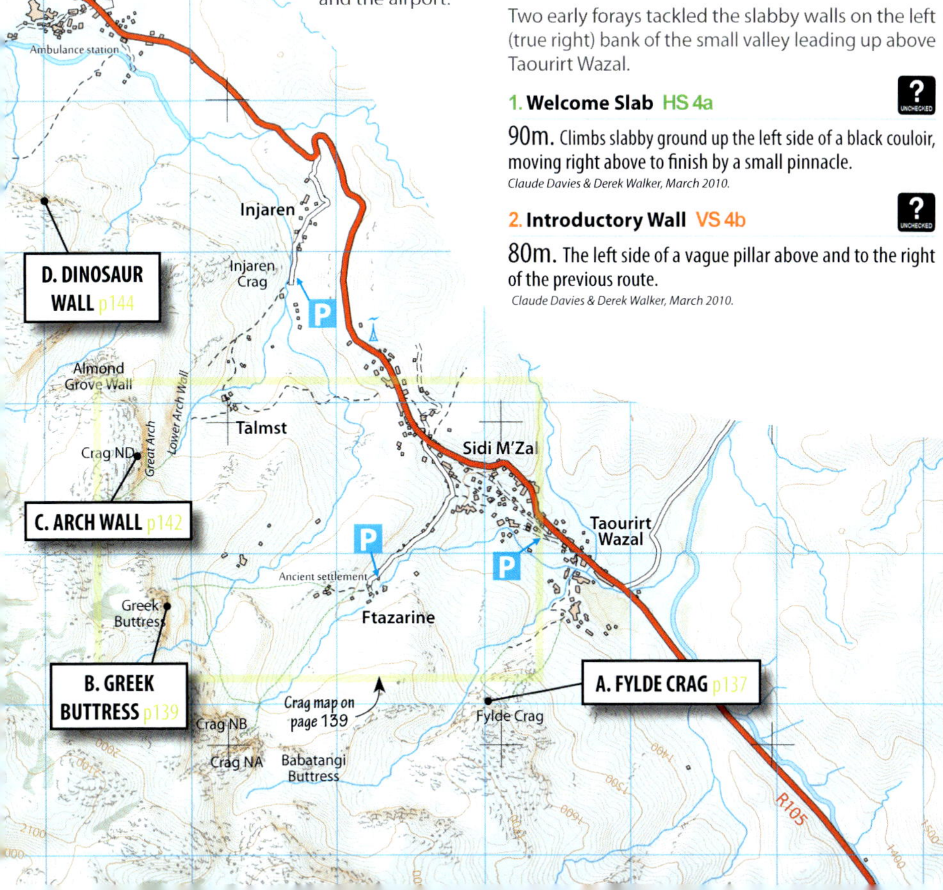

(A) FYLDE CRAG

Sun | Shade | Families | Hitch | Roadside

Drive from Tafraout: **30 minutes**
Walk-in: **30 minutes**

Fylde Crag (named after the Lancashire-based mountaineering club) is a pleasant, low-lying crag above the village of Taourirt Wazal, immediately south of Sidi M'Zal. It has seen limited development in recent years, but does provide a handful of pleasant climbs with an easy approach and friendly feel to them.

A small track leaves the main road just south of Sidi M'Zal, at the settlement of Taourirt Wazal. Park a short way along this, then walk back into the village to cross the outflow from the small valley beneath the Approach Walls. Ascend through prickly pears on the south side of the stream, next to houses, to gain a good trail which heads rightwards (southwest) beneath the Approach Walls.

THE APPROACH WALLS

Two early forays tackled the slabby walls on the left (true right) bank of the small valley leading up above Taourirt Wazal.

1. Welcome Slab HS 4a (? UNCHECKED)

90m. Climbs slabby ground up the left side of a black couloir, moving right above to finish by a small pinnacle.

Claude Davies & Derek Walker, March 2010.

2. Introductory Wall VS 4b (? UNCHECKED)

80m. The left side of a vague pillar above and to the right of the previous route.

Claude Davies & Derek Walker, March 2010.

Area Map
Crag Selector
Intro
The Climbing
How to Use
Suggested Climbs
Tafraout Granite
Anergui
Ameln Valley
Tarakatine Pass
Sidi M'Zal
Jebel Taskra
Idaougnidif
Afantinzar
Samazar
Aouguenz
Tagzene
Tagmout
History
Index

THE MAIN WALL

Continue along the path beneath the Approach Walls, turning left beyond them into a broad gully beneath an attractive northeast-facing wall.

3. Salam Alaykum E1 5b

? UNCHECKED

30m. This route climbs a curving wide crack near the left end of the cliff, but has not been positively identified. Scramble up to a belay where the crack forms a right angle, then ascend the wide crack until it is possible to move left into a flake crack. Continue with interest to a thread belay.

R.Smith & A.Taylor, October 2013

4. Sez Who? HVS 4c ★1

80m. The black streaks just right of the prominent dark gully, starting at a large boulder.

1) 50m (4c) Climb boldly up leftwards to gain a blocky groove. Follow this, then climb up to the left of a bulge to a small cave.

2) 30m (4b) Climb the exposed rib to the left of the groove.

Dave Wood & Hamish Legge, March 2012.

5. Woody Sez E1 5b ★2

100m. Very nice climbing up the centre of the wall. Start 5m left of the pink slab at start of *Sez Les*, 10m right of huge blocky pinnacles.

1) 30m (5b) Move up on good holds to a steepening. Climb straight up (crux) to a ledge on the left, then move diagonally right until it is possible to climb up to a large ledge and belay at the patch of vegetation (clearly visible from below).

2) 30m (4c) Go diagonally left from the stance to harder moves over a bulge landing on the "cannon stone". Continue leftwards to a huge stance.

3) 20m (-) Climb the slab right of the corner to the top.

Dave Wood, Martin Bennett & Alan Blackburn, March 2011.

DESCENT: Scramble leftward into broad gully

6. Cezanne HVS 5a ★1

95m. Start below a short left-facing corner.

1) 55m (5a) Climb the corner, then trend rightwards up slabs to a break. Traverse right into the corner of *Sez Les*, and move up to the stance as for that route.

2) 40m (4c) Move right onto the arête, then climb up steeply to a step right past a small vegetated groove and on to ledges. Go up an easier slab to a final wall on the right.

Martin Bennett & Ali Walsh (pitch 1), October 2013

Martin Bennett & Dave Cundy (pitch 2), November 2015.

7. Sez Les HVS 4c ★3

100m. This popular route climbs the big left-facing black and orange corner on the crag's northeast face, starting just left of the corner.

1) 55m (4c) Climb a rightward-leaning pink slab for 8m to ledges, then go over overlaps rightwards into the corner. This is followed to an obvious step around the right arête to a good stance and belays in the continuation corner.

2) 45m (4c) Climb the continuation corner on black rock to the final overhang which is avoided by rounding the rib on the left. It is possible to finish over the overhang directly at 5b (bold).

Martin Bennett & Dave Wood, March 2010.

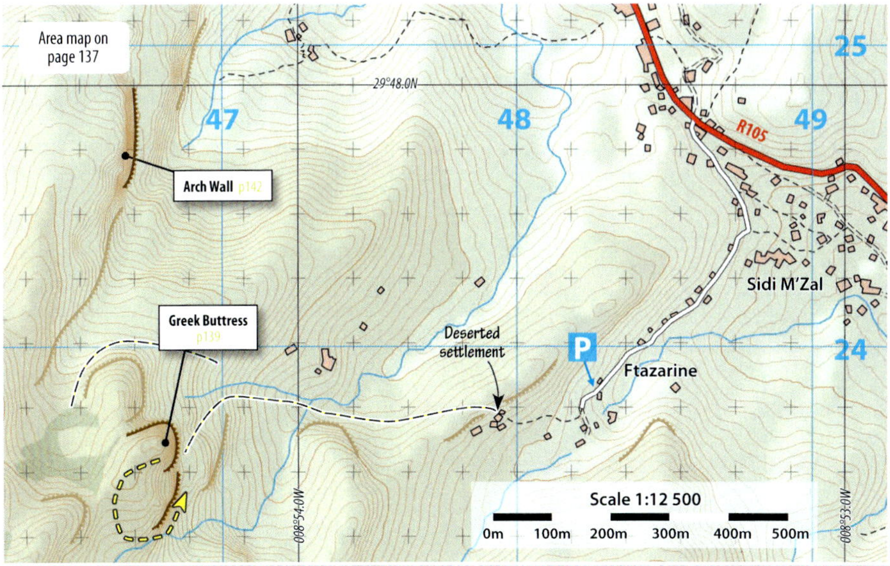

Area Map
Crag Selector
Intro
The Climbing
How to Use
Suggested Climbs
Tafraout Granite
Anergui
Ameln Valley
Tarakatine Pass
Sidi M'Zal
Jebel Taskra
Idaougnidif
Afantinzar
Samazar
Aouguenz
Tagzene
Tagmout
History
Index

B GREEK BUTTRESS (Crag NC)

Shade · Families · Hitch · Roadside

Drive from Tafraout: **35 minutes**
Walk-in: **50 minutes**

The tremendous dome-shaped crag to the left of Sidi's iconic Arch Wall is a major objective, offering serious climbs of great character. It was referred to in the original Cicerone guidebook as Crag NC, and has more recently adopted the name Greek Buttress. The crag faces southeast and is a spectacular sight in the morning sun, presenting a superb sweep of clean orange quartzite. The routes here are long, committing lines on good rock, making it one of the best venues on this side of the escarpment.

Approach is from the tiny village of Ftazarine (see map above). From the village, head uphill to a deserted settlement below a notch / col on the ridge above. Cross over the col and traverse down leftwards, passing beneath the right side of a crag (known as Twin Crags). Head up rightwards from here to pass beneath another band of rock, from where a steep ascent gains the base of the crag.

DESCENT: The best descent is to the left (south) side of the crag via open slopes some way behind the crag itself. Descend these slopes to a watercourse, then cut left along a narrow ramp. A shorter but more difficult alternative is to climb down into the gully on the right of the crag, or a third (long) option is to follow a good path well to the north.

1. Beta HVS 5a ★1

ADVENTURE

200m. This challenging climb takes the wall to the left of a right-facing corner high on the face, featuring a long and serious initial pitch.

1) 55m (5a) Start slightly to the left of the corner and climb the deceptively steep red wall to a ledge level with the top of the corner.

2, 3, 4) 145m (-) Follow easier angled ground to the right of the gully to the summit of the crag.

Chris Bonington, Les Brown & Derek Walker, March 2002.

2. Troy Boys E2 5b ★1

WIDE

195m. An alternative start to *Alpha*, that is low in the grade, but character-building nevertheless. Start beneath a striking crack about 30m left of *Alpha*.

1) 25m (4c) Climb flakes and cracks to a stance beneath the main crack.

2) 40m (5b) Bring out the big cams and fight up the wide crack and groove above.

3) 35m (5a) Head rightwards to a right-facing groove, then climb up this until forced steeply left to a niche below a chimney.

4) 25m (4c) Climb the chimney, exiting left at the top.

5) 40m (4b) Climb a groove, trending slightly right, to a belay below the final steepening.

6) 30m (4b) Take the weakness in the wall and finish up left to a final rib.

Paul Donnithorne, Pete Johnson & Mike Mortimer, November 2012.

Area Map
Crag Selector
Intro
The Climbing
How to Use
Suggested Climbs
Tafraout Granite
Anergui
Ameln Valley
Tarakatine Pass
Sidi M'Zal
Jebel Taskra
Idaougnidif
Afantinzar
Tasmazer
Aouguenz
Taqzene
Jagmout
History
Index

3. Alpha HVS 5a ★1

ADVENTURE

200m. The line of the first ascent gives an excellent and sustained climb up the fine steep wall, featuring about 8 pitches of climbing. The route starts by gaining and following a prominent rightward leaning corner before moving left into black grooves on the upper wall.

Derek Walker & Les Brown, March 2000.

4. Sailing the Aegean E3 5c ★3

180m. A superb, direct line up the front of the buttress, providing a sustained and trying experience with fine situations. Start 20m left of *Gamma*, below a left-facing corner.

1) 50m (5b) Climb the corner and follow a right-facing groove above. Continue to a ledge (optional belay) below a bulge, then move left around this to belay below a wall.

2) 50m (5c) A long, absorbing pitch.... Climb the wall above the belay, to another steep section. Overcome this via a short corner on the right, stepping left at the top to gain a crack. Belay on the good ledge above.

3) 30m (5b) Traverse right below the roof to enter an orange groove. This gives some technical climbing to a belay below a tree.

4) 50m (5b) Move right and climb a rib, then make exposed moves up left to gain easier ground. Scrambling remains to the summit.

Paul Donnithorne & Dan Donovan, April 2012.

5. Aphrodite E2 5b ★3

205m. A good companion route to *Eros* with tremendous, sustained and varied climbing. The route shares some ground with *Gamma* in its upper section. Start as for *Eros*.

1) 60m (5b) Start up the gangway and climb a few moves up the slab before breaking left to gain the fine crack in the wall left of the corner on *Eros*.
2) 30m (5b) Make a bold step onto the headwall just right of the bulge on *Eros*, then continue up rightwards into a small open groove on the right-hand side of the headwall. Pass a ledge and continue steeply to a good wide crack. Climb up to a ledge beneath a corner capped by a large roof.
3) 30m (5b) Go up the corner, moving left around the roof to gain an easier groove and shattered corner on the right. Climb this and step left past a bulge, then continue through a weakness to gain a niche below a chimney/corner.
4) 35m (5a) Climb the chimney to a tree on the left, then continue up the crack and slab above to a large ledge with blocks.
5) 50m (4b) Go up the rib on the right and finish up a wide groove and chimneys.
Paul Donnithorne & Emma Alsford, November 2012.

6. Eros E2 5b ★3

220m. A superb and varied climb starting up the right-facing corner just left of *Gamma*.
1) 50m (5b) Climb an easy gangway up right to a ledge. Trend right up a slab to the corner and follow it to a big ledge. Belay 3m right of the corner taken by *Linea D'Ombra*.
2) 35m (5b) Pull into an orange niche three metres right of the corner then undercut right around the bulge. Climb the right edge of a black streak then step left to a stance.
3) 30m (5b) Go up the rib on the left then a left-trending groove to enter a left-slanting slot. Squirm up this to a good stance below a black crack.
4) 45m (5a) The rib on the left leads to a deep chimney. Follow this to a ledge.
5) 60m (4b) Easier climbing to the right of a dark gully.
Paul Donnithorne & Emma Alsford, November 2012.

7. Gamma HVS 5a ★3

200m. A big classic climb up the grooves right of *Alpha*, from one of the strong teams of the early days of Anti-Atlas exploration.
1) 45m (5a) A superb steep corner crack provides a memorable introduction to the route. An optional stance is possible at 35m.
2) 15m (-) Easy climbing to below a steep black groove.
3) 15m (4c) The groove is difficult to start, and followed directly to a belay.
4) 15m (4b) Go around the arête on the left then up slabs to another belay.
5) 25m (4b) Step left once more to climb steep but rather broken rock.
6) 30m (4c) Go right up a steep finger crack through orange rock, past a bush and into an easier gully.
7) 50m (-) Continue up the easy gully to the top.
Derek Walker & Chris Bonington, March 2003

8. La Linea d'Ombra E1 5b ★2

230m. *The Shadow's Line* is yet another big outing with a classic mountaineering feel, following soaring dihedrals on perfect rock. The route starts as for *Gamma*, at a right-slanting ramp / corner.
1) 45m (5a) The long corner, as for *Gamma,* has the hardest moves near the top. Optional stance at 30m.
2) 10m (-) Move left to belay below the orange and black groove.
3) 35m (4c) Climb the long groove and belay beneath the orange roof.
4) 25m (4b) Go up the corner above the stance until it is possible to move left to a terrace. Traverse 5m left along the ledge to a belay.
5) 35m (5b) The beautiful orange wall above is perfectly situated, and leads to the left side of an orange chimney. Continue up to an easier groove and follow this to an airy perch on the prominent pinnacle.
6) 40m (4b) Follow easier ground on the right to gain a short chimney, then go up a corner to a belay on a block.
7) 40m (-) Traverse 3m left and climb a pleasant ridge to finish.
Alberto Rampini & Silvia Mazzani, November 2012.

9. Chukka HVS 4c

190m. The groove and wall just right of *Gamma*, starting on the right of a grey pinnacle.
1) 30m (4c) Climb the groove to a stance under the overhang.
2) 40m (4c) Step up left, then move back right above the overhang into a small groove. Continue trending rightwards up the wall to a belay on the arête.
3) 40m (4c) Go up right and climb an exposed flake, then easier ground to a tree.
4) 40m (4c) Climb slabs, then the corner above.
5) 40m (4c) Slabs and ribs lead to the top.
Paul Donnithorne & Dan Donovan, April 2012.

10. Zorba VS 4c

180m. Grooves and ribs up the right side of the cliff provide the easiest line of assault. Start on a rocky shoulder beneath a small roof.
1) 40m (4c) Climb a short orange corner, then traverse left under the roof to a crack. Pull into the crack and trend up left to a slabby groove leading up right.
2) 20m (4b) Go up the slabby groove to a large terrace overlooking the gully on the right.
3) 60m (4c) A long pitch that is probably better split... Move left and make nice moves around the arête to gain a crack. Follow this to a ledge, then step up right to climb the steep wall via a vague groove. This leads to a sloping ledge with a tricky wall behind. Surmount this and belay below a chimney on the left.
4) 15m (4c) Pull steeply up the corner to the right and pass a nose on its left. Belay on a ledge to the right.
5) 45m (4b) Grooves and ribs to the summit.
Emma Alsford & Don Sargeant, April 2012.

Area Map
Crag Selector
Intro
The Climbing
How to Use
Suggested Climbs
Tafraout Granite
Anergui
Ameln Valley
Tarakatine Pass
Sidi M'Zal
Jebel Taskra
Idaougnidif
Afantinzar
Samazar
Aouguenz
Tagzene
Igmoun
History
Index

C ARCH WALL (Crag ND)

Shade | Families | Hitch | Roadside

Drive from Tafraout: **35 minutes**
Walk-in: **1 hour**

Sidi M'Zal's Arch Wall is one of the most distinctive crags in the Anti-Atlas, and usually the first to catch the climber's eye on the journey to Tafraout from Agadir. Not surprisingly, this tremendous wall saw early interest from the Ameln pioneers, and despite some relatively poor rock underneath the arch itself, the crag has continued to attract adventurous teams ever since.

The best approach is from the village of Injaren, reached along a small track that leaves the main road at the bottom of the hill running north out of Sidi M'Zal. From an obvious parking area at the end of the track, cross a bridge and follow a good path towards ancient settlements. This path can be hard to follow at times, but it's worth taking care to stay on it. If in doubt, head for a tiny hamlet on the left of the stream – the path goes between the houses and climbs up onto the hillside to the south of the stream, heading for a gully at the left end of the Lower Arch Wall.

DESCENT: Down the left side of the crag. A 30m abseil may be required if descent is made too early.

1. Slabs Left VS 4b ★1 BOLD

150m. The slabs up the left side of the face provide some very good climbing on immaculate rock, but with a shortage of protection.

Les Brown & Pete Turnbull, April 1993.

2. Slabs Right VS 4b ★1 BOLD

150m. The north side's opening line is another bold route with a bit of a reputation.

Joe Brown & Claude Davies, April 1993.

3. Tree Chimney HS 4b ★1

200m. A fine mountaineering day out, marred only slightly by the eponymous tree.

1) 35m (4b) Climb the obvious vegetated chimney, with an awkward tree at about 20ft.

2) 40m (4b) Continue via the easiest line, passing a bulge and up to a belay.

3) 35m (4a) Climb a groove, with a bold upper section to a belay with big blocks beneath a smooth wall.

4) 10m (-) Move the belay 10m left.

5) 60m (4b) Climb the groove on the left, step over a pinnacle and continue up the left side of a pillar.

6) 15m (4a) A bold little finish leads to easier ground.

Derek Walker, Chris Bonington & Les Brown, March 2002.

4. The Great Corner E1 5b ★3

WIDE

200m. The large corner to the left of the arch is an infamous Tafraout classic, and one of many desperate offerings from Les Brown and Derek Walker in the 1990s. Like so many others, it has repulsed more than its fair share of aspirants, not helped by being wrongly named and wrongly graded in several guidebooks. The route features steep, sustained, wide crack climbing and is high in the grade.

1) The groove is entered awkwardly, one way or another, past a very prickly bush.

2) Direct up the off-width crack.

3) Climb the wall to the right of the crack.

4) Diagonally left to a stance above the corner.

5) Finish up the slabs above.

Les Brown & Derek Walker, March 1999.

5. Bowline E2 5b ★3

WIDE STEEP

200m. The first attempt at the arch was forced left after two pitches, but still provides an excellent route with fine exposed climbing. Follow the steep, strenuous corner for two emotional pitches (large cams required) until it is possible to break left up a steep grey wall. Climb grooves in the upper wall for three airy pitches to the top. Superb!

Les Brown & Derek Walker, March 1999.

6. Saif Din E3 6a ★2

WIDE LOOSE STEEP

200m. A staggering climb following the magnificent corner in its entirety. Parties should be prepared to encounter desperate wide cracks, difficult climbing with lots of exposure, and a fair helping of rotten rock....

Jim Fotheringham, Ben Wintringham & Derek Walker, March 2006.

7. Mashallah E2 5b

220m. The wall to the right of the arch, starting 50m right of *Saif Din* at a large triangular block resting on the face. Climb up left for 25m, then go diagonally left to a horizontal fault. Traverse back right here before climbing diagonally up right to another fault, reaching a tree below a pinnacle. Go easily up behind this to the top.

Ben Wintringham & Jim Fotheringham, March 2005.

D DINOSAUR WALL

Shade Families Hitch Roadside

Drive from Tafraout: **35 minutes**
Walk-in: **30 minutes**

This steep orange wall above Tagmout Ihouzine is a good choice if you're looking for strenuous, extreme-grade routes that stay in the shade most of the day. The crag can be identified by a sloping grey terrace at half-height on its left side (the Gallery), with a steep black gully running up the orange wall to the right.

Park anywhere in the village of Tagmout Ihouzine, from where the approach is obvious, taking about 30 minutes over easy terrain.

LEFT SIDE

Below and to the left of the Gallery is another tier of rock. The following route heads up this to gain a black mossy corner at the left side of the Gallery.

1. Pteradactyl E1 5b ★1

100m. An excellent climb, marred only slightly by the lichen. Start on the lower tier, below and left of the Gallery, about 6 metres right of a tree at the base of the cliff.

1) 50m (5a) Start up black slabby rock, heading up leftwards to gain a steep left-facing groove. Go up this to join a flake crack, and follow this to its end, going straight up to the base of the huge mossy corner.

2) 50m (5b) Climb up over a jumble of blocks to gain the corner, which leads with interest to an exit rightwards.

Emma Alsford & Paul Donnithorne, November 2014.

THE GALLERY

The next routes all start on the large sloping terrace halfway up the left side of the crag. Towards the left end of this are a series of striking cracks, which provide the first routes.

2. Treevolution E1 5b ★1

35m. Takes the crack and corner system to the left of *Reach for the Stars*. Start up a steep, overhanging groove leading to a small ledge. Traverse left into a shallow groove, and follow this and the crack above through trees to the top.

Paul Donnithorne & Emma Alsford, November 2014.

3. Reach for the Stars E3 5c ★3

45m. The soaring thin crack towards the left side of the Gallery, just left of the obvious off-width cracks. Start up a steep groove to access the crack which gives strenuous and technical climbing.

Emma Alsford & Paul Donnithorne, October 2014.

4. Whispering Crack E1 5b ★1

45m. The left-hand off-width crack, about 7m left of the obvious corner.

Emma Alsford & Paul Donnithorne, October 2014.

5. Right Off E2 5b ★2

45m. The right-hand off-width crack. Avoid the jammed block via moves out right.

Paul Donnithorne & Emma Alsford, October 2014.

Area Map
Crag Selector
Intro
The Climbing
How to Use
Suggested Climbs
Tafraout Granite
Anergui
Ameln Valley
Tarakatine Pass
Sidi M'Zal
Jebel Taskra
Idaougnidif
Afantinzar
Samazar
Aouguenz
Tagzene
Tagmout
History
Index

6. Poet's Corner E1 5b

60m. The central black corner.
1) 50m (5b) Climb the corner, moving right at the junction at 40m.
2) 10m (4b) Finish up the wide crack above.
Paul Donnithorne & Emma Alsford, October 2014.

7. Game of Thrones E3 5c

70m. An outstanding route, with two contrasting pitches, following the striking crackline up the left side of the impressive wall below the right-to-left curving overhang.
1) 40m (5c) Take the left-hand crack up white rock, following it as far as the left end of the roof. Jam leftwards along the break to a belay just below.
2) 30m (5c) Move up into a shallow groove and follow this for 6 metres until a committing stretch left gains a black crack. Follow this, then go up a right-slanting ramp until a step up rightwards gains a small ledge. Make an airy step left on good footholds above the overhang, before finishing delicately straight up.
Paul Donnithorne, Mike Turner & Emma Alsford, November 2014.

8. The Cave of Destiny E3 5c

145m. Climbs the soaring black groove at the right end of the Gallery. Gain the start of the route by scrambling up an open groove behind a tree.
1) 55m (4b) Easy climbing up slabs, exiting rightwards via an open corner.
2) 60m (5c) Climb the right face of the orange arête, moving right via a hanging flake to gain a black groove. Follow this past a small cave to belay in a larger cave.
3) 30m (5b) Traverse left for 10m until the angle eases. Climb up and then diagonally right to finish up an orange groove.
D.Lampard & B.Brewer, November 2014.

MAIN WALL

This is the right-hand part of the crag, to the right of the Gallery.

9. You Can Rest When You're Dead E4 6a

120m. Takes the line of curving flakes on the right of the terrace.
1) 33m (5a) Start directly below the central groove of the upper crag, and climb the left-hand crack to the terrace. Move right to belay below the arête on the left of the Great Flake. An alternative start is possible up the cracks 20m to the right.
2) 30m (5b) Move out right onto the arete, swinging round to the surprising flake system.
3) 15m (5a) Climb a juggy wall on the right in order to avoid the prickly bush. Go up to a stance on the right of the upper crack.
4) 30m (6a) Climb the overhanging crack, then move left into a slot, with a final pull to a cave belay.
5) 15m (5a) Leave the cave leftwards and finish up an excellent juggy wall.
B.Brewer & D.Lampard, November 2014

10. Café Negra E1 5b

80m. The obvious black streak. Start at a groove with some perched boulders a few feet up.
1) 45m (-) Climb the groove and ramp to a belay.
2) 35m (5b) Step up and climb the corner on the left side of the black streak.
P.Johnson & R.Turner, November 2014

11. Grumple Stiltskin E2 5b

65m. The black and orange wall, 10 metres left of a wide crack towards the right-hand end of the crag.
1) 30m (5a) Climb intermittent cracks directly below a prominent bulge, passing the bulge on its left. Step back right and continue to a ledge.
2) 35m (5b) A bold pitch. Climb the bulge above the belay, then follow a black and orange groove on worrying rock. Step right to continue more easily up the ridge, trending left to block belays and an abseil descent.
S.Bennett & O.Burrows, April 2015.

12. Grassy Jack's Verandah E1 5a

60m. The wall and rib to the right of the wide crack.
1) 30m (5a) Climb a slim slab, trending right to a good ledge.
2) 30m (4b) Climb awkwardly along a ramp above the belay, finishing up a rib above.
S.Bennett & O.Burrows, April 2015.

Map Page 137

Area Map
Crag Selector
Intro
The Climbing
How to Use
Suggested Climbs
Tafraout Granite
Anergui
Ameln Valley
Tarakatine Pass
Sidi M'Zal
Jebel Taskra
Idaougnidif
Afantinzar
Samazar
Aouguenz
Tagzene
Tagmout
History
Index

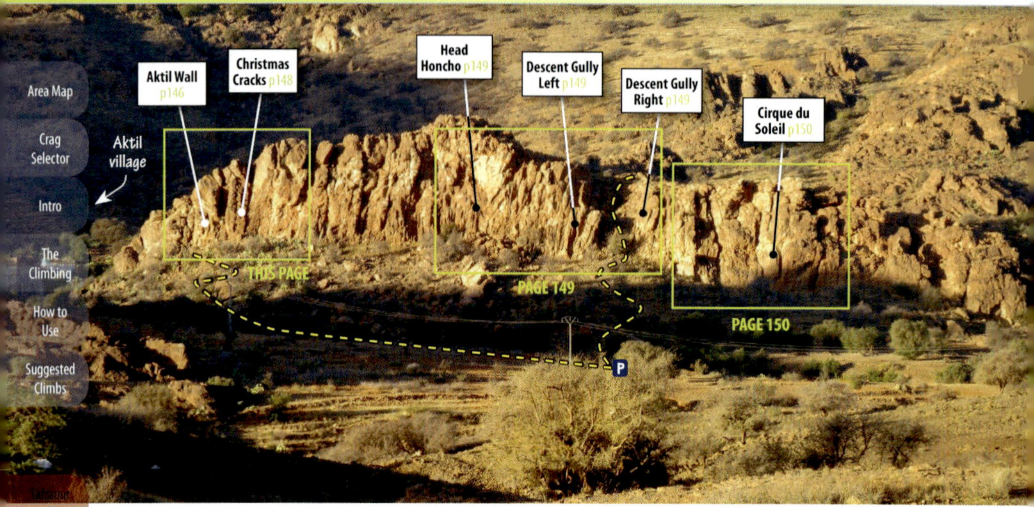

E TIZI GZAOUINE CRAG

Shade | Families | Hitch | Roadside

Drive from Tafraout: **40 minutes**
Walk-in: **5 minutes**

The small crags on the valley floor near Tizi Gzaouine provide a handful of fine climbs, right by the roadside, and can be a good choice for short days – indeed this is an ideal place to pass a few hours on the way to or from the airport. The crag faces southeast, so catches the sun in the morning but is pleasantly shady in the afternoons and has a very friendly atmosphere to it. It has also been referred to as Aktil Edge in some guidebooks.

Tizi sits right on the edge of the surface quartzite, and as a result there are substantial areas of friable rock throughout the crag, particularly under the numerous overhangs. Amongst this poorer rock, however, are some solid buttresses containing some very fine low- to mid-grade climbing.

A small track leaves the main road at a communications mast between Sidi M'Zal and the village of Tizi Gzaouine, marked by an Arabic road-sign pointing to villages at 3km, 4km and 6km. This track is rather rocky, but can be negotiated by 2WD vehicles. Turn left at the first junction to parallel the riverbed. The track eventually crosses the river and comes to a fork at a hairpin (park here for the lower access to Tizi Gzaouine Gorge). Bear left again and continue until the crag comes into sight on the right-hand side. There is a good off-road parking space for 2 or 3 cars on the left, from where the climbs are reached in a matter of minutes. It is also possible to reach the track along the river by turning off in Tizi Gzaouine village (see map page 137).

AKTIL WALL

This excellent buttress contains a handful of good-quality low- and mid-grade climbs on good rock. It is located at the far left end of the crag and is best gained by walking along the road until a vague trail breaks up right through terraces to the lowest rocks. The wall overlooks the small village of Aktil, from which it takes its name. An easy descent gully lies between *Aktil Rib* and *Aktil Wall* itself.

1. Aktil Rib V.Diff ★1

8m. The blunt rib to the left of the main wall is a fine little climb, with a tricky move at mid-height.
Steve Broadbent (solo), December 2009.

2. Aktil Wall Diff 1

15m. A little indirect, but worth it for the pleasantly exposed traverse. Start up easy ground to a large perched flake, from where a nerve-racking traverse rightward gains a large ledge. Finish up and left from here.

Steve Broadbent (solo), December 2009.

3. Prana VS 4c 1

BOLD

25m. A steep climb with some surprisingly big technical moves. Start up a vague groove in the corner behind a boulder and climb to the perched flake of *Aktil Wall*. Surmount this with difficulty (a lack of imagination will prove useful here) and continue up the bold wall above to a direct finish up the top block. A very photogenic, though escapable, pitch.

Steve & Katja Broadbent, February 2010.

4. Action Bop HS 4c 1

GEAR CRACK

15m. A good climb with well-protected moves on large holds. Climb the broken wall left of *Aktil Groove* to a ledge, then finish straight up the wall above via a wedged block.

Steve Broadbent (solo), December 2009.

5. Aktil Groove V.Diff 1

GEAR CRACK

12m. The groove up the front of the buttress has excellent holds and good protection, and leads to a difficult move to gain the ledge. From here it is possible to skulk off to the right, or finish up the next route....

Steve Broadbent (solo), December 2009.

6. Aktil Groove Direct MVS 4b 1

GEAR CRACK

15m. Follow *Aktil Groove* to the large ledge, then launch up the steep crack in the overhang above. Perfect protection and good holds await the confident.... A bail-out right awaits everyone else.

Steve Broadbent (solo), December 2009.

DESCENT: to the left, down the short gully between *Aktil Rib* and *Aktil Wall*.

CHRISTMAS CRACKS

The extensive left-hand crag contains large amounts of poor quality orange rock, but there are good climbs to be found amongst it. The first route starts just around the corner to the right of *Aktil Wall*:

7. Christmas Cracks HS 4b ★2 — GEAR, CRACK

25m. A very fine crack-climb, high in the grade but with perfect protection throughout. Climb the tempting jagged crack in the lower wall to a ledge. Easy broken ground then leads to an exposed finish rightwards up the wide corner-crack. Very merry stuff!

Steve Broadbent (solo), December 2009.

8. Argan Gully Very Difficult ★1

25m. Climb the broken gully past a tree to a fine finish in the upper corner.

Steve & Katja Broadbent, February 2010.

9. Rouble VS 4b — LOOSE

25m. The right side of the arête is technically mild but mentally challenging. Work rightwards from the gully to gain the shattered central groove, and follow this to an interesting finish left of the final steepening.

Steve & Katja Broadbent, February 2010.

10. Noodweer MVS 4b ★1

30m. An interesting and technical climb up the steep rib just left of a prominent clean slab high on the face. It is possible to escape into the gully at the top, but going directly up the rib provides a more satisfying finish.

Steve Broadbent (solo), December 2009.

11. Watersports HS 4b — PRICKLY

25m. Pleasant climbing up the gully right of *Noodweer*, immediately left of a tempting blank slab high on the wall. The route has some unfortunate vegetation in its upper section, which is bypassed via the left arête.

Steve Broadbent & Matt Mellor, February 2011.

12. Wall Street E1 5b ★3 — THIN

30m. Tremendous wall and crack climbing up the tempting south-facing wall high on the crag right of *Noodweer*. Climb the gully to gain the upper wall, which gives sustained climbing in a wonderful position. Low in the grade.

Steve Broadbent & Matt Mellor, February 2011. Photo front cover.

HEAD HONCHO

To the right is an area of poorer, more broken rock. The next route tackles a prominent blank wall and soaring arête some distance to the right.

13. Head Honcho E3 5c ★2

40m. Bold climbing up the blank wall left of the descent gully, with some poor rock low down but a fine finish up the arête,

1) 20m (5c) Go up a flake and shallow scoop to a poor belay below the blank wall.

2) 20m (5c) Traverse right along a horizontal crack to gain the superb flake to the top.

Paul Donnithorne & Dan Donovan, April 2012.

DESCENT GULLY LEFT

A short buttress just to the left (west) of the central descent gully holds the following climbs:

14. Rapunzel's Back Stairs Difficult

12m. The gully left of *Rapunzel's Tower*, moving right onto the wall at the overhanging block.

Jamie & Clare Wakeham, February 2010.

15. Rapunzel's Tower V.Diff ★1

12m. Lovely steep climbing up the narrow arête left of the central descent gully.

Steve Broadbent (solo), December 2009.

16. Lousy Mod Moderate

12m. The gully to the right of *Rapunzel's Tower* is nothing to write home about.

Jamie & Clare Wakeham, February 2010.

DESCENT GULLY RIGHT

A handful of short pitches up the right (true left) sidewall of the central descent gully.

17. Burka Boy Difficult

CRACK

8m. The short left-hand crack.

Steve Broadbent (solo), December 2009.

18. Clown Crack Hard Diff ★2

GEAR CRACK

10m. The tempting straight crack in the side-wall of the descent gully is a lovely little climb, with perfect rock, endless protection, and pleasant climbing throughout.

Steve Broadbent & Rachel Mellor, October 2009.

19. The Juggler Severe

10m. The wall to the right has a tricky start and leads to a large perched block. Surmount this to a stretchy crux finish.

Steve Broadbent (solo), December 2009.

20. Geology Corner MVS 4b

STEEP

10m. The short corner is accessed from the right via a difficult steep move, and exited left via another one. Finish as for *The Juggler*.

Steve Broadbent (solo), December 2009.

Area Map
Crag Selector
Intro
The Climbing
How to Use
Suggested Climbs
Tafraout Granite
Anergui
Ameln Valley
Tarakatine Pass
Sidi M'Zal
Jebel Taskra
Idaougnidif
Afantinzar
Samazar
Aouguenz
Tagzene
Tagmout
History
Index

CIRQUE DU SOLEIL

A superb buttress, with good long climbs...

21. Tired Blueberry HS 4a ★1

20m. Climb easily up initial blocks then tackle the smooth wall on excellent holds.
Steve & Katja Broadbent, Daniyal & Cecilie Mueenuddin, Zoe Bouras, Jan 2017.

22. Flashpump E1 5b ★3 STEEP GEAR CRACK

20m. Delicate climbing up a smooth lower slab leads to the intimidating steep crack which consumes energy and protection in equal amounts. A superb, strenuous pitch.
Steve & Katja Broadbent, February 2010.

23. Jonas HS 4a ★1

20m. The corner up the right side of the Flashpump Buttress is a pleasant, steep climb with some tricky layback moves and the occasional loose hold.
Steve & Katja Broadbent, February 2010.

24. Hall of Mirrors HVS 5a ★1 GEAR CRACK

30m. Surprisingly strenuous climbing up the high flake crack, which is reached with ease, and entered with great frustration....
Steve Broadbent & Rachel Mellor, October 2009.

25. Liquid Sunshine MVS 4b BOLD

40m. The arête to the right is marred by an avoidable move. Start up a crack leading left to the arête and climb up to a steepening. Overcome this on the left side and go up a short bold wall to large ledges (possible belay). Finish with a fine layback up the upper corner.
Steve Broadbent, Will Benfold & Cameron Hall, October 2010.

26. Samson and Delilah E2 6a ★1 STEEP WIDE

35m. The teasing off-width crack...

1) 18m (6a) Climb the overhanging crack to a belay below the upper chimney.
2) 17m (5a) Follow the chimney to a break, then traverse left to a fine finish up the arête.
Paul Donnithorne & Pete Johnson, April 2011.

27. Chasing Rainbows VS 4c ★3 STEEP GEAR

34m. Exquisite, three-dimensional climbing up the steep right-hand corner, with perfect protection throughout.
Steve & Katja Broadbent, February 2010.

28. The Lion Tamer HS 4b ★2 GEAR CRACK

30m. A good long pitch starting from the groove and following the fine flake-crack in the side wall.
Chris Bull, Paul Mainwood & Alison Parker, October 2009.

29. Sword Swallower HS 4b ★1 GEAR CRACK

30m. The face to the right of the flake crack.
Chris Bull, Paul Mainwood & Alison Parker, October 2009.

30. Trapeze Direct VS 4c ★2

30m. Start 2m left of *Cirque du Soleil*. Climb small finger pockets to a step right on good holds. Move up past a detached block to a small ledge, then finish direct.
Jim Slater, March 2014

31. Cirque du Soleil VS 4c ★3 GEAR CRACK

30m. A gem of a route. Difficult moves to gain the groove are almost enough to put you off, but lead to sustained, excellent and well-protected climbing above.
Chris Bull, Paul Mainwood & Alison Parker, October 2009.

32. High Wire HVS 4c ★1 BOLD

30m. The photogenic arête to the right is gained via a worrying traverse from the initial groove of the previous route.
Steve Broadbent & Rachel Mellor, October 2009.

33. Dolomismo Krak E4 6b

STEEP

17m. The overhanging crack to the right of *Cirque Du Soleil* is by far the hardest thing hereabouts.
A.Fairtlough & S.Paoros, October 2011.

RIGHT HAND END

The next two routes are located on short buttresses to the right of the steep orange overhangs.

34. Bimato Difficult

15m. The easy rib to a massive boulder.
Steve Broadbent (solo), March 2013

35. Bisarah Severe

BOLD

15m. The next buttress to the right. Start up a steep wall to gain easy climbing up the rib. Bold.
Steve Broadbent (solo), March 2013

F TIZI GZAOUINE GORGE

Shade · Families · Hitch · Roadside

Drive from Tafraout: **40 minutes**
Walk-in: **2 to 5 minutes**

This tiny gorge lies just off the trackside at the bottom of the concreted hairpins leading to Dotinzar, and provides a handful of short low-grade climbs in a pleasant environment. The seasonal river which carved the gorge has long since found an alternative course, leaving behind some steep walls that can provide entertainment for an hour or two for those passing along the main road through Sidi M'Zal and Tizi Gzaouine. A visit to Tizi Gorge can also be combined with climbing at the main Tizi Crags, which are only a few minutes' drive away.

Much like the main crag at Tizi, there is plenty of rotten rock here and lines are limited to a few isolated walls where the quartzite is perfectly sound.

To reach the crag, follow the rocky track signposted to villages at 3,4, and 6km as for the main Tizi Crags. Bear left at the first junction and follow the track until

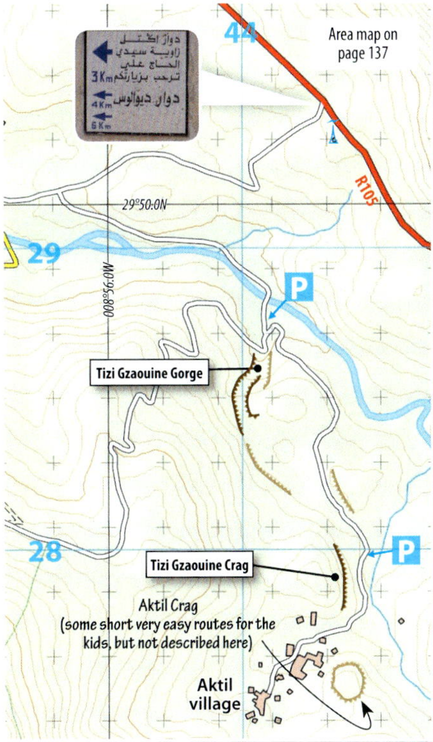

it crosses a riverbed just before the concrete starts at another junction. There is parking on the left at this point, from where the gorge is visible between the two concreted tracks ahead.

WELCOME WALL

This enticing south-facing sun-trap is located on the right-hand side at the entrance to the gorge. There are a number of very worthwhile pitches here, all on good rock with interesting moves.

1. The Aktil Undercut HS 4a ★

CRACK

12m. The undercut diagonal crack is a bit of a puzzler.
Steve Broadbent (solo), February 2010.

2. Bakalakadaka Severe ★

CRACK GEAR

12m. The prominent jagged crack on the left side of the wall.
Steve Broadbent (solo), December 2009.

3. Barry Sally Severe

GEAR

15m. A good steep route with nice positions. Start just left of the tree and traverse up and right on flakes to a difficult move near the top. Well protected throughout.
Steve Broadbent (solo), February 2010.

4. Ivory Pink MVS 4b ★1

12m. The blank-looking shallow groove up the front of the face is one of the most tempting lines on the crag.
Steve Broadbent (solo), December 2009.

5. Hammered with Mohammed HS 4a

12m. A good, varied climb up the centre of the wall. After a technical rightward traverse go back left to tackle the steep crack through the overlap.
Steve Broadbent (solo), December 2009.

6. Cricket Corner Mild Severe ★1 BOLD

10m. The obvious upper groove is accessed from the right via some rather bold climbing.
Steve Broadbent (solo), December 2009.

7. Formir Moderate

8m. The right arête should provide no trouble.
Steve Broadbent (solo), December 2009.

IZBEEP

This small tower lies on the north side of the gorge upstream from Welcome Wall, opposite *Apex*.

8. Izbeep VS 4a ★1 BOLD

12m. A bold and technical route with some questionable holds. Start up the arête then make tricky moves left onto the face. Climb the wall, trending left to an easier finish.
Steve Broadbent (solo), February 2010.

9. Immim Difficult ★1

12m. The slabby corner.
Steve Broadbent (solo), February 2010.

THE SOUTH WALL

The left-hand side of the gorge when approaching from the road is north-facing and generally less attractive for climbing. The following route has been climbed up the obvious leftwards slanting ramp-line opposite Welcome Wall.

10. Shadow Traverse Difficult

SLAB

15m. Pleasant slab climbing up the ramp gains an easy traverse left below steeper ground.
Steve Broadbent (solo), February 2010.

To the right of *Shadow Traverse* is a steep sandy section before the gorge swings round to the left into more slabby ground shown on the photo below. The next route climbs the steep wall just left of the rib where the gorge swings round.

11. The Paddy VS 4b

30m. Boulder up the steep wall left of *Apex*, then pull through the overhang to easier ground.
Geoff Hornby & Paul Seabrook, April 2012.

12. Apex Very Difficult ★1

SLAB

40m. Nice climbing up the edge of the slabby ground, starting from the toe of the buttress where the gorge swings around to the left. The climb has a low crux, with extended easy climbing above.
Steve Broadbent (solo), February 2010.

The slabs to the right provide lots of very easy climbs, of which the following has been reported.

13. Crescent Climb Moderate

SLAB

40m. The rightwards curving undercut is a pleasant way up the slabs.
Steve & Katja Broadbent, February 2010.

DESCENT: Walk off easily at either end of the gorge.

FESTIVAL WALL

This short southwest-facing wall lies at the very southern end of the gorge.

14. Tin Foil Teeth Severe

15m. Climb over slanting grooves to a perplexing finish up the hanging corner at the top of the wall.
Steve & Katja Broadbent, February 2010.

15. Tinsel Toes Mild Severe

15m. The central line on the wall is a lovely little climb over a couple of overlaps.
Steve & Katja Broadbent, February 2010.

16. Festival Fingers Hard Difficult

LOOSE

15m. Start up the right of a small black pillar and climb friable rock to finish up a small groove.
Steve & Katja Broadbent, February 2010.

Area Map
Crag Selector
Intro
The Climbing
How to Use
Suggested Climbs
Tafraout Granite
Anergui
Ameln Valley
Tarakatine Pass
Sidi M'Zal
Jebel Taskra
Idaougnidif
Afantinzar
Samazar
Aouguenz
Tagzene
Tagmout
History
Index

F THE BOAR WALLS

Shade, Families, Hitch, Roadside

Drive from Tafraout: **50 minutes**
Walk-in: **40 minutes**

Located on the hillside above Imiris, the Boar Walls are identified by a curious pinnacle (the Boar's Tusk) which can be clearly seen from the main road. The crag catches the morning sunshine and is a very pleasant place to climb – particularly the low-grade routes on the tusk itself.

Park in the village of Imiris, just before the last house, from where a good path leads up past water pipes to contour the terraced hillside above. The crag is reached in approximately 40 minutes.

1. The Gilt Edge VS 4b

105m. An unusual route following the ridge crest up the left side of the wall, left of *Big Bad Wolf*.
1) 60m (4b) Climb the grey rib up the left side of the wall to a summit.
2) 15m (4b) Descend down the other side of the ridge to a belay.
3) 30m (4b) Continue descending to the bottom of the ridge.
R.Neath & G.Neath, November 2015.

2. Big Bad Wolf E4 6a ★1

65m. Starts 10 metres left of *Deliverance*, below a large left-facing corner.
1) 35m (6a) Step off a boulder and trend leftwards up a technical slab past two peg runners. Reach right to good holds above the bulge, pulling up through this and continuing to the large corner. Follow this until a swing right at about 30 metres gains a flake belay.
2) 30m (5c) Climb the thin crack and black streak, heading steeply up right to a grey spike. Move up right, then back left to finish at a notch in the ridge.
Paul Donnithorne & Bob Brewer, October 2013.

3. Deliverance E4 5c ★3 BOLD

40m. A serious start up the shallow flake 3m left of *Piggy's Crack* gains a good crack. Follow this to a bold wall on the left, finishing up the rib above.
Dan Donovan, Paul Donnithorne & Neil Adams, March 2010.

4. Piggy's Crack E2 5b ★3 CRACK

40m. The striking crack leads to a flake. Follow this left to a descent rightwards into the gully.
Paul Donnithorne, Dab Donovan & Neil Adams, March 2010.

5. Pigging in the Rigging E2 5c ABSEIL CRACK

50m. This route starts in the descent gully from the previous routes, some 10m below a tree. Climb up rightwards via a vague groove to slabs, and belay beneath a steep crack. A second pitch up the crack gains a tree and abseil descent.
Paul Donnithorne & Pete Johnson, April 2010.

6. Porque Torque VS 4b ABSEIL

30m. The corner, 10m left of a large cleft.
Paul Donnithorne & Pete Johnson, April 2010.

THE BOAR'S TUSK

The next routes all climb the distinctive pinnacle.

7. Tenderloin VS 4c ★1 ABSEIL

20m. The corner and crack on the back side of the pinnacle (not visible on topo).
Neil Adams, Dan Donovan & Paul Donnithorne, March 2010.

8. Squealer Severe ABSEIL

25m. The left side of the pinnacle's slabby east face gives a pleasant climb.
Dan Donovan (solo), March 2010.

9. Tusker Severe ★3 ABSEIL

25m. The southeast arête is a tremendous little route, and well worth a visit.
Neil Adams, Dan Donovan & Paul Donnithorne, March 2010.

Andi Turner on *Piggy's Crack* (E2 5b) ➲
Photo: Pete Wilson

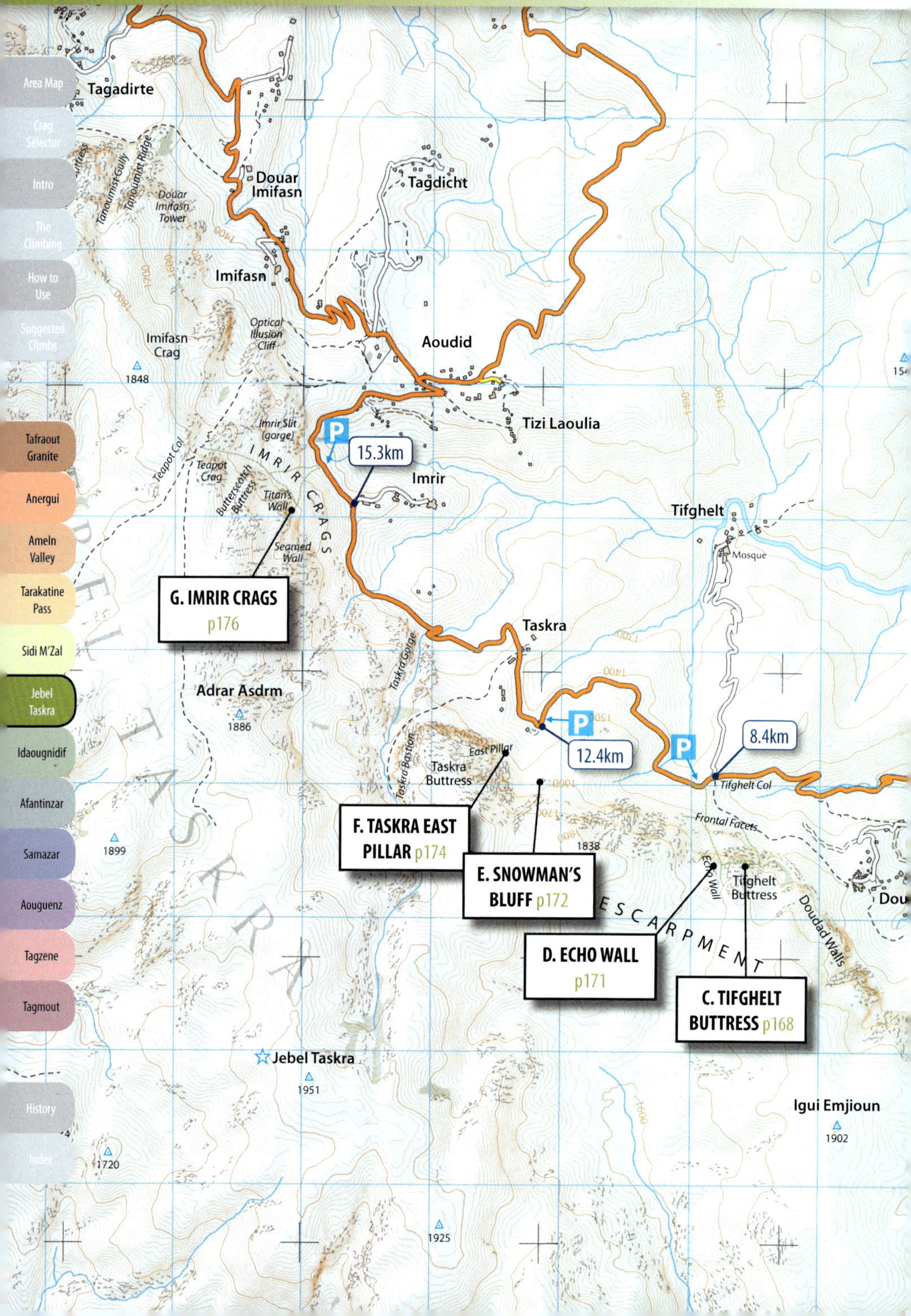
Tagadirte
Douar Imifasn
Tagdicht
Tanoumist Gully
Tanoumist Ridge
Douar Imifasn Tower
Imifasn
Optical Illusion Cliff
Aoudid
Imifasn Crag
1848
Tizi Laoulia
Imrir Slit (gorge)
15.3km
Imrir
Teapot Col
Teapot Crag
Butterscotch Buttress
Titan's Wall
IMRIR CRAGS
Seamed Wall
Tifghelt
Mosque
G. IMRIR CRAGS p176
Taskra
Taskra Gorge
Adrar Asdrm
1886
12.4km
8.4km
East Pillar
Taskra Bastion
Taskra Buttress
Tifghelt Col
Frontal Facets
F. TASKRA EAST PILLAR p174
1838
E. SNOWMAN'S BLUFF p172
Echo Wall
Tifghelt Buttress
Doudad Walls
1899
ESCARPMENT
D. ECHO WALL p171
C. TIFGHELT BUTTRESS p168
JEBEL TASKRA
Jebel Taskra
1951
Igui Emjioun
1902
1720
1925
Area Map
Crag Selector
Intro
The Climbing
How to Use
Suggested Climbs
Tafraout Granite
Anergui
Ameln Valley
Tarakatine Pass
Sidi M'Zal
Jebel Taskra
Idaougnidif
Afantinzar
Samazar
Aouguenz
Tagzene
Tagmout
History
Index

JEBEL TASKRA

and Tizi N'Takoucht Escarpment

Located to the north of Jebel el Kest, the Tizi N'Takoucht Escarpment of Jebel Taskra has plenty to offer the climber, particularly during hot afternoons when the northeast-facing crags come into their own. There's a superb mix of climbing here, from delightfully situated single-pitch routes to some long, full-day adventures.

When approaching the Anti-Atlas from Agadir, the long line of cliffs from Asseldrar in the east, to the high col above Imrir at the western end, make a superb vista and are usually the first crags to catch the eye of visiting climbers. The Tizi N'Takoucht escarpment itself is the northeastern front of the Jebel Taskra massif, which runs from the Kasbah at Tizourgane up to the tiny community of Tizi N'Takoucht on the far northern slopes of the Anti-Atlas. It is, therefore, quite a drive from Tafraout, taking between 1 and 1.5 hours by car. For this reason the escarpment was one of the most recent areas to be developed, only really seeing any significant development after the increase in popularity of the Kasbah Tizourgane as a climbers' base in 2009.

The Tizi N'Takoucht road, along which all of the climbing is located, leaves the main Agadir road just north of the Kasbah Tizourgane. Crags are described from east to west, the direction they are usually approached from Tafraout and the Kasbah Tizourgane. Distances shown on the map assume resetting the odometer as you turn off the main road at the Kasbah Tizourgane.

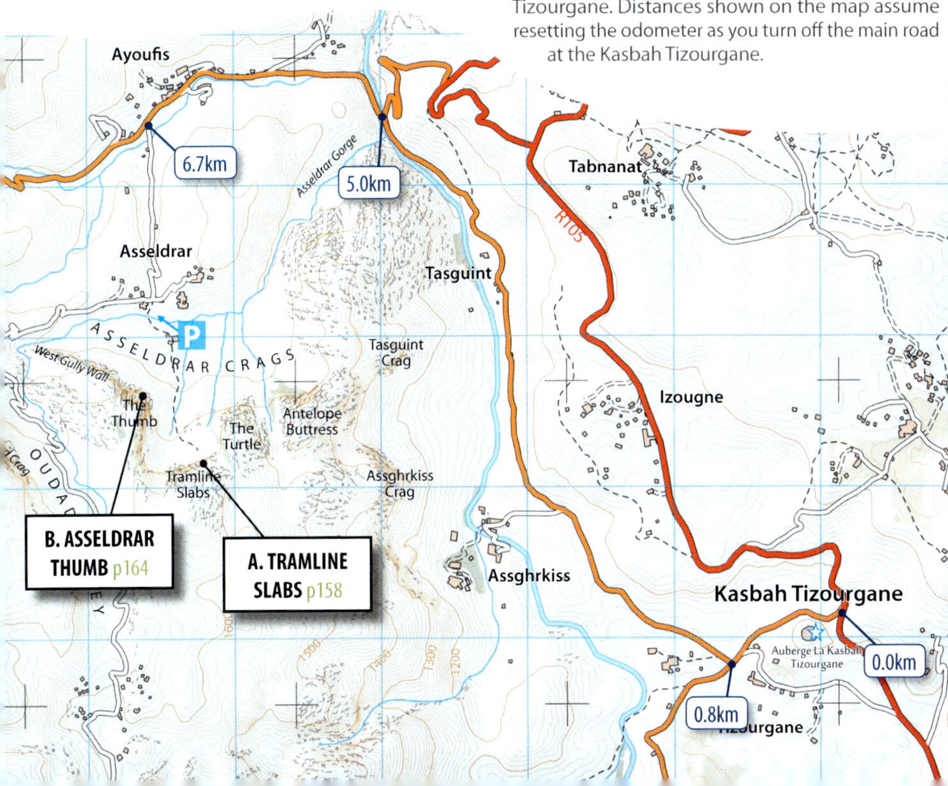

Area Map
Crag Selector
Intro
The Climbing
How to Use
Suggested Climbs
Tafraout Granite
Anergui
Ameln Valley
Tarakatine Pass
Sidi M'Zal
Jebel Taskra
Idaougnidif
Afantinzar
Samazar
Aouguenz
Tagzene
Tagmout
History
Index

A TRAMLINE SLABS

Shade · Families · Hitch · Roadside

Drive from Tafraout: **1 hour**
Walk-in: **40 to 45 minutes**

This fine crag is located up to the left of the main crag (The Thumb) at Asseldrar, and holds some excellent mid-length climbs that stay in the shade for much of the day. The crag takes its name from three distinctive parallel cracks, taken by *Going off the Rails*, *Senility Crack* and *Main Line*, which can be clearly seen from the approach.

Ample parking is available at the small junction in Asseldrar village, from where the crag is easily seen up to the left of the Thumb. Follow a good track to houses on the far side of a watercourse, then turn uphill, passing to the right of the buildings to pick up a small trail. This roughly follows the line of the stream running up between Tramline Slabs and the Asseldrar Thumb, arriving at the crag in approximately 40 minutes.

At the left-hand end of the slabs, a broad gully runs up between the Left Flank and Trainspotting Buttress.

TRAINSPOTTING BUTTRESS

This southwest-facing wall lies at the top left end of the main slabs, opposite the Left Flank.

1. Spud Very Difficult ☆1

10m. The straight flake crack, 1 metre left of the rubbly corner.

Amanda Turner & Alan Dickinson, October 2016.

2. Rent Boy Severe ☆1

20m. The chimney and continuation groove above.

Amanda Turner & Alan Dickinson, October 2016.

DESCENT: Trainspotting Buttress is a complicated crag with no easy descent routes, so parties may wish to set up abseil descents from any of these routes.

A) For routes 1 and 2, it is possible to descend down behind a large flake to the left.

B) From the top of the upper tier routes it is possible to scramble down the corner to the right of the prominent tower. This descent is marked by a small cairn, and leads to the mid-height terrace.

C) From the mid-height terrace it is necessary either to abseil, or down-climb the chimney of *Gameshows* (route 7).

3. Choose Life VS 4c ★2

30m. A fine climb, tackling the front of the prominent tower. Climb directly up to the central one of three blocks jutting out from the slab, then pull up left onto the ledge. Move up to excellent flakes in the headwall and finish up a final crack.
Alan Dickinson & Amanda Turner, October 2016.

The next routes lie on the lower tier and finish at the halfway terrace.

4. Watching Difficult

15m. The wide crack leading up to the mid-height ledge.
Amanda Turner & Alan Dickinson (solo), October 2016.

5. Mind-Numbing HVS 5a

10m. The left-hand crack in the wall just to the right.
Alan Dickinson & Amanda Turner, October 2016.

6. Spirit-Crushing VS 4c

10m. The crack and short wall just left of the chimney is something of an eliminate, but provides a pleasant way to the terrace. Use of the chimney is not allowed at this grade!
Amanda Turner & Alan Dickinson, October 2016.

7. Gameshows Difficult

15m. The chimney to the right also provides the easiest means of descent from the mid-height terrace.
Alan Dickinson & Amanda Turner (solo), October 2016.

↓ Alan Dickinson on the first ascent of *I Chose Something else* (E1) on Trainspotting Buttress at Tramline Slabs.
Photo: Amanda Turner

The next two routes are located on the upper tier, above the previous lines.

8. I Chose Not to Choose Life VS 5a ★2 GEAR

30m. The obvious left-facing corner is well protected, with a short crux section.
Alan Dickinson & Amanda Turner, October 2016.

9. I Chose Something Else E1 5b ★2

30m. Tackles the overlap in the centre of the wall. Start from the halfway terrace, just left of the base of a giant flake, climbing boldly up the slab to ledges. Gain the vertical crack above and climb it past two overlaps on the left, until a step left gains easier ground. Finish directly up the wall above.
Alan Dickinson & Amanda Turner, October 2016.

LEFT FLANK

The following routes have been climbed on the wall to the left of the main slabs, opposite Trainspotting Buttress. Approximately 40m up and left from the toe of the buttress a left-facing flake forms the left side of a shield of rock, taken by *First Class*.

10. Thomas the Menace HVS 5a ★1

40m. Climbs the wall 6 metres left of the shield, keeping 3 metres right of perched flakes, to gain easier ground. Go up a groove, then finish up the right-hand of two diverging cracks.
Paul Donnithorne & A.Price, October 2015.

11. First Class HVS 5a ★2

50m. The left-facing flake up the left side of a large shield of rock leads to a small ledge on top of the shield. From here, step right and climb a thin crack to ledges and finish up the superb rounded prow above.
Paul Donnithorne, October 2013

12. Business Class E1 5b ★1

40m. Gain the small groove forming the right side of the shield. Move up and right into a thin crack which leads to a ledge beneath the large orange roof. Pull through the left end of the roof, then swing back right to finish up a hanging groove.

Paul Donnithorne & Bob Brewer, October 2013

13. The Mechanic E3 5c ★1 GEAR ABSEIL

40m. A technical, but well-protected climb, starting a few metres down from the shield. Climb a thin seam to a good hold, from where it is possible to step up into a thin diagonal crack. Lean right into another thin crack and follow this to join a groove coming in from the right (taken by *The Passenger*). Move up right to climb the wall right of the large orange roof, then finish up leftward to the abseil anchors.

Bob Brewer & Paul Donnithorne, October 2013

14. The Passenger HVS 5a ★1 ABSEIL

40m. Pleasant climbing up the left-slanting groove leading up to the large orange roof. Pass the roof at its right-hand end via a thin finger flake, then finish up cracks above.

Paul Donnithorne & Bob Brewer, October 2013

15. The Flying Scotsman HVS 5a ★2 ABSEIL

40m. Start as for *The Passenger*, but continue straight up the slab 2m left of a black streak. This leads past a cave and small niche to finish up a knobbly groove and final slab.

Bob Brewer & Paul Donnithorne, October 2013

16. Up The Junction VS 4c ★1 ABSEIL

35m. This route starts up a crack a few metres left of the toe of the buttress, passing a tree to reach a block belay and abseil descent.

Paul Donnithorne & Bob Brewer, October 2013

17. The Bullet E2 5b ★2 ABSEIL

35m. Fine, intricate climbing up the arête above the toe of the buttress. Start up good flakes, then finish in a fine position up the rounded arête.

Paul Donnithorne, October 2013

18. Rabat Railway E1 5b ABSEIL

140m. Starts 5 metres right of the toe of the buttress, climbing up left of the *Marrakech Express*.

1) 35m (5a) Climb two corners trending right then follow a slabby crack to belay just above the top of *The Bullet*.

2) 30m (5b) Go up the steep crack just right of the arete, then take easier steps up the crest to below an overhanging wall right of a prominent fin.
3) 15m (5c) Step over a chimney, then climb an overhanging wall right of the arête. Continue up a crack to reach the crest.
4) 60m (4b) Finish up the stepped crest.
G.Cohen, A.Nisbet & G.Rooney, March 2014.

19. The Marrakesh Express E1 ★3 CRACK

105m. This excellent and popular climb follows a crack system in the steep orange buttress on the left side of the slabs.
1) 35m (5a) Start at the base of the corner and climb steeply to the crack in the buttress. Continue up to a spacious ledge.
2) 30m (5a) A first-class crack leads to a ledge. Continue trending right and climb up to another comfortable ledge.
3) 40m (5a) Follow the steep crack, stepping right towards a large overhang and finish up left of this.
Pete Johnson, Paul Donnithorne & David Barlow, December 2010.

THE MAIN SLAB

DESCENT: Either a two-pitch abseil down the line of *Going off the Rails* (40m, 60m), or walk down the gully to the right.

20. Edgeware Road VS 4c ★1 ABSEIL

90m. A good route up the corner at the far left-hand side of the slabs.
1) 50m (4a) Climb the corner-crack to a belay on sloping ledges. The original way followed the right-hand crack with a blank section at 4c.
2) 40m (4c) Move right and climb a vague crack up the slab to a small roof, passing this on the right. Continue up to large ledges and either scramble up to finish or move across right to the abseil point.
Pete Johnson, Paul Donnithorne & David Barlow, December 2010.

21. Day Tripper VS 4c ★1 BOLD WIDE ABSEIL

80m. A varied route starting some 10 metres right of *Edgeware Road*.
1) 45m (4c) Climb boldly up rightwards to a thread, then follow discontinuous cracks to the left of an A-shaped niche. Climb the steep wall left of the niche and follow a crack to a ledge.
2) 35m (4c) Step up right to a crack, then continue to a finish up a wide left-trending crack.

22. From the Bat Cave VS 4c ★2 ABSEIL

80m. An exciting alternative finish to the previous route. Start up pitch 1 of *Day Tripper* to the ledge below a tree in the Bat Cave.
2) 35m (4b) From the tree, climb up to the roof of the cave, then traverse out left to finish up a shallow groove.

23. Ticket to Ride E1 5b ★2

95m. An elegant climb, starting 20m right of *Edgeware Road*.
1) 30m (5a) Follow a left-trending diagonal crack and slabs to a cave. Pull into the groove above and continue to a bollard belay on a ledge.
2) 35m (5b) Move right and climb the fine black wall on big holds. Continue up a slab to a chimney, which leads through a notch to a ledge.
3) 30m (4c) Climb a narrow slab on the right, then step left and pull through a niche in the overhang to easier ground.
Paul Donnithorne & Marion Wintringham, March 2013.

24. Thomas the Tank Engine VS 4c ★2

90m. A good outing, with some varied climbing. Start at an obvious black streak to the left of a buttress leaning against the cliff.
1) 35m (4b) Follow the black streak to a steepening, then go up slightly left to a good ledge below an orange and black groove.
2) 55m (4c) Climb the groove, then continue up a big flake chimney (possible belay above this). Move rightwards up the wall above via a vague flake line, then scramble up right to the abseil point.
Emma Alsford & Pete Johnson, March 2013.

Main Slab
SHADE 40m

Area Map
Crag Selector
Intro
The Climbing
How to Use
Suggested Climbs
Tafraout Granite
Anergui
Ameln Valley
Tarakatine Pass
Sidi M'Zal
Jebel Taskra
Idaougnidif
Afantinzar
Samazar
Aouguenz
Tagzene
Tagmout
History
Index

25. Sleeper HVS 5b ★2

60m. Good climbing, starting up a buttress leaning against the face. Climb the crack in the left side of the leaning buttress to below an obvious white flake/nose above. Go up a crack on the right, then move left below the nose into another good crack. Follow this, moving onto the right wall to avoid vegetation, and continue to a small stance (possible belay). Climb up diagonally right from here to ledges and the mid-height abseil point.

Emma Alsford & Pete Johnson, March 2013.

26. Midnight Express E2 5a ★2

BOLD

60m. The scoop and black wall between *Sleeper* and *GOTR* gives some bold climbing. Trend up left to a hollow flake, then race up the black wall above to reach protection at a thin crack. Continue directly above to the abseil point.

Emma Alsford & Pete Johnson, March 2013.

27. Going off the Rails E2 5b ★3

100m. The left-most of the three main crack lines gives a magnificent climb with an infamous initial pitch.

1) 60m (5b) Climb the crack until it fades. Step left then climb boldly upwards to rejoin the line. Belay on the ledge above.

2) 40m (5a) Climb rightwards up a steep wall and thence up a crack to an overhang. Climb up to the left side of this, pulling through to finish up a groove on the right.

David Barlow & Pete Johnson, December 2010.

28. Supertram E3 5c ★3

60m. The intermittent cracks between *Going off the Rails* and *Senility Crack* are awkward to protect but give some excellent climbing.

Paul Donnithorne & Emma Alsford, December 2010.

29. Senility Crack HVS 5a ★1

CRACK

120m. The central of the three main crack lines is climbed in three pitches. Finish up a chimney.

Pete Johnson & David Barlow, December 2010.

30. One Track Mind E1 ★1

120m. The crack between *Senility Crack* and *Main Line*.

1) 50m (5a) Climb the deep crack right of a large boulder to an airy stance on the left.

2) 55m (5b) Continue climbing up the crack and then take a shallow groove to a belay under the roof.

3) 15m (5a) Step left around the roof and climb the right wall of the chimney taken by *Senility Crack*.

Pete Johnson & Paul Donnithorne, November 2011.

31. Main Line HVS ★1

120m. The right-most of the three main crack lines.

1) 40m (5a) Climb the face to a pinnacle belay.

2) 40m (4c) Step left and climb the right-hand crack through a bulge to a small stance.

3) 40m (4c) Move right to tackle the bulge (or take it direct up the crack at E3 5c) and finish up the wall above.

Paul Donnithorne & Emma Alsford, December 2010.

The next route climbs a vague rib to the right of the main slab, at the point where the main path reaches the foot of the cliff.

32. Qeso VS 4c ★1

ABSEIL

40m. An attractive climb up the vague buttress. Climb up easy ground to the left to beneath a steep crack on the left side of the buttress. Make an exciting step right here to finish with interest up the front face. Descend by abseil.

Steve & Katja Broadbent

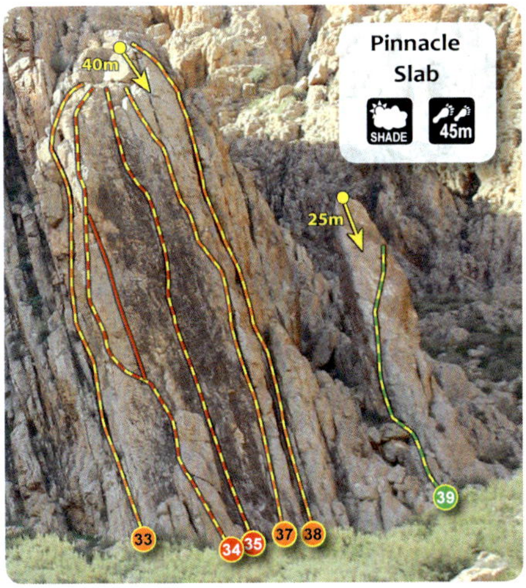

Photo by Brian Davison

THE PINNACLE SLAB

The following climbs are located towards the right side of the crag, at an attractive smaller slab with a huge flake leaning against its left side.

DESCENT: Make a 40m abseil from the top of the slab.

33. Clickety Clack HVS 5a ★1 ABSEIL

40m. The groove up the left side of the buttress, starting just left of the huge perched flake.
Paul Donnithorne & Marion Wintringham, March 2013.

34. Chancery Lane E2 5b ★2 ABSEIL

40m. Excellent climbing up the flake and arête. Start up a crack in the front of the flake to gain a good ledge on its top. Step left to gain the arête, which is climbed with interest first on the left, then on the right. Alternatively, continue straight up the crack to the right of the arête at E3 5c.
Paul Donnithorne & Emma Alsford, March 2013.

35. Night Train to Munich E2 5b ★3 ABSEIL

40m. A brilliant face-climb up the centre of the slab, starting just right of the big flake. At the top of the chimney forming the right side of the flake, step right to follow a crack up leftwards to a spike close to the left arête. Committing moves up right eventually gain better protection and a final crack to the top.
Paul Donnithorne & Emma Alsford, March 2013.

36. Last Train to Clarksville E3 6a BOLD

40m. Start up *Orient Express* until it is possible to step left into a hanging corner. Follow this to a ledge, then make bold moves up the wall right of *Night Train* to a good handhold. Move up right to a thin vertical crack, and continue up to a final wider crack.
Brian Davison & Paul Wood, December 2014

37. The Orient Express VS 4c ★3 ABSEIL

40m. The attractive crack up the right side of the slab, moving left at the top.
Paul Donnithorne & Marion Wintringham, March 2013.

38. Great Western VS 4c ★1 ABSEIL

40m. The chimney to the right is better than it looks.
Paul Donnithorne & Marion Wintringham, March 2013.

TRAM SPIRE PINNACLE

This is the obvious pinnacle at the right-hand end of the crag.

DESCENT: Make a 25m abseil from the top of the pinnacle.

39. Tram Spire Severe ★3 ABSEIL

25m. The prominent crack and right-trending flake up the pinnacle give some superb and atmospheric climbing.
Paul Donnithorne & Marion Wintringham, March 2013.

40. Tram's Late HS ★1 ABSEIL

22m. This route climbs the west face of the pinnacle (facing into the gully). Take the left-hand crack to a niche, then step right to a hollow flake. Pull through the bulge and continue more easily to the top.
T & M Cruse, March 2013.

Area Map
Crag Selector
Intro
The Climbing
How to Use
Suggested Climbs
Tafraout Granite
Anergui
Ameln Valley
Tarakatine Pass
Sidi M'Zal
Jebel Taskra
Idaougnidif
Afantinzar
Samazar
Aouguenz
Tagzene
Tagmout
History
Index

B THE ASSELDRAR THUMB

Shade | Families | Hitch | Roadside

Drive from Tafraout: **1 hour**
Walk-in: **30 minutes**

This giant monolith, towering above the village of Asseldrar, epitomises Anti-Atlas adventure climbing and is one of the most iconic pieces of rock in the whole region.

For visitors approaching Tafraout from Agadir and the North, the long line of cliffs that form the Tizi N'Takoucht escarpment are the first real hint of what the Anti-Atlas has in store, and tucked away at the extreme eastern end of those cliffs is the tremendous 'Thumb' at Asseldrar – home to some of the region's most inspiring, difficult, and significant routes.

The crag provides a full 300m of vertical and overhanging quartzite, catching the sun in the morning and remaining shady during the heat of the day. It has an easy approach, and some truly sensational climbing, most of which is well into the extreme grades. This fact, combined with the length and high level of commitment of these routes, means that Asseldrar can only be recommended for competent teams who are operating well within their capabilities. All routes are major undertakings, requiring early starts and a confident approach.

The crag is accessed from the village of Asseldrar (Assandrar) in approximately 30 minutes. Take the turn-off at Ayoufis and follow the track to parking at a junction in the village itself, from where the crag is ominously obvious.

DESCENT: Scramble off down either side. The right-hand (west) gully is shorter but requires a 20m abseil or tricky downclimb. The left-hand (east) gully is slightly longer but more straightforward.

1. Assandrar Welcome VS 4c ★2 (ADVENTURE)

350m. A Tafraout classic, and one of the first routes up this tremendous cliff. Start under a rib, just left of a dark left-slanting crack at the left side of the face.

1) Climb the rib left of the crack to a tree.
2) Stride across the crack, then climb up rightwards to ledges.
3-4) Climb cracks and corners to the base of a large slab.
5) Climb the right side of the slab until it is possible to move left to a ledge.
6) Gain the rib on the left, following it to a large ledge on the right side of a big couloir.
7) Move up to the ridge on the right and climb it to ledges.
8-9) Continue up the ridge to the top.

Les Brown & Derek Walker, March 2001.

2. Sungold E2 5b ★2 (ADVENTURE)

270m. A superb climb, featuring continuously interesting and sustained climbing up the left side of the front face. The route is at the top of its grade, and many parties have difficulties with route finding, resulting in epic long days. Start at the right side of a cave below a left-slanting crack.

1) 55m (5b) Climb through the slanting corner and go up flakes leading up to the right side of a big corner / roof. Belay 10m higher on a vague ledge.
2) 55m (5a) Go up diagonally rightwards from the right end of the ledges, making surprisingly easy moves through a weakness in the big bulges above. Continue up and right to a ledge below obvious cracks.
3) 60m (5b) Good jamming up the crack leads to bold moves out left to gain a vegetated groove left of the white slab. After about 10m move back right onto the white slab and follow a shallow groove to an airy stance at orange rock below steeper ground above.
4) 20m (5b) Step left to follow a vague crack through the steepening, then go diagonally left to the foot of an impressive orange corner.
5) 30m (5b) Move up left into the corner and follow this in an excellent position to its top.
6) 50m (5b) From the centre of the ledge, pull through an overlap and follow a left-trending crack, until moves back rightwards through a vague groove lead to a final slabby wall.
7) Scrambling to the top.

Emma Alsford & Paul Donnithorne, March 2009.

3. Rhythm and Stealth E3 5c ★3 (ADVENTURE)

350m. The smooth grey pillar high on the wall gives one of the best routes at this grade in the area (though see below...) Start directly below the pillar, at the base of the left-hand of two cracks forming an inverted-V.

1) 30m (5b) Climb the crack to an area of steep shattered rock, then pull up right to a poor sloping stance.
2) 50m (5c) Step up right and climb the groove and wall above through bulges and overlaps to a belay on a good ledge.
3) 50m (5a) Continue more easily past a chimney-flake to the base of the grey pillar. Climb a vague groove to gain and follow a giant flake, belaying on its top.
4) 50m (5b) A beautiful pitch. Weave gingerly up the pillar until a shallow groove leads right to a belay beneath steeper, orange rock.
5) 30m (5c) Climb thin overhanging cracks above, then trend right and back left to gain a slabby groove. Follow this to the base of a severely overhanging crack.
6) 40m (5c) Gain and follow the crack for a short way, until common sense dictates a tricky move up left into a groove instead. Follow this steeply up left to ledges beneath a broad wall.
7) 50m (5a) Climb the right side of the wall in a fine position to easier ground.
8) 50m (-) Easier climbing and scrambling to the top.

Guy Robertson & Trevor Woods, October 2003.

4. The Orgasmatron E3 5c ★★★

320m. The direct assault of the front wall is a scintillating climb, and one of Morocco's great E3 adventures, finding an inspired line up some seriously big ground. Start 10m left of *Adventures Beyond the Ultraworld*, just left of a diagonal fault line.

1) 50m (5b) Follow the line of weakness rightwards past a block in the fault line, then continue up to cross the line of *Adventures* to a good stance below a distinctive corner.

2) 30m (5c) Follow the corner to a cave ledge.

3) 20m (5a) From the right end of the ledge step up onto a boss of rock and haul up jugs to a ledge.

4) 55m (5a) Step right and continue up slabby walls, past a big flake, over blocks and then up an off-width crack to belay right of boulders, beneath a slim orange groove.

5) 40m (5b) Climb the wall 2m right of the steep orange groove, with an awkward start.

6) 25m (5c) Climb the steep groove above to a jug. Pull over the bulge and move up to a stance below twin orange grooves.

7) 40m (5b) Climb the right-hand groove and continue to ledges.

8) 60m (5a) Go up to a blocky overhang and weave through this, then continue up bulges to a slab. Climb up the slab, stepping left to finish up a wide crack.

Pete Johnson & Paul Donnithorne, October 2010.

5. Adventures Beyond The Ultraworld E5 6b ★★★

350m. This tour-de-force up the high prow in the centre of the face gives one of the hardest and best climbs in the Anti-Atlas. Start in the centre of the smooth orange wall, at cracks leading leftwards.

1) 40m (6a) Climb the cracks to a break, then step up right. Make hard moves to gain and follow a vague groove directly up to another break below the overhang. Hand-traverse left to a prominent groove and follow this up rightwards to a good ledge.

2) 25m (5b) Continue directly up the centre of the wall to another ledge.

3) 25m (5b) Climb the wall above, then a couple of awkward grooves to a niche.

4) 40m (6b) Climb a flake out right, then step back left to climb the bold black wall to a groove. Follow this up left to a large ledge.

5) 30m (5a) Traverse the blocks leftwards to a step down, then climb a steep groove leading to a prominent red chimney.

6) 20m (5a) Continue up the excellent chimney to a ledge on the crest.

7) 30m (5c) Climb the wall directly to a sloping ledge, then step right to a crack. Continue more easily to a belay in a big bay.

8) 20m (5b) Climb blocks, slightly rightwards, then move left to climb a little flying groove in the crest.

Area Map
Crag Selector
Intro
The Climbing
How to Use
Suggested Climbs
Tafraout Granite
Anergui
Ameln Valley
Tarakatine Pass
Sidi M'Zal
Jebel Taskra
Idaougnidif
Afantinzar
Samazar
Aouguenz
Tagzene
Tagmout
History
Index

9) 25m (5c) Continue directly to an overhanging crack / groove and follow it with some difficulty to a fine perch.
10) 35m (5c) Climb the bulging wall using a crack on the left, then traverse right to a flake. Climb left around the edge to gain an exposed wall which leads to easier ground up right.
11-12) 75m (4c) Climb a groove, then easier rock to the top.
Guy Robertson & Trevor Woods, October 2003.

6. Eagles and Doves E2 5c ★2 ADVENTURE STEEP

300m. A lonely lead up the centre of the imposing wall. An unappealing shallow cave system is the only weakness in the lower wall, and this route starts at the blunt arête to its right.
1) 30m (5c) Climb the arête rightwards, then back left and move up to gain a short groove. Go up this to a ledge on the right.
2) 20m (-) Move easily up right to below red bulges.
3) 50m (5a) Climb up through a break in the bulges, then continue more easily up rightwards to belay on a huge flake below bushes.
4) 40m (4c) Climb the wall left of the bushes, then go up steps to a belay on a shelf at the start of a right-trending fault line in the headwall.
5) 30m (4c) Climb up the fault to a pedestal.
6) 20m (5b) Go up a crack until it fades, then step up right before moving back left and up to a narrow ledge. Move 5m right to belay by a huge flake.
7) 20m (5b) Go back left along the ledge and climb up to a bulge left of the big roof. Climb through this and move 5m right to a belay.
8) 40m (4c) Go up a short crack and then trend more easily up leftwards.
9) 30m (5a) Head up towards a slot on the skyline, then step up right onto a large detached nose before scrambling up to easy ground.
10) Further scrambling remains to the top.
C.Henderson & R.Durran, April 2003.

7. The Big Marhaba E3 5c ★1 ADVENTURE

300m. A good climb, with two magnificent initial pitches but poorer climbing above. Start at the middle of the base of the wall, just left of a tree.
1) 40m (5c) Climb up to prominent flakes and jugs, then move right and up to gain and follow a crack through the overhang. Belay at a big break.
2) 40m (5c) Continue up the bulging orange wall above with sustained interest.
3-4) 70m (-) Scramble up right, heading for the big arching overhang. Belay on a spacious ledge below the rib on its left.
5) 50m (5a) Climb the rib to a huge block and bushy recess.
6) 40m (5b) Step across onto the wall and climb directly up to belay below a wall and left-slanting groove.
7-8) 60m (5a) Climb the wall and groove, then easier ground to the top.
Guy Robertson & Trevor Woods, October 2003.

8. Rust Never Sleeps E2 5b ★3 ADVENTURE BOLD

300m. An excellent route with some hard, bold climbing and fine positions. Starts to the right of the *Big Marhaba* at a grey cone of rock, left of the big corner.
1) 50m (5b) Bold moves up left gain easier ground heading up right to a small bush.
2) 20m (4a) Move left along the ledge, then up through a groove to a belay.
3) 50m (4b) Climb directly up easier ground.
4) 50m (4c) Follow a succession of steps and corners to the left of the obvious black streak, heading rightwards all the time to a tree on easier ground.
5) 20m (4b) Move up to belay beneath the upper wall.
6) 50m (5b) Another bold pitch. Go up the crackline past a small block and overhang, then continue up the thin wall above to easier ground and ledges.
7) 50m (4b) Move left then up a square red groove to finish up several steps above.
Brian Davison & Geoff Hornby, October 2005.

9. Crazy Horse HVS 4c ★2 ADVENTURE

300m. The huge corner / groove is a good climb, but like many hereabouts features considerable route-finding difficulties. The route climbs up to a prominent arched overhang half-way up the face.
1) 50m (4a) Climb the corner.
2) 50m (-) Continue up ledges and walls to belay beneath the arched overhang.
3) 50m (-) Climb up to the right of the arched overhang, over easy blocks and ledges.
4) 45m (4c) Traverse horizontally left to gain a groove, which leads to further grooves above.
5) 35m (4a) Pleasant face-climbing leads to a large block on a ledge.
6) 50m (4c) Climb up to a left-facing groove to the right of a black line.
7) 20m (-) An easier finish over blocks and ledges.
Geoff Hornby & Paul Seabrook, March 2007.

10. Overture VS 4c ★1 ADVENTURE

250m. The clean sweep of rock on the right-hand side of the front face gives another typically adventurous route. Start in the gully on the right of an easy left-trending break.
1) Climb up left and continue easily to good ledges.
2) Climb upwards, heading for a prominent crack / chimney and passing overhangs on the right.
3) Go up to a large ledge-system beneath the steeper walls above.
4) Climb a crack, then traverse up rightwards across slabs to gain the prominent crack.
5-6) Climb the crack, which widens into a wide chimney, capped by an overhang.
7) Surmount the overhang and continue more easily to the top.
Les Brown, Pete Turnbull & Roy Warner, March 1999.

4
5
6
7
8
9
10
Asseldrar Thumb
AM
25m
WARNING: Approximate lines only!

Area Map
Crag Selector
Intro
The Climbing
How to Use
Suggested Climbs
Tafraout Granite
Anergui
Ameln Valley
Tarakatine Pass
Sidi M'Zal
Jebel Taskra
Idaougnidif
Afantinzar
Samazar
Aouguenz
Tagzene
Tagmout
History
Index

C TIFGHELT BUTTRESS

Shade | Families | Hitch | Roadside

Drive from Tafraout: **1:10**
Walk-in: **25 to 40 minutes**

Beyond Ayoufis and the turn-off to Doudad, the Tizi N'Takoucht road climbs up to the Tifghelt Col, from where a superb array of crags are visible. The highest of these, guarded by the two Frontal Facets, is Tifghelt Buttress, which provides a tremendous variety of climbing, from long adventures to short technical masterpieces. The various faces provide plenty of options to find or avoid the sunshine, making this one of the most popular venues on the escarpment.

Parking is available at the col, from where all buttresses can be accessed.

THE EAST BUTTRESS

In the left side of the crag is a hidden gully, with a prominent orange arête (*Survival of the Fittest*) below and to the left. The north-facing wall which overlooks this gully is known as the East Buttress, and can be accessed in one of two ways:

1) The lower approach – traverse the hillside leftwards from the col, below the frontal facets, until it is possible to head up the gully to the foot of *Survival of the Fittest*.

2) The upper approach – go up the broad gully between Tifghelt Buttress and Echo Wall, then scramble up to the Upper West Walls (page 170). From here it is possible to scramble around the north face of the crag to the top of the hidden gully underneath the East Buttress routes.

DESCENT: Head up rightwards to the summit, from where it is possible to scramble down the Upper West Walls descent. This leads to the horizontal traverse (shown below), which can be followed back to the East Buttress.

1. Natural Selection E2 5b ★2

85m. Testing climbing up the face left of *Survival of the Fittest*.
1) 20m (5b) Ascend an open corner on the left side of the face to a crack. Climb this through two bulges to reach a large recess on the left.
2) 30m (5a) Climb up the right side of the recess and move right onto the face. Climb up the steep blocky crack on the right to reach a faint groove, passing right of an overhang. Belay five metres below a square roof.
3) 35m (4c) Climb up to the right of the roof and up a corner. Finish directly up the face.
Dan Donovan & Neil Adams, February 2012.

2. Survival of the Fittest E2 5c (3 stars)

80m. The outstanding orange arête high up on the left side of the cliff.
1) 30m (5b) A sustained pitch. Climb up a few metres and move right to a short but tricky groove. Exit left at the top of this, and climb up and right to a hanging belay on the arête.
2) 30m (5c) Continue climbing the arête, chiefly on the left side. Belay in a groove above the difficulties.
3) 20m (4c) Climb leftwards to a corner and follow this to easier ground.
Pete Johnson, Ben & Marion Wintringham, March 2009.

3. Voyage of the Beagle HVS 4c (3 stars) THIN

105m. An excellent, sustained, and intimidating route taking the thin crack above the lowest boulder choke in the gully.
1) 55m (4c) Climb the thin crack past small ledges to belay at a spacious ledge below an orange roof.
2) 50m (4c) Climb the wall above just right of the overhangs (hidden pocket) for a few metres and then move left following breaks to a small ledge. Climb straight up, passing a small overhang on its left, to reach white ledges. Move right and climb the serrated orange and black flake to finish.
Dan Donovan & Neil Adams, February 2012.

4. Puffing Billy E2 5b (1 star)

55m. Climbs a crack up the left side of the hanging arête at the top of the wall. Start below a boulder, stepping up left onto the slab. Climb this leftwards to a superb position on the arête, then pull around the roof to finish up the crack.
Dan Donovan & Neil Adams, February 2012.

5. Sunseeker E1 5c (2 stars)

55m. Another very good climb, this time taking the right side of the huge hanging flake. Follow *Puffing Billy* to beneath the overhanging orange and black wall, then break out right and climb the crack up its right side.
Neil Adams & Dan Donovan, February 2012.

6. The Selfish Gene E2 5c (1 star)

55m. Follow Puffing Billy for 10m, then move right into a steep crack. Climb this past a good rest to join *Sunseeker* for its final corner.
Neil Adams & Dan Donovan, October 2012.

7. Captain Bluebear HVS 5a (3 stars)

55m. A tremendous climb up the wall right of *Sunseeker*, defining the upper limit of the grade. Start up the easy slab as for *Puffing Billy*, moving up right onto the wall after about 8m into an open groove. This leads to a big flake with a dead tree, (crux) from where it is possible to step up right with some difficulty into a black groove. Follow this, passing left of a bulge to a fine finish.
Neil Adams & Dan Donovan, February 2012.

8. The God Dilemma E4 5c (2 stars)

50m. A fine, challenging wall climb. Pull onto the wall under the boulder (as for *Brown Eyed Girl*) then step left to the rib. Climb good cracks, then go up the rib on the right. Go up the centre of the wall above, past small ledges to a groove. Hand traverse 2m left then finish up a crack.
Neil Adams & Dan Donovan, October 2012.

9. Brown Eyed Girl E3 5b (2 stars)

50m. Start as for *Puffing Billy* and climb up underneath a boulder to reach the wall above. Step immediately left and climb rightwards up a black slab. About 4m before the big chimney it is possible to step left into a crack – climb this up left, through a groove and into a left-facing orange corner to finish.
Dan Donovan & Neil Adams, February 2012.

Area Map
Crag Selector
Intro
The Climbing
How to Use
Suggested Climbs
Tafraout Granite
Anergui
Ameln Valley
Tarakatine Pass
Sidi M'Zal
Jebel Taskra
Idaougnidif
Afantinzar
Samazar
Aouguenz
Tagzene
Tagmout
History
Index

THE UPPER WEST WALLS

Situated high on the northwest front of the buttress, this superb and popular little crag offers a handful of excellent single-pitch climbs that remain in the shade throughout the day. This fact, combined with the relatively high altitude, makes the Upper West Walls a good choice on hot days. They are easily approached in about 25 minutes up the broad gully between Tifghelt Buttress and Echo Wall.

10. New World HS 4b (GEAR)

20m. Nice climbing up the left-hand crack.
Dan Donovan (solo), February 2012.

11. Temptress E1 5b (3 stars)

30m. The amenable face between the two cracks is one of the most popular extremes on the escarpment, though it's no pushover.
Dan Donovan & Neil Adams, March 2011.

12. Dead Parrot Crack VS 4c (2 stars) (GEAR, CRACK)

35m. The awkward right-hand crack is another popular route, giving good climbing up from the ledge behind the bush.
Neil Adams & Dan Donovan, March 2011.

13. New Year's Play E1 5b

40m. Climb the crack, rib and groove to the left of *Honker* and finish up the rib on the right (as playfully as you can).
Paul Donnithorne & Sue Hazel, January 2012.

14. Honker E2 5b (3 stars) (GEAR, WIDE)

35m. The brilliant corner is surely too much to resist? Waltz up the slab to a couple of technical moves past the overhang, where good gear and good jams just about make up for an amusing lack of footholds. The upper part is easier, but still feels like a battle with tired arms...
Dan Donovan & Neil Adams, March 2011. Photo page 37.

15. Three's Company Severe (1 star)

45m. Nice climbing up the front face to the right. Start with an airy traverse rightwards to gain the arête, then climb straight up to pull through the overhang at a wide crack.
Steve Broadbent, Helen Copeland & Katja Broadbent, March 2013.

DESCENT: Scramble down leftwards to gain the ledges at the top of the main buttress (one short awkward step).

D ECHO WALL

Shade Families Hitch Roadside Drive from Tafraout: **1:10** Walk-in: **20 minutes**

This is the attractive wall on the right side of the broad gully, directly opposite the Upper West Walls on Tifghelt Buttress. The wall faces east and gets plenty of shade during hot afternoons, making it a good choice during periods of warm weather. Approach in about 20 minutes from Tifghelt Col, via the obvious broad gully.

Several routes have been climbed on the main wall, though the best climbing is found around the striking corner at the right-hand (lower) end of the crag (Echo Corner).

DESCENT: Abseil from a small notch above *Life and Fate*.

1. If Only they Sold Beer E1 5b ★2

70m. Good climbing up the left sidewall of *Echo Corner*.
1) (5a) Climb an open crack to its end, then go right to a square block.
2) (5b) Traverse right, then move up into the groove. Climb this for 3m before escaping rightwards into *Echo Corner*. Climb up 6m to a belay.
3) (5b) Finish up *Echo Corner*.
J.Buckley & T.Madden, March 2013.

2. Echo Corner E1 5b ★3

ABSEIL MOSSY

65m. The epic corner, climbed in two magnificent pitches, needs little introduction, but can be rather mossy at times.
Neil Adams & Dan Donovan, March 2011.

3. Good Vibrations HVS 5a ★1

65m. Climbs the wall and arête to the right of *Echo Corner*.
1) 40m (5a) Follow the prominent diagonal ledge system rightwards. At the end of the overlap go up steep scoops to the arête and climb a vertical crack at the top.
2) 25m (4c) Step right and follow the arête above the gully to an abseil point.
Neil Adams & Dan Donovan, October 2012.

4. Life and Fate E5 6a ★3

55m. An excellent and sustained pitch up the superb wall right of *Echo Corner*. Start up the diagonal line of *Good Vibrations*. Climb 10m to a bush then traverse left under the roof and pull up onto the wall. Climb a crack above then move left and make difficult moves up to a break. Finish up a thin crack system to the notch.
Dan Donovan & Neil Adams, October 2012.

5. Gaddafi's Gold E3 5c ★3

ABSEIL

65m. Another tremendous route up the right wall of the corner.
1) 30m (5b) Climb the vertical crack in the centre of the wall, go past a bushy ledge and climb a steep wall. Step left and belay on a small ledge above.
2) 35m (5c) Angle up left across the wall to reach a crack which resembles an arrow pointing downwards. Climb the crack and step left to a roof, pull round its right side and finish up the arête.
Neil Adams & Dan Donovan, March 2011.

6. Bob's Arête E1 5b ★1

ABSEIL BOLD

65m. The direct start to *Good Vibrations* tackles the tempting arête, with a bold and serious start. Finish more easily above.
T.Madden & J.Buckley, March 2013.

E SNOWMAN'S BLUFF

Shade · Families · Hitch · Roadside

Drive from Tafraout: **1:15**
Walk-in: **20 minutes**

This excellent little outcrop is a good choice on hot days, giving a number of very fine, steep crack climbs that stay in the shade all day. Park as for Taskra East Pillars and walk up the track as far as the first house. Head up terraces from here, towards the East Pillars, until a good path is reached, running back left towards Snowman's Bluff.

1. High Plains Drifter E1 5b ★1

25m. Starts on a large block some 30 metres up and left of the chimney of *A River Runs Through It*. Climb a crack, then step left and pull into a corner. Go up this, stepping left again to finish up a groove.

P.Donnithorne & G.Desroy, November 2015.

2. A River Runs Through it VS 4c ★2

50m. Climbs the chimney near the left side of the cliff.

1) 30m (4c) Climb the chimney past chockstones to a stance up and right.

2) 20m (4b) Pull over the left side of a jutting roof to climb a slim corner, then finish up a short wall to the top. Descend leftwards around boulders to gain the easy rake.

P.Donnithorne & G.Desroy, November 2015.

3. Tyreless Tony E1 5b ★1

70m. Pleasant climbing up the right edge of the slabby wall, about 15 metres left of the bending orange crack in the middle of the face.

1) 55m (5b) Start up a short crack then climb the right side of the wall past horizontal breaks to a small ledge. Pull up left onto the slab and continue to a block belay.

2) 15m (5a) Finish up the left-hand crack above.

P.Donnithorne & S.Whitehouse, March 2015.

4. Meltdown E2 5b

ABSEIL

40m. Unusual climbing up the left-slanting orange corner in the centre of the crag. Follow the corner to a large block, then pull steeply off this, trending awkwardly right to a balancy finish.

G.Desroy & P.Donnithorne, November 2015.

5. Freewheelin' E1 5b ★2

CRACK · ABSEIL

50m. An excellent climb, starting up the buttress right of the central orange crack.

1) 25m (5a) Climb the crack past a bush to the top of the buttress.

2) 25m (5b) Continue up a wide crack to a step left, then move back up right to gain a square-cut corner to a ledge. Abseil from a tree down and right.

J.Wigg, P.Donnithorne & G.Desroy, November 2015.

6. Walking in the Air E1 5b ★3

CRACK · ABSEIL

50m. Brilliant climbing up the striking crack. Follow the crack to a steepening at 20 metres, then trend up left into a white scoop. Climb this, then swing back right to finish up the crack.

J.Wigg, P.Donnithorne & G.Desroy, November 2015.

7. Cold Case E1 5b ★2

WIDE · ABSEIL

35m. An absorbing route up the crack just right of the right-hand toe of the crag. Bridge up the initial section to reach exposed moves up the final wide crack.

P.Donnithorne, March 2015.

8. Snow Patrol E1 5b ★2

CRACK · ABSEIL

45m. Starts up an attractive right-facing white flake.

1) 35m (5b) Climb the flake, then step left and follow the crack up rightwards to circumnavigate the large roof. Continue up a short groove to a ledge.

2) 10m (4c) Finish up the corner to blocks and an abseil descent.

P.Donnithorne & S.Whitehouse, March 2015.

Dave Rogers and Martin Skinner on *A Few Pillars More* (HVS 5b) at Taskra (page 174)

Photo: Paul Bennett

Area Map
Crag Selector
Intro
The Climbing
How to Use
Suggested Climbs
Tafraout Granite
Anergui
Ameln Valley
Tarakatine Pass
Sidi M'Zal
Jebel Taskra
Idaougnidif
Afantinzar
Samazar
Aouguenz
Tagzene
Tagmout
History
Index

F TASKRA EAST PILLARS

Shade · Families · Hitch · Roadside

Drive from Tafraout: **1:15**
Walk-in: **15 minutes**

The tiny village of Taskra sits on a small hilltop just above the road, dominated by some huge cliffs that have seen only limited exploration by climbers. At the left side of these cliffs are the 'East Pillars' – home to a collection of excellent long climbs with short walk-ins.

DESCENT: Descent can be made down the gully to the left of the crag, or by continuing left over a dome-shaped hill to pick up a good path that returns to the road in about 1 hour.

1. Pan's Labyrinth HS 4b ★3 (GEAR) (ADVENTURE)

235m. An excellent adventure, giving sustained enjoyable climbing on good rock. Start at the left edge of the cliff, next to the vegetated descent gully as for *A Few Pillars More*.

1) 60m (4b) Trend up and right, passing the first bush, then pull right onto the rock lozenge below the second bush. Belay in a gully to the left of the second bush.

2) 55m (4b) Climb the chimney for 10 metres, then move left onto the slab and follow this to a large cave.

3) 30m (4b) Traverse horizontally rightwards out of the cave at the height of the top of the boulders, regaining the central pillar. Continue up this to a large flat stance with several boulders.

4) 60m (4a) Walk to the main buttress, ignoring the tower on the left. To the left are several clean ribs, left of a mossy face. Climb the first rib, which has a deep cleft to its left. From the flat top of the rib, step left across the cleft to rejoin pitch 4 of *A Few Pillars More*.

5) 30m (4b) Finish as for pitch 5 of *A Few Pillars More*.

Alan Dickinson & Amanda Turner, October 2016.

1. A Few Pillars More HVS 5b ★2 (ADVENTURE)

220m. The original way up the left-hand pillar provides lots of easy climbing with a difficult but well-protected crux on pitch 2, and a spectacular finale. Start at the left edge of the cliff, next to the vegetated descent gully.

1) 60m (4b) Trend up and right, as for the previous route, but climb the lozenge to belay above the second bush.

2) 30m (5b) Climb the right edge of the pillar to a ledge (crux) then continue up the edge and wall above to a rock ledge.

3) 45m (4a) Follow the edge of the pillar to a small ledge.

4) 55m (4a) Continue to reach a narrow gap between the pillar and the wall above. Step down and across the gap, then move up to climb a rib to a blocky ledge. Walk left into a deep rift.

5) 30m (4b) Climb out of the deep rift via a spectacular chimney, finishing up the right wall to reach a big ledge below an ancient yew tree. Fifteen minutes of scrambling and walking leads to the top.

Graham Little, Jim Lowther & Mike Rhodes, March 2013. Photo previous page.

3. A Fistful of Pleasure HVS 5b ★1

240m. Start mid-way between *A few Pillars More* and *Multiple Pillars of Pleasure* at a pointed boulder below the centre of a broad slab.

1) 55m (4b) Climb a shallow black groove just right of the pointed boulder to gain a grassy crack at 10 metres. Climb the slab just right of the crack to a ledge 10 metres below the centre of a large roof.

2) 30m (5b) Climb up leftwards to gain a left-trending flake and follow this to a stance.

3) 45m (4c) Climb the crack above, then continue more easily to belay just right of a tower.

4) 55m (4a) Move left for 8 metres and climb the long, easy rib to belay below a huge tower.

5) 55m (5a) Walk right for 10 metres and climb up from a high ledge past a small thread to a big cam slot. Go up left to finish up easier ground.

Paul Donnithorne & Bob Brewer, October 2013

4. The Good, The Bad, and The Ugly HVS 5a ★1 (UNCHECKED)

230m. Starts 5 metres right of *A Fistful of Pleasure*, and 5 metres left of a huge chimney. Unfortunately, details of the exact line above pitch 3 are somewhat vague.

1) 50m (4a) Trend easily up right to a good ledge below a steep crack in the orange wall.

2) 30m (5a) Follow the crack up left, then move up right up the hanging wall to a ledge on the right. Continue up a crack to a block ledge.

3) 40m (5a) Follow the rib above, moving slightly left into a groove. Pull through a steep bulge above to gain a slab, then move up to belay at the top of a sloping ledge.

4) 20m (4c) Trend rightwards up the attractive wall to gain the top of the tower.

5) 40m (5a) Bridge across the chasm into a thin crack, and climb up to gain a vague groove on the left. Continue to a large boulder-covered ledge, below and left of a huge chimney.

6) 50m (5a) Move the belay into the chimney, then bridge up the chimney a few metres right of *A Few Pillars More*. Move right, pulling through the right side of an overlap to reach easier ground.

Emma Alsford & Paul Donnithorne, March 2014.

5. Keep Taking the Pillars E1 5a ★2 (UNCHECKED)

280m. The wall to the left of *Multiple Pillars of Pleasure* gives 7 pitches of excellent climbing, sharing the step across from the final pillar with that route. Details of the exact line are somewhat vague.

1) 50m (5a) Climb the arête left of *Multiple Pillars of Pleasure*, heading for the right side of the roof. Continue up the arête to a crevasse stance.

2) 50m (5a) Continue up the excellent arete on large holds.

3) 40m (5a) Go up the wall above and climb just right of a crack to gain a small stance.

4) 20m (5a) Continue up the wall above to below a steepening.

5) 30m (5a) Move left, climb a corner, then swing right to climb up a wall to gain the terrace.
6) 15m (5a) Climb onto the big boulder and make a bold move across the gap to reach small holds. Climb up to another terrace.
7) 50m (5a) Walk right and re-belay below a black wall. Climb a steep left-leaning flake up the wall just left of *Multiple Pillars*, finishing more easily on chicken-heads.
Mike Turner, Nigel Braggins & Martin Bischoff, April 2014.

6. Multiple Pillars of Pleasure HVS 5a

255m. An Anti-Atlas classic. The series of overlapping pillars near the left side of the crag gives a magnificent and adventurous day out that is low in the grade, with mostly VS climbing in a committing situation. Start at the left edge of the tapering pillar just right of a deep chimney.
1) 55m. (4b) Follow a right-trending line on fine rock to a block belay overlooking the chimney on the right.
2) 15m (4b) Move left onto the face of the main pillar and climb up to reach another block belay on top of a smaller pillar.
3) 40m (5a) Step across to climb the narrowing pillar (crux) to its top.
4) 20m (4a) Step across again and climb up to a vegetated ledge directly above. Belay at the left end.
5) 35m (4b) Go up a dark wall to reach a wide ledge and climb a huge block.
6) 45m (4b) Cross the gap and climb a short wall. Negotiate the vegetation to reach an orange groove.
7) 45m (4c) Follow first-class climbing up the steep orange groove and the face above to easier terrain. From here fifteen minutes of scrambling and walking should gain the summit.
Graham Little & Chris Bonington, March 2010.

7. The Second Coming HVS 5a

140m. Starts just right of *Multiple Pillars of Pleasure*.
1) 30m (5a) Climb a corner crack and surmount a bulge to reach a belay high in the groove above.
2) 40m (4b) Move right onto the arête and follow shallow grooves up this to awkward moves onto a slab. Belay below and left of a large orange cave.
3) 40m (4b) Traverse up leftwards to reach a groove, which leads to a belay in a scoop.
4) 30m (4a) Follow the arête to rejoin *Multiple Pillars of Pleasure*.
R.Keet, R.Creamer & C.Keefe, November 2014

Area Map
Crag Selector
Intro
The Climbing
How to Use
Suggested Climbs
Tafraout Granite
Anergui
Ameln Valley
Tarakatine Pass
Sidi M'Zal
Jebel Taskra
Idaougnidif
Afantinzar
Samazar
Aouguenz
Tagzene
Tagmout
History
Index

G IMRIR CRAGS

Shade · Families · Hitch · Roadside

Drive from Tafraout: **1:15**
Walk-in: **25 to 40 minutes**

Beyond Taskra the road passes over a small shoulder into a vague cirque of excellent crags above the little village of Imrir. These well-developed crags are amongst the best on the escarpment, and a visit here is highly recommended, particularly during spells of warm weather when the high-altitude, north- and east-facing crags really come into their own. All of the climbs here are in excess of 1500m above sea level, and the views across to the High Atlas mountains are correspondingly spectacular on clear days.

IMRIR UPPER BUTTRESS

This tremendous little wall of perfect quartzite lies up and left of Titan's Wall, partially hiding in a shady gully behind unclimbed lower crags. It offers plenty of shade, a magnificent outlook, shelter from the wind, and some of the best mid-length, mid-grade crag routes in the area. It is reached fairly easily up the steep hillside in approximately 40 minutes from the road.

DESCENT: For routes left of *Raindrops* the best option is a 50m abseil down *Butch Cassidy* (steel cable in place). For routes to the right, an entertaining abseil can be made down the huge cleft to the left of *Flakeaway*.

1. Left Choice E1 5b ABSEIL

50m. Climb the left-hand crack at the far left end of the upper wall, near the top of the gully. There is an awkward bulge at one-third height.

Paul Donnithorne & Emma Alsford, April 2009.

2. Right Choice E1 5b ★1 ABSEIL

30m. The crack to the right of *Left Choice*, surmounting an overhang at the top.

Paul Donnithorne, Ben & Marion Wintringham, April 2009.

3. Sundance E3 5c ★3 ABSEIL

30m. This excellent face climb takes a right-to-left diagonal line up the fine wall just right of *Right Choice*. Climb up to a ledge at 4m, up through an overlap and then angle left to get through the second overlap at a weakness. Continue up left then trend back right at the top.

Emma Alsford & Paul Donnithorne, April 2009.

4. Cowgirl Groove HVS 5a ★1 ABSEIL STEEP

40m. Nice climbing up the prominent groove immediately right of *Sundance*, finishing steeply through the upper overhang.

Pete Johnson & Lun Roberts, March 2013.

5. The Crossing HVS 5a ★2 ABSEIL

45m. A fine counterpart to *Butch Cassidy*, starting a few metres up and left of that route. Climb diagonally up rightwards to the first belay of *Butch Cassidy*, then follow a vague groove and pleasant wall above.

Pete Johnson & Lun Roberts, March 2013.

6. Butch Cassidy VS 4c ★3 ABSEIL

60m. The central groove gives a memorable and very varied climb, and one of Tafraout's best VS crag routes.

1) 20m (4c) Climb the left-slanting groove to a stance on ledges. Amusing antics in the crack are best avoided.

2) 40m (4c) Continue up the groove then pull up to a ledge on the right. The wall above looks daunting, but is climbed trending leftward with an increasing sense of delight.

Paul Drew, Kevin Sales & Mike Mortimer, October 2010.

7. Raindrops HVS 5a ★1 ABSEIL

40m. Start from ledges in the centre of the wall below the large vegetated corner. Climb up 6m to a ledge, trend right up steep ground on good holds, then back left past a delicate move until the angle eases. Finish straight up a steep wall to the large ledge.

Mike Mortimer, Paul Drew & Kevin Sales, October 2010.

8. Rockwarrior HVS ★1

ABSEIL

60m. Start below the central crack/ groove.
1) 30m (5a) Follow the crack/ groove up left then climb a short wall to a belay on the right.
2) 30m (4b) Follow the wall and vague prow to the top.

The next routes climb a pillar to the right of a prominent deep gully, which provides the line of an exciting abseil descent.

9. Flakeaway E3 5c ★1

ABSEIL

60m. A challenging line with a difficult crux up the right wall of the huge cleft.
1) 30m (4c) Start up the chimney groove beneath overhangs, passing these on the left to a belay.
2) 30m (5c) A difficult flakey groove up the left side of the buttress.
Neil Adams, Paul Donnithorne & Dan Donovan, March 2010.

10. Imrir Arête E2 5b ★2

ABSEIL

65m. The right arête of the upper black wall is a justifiably popular climb with fine positions.
1) 35m (5b) Climb steep cracks just left of the arête, then continue up the arête to a ledge.
2) 30m (5b) More steep cracks on the left of the arête, once again finishing up the arête itself.
Pete Johnson & Lun Roberts, March 2009.

Area Map
Crag Selector
Intro
The Climbing
How to Use
Suggested Climbs
Tafraout Granite
Anergui
Ameln Valley
Tarakatine Pass
Sidi M'Zal
Jebel Taskra
Idaougnidif
Afantinzar
Samazar
Aouguenz
Tagzene
Tagmout
History
Index

TITAN'S WALL

This impressive orange cracked wall is clearly visible from the road, at the top of the steep approach gully. Relentless overhangs and awkward cracks provide extreme workouts on some unlikely looking lines, making this a good place to head if you've become 'disillusioned with the easy-angled romps' elsewhere in the range...

The crag is frequently home to nesting birds of prey, and should be avoided if birds are present.

DESCENT: A 60m abseil down the line of *Cracktastic*.

11. The Clash E2 5b ★2

ABSEIL STEEP

50m. A series of corners up the rib overlooking the gully at the left side of the cliff, giving excellent sustained climbing with adequate protection.

1) 30m (5b) Climb the gully for 3m then step left onto the rib. A series of grooves leads up to a belay 4m below the roof.

2) 20m (4b) Make an exposed traverse rightwards for 10m and finish up the clean rib above.

D.Ryden & M.Pycroft, March 2013.

12. Pulling Like a Tractor E2 5c ★2

ABSEIL STEEP

80m. The wall and corner left of *Titan's Chimney* has good gear, great rock, and some excellent steep climbing.

1) 25m (5b) Climb the chimney groove left of *Titan's Chimney* for 15m, then make an exposed traverse right and swing around the corner to a belay.

2) 20m (5c) A hard pull over the bulge leads to some fine climbing up the wall to a small ledge.

3) 55m (5a) Climb up and pull into a black corner. Follow this until the angle eases and it is possible to move up chicken-heads on the superb right arête.

Twid Turner, Ed Lansing & Pat Lindenbach, March 2013.

13. Titan's Chimney E1 5b ★3

ABSEIL STEEP

90m. The ridiculous-looking corner and hanging chimney is a 'marvellous route' for those who like that kind of thing.

1) 35m (5a) Start up a right-trending ramp to gain the corner, going up steeply through a pod to a fine spike belay. A direct start up cracks to the right has also been climbed at the same grade.

2) 55m (5b) Continue up the corner to gain the wild chimney above, following it with surprising ease to a ledge system.

Emma Alsford & Paul Donnithorne, April 2009 (original start)
Paul Drew & Kevin Sales, October 2010 (direct start).

14. Cosmic Corner E3 6a ★1

ABSEIL STEEP

80m. The overhanging corner and crack, midway between *Titan's Chimney* and *Cracktastic*. Start 5m left of an ugly off-width corner crack.

In order to minimise distress to both climbers and birds, please do not climb this route when birds of prey are nesting in the crack.

1) 25m (5b) Climb the groove up rightwards to a bulge, and pull through this, up left to a block belay.

2) 55m (6a) The overhanging corner provides considerable difficulty. Pull through the right side of the roof above and follow cracks trending rightwards to the top.

Pete Johnson & Paul Donnithorne, October 2010.

15. Titanic E5 6b ★2

ABSEIL WIDE STEEP

80m. Audacious climbing up the crack and roof to the right of *Cosmic Corner*. Start 5m right of *Cosmic Corner* at the base of a wide crack / chimney.

1) 25m (5b) Breeze up the off-width crack, moving left at the overhang, then continue straight up to belay on a wide ledge.

2) 55m (6b) Climb the steep corner to an awkward rest beneath the overhang. Move left here, then make difficult moves over the lip to better holds. Finish up the crack and groove above.

Peter Blackburn & Chris Parkin, March 2013.

Titan's Wall

AM 25m

Overview Page 176

THE WHITE TOWER

This is the right-hand (north-facing) wall immediately right of Titan's Wall, providing yet more first class climbs in the upper grades.

DESCENT: A 60m abseil down the line of *Cracktastic*.

16. G&T Special E2 5c ★2 ABSEIL

70m. Sensational, steep climbing.
1) 20m (4c) Climb the crack and wall 3m left of *Cracktastic*.
2) 20m (5c) Climb a short crack (as for *Cracktastic*), moving left after 5m to gain a leaning groove. Follow this to a niche belay beneath the roof.
3) 30m (5b) Go up to the big roof, swing right and climb the upper wall, trending right and then back left.
Pete Johnson & Paul Donnithorne, March 2010.

17. Pussyfooting E5 6a ★3 GEAR ABSEIL STEEP

60m. The upper wall between *G&T Special* and *Cracktastic* gives a well-positioned climb that is steep, strenuous, and well protected.
1) 20m (4c) As for *G&T Special* pitch 1.
2) 40m (6a) Climb up left into the niche of *G&T Special*, then step up right over a roof. Strenuous moves up a groove gain easier climbing towards the top.
Dan Donovan & Neil Adams, March 2011.

18. Cracktastic E1 5b ★2 ABSEIL CRACK

60m. A fine climb up the jagged crack.
1) 15m (4c) Climb a wide flake crack to a crevasse belay.
2) 45m (5b) Climb a short crack, then step left and up into a shallow groove. After a few metres move up right into the crack proper, following it through two bulges.
Emma Alsford & Paul Donnithorne, March 2009.

19. Statement of the Bleeding Obvious E3 6a ABSEIL STEEP

115m. The rib to the right of *Cracktastic*.
1) 45m (5c) Climb a shallow groove to gain a steeper groove on the right. Follow this, then traverse rightwards along a horizontal crack until it is possible to move back up left, continuing up the rib to a spike belay.
2) 40m (5b) Continue up the left side of the rib to a ledge.
3) 30m (5a) Climb the corner behind the tree for a few metres, then trend up right and pull around the right side of the overhang.
Dan Donovan, Paul Donnithorne & Neil Adams, March 2010.

20. Moonbeam E2 5c ★2 ABSEIL

110m. An interesting meander up the centre of the wall, with some good climbing throughout. Start below the left-hand corner crack, just right of a big V-groove.
1) 50m (5b) Climb up past a small tree, then go up a corner crack to gain a pedestal on the left. Make a committing move rightwards across the wall to a belay ledge.
2) 60m (5c) A big pitch. Climb up a crack, then undercling the roof and pull up rightwards to a ledge. Climb a hidden flake crack to the right of the arête, before moving left along a ledge and up to a bigger ledge with a tree. Step left from here to finish up the prow above.
Emma Alsford & Paul Donnithorne, March 2009.

21. Wacky Races E1 5b ★2 ABSEIL

110m. Another good climb, starting just right of *Moonbeam*.
1) 30m (5a) Climb the right-hand corner crack to a ledge.
2) 30m (5b) Move up and traverse rightwards along a break to gain a groove. Climb this into a chimney, belaying at its top.

The White Tower
SHADE 30m
Overview Page 176

Area Map
Crag Selector
Intro
The Climbing
How to Use
Suggested Climbs
Tafraout Granite
Anergui
Ameln Valley
Tarakatine Pass
Sidi M'Zal
Jebel Taskra
Imighzhidir
Afantinzar
Samazar
Aouguenz
Tagzene
Tagmout
History
Index

3) 50m (5a) Climb a big flake and move up to a vegetated ledge. Climb a wide crack to finish just left of a large jutting block.

Emma Alsford & Paul Donnithorne, March 2009.

22. OCD E4 6a ★★

110m. The front of the buttress to the left of the *Meteor* chimney.

1) 25m (6a) Climb up past a large detached block to gain the overhanging groove and crack. Follow this to a good ledge on the left.

2) 45m (5c) The steep white wall above leads to a flake crack. Follow this and the corner above to a vegetated ledge and small tree.

3) 40m (5a) Climb the groove on the right, then move left onto the left side of the tower, finishing direct on good rock.

Paul Donnithorne & Pete Johnson, October 2010.

23. Meteor E1 5b

55m. The obvious chimney is climbed in two pitches, with a fine stance beneath a flake at 20m.

Pete Johnson & Paul Donnithorne, March 2010.

24. Inglorious Basterds E1 5b

55m. Start 10m right of *Meteor*, just right of a large boulder.

1) 20m (4c) Climb a flake crack to a ledge.

2) 35m (5b) Go up a sharp flake, then up rightwards to a ledge. The rib on the right has a hard start, and leads to an abseil descent from the top of Meteor.

Pete Johnson & Paul Donnithorne, March 2010.

Katja Broadbent on *Butch Cassidy* (VS 4c) on the Upper Buttress at Imrir... one of the best routes at this grade on the escarpment.
Photo: Steve Broadbent

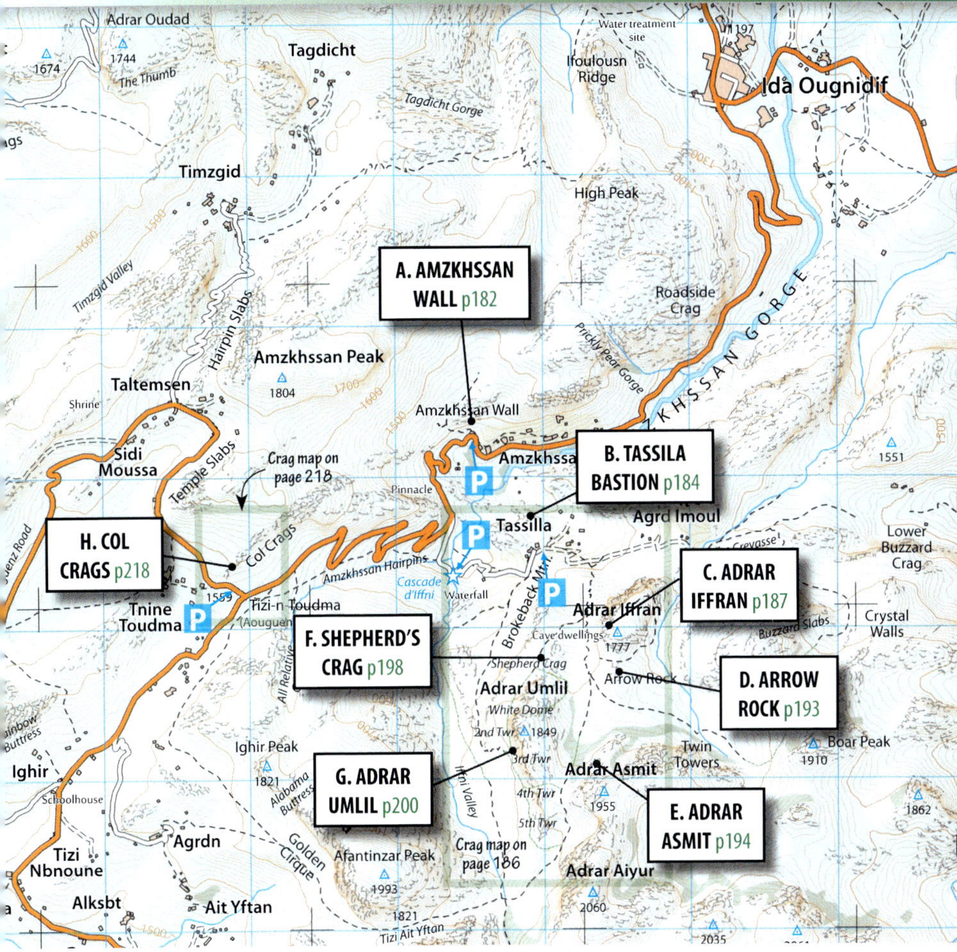

THE IDAOUGNIDIF AREA

With a high concentration of first-class rock climbs, breathtaking views, and a touch of mountain solitude, the rocky summits above Idaougnidif are a justifiably popular climbing destination. These high peaks escape the worst of the daytime heat, are generally moss-free, and hold some of the best multi-pitch climbing on the whole massif.

The small town of Idaougnidif lies just off the main Tafraout to Agadir road, and is reached in approximately one hour by car from Tafraout, or a few minutes from the Kasbah Tizourgane. The town's full name, '*El Khemis Ida Ougnidif*' is normally shortened to the more convenient 'Idaougnidif' (*Id-owg-nid-if*) by the local people, but is still seen on several road-signs.

When approaching from Tafraout take the left turn just after Madao (see overview map on page 5) and follow it into the centre of Idaougnidif, from where a good road (signposted to Tnin and Tanalt), winds its way up the impressive Amzkhssan Gorge to the small village of Amzkhssan, and then onwards to the Aouguenz junction and Afantinzar. Although there are dozens of crags scattered around these hillsides, it is the impressive high peaks to the south, above Tassila, which are of most interest to the climber.

These peaks are accessed via the poor, unsurfaced track that leaves the road 5.2km from the junction in Idaougnidif, descending to the eye-catching Cascade d'Iffni waterfall.

A AMZKHSSAN WALL

Shade Families Hitch Roadside

Drive from Tafraout: **1 hour**
Walk-in: **2 to 5 minutes**

This deceptively large roadside crag of compact low-angled quartzite lies on the north side of the road above the village of Amzkhssan. It is home to a handful of worthwhile easy climbs on good rock, and although some of them are disconcertingly bold, big holds usually abound and the routes are not particularly committing.

There is parking at a bend as the road leaves the village, from where the crag is reached in a matter of minutes through the trees. Identifying lines can be difficult, and many parties find themselves going 'off-route' here. Fortunately the wall can be climbed pretty much anywhere, and you're unlikely to get into too many unexpected difficulties.

DESCENT: From the top of the crag continue down the far side to gain a good path heading back left (west). This path swings round the western end of the crag and returns to the road near the start of the routes. It is also possible to descend the eastern end of the crag.

1. Super Shape Work HVS 4c ★1

40m. An interesting climb up the short left arête, with a distinct crux. Enter the initial groove in the lower arête with some difficulty, and follow it to ledges (possible belay). Go straight up above to a difficult groove through the roof. Finish on the ridge, then run away bravely down slabs on the left.

Steve Broadbent & Anna Piotrowski, October 2013.

2. Donkeys Stole my Droids Very Difficult

UNCHECKED

150m. This route starts up a small buttress in front of the main cliff, below and left of a large curving overlap with an S-shaped crack high above it. Unfortunately the exact line has not been located.

1) 60m (-) Climb the easy buttress and continue to a big ledge.
2) 60m (-) Follow the easiest line up to another ledge system.
3) 30m (-) Finish up a crack to the top.

R.Eckersley & B.Carter, May 2013.

3. Zig Zag HS 4b

BOLD

130m. Starts up a right-slanting ramp-line towards the left side of the wall.

1) 50m Easy climbing up the ramp.
2) 40m Go left up a crack then straight up to the right of an overhanging block.
3) 40m Move right to avoid the steep pale wall, then climb straight up to capping overlaps.

Jan Van Winkel & Tim Vercauteren, February 2010.

4. Amzkhssan Wall Severe

BOLD

120m. Climbs the centre of the wall directly from the lowest point. Good positive holds make up for a complete lack of protection.

1) 35m. Easy climbing to a good belay on the right-slanting ledge system.

2) 30m. Climb a weakness in the steeper left wall, then step right to a belay.
3) 20m. Climb steeply leftwards (crux) from the belay, then move right onto a ledge.
4) 35m. Go straight up past the left side of the final overlap.
Steve & Katja Broadbent, October 2008.

5. Amzkhssan Rib Very Difficult ★

130m. A good climb up the rib immediately right of a right-slanting ramp/gully, following one of the few natural lines on this otherwise featureless wall. The difficult section is well protected, making this route a good introduction to the region. Start from the lowest point of the crag, nearest to the road. After a tricky start just right of the gully the rib is climbed with ease (numerous belay possibilities along the way). A final 40m pitch through steep ground at the top of the route provides the highlight of a very enjoyable climb.
Steve Broadbent, Katja Broadbent & Niall Hedderley, December 2009.

6. Pinnacle Slab Difficult ★

120m. The slabs to the right of Amzkhssan Rib can be climbed pretty much anywhere, and provide a pleasant low-grade ascent on immaculate rock. The line described here starts up slabby ground about 10m right of Amzkhssan Rib and goes straight up towards a rectangular black overhang with a crack through its centre, high on the wall. Turn the overhang on the right and move up to a pinnacle beneath a small overlap. Step off the pinnacle to surmount the overlap and continue straight up to the top of the crag.
Steve Broadbent & Peter Hill, December 2010.

7. Greem Difficult

120m. This route climbs a vague black buttress halfway between *Pinnacle Slab* and the *Amzkhssan Simul-Solo.* On the approach the trail is squeezed up against the crag – start here at a cairn by the lowest rocks. Climb easily up the front of the vague buttress, generally trending rightwards.
Will Benfold & Steve Broadbent, February 2012.

8. The Amzkhssan Simul-Solo Difficult ★

120m. Consistently interesting easy climbing up the right side of the crag. There is an area of vegetation at half-height with a short corner above it, just right of a lone tree near the top of the wall. Climb up to the right side of the vegetated area, then head straight up to a fine finish up the corner.
Steve Broadbent & Caroline Culwick, April 2011.

9. Logan Lovin' Very Difficult ★

120m. This pleasant climb follows the rib to the right of a vegetated gully high on the face. Start beneath a pale patch of rock under steep black rock, immediately left of an orange overhang. Go up some difficult black rock left of the overhang to an oasis. Move up right, then head back left to finish up the fine steep rib, or more easily on the right.
Will Benfold & Steve Broadbent, February 2012.

Will Benfold, solo on *Logan Lovin'* (V.Diff) ➲
Photo: Steve Broadbent

Area Map
Crag Selector
Intro
The Climbing
How to Use
Suggested Climbs
Tafraout Granite
Anergui
Ameln Valley
Tarakatine Pass
Sidi M'Zal
Jebel Taskra
Idaougnidif
Afantinzar
Samazar
Aouguenz
Tagzene
Tagmout
History
Index

Area Map
Crag Selector
Intro
The Climbing
How to Use
Suggested Climbs
Tafraout Granite
Anergui
Ameln Valley
Tarakatine Pass
Sidi M'Zal
Jebel Taskra
Idaougnidif
Afantinzar
Samazar
Aouguenz
Tagzene
Tagmout
History
Index

B TASSILA BASTION

Shade Families Hitch Roadside

Drive from Tafraout: **1 hour**
Walk-in: **10 minutes**

A pleasant cragging venue, with an easy approach from parking in Tassila village, opposite a large gated house (see map on page 186). Walk around the right-hand side of the large house to follow a small path running leftwards to the crag. Follow this path along the full length of the crag – the routes are located at the far left-hand end.

DESCENT: Scramble down the left-hand end of the crag.

1. Carter Crack Severe

30m. The shady corner, then cracks up leftwards.
R.Eckersley & M.Newbury, March 2014

2. Wannabe HS 4b

30m. Climb the corner by a tree to the left of the wall. finish up a steep wide crack above.
E.Alsford & P.Donnithorne, March 2014

3. Chewbacca Crack HS 4c

30m. Start two metres right of the tree in the shady corner and follow the crack to the top.
M.Newbury & R.Eckersley, March 2014

4. Katreen Severe

30m. The left-slanting crack 2m left of *Mrs Sausage Casserole*. Step right after the crack and finish direct.
K.Lyle, May 2013

5. Mrs Sausage Casserole HVS 5a

30m. Start under a hanging block, which is gained with some excitement. Climb the arête on its right and finish up an easy slab.
R.Eckersley, May 2013

6. March of the Pencil HS 4c ★2

30m. A good climb, starting just left of a small stone wall in a corner at the base of prominent twin cracks. Gain the left-hand crack and follow it to the top.
R.Eckersley, April 2013

7. The Bastion VS 4c ★2

30m. Good climbing up the right-hand crack.
R.Eckersley, April 2013

8. Pisses pas sur mes Frites VS 4c ★2

30m. An excellent little route. Start as for *The Bastion*, but continue straight up via cracks, passing a bush on the left.
F.Richard, May 2013

9. Shard Dancer HS 4b ★1

30m. Follow *The Bastion* for 10 metres, then traverse right to climb a wide groove. Trend up right past a hanging block to easier ground.
B.Carter, May 2013

10. The Egotist HVS 5a ★1

30m. Starts at a bush in a short groove. Climb the groove then swing left onto the wall, following cracks to the upper overlap. Pull through this and finish up a thin crack.
P.Donnithorne & E.Alsford, March 2014

11. Arch Enemy E1 5b ★1

30m. The groove leading to the arched overhang is better than it looks. Move delicately right at the overhang and pull steeply through its right-hand side. Continue more easily via a bulge and crack at the top.
E.Alsford & P.Donnithorne, March 2014

12. Flanking Attack HVS 5a ★1

40m. The groove 30 metres right of *Arch Enemy*, pulling through two bulges at the top.
P.Donnithorne & E.Alsford, March 2014

13. Wheeler's Wisdom HVS 4c

40m. Start just right of the groove taken by *Flanking Attack*. Follow a vague arête, trending up and right through a steep section to easier ground. Finish with a steep pull through the upper bulge.
A.Chubb & G.Hustinx, March 2015.

The Golden Compass (E1) on the Third Tower of Adrar Umlil (page 208). Will Benfold climbing. ➲
Photo: Steve Broadbent

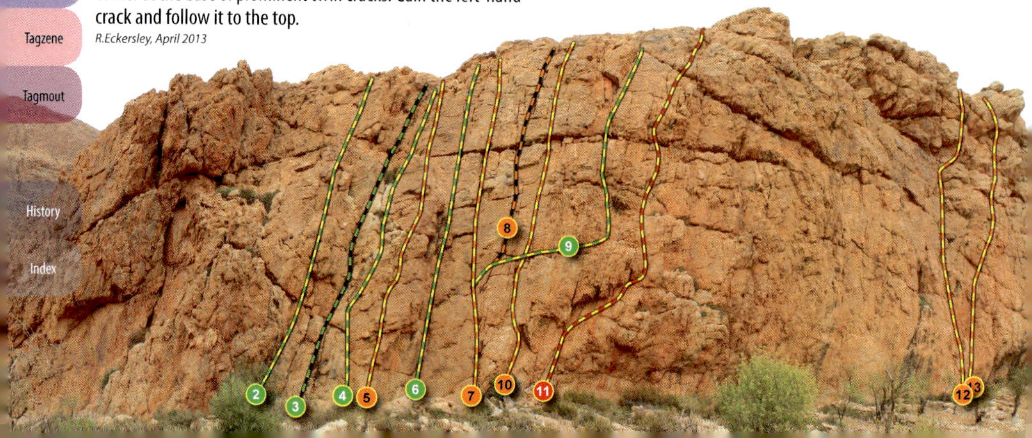

THE AMZKHSSAN SUMMITS

The magnificent summits and crags on the south side of the valley above Amzkhssan are home to some of the finest multi-pitch routes in the region, and have become a justifiably popular destination in recent years. These high crags offer first-class routes throughout the grade range, from long mountain classics to Anti-Atlas test-pieces, all in a wonderful mountain setting.

Most of the crags are accessed via a very pleasant approach walk of 30–60 minutes through some stunning scenery. Reaching altitudes of almost 2000m above sea level, the Amzkhssan summits are a good choice during spells of hot weather, when they often provide an escape from the heat without the moss that is often a feature of other cooler venues.

A poor unsurfaced track leaves the Afantinzar Road just after the first set of hairpins above Amzkhssan, at a blind junction signposted to Tassila and Agrd-Imoul. This track descends to an attractive waterfall (the *Cascade d'Iffni*) before climbing back up to a collection of large houses beneath low crags. This is Tassila village, and paths leave this point for Adrar Iffran, Arrow Rock, Adrar Asmit, and Adrar Umlil. Above Tassila the rough track continues to the ancient village of Agrd Imoul – the access to Buzzard Crag and the north face of Adrar Iffran.

Parking in Tassila is limited, and on private ground. If it is full, please park at the *Cascade d'Iffni* waterfall (10 minute walk).

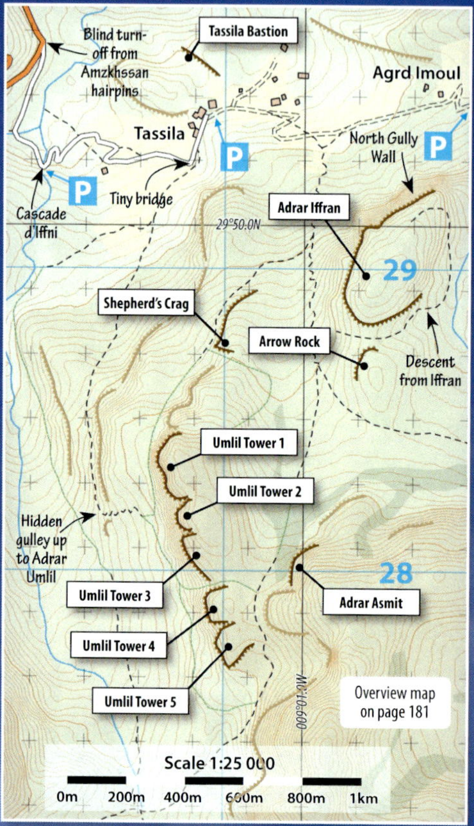

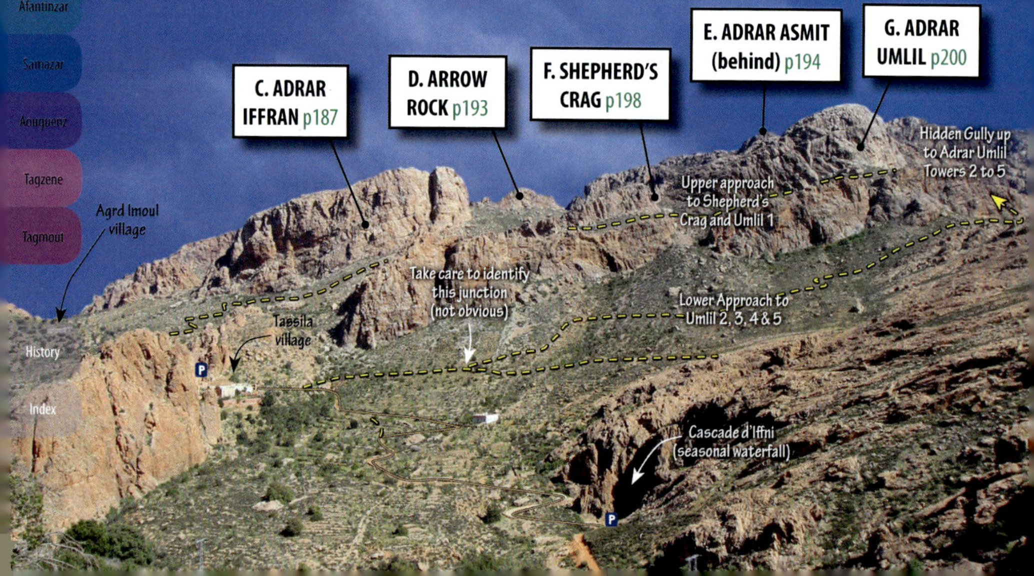

C ADRAR IFFRAN

Sun Shade Families Hitch Roadside

Drive from Tafraout: **1 hour**
Walk-in: **15 to 45 minutes**

The left-hand of two dominant peaks on the south side of the valley overlooking Amzkhssan has a prominent square-cut notch on its west face. This is the tremendous crag of Adrar Iffran (The Peak of the Caves) which once provided a fortified dwelling for early settlers. The summit is guarded on four sides by steep crags, and although much of the rock is not attractive for climbing there are a number of very high-quality routes here that are well-worth a visit. The mountain has two faces of real interest to the climber – the fearful north face, overlooking the village of Tassila, and the sunny southwest face above the high mountain pastures.

NORTH GULLY WALL

The extensive and impressive north face, with its intimidating and loose-looking overhangs, towers over Tassila village. North Gully Wall is the upper-left part of the face behind a blind gully, and is best approached from the higher village of Agrd Imoul.

DESCENT: Descend via the rock ramp to the left of *Lone Tree Rib*, or abseil from the top of *The Mighty Logan*.

1. Lone Tree Rib HS 4a ★2

90m. This is the first rib on the left side of the face, reached by stepping in from the right. Climb the rib to a jammed boulder, where a step over the cleft gains a groove leading to the lone tree. Scramble easily off to the left.
Ben Wintringham, Mike Mortimer, Marion Wintringham, October 2009.

2. Jekyll & Hyde E1 5b ★1

90m. The obvious chimney 20m up North Gully Wall is strangely compelling...
1) 55m (5a) Climb the chimney.
2) 35m (5b) Trend left to gain a steep crack leading to an easier finish.
Paul Donnithorne & Pete Johnson, March 2010.

3. What a Cheek HVS 5a BOLD LOOSE

80m. The steep wall to the left of *Em's Cleft* is a worrying route on fragile rock, climbed in 3 pitches 5a, 4c, 4c to finish up a prominent V-notch.
Ben & Marion Wintringham, October 2009.

Area Map
Crag Selector
Intro
The Climbing
How to Use
Suggested Climbs
Tafraout Granite
Anergui
Ameln Valley
Tarakatine Pass
Sidi M'Zal
Jebel Taskra
Idaougnidif
Afantinzar
Samazar
Aouguenz
Tagzene
Tagmout
History
Index

Area Map
Crag Selector
Intro
The Climbing
How to Use
Suggested Climbs
Tafraout Granite
Anergui
Ameln Valley
Tarakatine Pass
Sidi M'Zal
Jebel Taskra
Idaougnidif
Afantinzar
Samazar
Aouguenz
Tagzene
Tagmout
History
Index

4. Em's Cleft E1 5a

70m. Fine, traditional stuff up the delightful cleft.
1) 35m (5a) Climb the cleft to a ledge.
2) 35m (5a) Go up a big flake, climb a chimney and squeeze behind a chockstone.
Paul Donnithorne & Mike Mortimer, October 2009.

5. The Mighty Logan E4 5c

75m. The flake in the centre of the wall is a classic testpiece, and one of the best routes of its grade in the area. Start 12m right of *Em's Cleft* beneath a leaning black and orange groove.
1) 30m (5c) Gain the groove and follow it to a bulge. Surmount this, then trend up left to a flake crack, which leads to a good stance.
2) 30m (5b) Climb a steep flake, then a slabby groove to a small stance.
3) 15m (5a) Super climbing rightwards along a crack above the roof to gain the first groove. Follow this to the top.
Adam Mulholland & Paul Donnithorne, October 2009.

6. Wandering Star E2 5b

90m. This route wanders its way up to and around the huge curving corner, providing another fine outing.
1) 40m (5b) Start up a crack, which leads to a bulge. Traverse left above this (bold) to a vague groove, and follow this until it is possible to climb back rightwards to gain the alluring corner.
2) 30m (5b) Climb the crack for 5m, then move up left to the roof. Traverse to a stance at the end of the roof.
3) 20m (5a) Step up left around a rib to a steep finish up a wall.
Ben & Marion Wintringham, October 2010.

7. The Lixt Crack E2 5c

100m. Further up the blind gully is a series of cracks. This route climbs the right-hand, most continuous crack, trending right to a steep corner crack and chimney with large chockstones. 3 pitches, 5b, 5c, 4c.
Paul Donnithorne & Mike Mortimer, October 2009.

THE NORTH FACE

The ferocious north face of Iffran sees little traffic, and the following climbs are all likely to be adventurous routes suitable only for strong parties. The first lines tackle the wall below North Gully.

DESCENT: Descend from the first two routes down North Gully.

8. The Gongscourers HVS

60m. A rather disappointing route, starting just right of the east end of the cliff.
1) Climb a black groove to a tree.
2) Go right along the ledge to a rib right of a chimney. Climb the rib until it is possible to move left into the chimney, which is followed to an easy descent down North Gully.
Mike Pycroft, Pete Johnson & Paul Donnithorne, October 2010.

9. Light My Fire E3 5c

75m. The first pitch opened on the north face is a modern classic, giving beautifully sustained, technical and exposed climbing. It is gained by scrambling 50m up white slabs to a terrace below the roof.
1) 35m (5c) Start up the corner directly underneath the roof and go right via a wide crack when the holds run out. From the alcove take the lowest fist-sized diagonal crack and fight

your way up it with technical hand jamming, great moves and small footholds. At the end of the wall go up a wide groove to a diving-board belay with large cams.

2a) *The Central finish* 40m (5a) The best finish heads straight up the rib above the belay to a steep short corner. Finish up an easy slab to the right.

2b) *The Right Hand Finish* 40m (5a) This inferior, but still pleasant, alternative traverses steeply rightwards off the belay for 3m to pull over the lip of the overhang into a final groove.

Emmanuel Freudenthal & Arnaud Viel, October 2009.

The next routes climb the full height of the north face, finishing on the summit of Adrar Iffran.

DESCENT: Descent from the summit can be awkward. Head to the north-eastern corner of the summit plateau, where the ancient remains of buildings mark the start of a man-made trail heading initially south across the slabs of the east face. Continue south on a vague path, ascending slightly to regain the small col between Adrar Iffran and Arrow Rock. See map on page 186.

10. The Nibbler E4 5c ★2 BOLD

200m. The line of lines... The most direct, uncompromising and fearsome line on the north face is a mighty impressive climb and one of the region's big E4 ticks. It takes the central, overhanging rib, which is an irresistible impossibility in the evening light. Stunning.

Adam Mulholland & Lorna Jones, October 2009.

11. Rainy Day Dream Away E1 5a ★1 BOLD

180m. A brave endeavour with lots of average climbing and a very bold crux high on the face. Start at a small roof at the base of grey slabs in the centre of the face.

1) 45m (-) Go up the right side of the roof then move left into a shallow groove to a ledge.

2) 30m (4a) Go up and left below a roof, then step up into a crack to another ledge.

3) 10m (-) Walk right along the ledge to beneath a black streak.

4) 35m (5a) A bold pitch up the black streak.

5) 55m (4c) Follow the groove on the right to a tree.

Pete Johnson & Mike Mortimer, October 2009.

THE NOTCH

The square-cut notch on the west face of the mountain is a prominent feature marking the right-hand end of the north face.

12. Oriental Orbits HVS 5a ★2 BOLD

185m. A worthwhile outing starting about 30m left of the square-cut notch.

1) 30m (4b) Keep to the left of the large gully and follow a simple-looking crack. Once over the top continue for 15m to a large ledge.

2) 30m (4c) Leave the subsidiary tower, taking the main face to the right for sustained VS climbing.

3) 40m (4c) Continue up the near-vertical face but duck out right when the going gets tough. Belay just round the corner in the gully.
4) 60m (5a) Head vertically upwards, tackling a steep sequence of HVS moves followed by some easier ground and an interesting slab.
5) 25m (4a) An easy crack heads off to the left – take this and go for the summit, topping out with excitement and celebrations.
Adam Bradley & Graham Lee, March 2009.

13. Recessed Wall HVS 4c ★2

185m. A wandering line that was just waiting to be climbed, taking the back wall of the notch.
1) (4b) Start left of the centre of the wall, trending up and right to belay in the gully on the right.
2) (4b) Climb left of the gully, behind a tree, and back onto the face to a ledge.
3) (4c) A rising traverse from the right end of the ledge leads to bold moves leftwards to a narrow ledge.
4) (-) Easier climbing from the left end of the narrow ledge.
Chris Bull & Alison Parker, October 2009.

14. The Golden Pillar of Askabhan E2 5b ★1

150m. The left arête of the southwest face, climbed in three long pitches.
1) 60m (5a) Start just right of the arête, climb a vague crack in the slab then move up to a large ledge. Move right onto a bulge, then pull over the overhang to belay on top of a pinnacle.
2) 30m (5b) Climb the groove above, moving left to the arete. When possible, traverse back right past a good ledge to belay below an overhanging crack / groove.
3) 60m (5a) Climb the steep crack then move left to the arete. Continue up this in a fine position to a summit pinnacle.
Bob Brewer & Dai Lampard, March 2014.

THE SOUTHWEST FACE

To the right of the Notch the face swings round towards a small col between Adrar Iffran and Arrow Rock. This superb, sun-drenched wall is home to some of the finest mid-grade climbs on the mountain, featuring exposed climbing on generally sound rock. There is a small pillar at the base of the face, and to the right of this a low white ledge from where Goldrush begins.

DESCENT: As for the north face (see previous page).

15. West Face Indirect VS 4c ★2

125m. A devious route that gains and climbs the attractive clean wall above the overhangs, with some excellent face climbing and intricate route-finding. Start from the left end of a pale rock ledge at the right side of the west face.

1) 30m (-) Climb up a straightforward gully, exiting left to ledges.
2) 30m (4c) Go up to a difficult move to gain the excellent corner crack. Follow this for 6m then step left onto the white face, which provides superb climbing to a small overhang. Go left beneath this into a vegetated bay.
3) 10m (-) Walk left across the vegetated bay to belay near the arête.
4) 20m (4a) Climb left onto the arête and gain a narrow ledge that traverses left across the face. Follow this for 7m to a groove, then work back up and right to a stance with vegetation.
5) 30m (4a) Climb the crack / groove to a large bay, and exit left up some worrying tottering blocks to what appears to be the end of the climb.
6) 5m (-) Move right and finish up the crack in the short wall.
Steve & Katja Broadbent, October 2008.

16. Bubble and Squeak E1 5b

? UNCHECKED

130m. This route starts 8 metres left of *Ruby Groove* at a wide crack/chimney, but has not been positively located.
1) 30m (4c) Climb ramps and the chimney to a large ledge.
2) 45m (5a) Take the weakness through the roof above, then trend right and up to a stance.
3) 55m (5b) Climb up for 4m, taking the roof on its right side. Traverse right to a crack, and follow this to a corner. Climb up diagonally below the large roof to the arête, then finish up a final crack.
R.Barr, T.Penning, November 2015.

17. Guillotine Direct VS 4c ★3

105m. The central groove line is an Anti-Atlas classic, giving fine, varied, and sustained climbing. The groove to the left of pitch 1 gives an alternative start (*Ruby Groove*, 4c).
1) 30m (-) A straightforward gully leads to large ledges as for *West Face Indirect*.
2) 35m (4c) Go straight up the corner to a steepening, where an excellent undercut layback traverse leads out to the right. Regain the corner above this and follow it to a narrow rock ledge.
3) 40m (4c) Continue up the corner-crack with increasing difficulty to a sequence of bold moves beneath the capping overhang (the Guillotine). This is avoided by a hand-traverse left as for *Goldrush*.
Steve Broadbent & Iza Pstrucha, February 2009.

18. Pinky and Perky HVS 5a ★2

130m. A good climb, taking an improbable line through the huge overhangs. Start 2m right of *Guillotine Direct*.
1) 55m (4c) Climb shallow grooves in the wall right of the corner to a stance on the slabs.
2) 40m (4c) Go easily up and right to the stepped crack through the first overhang. Climb this before a traverse right leads to a belay beneath the upper overhang.
3) 35m (5a) Traverse horizontally right, then cross a bold white wall to gain a final rib.
Pete Johnson & Paul Donnithorne, March 2010.

19. Goldrush HVS 5a ★2

GEAR

115m. The line of the first ascent is a superb and popular climb with great variety, starting up the vague rib between the west and southwest faces and finishing through steep ground left of the upper overhangs. Some questionable rock requires a careful approach, but the climb is generally low in the grade.
1) 20m (-) Enjoyable easy climbing up the front of the buttress to a good ledge.
2) 15m (4b) The wide crack above the ledge has a couple of tricky moves. Continue rightwards until a short traverse back left gains a small rock ledge.
3) 30m (4a) Go straight up steep ground on excellent jugs until the angle eases to a large ledge beneath the upper overhangs.
4) 25m (5a) Climb a weakness in the steepening, heading for the left side of the roofs. Once over the steep section step left to a very poor stance.
5) 25m (4c) Follow the excellent rib until forced left into the corner, then hand-traverse left under the final overhanging block.
Steve & Katja Broadbent, October 2008. Photo next page.

20. Voyager E2 5b ★3

GEAR

130m. A superb, dramatic climb with gradually increasing interest and magnificent positions. Start immediately left of a large, shallow orange cave at the foot of the face.
1) 35m (4a) Climb up the left side of the cave to a ledge on the right.
2) 35m (-) Go up a groove then trend up right to a stance by a 'slab' weakness in the first roof.
3) 30m (5a) Pull up onto the slab which leads up through the first roof. Easy climbing above to a belay in the corner below the upper roof.
4) 30m (5b) Climb slabs into a steep corner, then pull left onto the hanging hand-traverse. Follow this to a finish up a bottomless corner/groove.
Will Benfold & Steve Broadbent, October 2014. Photo page 197

21. Curious HVS 5b ★1

105m. An alternative start to *Catastrophe and the Cure*, giving another worthwhile climb.
1) 50m (5b) Climb up the crack before moving up onto a wall. Follow this to a ledge.
2) 55m (-) Upwards through very steep but easy ground.
Chris Bull & Alison Parker, October 2009.

22. Gabion in a Basket E4 6a ★1

95m. A fine, challenging climb, starting just right of *Curious*.
1) 15m (5c) Climb the obvious splitter crack.
2) 35m (6a) Traverse right for 5 metres, then climb directly up onto a nose (crux). Swing around the nose and trend left, continuing more easily to a stance by a square block below a roof.
3) 40m (6a) Climb through the double roof via a large slot and continue to the top.
R.Barr, T.Penning, November 2015.

Area Map
Crag Selector
Intro
The Climbing
How to Use
Suggested Climbs
Tafraout Granite
Anergui
Ameln Valley
Tarakatine Pass
Sidi M'Zal
Jebel Taskra
Idaougnidif
Afantinzar
Samazar
Aouguenz
Tagzene
Tagmout
History
Index

23. Catastrophe and the Cure VS 4c ★1

125m. The big crack to the left of the huge cave is easier than appearances suggest, and leads to easier ground in-between the overhangs.

1) 35m (4c) Climb the crack to a small ledge beneath the overhangs.

2) 55m (4b) Traverse left under the overlap to a bold finish up steep blocks left of the vegetated corner.

Jayson Orton & Elie Dekoninck, October 2008.

24. Eye of the Lion VS 4c ★2

55m. A worthwhile excursion to the '*Eye of Allah*' cave.

1) 40m (4c) Climb ramps up leftwards onto the wall until an easy traverse right gains a corner. Follow this to the cave.

2) 15m (4c) Step right onto a dry stone wall and finish up the obvious crack above.

R.Barr, T.Penning, November 2015.

25. Eyebrow Arête Very Difficult

ABSEIL

70m. The curving arête over the Eye of Allah cave leads to an abseil descent.

D.Medcalf & C.Woodhead, March 2013.

Katja Broadbent making the first ascent of Adrar Iffran via the popular *Goldrush* (HVS 5a) ➲

Photo: Elie Dekoninck

D ARROW ROCK

Shade

Drive from Tafraout: **1 hour**
Walk-in: **45 minutes**

The small triangular buttress to the south of Adrar Iffran is home to some high-quality and delicate pitches on immaculate rock that remain in the shade for much of the day. This makes it an excellent choice on hot afternoons. It is approached in about 45 minutes up a good path from Tassila (as for Adrar Iffran). See overview on page 186

1. Surrender Monkey VS 4b

40m. Climb the lower slab and groove above

Jayson Orton & Elie Dekoninck, October 2008.

2. Silverback VS 4c ★1 BOLD

75m. An interesting climb, taking a right-slanting diagonal line from the left side of the grey slab.

1) 50m (4a) Climb up to the headwall and follow the ramp rightwards, moving up to a ledge between the two main cracks .

2) 25m (4c) Make a committing move from the block on the right, stepping down across the void and onto the slab. Traverse rightwards to finish up the arête.

C.Ford & E.Wright, October 2013.

3. Baby Killing Box VS 4b ★3 SLAB

40m. A superb climb, and one of the best pitches of its grade in the area. Follow a thin crack up the initial slab until a difficult move gains an L-shaped recess which is climbed to the top.

Jayson Orton & Elie Dekoninck, October 2008.

4. Dilapidated Eyes & Sexy Sighs E2 5a ★2 BOLD

40m. A good test of climbing nerve. Gain a thin diagonal crack then follow the slab left of the gully to a short pillar. The headwall above is very bold, and barely protected by a poor wire runner.

Jayson Orton & Elie Dekoninck, October 2008.

5. Technique is for Girls E2 5c ★3 SLAB

45m. This magnificent pitch features one of the best slabs in the area, with technical climbing throughout. Reachy moves up the smooth slab behind the boulder lead to the blunt arête. Climb this to a small ledge below the headwall and continue up a recess, finishing left.

Jayson Orton & Elie Dekoninck, October 2008.

6. Wool Carpet Good for Jiggy Jiggy HVS 4c / Severe

45m. Climb the groove / crack, going left around the first bulge and right around the second. Continue into the big groove and finish up the wall to the right. An escape up the big cleft is also possible, reducing the grade to Severe (4a).

Jayson Orton & Elie Dekoninck, October 2008.

7. Desperate Donkey VS 4c

50m. Start up the shallow right-facing corner then move up and right into the big groove. Follow this until forced left, before regaining the groove and swinging right to finish on the right wall.

Jayson Orton (solo), October 2008.

8. Straight as an Arrow E2 5b

50m. The blunt arête right of *Desperate Donkey*, finishing up the corner as for that route.

Brian Davison & Paul Wood, December 2014.

9. Quiver Me Timbers! MVS 4b ★1

35m. The rib and groove just right of the large overhang requires a fairly confident approach. Start up a steep crack to join the rib from the left side. Follow this to a technical finish up the upper groove.

Steve Broadbent & Iza Pstrucha, February 2009.

E ADRAR ASMIT

Shade · Families · Hitch · Roadside

Drive from Tafraout: **1 hour**
Walk-in: **1 hour**

This minor peak forms the westerly end of a long line of cliffs above and behind Adrar Iffran and Adrar Umlil, but is not easy to see or identify from the Amzkhssan valley. It is, however, surprisingly easy to access by following the good shepherd's path from Tassila, as if walking to Adrar Iffran or Arrow Rock. Beyond Arrow Rock the path becomes rather small and indistinct, but can be followed with care towards a pass on the right skyline, with the back side of Adrar Umlil on the right. Adrar Asmit is the buttress to the left of the pass, reached in about 15 minutes from Arrow Rock (1 hour from the road).

Routes here have a superbly remote feel to them, and will suit climbers looking for a slightly 'out of the way' mountain adventure. The rock is generally excellent, and the views cannot fail to inspire exploration of this superb mountain landscape. Indeed, for climbers operating in the lower grades Adrar Asmit provides some of the best mountain routes in the area and a visit to this fine viewpoint more than justifies the rather lengthy approach.

DESCENT: Descent from the summit is simple, if a little prickly. Drop down into the notch between the top of the crag and the mountain behind, then turn left and descend a broad vegetated gully. At the bottom, cut back left to regain the base of the north face.

THE NORTH FACE

This deceptively steep wall lies on the left side of the crag when viewed from the walk-in.

1. Thin Air E4 5c ★2 CRACK STEEP

85m. The striking crack-line up the left side of the north face gives a tremendous and strenuous journey... Who said this was a friendly place to climb?
1) 20m (5c) The steep crack leads to a belay on the white flake.
2) 25m (5c) Continue (if you can) up the crack to a belay on the right beneath an off-width crack.
3) 40m (5b) The off-width provides respite only for those who like that kind of thing, but does lead to easier ground eventually.
Paul Donnithorne & Pete Johnson, March 2012.

2. High on Crack E2 5c ★2 UNCHECKED CRACK STEEP

90m. This route reportedly starts 7 metres left of *Childbirth*, below a stepped ramp, but the exact line has not been identified.
1) 30m (4c) Climb the ramp, then trend left up a broken groove system to ledges.
2) 60m (5b) Step right and climb up a steep rib, left of a groove. Continue to gain and climb an overhanging crack line on the left, which leads to a ledge below a wall (possible belay). Climb up the wall to finish up twin vertical cracks.
A.Price & R.Neath, November 2011.

3. Childbirth E1 5b ★1

LOOSE CRACK STEEP

100m. A long and brutal battle up the wide crack at the right side of the north face, featuring a whole spectrum of difficulties, moss, and loose rock... as well as some magnificently steep climbing that is consistently harder than it looks. The star is deserved with the benefit of hindsight.

1) 25m (5b) The climb begins as it means to go on... with great difficulty. The initial crack leads to some steep climbing on the fragile left wall before the relief of belay ledges.

2) 25m (5b) Wildly steep climbing up the overhanging crack leads to a chimney. Traditional technique then lands one on another very welcome ledge.

3) 30m (5a) The continuation of the chimney is somewhat easier until a step left gains a very fine corner crack to a left-slanting ramp. Follow this in a magnificent position to a belay stance beneath a steepening.

4) 20m (5a) Continue leftwards up the ramp to some bold and steep moves, then finish leftwards to an enormous boulder.

Steve Broadbent & Rachel Mellor, October 2009.

THE NORTHWEST FACE

To the right of the north face the rock swings round on to the northwest face and becomes more gently-angled. This excellent climbing ground looks broken and unattractive from below, but catches the afternoon sun and is home to some tremendous easy climbs on immaculate rock.

4. West Side Story Severe ★2

140m. A very agreeable climb up the vague rib between the north and northwest faces, with continual exposure and a challenging crux. The route starts up a smooth rib just to the left of the left-hand of two low trees.

1) 45m (-) Climb the rib easily to a tree behind a large pinnacle (possible belay on a ledge at 30m).

2) 35m (4a) Step up onto the wall behind the tree and make a rising leftwards traverse to a small tree in a niche beneath a vegetated groove.

3) 50m (-) Step left onto the fine rib and follow it to the top of the crag with some superb positions.

Steve Broadbent & Sally Fitton, March 2010.

5. The Shepherd's Song / Pastorale MVS 4c ★1

150m. *Pastorale* follows a direct and at times unlikely line up the northwest face, straightening out three of the original routes.

1) 30m (-) Start as for *West Side Story*, gaining the sloping ledge with prominent tree. Climb the wall to the right to gain a detached block above the tree, then continue to a belay under a vague crack.

2) 35m (4c) Climb straight up to a red pillar and make an overhanging move to a belay on its top.

3) 25m (4a) Climb the wall on the right to the top of a small tower (as for Culture Shock).

4) 25m (4a) The steep headwall is an intimidating prospect, but has good holds and leads to a very exposed belay on a small pulpit.

5) 40m (-) Move up right to join the upper section of *Wild Country* above the *Black Groove*, with a possible belay as for that route if required.

Alberto Rampini & Silvia Mazzani, October 2010.

6. Central Slabs Severe ★1

145m. A pleasant, low-commitment route featuring lots of easy climbing and an avoidable crux right at the top, allowing the route to be ascended at Very Difficult standard.

1) As for *Culture Shock*.

2) 30m Climb slabby ground left of the steep buttress to a belay on the side of the gully.

3) 30m Cross the gully and climb a pleasant rib to a good belay ledge left of the bush.

4) 30m Up the continuation rib for 20m then step right at a chockstone to gain another rib to a good ledge.

5) 25m Climb a steep crack through poor-looking orange rock left of the gully. This can easily be avoided on the left, reducing the overall grade to Very Difficult.

Steve Broadbent & Rachel Mellor, October 2009.

Area Map
Crag Selector
Intro
The Climbing
How to Use
Suggested Climbs
Tafraout Granite
Anergui
Ameln Valley
Tarakatine Pass
Sidi M'Zal
Jebel Taskra
Idaougnidif
Afantinzar
Samazar
Aouguenz
Tagzene
Tagmout
History
Index

7. Culture Shock HVS 5a ★1 BOLD STEEP

150m. An adventurous outing up the centre of the face, with some pleasant easy climbing lower down, and an excitingly exposed crux high on the route.

1) 25m Start in between two trees low on the right side of the face and climb a left-slanting diagonal crack up the initial white wall to a ledge and huge thread.

2) 25m Scramble straight up to a ledge and small bush beneath a steep orange tower.

3) 15m (4a) ***The Red Pillar*** – The tower is climbed steeply to a small rock ledge.

4) 25m Easy ground straight up to a terrace beneath the steep orange wall.

5) 27m (4a) ***The Orange Wall*** – From chockstones at the upper left end of the terrace, go up suspect-looking steep ground to gain a left-trending ramp. Follow this with excellent exposure to a poor belay around the corner. The way ahead looks unlikely...

6) 10m (5a) A serious pitch. Move out left onto an exposed nose, then make a tricky traverse back right to gain the crack in the niche. Climb this to a stance.

7) 23m (4a) Continue up the groove-line trending up and left to an excellent steep finish on black rock.

Steve Broadbent & Iza Pstrucha, February 2009.

8. Wild Country Very Difficult ★3 BOLD

145m. With a remote setting, easy approach and descent, solid rock, large belay stances and some tremendous climbing, this is one of the finest easy routes in the Anti-Atlas. Commitment is generally low, though parties should be prepared to encounter some bold climbing as well as a technically challenging crux high on the route.

1) 35m Start just right of a tree in a small bay on the right side of the face. Climb easily up white rocks, with one tricky move off a ledge, until the angle steepens and the rock takes on a pinkish brown hue. Step right to a good ledge.

2) 20m Move back left onto the brown rock and climb straight up to a ledge with a bush.

3) 20m The wall above offers a number of possible lines, though some are rather bold. Options to the left are generally easier and better protected. Boulder-belay on a large ledge below and right of the steep orange wall.

4) 10m Go rightwards up a cracked wall to belay by a bush in a left-slanting groove system.

5) 30m ***The Black Groove Pitch*** – first class climbing up the slanting groove system above the steep orange wall, with perfect protection and superb exposure. Interest is maintained throughout, until a distinct crux marks the end of the difficulties at 25m. From here an easy ramp leads 5m left to a stance.

6) 30m Easy scrambling, with big holds, good rock, and lots of exposure.

Steve & Katja Broadbent, October 2008.

Will Benfold on the airy traverse of *Voyager* (E2 5b), page 191 ➲

Photo: Steve Broadbent

F SHEPHERD'S CRAG

Shade Families Hitch Roadside Drive from Tafraout: **1 hour** Walk-in: **20 minutes**

This pleasant crag is located to the left (East) of the Left Wing of Adrar Umlil. All climbs to date are located at the right-hand end of the crag, where it swings round onto the west-facing sidewall of one of the White Dome descent gullies. Approach from Tassila village initially as for Adrar Iffran, but take a path heading rightwards over a small col towards Tower 1 of Adrar Umlil (The White Dome). The approach takes approximately 20 minutes along good paths (see overview on page 186).

THE FRONT FACE

For the most part, the crag's 'front' (northwest) face consists of very compact rock, and although there are many possible lines, protection is almost non-existent. At the right-hand end of the crag, however, just before the broad descent gully, the following lines are much more amenable:

DESCENT: Scramble up and right to reach a short down-climb into a broad descent gully.

1. Vandal HS 4a ★

40m. The left-hand groove, to join the next route at two-thirds height.
Dave Arthur, Will Benfold & Mary Slingo, October 2014

2. The Van of Life MVS 4b ★

35m. Good climbing up the thinner, left-hand crack up the front of the tower.
Mary Slingo, Will Benfold & Dave Arthur, October 2014

3. Golden Gate Crack MVS 4a ★

35m. The wide crack gives some excellent bridging, and is much less of a struggle than appearances suggest.
Steve Broadbent & Caroline Culwick, October 2014

THE WEST FACE

This attractive face forms the side-wall of a broad descent gully.

4. Pimp Pethera MVS 4b ★

35m. The right-hand side of the buttress just right of the chimney, heading for an upper crack to a pinnacle.
Will Benfold, Mary Slingo & Dave Arthur, October 2014

5. Yan Tan Tethera HVS 5a ★

35m. Excellent climbing, straight up to the obvious small roof. Pull rightwards through this and then step back left on to the short face above.
Steve Broadbent & Caroline Culwick, October 2014

6. Pip Dick Bumfit Jigget VS 4b

35m. Start as for the previous route, but move right to climb a broken groove.

Caroline Culwick & Steve Broadbent, October 2014

7. Silverline HVS 4c

30m. The left-hand of two vague cracks up the narrow square buttress. Difficult, bold moves gain the crack through a steepening.

Caroline Culwick & Steve Broadbent, October 2014

8. Master of Magnesium HS 4a

30m. Pleasant climbing up the right-hand of two vague cracks.

Steve Broadbent & Caroline Culwick, October 2014

9. The Van of Death VS 4c

25m. The steep groove and corner crack immediately left of a vegetated gully.

Mary Slingo & Will Benfold, October 2014

10. Edero Bumfit Very Difficult

25m. The wall to the right of the gully is a poorly protected pitch, but gives some nice enough climbing.

Steve Broadbent & Caroline Culwick, October 2014

11. Methera Bum Very Difficult

20m. The vague groove just to the right...

Steve Broadbent & Caroline Culwick, October 2014

12. Ginhaler Very Difficult

20m. The narrow face in between two grooves.

Steve Broadbent & Caroline Culwick, October 2014

13. Ten Climb Challenge Difficult

15m. The easy groove eases rapidly towards the top...

Steve Broadbent & Caroline Culwick, October 2014

14. Inadequate Gin Difficult

15m. The escapable rib.

Caroline Culwick & Steve Broadbent, October 2014

Area Map
Crag Selector
Intro
The Climbing
How to Use
Suggested Climbs
Tafraout Granite
Anergui
Ameln Valley
Tarakatine Pass
Sidi M'Zal
Jebel Taskra
Idaougnidif
Afantinzar
Samazar
Aouguenz
Tagzene
Tagmout
History
Index

G ADRAR UMLIL

Shade Families Hitch Roadside

Drive from Tafraout: **1 hour**
Walk-in: **1:00 to 1:20**

Towering above Amzkhssan and Tassila, Adrar Umlil is one of the most significant crags in the Idaougnidif area. The Berber 'Adrar Umlil' means '*the White Mountain*', and indeed when viewed from the Afantinzar Road above Amzkhssan, it appears as an isolated, pale, dome-shaped summit. In reality, however, this is merely a glimpse of an extensive and varied crag that comprises five independent towers and some of the very best multi-pitch routes in the region.

Umlil once had a reputation for being the preserve of the extreme climber, and indeed many of the climbs here are in the upper grades. The development of the southern towers, however, has revealed some equally spectacular lower-grade routes up some impressive ground, and the crag now has plenty to offer throughout the grade range. Most of these are big routes, on immaculate rock, with some sensational climbing and high levels of commitment. Add to that a remote mountain environment, spectacular views, and availability of sunshine and shade throughout the day, and you've got one of the very finest crags in the Anti-Atlas.

Approach from Tassila village is not as arduous as first appearances suggest, provided the correct path is located. Both approaches start from the village, where there is very limited parking on private land. Climbers are therefore advised to park at the Cascade d'Iffni and walk up the track to Tassila (10 minutes). See page 186 for area overview details.

For climbs on Tower 1 (the White Dome itself, and the most northerly of the five towers) it is best to start the approach as for Adrar Iffran, up a good path that leaves the dirt road just above the village. After 15 minutes or so a narrow trail bears right, cutting under a line of low crags (Shepherd's Crag) to reach the foot of the north face.

For climbs on all other towers a much better approach leaves the dirt road at a small bridge 30 yards beneath Tassila village. The path climbs gradually through terraces (some cairns) to a final steep ascent up to the west face of the mountain (See overview on page 186).

TOWER 1 (THE WHITE DOME)

The dome-shaped Tower 1, from which this extensive crag takes its name, is the most obvious from the road and was the first to be climbed. It is comprised of high-quality, compact white quartzite, giving rise

to mostly upper-grade climbs. The north face remains in the shade for much of the day, but generally only suffers from moss following particularly wet spells. This tower is best approached via the upper approach from Adrar Iffran (see crag details on opposite page and map on page 186).

DESCENT: A terrace runs across the face at about 2/3 height, on which most of the climbs terminate - A single 55m abseil can be made from a variety of in-situ tat to regain the base of *Michael Burka*.

From those routes which continue to the summit the easiest descent is to walk east towards Adrar Iffran, though this does not return to the base of the routes. For climbers wishing to return to the start of the climbs it is possible to descend down the gully next to *Jaws*, or more easily via Shepherd's gully to the left of the Left Wing (shown on photo opposite).

1. Shark Fin Soup E2 5b ★2 WIDE BOLD

70m. The fin to the left of *Jaws* is an even more fearful proposition than that route.
1) 35m (5b) Follow *Jaws* to the mid-way belay.
2) 35m (5b) Climb diagonally left up the left wall to gain a ledge on the arête. Go up left across the steep slab (cam) then head up and right back to the arête. Pull left through overhangs to finish.
James Marshall & Brian Bigger, October 2009.

2. Jaws E1 5b ★3 WIDE BOLD

70m. The man-eating chimney at the left side of the face is the obvious line of the crag, but on closer inspection is likely to deter all but the bravest. Two 35m pitches of 5b and an array of large cams give access to the terrace.
Paul Donnithorne & Pete Johnson, October 2008.

3. The Beckoning E3 5c ★3 SLAB BOLD

120m. The desperate-looking blank slab to the right of *Jaws* is another first-class climb, and a local classic.
1) 25m (5b) Go up rightwards to a groove and follow it left to a stance.
2) 15m (5b) Cracks on the left to a ledge.
3) 40m (5c) A big pitch that tackles the harrowing slab, after a steep start on the right.
4) 20m (5c) A crack and final off-width chimney gain a ledge, from where it is possible to scramble rightwards to the *Michael Burka* abseil, or finish up *Rock the Kasbah*.
Paul Donnithorne & Pete Johnson, October 2008.

4. Jumping Jack Flash E1 5b ★2

85m. An audacious climb, tackling the right side of the *Beckoning* slab. Start at a small tower of blocks with a rosebush at the top.
1) 35m (5a) From the top of the blocks an impossible reach gains good holds. This can be achieved either with creativity

or combined tactics. Climb up to a left-trending flake which leads to a crack before joining *Rock the Kasbah*. Follow this to a belay on top of a chockstone.
2) 30m (5b) Continue up *Rock the Kasbah* for 10m, then step left into an obvious groove in the slab. Follow this to belay on a large ledge.
3) 20m (5a) Continue up the slab to a cracked-block overhang. Surmount this and climb to a ledge with a large perched block. from here it is possible to traverse right to the abseil descent, or continue up *Rock the Kasbah*.
Pete Johnson & Paul Donnithorne, November 2010.

Map Page 181 &186

Area Map
Crag Selector
Intro
The Climbing
How to Use
Suggested Climbs
Tafraout Granite
Anergui
Ameln Valley
Tarakatine Pass
Sidi M'Zal
Jebel Taskra
Idaougnidif
Afantinzar
Samazar
Aouguenz
Tagzene
Tagmout
History
Index

5. Rock the Kasbah E1 5b ★3 (GEAR, WIDE)

140m. Another magnificent and varied climb of great character, following the prominent left-facing groove in the left side of the north face. It is the only route to tackle the full height of the cliff. All of the difficult sections give very well-protected but strenuous climbing. Start at a large left-slanting slab.

1) 30m (-) Trend left up easy slabs to belay in a corner.
2) 30m (5a) Step back right and climb a blocky chimney to gain a steep corner crack. This provides excellent jamming and eventually widens to a narrow chimney before a belay in a large niche.
3) 30m (5b) The wide crack above is steep and difficult, and leads to a sloping ledge. Above the ledge it is steeper, more difficult, and requires some creative thuggery. Continue up an easier chimney above, and make a short hand traverse left to belay on a good ledge with a boulder. It is possible to split this pitch if the overhanging crack is all getting a bit too much...
4) 25m (-) Trend left up a slab then go straight up broken ground to belay below a large blank wall.
5) 25m (4b) The wall on its right side is thankfully easier than it looks.

Steve & Katja Broadbent, April 2008.

6. Michael Burka E1 5b ★2 (CRACK, ABSEIL)

50m. The excellent flake crack to the right of *Rock the Kasbah* is a classic of its type, low in the grade and well-protected. The start is accessed along a ledge from the right, and descent is by abseil down the line of the route.

Ed Bulman & Steve Pack, October 2008.

7. The Mysterons E3 5c ★2 (THIN, STEEP, ABSEIL)

75m. A challenging eliminate, for which small cams and microwires are required.

1) 55m (5c) Climb the smooth wall to a left trending crack. Follow this, keeping left of the bush, to a hard move to gain the slabs. Follow *Bishop's Climb* to belay below a groove/crack
2) 20m (5c) Climb the groove/crack then go boldly up the wall above to join *Bishop's Climb* where it finishes.
Dave Barlow & Pete Johnson, December 2010.

8. Captain Scarlet VS 4c ★1 ABSEIL

75m. This good route starts at a crackline below the sloping ramp system.
1) 55m (4c) Climb the crack, then go up the slabs to belay in the top left corner.
2) 20m (4c) Follow the dog-leg corner-crack to the big ledge.
Dave Barlow & Pete Johnson, December 2010.

9. Captain Black E2 5c ★2 BOLD ABSEIL

85m. Another worthwhile eliminate up grooves above *Bishop's Climb.*
1) 45m (5a) Start up the initial crack of *Captain Scarlet*, 20m left of *7-Up.* Move out right onto the bold wall and climb it to easy ground on the terrace of *Bishop's Climb*. Continue above this to a belay ledge.
2) 40m (5c) Go left up easy ground to a pillar/flake. From the top of this climb the difficult wall on the left, then move right to climb a bold rib up the left side of a groove.
Pete Johnson & Lun Roberts, October 2011.

10. Belay Bunny's Birthday Treat HVS 5b ★1 CRACK ABSEIL

85m. Yet another good route, gaining and climbing the tempting red chimney high on the face above *Bishop's Climb.*
1) 50m (4c) Start up a crack, cross easy ground, then continue to a belay left of the chimney.
2) 35m (5b) Go up the fine chimney, then finish up cracks above to reach the terrace.
Pete Johnson & Lun Roberts, October 2011.

11. Bishop's Climb HS 4b ★1 ABSEIL

95m. The leftwards-slanting ramp system is the only 'easy' climb on this tower, and provides a pleasant route up a big face. The first pitch is by far the most difficult, and some parties may wish to belay before the traverse left to avoid rope-drag.
1) 40m (4b) Climb the steep crack of *7 Up* as far as a ledge (possible belay). From here traverse left then step down to gain the left-slanting vegetated ramp which is climbed to a belay by a bush on a large ledge.
2) 35m (-) Work leftwards up slabs and onto the prominent ramp. Belay on the second of two good ledges.
3) 20m (4a) Continue left in a fine position until a final short wall forces a traverse right to finish close to the abseil point.
Steve & Katja Broadbent, December 2008.

12. 7 Up HVS 5b ★1 CRACK ABSEIL

100m. The left-hand of two prominent cracks on the right side of the north face. Follow the crack and left-slanting ramps for two pitches to the terrace.
Paul Donnithorne & Mike Mortimer, October 2008.

13. The Real Thing E1 5a CRACK ABSEIL

100m. The right-hand of the two crack-lines gains the terrace in two pitches.
Ben & Marion Wintringham, October 2008.

The face now begins to swing round to a more westerly aspect, becoming somewhat steeper and more intimidating as it does so.

14. The Fairest E1 5b ★2 ABSEIL

90m. Starts below thin slabby cracks, 6m left of *Snow White.*
1) 30m (5b) Climb the slabby cracks, then swing up right past a groove and into another thin crack. Traverse left in between two roofs to a fine belay at the left end of the upper roof.
2) 30m (5b) Climb up right through a niche and continue up to a groove. This leads to a good stance on the right.
3) 40m (5a) Climb a crack up left to the terrace.
Mike Mortimer & Paul Donnithorne, October 2009.

15. Snow White E3 5c ★3 WIDE

100m. A fine climb, with magnificent and challenging climbing up the prominent groove forming the boundary between the north and west faces. Follow the groove (vegetated low down), moving left beneath the second huge overhang.
Paul Donnithorne & Mike Mortimer, October 2008.

16. London Calling E2 5b ★2 BOLD ABSEIL

100m. A bold route, starting 20m right of *Snow White.*
1) 30m (5a) From the top of a large flake at 15m climb an excellent jamming crack and move up and right to a belay.
2) 45m (5b) Step back left to climb a short, difficult groove. This is followed by 10m of easier ground, then work right to the right side of the overhangs. Climb through these to a stance.
3) 25m (-) Easy climbing to the terrace.
Paul Donnithorne & Pete Johnson, October 2008.

17. The Three Dwarfs E1 5b ★3 ABSEIL

100m. A brilliant climb, following a strong line. Start below a groove between *Fairest of All* and *London Calling.*
1) 30m (5a) Climb the groove, then cracks to a roof. Swing left and climb up a steep wall to a ledge beneath the arching groove.
2) 20m (5b) Make a tricky pull into the groove and follow it to a fine slab / corner. Belay on a good ledge above.
3) 50m. Move right and follow *The Fairest of All* through the roof. Swing right into a magnificent crack system to the top.
Twid Turner, Ed Lansing & Pat Lindenbach, March 2013.

18. The Fairest of All E3 5c STEEP ABSEIL

110m. A very steep and strenuous start gives way to more slabby climbing to the terrace... Adventurous, as few details are known!
Ben & Marion Wintringham, October 2008.

19. Comes the Berber E4 6a STEEP ABSEIL

100m. A technical climb tackling the intimidating west face. Start at a perched block.

Area Map
Crag Selector
Intro
The Climbing
How to Use
Suggested Climbs
Tafraout Granite
Anergui
Ameln Valley
Tarakatine Pass
Sidi M'Zal
Jebel Taskra
Idaougnidif
Afantinzar
Samazar
Aouguenz
Tagzene
Tagmout
History
Index

Area Map
Crag Selector
Intro
The Climbing
How to Use
Suggested Climbs
Tafraout Granite
Anergui
Ameln Valley
Tarakatine Pass
Sidi M'Zal
Jebel Taskra
Idaougnidif
Afantinzar
Samazar
Aouguenz
Tagzene
Tagmout
History
Index

1) 50m (6a) Climb the orange corner left of the perched block to overhangs and a belay.
2) 50m (4c) The crack above leads through an overlap to easier ground.
Ed Bulman & Steve Pack, October 2008.

20. Bacon Double Cheese Burger E2 5b

ABSEIL

100m. An 'easier' proposition from the perched block...
1) 50m (5b) Climb the S-shaped crack to the right of the block and follow a thin seam to a ledge.
2) 50m (5b) Continue up a crack through an overlap to the terrace.
Ed Bulman & Steve Pack, October 2008.

21. Grumpy HVS 5a

STEEP ABSEIL

100m. The right-hand side of the face is an audacious line at this grade.
Mike & Marjorie Mortimer, October 2008.

22. Proposal to the Wise E3 5c ★1

120m. A fine climb with some superb positions. Start just left of the largest boulder beneath the massive overhang at the right side of the face.
1) 30m (5a) Climb the corner until it is possible to traverse right and move up into the next corner. Follow this to the overhang, then move left to good but fragile holds, going up the face to a small stance.
2) 30m (5c) Traverse left to a good side-pull and cam placement. Pull into the groove above before moving left to the arête in an spectacular position. Continue more easily to a belay in a niche.
3) 60m (5b) Climb over a bulge and continue directly to a vegetated ledge. Move right and climb the hanging slot to easier ground.
T.Penning & R.Barr, March 2013.

23. Running on Empty HVS 5b

115m. The attractive slabby face is gained via a difficult wall. Belay in the gully at the top of this, then move left and finish straight up the wall to a big ledge.
Chris Allen & Peter Hill, October 2010.

The next two climbs are located on the slabby south face of Tower 1, overlooking the gully between towers 1 and 2. They are accessed by scrambling up the gully, underneath an enormous boulder and then onto a ledge on the left wall.

DESCENT: It is not easy to descend the gully between Towers 1 and 2, so descent is either by abseil or a long walk over the summit to descend as for routes on the north face.

24. A Taste of Africa VD ★1

70m. A pleasant easy climb on good rock.

1) 30m. Climb up left, heading towards an oasis.

2) 40m. Go up right, following the obvious groove system.

Steve Broadbent & Anna Piotrowski, March 2012.

25. Poles Apart Severe ★2

60m. A very fine climb with some superb steep moves on excellent holds.

1) Start heading up left as for the previous route, but then climb up right to a block belay.

2) Climb straight up on excellent rock.

Steve Broadbent & Anna Piotrowski, March 2012.

TOWER 2

Guarded by smooth slabs and fearsome overhangs, the beautiful second tower was the last of the five to be climbed, and is famously home to 'dozens of unclimbable lines'. It also provides the true summit of the mountain.

The first routes lie on the shady north face, overlooking the narrow gully between it and the first tower. Approach by scrambling up the gully underneath enormous chockstones. There are a couple of short technical sections before it is possible to climb up behind the largest boulder and belay on its top.

DESCENT: The best descent is to walk northeast and descend as for the summit of Tower 1 – either take the first gully on the skyline (descending the steep gully left of *Jaws*), or go a little bit further to an easier, broader gully, visible as a notch on the skyline (Shepherd's Gully). See page 200.

26. Prince of Persia HVS 5b ★2 BOLD CRACK

145m. A tremendously varied climb up the northwest face, featuring some strenuous chimneying, bold slabs, and exposed wall-climbing. The route takes an intricate line and route-finding problems are not uncommon, though a superb, panoramic top out awaits the successful. Start on the enormous chockstone, beneath an ominous (enticing?) chimney on the right wall.

1) 45m (5b) Make an alarming stretch from the boulder, straight into difficult moves to get established in the chimney. This is followed to a tricky exit. Move up left onto a slabby ramp and follow this very boldly to a belay in another chimney.

2) 35m (4c) Teeter left in a fine position, then follow a line of holds up right until it is possible to move back right into the chimney. Climb the corner to a cave and good ledge on the left. (An alternative finish directly up the slab is inferior).

3) 40m (5a) Pull steeply up a flake crack and power through to a vegetated groove. Go up this, then climb excellent walls above to a belay in the chimney.

4) 25m (5a) Another intimidating pitch that is not as bad as it looks. Move up left to gain a vague groove to steeper ground. Traverse 2m right to finish up a broken crack with a magnificent top-out.

Will Benfold & Steve Broadbent, February 2012.

27. Jafaar HVS 5b ★2 CRACK

135m. The continuation crack above the 1st pitch of *Prince of Persia* has a superb second pitch, but more scrappy climbing above.

Area Map
Crag Selector
Intro
The Climbing
How to Use
Suggested Climbs
Tafraout Granite
Anergui
Ameln Valley
Tarakatine Pass
Sidi M'Zal
Jebel Taskra
Idaougnidif
Afantinzar
Samazar
Aouguenz
Tagzene
Tagmout
History
Index

Area Map
Crag Selector
Intro
The Climbing
How to Use
Suggested Climbs
Tafraout Granite
Anergui
Ameln Valley
Tarakatine Pass
Sidi M'Zal
Jebel Taskra
Idaougnidif
Afantinzar
Samazar
Aouguen
Tagzene
Tagmout
History
Index

1) 25m (5b) Climb the chimney as for the previous route, but step right to a ledge where that route goes up left.
2) 25m (5b) The steep crack above is an exquisite pitch involving some exposed contortions. Belay on a large ledge.
3) 35m (4c) Head up left, then back right across shattered rock to regain the crack-line. This leads to a ledge, from where some scrambling up another step gains a higher stony ledge (belay 6 of *The Lion King*).
4) 30m (4b) The left arête of the upper gully.
5) 20m (4b) Finish up a pleasant groove.
Steve Broadbent & Anna Piotrowski, March 2012.

28. Beacon E3 5c ★2

190m. The impressive front face of the tower gives a climb of significant difficulty. Start at the foot of the lower slabby wall beneath overhangs.
1) 30m (4b) Climb up boldly to a stance below the roof.
2) 40m (5c) Go up a corner, passing the roof on its left, and continue up a steep wall above to a stance.
3) 45m (5b) Continue straight up the fine face to easier ground on the left side of the tower. Scramble up to belay above the tower as for *Jafaar*.
4) 35m (4c) Climb rightwards, passing the chimney to a stance beneath the roof.
5) 40m (5c) Go right, then make committing moves up the arête before finishing up the face to the left. An escape up the corner is possible on the right.
S.Mayers & E.Jones, November 2011.

29. Bat Out of Hell HVS 5b

185m. An optimistic line up the groove in the front of the tower left of *The Lion King*.
1) 40m (4c) Climb a vegetated crack left of the large chimney, then move up through vegetation to the foot of the *Lion King* corner.
2) 30m (5b) Start up the corner, but then traverse out left across the slab to belay on a ledge below a crack.
3) 60m (4c) Climb the long crack / groove to a belay on top of the tower.
4) 40m (4c) Continue up grooves in the rib to the left of the chimney (or take the chimney at the same grade).
5) 20m (4a) A final groove leads to the top.
Pete Johnson & Paul Donnithorne, November 2011.

30. The Lion King HVS 5b ★3

CRACK GEAR

185m. The exhilarating long corner up the west face is a big climb up a strong natural line, providing the line of the first ascent and one of Tafraout's most popular HVS routes. Start in a deep gully at the right side of the tower.
1) 15m (-) From the deep chockstone-capped gully climb a wide crack on the right wall to a large ledge.
2) 20m (-) Move up and left through vegetation and a couple of rock ribs to belay at the foot of the enticing long corner.
3) 15m (5b) Pull up from the belay to gain the corner and follow it with some difficulty to a stance above a steepening.

4) 25m (5a) Go up past some questionable blocks, moving right to gain the continuation corner. Climb this on excellent holds to a stance below vegetation.
5) 35m (4c) ***The Bat Cave Pitch*** – Bridge over the bush with surprising ease and climb right up into the cave. Exit left at the top and continue up the corner, passing several ledges to a superb belay on the top of the lower tower.
6) 15m (-) Easy climbing to gain a pleasant, flat, stone-covered ledge.
7) 50m (4c) Go up the gully above with increasing interest to a superb finish on good holds. Numerous belay possibilities en-route.
Steve Broadbent & Sally Fitton, March 2010.

TOWER 3

The broad third tower is easily identifiable by an extensive area of slabs on its right side. These provide a handful of easy pitches, but the main attraction is the superb steep buttress to the left, split by a prominent diagonal terrace taken by *Carousel*. This buttress is crisscrossed by a brace of classic extremes, giving some of the best climbing in the range.

DESCENT: A straightforward scramble down the gully between towers 3 and 4 (Staghorn Gully), or an abseil from the top of *Central Arête*.

31. Merry-Go-Round VS 4c ★2

170m. Interesting climbing up the left-hand face of the third tower, starting some 10 metres right of *The Lion King*.
1) 30m (4c) Climb up the right-hand side of a large tilted flake, then squirm left past a block to a block belay.
2) 30m (4c) Climb up a left-facing groove to a platform.
3) (-) Scramble up behind large boulders, then drop down to the foot of the fine slab on the right.
4) 50m (4c) Climb the centre of the slabby wall, roughly following the prominent black streak, first on its left then to

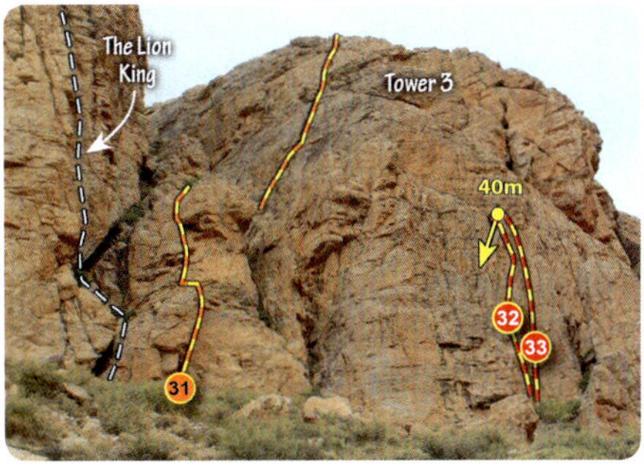

the right. Gain a good ledge and move left to belay beneath a black streak through the bulge.
5) 60m (4c) Pull through the bulge at the black streak to finish up an easy shallow groove and chimney.
Emma Alsford & Paul Donnithorne, April 2014.

32. 3rd Rock From The Sun E2 5b

ABSEIL

50m. The crack / groove 5m left of *Leaving Las Vegas* is gained from the right side. After 35m trend right, almost into the groove of *Leaving Las Vegas*, before pulling up left over bulges. Descend by abseil.
Paul Donnithorne & Emma Alsford, December 2010.

33. Leaving Las Vegas E1 5b ★3

GEAR ABSEIL

40m. The brilliant corner-crack is a Tafraout classic, with sustained bridging and excellent positions throughout.
Steve Broadbent & Paul Mainwood, October 2009.

34. Crag Swag E3 5c ★3

THIN ABSEIL

60m. The arête 5 metres right of *Leaving Las Vegas* gives another brilliant technical pitch. Small wires useful.

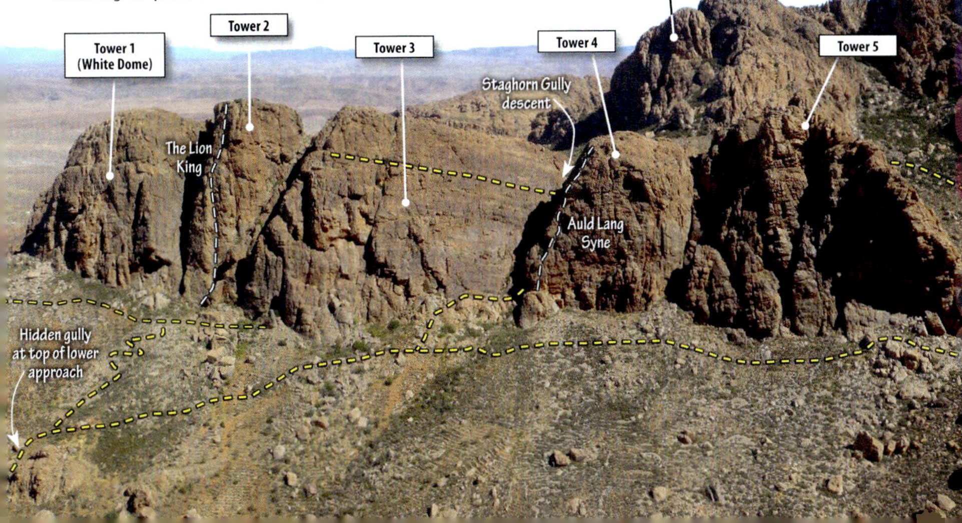

1) 40m (5c) Gain the arête from the right and follow a crack until it fades. Move up to a good hold above a bulge, then pull back up right to the arête and a good ledge. Step right, following the arête on superb holds. Go past a ledge to a good belay 5m higher up.
2) 20m (5a) Pull over the overhang above and follow broken rock to easy ground. Move right to belay at the abseil point.
Dan Moore & Shauna Clarke, March 2013.

35. Some Like it Hot E3 5c ★3 ABSEIL

55m. An excellent technical pitch, starting halfway up the slope behind the bullet-head pinnacle, 20m right of *Leaving Las Vegas*. Start up a short initial groove to a ledge, then climb a smooth wall. Step left to a groove, which is followed until it's possible to move right and climb steep cracks to a final slab. Abseil descent from the base of the prow above.
Emma Alsford & Paul Donnithorne, December 2010.

36. Sugar Kane E3 5c ★ ABSEIL

40m. A direct line up the wall right of *Some Like it Hot*, following the line of the abseil and providing some sustained climbing with generally good protection. Start up the low, crux wall of *Some Like It Hot* but pull straight through the roof into a hanging ramp. Follow this, then shallow grooves to the top.
Niall Grimes & Andy Scott, March 2013.

37. The Amber Spyglass HVS 5a ★2 BOLD

115m. Superb varied climbing, combining the famous first pitch of *The Golden Compass* with an interesting alternative finish. Start near the top of the slope behind the bullet-head pinnacle, at a striking golden corner.
1) 50m (5a) A big 3-star pitch, requiring stamina. Climb a short corner until a step right gains the superb flake. Follow this with continued interest to an easier finish on the sloping terrace. Continue up left to a belay in the chimney.
2) 45m (4b) Start up the steep wall left of the gully, moving right to follow the rib to easier ground after about 15 metres. Continue up the easy slab above to belay beneath steeper ground and an attractive wall on the right.
3) 20m (4c) Excellent technical climbing up the wall on the right provides a bold finale. Walk off rightwards.
Steve Broadbent & Lina Arthur, October 2016.

38. The Golden Compass E1 5b ★3 BOLD

100m. Yet another tremendous classic climb from behind the bullet-head pinnacle, providing one of the most popular extremes in the range.
1) 50m (5a) As for the *Amber Spyglass*.
2) 50m (5b) A rather bold pitch, wandering up the sidewall of the central tower. Step up right and climb the fine wall rightwards to a crack. Continue boldly, trending generally rightwards.
Emma Alsford & Paul Donnithorne, December 2010. *Photo page 185.*

39. Bread and Jam E3 5c ★2 LOOSE

85m. A good route tackling the grooves between the second pitches of *Central Arête* and *Giant*, unfortunately marred by poor rock in places.
1) 25m (4c) Climb the crack in the middle of the buttress, 2m left of *Central Arête*, belaying as for that route.
2) 25m (5c) Make a thin pull to a small ledge and protection on the right side of the arête. Climb the groove and crack above to a hard exit left onto a slab, moving right up this to a large groove. Bridge steeply up through poor rock to another hard step left at a horizontal break
3) 25m (5b) Step left, then move up and climb the left-trending ramp to easier ground, finishing up an easy groove on the left.
Tim Monks & Emma Postlethwaite, December 2012.

40. Central Arête E2 5c ★2 BOLD STEEP

75m. An impressive line up the towering prow, giving some steep climbing. Start at the highest point behind the pinnacle.
1) 30m (4c) Climb a good crack through the initial wall to a belay at the foot of the upper arête.
2) 45m (5c) Climb the right side of the arête to gain a crack. Climb up the wall and trend left beneath the roof, swinging left around the arête in a tremendous position. Layback up a crack on the left side of the arête, then finish up a short steep crack above.
Neil Adams & Dan Donovan, March 2011.

41. Giant E2 5c ★3 CRACK STEEP

110m. The irresistible chimney is one of quartzite's great thrutching adventures.
1) 35m (5b) Climb a steep jamming crack rightwards, passing a bulge and continuing up slabs to belay 5 metres below the chimney.
2) 25m (5c) The totally overhanging chimney is 'in there', 'out there' and desperately energetic but thankfully well protected.
3) 50m (5a) Continue up the chimney, climb a short crack and corner to a roof, then step left to a final crack.
Paul Donnithorne & Emma Alsford, March 2011.

42. Ear Nose And Throat E1 5b ★2 STEEP

110m. A big climb, at the top end of its grade, that tackles the intimidating upper overhangs. Start 20m right of the top of the slope.
1) 50m (4c) Climb the obvious corner, moving rightwards up slabs to a belay beneath a nose-shaped flake.
2) 30m (5b) Climb steeply to gain the nose, then follow the continuation crack to a cave belay.
3) 30m (4b) Finish up a chimney, passing a chockstone to reach the top.
Emma Alsford & Paul Donnithorne, December 2010.

43. Carousel MVS 4a ★1 BOLD SLAB

210m. A route of two halves, with some exquisite slab climbing in the lower section, marred slightly by extensive easy climbing above. The climb gains and follows a ramp system running round from the west face onto the shady north face.

Umlil 3
Left Side
PM
60m
Overview Page 207
55m
37
38
Side wall of central arête, showing second pitch of Golden Compass
Walk off rightwards to descend Staghorn Gully
55m
37
38
50m
40m
35
36
37
39
40
41
42
Bullet-Head Pinnacle
32
33
43

1) 30m (4a) Climb sandy rock for 20m to a stance then move up trending slightly left up the slab with a tricky move cruelly below good gear. Belay on a small stance.
2) 40m (4a) Go up the corner above, exiting rightwards at the overlap. Traverse left from here across the exposed slab with spaced gear, crossing a gully at 30m to reach a good hidden belay ledge with a shrub. This pitch is easier than it looks, but is equally challenging for leader and second.
3) 40m (-) Continue traversing left under the big overhangs to a belay around the corner.
4) 50m (-) Keep going along the ledge to a belay at a boulder.
5) 30m (4a) Now on the shady north face, the route climbs a steep wall with a tricky move over a low overhanging step to a belay on a vegetated ledge.
6) 20m (-) Climb the slanting chimney above, then finish up easy ground.
Steve Broadbent & Rachel Mellor, October 2009.

44. Fiddler Under The Roof E3 5c ★1 STEEP

130m. A character-building excursion, following an intricate line through the tremendous stepped roofs.
1) 55m (4b) Start as for *Carousel*, but move up right on the slabs to a belay beneath the right side of an overhanging wall, left of the tree.
2) 45m (5c) A big pitch. Climb the groove just left of the chimney then follow cracks to the roofs. Follow these leftwards to gain a ledge with some relief.
3) 30m (-) Climb up right to gain the arête which leads pleasantly to the top of the crag.
Pete Johnson & Dave Barlow, December 2010.

45. House of Cards VS 4c LOOSE

100m. This route takes the left-hand weakness in low overhangs to gain the upper left side of the large slabs.
1) 30m (4a) Bold climbing up the ramp above vegetation gains a ledge beneath a steep corner.
2) 30m (4c) The corner through the overhangs has some worrying loose flakes before some fine exposed moves lead through to the slab.
3) 40m (-) Very easy climbing up the slab to a belay. A further 20m of scrambling then gains the terrace.
Steve Broadbent, Cameron Hall & Will Benfold, October 2010.

46. Cabaret HS 4b ★2 SLAB

125m. Excellent, varied climbing. Start at a short flake groove below overhangs with a wide vegetated crack.
1) 25m (4a) Climb the flake groove to reach the overhang, then head up right via a fine hand crack to a sloping stance.
2) 35m (4a) Follow the centre of the excellent slab to a ledge below two cracks.
3) 15m (4b) Climb the right-hand crack to reach easy ground (The left-hand crack is an alternative at 5a). A further 50m of scrambling reaches the terrace.
Emma Alsford & Paul Donnithorne, October 2014.

47. Cabernet MVS 4b

115m. The short off-width crack to the right of *Cabaret*.
1) 20m (4b) Climb the wide crack to a belay.
2) 55m (4b) Go diagonally rightwards to reach the arête, then follow pleasant slabs above.
3) 40m (-) Easy scrambling.
Will Benfold, Katja Broadbent & Dave Arthur, October 2016.

Area Map
Crag Selector
Intro
The Climbing
How to Use
Suggested Climbs
Tafraout Granite
Anergui
Ameln Valley
Tarakatine Pass
Sidi M'Zal
Jebel Taskra
Idaougnidif
Afantinzar
Samazar
Aouguenz
Tagzene
Tagmout
History
Index

The next routes start from a ledge system at the base of large slabs.

48. So Much for Sundowners Severe ★2 SLAB

125m. A very fine climb up the left side of the slabby face, with the first two pitches giving some of the best easy slab climbing in the region. Start at the left side of the low ledge.
1) 25m. Go up the cracked flake buttress with some superb friction moves to a good block belay.
2) 30m. Step left onto the brilliant upper slab and follow it to a stance beneath steeper ground.
3) 35m. Go up over a huge flake to an interesting move over the overlap. Further easy climbing leads to a belay.
4) 35m. Scramble rightwards up very easy ground underneath a right-trending overlap to the large grassy ledge.
Steve Broadbent & Sally Fitton, March 2010.

49. Hissing Sid's Staircase Difficult ★1 SLAB

100m. The vague groove system up the centre of the slabby face gives a pleasant climb with big belay ledges and little commitment.
1) 35m. Start from a large boulder just right of the centre of the low ledge and climb easy ground to a large sloping ledge.
2) 35m. Good climbing up the broken gully to another large ledge.
3) 30m. Easy climbing up a vague gully to the large grassy ledge.
Sally Fitton & Steve Broadbent, March 2010.

THE SOLARIUM SLABS

A number of easy pitches exist on the slabby wall between two terraces at the right side of this tower. This area, known as the Solarium, lies immediately right of the second pitch of *Hissing Sid's Staircase*, and, were it not for the hour-long approach, would be an ideal venue for learning to lead, thanks to perfect rock and plentiful gear placements. It can be accessed either up *Hissing Sid's*, or by traversing in from the 3-4 descent gully.

50. Sunspot HS 4b ★1

35m. The blank slab and overlaps above provide some very nice climbing, and can easily be used as an alternative second pitch to *Hissing Sid's*.
Steve Broadbent & Sally Fitton, March 2010.

51. Matt's Route Mild Severe ★1 GEAR

35m. The low overlap just right of pitch 2 of *Hissing Sid's* gives a very pleasant climb with some interesting moves.
Matt Mellor (solo), February 2011.

52. Solero Severe ★1 GEAR

35m. The smaller, higher overlap to the right is overcome by a tricky little move. Finish through the obvious weakness in the upper overhang.
Steve Broadbent (solo), February 2011.

53. Solarium Difficult ★2 GEAR

35m. A superb and varied beginner's climb, with perfect rock, good holds and plentiful protection. Start up the smoothest part of the slab, climbing a narrow crack up to the overhang. This is surmounted with surprising ease to the left of a prominent block.
Steve Broadbent (solo), October 2010.

54. Idaougni Difficult ★1 GEAR

35m. The wide crack just to the right is another pleasant climb, gaining the overhang at the right side of the hanging block. Pull up left onto the block to finish.
Steve Broadbent (solo), October 2010.

55. Inaccurate Punctuation Difficult

30m. The broken crack up the right side of the slab, avoiding the upper overhangs on the right.
Steve Broadbent (solo), February 2011.

Area Map
Crag Selector
Intro
The Climbing
How to Use
Suggested Climbs
Tafraout Granite
Anergui
Ameln Valley
Tarakatine Pass
Sidi M'Zal
Jebel Taskra
Idaougnidif
Afantinzar
Samazar
Aouguenz
Tagzene
Tagmout
History
Index

TOWER 4

The fourth tower has seen marginally less interest from climbers, but is home to some excellent climbs, particularly in the lower grades. It has two distinct faces: the smaller, shady, northwest face above the Staghorn Gully, which has a couple of excellent short multi-pitch climbs on good pale rock; and the much bigger west face, characterised by continuously overhanging, crumbling orange rock. Dividing the two is a vague rib, taken by the magnificent *Auld Lang Syne*.

DESCENT: Walk leftwards and descend Staghorn Gully (between towers 3 and 4).

56. The Tyrolean Snake Escape VS 4c ★1 CRACK

45m. The zigzag crack near the top of Staghorn Gully is often wet, but provides a good long crack pitch when dry.

Steve Broadbent & Sally Fitton, March 2010.

57. Sunset Boulevard Severe ★1

90m. A terrific and popular face climb on good rock, giving a relaxed introduction to one of Tafraout's best crags. The route has a friendly feel to it, and is a much shorter endeavour than many of the climbs hereabouts.

1) 25m. Start up the face 3m left of the initial crack of *NW Face* to a black streak. Climb this on good holds to a belay at vegetation.
2) 25m. Easy climbing up the groove, then move up right on the fine face to a block belay.
3) 25m. Climb straight over steep ground and continue up to a ledge.
4) 15m. Finish up the wall above (this can be combined with the previous pitch if required).
Will Benfold, Steve Broadbent & Cameron Hall, October 2010.

58. Northwest Face Mild Severe 1 BOLD

95m. The centre of the shady wall gives an excellent but bold climb of great character, somewhat reminiscent of routes in the English Lake District. It is slightly easier than *Sunset Boulevard*, just as good, but rather more serious. Start up a prominent left-facing corner-crack about half way up the 3-4 descent gully.
1) 20m. Superb, well-protected climbing up the wide corner crack to a vegetated ledge.
2) 25m. Go straight up the groove above, stepping right then back left to gain a fine wall to a good ledge with a small bush and poor belays.
3) 15m. Make a bold and airy traverse up and right to the rib, which is followed to a ledge.
4) 35m. Fine, open and exposed face-climbing following the easiest line to the top with little in the way of protection.
Sally Fitton & Steve Broadbent, March 2010.

59. War of the Roses HS

115m. Start at a rose bush, a few metres left of a wide crack some 50m up Staghorn Gully. Climb up left of seepage and continue up the easiest line above.
Chris Bull & Jen Booys, November 2013

60. Footloose HVS 5a 2

135m. Excellent climbing up the left side of the rib that separates the northwest and west faces. Start in Staghorn Gully, left of *Auld Lang Syne*, at a dirty corner.
1) 35m (5a) Climb the wall to the left of a dirty corner to gain the arête. Follow this until things get steep, then move right to climb slabs to a ledge.
2) 25m (4c) Climb broken orange rock through a gap in the roof and continue to the shoulder below the 'perched flake'.
3) 45m (5a) Bold climbing to the top of the perched flake, from where an alarming move gains the slab on the main face. Follow this, trending leftwards to a large ledge.
4) 30m (4b) Climb the wall above the ledge and surmount overhangs to reach the summit.
Caroline Culwick & Patrick Timoney, March 2012.

61. Auld Lang Syne HS 4c 3 GEAR

110m. One of the best routes at this grade in the Anti-Atlas, with interesting climbing and obvious commitment throughout. For a great mountain link-up, the route can be continued up *Wild Country* (page 196). All difficulties are well protected, but the route is a serious undertaking at the top end of its grade. There is a smooth tower at the foot of the northwest buttress, and the route starts up a corner up the right side of the ridge, above this lower tower.
1) 25m (4c) Climb the prominent corner on the south side of the ridge to a belay below some large trees. The groove to the right is an alternative start: ***Auld Lags' Start*** (VS 4c).
2) 30m (-) Work rightwards up flakes, heading for the right side of an enormous perched flake. Belay in an alcove beneath this.
3) 25m (4c) An intricate pitch. Climb the wall to the right of the perched flake, pulling through steep ground on the right. Step left and make more steep moves to gain a rightwards rising traverse to a good runner in the undercut crack. From here traverse left across sandy rock to easier ground on the left face, then climb up 5m to a belay stance.
4) 30m (4a) Step right and climb steep ground up the front of the ridge. This soon gives way to easy climbing staying right on the rib to a final difficult undercut move to the top.
Steve & Katja Broadbent, February 2010.

Area Map
Crag Selector
Intro
The Climbing
How to Use
Suggested Climbs
Tafraout Granite
Anergui
Ameln Valley
Tarakatine Pass
Sidi M'Zal
Jebel Taskra
Idaougnidif
Afantinzar
Samazar
Aouguenz
Tagzene
Tagmout
History
Index

Right of here the crag swings round onto the intimidating, overhanging west face and the quality of the rock deteriorates somewhat.

62. The Fourth Dimension HVS 5a ★1

150m. The broken groove-line up the centre of the west face is the most striking line hereabouts, although it deterred several attempts over the years before its first ascent.

1) 45m (4c) Climb a groove, passing a tree on the left, to a good ledge.

2) 30m (5a) Continue up the groove to a stance below a steepening.

3) 50m (5a) Power up the steep, overhanging crack, continuing up the groove above to a ledge.

4) 25m (4a) Either continue in the same line or follow slabs rightwards to the top.

Paul Donnithorne, Emma Alsford & Don Sargeant, March 2013.

63. Jumanji E1 5b ★1

LOOSE BOLD

130m. This very serious climb tackles the steep west face of the 4th Tower, and features technical climbing in superbly exposed positions. The route gains and follows a curving ramp beneath an orange and black wall high on the right side of the face. It is a major undertaking due to sustained difficulties on shattered rock, from which retreat is almost impossible. Add to this a number of challenging traverses and you have a committing climb that is bold for both leader and second. A route not to be underestimated!

1) 25m (4c) Climb disappointingly blank grooves up the right side of the face to a stance.

2) 25m (5b) Step up right onto a small pillar with a vegetated crack up its left side. From the top of this make steep moves up the overhanging groove to slightly easier ground. Continue up the corner for 5m then make a tricky traverse left to a hidden belay.

3) 30m (5b) The groove above the belay continues steeply to overhangs. Go over the small lower overhang to protection, then traverse left, stepping down across a groove to gain the start of a large black flake. Follow this onto the large ramp system.

4) 25m (5a) The steep corner at the top of the ramp is very rotten, so the route escapes left here. Move up the ramp for 5m to an easy traverse left. Some tricky moves around the corner to the left, underneath the overhangs, gain another hidden belay on a vegetated ledge.

5) 25m (4a) A bold, but excellent pitch on good rock. Step up and right onto a small slab then climb the groove above to the top of the crag.

Steve & Katja Broadbent, February 2010.

TOWER 5

The most southerly of the five towers comprises a very steep, orange, west face, split by numerous gullies and buttresses. At the right side of the face is the steep South Ridge, where the crag swings round on to the much friendlier south face: home to a handful of delightful easy climbs. Routes on the west face are described first.

DESCENT: Scramble off the back side to regain the hillside in front of Adrar Asmit. Turn right and cross a col, descending a small path below the north face of Adrar Aiyur before cutting right to regain the base of the cliff.

64. Fur Elsie HVS 5a ★2

130m. A varied climb up the left side of Tower 5, starting in the gully between the fourth and fifth towers.

1) 45m (5a) Start at the lowest point of the initial slab and climb up its centre. Tackle the headwall via a finger crack on the right, then step left at the top. Belay back and right near a curving wide crack.

2) 35m (5a) Climb the crack and its continuation, stepping left to exit at a chockstone.

3) 50m (5a) Head up and right to a black-streaked wall, stepping left over a bulge just before the wall. Climb the black streak, taking the steep right-hand fork to the top.

Jonnie Williams & Carol Goodall, November 2013.

65. Ice Age Hard Severe ★1

175m. Nice climbing up the broad buttress at the left side of the rambling 5th tower. There is a prominent tree high on the left wall, and this route follows generally slabby ground to reach the tree at the top of pitch 4. The line can also be identified by a jagged crack low down, clearly seen from the approach. Start on large white blocks that abut the overhanging base of the face.

1) 35m (4b) From the high point of the blocks make a steep pull onto the face and climb up to a wide crack. Follow this more easily and continue to a good ledge below the wide jagged crack.

2) 20m (4a) The wide crack provides a fine layback and leads to a pinnacle belay.

3) 50m (-) The prominent high tree is just about visible above... Climb easy but bold rock heading for the tree, until a small vegetated ledge provides a belay at 50m.

4) 35m (-) Go up a vague groove until the rock becomes more shattered. From here traverse right onto the rib just below the tree. Belay in the gully.

5) 35m (4b) From behind the tree step up into a worryingly broken groove, then make bold moves out right to gain easier ground. Finish up the right-hand of two upper cracks, which provides a strenuous sting in the tail.

Steve Broadbent & Matt Mellor, February 2011.

66. Event Horizon HVS 5a ★3

STEEP

150m. The steep central buttress gives a superb and atmospheric climb of great character, which is consistent throughout and generally low in the grade. There are four brilliantly steep and exposed pitches featuring excellent climbing on good rock. Start by scrambling up clean rock in the bed of the gully right of *Ice Age*, belaying at the foot of a steeper rib of rock.

1) 25m (4a) Start up the right-hand gully until it is possible to step left onto the fin. Follow this to its top, then climb a steep crack on the right wall of the chimney to a small ledge.
2) 20m (5a) Step left across the gully and traverse up left to an exposed step left around the arête. Difficult and very exposed moves then follow to a belay up left in a small niche.
3) 30m (4c) Move left and climb up to slabby ground below overhangs. Work right to gain a prominent steep flake which provides an airy way through the first overhang. (It is possible to avoid this via a traverse right under the fin of white rock). At the top of the flake move right to a stance, then up steep ground to a good ledge.
4) 40m (4c) Climb a grassy gully until a step right gains the front face. Continue up the left side of the buttress, pulling through several overhangs to a ledge below a wide crack.
5) 35m (4b) The steep, wide crack provides a brilliant finale, finishing up grooves and flakes in the final tower.
Steve Broadbent & Caroline Culwick, March 2011.

67. Vanishing Point VS 4c ★2

175m. An intriguing climb, following an intricate line through some steep ground. Start at a crack, just left of a gully.
1) 45m (4b) Climb the vague crack with an awkward layback to an optional belay by vegetation on the right. Tricky steep climbing through cracks on the arête leads to a ledge. Continue to a second, larger ledge.
2) 40m (4b) Go up a short gully on the left side of the buttress, then a nice wall to regain the crest. Work up right across a slab to an oasis.
3) 30m (4c) From the front left corner of the ledge down-climb a narrow ledge-system into the clean chasm on the left. Step across (if you dare) onto a slab, then move up right to gain a ramp leading left under the overlap. Go along this to a tricky move at the arête, before continuing more easily to belay at vegetation on the right.
4) 30m (4c) Go up past an overlap to a ledge beneath overhangs. Make a few steep bouldery moves through the first roof, heading for a roof crack above. This is avoided on the right to gain a belay above.
5) 30m (4c) Climb up to the left side of the even bigger roof above, from where it is possible to make a fun traverse rightwards, out across the sidewall. Break through a weakness on the front of the overhang to gain an easy slab to the top. Phew!
Will Benfold & Henry Northern (pitches 1 & 2), February 2011.
Steve Broadbent & Cameron Hall (pitches 3,4,5), October 2011.

68. The Fifth Element E4 6a ★3

150m. Varied climbing up the attractive golden groove, 5m left of *Crag Hill Dream*.
1) 30m (4b) Climb the easy-angled slab to a stance below the golden groove.
2) 25m (6a) Continue up the groove with considerable difficulty to gain a good ledge.

Area Map
Crag Selector
Intro
The Climbing
How to Use
Suggested Climbs
Tafraout Granite
Anergui
Ameln Valley
Tarakatine Pass
Sidi M'Zal
Jebel Taskra
Idaougnidif
Afantinzar
Samazar
Aouguenz
Tagzene
Tagmout
History
Index

3) 40m (5b) From the left end of the ledge, move up then rightwards to a steep wall. Climb this, then follow a groove to a small ledge below a sentry box.
4) 30m (5a) Climb the sentry box, moving up left to an exposed hanging rib just left of a chimney flake. Pull around to the left and continue to a large ledge.
5) 25m (5b) Layback the steep flake above the centre of the ledge, then traverse easily rightwards to the ridge.
Paul Donnithorne & Bob Brewer, October 2013.

69. Crag Hill Dream E2 5c ★2

140m. An optimistic endeavour up the steep wall at the right side of the face. Start 30m left of an enormous boulder beneath the steepest part of the face.
1) 50m (5c) Climb easy slabs to gain thin twin cracks up steeper ground above. Or should that be twin thin cracks? Either way, they lead to a chimney, which is climbed to a ledge.
2) 30m (5b) Step back down and make exposed moves up right across the wall to a ledge. Continue more easily to a stance.
3) 60m (5b) Follow a left-trending groove until it is possible to swing right, then back left into the huge slabby corner leading to a notch on the *South Ridge*.
Paul Donnithorne & Dave Noddings, March 2011.

70. Vulture Squadron E4 6a ★3

145m. A spectacular effort up the overhanging orange wall at the right side of the face. Start 10m right of the previous route.
1) 15m (4c) Climb the left-facing flake to a stance under the roof.
2) 25m (5c) A superb but strenuous hand-traverse out right leads to a steep groove.
3) 40m (5b) Step left and continue up the groove for 15m, until it is possible to teeter rightwards to a corner stance.
4) 25m (5b) Continue up to another corner and follow it to a fine stance.
5) 20m (6a) Climb a steep groove to the left of the prominent chimney.
6) 20m (-) Finish easily with relief.
Paul Donnithorne & Bob Brewer, October 2011.

71. South Ridge Severe ★2

165m. Viewed from the southwest the *South Ridge* is an impressive sight, appearing as a steep and intimidating tower. This very fine climb takes the easiest line up the ridge, with immaculate white rock and good belay stances. A beautifully exposed route.
1) 30m. Start from the toe of the buttress and follow the crest, keeping as far left as possible to a good ledge at a major notch in the ridge.
2) 8m. Make a horizontal traverse right to a belay ledge, or tackle the overhang direct at HVS.
3) 17m. Steep climbing up leftwards to regain the front of the buttress. Belay on a ledge beneath a corner.
4) 30m. A pleasant pitch up the wall left of the corner.
5) 40m. Continue easily up the ridge.
6) 40m. Scrambling remains to flat ground below the summit. It is possible to continue right to the top, but a more popular option is to scramble rightwards down vague terraces across the south face (shown opposite).
Steve Broadbent & Sally Fitton, December 2009.

The next routes lie on the sunny south face:

72. Always Neverland Very Difficult ★2

115m. An excellent, well-protected climb with plenty of exposure. Start under a huge left-to-right diagonal crack under a dark streak.
1) 45m. Climb the crack to a half-height ledge.
2) 25m. Follow the crack rightwards to a block belay.
3) 45m. Climb up the crack above, then make an airy step left onto a slab. Climb up past bushes to another block belay.
R.Eckersley & M.Newbury, March 2014.

73. Cefn Garw Severe ★2

80m. The rib immediately left of *Starlight Express* gives a brilliant low-grade climb with big holds, immaculate rock and nice positions. Start from a tree behind a large boulder.
1) 45m. Go leftwards up a blocky groove to gain the front face. Trend right with some steep moves to a tremendous romp up jugs to a belay ledge level with the crux of *Starlight Express*.
2) 35m. A steep wall directly above the ledge leads to another good ledge (possible belay). From here step right and finish up a fine rib to the top.
Steve Broadbent & Matt Mellor, February 2011.

Area Map
Crag Selector
Intro
The Climbing
How to Use
Suggested Climbs
Tafraout Granite
Anergui
Ameln Valley
Tarakatine Pass
Sidi M'Zal
Jebel Taskra
Idaougnidif
Afantinzar
Samazar
Aouguenz
Tagzene
Taghoute
History
Index

74. Starlight Express HS 4c ★2

105m. The tempting right-facing corner up the middle of the southeast face is a good line, with lots of easy climbing and a short, brutal crux at the top end of its grade. Start from a shady den behind an enormous boulder.

1) 20m (-) Climb easy angled ground to the right of the corner to a flake belay.

2) 30m (-) Excellent climbing up the corner to a small stance beneath overhangs.

3) 55m (4c) Move up left towards the overhang, then make a very difficult rockover rightwards onto the front of the enormous flake. Go up to the wide handrail under the overhang and follow it rightwards to easy ground. Easy climbing up and right leads to a final steep section that is overcome with surprising ease. Descend rightwards down a vague ramp that traverses back to the foot of the face.

Steve Broadbent & Sally Fitton, February 2010.

75. Evening Wall Very Difficult ★2

85m. Another excellent route at this grade, starting down and left from a low curved roof.

1) 33m. Go up easy ground to the left end of an easy ramp above the curved overhang. Climb straight up the superb steep wall above to a belay.

2) 30m. Go up, trending right to a weakness in the overlap above. Pull through this, then follow easier ground to a ledge.

3) 20m. Go up the right side of a huge flake to reach the descent ledge.

Steve Broadbent & Cameron Hall, October 2011.

Sally Fitton on the superb rock of Adrar Umlil's *South Ridge* (Severe) during the first ascent.

Photo: Steve Broadbent

DESCENT: A convenient, exposed, and somewhat devious scramble cuts back across the south face as shown below:

Umlil 5
South Face
1:20
Overview Page 207

Area Map
Crag Selector
Intro
The Climbing
How to Use
Suggested Climbs
Tafraout Granite
Anergui
Ameln Valley
Tarakatine Pass
Sidi M'Zal
Jebel Taskra
Idaougnidif
Afantinzar
Samazar
Aouguenz
Tagzene
Tagmout
History
Index

H COL CRAGS

Shade | Families | Hitch | Roadside
Drive from Tafraout: **1 hour**
Walk-in: **10 minutes**

A collection of rather scrappy crags lie above the road at the top of the Amzkhssan Hairpins, accessed easily from parking just north of the Aouguenz junction. Good Book Buttress is the most prominent of the crags, identifiable by a large open-book corner high on its southwestern flank.

The layout of the crag is somewhat confusing, not helped by many of the routes starting from inaccessible ledges, gained only via other climbs. That said, there are some pleasant pitches with short walk-ins, and the crag still has something of an adventurous feel to it.

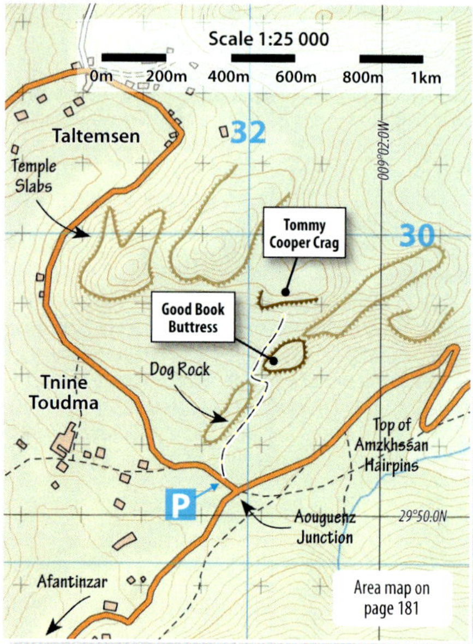

GOOD BOOK BUTTRESS

The first routes start up the left side of Little Donkey Tower, although the exact lines are somewhat unclear.

DESCENT: Abseil descent from behind the tower.

1. Donkey Screams VS 4a ★1 UNCHECKED

30m. Start up the left side of the west-facing tower (Little Donkey Tower) beneath a thin crack. Follow the thin crack to the top of the tower. Escape left to the Good Book Col or continue up *Happy Donkey*.
S.Smidt & A.Vilen, January 2013.

2. Donkey Walk Severe 4a UNCHECKED

55m. Start in the crack-line a few metres to the right of *Donkey Screams*. Follow the crack to the top of the tower (abseil boulder) and continue straight up to the top of Big Donkey Pinnacle.
S.Smidt & A.Vilen, March 2013.

3. Happy Donkey VS 4c ★1 UNCHECKED

25m. Start at the top of Little Donkey Tower, at the top of *Donkey Screams*. Climb up the left side of an overhang and move right into the crackline, climbing to the summit of Big Donkey Pinnacle.
S.Smidt & A.Vilen, January 2013.

The next routes climb up the right-hand side of Big Donkey Pinnacle to reach a col below the prominent 'Good Book Corner'.

4. Donkey's Way Severe 4a

75m. Start at the lower left corner of the crag close to a boulder beneath a clean buttress.
1) 40m. Climb the buttress and move right to the curving crack. Follow this rightwards past ledges to a belay at cactus.
2) 35m. Continue up the slab via a blind crack and scramble to a belay at the bottom of the big dihedral.
S.Smidt & A.Vilen, January 2013.

5. The Story E1 5c ★1

40m. Low down on the crag is a dihedral capped by a little roof. To the left of this is an overhanging crack and this route climbs a second crack, 2 metres left of the overhanging crack. At the top of the crack traverse right underneath a wall then finish up this wall with some difficulty. Belay at the bottom of *The Good Book*.
S.Smidt & A.Vilen, January 2013.

6. The Short Story E1 5b ★2 ABSEIL

25m. Scramble up ledges beneath a short, clean dihedral in the middle of the lower part of the south face. Climb the dihedral to the capping overhang, then traverse right around the corner to a belay. Descend by abseil, or continue up *Honkey Donkey*.
S.Smidt & A.Vilen, March 2013.

7. Donkey Chimney HS 4b

20m. Start at the left side of the broad chimney and climb the wall left of the chimney, continuing to a ledge with big boulders below an orange wall.
S.Smidt & A.Vilen, January 2013.

8. Honkey Donkey Severe 4a

55m. Follow the huge left-curving corner up the orange wall above *Donkey Chimney*. Belay at the bottom of *The Good Book* dihedral.
S.Smidt & A.Vilen, January 2013.

9. Blowing in the Wind HS 4a

15m. This short route climbs the crack in the centre of the west face, round to the left of *The Good Book*.

The following routes start from Good Book Col, at the base of the obvious open-book corner.

DESCENT: Either make a 45m abseil down the north side, or continue scrambling over the top until it is possible to scramble northwards.

10. The Good Book HVS 5b ★2 WIDE

35m. Climb the crack in the characteristic open-book corner. Long slings for the chockstones or big cams required.
S.Smidt & A.Vilen, January 2013.

11. Your line HVS 5a UNCHECKED

35m. Start from the base of *The Good Book* dihedral and climb up to gain the higher of two right-slanting cracks. Follow this to its end then go straight up the wall to the top. Descend as for *The Good Book*.

12. Leguan Fewer HVS 5b UNCHECKED

30m. Start from the Good Book Col on the face between *The Good Book* and *White Pages*, climbing straight up the face towards a small dihedral.
S.Smidt & A.Vilen, March 2013.

13. White Pages HVS 5b UNCHECKED

30m. Starts below the belay for *The Good Book* at The Good Book Col. Climb up past an overhang and continue up the wall moving right to the lower of two right-slanting cracks. Follow the crack up right to the crest and climb the left side of this to join *Your Line*.
S.Smidt & A.Vilen, January 2013.

The next routes are located further right, near a 40m-high pinnacle in the centre of the south face of the crag.

DESCENT: For the first four routes, a long abseil down the line of Trapeze regains the gully behind the pinnacle. For routes further right it is possible to walk off rightwards.

14. Cactus Garden E1 5a ★1 ABSEIL

60m. Follows the ramp-line and flakes 10m left of the pinnacle.
1) 30m (5a) Start up a short crack to gain an easy slab, then pull awkwardly up left to gain the second slab. Follow a ramp up right to a ledge, belaying in a corner on the left.
2) 30m (4c) Climb the corner / flake to where it narrows. Move boldly to the right side of an overlap and follow the groove to a ledge.
T.Monks & E.Postlethwaite, January 2013.

Area Map
Crag Selector
Intro
The Climbing
How to Use
Suggested Climbs
Tafraout Granite
Anergui
Ameln Valley
Tarakatine Pass
Sidi M'Zal
Jebel Taskra
Idaougnidif
Afantinzar
Samazar
Aouguenz
Tagzene
Tagmout
History
Index

Area Map
Crag Selector
Intro
The Climbing
How to Use
Suggested Climbs
Tafraout Granite
Anergui
Ameln Valley
Tarakatine Pass
Sidi M'Zal
Jebel Taskra
Idaougnidif
Afantinzar
Samazar
Aouguenz
Tagzene
Tagmout
History
Index

15. Trapeze E1 5c ★★★ ABSEIL

55m. An excellent route up the fine-looking corner just left of the Preface Pinnacle. Pitch 2 offers some committing climbing at the top end of its grade. Start 3m left of the pinnacle.

1) 30m (5b) Start up slabs, trending slightly rightwards to a ledge. Move up left to a thin crack, which leads to a further ledge. Move right to belay in the corner.

2) 25m (5c) Follow the corner to its top, then teeter leftwards along the ledge. Move up past two pegs to gain the magnificent wide crack to the top.

Emma Alsford & Paul Donnithorne, January 2014

16. No Resolution HVS 5b ★★ GEAR

50m. Follows the distinctive crack in the groove behind the pinnacle, starting left of a small tree at the top of the gully. Climb cracks to reach a ledge then step right and make a steep pull to gain the right-trending ramp. Follow this to a good ledge at the top.

T.Monks & E.Postlethwaite, January 2013.

The next routes are located on the wall to the right of the pinnacle.

DESCENT: Walk off rightwards.

17. Well Read E1 5b ★

50m. Start 5 metres right of *No Resolution,* behind the pinnacle. Climb a right-trending ramp then continue up brown slabs to a steepening. Climb a thin crack to a vegetated ledge, then move right and surmount a bulge. Step left and finish up the steep headwall above.

Paul Donnithorne & Emma Alsford , January 2014

18. Between the Lines HS 4b ★

50m. Pleasant climbing, starting half way up the gully behind the pinnacle. The route starts up a groove, then tackles the blankest section of the slab above, moving left under a bulge to a ledge. Climb up steeply from here, trending back rightwards before finishing direct over a final bulge.

Emma Alsford & Paul Donnithorne, January 2014

19. Underline Very Difficult ★

55m. Starting from the foot of the gully behind the pinnacle, climb a flake and slab to the left of cactus. Pull up left through steeper ground to a boulder belay and easy finish.

D.Sargeant & J.Hornsby, January 2014

20. Margin Severe 4a ★

55m. Start just right of black streaks, climbing a blunt rib and slab towards a steep black crack. Climb this, then scramble up easier ground to the top.

J.Hornsby & D.Sargeant, January 2014

21. Kindle Fire Severe 4a ★

60m. Start by a stumpy pinnacle, some 15 metres right of the main pinnacle.

1) 30m (4a) Climb an attractive groove to a stance.

2) 30m (-) Continue over bulges, passing to the right of a large block.

Emma Alsford & Paul Donnithorne, January 2014

22. Preface Pinnacle HVS 5a ★★ ABSEIL

40m. An excellent pitch, taking the groove on the southwest arête of the pinnacle. Follow the arête above the groove to a good platform, then abseil from a spike at the summit.

Emma Alsford & Paul Donnithorne, January 2014

TOMMY COOPER CRAG

A very pleasant single-pitch cragging venue, with a remote feel despite easy access from the Aouguenz junction at the top of the Amzkhssan hairpins.

From parking immediately north of the junction on the col, follow a small path towards Good Book Buttress, passing beneath Dog Rock to gain the col between Good Book and Dog Rock. Cross over this, then bear right towards the attractive quartz-striped crag. See map page 218.

1. Spider Sam and the Sun-kissed Goddess HVS 5a ★2

40m. Start 10m left of an obvious S-shaped gully. Climb cracks, moving slightly left to pull over a bulge. Continue up the crack in the black wall, then move right to finish up two short corners.
G.MacCauley & S.Crossley, March 2014.

2. Cooper's Corner E2 5c ★1

35m. Climbs the central square corner high on the cliff. Start 5m right of the S-shaped gully.
1) 20m (5c) Gain a bulge at 10m, then jam steeply leftwards to reach a small ledge. Step right and pull up to a large ledge beneath the corner.
2) 15m (5c) Climb the excellent corner, moving right at the top to an easier finish.
P.Donnithorne & B.Watson, January 2015.

3. Just Like That VS 4b ★1

30m. Start beneath the smooth corner, climbing the bulging wall to gain its base. Step left to finish up the left-hand wall.
S.Crossley & G.MacCauley, March 2014.

4. Smoke and Mirrors VS 4c ★2

35m. The right-facing flake a few metres right of *Cooper's Corner* has some nice moves. Gain the flake, climb it, then exit left to a ledge. Step awkwardly off a block to finish up an interesting flake corner.
P.Donnithorne, B.Watson & D.Sargeant, January 2015.

5. Fez Very Difficult ★1

30m. The short corner, 10 metres right of *Just Like That*.
S.Crossley & G.MacCauley, March 2014.

6. Fork, Spoon Severe

30m. Start 10 metres right of *Fez*. Gain and climb a left-slanting flared groove, then move left to finish up a blocky wall.
G.MacCauley & S.Crossley, March 2014.

7. Not Like That HVS 5a

35m. Climb up to a short ramp in a bulge 3 metres right of *Fork, Spoon*. Pull up to a ledge, then climb a shallow groove, stepping right at its top to finish up a thin flake.
P.Donnithorne & B.Watson , January 2015.

8. Like This HS 4b ★1

35m. Start 2m right of *Not Like That*, below a chunky left-facing corner. Climb a short corner, then step right. Pull up and back left and finish up the corner.
B.Watson & P.Donnithorne, January 2015.

Area Map
Crag Selector
Intro
The Climbing
How to Use
Suggested Climbs
Tafraout Granite
Anergui
Ameln Valley
Tarakatine Pass
Sidi M'Zal
Jebel Taskra
Idaougnidif
Afantinzar
Samazar
Aouguenz
Tagzene
Tagmout
History
Index

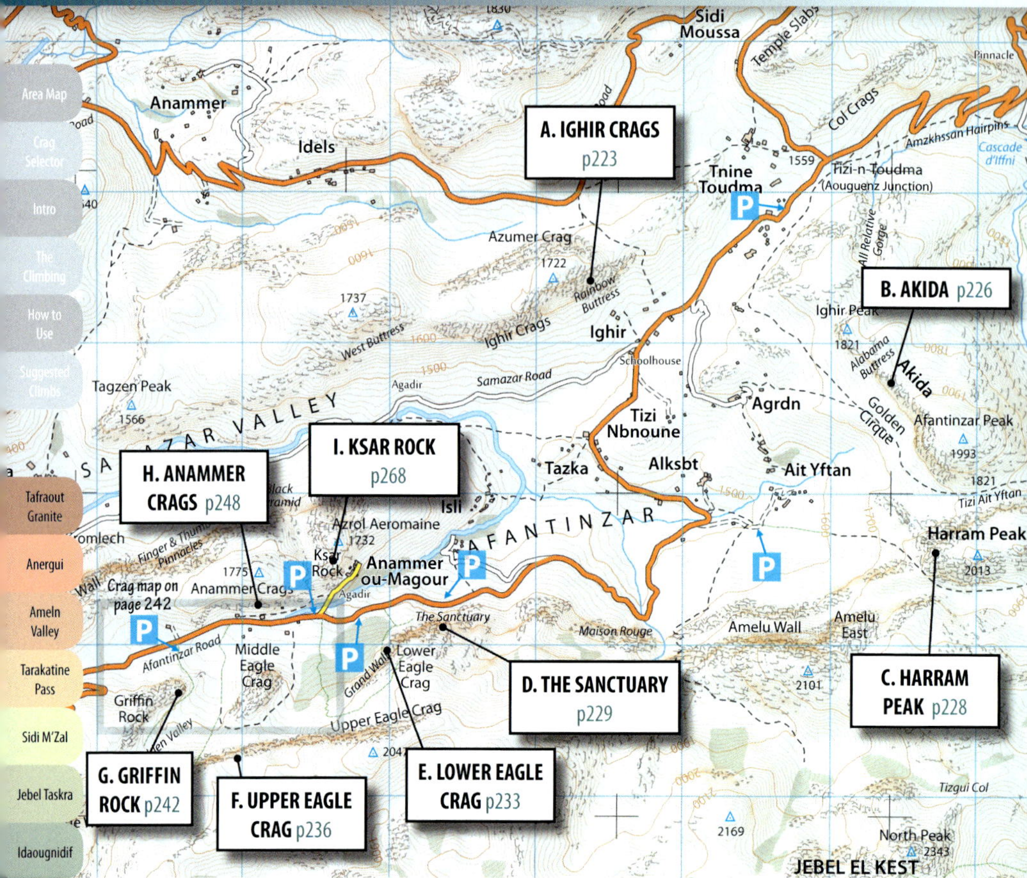

Area Map
Crag Selector
Intro
The Climbing
How to Use
Suggested Climbs
Tafraout Granite
Anergui
Ameln Valley
Tarakatine Pass
Sidi M'Zal
Jebel Taskra
Idaougnidif
Afantinzar
Samazar
Aouguenz
Tagzene
Tagmout
History
Index

AFANTINZAR

The high mountain valley of Afantinzar is one of the most important and historic climbing areas of the Anti-Atlas, with a huge variety of routes from single pitch to full-day outings spanning the full spectrum of grades.

The valley is best approached from Tafraout via Idaougnidif by continuing over the pass above Amzkhssan (this pass is known as Tizi-n-Toudma, or the 'Aouguenz Junction'). The drive from Tafraout takes approximately 1 hour and 15 minutes, but fortunately whilst the drive is rather long, the walk-ins tend to be conveniently short and many of the crags have a fairly roadside feel to them. Parking areas and approaches to the crags are usually obvious on a first visit.

Beyond Anammer and Griffin Rock the road crosses a pass into Tagzene (this is the pass of Tizi-n-Tagnit) and continues towards Dwawj and Tanalt. It is possible, though slightly longer, to approach the valley this way from Tafraout via Tanalt.

The Afantinzar valley sits about 500 metres higher than Tafraout and so remains somewhat cooler than most venues described in this guide. It is, therefore, a good choice during early and late season when the crags of the Ameln Valley are unbearably hot.

Crags are described in a clockwise direction from the tiny hamlet of Ighir.

A IGHIR CRAGS

Shade Families Hitch Roadside
Drive from Tafraout: **1:15**
Walk-in: **15 to 30 minutes**

The attractive south-facing crags above the village of Ighir were a surprisingly late discovery, escaping the interest of climbers until 2011 despite their obvious and easily accessible position at the start of the Samazar Road. For climbers seeking mid-grade multi-pitch routes in the sunshine, Ighir is an ideal venue with perfect orange quartzite and reliably high-quality climbing, including a number of local classics.

The main buttress, Rainbow Buttress, was the first to be climbed, and although it is located in Afantinzar, it is accessed from the Samazar road: take the small turning onto the Samazar Road in Ighir, following the dirt track to a small pull-out just in front of Rainbow Buttress. Several poor trails leave the road hereabouts, reaching the crag in about 20 minutes.

RAINBOW BUTTRESS

This is the main buttress, closest to Ighir, containing a handful of excellent mid-length climbs.

DESCENT: Descend a vegetated gully to the right of the crag.

1. Crock of Gold HVS 5a ★2

UNCHECKED STEEP

140m. Four pitches of excellent climbing, starting 5m left of *Crooked Eclipse*.

1) 40m (5a) Climb stepped cracks to belay in a large niche.
2) 35m (5a) Take the overlap above the belay on the right, then traverse left into a corner. Pull up onto a rib and climb the centre of the wall to belay on a ledge below another corner.
3) 35m (5a) Climb thin cracks in the corner, then go up blocks and ledges to belay by a bush beneath a corner and cracked roof.
4) 30m (4c) Go up the awkward corner to an easier finish.
Kev Sales & Paul Drew, March 2013.

2. Crooked Eclipse HVS 5b ★3

STEEP

135m. A steep and sustained outing up the left side of the buttress, providing considerable difficulty. The route starts some 5m left of a big gully, guarded by prickly pears.

1) 30m (4b) Climb easily up the left side of a black streak (or take the streak directly at 5b, bold), then move back right and follow a black crack to a belay beneath twin bulging cracks.
2) 50m (5b) Climb the overhanging cracks with difficulty to gain easier ground to a large terrace. Belay at the base of a black crack, close to a prickly pear.
3) 35m (5a) Climb the steep corner crack, moving right at the top into the continuation corner. Follow this to an easier groove and continue to a belay beneath an overhang-capped wall.
4) 20m (5a) Step left and follow a crack leading to the left side of the overhang. Climb this and the crack above to the top.
Tony & Ulla Pearson, January 2013.

3. Orange Rocket VS 5a ★2

160m. A super climb up the obvious orange pillar in the centre of the buttress. The route is mostly fairly easy, on good rock, with a short, hard crux on pitch 2. Start below a spur on the right of a vegetated gully.

1) 35m (4a) Climb the spur, then enter a right-slanting chimney to a small terrace.
2) 30m (5a) Go up to a pillar, then slant up left to the main wall and climb a fine dihedral crack up the second corner. Belay at a block on the large terrace beneath the upper orange tower.
3) 40m (4a) Climb easy rocks to an upper terrace on the left, then climb a fine carved crack up the left side of the tower.
4) 25m (4b) Easy climbing leads to a short corner. Follow this to join *Afantinzar Dogs* for the last pitch.
5) 20m (-) A red slab and easy climbing to the top (as for *Afantinzar Dogs*).
Alberto Rampini & Silvia Mazzani, November 2011.

4. The Main of Light HVS 5b ★3

190m. A superb series of corners and cracks following a direct line up the buttress. Start above some rock steps with an almond tree gully to the right.

1) 30m (4c) Climb the black cracked corner past a bush to a large vegetated ledge.
2) 30m (5b) Move left into a runnel and climb up the right side of this to a crack. Continue with some difficulty to a belay beneath a prominent cracked orange corner.
3) 50m (4b) Climb the groove until it is possible to step right onto the wall. This leads more easily to a large ledge and prickly pears. Scramble up to the base of an enticing corner crack.
4) 45m (5a) Climb the excellent crack to the left of the corner, then continue more easily straight up to a wide crack. Belay on a terrace.
5) 35m (-) Continue in a direct line, following the right side of the chimney and crossing a wide ledge to finish up a short corner.
Tony & Ulla Pearson, January 2013.

5. Sweet Sweet Afantinzar Dogs VS 4c ★2

175m. A very fine climb on excellent rock. Start below a chimney near the lowest point of the buttress. The first ascent team described the following pitches, though other parties have reported a number of pitch variations that may be preferable.

1) 30m (4a) Climb the left edge of the chimney, then move left and follow a short crack, returning right to belay at a jammed block inside the chimney.

2) 35m (4c) Take the secondary chimney to the left, then climb a short crack and vague edge to a stance beneath flakes.
3) 35m (4b) Go up to a terrace and climb flakes on the right, then a shallow crack system before moving left to a smooth chimney. Climb the left edge of this to belay on a wide stance at the top of the pillar.
4) 30m (4c) Walk left to a short corner, following this to another wide-angled corner. Climb this until forced into a leftwards traverse to a stance on the ridge.
5) 30m (4c) A series of grooves leads to crux moves through the overhanging corner. Gain easy ground above.
6) 20m (-) A short red slab and easy scrambling to the top, as for *Orange Rocket*.
Alberto Rampini & Silvia Mazzani, November 2011.

6. Route 66 VS 4c ★2

185m. The black streak to the right of *Sweet Afantinzar Dogs* gives yet another very fine climb – one of the most enjoyable hereabouts. Start just right of a bush.
1) 35m (4b) Trend up right to a short pillar at the left edge of the black streak. Continue up the left edge to a ledge on the right.
2) 35m (4b) Continue up to pass through a square notch, following the line of the black streak. Cross a ledge and move up to a crevasse belay below a short pillar.
3) 35m (4c) Climb the pillar, then move left to twin diagonal cracks, following these to the right side of a nose. Traverse right on good flakes until close to a ledge, then go straight up on good holds to a block belay on the large ledge.
4) 40m (4c) Move to the right end of the ledge, where a steep move left of a square block gains a groove. Climb up this to a further groove on the left, followed by a final corner to a large bay.
5) 40m (-) Scramble up left to finish up an orange slab.
Joan & Andy Prickett, March 2015.

7. Rouster Wall HS 4c ★2

120m. A good climb up the central walls, starting at a crackline some 100m left of *Rainbow Bridge*.
1) 30m (4a) Climb the obvious crack, avoiding a tree at half-height, to a belay by two large blocks.
2) 30m (4b) Climb leftwards off the ledge, up the block and over small overhangs on good holds. Easier ground then leads to a small ledge.

3) 30m (4a) Climb directly, then follow a ramp up right to a large ledge.
4) 30m (4c) Move the belay up to a crack on the wall above. Make a difficult move off the ledge, then follow the large crack to a sloping ledge. A tricky move over a block then gains easier ground and scrambling to the top.
Andy Foster & Lucy Rouse, February 2013.

8. Hee-Haw E1 5a ★3

175m. Another superb route, taking the centre of the buttress. Start at the obvious corner crack.
1) 35m (4a) Climb the corner to a good ledge.
2) 40m (4b) Go up a curving crack leftwards, then follow slabby rock rightwards to a small pinnacle. Belay on a ledge up and left of this.
3) 30m (4a) Climb directly up to a large ledge.
4) 40m (5a) Climb up left initially, then go back right to the arête on the left of the corner. Excellent moves up left gain a ledge. Move right and climb a groove in the well-positioned arête, stepping left at the top onto a ledge. Scramble up above blocks to belay below an overhang.
5) 30m (4c) Pull awkwardly over the overhang and climb more easily to gain a right-trending crack-line in the headwall. Follow this with interest to the top.
Ron & Catherine Kenyon, November 2012.

9. La Quartzite ca M'Excite! E2 5c

175m. This is a minor variation to *Hee-Haw*. Start up the rib to the left of that route, and join it for the middle section to the ledge. Climb up rightwards through steep ground at the top (5c)
Marie Agnes, Didier Clouzure & Simon Destombes, March 2015

10. Rainbow Bridge HVS 5b ★1

200m. The walls up the right side of the buttress give an adventurous climb on good rock. Many parties have difficulties with route-finding, with pitch five traditionally causing its fair share of epics... Start below a small wall between huge blocks on the left and some trees on the right.
1) 30m (-) Climb the small wall, cross a ledge and take a crack to a stance below a big block.
2) 30m (4a) Go up to the block and the big terrace, then take a corner on the left to a fine orange wall. This is climbed on good holds to a final short crack.
3) 35m (-) Climb another orange wall to a wide terrace.
4) 30m (4c) The orange wall above is split by two parallel cracks: climb the left-hand one to belay on a large ledge.
5) 20m (5b) From the right side of the ledge climb a smooth corner to another magnificent orange wall. Take the left-hand crack to belay on an exposed rock step.
6) 30m (4c) Traverse 2m left to climb an edge and some little walls to reach the top of the pillar. Scramble down 2m to a belay.
7) 25m (-) The easy ridge above.
Alberto Rampini & Silvia Mazzani, November 2011.

An alternative to pitch five follows the wall to the left of the original way at 5b/c, providing something of a trap for those who go off route.

11. Chocolate Orange HVS 5a

140m. A variation start to *Rainbow Bridge*, giving some pleasant climbing. Start by scrambling up the gully on the right.
1) 25m (-) Climb easy cracks to a stance below a flake crack.
2) 25m (4b) Climb the right side of the wall above.
3-7) Finish up *Rainbow Bridge*.
Mike Mortimer & Pete Johnson, November 2012.

12. Inverted V VS 4c ★2 WIDE

130m. Climbs the wall on the right side of the crag, giving excellent and sustained climbing. The route starts at a large ledge with a huge perched boulder at its left end, some 70m beneath a prominent black inverted 'V'.
1) 25m (4c) Climb the groove and crack, then move steeply up left to a good ledge above the vegetated ramp.
2) 40m (4a) Follow grooves and cracks to a huge ledge below the 'V'.
3) 10m (4c) Enter the 'V' and exit left (large cam useful).
4) 25m (4c) Climb up the corner on the right for a few metres, then traverse leftwards along a foot ledge to gain steep cracks. Follow these, and a curving groove, to easier ground.
5) 30m (-) Easy climbing to the top.

13. Almonds are Forever Severe ★2

130m. A pleasant route on excellent rock. Start 10m right of *Inverted V*, at a black crack by an almond tree.
1) 35m (-) Climb the black crack, then continue up easier ground to a belay on the right side of the overhang.
2) 30m (4a) Climb a crack to the left of a smooth wall. Continue more easily to a ledge with a boulder.
3) 30m (4b) Go up an awkward short wall, then continue to another ledge.
4) 35m (4a) Climb the steep buttress to the top.
David Medcalf & Cathy Woodhead, March 2015

14. Yankee Tom Severe

This route climbs a pinnacle at the right-hand side of the crag. Start up a pleasant slab to gain the upper arête, belaying on top of the pinnacle.

Area Map
Crag Selector
Intro
The Climbing
How to Use
Suggested Climbs
Tafraout Granite
Anergui
Ameln Valley
Tarakatine Pass
Sidi M'Zal
Jebel Taskra
Idaougnidif
Afantinzar
Samazar
Aouguenz
Tagzene
Tagmout
History
Index

Map Page 222

Area Map
Crag Selector
Intro
The Climbing
How to Use
Suggested Climbs
Tafraout Granite
Anergui
Ameln Valley
Tarakatine Pass
Sidi M'Zal
Jebel Taskra
Idaougnidif
Afantinzar
Samazar
Aouguenz
Tagzene
Tagmout
History
Index

B AKIDA – The Golden Cirque

Shade Families Hitch Roadside

Drive from Tafraout: **1:15**
Walk-in: **35 minutes**

The West Face of Afantinzar Peak, bounding the eastern end of the Afantinzar valley above Ighir, forms a tremendous cirque of towers that provide a varied array of climbing.

The approach is straightforward, taking about 30-45 minutes from the Afantinzar Road. Park just before the first house on the left as the road descends into Afantinzar from Amzkhssan. Walk up a track past this house, heading uphill to gain a path that gently climbs up rightwards towards an isolated settlement. Just before reaching this settlement a small path strikes left uphill, heading for a broad col. Ighir Peak is visible on the left, but the first few yards of this path are hard to spot.

An alternative approach can be made by driving up a narrow track a little further along into Afantinzar. This track climbs to the small village of Agrdan, from where the walk-in is somewhat shorter. However, as the parking for this approach is on private land and is somewhat intrusive, climbers are asked to follow the approach described above from the Afantinzar Road.

Although climbing has been recorded on all thirteen buttresses, only the Alabama Buttress is described here, as this has the highest concentration of high-quality routes.

DESCENT: There is an easy descent down the gully to the right.

1. Rockin' Biougra HS 4b ★2 THIN

90m. The rib left of *Mojo* is a good climb, never too difficult but requiring a thoughtful approach throughout. Start immediately left of *Mojo*.
1) 25m (4b) Climb the rib with some excellent steep moves to a stance. Small gear protects.
2) 35m (4b) Continue straight up over bulges on the front of the rib to a final steep tower. Traverse left here and climb a short wall to ledges.
3) 30m (4a) The rib above the belay, left of the gully, has some questionable rock low down but finishes easily on excellent rock in a fine position.
Caroline Culwick & Steve Broadbent, March 2011.

2. Mojo Severe ★2 STEEP

105m. An excellent climb up one of the most impressive lines in the cirque. The long initial pitch can be split, but intermediate belays are very poor.
1) 60m. The big slabby corner is climbed to an overhang at 30m, which is overcome on good holds. Continue to a second steepening, and exit rightwards above this to a big ledge.
2) 45m. Take the left side of the upper buttress, right of a vegetated gully. A final difficult crack is avoided on the right to gain a large ledge. From here it is possible to walk off rightwards or continue to the summit (50m scrambling).
Matt Mellor & Steve Broadbent, February 2011.

3. Sweet Home Alabama VS 4c ★2

105m. A good climb with lots of character, tackling the front of the buttress right of the prominent corner. The long first pitch, an archetypal quartzite VS, is intricate and sustained though technically mild.
1) 45m (4c) Climb the shallow corner / groove up the front of the buttress, with difficult moves through the initial steep

section. Move leftwards at the roof to follow a ramp up left to the arête, turning the large upper overhang on the left. Above this traverse back right onto the front face in a fine position to a good ledge.
2) 15m (-) The short wall above the ledge leads easily to another large belay terrace.
3) 45m (-) Climb the right side of the upper buttress to the top.
Steve Broadbent & Matt Mellor, February 2011.

4. The Alabama Buttress HS 4a ★2

110m. A classic of its type, the *Alabama Buttress* takes in some very pleasant ground at an amenable grade, and is at its very best late in the day, when the rock glows orange in the evening sunlight. Start at the toe of the buttress as for the previous route.
1) 60m (4a) From the base of the shallow groove head up rightwards onto the rib. Climbers with 50m ropes should belay here. Go up the easy-angled ground heading up left to overhangs, which are turned on the right, before interesting technical moves lead further rightwards to the top of a prominent wide crack. Cross this and belay on the right side.
2) 50m (4a) An excellent traverse rightwards across slabs leads to a wide crack through the steep ground above. Move up right from here into a vague groove, then finish up the excellent and slabby right wall above. Unless you've protected this pitch very carefully, it might be worth splitting to avoid rope drag.
2b) For those in search of more exposure, the very fine alternative finish (VS 4b) traverses out leftwards above the roof from the base of the steep wide crack, before finishing up easier ground above.
Matt Mellor & Steve Broadbent, February 2011.

5. Alabama Groove HS 4c ★2

75m. The obvious steep wide crack to the right of *Alabama Buttress*. Start by scrambling up easy ground to a small ledge on the right wall.

1) 30m (4c) Climb the crack on good holds, stepping right at the top to belay as for *Alabama Buttress*.
2) 45m (4c) Step right then climb the chimney groove through the overhangs above.
Caroline Culwick & Steve Broadbent, March 2011.

Area Map
Crag Selector
Intro
The Climbing
How to Use
Suggested Climbs
Tafraout Granite
Anergui
Ameln Valley
Tarakatine Pass
Sidi M'Zal
Jebel Taskra
Idaougnidif
Afantinzar
Samazar
Aouguenz
Tagzene
Tagmut
History
Index

C HARRAM PEAK

Shade · Families · Hitch · Roadside

Drive from Tafraout: **1:15**
Walk-in: **1 hour**

Harram (meaning Pyramid) Peak is the attractive triangular summit at the eastern end of Afantinzar, providing a handful of excellent mountain routes.

The mountain is actually a long ridge, of which only the steep west face is visible from this direction, and it is this face that holds the good climbing. Follow the road from Idaougnidif through Ighir as far as a sharp bend in the road beyond the red house. Just after this there is a track on the left that leads up to houses. Park as high as possible, and then the peak is gained in about 1 hour.

DESCENT: Continue east over the highest summit and on to the plateau, then drop rightwards into a hanging valley lying to the south of the summit ridge. Follow a vague path westwards along this, turning right to cross through a narrow rocky pass to the foot of the routes.

1. Pharaoh's Buttress HVS 5a ★2

145m. Good climbing up the buttress on the left side of the Afantinzar Face with some excellent varied pitches and an exciting twist at the end.

1) 15m (4b) Starting at a steep slab at the lowest point of the buttress traverse up and left to gain flakes and cracks to a belay ledge.

2) 20m. Easy climbing up the rib to belay at a huge boulder.

3) 30m (5a) Climb onto the boulder and then step left onto the very steep wall above. Follow difficult cracks to easier ground.

4) 30m (4a) Go up a groove / crack for 5m and then step right onto the face. This provides brilliant easy face-climbing to a belay by a large boulder overlooking the vegetated gully.

5) 20m Steep moves then easy ground to a two-tiered ledge.

6) 20m (4c) The cracks in the square-cut groove are awkward, and lead to a belay behind a pinnacle.

7) 10m. Climb pinnacles, mostly on the right side to the highest tower. From here a 15m abseil gains the vegetated gully. The west summit is then reached by a 100m scramble trending rightwards.

Steve & Katja Broadbent, October 2007.

2. Raving Sax Machine HVS 5a ★1 CRACK

130m. A direct line up the centre of the west face, crossing a large diagonal terrace at the top of the first pitch.

1) 50m (4b) Climb a leftwards slanting corner then continue up the arête to the terrace.

2) 30m (4c) Start just left of a bulge and climb up slabs aiming for twin cracks above. After about 25m step left to a vegetated crack before moving back right to a belay at the base of more cracks.

3) 35m (5a) From the belay an awkward move gains the cracks. Climb these past a well-protected mantel (technical crux) then steeper ground to hollow flakes and an easy finish. Belay on a ledge beneath a large boulder.

4) 15m (4b) Climb from the boulder, about 1m left of a wide crack.

Chris Bull & Elie Dekoninck, February 2009.

D THE SANCTUARY

Drive from Tafraout: **1:15**
Walk-in: **20 minutes**

The prominent gorge of The Sanctuary is clearly visible on the left side of Lower Eagle Crag when entering the valley from the east above Ighir. The gorge is dominated on three sides by vertical walls and slabs and provides some steep, atmospheric climbing. The main wall receives very little sun, and so whilst this is a good choice on hot days it can be very mossy or wet during winter months.

The routes are easily reached in about 20 minutes from roadside parking via a vague path. This old hunters' path can be followed up the gorge to the top of the crag via scrambling and steep chimneying through some spectacular scenery.

DESCENT: It is possible to descend the broad vegetated gully on the eastern edge of Eagle Crag, but care must be taken to spot the slabby ramp on the left (facing out) to avoid the very vegetated lower section. Alternatively, continue over the top of Lower Eagle Crag and follow the easy descent to the west.

THE EAST WALL

The left-hand wall of the gully holds a single magnificent climb.

1. The Sword of Damocles E2 5c ★3

150m. This tremendous route climbs the west-facing wall on the left of The Sanctuary. Start from the top of a rock step.
1) 60m (4c) Step onto the wall then follow easy grooves to belay on a ramp.
2) 30m (-) Scramble right across the ramp to a bollard belay.
3) 60m (5b) Climb the shallow groove in the arête, trending slightly rightwards, then move precariously back left past a large hanging block. Follow the arête to a big ledge and belay under a roof.
4) 50m (5c) Move right to a large crack. Step up left onto the face and follow a perfect crack, continuing in the same line past a roof-crack and tree to the top.
Pete Johnson & Paul Donnithorne, April 2008.

Area Map
Crag Selector
Intro
The Climbing
How to Use
Suggested Climbs
Tafraout Granite
Anergui
Ameln Valley
Tarakatine Pass
Sidi M'Zal
Jebel Taskra
Idaougnidif
Afantinzar
Samazar
Aouguenz
Tagzene
Tagmout
History
Index

THE SANCTUARY WALL

The West Wall, otherwise known as The Sanctuary Wall, is the steep east-facing wall with two black streaks, clearly seen from Ighir in the morning light when approaching the valley from the east.

2. Double Overhang E2 5b

150m. The left-hand line that heads for a break in the huge double roof. Start up a silver-grey pillar and follow slabs up to the weakness in the roof, where pulling through the steep ground is easier than it looks.

Paul Donnithorne & Steve Findlay, 2008.

3. Sanctuary Slabs E1 5b

MOSSY

200m. This route starts as for *Saladin*, but breaks left to finish up the left side of the double overhang. From the start of *Saladin's* black groove head up left across the wall with difficulty to a stance and easier ground. Climb slabs and move to the left of the overhangs at the top.

Mike & Marjorie Mortimer, Derek Walker, March 2008.

4. Saladin E1 5a ★2

MOSSY

200m. The left-hand black streak gives good climbing in its upper section, despite some moss on the initial pitches.

1&2) 60m (4b) Climb the lower slabs until an easy traverse leads left to an excellent stance on the black streak.

3) 25m (5a) Step left and climb the interesting slabby rib to an overlap. Pull over this to a stance.

4) 25m (5a) Continue up the black rock to another stance.

5) 30m (4c) Climb the groove until big flakes allow a steep pull to be made out right. Follow the orange rock to an easy but very exposed traverse left back to the black streak.

6) 30m (5a) Ascend the delightful wall, heading for the overhang. After placing protection to the right of the bulge take the steep ground direct with a couple of strenuous pulls, leading to good runners and an exit right to easier ground. Belay at the foot of a crack on the right.

7) 30m (4b) Climb easily to large ledges.

Mike & Marjorie Mortimer, October 2007.

5. Juggulator E1 5a ★2

MOSSY

200m. Exposed jug-pulling up the prominent rib between the two black streaks.

Ben & Marion Wintringham, October 2007.

6. Iago HVS 5a ★1

STEEP MOSSY

190m. A spectacularly steep route, but unfortunately often wet.

1&2) 55m (4b) Climb the lower slabs to a stance beneath the upper wall.

3) 30m (5a) Go easily to the right before moving back left across more brittle rock, then climb steeply to a stance.

4) 25m (4c) Trend rightwards to belay below the arête.

5) 35m (4c) Continue rightwards until it is possible to move back left onto the arête and follow this on large holds to a stance.

6) 45m (4b) Take the easiest line to ledges and the top.

Mike Mortimer & Jim Fotheringham, October 2007.

7. Otello E1 5a

STEEP MOSSY

200m. The right-hand black streak is low in the grade and unfortunately mossy.

1&2) 60m (4b) Climb lower slabs to reach a stance at the foot of the black streak.

3) 25m (5a) The start of the black streak is very steep, but is followed until the line is forced out right onto orange rock. This is climbed on excellent holds to a step back left onto the black rock and a fine stance.

4) 35m (5a) Ascend the groove for a few metres until excellent holds lead steeply out left. Awkward moves then give access to smoother rock moving back right to another good stance.

5) 35m (5a) Follow a black groove until forced right again onto the orange rock, where a few fingery moves lead to a traverse back left to an ingenious belay.

6) 45m (5a) Traverse awkwardly left to much easier ground leading up to a ledge.

Mike & Marjorie Mortimer, October 2007.

8. Kids in the Toy Shop E1 5b ★2

MOSSY STEEP

210m. The steep wall to the right of the right-hand black streak.

Ben & Marion Wintringham, April 2008.

9. Butcher Bird HVS 5a

MOSSY

200m. The chimney to the left of *Beauty and the Beast* has some nice climbing in the first few pitches.

1) 30m (4c) Climb straight up cracks and ribs to a belay below the overhang.

2) 40m (5a) Move easily over the overhang and up into a groove below a large roof. Climb rightwards across the slabby lichenous wall and up into a steep niche. An awkward crack leads from here to a good stance in the big chimney line.

3) 40m (-) The left wall of the chimney.

4) 30m (-) Continue easily up the chimney.

5) 60m (-) Pull out onto the rib on the right to finish via scrambling as for *Beauty and the Beast*.

Steve Burns & Valerie Partington, March 2012.

10. Beauty and the Beast E1 5a

PRICKLY MOSSY

140m. Climbs a vague groove just left of the steep orange wall at the entrance to the Sanctuary Gully, just right of two converging black chimneys. Start behind the left-hand of two small trees, just right of the toe of the buttress.

1) 50m (5a) Climb vegetated cracks, grooves, and ribs rightwards to an overhanging v-shaped chimney with a streaky left wall. Climb this and belay at its top.

2) 50m (5b) Pull over the roof above and follow the groove until forced left into another groove. Make tricky moves left to a flake, and step off this leftwards to gain a ledge below a steep flake crack (possible belay). Climb the crack, then over a bulge to gain a large ledge.

3) 40m (4c) Continue up right of the chimney to gain a large platform. The top of the crag is then reached by 180m of scrambling.

Emma Alsford & Chris Bonington, April 2008.

Area Map
Crag Selector
Intro
The Climbing
How to Use
Suggested Climbs
Tafraout Granite
Anergui
Ameln Valley
Tarakatine Pass
Sidi M'Zal
Jebel Taskra
Idaougnidif
Afantinzar
Samazar
Aouguenz
Tagzene
Tagmout
History
Index

GRIVEL

E LOWER EAGLE CRAG

Drive from Tafraout: **1:15**
Walk-in: **20 minutes**

One of the most important 'big' crags in the area, the iconic northwest-facing wall above the village of Anammer is a beautifully tempting piece of rock that catches the sun from mid-afternoon, and holds many good long climbs throughout the grade-range. Locally known as Azrol Doutmda, it is commonly referred to by western climbers as Lower Eagle Crag. The rock is mostly solid, though it can be rather mossy during winter months.

DESCENT: From the top of the climbs head rightwards over the highest point of the crag, then follow a well-cairned trail down the west end (take care not to descend too early).

THE GRAND WALL

The tremendous clean sweep of rock that forms the crag's northwestern front dominates the upper Afantinzar valley, and is one of the most frequently climbed and photographed pieces of rock on the massif. Although many of the routes here feature large amounts of moss this does not detract from the crag's popularity amongst climbers in search of high-quality full-day adventures. The afternoon sun hits the left side of the face early in the afternoon and gradually spreads across all the routes by the end of the day, when the wall is a magnificent sight in the evening light.

Routes near the left end are easily approached in about 15 minutes from the Afantinzar road. Routes further right require some rather more adventurous bushwhack and are best approached from well to the left...

Jen Booys and Kerry Mellor on *Pink Lady* (VS), page 235.
Photo: Steve Broadbent

1. Great White E1 5a

250m. Starts at a crack just right of some very smooth compact slabs.
1) 45m (4c) Climb the crack and go up easier ground to a ledge.
2) 45m (4c) Go up the slab to reach an easy gully and follow this to the foot of a black cracked groove. Climb this to its top and then step up left to a good stance.
3) 45m (4c) Go straight up and climb over a bulge, then continue slightly rightwards on easier ground to good belays.
4) 30m (4a) Climb easily to the left of, and slightly above, the foot of a tower.
5) 30m (5a) Step right onto the tower and go up for a few metres until a bold move leads to a traverse right into a groove. Climb up to a ledge, then steeply right to another good ledge.
6) 45m (4c) Up the left edge to the top of the tower.
7) 15m (-) Finish up the slab to easy ground.
Derek Walker, Mike & Marjorie Mortimer, March 2007.

2. Fifty Shades of Grey E1 5b ★2

240m. Starts just uphill from the *Great White* at an attractive white rib, just right of a corner with a small tree at its base.
1) 35m (4a) Climb the rib to a belay.
2) 30m (-) Scramble up the rake to belay right of a black streak.
3) 55m (4b) Climb the crack in the slab left of the dirty corner, then trend left across slabs to climb a crack in the small overlap.
4) 30m (4b) Continue directly to a large ledge.
5) 30m (5b) Climb the corner crack then step up and right over bulges. Move up, then climb boldly up leftwards to belay at the base of a prominent dog-leg crack.

Area Map
Crag Selector
Intro
The Climbing
How to Use
Suggested Climbs
Tafraout Granite
Anergui
Ameln Valley
Tarakatine Pass
Sidi M'Zal
Jebel Taskra
Idaougnidif
Afantinzar
Samazar
History
Index

Area Map
Crag Selector
Intro
The Climbing
How to Use
Suggested Climbs
Tafraout Granite
Anergui
Ameln Valley
Tarakatine Pass
Sidi M'Zal
Jebel Taskra
Idaougnidif
Afantinzar
Samazar
Aouguenz
Tagzene
Tagmout
History
Index

6) 35m (4c) Climb the crack, then step right and make steep moves up to a stance at a crevasse.
7) 25m (5a) Make a tricky step onto the wall then trend up right past a flake to the top.
Mike Mortimer & Pete Johnson, November 2012.

3. Donkey Serenades Very Difficult ★1

300m. An easy meander up slabby ramps at the left side of the face, providing a pleasant way up the crag.
1) 20m Scramble up an easy ramp to a belay ledge at the base of grey slabs.
2) 30m Climb the slabs, trending left towards a large tree. Belay beneath an overlap.
3) 40m Go past the overlap to a huge ledge, and continue up slabs on the right.
4) 10m Walk left to the foot of black-streaked slabs.
5) 30m Climb the black slabs on the right side.
6) 15m Walk left along a terrace beneath the huge overhanging wall.
7) 40m Climb up slabs to the left of the overhanging wall.
8) 30m Trend left to an exciting belay by a corner, below a steep final wall.

9) 30m The headwall is avoided by continuing left to gain easy slabs.
10) 60m Easy scrambling to the top.
Sesh Nadathur & Caroline Culwick, April 2008.

4. Pink Lady VS 4c ★3

230m. A tremendous way up the face, giving one of the most popular routes of its type in the Anti-Atlas. The climbing is not sustained, but features a couple of short cruxes in splendid situations. It is described here with the full 9 pitches in order to provide options in case of traffic jams, as this is one of very few routes in Tafraout where queues have been known to develop. In reality, parties usually complete the climb in 5 rope-lengths.
1) 30m (-) Easy climbing up a short groove, then make an airy step left and climb an easy slab to a narrow grassy ledge.
2) 20m (4a) Follow pleasant slabs to a poor stance at the foot of the chimney groove.
3) 20m (4c) Excellent technical climbing up the chimney leads to a large ledge (The ***Partytime Belay***).
4) 25m (-) Continue up the easy groove above the ledge, then trend up right to a stance below the steep pillar.
5) 25m (4a) Good climbing, trending slightly right to a belay beneath a black wall (The ***Black Wall Belay***).
6) 25m (4c) A superb rising traverse left, up the obvious groove, leads to the arête. Step back right and go up a short groove to a dead-end at the overhang. Unlikely moves rightwards hopefully reveal a hidden jug above the overhang, which facilitates an airy swarm onto a sloping ledge (The ***Snoggers' Perch***).
7) 30m (4b) Bridge up the black chimney, exiting left at the top. Finish straight up steep ground on good holds to a large ledge system (the ***Lunchtime Ledge***).
8) 15m (-) Scramble up an easy groove to belay below the left end of the arching overhang.
9) 45m (4b) Climb up to the right of a right-facing undercut corner to gain a fascinating hand-traverse left under the roof. This leads to another unlikely move, pulling steeply through the overhang at a weakness into a right-trending groove and easier finish.
P.Johnson & E.Roberts, April 2008. Photo page 232.

5. Immaculardet HVS 5a ★2 STEEP

210m. The tempting steep orange line, starting 20m left of the major black streak. Follow a crack to a ledge with a bush on the arête. From here continue straight up the arête, using the left wall whenever the ground gets too steep.
Ben & Marion Wintringham, March 2007.

6. Black Beauty E1 5b ★2

210m. The obvious broad black streak provides a superb natural line. Start beneath a crack on the right side of the black streak, about 5m left of a chimney.
1) 15m (5a) Go up a right-trending crack, breaking left to ledges, then traverse up left to a groove with a good stance.
2) 35m (5b) A superb, committing pitch with just about enough protection. Climb straight up the black streak until it is possible to move right into a groove. Continue directly to a stance on the left of the black streak.
3) 50m (5a) A tricky start gains easier climbing above. Continue up to a corner, then follow this through a bulge to belay below a tree.
4) 50m (5b) Move up right into a technical groove, then make tricky moves onto the right-hand rib. Continue up a crack and weakness in the overhang, then climb up slabs above, heading up left to reach a big ledge.
5) 60m (4c) Finish up a groove line left of the overhangs.
Emma Alsford & Paul Donnithorne, March 2007

7. Moroccan Gold E2 5b ★3

210m. The chimney and grooves 5m right of the black streak give another good outing.
1) 25m (4c) ***Emma's Chimney*** – Climb the chimney to a small stance on the right.
2) 30m (5b) Climb up then move left into a hanging groove. Follow this, and a second groove to a fine ledge.
3) 55m (5b) An excellent and involved pitch, taking slabs and grooves to bulges. Go up through these to a ledge below an orange bulge.
4) 50m (5a) Follow a diagonal crack on the right, then trend up leftwards over slabs and bulges to a ledge.
5) 50m (4b) Finish directly.
Emma Alsford & Paul Donnithorne, March 2007.

8. Pale and Interesting E1 5a ★2

200m. Another direct line up the wall, starting up the first pitch of *Moroccan Gold*.
1) 25m (4c) ***Emma's Chimney*** – Climb the chimney to a small stance on the right.
2) 30m (4c) Traverse horizontally right until difficult moves lead up a steep crack to a ledge.
3) 30m (5a) Step left and climb the steep wall over two bulges to a ledge under the obvious roof. Pull over the right side of the roof and follow a groove to a good ledge.
4) 45m (4c) Continue in the same line.
5) 45m (4a) Easier climbing to another ledge.
6) 25m (-) Easy ground to the top.
Jim Fotheringham & Mike Mortimer, March 2007.

9. Infinity E4 5c ★3 STEEP

190m. Two wonderfully contrasting hard pitches providing one of the best and most difficult big climbs in the valley. Start from behind a large boulder.
1) 30m (5c) Gain a tiny groove then trend boldly up and right to a break. Power up the superb flake crack above to a spike belay in a groove.
2) 40m (5b) Swing right and follow the fine flake for 15m before another steep move rightwards through a bulge. Climb an overhung flake to belay on the left end of a large ledge.
3) 60m (4c) Continue in the same line through black and brown bulges.
4) 60m (5a) Direct to the top.
Emma Alsford & Paul Donnithorne, April 2008.

Area Map
Crag Selector
Intro
The Climbing
How to Use
Suggested Climbs
Tafraout Granite
Anergui
Ameln Valley
Tarakatine Pass
Sidi M'Zal
Jebel Taskra
Idaougnidif
Afantinzar
Samazar
Aouguenz
Tagzene
Tagmout
History
Index

F UPPER EAGLE CRAG

Shade · Families · Hitch · Roadside

Drive from Tafraout: **1:15**
Walk-in: **25 to 35 minutes**

High on the south side of the valley is the enormous wall of Upper Eagle Crag, stretching for over a mile from the summit of Lower Eagle Crag at its eastern end to the Hidden Valley behind Griffin Rock. This sombre, north-facing wall is home to long, remote, and adventurous routes mostly in the upper grades, although the approach and descent are not as arduous as first appearances might suggest.

To date most of the climbing has been focussed around the right-hand end of the crag, close to an easy descent gully. This area is approached in about 30 minutes from a cleared area opposite the last house before the Afantinzar road starts climbing up to the pass. From here a small track runs up past the left side of Griffin Rock into the Hidden Valley, from where most of the climbs are visible. See Griffin Rock approach on page 242.

DESCENT: The broad descent gully towards the right-hand side of the crag provides a simple return to Hidden Valley.

THE LOST WORLD

The left side of the wall behind Lower and Middle Eagle Crags has seen little attention from climbers, being both far from the road and far from the descent gully. There is almost certainly scope for further exploration here, though much of the rock is likely to be mossy and the routes somewhat esoteric. This vegetated area, christened by the first-ascent team as 'The Lost World', but whimsically named 'The Stockade' by some, can be accessed in about 40 minutes from the road, passing either side of Middle Eagle Crag. Both approaches have their merits, we're just not sure what they are. A prominent pinnacle (*The Tower of Babel*) is located some 100m east of the fence behind Middle Eagle Crag.

1. Le Petit Ramoneur E2 5c ★2 WIDE

120m. A tempting climb up a very logical line, and a special treat for off-width connoisseurs. The route starts directly underneath a distinctive flared triangular niche, about 10m right of two small detached towers, 50m left of the pinnacle.
1) 35m (5c) Head boldly up the initial slab to reach the flared niche and follow the fierce off-width crack to a belay.
2) 25m (4b) Bridge up the widening crack to a ledge.
3) 15m (-) Scramble over the ledge.
4) 45m (5a) Go up the crack into the black corner and follow it to an amusing roof. Finish up a delicate flared chimney.
Arnaud Viel & Emmanuel Freudenthal, October 2009.

DARKSIDE

This sector is located some 50-100m to the right of a dry stone wall behind Middle Eagle Crag.

2. The Orange Groove E3 5c (2) BOLD STEEP

180m. The prominent orange groove is a testing route with some exposed hard climbing.

1) 55m (5a) Start up a groove / crack and surmount a chockstone to belay on top of the pinnacle.

2) 60m (5b) Step up and right to gain the orange groove, which is followed to a belay.

3) 30m (5c) Cross the exciting steep wall on the left before moving back right to the groove above the overhang (bold). Continue up to a stance.

4) 35m (4c) Follow the easiest line to the top.

Pete Johnson & Paul Donnithorne, April 2008.

3. All's Well that Ends Well E3 5c (2) ABSEIL

75m. A superb route that attempts the steep wall right of the *Orange Groove*. Start just right of a wide crack.

1) 30m (5b) Climb up to a steep flake, and go up this to a ledge.

2) 45m (5c) Trend left up a vague ramp to the arête then climb a steep crack to a spike. Finish up and right to a good ledge and descend by abseil.

Paul Donnithorne & Pete Johnson, October 2008.

4. Mosside Story E1 5b

175m. Follows the left hand arête of a major black groove. Start up the black groove until it is possible to break left onto the arête, which is followed to the top of the crag.

Ben & Marion Wintringham, March 2007.

5. The Dark Side E3 5c (1) MOSSY STEEP

175m. A climb of great character on mainly excellent, but dirty, rock.

1) 30m (4c) Go leftwards up slabby rock to a stance left of the corner.

2) 30m (4c) Climb straight up, cross the corner, and go steeply over a bulge to a stance on the right.

3) 25m (4c) Go up to belays left and below the obvious chimney crack.

4) 40m (4c) Move right around the rib to gain another crack to a big ledge at the foot of the final corner.

5) 50m (5b) Climb the steep corner with occasional deviations onto the left wall.

Jim Fotheringham & Mike Mortimer, March 2007.

6. The Corner of Brilliant Things E3 5c (1) STEEP

155m. Starts mid way between *The Dark Side* and *Double Zero*, below and 20 metres right of a square-cut, right-facing orange corner high on the face.

1) 50m (5a) Start up a wide crack to reach a vegetated ledge. Continue over a bulge to a terrace with trees.

2) 25m (5c) Climb a vague groove in a black wall, then move left and make a bold step down. Continue diagonally up left to belay below the groove.

3) 30m (5c) Climb the groove with increasing interest. Pull around a bulge and continue up the right-hand crack to belay in a groove below a black overhang.

4) 50m (5c) Go up through the overhang and continue up the wall above. Finish up grooves and open black corners to the top.

Bob Brewer & Dai Lampard, March 2014.

Area Map
Crag Selector
Intro
The Climbing
How to Use
Suggested Climbs
Tafraout Granite
Anergui
Ameln Valley
Tarakatine Pass
Sidi M'Zal
Jebel Taskra
Idaougnidif
Afantinzar
Samazar
Aouguenz
Tagzene
Tagmout
History
Index

DOUBLE ZERO AREA

To the right of Darkside is a steep orange wall above lower, grey rocks. An old route, Double Zero, tackled the centre this steep wall on dubious rock, ending in a scary abseil from poor anchors. A more satisfactory offering starts in a similar position:

7. The Eagle Has Landed E4 6a ★★★

150m. Starts up the grey wall beneath a steep orange section of cliff.

1) 30m (5a) Climb an open groove to a block belay on the large ledge.

2) 30m (5c) Climb up left-trending diagonal cracks to a ledge system. Move up right for 5 metres to belay beneath a groove and prow.

3) 30m (6a) Climb the groove until forced left into an overhanging square-cut corner. Follow this then step left to tackle an off-width crack. Continue until the angle eases.

4) 30m (5a) Climb grey rock towards a terrace on the skyline.

5) 30m (4b) Gain the ridge and follow it rightwards to the top.

B.Brewer & D.Lampard, March 2014.

8. Fantastic Mr.Fox E1 5b ★★

85m. The slabby sidewall...

1) 30m (5b) Start up the crack of *Pteradon*, moving out left onto the slab and rib past an abseil point. Continue up the arête to an alcove belay beneath the upper slab.

2) 55m (5b) Climb onto the slab and follow intermittent cracks up leftwards towards a bulge with a crack. Follow this crack to the top. An abseil point is located up and right.

S.Bennett & B.Brewer, March 2015.

9. For Whom the Bean Tolls E1 5b ★★

85m. Follows the corner to the right.

1) 25m (5b) Follow *Fantastic Mr.Fox* to an abseil point.

2) 60m (5b) Climb the crack right of the abseil point and continue up to a slab. Take a central line, heading for a black corner and large crack, which is climbed to an exit rightwards.

B.Brewer & S.Bennett, March 2015.

10. Pteradon E3 6a ★★★

130m. Starts 20 metres left of the left side of a large orange overhang.

1) 50m (4c) Climb a crack, and continue past an abseil anchor. Move right and climb an orange leaning crack until forced left into an open groove. Follow this, taking the overhang on its right, then trend up left over blocks to a ledge below a steep wall.

2) 30m (6a) Climb the wall, moving left past a surprising crux and continue to belay on black rock.

3) 15m (4b) Climb an open groove, trending left to the top.

B.Brewer & D.Lampard, March 2014.

INSHALLAH BUTTRESS

The biggest unbroken wall on the crag is situated 200-300 metres left of the descent gully. The first route takes a prominent area of black rock at the left side of the steep Inshallah wall.

11. Riding Dirty HVS

150m. This route starts up a diagonal crack with a tree at 15m, then climbs the large area of dark rock. It is described as a good, steep climb, but perhaps only if you like moss...

1) 35m (4c) Climb the crack to a stance.
2) 30m (5a) Follow a cracked groove.
3) 25m (4c) Climb black rock to belay at the foot of a chimney.
4) 35m (5a) Traverse right to climb a mossy corner and short off-width crack.
5) 25m (4a) Easier climbing to the top.

Jim Fotheringham & Mike Mortimer, October 2007.

12. With a Little Help from my Friends E1 5c

150m. The groove and crack a few metres left of *Clay Pigeon Shoot* has a short, hard section at one third height.

C.Binington & R.Hazsko, April 2008.

13. Clay Pigeon Shoot E3 5c

150m. The wall left of *Inshallah* is a climb of sustained difficulty...

1) 30m (5b) Start 7m left of *Inshallah*, just left of a large thorny bush. Climb steeply to a flake stance, and continue up the wall to a fine ledge.
2) 20m (5c) Move left, then go back right on a big flake to gain the left-slanting overhanging crack.
3) 40m (5b) Step right and go up grooves to a stance below an overhang.
4) 60m (5c) Pull left over the overhang before trending right to gain grooves to the top.

Graham Little & Paul Donnithorne, April 2008.

14. Inshallah E2 5b

120m. A big route, and one of the most popular on the crag. Start 10m right of a large fin of rock embedded in the ground at the foot of the crag, directly below an orange chimney high on the wall.

1) 30m (5b) Climb steeply for 10m past a small corner on the right to a ledge. Move left for 5m then straight up a groove / crack to a stance.
2) 25m (5b) Climb the orange corner on the right, moving left under the roof to gain the crack above. Belay on a large ledge below the chimney.
3) 35m (5b) Traverse right, then move up to a wide crack. Move left around a steep nose, then up into the groove above. Continue awkwardly up a second hanging groove to gain a ledge on the left.
4) 30m (5b) Traverse right and continue up a crack to finish up a wide chimney.
4a) 30m (5b) A better finish follows the diagonal crack straight up from the final belay.

E.Alsford & E.Roberts, April 2008 (Original finish).
J.Rushbrooke & P.Donnithorne, March 2012 (Direct finish).

15. Condor E4 6a

130m. A superb climb up the intimidating wall right of *Inshallah*. Start midway between *Inshallah* and *Sunshine Superman*, at a boulder beneath a right-curving flake.

1) 35m (6a) Step off the boulder and climb up to gain the curving flake. Follow this rightwards to a roof, which is climbed to a small ledge. Continue steeply to a stance on the left.
2) 25m (5b) Climb a slim orange groove to a ledge in the chimney on the left.

Area Map
Crag Selector
Intro
The Climbing
How to Use
Suggested Climbs
Tafraout Granite
Anergui
Ameln Valley
Tarakatine Pass
Sidi M'Zal
Jebel Taskra
Idaougnidif
Afantinzar
Samazar
Aouguenz
Tagzene
Tagmout
History
Index

3) 30m (5b) Follow the chimney, then climb the left wall to a ledge.
4) 40m (5c) Continue in the same line and climb a groove and wall to reach the vegetated ledge below the final chimney of *Inshallah*. Move left and climb the excellent rib up left, pulling directly through bulges to gain easier ground.
Bob Brewer & Paul Donnithorne, October 2013

16. Sunshine Superman E2 5b 2

MOSSY STEEP

130m. Nice climbing up the groove to the right.
1) 35m (5b) Climb a rounded groove to a stance above a spike.
2) 40m (5b) Climb the steep right-hand groove, then step left to avoid a vegetated chimney. Climb a short crack to a ledge.
3) 55m (5b) Go up the grooves and ribs to the top
Paul Donnithorne & Sue Hazel, January 2012.

DESCENT GULLY AREA

A series of long ribs and arêtes, close to a prominent descent gully towards the right-hand side of the crag.

17. Jiggery Pokery E2 5b

MOSSY STEEP

150m. A tour-de-force following a blunt rib about 150m left of the descent gully, identified by a groove capped by a triangular overhang low down on the wall. The first ascent was made over two days in October 2007 – one day to the large spike, which was regained by abseil for the second day of climbing.
1) The initial scrappy wall is climbed via a groove to a vegetated ledge.
2) Step down and left to gain a crack into the main groove, which is followed to the triangular overhang. This is overcome with substantial difficulty, before a cracked arête leads to a large spike.
3) Step left onto the blank wall above and climb up and slightly right to easier ground on a large detached ledge. This section is rather mossy and quite difficult.
4) Step across and climb the easy groove on the left to the top.
Ben & Marian Wintringham, October 2007.

18. Eye of the Needle E2 5b 2

160m. The rib to the right of *Jiggery Pokery* gives another worthwhile climb.
1) 30m (5a) Step up from flakes and climb the chimney to the top of the buttress.
2) 40m (5b) From a tree belay at the col, climb the rib and groove to gain a superb flake. Climb this to reach a stance by a large block.
3) 20m (4c) Continue up, passing a pinnacle to gain the col beyond, belaying on a ledge beneath a chimney.
4) 25m (5a) Follow a ramp up leftwards and pull through a notch. Continue to a large ledge with thread belays.
5) 45m (5a) Climb a clean rib, moving up left to a small ledge. Pull up right onto a slab and climb this passed a block. Gain the top of a sharp pinnacle, then finish more easily above.
Bob Brewer & Paul Donnithorne, October 2013.

19. Cardiac Arêtes E3 5c 2

BOLD

100m. The striking arête tucked away at the left side of the Descent Gully Area gives a classic climb. It starts in the gully left of *Magical Mystery Tour* and follows the soaring arête on the left in three pitches.
1) 50m (5b) Go up a chimney then grooved ribs and cracks to a hanging stance just right of the base of the first arête.
2) 25m (5c) Step left around the arête, then follow flakes and cracks up and right back to the arête at a huge thread. Step right and climb a crack to a ledge.
3) 25m (5b) Climb the final arête directly, protected by thin slings and wires.
Paul Donnithorne & Pete Johnson, April 2008.

Katja Broadbent on the excellent *Grasshopper Arête* (VS) at Griffin Rock, page 243. ➲
Photo: Steve Broadbent

Area Map
Crag Selector
Intro
The Climbing
How to Use
Suggested Climbs
Tafraout Granite
Anergui
Ameln Valley
Tarakatine Pass
Sidi M'Zal
Jebel Taskra
Idaougnidif
Afantinzar
Samazar
Aouguenz
Tagzene
Tagmout
History
Index

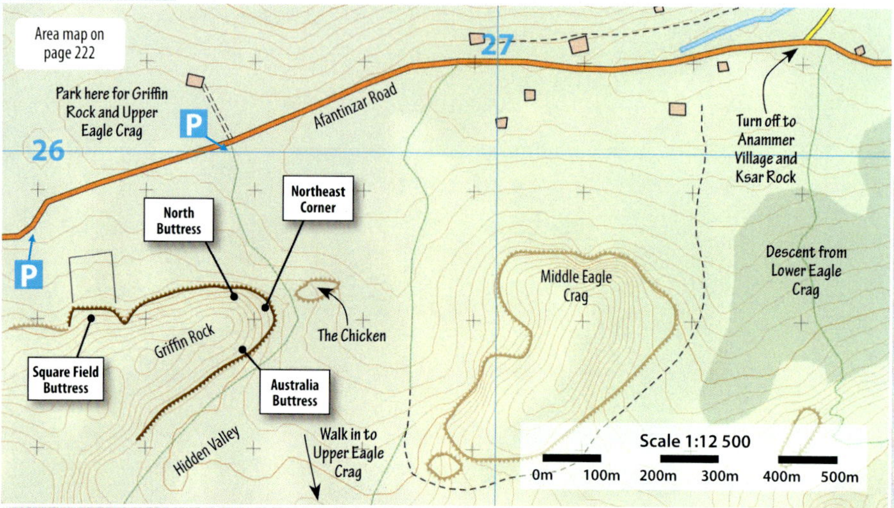

G GRIFFIN ROCK

Shade · Families · Hitch · Roadside

Drive from Tafraout: **1:15**
Walk-in: **5 to 10 minutes**

This popular cragging venue lies on the ridge between the Afantinzar road and a hidden valley below the western end of Upper Eagle Crag, with climbing on both the south face (overlooking the Hidden Valley) and the north face (overlooking the Afantinzar Road). There are some longer and more adventurous pitches here than at neighbouring Anammer, and the rock here is more typical of that found on the bigger multi-pitch routes.

Griffin Rock is one of the highest roadside crags in the Anti-Atlas, so whilst it is the first to catch poor weather in the winter, it can be a good option on hot days, particularly as many of the routes face north and stay out of the sun.

Park on the roadside opposite the last house before the road starts climbing up to the pass. A small trail leads up to the eastern end of the rock (about 10 minutes) and on into the Hidden Valley. Most of the best climbing is focussed around the eastern end of the ridge, and only the better sectors are described here.

DESCENT: Most routes here require an abseil descent, and some have seen little traffic. Climbers should therefore be prepared to replace abseil anchors when climbing here.

AUSTRALIA BUTTRESS

This southeast-facing buttress is reached by following a vague trail around the eastern end of the crag, between Northeast Corner and the Chicken.

1. The Inquisitive Velociraptor HVS 5b ★ ABSEIL

30m. Start left of the chockstone gully just below a long broken crack. Gain the crack with difficulty, then follow it more easily to a step right into a bulging crack. Keep right of a bushy cleft and continue to a final gully.

R.Eckersley, March 2014.

2. Samaa Zarka HS 4b ★★ ABSEIL

40m. Start just left of the jammed boulder gully, directly below a nose at three metres. Climb up to the right of a corner, stepping left underneath the nose into a crack. Climb this, and the buttress to its right, to a diagonal crack through a roof. Step left onto the orange wall and climb up rightwards to a groove and easier rock above. Descend by walking east to the top of *Ten Pound Pom*.

Tim Gledhill & Nick Eaton, January 2013.

3. Kangaroo Rib E1 5b ★ LOOSE ABSEIL

50m. The left arête gives a good long pitch, though care is required with suspect rock.

Paul Donnithorne & Steve Findlay, October 2007.

4. Arapiles Calling E2 5b ★ BOLD ABSEIL

50m. A good climb up the centre of the small face and line of the abseil descent. A bold start leads to easier ground and cracks in the final brown wall.

Steve Findlay & Paul Donnithorne, October 2007.

5. Bridge Over the River Kasbah VS 4c

55m. Starts as for *Ten Pound Pom*, just left of a small recess.
1) 15m (4c) Climb the wall and large crack to belay on large blocks just right of the huge chockstone.
2) 25m (4b) Cross the chockstone bridge, traverse right, then move left and up to a belay beneath an overhanging crack.
3) 15m (4a) Move left and finish up a groove to a block belay.
R.Eckersley & M.Newbury, March 2014.

6. Ten Pound Pom HVS 5a

50m. Start up the right-hand rib, until a step left leads up the groove to a ledge. Step back onto the arête and follow it to a final crack.
Ben & Marion Wintringham, October 2007.

7. Mike's Route HVS 5a

50m. The slabby right-hand wall has some dubious rock. Finish left onto the arête and up the final crack of *Ten Pound Pom*.
Mike & Marjorie Mortimer, October 2007.

8. Dennis the Menace HVS 5a

35m. Good climbing up a vague streaked-crack up the left side of the buttress. Climb up to a ledge, then step left into the upper crack.
E.Roberts & E.Alsford, April 2008.

9. Berber Ella HS 4b

35m. Start up a leftward trending flake to a ledge. From here move slightly right and climb a shallow groove to an abseil descent.
E.Roberts & E.Alsford, April 2008.

10. Grasshopper Arête VS 4b

40m. The right-hand arête gives some super, steep climbing to mid-height ledges. Step right from here for a bold move onto the upper arête.
E.Roberts & E.Alsford, April 2008. *Photo previous page.*

11. Amphitheatre Buttress E1 5a

50m. Start from a chimney with a jammed block, climbing a dark stain and then groove up right to a ledge. Go up slabby ground to a final flake corner.
P.Donnithorne & L.Brown, October 2010.

12. Crackerjack E3 5c

50m. Safe but strenuous climbing up the obvious overhanging corner, giving one of the valley's classic E3 pitches.
1) 25m (4a) Climb easily up to a ledge below the wide crack.
2) 25m (5c) Power up the wide crack, then pull up right to a fine finish on the upper wall. Low in the grade.
E.Roberts & E.Alsford, April 2008.

13. Kangoo Corner VS 4b

60m. Climbs a crack just left of the arête to gain a large ledge. Traverse left and finish up a prominent chimney to a step across to the top.
Jim Fotheringham, Ben & Marion wintringham, October 2007.

14. Rest Day Rendezvous HVS 4c

60m. Starts on the right side of the bay, close to *Kangoo Corner*.
1) 30m (4c) Climb the crack in the prow up to a prominent ledge. Step right here and go up a short corner to a spike belay.
2) 30m (4b) Step right and follow the off-width crack to join the final section of *Kangoo Corner*.
Paul Donnithorne & Pete Johnson, October 2010.

Area Map
Crag Selector
Intro
The Climbing
How to Use
Suggested Climbs
Tafraout Granite
Anergui
Ameln Valley
Tarakatine Pass
Sidi M'Zal
Jebel Taskra
Idaougnidif
Afantinzar
Samazar
Aouguenz
Tagzene
Tagmout
History
Index

Map Page 222

NORTHEAST CORNER

A collection of excellent harder climbs is located at the very eastern end of the Ridge, where the path passes between Griffin Rock and The Chicken, and then on into the Hidden Valley.

15. A Profusion of Protrusions E1 5b ★2 CRACK STEEP ABSEIL

50m. A brilliant steep route with large holds, following a series of jamming cracks and bulges. It is low in the grade and can be split into two pitches if required to avoid rope-drag.

Paul Donnithorne & Steve Findlay, October 2007.

16. Seven Years E2 5b ★1 CARE!

50m. A very fine climb, marred slightly by a rather dangerous top section. Follow a left-leaning ramp, then go straight up the wall to a ledge with a block and possible belay. Step right onto the rib and climb up the left arête of a short chimney. This section is poorly protected, and features some worrying holds (a runner high in the previous route is recommended to keep the rope off the sharp edge below). At the top step right again and climb the brilliant steep arête on jugs.

Steve Findlay & Paul Donnithorne, October 2007.

17. Sound of One Flip-Flopping E3 5c ★1 CRACK STEEP ABSEIL

60m. A direct start to *North East Corner*, climbing an overhanging crack to a vague left-slanting groove.

Steve Pack & Ed Bulman, October 2007.

18. North East Corner E1 5b ★2 CRACK STEEP ABSEIL

60m. The third in a trio of tremendous climbs, taking the deep groove to a belay ledge at 30m. From here climb a crack and short chimney to gain a superb traverse out right, then finish up a groove.

Steve Findlay & Paul Donnithorne, October 2007.

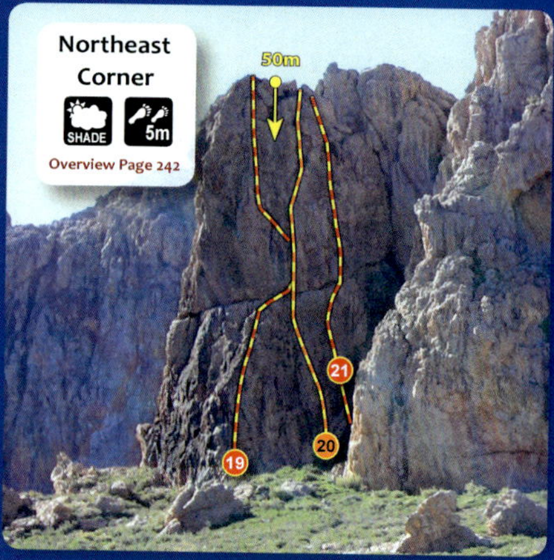

19. Two Left Feet E2 5b ★1 BOLD ABSEIL

70m. Another worthwhile but bold climb, starting a few metres right of *Northeast Corner*.

1) 30m (5b) Climb up right through bulges to spike belays.

2) 30m (5b) Cracks on the right lead to a cave, from where a step left gains an exposed ramp to finish.

Bob Brewer, Paul Donnithorne & Pete Johnson, October 2011.

20. Pot Black HVS 5b

60m. Shady climbing up the north-facing wall. Start up a deep groove and climb steep cracks into the chimney. Follow this to the top.

Bob Brewer, Paul Donnithorne & Pete Johnson, October 2011.

21. Perfect Partners E1 5b ★2 ABSEIL

50m. Start up the right-hand of two steep flake-grooves on the left wall of the gully. At the top of the groove step right and pull through a bulge onto the upper wall.

Paul Donnithorne, April 2008.

NORTH BUTTRESS

To the right of The Northeast Corner the crag swings round to a steep orange and black north-facing wall overlooking the Afantinzar road. This is the North Buttress, home to the hardest collection of routes in the valley, all with abseil descents.

22. Moussem E5 6a ★2 ABSEIL

25m. A superb modern test-piece up the face 50 metres right of *Northeast Corner*. Climb rightwards to an obvious pocket at 4 metres then step left and go up to a large thread on the bulge at 15 metres. Descend by abseil from a spike.

Pete Johnson & Paul Donnithorne, March 2010.

23. Bossy Boots E4 5c BOLD ABSEIL

60m. Steep scoops followed by easier climbing up the corner and lumpy pillar to the right of *Moussem*. Start just left of a low cave.

1) 30m (5c) Climb the scoop past two peg runners before moving right to a ledge. From here go up left to belay below a large circular niche.

2) 30m (5b) The corner forming the right side of the niche leads to a swing right onto the pillar, which is followed to the top.

Paul Donnithorne & Pete Johnson, March 2010.

24. Funky Town E1 5a ABSEIL

60m. This rambling pitch starts some 20 metres right of *Bossy Boots*, and has a black chimney above it. No further details are known.

Paul Donnithorne & Amy Colson, November 2009.

25. Blackout E4 5c ABSEIL

40m. A testing pitch, taking the right side of the mid-height roof. Climb scoops to the overhang then pull through into a shallow groove. Finish up a weakness trending left to the top.

Dan Donovan & Neil Adams, March 2010.

26. Knit One Perl One E1 5b ★1 ABSEIL

50m. The vague black streak to the right of an area of orange rock is a good pitch.

Ben & Marion Wintringham, April 2008.

27. The Rainmaker E1 5a ABSEIL

50m. Climb black rock on the left wall heading for a vegetated ledge until moves can be made up right to the pinnacle. Low in the grade.

Ben & Marion Wintringham, April 2008.

28. Kasbah Tizourgane E3 5c ★2 ABSEIL

50m. An excellent pitch taking the wall just left of the crack, with a possible lower-off from a spike at 25m. Low in the grade.

P.Johnson & E.Roberts, April 2008.

29. Cornish Cream E1 5b ★1

80m. Good climbing, providing a longer finish to *Green Plastic Dinosaur Crack*.

1) 45m (5b) Follow *G.P.D.C*, but where that route breaks right continue straight up the wide black corner to belay by the pinnacle.

2) 35m (4c) Step off the boulder and climb a slab leftwards towards the arête. Follow this to pinnacles and scramble rightwards to finish.

B.Bigger & J.Marshall, November 2009.

30. Green Plastic Dinosaur Crack E2 5b ★2 CRACK ABSEIL

50m. Climb the deep crack 10 metres left of the arête, as for *Cornish Cream*. This time, break right up a shallow technical groove to a hole, then jam your way to glory!

Paul Donnithorne & Steve Findlay, October 2007.

Area Map
Crag Selector
Intro
The Climbing
How to Use
Suggested Climbs
Tafraout Granite
Anergui
Ameln Valley
Tarakatine Pass
Sidi M'Zal
Jebel Taskra
Idaougnidif
Afantinzar
Samazar
Aouguenz
Tagzene
Tagmout
History
Index

31. Silver Arête E1 5b

40m. Start as for *Silver Wall*, but after 3m trend left to a spike on the arête. Continue left and up big flakes to the top.
Paul Donnithorne & Steve Findlay, October 2007.

32. Silver Wall E1 5b

30m. The west-facing wall just left of the pinnacle.
Paul Donnithorne & Steve Findlay, October 2007.

33. Srebrny E2 5c

25m. Starts right of *Silver Wall*, below a thin crack. Gain the crack and follow it on side-pulls to a direct finish above.
W.Calvert & J.Mothersele, October 2016.

THE FIRST BAY

34. The Left Edge E2 5b

50m. Climb up a brown wall, then left to the arête and finish up the central groove.
Paul Donnithorne & Steve Findlay, October 2007.

35. The Beak E1 5b

50m. Climb a smooth groove to pass the beak on the right, before moving back left to stand on it. Finish up a steep crack and shallow groove.
Paul Donnithorne & Steve Findlay, October 2007.

36. Tuffroute E4 5c

50m. The tower's right arête. Start up *The Beak* then follow the undercut right-leaning crack to the right-hand arête.
Steve Findlay & Paul Donnithorne, October 2007.

37. Galloping Trots E1 5a

20m. A vague crack line to the left of the chimney.
P.Johnson & E.Roberts, April 2008.

38. The Italian Job E1 5b

45m. Climb the straight crack in the back wall of the gully to finish between two large spikes.
Paul Donnithorne & Emma Alsford, April 2008.

SQUARE FIELD BUTTRESS

DESCENT: Descend from the first two climbs by continuing up left until it is possible to scramble down.

39. Broccoli Meet Thy Doom VS 5a

40m. Starts just left of the central orange pillar. Climb a crack to an overhang at 15 metres and surmount this with difficulty to an easier finish.
Adam Bradley & Graham Lee, March 2009.

40. But Señor, There is no Sun! HS 4b

40m. The central orange buttress, starting from the right side, is a somewhat shady affair.
Graham Lee & Adam Bradley, March 2009.

41. Chasing Sunset HS 4b

20m. This route lies on the opposite side of the gully from a prominent black wall. It climbs an attractive golden wall, initially leftwards, then back right up an open scoop to the top. Walk off the back and bear right down a rock gully.
Emma Alsford & Paul Donnithorne, March 2013.

The next two routes are on the prominent red buttress in the middle of the bay.

42. Consolation Crack E4 6a

30m. The left-slanting crack has some tricky moves, and

leads to a wobbly pinnacle on the arête. Finish easily above, taking care with loose blocks at the top. Descend by scrambling off over the top.
P.Johnson & E.Roberts, March 2013.

43. The Mad Dash E3 5c ★2 CARE!

30m. The right side of the red buttress, starting as for the previous route. Gain the initial groove of *Consolation Crack*, then move up right to a ledge on the arête. Airy moves up left lead to a pinnacle, from where a fine finish up the arête gains the top.
P.Donnithorne & P.Johnson, March 2013.

To the right of the red buttress is a black wall with two prominent crack lines.

44. The Prize E2 5b ★3

30m. A magnificent climb up the left-hand crack. Bridge up the open chimney for 5 metres to an in-situ thread. Reach into the crack and continue steeply to the top.
Emma Alsford & Paul Donnithorne, March 2013.

45. Free Gift E1 5b ★2

30m. The right-hand crack has some creaky flakes, but offers good, well-protected climbing.
Paul Donnithorne & Emma Alsford, March 2013.

TIGER BUTTRESS

This super little wall of good orange quartzite is located at the far western end of the north face of Griffin Rock, and is best approached by parking at the second hairpin on the road up to the col at the top of Afantinzar, from where it is clearly visible to the east. The buttress is approached easily in about 5 minutes from the road.

46. Over the Shoulder HVS 5a ★2 GEAR

30m. Start up the right-facing corner in the left side of the wall. Continue up a pale streak and shallow groove to the top.
D.Rumney & T.Rumney, March 2013.

47. A Hole Full of Protein E1 5b ★2

30m. The left-facing corner in the centre of the face is a strong line, well-protected with slings. Trend up left when things get steep to access the upper black-streaked groove.
D.Rumney & T.Rumney, March 2013.

48. Boulder Holder VS 4c ★1

30m. The ominous dark cleft is better than it looks.
D.Rumney & T.Rumney, March 2013.

Area Map
Crag Selector
Intro
The Climbing
How to Use
Suggested Climbs
Tafraout Granite
Anergui
Ameln Valley
Tarakatine Pass
Sidi M'Zal
Jebel Taskra
Idaougnidif
Afantinzar
Samazar
Aouguenz
Tagzene
Tagmout
History
Index

H ANAMMER CRAGS

Shade Families Hitch Roadside

Drive from Tafraout: **1:15**
Walk-in: **5 to 10 minutes**

The south-facing outcrops at Anammer offer some of the best single-pitch cragging in the region, and have become a justifiably popular destination. If you're looking for low-grade, low-commitment cragging in the sunshine then you need look no further than Anammer, where an almost non-existent walk-in, simple descents, perfect rock, and huge diversity of routes combine to create a friendly and varied crag. Novice climbers can cut their Moroccan teeth on the delightful routes of Banbury and Cinnamon Buttress, VS leaders will lose themselves amongst the dozens of three-star classics, whilst extreme climbers entertain themselves on the superlative *Park End*.

The crag is quite extensive, and is split up into several distinct sectors as seen in the diagram below. There is much broken rock on this hillside, and the Afantinzar road provides the best spot from which to identify particular areas – the low triangular wall of Continental, as well as the isolated houses provide good reference points.

A long horizontal path runs along the bottom of the crags, linking the houses and providing a convenient means of transiting between areas. Despite this, however, it's still worth picking the parking spot nearest to your chosen area, as the whole crag extends for over half a kilometre from Cindies to The Purple Turtle.

There is ample parking along the roadside, and approaches are obvious on a first visit. Please be respectful of the local agriculture and avoid trampling fields or damaging terrace walls – a number of small trails exist and should be utilised to avoid damaging the planted land near the road. Almost all of the climbs here also overlook houses, so please adopt a low impact approach, keep noise to a minimum, and avoid climbing in large groups. Although the local people are very friendly to visiting climbers, care must be taken to maintain this good relationship.

CINDIES

The excellent and secluded buttress of Cindies is somewhat detached from the rest of the Anammer areas, but the climbs here are well worth seeking out. The crag is easily approached in about 5 minutes straight up from the road, or can be accessed by traversing along from Jericho and the Double Buttress.

1. A.T.B. HVS 4c ★1 LOOSE

20m. Steep climbing up the rickety crack leads to a bold rock-over to the left. The route is easy for the brave, and for those willing to ignore some slightly dubious rock.
Steve & Katja Broadbent, April 2008.

2. The Puppies of Wrath HS 4a LOOSE

20m. The buttress has some suspect rock lower down and eases considerably above.
Steve & Katja Broadbent, April 2008.

3. Adelante! E2 5c BOLD

20m. Follow *Ecuador* until just before the easier wide crack, then step left and finish up the face, trending left.
D.Jeff & S.Capewell. October 2015.

4. Ecuador HVS 5b ★2 GEAR CRACK

20m. The thin crack in the impending wall is a superb and photogenic test-piece. From good protection at the overlap make awkward moves to gain the diagonal crack and follow it to the easier wide crack above. Difficult but safe climbing that sees its fair share of air-time and almost makes it into the E1 grade.
Steve & Katja Broadbent, April 2008.

5. Sunshine Arête E2 5a ★2 BOLD

20m. The excellent arête on its right side is unprotected and has a high crux.
Steve & Katja Broadbent, April 2008.

6. Scorpion Stripper VS 4b

25m. The wall to the right, finishing up the off-width crack above.
Graham Lee & Adam Bradley, February 2008.

7. We Are But Men Severe ★1 WIDE

30m. The tempting off-width crack is easier than it looks, with some excellent hidden holds.
Adam Bradley & Graham Lee, February 2008.

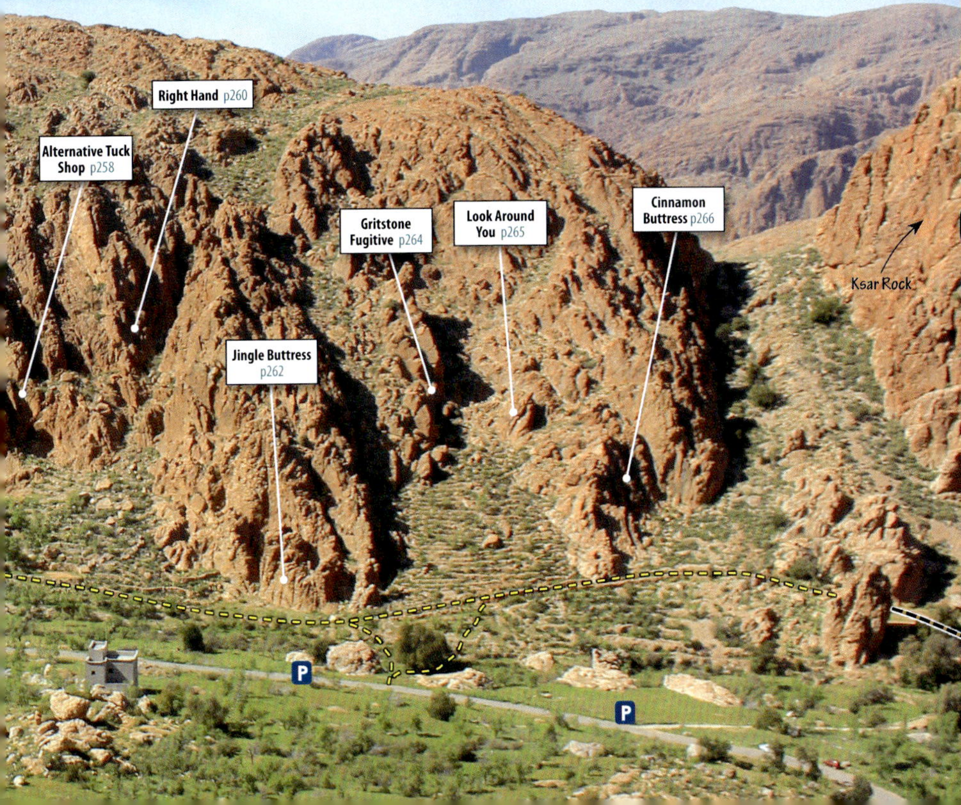

Area Map
Crag Selector
Intro
The Climbing
How to Use
Suggested Climbs
Tafraout Granite
Anergui
Ameln Valley
Tarakatine Pass
Sidi M'Zal
Jebel Taskra
Idaougnidif
Afantinzar
Samazar
Aouguenz
Tagzene
Tagmout
History
Index

8. Heart of Asia MVS 4b

25m. The buttress leads to an awkward wide crack. A very short second pitch may be required before walking off to the left.

Steve & Katja Broadbent, April 2008.

9. The Sheriff HVS 5a ★1

25m. Follow the crack to the right of the previous route.

Louis Hume & Jenny Hall, April 2012.

10. Be You Angels VS 4c ★2

30m. Another excellent pitch. Start on a square block and make well-protected moves up to a ledge. Continue through the cruxy arête on the right to a belay.

Adam Bradley & Graham Lee, February 2008.

THE BALCONY

High on the left side of the crag is a small wall with a short clean slab at its right side. These short routes are best approached from below Jericho and the Main Bay, scrambling up left as for the descent from Double Buttress.

11. Essex Street Difficult

15m. The easy-looking buttress has excellent holds and is climbed direct to a short pinnacle.

Steve Broadbent (solo), December 2008.

12. Chaffinch Walk Difficult (SLAB)

15m. The pleasant slab to the right has some nice moves.

Steve Broadbent (solo), December 2008.

13. Blockhead Mild Severe (UNCHECKED, SLAB)

18m. Climb a crack for 2m, then move up right past suspect blocks. Finish up stepped walls.

Dave Wilkinson & Alex Wellings, February 2016.

14. Chaffinch Walk V.Diff (UNCHECKED, SLAB)

17m. Start from a small ramp, trending slightly left then back up right.

Dave Wilkinson & Alex Wellings, February 2016.

15. Tom Tower Very Difficult

15m. The rib can be tackled direct, though easy escapes leftwards are always possible.
Steve Broadbent & Elie Dekoninck, December 2008.

16. Cheney Lane Very Difficult ★1

15m. The short narrow buttress left of the prominent small slab has interesting moves above the overlap.
Steve & Katja Broadbent, October 2008.

17. Learning to Fly E2 5b ★1 SLAB BOLD

10m. The small slab provides sustained difficulties, disappointing holds and poor protection, and is a much bigger lead than its height might suggest.
Steve & Katja Broadbent, Elie Dekoninck, December 2008.

DOUBLE BUTTRESS

This narrow stepped buttress lies on the left side of the Main Bay and holds a number of good climbs.

DESCENT: The descent from Double Buttress is straightforward but relatively long. Head left from the top of the climbs and descend to a vague path cutting back across rocks to the base of the routes.

18. Iffley Road E1 5b ★2 BOLD

25m. A bold climb up the very blank-looking wall set back to the left of the Double Buttress. Climb the initial wall via an interesting mantel and hard, unprotected moves to a good break beneath the overlap. Pull through the roof using good holds and cracks, and continue easily to the top.
Steve & Katja Broadbent, February 2007.

19. Cornmarket VS 4b ★2 CRACK

25m. Good crack climbing and bridging up the hidden corner right of the previous route.
Steve & Katja Broadbent, February 2007.

20. Rose Lane HVS 5a ★1 BOLD

70m. A fine and varied climb up the left side of the double buttress. Climb the smooth face to a ledge, and continue boldly up the short wall behind. The overhang is then taken direct with good protection and large holds to a belay on boulders. The second pitch gives pleasant steep climbing to the top.
Steve & Katja Broadbent, February 2007.

21. Golden Road Very Difficult ★2

70m. A good face climb on immaculate rock. Start up the corner and follow good cracks to belay on a large ledge. The upper wall looks daunting, but is overcome easily on excellent holds.
Steve & Katja Broadbent, February 2007.

Area Map
Crag Selector
Intro
The Climbing
How to Use
Suggested Climbs
Tafraout Granite
Anergui
Ameln Valley
Tarakatine Pass
Sidi M'Zal
Jebel Taskra
Idaougnidif
Afantinzar
Samazar
Aouguenz
Tagzene
Tagmout
History
Index

THE MAIN BAY

Tucked at the back of a large bay between Double Buttress and the pinnacles of Jericho are a series of rather rambling walls that appear less attractive than the neighbouring rock. On closer inspection, however, this bay holds a number of pleasant mid-grade routes that provide an excellent day out for those operating in the HS to HVS grade range.

22. Floral Dance MVS 4b ★2

25m. A brilliant route, sustained at the grade with good holds and adequate protection. Climb the left side of the buttress until it is possible to step right onto a ledge beneath the final overhang. Pull through this at the obvious weakness.

Steve & Katja Broadbent, April 2007.

23. Beaumont Street HVS 5b ★1

25m. The right hand crack line is a pleasant route with a distinct crux. Follow the crack easily to an awkward break in the overhang, where a loose jug hinders progress. This is overcome athletically to an excellent finish up the wall above.

Steve & Katja Broadbent, April 2007.

DESCENT: Traverse up left past the top of Double Buttress, then descend further left as for routes there.

24. B3 MVS 4c ★3

GEAR CRACK

25m. A superb pitch, tucked away in the vegetated gully right of *Beaumont Street* featuring some fine crack climbing and bridging. Start by scrambling in from the right to a good ledge between the two bushes. Step across the gully and climb the lower corner crack until an easy traverse right gains the right-hand upper crack. This is entered with difficulty, then followed to a fine steep finish on jugs.

Steve & Katja Broadbent, October 2008.

25. Headington Hill MVS 4b ★1

25m. A worthwhile climb up the left side of the back wall. Gain the starting ledge by scrambling leftwards from the gully at the foot of *Woodstock Road*. Start up a short corner then move left up the wall to gain the obvious crack. This has one difficult section near the top.

Steve & Katja Broadbent, October 2008.

26. Woodstock Road HS 4b ★1

35m. The crack up the back wall is started from a narrow gully and has some tricky moves above the half-height ledge. Finish up a small groove left of the tree.

Steve & Katja Broadbent, October 2008.

27. Knights of the Kasbah HVS

30m. The wall between *Woodstock Road* and *Bridge of Sighs*, starting up the latter route before moving left to tackle the centre of the wall.

Ron Kenyon, November 2012.

28. Bridge of Sighs HS 4a ★1

30m. Nice bridging out of the gully gains a left-slanting ramp. Climb this to a steep finish up the prominent upper crack. The climb finishes on a flat rock ledge which can either be exited by scrambling up the corner crack to the left, or better via the...

10m. ***Direct Finish*** (HS 4b) – The vague thin crack-line through the small overlap above the ledge.

Steve & Katja Broadbent, Elie Dekoninck, December 2008.

29. High Street Severe ★2

30m. Good climbing on the highest tier of the crag. Best approached by a combination of pitches up through Jericho, and then up *Baby Eric*. Climb a crack system to a small ledge, below and right of a prominent short chimney. Go up the arête, then step right for an excellent steep finish up the wall.

Steve & Katja Broadbent, April 2007.

30. Baby Eric VS 4c

12m. The short arête at the back of the Main Bay is harder than it looks with good gear up to the block. Finish direct, avoiding the temptation to skulk off left.

Steve & Katja Broadbent, April 2007.

31. Knight's Move E1 5b ★2 BOLD

10m. The blank wall right of *Baby Eric* is a bold and technical climb for its grade, but fortunately is not sustained. From the ledge, toe-traverse left to gain a good runner before sprinting up and right on tiny holds. Poor, small gear protects. A direct start from the ground has also been climbed at the same grade.

Steve & Katja Broadbent, Elie Dekoninck, December 2008.

32. Pygmy Crack Severe

10m. The short crack has an interesting exit.

Steve & Katja Broadbent, October 2008.

JERICHO (FIRST TOWER)

The towers and faces of the central crag provide some excellent and steep mid-grade routes. The area can be identified by two towers with a grassy bay between them, and the prominent orange overhangs of *Radcliffe Corner* behind. The first routes climb the First Jericho Tower

DESCENT: A short scramble off the back gains the notch.

33. Cranham Street VS 4b ★1

30m. Climbs the south face of the First Tower. Start up steep rock to gain a crack in the centre of the face. Follow this past a large ledge to a tricky direct finish.

Steve & Katja Broadbent, April 2007.

34. Folly Bridge Severe ★2

30m. The obvious crack / groove in the south face leads to some superb bridging in the upper chimney.

Steve & Katja Broadbent, April 2007.

35. Anzar HVS 5a ★1 GEAR STEEP

25m. The overhanging rib on the right side of the Tower's south face is a photogenic pitch that is low in the grade and has excellent protection. Taller climbers will find the route considerably easier.

Steve & Katja Broadbent, April 2007.

36. Wall of the Early Morning Light VS 4c BOLD

30m. The intimidating east face of the First Jericho Tower is a steep climb with a bold section at half height. Start up a crack at the right side of the face, step left and climb the centre of the face before an easier finish onto the south face.

Steve & Katja Broadbent, February 2007.

JERICHO (BACK WALL)

The next routes are located on the wall behind the two towers.

37. Kingston Road Mild Severe ★2 STEEP

35m. Excellent steep climbing up the buttress behind the First Tower. Follow the natural weakness slanting up and left, before some very steep moves lead to an easier rightwards-slanting wide crack. Descend via a short down-climb on the summit's eastern end.

Steve & Katja Broadbent, February 2007.

38. Farmboy's Mum HS 4b ★1 STEEP

30m. An eliminate on *Kingston Road*, taking the wall direct, rather than following the slanting crack.

Graham Lee & Adam Bradley, February 2008.

Area Map
Crag Selector
Intro
The Climbing
How to Use
Suggested Climbs
Tafraout Granite
Anergui
Ameln Valley
Tarakatine Pass
Sidi M'Zal
Jebel Taskra
Idaougnidif
Afantinzar
Samazar
Aouguenz
Tagzene
Tagmout
History
Index

39. Amazir Crack HS 4a ★1 WIDE

25m. The wide crack at the back of the Jericho Bay is gained via ledges, starting just left of the arête of *Little Clarendon Street*.

Steve & Katja Broadbent, April 2007.

40. Little Clarendon Street Mild Severe

10m. The short arête at the back of the grassy bay between the two towers is a pleasant climb with good holds and well-spaced protection.

Steve & Katja Broadbent, February 2007.

41. Walton Street VS 4c ★1 CRACK

25m. The meandering line up the buttress above *Little Clarendon Street* is considerably better and more technical than appearances would suggest. From the ledge at the top of *LCS* climb grooves and cracks up the blunt rib to a small block stance on the arête. Step left into the corner, which is climbed strenuously to a cave belay. Escape leftwards.

Steve & Katja Broadbent, February 2007.

42. Radcliffe Corner E1 5c ★2 PRICKLY WIDE

35m. The stunning overhung corner behind the Jericho Towers is one of the crag's big ticks... vegetated low down and very strenuous above. Layback desperately up the corner to difficult moves left past the huge block. Exit with relief onto a ledge (possible belay) and then step back left onto the fine upper wall, passing a worryingly wobbly perched boulder. A difficult climb, even with a rack of large cams...

Steve & Katja Broadbent, April 2007.

43. Plantation Road MVS 4b

40m. The buttress to the right of the big orange corner gives a good climb, marred only slightly by the vegetation. Climb the lower buttress easily on excellent large holds until a tricky reach rightwards gains the overhung crack. Follow this up to the roof, which is overcome easily on huge perfectly placed holds. Continue via a variety of ramps and walls (depending on how much rope-drag you've developed).

Steve & Katja Broadbent, February 2007.

JERICHO (2ND TOWER)

The next two routes climb the slender 2nd Tower.

44. Kraminssn HVS 5a ★1 ABSEIL

15m. A direct line up the west face of the Second Jericho Tower. Start on the west side of the notch and climb straight up past a block until the crack, good holds, and protection run out... finish with flair.

Steve & Katja Broadbent, February 2007.

45. Jericho VS 4c ★3 ABSEIL

35m. The centre of the Second Tower's south face gives a popular, steep pitch with a bold start and well-protected exhilarating climbing above.

Steve & Katja Broadbent, February 2007.

DESCENT: From the Second Tower a 20 metre abseil can be made down the overhanging east face.

PARK END

This immaculate tilted block provides some of the very best pitches at Anammer and is seen clearly from the Afantinzar Road.

DESCENT: A tricky scramble down the right-hand side.

46. Park End Chimney HS 4a ★2

20m. The deep chimney is climbed using small holds as well as more traditional methods... Excellent for those who like that kind of thing.
Katja & Steve Broadbent, February 2007.

47. Park End E3 5b ★3 BOLD

25m. The photogenic arête features mercifully easy climbing a long, long way above low protection in St.Clements. Follow the arête directly with increasing commitment to a cathartic finale that is sure to stand the test of time. Best climbed ground-up with much bottle and no side runners...
Steve & Katja Broadbent, February 2007. *Photo page 256.*

48. St.Clement's HVS 4c ★3

25m. An excellent sustained pitch. Start from the arête and follow a right-slanting crack-line to an amazing bold finale on perfect edges.
Steve & Katja Broadbent, February 2007.

49. St.Aldate's HVS 4c ★2

25m. The left-slanting crack is easy to start, but runs out near the top. Place good gear and levitate up to the top on excellent small holds.
Steve & Katja Broadbent, February 2007.

50. Black Crow Crack E1 5a ★1 BOLD

25m. The thin crack up the wall has a bold start, stepping off a block.
Peter Riley & Charlie Boscoe, November 2011.

51. Greyhound Crack HVS 4b ★1 BOLD

25m. The tempting wide crack up the centre of the face is poorly protected and can be a bit of a struggle... Easier, but bolder, if you don't get inside it!
Steve & Katja Broadbent, February 2007.

52. Angel Crack VS 4b WIDE BOLD

25m. The right-hand crack has some bold moves in the middle, but a surprising amount of protection higher up. The right-hand variation start is a strenuous 5c jamming crack.
Steve & Katja Broadbent, February 2007.

THE CONTINENTAL WALL

The front of the broken triangular buttress closest to the road holds a number of easier lines with a very short approach and simple descent. Please be careful not to trample the small fields when accessing this wall.

53. An Australian Werewolf in Morocco VD

25m. The left-facing crack and the left end of the wall, with a steepening at 2/3 height. Avoid the bush on its left.

A.Stanley & T.Cooksey, December 2013

54. India Rib Very Difficult

20m. The wide rib to the right of the previous route, with a step left at 12 metres to avoid the steepening.

P.Baxter & D.Sim, December 2013

55. Intercontinental Mild Severe ★1 STEEP BOLD

35m. The right slanting crack-line is a good long pitch that can easily be split with a half-height belay. Bold climbing with several steep sections on good holds.

Steve & Katja Broadbent, October 2008.

56. Ants of Antarctica Severe

35m. A central line up the triangular face. Climb straight up to the half-height ledge, then step right and trend left to finish left of the highest point.

Elie Dekoninck & Jayson Orton, October 2008.

57. Eurobunny V.Diff STEEP

35m. Gains and climbs the left-trending ramp above the half-height ledge, finishing directly up steep ground.

Elie Dekoninck & Jayson Orton, October 2008.

58. Go Your Own Way Severe ★1 ? UNCHECKED

35m. Takes a line up the wall to the left of the bulges, finishing between *Intercontinental* and *Hardcore African*. The climbing is well-protected throughout.

A & J Prickett, March 2013

59. Hardcore African VS 4b

35m. Good climbing up the steeper right-hand section of the wall, with an optional belay on the ledge at 25m.

Elie Dekoninck & Jayson Orton, October 2008.

60. Isis VS 4c ★2 GEAR

35m. An excellent climb up the right hand side of the low triangular face, with plenty of protection, large holds, and some exhilarating steep moves.

1) 25m Follow a vague crack-line through the overlap to a comfortable ledge.

2) 10m Make a tricky move straight off the belay and finish direct.

Steve & Katja Broadbent, February 2008.

61. Asian Fever Severe

35m. The right arête of the triangular face, with an optional belay on the ledge at 25m.

Elie Dekoninck & Jayson Orton, October 2008.

⊂ Steve Broadbent, solo on the superb arête of *Park End* (E3 5b), page 255.
Photo: Katja Broadbent

62. **Pillar of America** V.Diff

35m. The large flake crack up the pillar just right of the arête.
Elie Dekoninck & Jayson Orton, October 2008.

63. **Cherwell Street** HS 4a ★

30m. Good climbing up the narrow buttress just right of the low triangular face. A bold start is followed by some fine steep rock.
Steve & Katja Broadbent, February 2008.

Above the Continental Wall is another shorter wall that can be accessed either by climbing one of the preceding routes or by scrambling up from the left. It holds the following climbs...

64. **Osiris** VS 4c ★ BOLD

20m. The short broken wall above *Isis* makes a good continuation to that route, featuring nice steep moves on worrying rock.
Steve & Katja Broadbent, February 2008.

65. **Ears Between** Mild Severe

20m. From the large ledge at the top of *Isis* and *Cherwell Street*, make a tricky traverse rightwards and climb up into the good easy corner above.
Steve & Katja Broadbent, February 2008.

66. **One in Five Aint Bad** VS 4b ? UNCHECKED

20m. Starts on a grassy ledge on the NE-facing side of the tower to the right. Climb past a quartz band to reach a groove.
Dave Williams & Carol Umarova, March 2016.

Area Map
Crag Selector
Intro
The Climbing
How to Use
Suggested Climbs
Tafraout Granite
Anergui
Ameln Valley
Tarakatine Pass
Sidi M'Zal
Jebel Taskra
Idaougnidif
Afantinzar
Samazar
Aouguenz
Tagzene
Tagmout
History
Index

BANBURY

This is the left wall of the broad bay to the right of the lowest triangular face (Continental Wall).

DESCENT: Continue west towards Park End, then drop down to the left of Continental Wall.

67. Full of Fish Severe

25m. The overhung rib is much easier than it looks if the wide corner crack is used to overcome the steep section.
Steve & Katja Broadbent, October 2007.

68. Banbury Road VS 4b ★1

30m. The easy rib gives a good climb with tricky moves to finish.
Steve & Katja Broadbent, October 2007.

69. Samba E2 5b ★3 BOLD

25m. An excellent route with some bold and technical moves up the attractive clean buttress high on the crag. The start of the route is best approached by abseil to a comfortable belay ledge. Step left onto the arête and climb this with well-spaced gear to an escape left up the smooth groove. The direct finish up the arête is less satisfying, but no more difficult.
Steve & Katja Broadbent, October 2007.

THE ALTERNATIVE TUCK SHOP

Just right of an unclimbed triangular wall is a short east-facing wall with parallel cracks.

DESCENT: Either abseil or downclimb *Popeye's Pipe* (easier than it looks!)

70. Time to Burn E1 5a ★2 BOLD ABSEIL

20m. The buttress left of the cracked wall gives steep climbing with a very bold crux above the back-breaking mid-height pinnacle.
Steve Broadbent, Iza Pstrucha & Leanne Common, February 2009.

71. Holywell Street HS 4b ★2 CRACK ABSEIL

20m. The thin left-hand crack is a good climb, though frustratingly short.
Steve Broadbent, Iza Pstrucha & Leanne Common, February 2009.

72. Popeye's Pipe Difficult ★1 ABSEIL

20m. A chthonic excursion up the entertaining chimney, finishing behind the chock-stones. Unfortunately this route is also the easiest descent from these climbs.
Steve Broadbent (solo), February 2009.

73. Third Rib Severe

ABSEIL

20m. The narrow rib to the right of the wide crack is something of an eliminate.
Aeron Buchanan (solo), October 2007.

74. Third Crack Difficult

ABSEIL

20m. The third crack from the left, suprisingly!
Leanne Common, October 2007.

75. Hornpipe Hard Difficult 1

ABSEIL

20m. Fun, steep jug-pulling up the next buttress to the right.
Steve Broadbent (solo) October 2009.

76. Piece of Cake V.Diff 1

BOLD ABSEIL

20m. The right-hand rib has very sparse protection but good holds.
Iza Pstrucha, Leanne Common & Steve Broadbent, February 2009.

The next two routes are located on the south-facing wall just to the right...

77. Alternative Tuck Shop Difficult

18m. The short face to the right poses no problems.
Leanne Common & Niall Hedderley, October 2007.

78. Sherbert Dip Difficult

15m. A direct line up the wall, 4m right of the corner. Trend right at the top to belay in the groove.
Niall Hedderley, Leanne Common & Aeron Buchanan, October 2007.

Area Map
Crag Selector
Intro
The Climbing
How to Use
Suggested Climbs
Tafraout Granite
Anergui
Ameln Valley
Tarakatine Pass
Sidi M'Zal
Jebel Taskra
Idaougnidif
Afantinzar
Samazar
Aouguenz
Tagzene
Tagmout
History
Index

Area Map
Crag Selector
Intro
The Climbing
How to Use
Suggested Climbs
Tafraout Granite
Anergui
Ameln Valley
Tarakatine Pass
Sidi M'Zal
Jebel Taskra
Idaougnidif
Afantinzar
Samazar
Aouguenz
Tagzene
Tagmout
History
Index

RIGHT HAND BAY

The large bay between Banbury and Jingle Buttress has a lot of rather broken rock, but hidden amongst it are some excellent and varied lines to suit most grades and tastes. The unique slab of *Y Mixi Mique*, the excellent grooves of *The Oxford Story*, and the tricky wall of *Sounds of the Zodiac* are all well-worth seeking out.

DESCENT: Descent from the first two routes involves either a difficult downclimb or an abseil from the first belay of *Cinderella*.

79. Belvedere Road Severe ★1 STEEP ABSEIL

35m. An excellent steep buttress that is much easier than it looks. Descend by scrambling down and right, crossing *Cinderella* at the belay (possible abseil from this point).

1) 15m Follow the right side of the buttress to a large belay ledge. Easier variations are available on the left.

2) 20m Take the steep ground above the belay directly on excellent holds.

Steve & Katja Broadbent, February 2008.

80. Cinderella Difficult ★3 ABSEIL

45m. A good easy climb up the narrow rib left of the *Y Mixi Mique* slab. Descend leftwards to the top of *Belvedere Road*, then scramble back down to the mid-height belay. From here either downclimb in the gully or abseil back to the base.

1) 25m Start up the corner before moving left onto the slab. Follow this to a good belay ledge.

2) 20m A superb steep pitch up the crest of the rib.

Steve & Katja Broadbent, February 2009.

DESCENT: The next two routes finish right at the top of the crag, and descent is via a long walk leftwards to Park End, then down the left side of Banbury.

81. Y Mixi Mique HVS 4c ★2 SLAB BOLD

50m. The curving orange slab high on the crag is a big, bold lead. The route is low in the grade, and the climbing is never difficult nor dangerous, but this long pitch will require a steady nerve. Scramble up to a small ledge below the slab and climb up its centre, avoiding an escape to the crack out right. Finish directly up steeper but easier ground.

Steve & Katja Broadbent, February 2008.

82. J'aime La Crème MVS 4b ★2 STEEP

27m. A hidden gem up the buttress high in the gully, with steep climbing on large jugs.

Steve & Katja Broadbent, February 2009.

The next climbs lie on the right side of the gully, up a series of huge stacked flakes.

DESCENT: From the top of the routes descend rightwards until a short scramble below *Dangermouse* leads back to the base of the climbs.

83. The Oxford Story VS 4b ★3 GEAR

40m. An excellent climb that is considerably better than it looks. Pleasant bridging up a series of corners leads to a steepening where the route is forced left into the main corner above the vegetation. Continue up this (possible belay en-route) to a step left beneath the capping roof.
Steve & Katja Broadbent, October 2007.

84. Numa Numa Severe ★1 STEEP

25m. The small buttress just left of *The Turf Tavern* is a good steep pitch with reassuringly large holds and well-positioned protection.
Steve & Katja Broadbent, February 2008.

85. The Turf Tavern HS 4b ★1 GEAR

25m. The chimney immediately left of *Sounds of the Zodiac* is a well-protected climb with some interesting moves.
Steve & Katja Broadbent, February 2008.

86. Sounds of the Zodiac E1 5b ★1 GEAR

30m. The huge first rib on the west side of Jingle Buttress is a technical route with a well-protected crux and bold middle section. Climb the arête until difficult moves lead right into the broken crack. Follow this to a welcome rest back on the arête, before a steep but easy finish.
Steve & Katja Broadbent, October 2007.

87. Dangermouse Very Difficult

20m. The prominent flake has some excellent steep moves low down, and a hollow finale.
Steve Broadbent (solo), October 2009.

Area Map
Crag Selector
Intro
The Climbing
How to Use
Suggested Climbs
Tafraout Granite
Anergui
Ameln Valley
Tarakatine Pass
Sidi M'Zal
Jebel Taskra
Idaougnidif
Afantinzar
Samazar
Aouguenz
Tagzene
Tagmout
History
Index

JINGLE BUTTRESS

Towards the right hand side of the crags are two long ridges that provide fun warm-ups or scrambles. At the foot of these ridges is a very accessible and attractive wall with an excellent selection of lower-grade climbs.

DESCENT: Behind the lower wall is a chockstone chimney (moderate) that provides a speleological descent for all but the well built.

88. Bevington Road VS 5a

15m. The left-hand arête has some technical moves.
Felicity Soper & Dan Shacklock, February 2008.

89. Jackdaw Lane Severe ★1

15m. Pleasant climbing up the right-to-left slanting crack-line, with one tricky move at a steepening.
Steve & Katja Broadbent, April 2007.

90. Keble Road Very Difficult ★2 BOLD

15m. The slabby east face of the left-hand pillar is a good route on perfect rock, but with very sparse protection. Downclimb to the notch then descend to the left (west).
Steve & Katja Broadbent, April 2007.

91. Littlegate HS 4a

20m. The smooth-looking narrow slab above *Jackdaw Lane*, passing to the left of a small nose.
Steve & Katja Broadbent, October 2007.

92. Hither and Thither Very Difficult

30m. A meandering outing following the easiest line up the face above the left-hand tower.
Aeron Buchanan & Leanne Common, October 2007.

93. Mitranan HVD ★2

50m. The obvious groove / chimney is a good long pitch, sustained at the grade with gradually increasing difficulties all the way to the top. Descend to the right.
Steve & Katja Broadbent, October 2007.

94. Isuzu E1 5a ★1 BOLD

15m. A bold outing up the small west-facing wall at the bottom of the chockstone gully. Start on the arête at the bottom of the gully and make an unprotected swing right to a sequence of steep face moves to a flake and protection at 5m. Traverse right to a small ledge on the arête, before moving up to a leftwards traverse back across the face.
Steve & Katja Broadbent, April 2007.

95. Iziki HS 4b ★2 STEEP

15m. The crack just right of the left arête is a brilliant steep pitch. Enter the crack from the right with difficulty and follow it to excellent finishing moves out right.
Steve & Katja Broadbent, April 2007.

96. Campbell Road Severe ★1

20m. From the chockstone at the top of Jingle Buttress head left and climb up a crack system in a fine position.
Steve & Katja Broadbent, October 2007.

97. Touareg VS 4c

15m. The thin crack has more holds and protection than appearances would suggest, but features a tricky steep finish past a large triangular niche.
Steve & Katja Broadbent, April 2007.

98. Magic Bop VS 4c

12m. The narrow wall to the left of the crack is something of an eliminate, with tricky moves low down and easier climbing to finish.
Steve Broadbent (solo), October 2009.

99. Dish Dash Difficult ★1 CRACK

12m. The right hand crack is a nice easy pitch, walking right to finish.
Steve & Katja Broadbent, October 2009.

100. Mmm Bop Difficult

10m. The short wall just left of the perched boulder.
Steve Broadbent (solo), October 2009.

101. Da Pa Do Wap Difficult

10m. The groove up to the perched boulder has a few tricky moves leftwards to finish.
Jenny Burrow & Niall Hedderley, October 2009.

102. Jingle Ridge Moderate

140m. The long ridge at the right side of the crag is climbed in about 4 pitches and is a pleasant warm up. Difficulties can be varied to suit, and a better start is possible up *Dish Dash*. Descent to the right (east).
Steve & Katja Broadbent, April 2007.

103. Nutcracker VS 4c ★2 CRACK

15m. Lovers of hand-jams need look no further than this gem of a pitch up the front of *Pinnacle Ridge's* lower buttress.
Steve & Katja Broadbent, October 2009.

104. Pinnacle Ridge Difficult

130m. The ridge just right of the previous route has some interesting exposed climbing up or around sharp pinnacles in the lower section, including an avoidable Hard Severe crack. Start from behind a slender pinnacle at the base of the crag, and choose the most interesting line above.
Steve & Katja Broadbent, April 2007.

105. Catte Street Difficult

30m. Climbs a deep groove (with a tree at the top) below a nose on the east side of *Pinnacle Ridge*, about 15 metres uphill from the pinnacle.
Niall Hedderley (solo), October 2007.

Map Page 222

GRITSTONE FUGITIVE

Although this minor buttress lies somewhat isolated in the large bay between *Jingle Ridge* and *Cinnamon Buttress*, *Gritstone Fugitive* is one of the crag's finest routes and is well worth seeking out. The climbs here are short, on good rock, and with a straightforward descent.

DESCENT: Scramble up and right, then descend to the right of the buttress. A descent to the left is also possible via a short down-climb.

106. Gritstone Fugitive E1 5b ★3 BOLD

23m. Excellent, exposed climbing in a fine position, with a challenging and notorious crux move. Start easily up the lower wall to good protection below the steep part of the arête. Overcoming this section traditionally requires pause for thought and a reasonable amount of soul-searching. Above this things get much easier, with pleasant moves leftwards across the face to regain the arête. Follow this to the top in a tremendous position.

Steve & Katja Broadbent, October 2009. Photo opposite.

107. The Primates Game HVS 4c ★1 STEEP

20m. Very strenuous climbing up the right side of the buttress. Start up the creaky flake to reach a ledge above the bush. Easier climbing then leads rightwards up cracks to the top.

Steve & Katja Broadbent, Alison Parker, October 2009.

108. Rich Very Difficult

20m. A pleasant route taking the broken corner and rib to the right.

Alison Parker & Rachel Mellor, October 2009.

109. Matt HS 4a STEEP

12m. The third rib has a very steep start with pleasant jug-pulling above. Difficulty can easily be varied as required.

Rachel Mellor, Alison Perker & Steve Broadbent, October 2009.

110. Captain Carpet Severe ★1

15m. A surprisingly good climb starting up the pale slab to a steepening. Pull through this then move right to finish with difficulty up a steep groove.

Steve Broadbent (solo), October 2009.

111. Mornington Crescent VS 4b ★1

20m. The centre of the long face to the right is curiously difficult, with some steep and thought-provoking climbing throughout.

Steve Broadbent, Alison Parker & Rachel Mellor, October 2009.

LOOK AROUND YOU

An even smaller buttress at the back of the bay in between Jingle Ridge and Cinnamon Buttress. This short triangular wall is recognisable by a shallow slabby corner running up the middle of it. It holds a handful of very short, but worthwhile amusements...

112. "" Mild Diff

10m. The broken wall to the left of the corner. This route does have a name, but it's silent.
Steve Broadbent (solo), October 2009.

113. Look Around You HS 4a ☆1

10m. A very pleasant micro-gem up the overlapped corner. Have you worked out what you're looking for yet?
Steve Broadbent (solo), October 2009.

114. Synthesizer Patel Difficult

10m. The right-hand arête is a pleasant pitch with big holds, but worth trying nevertheless.
Katja Broadbent & Jenny Burrow, October 2009.

Rachel Mellor on the upper arête of *Gritstone Fugitive* (E1 5b), having overcome the notorious crux overhang. ➲
Photo: Steve Broadbent

CINNAMON BUTTRESS

An excellent concentration of low-grade climbs on a series of slabby pillars at the far right side of the crags, close to the gully between Anammer and Ksar Rock. An easy approach, good rock, and a plethora of big holds makes this an ideal spot for soloists or beginners.

115. Speculaas Difficult

20m. Straightforward slabs at the left side of the buttress lead to a steeper finish, well-protected with slings.
Steve Broadbent (solo), October 2009.

116. Ground Nutmeg Hard Difficult ★1

20m. The left-hand rib is usually gained from behind a low tower, though it is also possible to extend the route by starting up this tower.
Katja Broadbent (solo), October 2009.

117. Burnt Sienna Difficult ★1

20m. The second rib, starting from the left.
Steve Broadbent (solo), October 2009.

118. Cracked Pepper Difficult ★1

20m. Good bridging up the well-protected gully.
Niall Hedderley & Steve Broadbent, October 2007.

119. Bagel Down Hard Difficult ★1

20m. The centre of the right-hand buttress.
Steve Broadbent (solo), October 2007.

120. Apple Pie Difficult

20m. The right-hand groove has a couple of questionable holds, but is straightforward and escapable.
Niall Hedderley & Katja Broadbent, October 2007.

121. Cinnamon Gully Moderate

20m. The gully at the right side provides a convenient descent.
Niall Hedderley (solo), October 2007.

122. Danish Pastry Hard Difficult ★1

20m. The slabby rib right of *Cinnamon Gully* is much better than it looks, giving a fine climb with a bold upper section.
Steve Broadbent & Jenny Burrow, October 2009.

Rachel Mellor and Katja Broadbent on *Desert Man* (Severe), one of Ksar Rock's classic low grade routes (page 274). ➲
Photo: Steve Broadbent

DESCENT: Either walk off leftwards or downclimb the fairly straightforward *Cinnamon Gully*.

Cinnamon Buttress
AM 5m
Overview Page 248

Area Map
Crag Selector
Intro
The Climbing
How to Use
Suggested Climbs
Tafraout Granite
Anergui
Ameln Valley
Tarakatine Pass
Sidi M'Zal
Jebel Taskra
Idaougnidif
Afantinzar
Samazar
Aouguenz
Tagzene
Tagmout
History
Index

KSAR ROCK

Shade | Families | Hitch | Roadside

Drive from Tafraout: **1:15**
Walk-in: **5 to 10 minutes**

With a short walk-in, picturesque setting, and great variety of high-quality routes, Ksar Rock has justifiably become one of the most popular cragging destinations in the Anti-Atlas, with routes to suit most tastes and abilities. The Rock, known locally as Azrol L'Modda, stands above the small village of Anammer by the side of the Afantinzar road, and is approached in a matter of minutes from roadside parking.

Ksar, meaning 'Castle' is home to the highest concentration of 3-star routes in the range, so if you're only going to visit one crag during your stay in Morocco then this is the place to go.

Routes on Ksar vary from delightful single pitch outings to half-day adventures, and in many cases it is possible to link a variety of pitches up the full height of the crag, providing endless combinations. Despite its friendly 'crag' atmosphere, however, parties visiting for the first time should be aware that link-ups can often be deceptively long, and indeed the crag has been the scene of a number of near benightments. Fortunately descent from the summit is straightforward.

Despite its diminutive size when compared with some other Anti-Atlas crags, Ksar Rock has a somewhat complex structure, and many of the good lines are not immediately obvious.

For simplicity the rock can be considered to have three faces of interest to the climber – the west face, with its long steep ridges; the south face, with the prominent Cannon Tower; and the shady east face, with huge soaring arêtes and foreboding corners. The north face is more gently angled and offers a convenient scramble descent down to the West Col, from where a small trail leads back to the base of the south face.

KSAR ROCK GUESTHOUSE

For those wishing to spend a few days exploring the tremendous wealth of climbing on Ksar Rock there is a traditional Berber guesthouse offering accommodation in Anammer village, just yards from the foot of the climbs. For more details, see the introduction, page 21.

DESCENT FROM CANNON TOWER:

A) King's Chimney Rappel (35m) from a steel cable at the top of *King's Chimney* and *Morocco Coco*, into Cannon Tower Gully.

B) Days of Thunder Rappel (26m) from a steel chain at the top of Day's of Thunder, down to the bay with the huge boulder. To reach this rappel from the left-hand side of the Cannon Tower it is necessary to scramble up under the chockstone, as shown on page 273.

DESCENT FROM PALADIN:

C) Paladin Rappel (35m) from thin threads and tat at the top of Paladin, back to the bottom of the route.

DESCENT FROM THE CATWALK:

Either scramble up to the summit and walk over the north side to the West Col, or traverse left along the Catwalk. This has a very bold exposed step just before Central Gully. Continue left to vegetation and an abseil point:

D) Catwalk Rappel (20m) from a steel cable at the left-hand end of the catwalk. Continue diagonally past the Paladin Rappel to reach the top of the Cannon Tower, then descent (B).

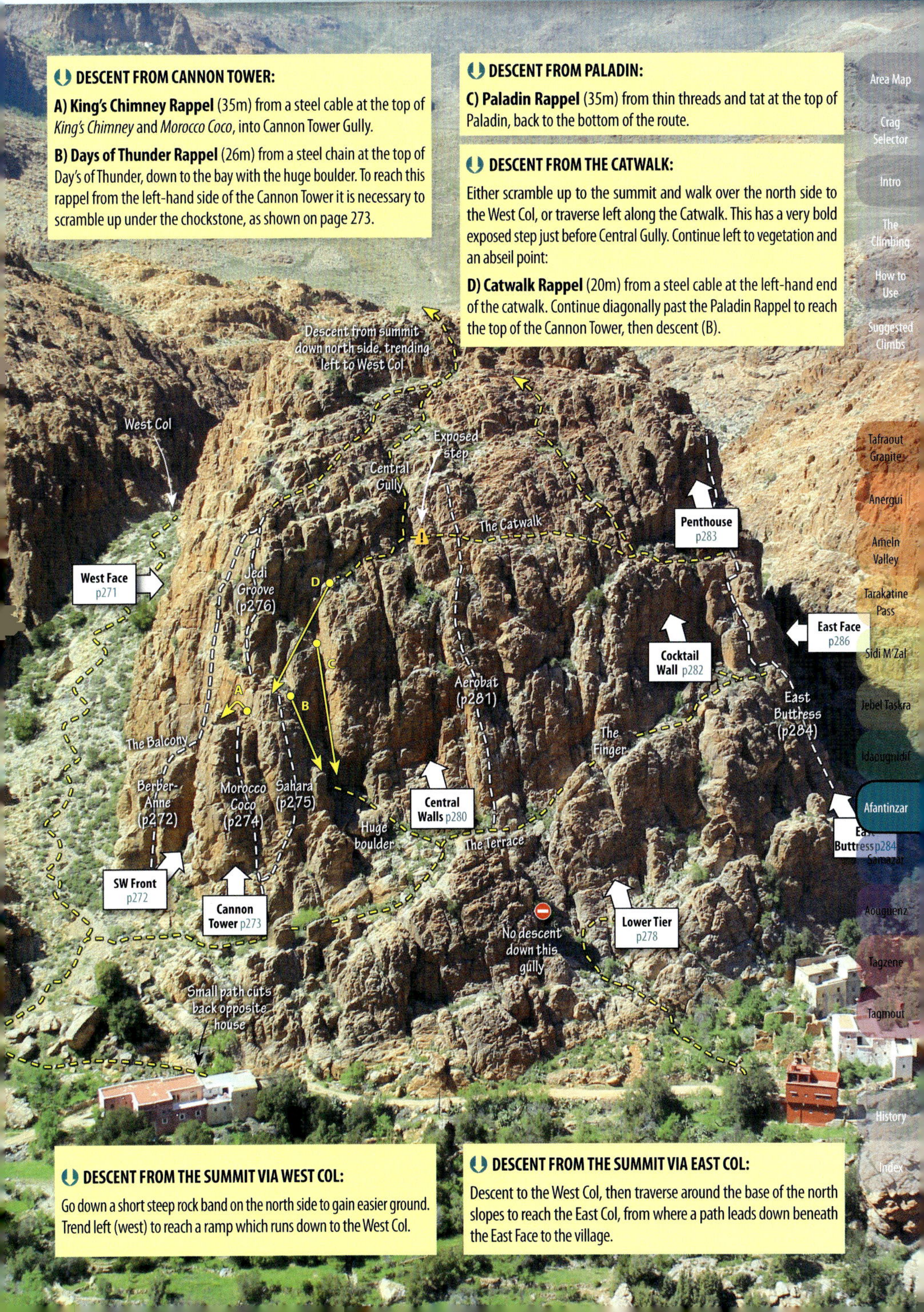

DESCENT FROM THE SUMMIT VIA WEST COL:

Go down a short steep rock band on the north side to gain easier ground. Trend left (west) to reach a ramp which runs down to the West Col.

DESCENT FROM THE SUMMIT VIA EAST COL:

Descent to the West Col, then traverse around the base of the north slopes to reach the East Col, from where a path leads down beneath the East Face to the village.

THE WEST FACE

The sunny west face of Ksar Rock is best viewed from Anammer Crags, from where several long steep ridges are evident. This face has not achieved the popularity of the south face due to a fair amount of friable rock, although there is some of good climbing to be found amongst it.

1. The Tethered Donkey VS 4c

50m. The right-hand side of the left-hand buttress has some pleasant climbing on good holds. Start at the lowest point of the face at a black streak, and climb to a ledge at 5m. Go up the crack above to the top of the buttress.

Haydn Griffiths & Ali Taylor, March 2013.

2. Give me your Hand HVS 5a

LOOSE CRACK

55m. A good climb up the buttress second from left, split by an obvious left-slanting crack.

1) 25m (5a) Climb the crack to belay on a ledge in the gully.

2) 30m (4b) Go up the face on the right before trending left at a shattered wall, crossing the gully to a loose finish on the left.

A.Morris & C.Cooper, February 2009.

Tim Culwick getting stuck into *Kingpin* (HVS), one of Ksar's many classic 3-star pitches (page 273).

Photo: Steve Broadbent

3. Sunlight Buttress VS 4c ★1

LOOSE

100m. This long and varied climb up the third buttress from the left was the first route on Ksar Rock, and provides a pleasant outing.

1) 20m Gain the arête on initially poor rock and follow it to a stance at 20m. The right hand start is somewhat bold and pleasantly technical. From the left is easier, but involves clambering over a bush...

2) 30m (4b) Follow the steep arête, passing difficulties on the left side to a block belay next to a large vegetated bay.

3) 10m (4c) Step up from a block onto the steep right wall of the bay. A few bouldery moves lead to easy ground and a belay.

4) 40m (-) Easy ground up and right leads to a pleasant steep corner to the top.

Steve & Katja Broadbent, April 2007.

4. Camel Ot HVS 5a ★1

CRACK

100m. The wall to the right of *Sunlight Buttress* is gained via a corner crack.

1) 25m (4c) Climb the corner crack to sloping ledges.

2) 25m (5a) Take a vertical crack behind a prickly bush to belay on the ridge of the previous route.

3) 50m (4c) Finish up *Sunlight Buttress*.

Dan Shacklock & Feleicity Soper, February 2008.

5. Speed is Everything E1 5b ★2

STEEP

80m. A popular and varied climb up the steep arête at the right side of the face.

1) 35m (5a) Start in a wide crack on the right side of the buttress. Steep climbing on good holds leads to the point where the crack becomes an off-width and joins the arête. From here step right around the arête and climb the face to a belay at a large platform.

2) 35m (5a) Climb the short wall on the left of the platform, then head towards an obvious leaning layback corner crack. This is climbed strenuously to a ledge (possible belay). Finish up the finger crack in the block on the right.

3) 10m (5b) Delightful technical climbing on the face to the left leads to a belay. Scramble to the summit.

Chris Bull & Sesh Nadathur, January 2009.

Overview Page 269

For descent details, see crag overview on page 269.

Map Page 222

THE SOUTHWEST FRONT

At the right side of the west face, the rock swings round onto the south face in a series of very complex walls, towers and ledges. This is home to the Cannon Tower – one of Ksar's greatest features, though rather difficult to identify from some angles. The first three climbs tackle the wall to the left of the Cannon Tower, starting from a prominent vegetated gully.

6. Serendipity E1 5b ★2

110m. Good homogenous climbing up the left side of the face from the Balcony.
1) 30m (5b) Gain the Balcony by following *Mojitos in the Sky* or *Berber-Anne*.
2) 50m (5b) Traverse left to a corner, then climb this to a horizontal break. Climb rightwards and finish up a dark, pocketed wall to a ledge.
3) 30m (5b) Climb the crack rightwards, then back left to finish up an arête.
Paul Bennett & Mick Nunwick, March 2013.

7. Berber-Anne E2 5c ★2

105m. A difficult climb, starting some 10m left of the Cannon Tower at a corner crack in the buttress to the left of Cannon Tower Gully.
1) 30m (5a) Climb the corner and groove to a huge platform.
2) 45m (5c) Step right onto the clean face, climb its centre to half-height and then trend slightly leftwards aiming for a pale crack-line. This is followed past a first ledge to a belay on the second ledge.
3) 30m (4c) Climb the zigzag crack directly above and turn the large block on the right. Easy ground then leads to the top.
Henward Nind, Topher Dagg & Euan Strachan, February 2010.

8. Mojitos in the Sky E3 6a ★3

100m. A good, sustained route that provides one of the most difficult 'long' climbs on the crag.
1) 30m (5b) Follow *Berber Anne* for 3m until it is possible to break right to the arête. Follow this to a large platform (The Balcony).
2) 30m (6a) Step down right and follow the crack in the pillar to join *Pelez*. Move right again to gain the tempting slim groove that provides the crux of the climb. Belay on The Oasis.
3) 20m (5b) Move right beneath The Pulpit and climb a steep corner crack to belay on The Pulpit.
4) 20m (5b) Finish up the arête and impressive slim slabby groove right of *Jedi Groove*.
Dave Noddings & Paul Donnithorne, March 2011.

9. Pelez E1 5b ★3

35m. This superb and audacious climb tackles the tempting orange wall behind Cannon Tower Gully, and forms the first pitch of one of Ksar's most sought-after link-ups. Start from a large rock at the top of the gully, and make aesthetic moves above a large undercling to gain the elegant corner finger-crack. This is followed to a detached block at mid-height, from where technical moves leftwards up the steep face gain a good belay on the left end of The Oasis. From here the obvious and classic finish is to continue up *Pour Manger* (Route 29, p276).
Arnaud Viel & Emmanual Freundenthal, October 2009.

CLIMBS UP THE CANNON TOWER

This tremendous broad tower, sitting up against the southwest front of the mountain, is perhaps the showpiece of this magnificent crag. It is separated from the main rock by a deep chockstone gully on the left (Cannon Tower Gully), and a broader bay to the right (*Days of Thunder* area). A shallow orange cave at the bottom of the tower's south face aids identification of routes.

DESCENT: Two convenient abseil descents exist from the Cannon Tower as follows:

1) The Days of Thunder Rappel: From the Cannon itself a 26m abseil can be made down the wall right of *Days of Thunder* (Steel chain in place). Routes right of *Iron Maiden* all top out on this upper platform, but from routes to the left it is necessary to scramble up behind the Cannon to reach the chains (as shown on the illustration opposite).

2) King's Chimney Rappel: A steel cable at the top of *Kingpin* allows a 35m abseil into Cannon Tower Gully.

A third abseil line down *Morocco Coco* is not recommended due to the possibility of getting ropes stuck. The anchor has been missing since 2015.

Routes up the Cannon Tower are described from left to right, starting in the Cannon Tower Gully, where two intimidating wide cracks cleave the tower's west face...

10. King's Chimney E1 5b ★2 ABSEIL BOLD

30m. The left hand 'crack' is in fact one of the finest (and hardest) real chimney climbs in the valley, requiring bold back and footing and a well-developed sense of humour. Some fragile rock detracts slightly from what would otherwise be yet another 3-star Ksar classic.

Steve & Katja Broadbent, October 2009.

11. Kingpin HVS 5a ★3 ABSEIL WIDE

30m. The right-hand crack is a 'marvellous' climb with holds just where you need them, until a short off-width section provides a bit of a struggle. Combined with a finish up *Cannon Crack*, this climb provides one of Morocco's best wide-crack routes. Sport-climbers and the uninitiated should look elsewhere...

Steve & Katja Broadbent, October 2009. *Photo page 270.*

12. Solar Event E2 5c ★3 ABSEIL CRACK

55m. A very varied climb up the tempting overhung corner and thin groove above. The difficult traverse is very well-protected with medium-sized cams, but the (easier) upper groove has some more bold moves.

1) 30m (5c) From a large rocky ledge at the bottom of the Cannon Tower climb a very difficult steep crack to a vegetated ledge. Swing right into the main corner and follow this to an uncomfortable stance below the capping roof (possible belay). Traverse left under the roof on brilliant undercuts with a difficult move to gain a foothold on the

arête. From here it is advisable to down-climb a metre or so to a comfortable rock ledge.
2) 25m (5a) A brilliant pitch up the upper groove with a delicate and rather bold middle section before a powerful finish on jugs.
Steve & Katja Broadbent, October 2007.

13. Northern Lights E1 5b

25m. A pleasant but bold pitch. From the belay at the top of pitch one of *Solar Event*, climb straight up the face to the left of the groove.
Mike & Linda Engle, December 2014.

14. Cannon Buttress Direct E1 5b

40m. A continually interesting climb, taking a commanding line up the front of the Cannon Tower and featuring two varied pitches.
1) 20m (5b) Start from a flat rock ledge just right of the wide gully. Climb 3m to a ledge on the right wall (bold), and make an exposed move right, around the arête, onto the front face. The magnificent crack is then followed with increasing difficulty to a sequence of steep moves onto a poor hanging stance.
2) 20m (4b) Go up blocks on the left wall until it is possible to move back right onto the front face with delightful easy climbing to the top of the Cannon Tower.
Steve & Katja Broadbent, April 2007.

15. The Circle Of Life E2 5c

ABSEIL CRACK

60m. The notorious crack up the front of Ksar's Cannon Tower had become something of a 'last great problem', attracting more than its fair share of failures. The route is steep, sustained, and intimidating, with few comfortable rests, making it a major undertaking for its size.
1) 20m (-) Climb easy ground to the right of the circular cave, then traverse left to a disappointing belay above the roof.
2) 20m (5c) Make hard moves up left onto the front face to gain an awkward thin crack. Follow this with considerable difficulty to good runners in the overlap. Undercling leftwards (safe, but difficult) to reach the start of the wide crack, which is entered with further difficulty and followed with ever diminishing strength to an overhung belay ledge on the right.
3) 20m (4c) Pull steeply up a good overhanging crack directly above the belay and climb to a small overlap. Surmount this on the arête, then finish more easily.
Steve Broadbent & Peter Hill, October 2010.

16. Desert Man Severe

ABSEIL GEAR

55m. Excellent, well-protected climbing in a fine position with a wonderfully exposed second pitch above the cave.
1) 15m. Climb a blunt arête, or scramble easily to sloping ledges right of the Orange Cave.
2) 20m. Traverse left and climb the fine wall above the cave on perfect holds to a comfortable ledge.

3) 20m. Pull straight up through steep ground and continue up the buttress to belay on a large ledge below the Cannon.
Steve & Katja Broadbent, April 2007. Photo page 266.

17. Morocco Coco VS 4c

ABSEIL GEAR

65m. Yet another first-class climb, this time following the long corner right of *Desert Man*, with some superbly positioned climbing and good protection.
1) 15m (-) As for *Desert Man*.
2) 30m (4a) Excellent bridging straight up the corner to a good belay ledge.
3) 20m (4c) The upper corner-crack is wide, steep, and provides something of a sting in the tail.
Steve & Katja Broadbent, October 2009.

18. Central Buttress HS 4a

ABSEIL

65m. The central rib above the initial belay ledge was originally climbed as part of the following route, but can be continued directly to the top via this variation.
Paul Mainwood, Chris Bull & Alison Parker, October 2009.

For descent details, see crag overview on page 269.

19. Fortune and Fame E1 5b ★

ABSEIL

60m. Another worthwhile route with lots of good easy climbing and a short but superbly positioned technical traverse. Low in the grade.

1) 15m (-) The blunt arête as for *Desert Man*.

2) 30m (4a) Continue straight up the central slabby rib above to a small ledge below a blank wall.

3) 15m (5b) Difficult moves gain and follow the break rightwards across the steep wall to a welcome rest on the arête. Finish easily up the arête's right hand side.

Steve &Katja Broadbent, October 2007.

20. The Stage Door Variation VS 4c

ABSEIL

55m. This inferior alternative to *Fortune and Fame* traverses right along a low break to gain *Sahara*.

21. Iron Maiden E1 5b ★★

ABSEIL GEAR STEEP

55m. Steep climbing up the crack in the sidewall above the initial belay ledge, with increasingly difficult moves to a desperate crux through the overlaps at *Fortune and Fame*, where flexibility, brute force, or assistance from the rope may well be called upon .

Steve Broadbent & Rachel Mellor, October 2009.

22. Sahara MVS 4b ★★★

ABSEIL

55m. The long and absorbing pitch up the right-hand side of the buttress is a quartzite classic on perfect rock, but requires a steady nerve. The combination of *Sahara* and *Jedi Groove* has become one of the most popular routes in the valley, providing a tremendously exposed and varied way to the top of Ksar.

1) 15m (-) Climb the blunt arête to ledges as for *Desert Man*.

2) 40m (4b) Work right from the belay to gain the centre of the face, which is climbed on amazing large holds to a belay on top of the Cannon Tower. The huge chockstone, and start of *Jedi Groove* is now easily reached around the right side of the Cannon.

Steve & Katja Broadbent, October 2007.

23. Populous VS 4c ★★

ABSEIL BOLD

20m. A good pitch with some bold moves on creaky holds. Start at the left side of the short tower below and right of *Sahara*. Climb the arête to gain a right-slanting upper crack which is followed to a ledge. Walk off to the right from here, or continue up the upper pitches of *The Knight's Quest* to reach the Cannon.

Steve & Katja Broadbent, October 2009.

24. The Knight's Quest HS 4b ★

ABSEIL BOLD

47m. Three varied pitches up the east side of the Cannon Tower, starting on the small tower below *Sahara* and finishing up a fine bold chimney.

1) 12m Climb cracks up the right side of the Populous Tower, with a couple of surprisingly difficult steps along the way.

2) 20m Go up flakes around the right side of the next tower then climb the left hand crack up the side wall to a large ledge.

3) 15m The narrow chimney in the corner above is somewhat intimidating, and provides a good test of both technique and nerve. The route finishes at the top of *Days of Thunder*, where a steel chain provides an easy descent.

Steve & Katja Broadbent, October 2009.

25. Days of Thunder E3 6a ★★

ABSEIL

25m. The beautiful rounded rib at the back of the bay has a lurking flake crack in its upper section, but turns out to be one of the hardest climbs on the crag. A poorly protected initial groove is tackled directly via a technical sequence of slaps, heel-hooks and side-pulls to the relief of a good hold (bridging to the right is not allowed!) Finish up glorious jugs with a modicum of relief to a convenient abseil descent.

Steve & Katja Broadbent, October 2009.

26. The Lunatic Fringe E3 5c ★

ABSEIL BOLD

20m. The blank wall right of *Days of Thunder* provides some emotional climbing up the line of the abseil. Start easily up a short wall right of the gully to gain a large ledge, from where a good flake leads to steep moves up left to the arête. Place good cams, then move back right into the centre of the wall for a 'delightful' finish on small holds. A poor skyhook protects...

Steve Broadbent & Caroline Culwick, March 2011.

Area Map
Crag Selector
Intro
The Climbing
How to Use
Suggested Climbs
Tafraout Granite
Anergui
Ameln Valley
Tarakatine Pass
Sidi M'Zal
Jebel Taskra
Idaougnidif
Afantinzar
Samazar
Aouguenz
Tagzene
Tagmout
History
Index

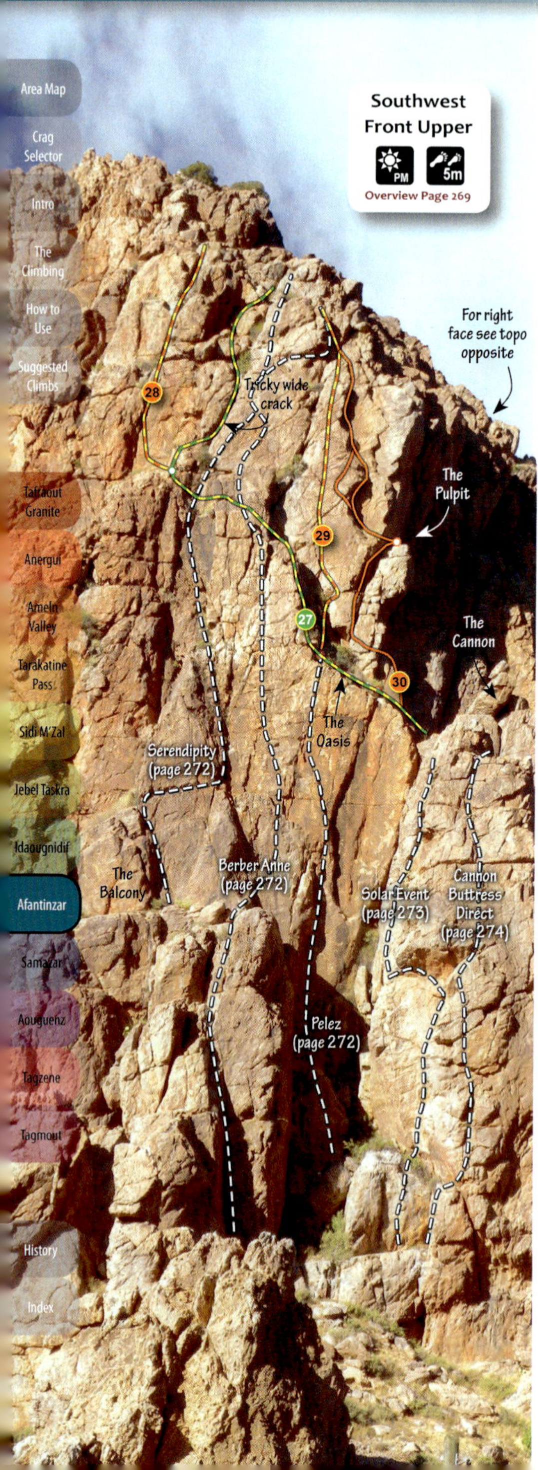

ABOVE THE CANNON TOWER

There are few easy ways from the top of the Cannon Tower up to the summit of Ksar Rock, resulting in many parties experiencing off-route adventures attempting to follow the notorious *Oasis* route to the top. For those willing to try something a little more challenging, however, the routes here offer some superbly-positioned continuations to the summit.

27. Oasis Severe

BOLD PRICKLY

50m. The easiest way upwards from the Cannon Tower features some prickly vegetation and some good climbing on the upper rib, but route-finding errors can easily lead to difficulties.

1) 30m. From a belay on the chockstone make awkward moves left of the patch of vegetation to gain a blocky staircase. Climb this, and then traverse further left over blocks to a belay ledge. Those who try to avoid exposure by skirting the vegetation on the right will suffer a prickly fate.

2) 20m (4a) Make a tricky step rightwards from a large boulder to gain a hidden wide crack above. This looks impossible, is bold to start, but has good holds and protection higher up. Follow the rib on the right of the crack to a ledge, and then make an interesting steep move onto the upper ledge. Disbelieving leaders who opt for the easier-looking ground to the left of the 2nd pitch will find themselves on the more exciting alternative...

Steve & Katja Broadbent, April 2007.

28. Sunset Race Finish VS 4c

BOLD PRICKLY

20m. For those who dismiss the wide crack on the second pitch of *Oasis* as impossible, the groove to the left provides a bold, vegetated, and altogether more epic finish to the route.

Aeron Buchanan & Leanne Common, October 2007.

29. Pour Manger HVS 5b ★3

40m. The blank-looking orange wall above The Oasis gives magnificent climbing on perfect rock, and makes a natural finish to *Pelez* (see page 272).

1) From the belay of *Pelez*, step over bushes to a boulder on the right and an unusual and committing move back left above the belay. Continue in a straight line in the middle of the steep and technical face with exhilarating moves on good holds.

30. Jedi Groove HVS 4c ★3

40m. A brilliant classic climb up the steep stepped corner above and left of the Cannon Tower, with some wild bridging in the upper section. Combined with an ascent of *Sahara* this route offers one of the finest ways to the summit.

1) 20m (4b) From a belay on the chockstone climb mostly on the left face, before moving right to a remarkable flat rocky belay ledge (The Pulpit) below an impending hanging arête.

2) 20m (4c) An airy step left gains the corner system. The first steepening is often avoided by bold moves on the left face to regain the corner below the second steepening,

though it can also be climbed direct at 5a. The upper corner offers some sublime climbing with good holds, perfect gear, and lots of exposure.
Steve & Katja Broadbent, April 2007.

The next two routes climb from the top of the Cannon Tower up to an intermediate ledge system with very poor belays.

31. Marmalade Crack MVS 4b ★2 CRACK

12m. The short jam-crack on the right wall above the Cannon Tower is a delightful little pitch that is easier than it looks.
1) 12m (4b) From the top of the Cannon Tower climb the crack using good holds on the right wall to a ledge with no belays.
Steve & Katja Broadbent, April 2007.

32. Marmalade Rib Severe ★2

12m. The rib to the right of *Marmalade Crack* is a beautifully exposed pitch.
1) 12m Step right to gain instant exposure and plentiful holds on the front of the rib. Follow this to a ledge with no belays, and then scramble left to gain the pulpit, or right to the Paladin abseil.

The next climbs begin from an airy belay on the Pulpit...

33. Cannon Crack E1 5b ★3 WIDE

23m. The peerless off-width above the Pulpit overhangs in every dimension imaginable and provides a memorable struggle with unparalleled exposure. A love of wide cracks, a brace of big cams, and a good head for heights are all advised for what is one of the finest climbs of its type in Morocco. It's only just E1 to climb, but more like E4 to look at...
Steve Broadbent, Rachel Mellor & Paul Mainwood, October 2009.

34. Castles in the Sky E2 5c ★2 GEAR STEEP

20m. The steep hanging rib to the right of *Cannon Crack* is a well-protected but desperately strenuous climb in a commanding position high on the crag. It is gained either by climbing the first pitch of *Jedi Groove*, or scrambling in from the top of *Marmalade Crack / Rib*.
1) 20m (5c) Use the chimney to gain the undercut wall with considerable difficulty. Climb steep cracks until a good flake can be followed rightwards to a magnificent and welcome finish up the right wall.
Steve & Katja Broadbent, April 2007.

The final routes start on the intermediate ledge at the top of *Marmalade Crack*.

35. Spacewalk HVS 4c ★1

30m. A meandering finish, connecting some nice varied climbing.
1) 30m (4c) Make a tricky step right from the ledge to gain a shallow square-cut groove on the right wall. This is climbed with good finger-locks and bridging to a rightwards exit... but it's not over yet! From the arête make an exposed traverse

right on good holds to below a steep wall between two wide cracks, just before a shallow gully. Finish directly up this unlikely-looking wall.
Steve & Katja Broadbent, October 2007.

36. Bushcraft E1 5b PRICKLY

25m. A rather arboreal alternative, linking the groove of *Spacewalk* with the upper wall of *Castles in the Sky*.
Paul Donnithorne & Dave Noddings, March 2011.

For descent details, see crag overview on page 269.

Area Map
Crag Selector
Intro
The Climbing
How to Use
Suggested Climbs
Tafraout Granite
Anergui
Ameln Valley
Tarakatine Pass
Sidi M'Zal
Jebel Taskra
Idaougnidif
Afantinzar
Samazar
Aouguenz
Tagzene
Tagmout
History
Index

Area Map
Crag Selector
Intro
The Climbing
How to Use
Suggested Climbs
Tafraout Granite
Anergui
Ameln Valley
Tarakatine Pass
Sidi M'Zal
Jebel Taskra
Idaougnidif
Afantinzar
Samazar
Aouguenz
Tagzene
Tagmout
History
Index

THE LOWER TIER

A handful of pleasant pitches located on the lower walls beneath the Terrace. Follow the track into the village, passing beneath some steep walls right above the trackside. These walls have been left unclimbed to preserve the privacy of the local people. Beyond the initial walls a vague bay is reached and a short scramble gains the start of the routes.

Descend easily leftwards down the Terrace past the foot of the Cannon Tower. Do not attempt to descend any of the steep gullies on the lower walls as they have vertical sections with loose rock.

37. Left Edge Very Difficult

30m. The easiest line up the left side of the wall is a straightforward route that sees few ascents.

Leanne Common & Iza Pstrucha, February 2009.

38. Lady X MVS 4b ★3 GEAR

40m. A tremendous little climb up the obvious weakness in the overlap, with excellent holds and good protection. Start on immaculate rock near the lowest point of the tier and head through steeper ground to a short vertical crack. The original way went rightwards from here, but a finish left up the easier ground is more popular.

Sesh Nadathur & Sally Fitton, January 2009.

39. Brandenburg VS 4c ★2 BOLD

30m. A steep, bold outing up the centre of the wall. Climb easily to good high runners, then race left through the steep ground on jugs. Continue straight up the final slab to a tricky finish up a short crack.

Steve & Katja Broadbent, February 2009.

40. Battenburg HS 4c ★1

30m. A worthwhile route that tackles the obvious corner-crack. A very technical start in the groove is significantly harder than anything above, and leads to the excellent left-slanting crack.

Steve & Katja Broadbent, February 2009.

41. Rio Grande VS 4c ★2

33m. A tricky little pitch taking the steep wall to the left of *Hangover Crack*. Start up the rib to a ledge beneath *Hangover Crack*, then move left across the wall with some thought-provoking moves to gain a vague groove up the left arête.

Steve Broadbent & Sally Fitton, December 2009.

42. Hangover Crack E1 5b ★1 CRACK STEEP

45m. The soaring crack-line in the upper part of the wall has a loose chockstone above the final steep section, but gives a fine strenuous climb.

Chris Bull & Elie Dekoninck, January 2009.

43. Cactus Crack MVS 4b ★2 WIDE

25m. This is the wide curving crack hidden in the groove to the right of *Hangover Crack*. It is a very pleasant pitch, gained by scrambling up to the upper ledge right of *Rio Grande*.

Steve Broadbent & Sally Fitton, December 2009.

44. What is String Theory? VS 4c ★2 BOLD

30m. A somewhat bold and technical outing up the wall to the right of the previous route, with some tricky moves on small holds.

Steve Broadbent & Sally Fitton, December 2009.

Rachel Mellor in the long corner of *Paladin* (VS), on Ksar's South Face (page 280). ➲
Photo: Steve Broadbent

Area Map
Crag Selector
Intro
The Climbing
How to Use
Suggested Climbs
Tafraout Granite
Anergui
Ameln Valley
Tarakatine Pass
Sidi M'Zal
Jebel Taskra
Idaougnidif
Afantinzar
Samazar
Aouguenz
Tagzene
Tagmout
History
Index

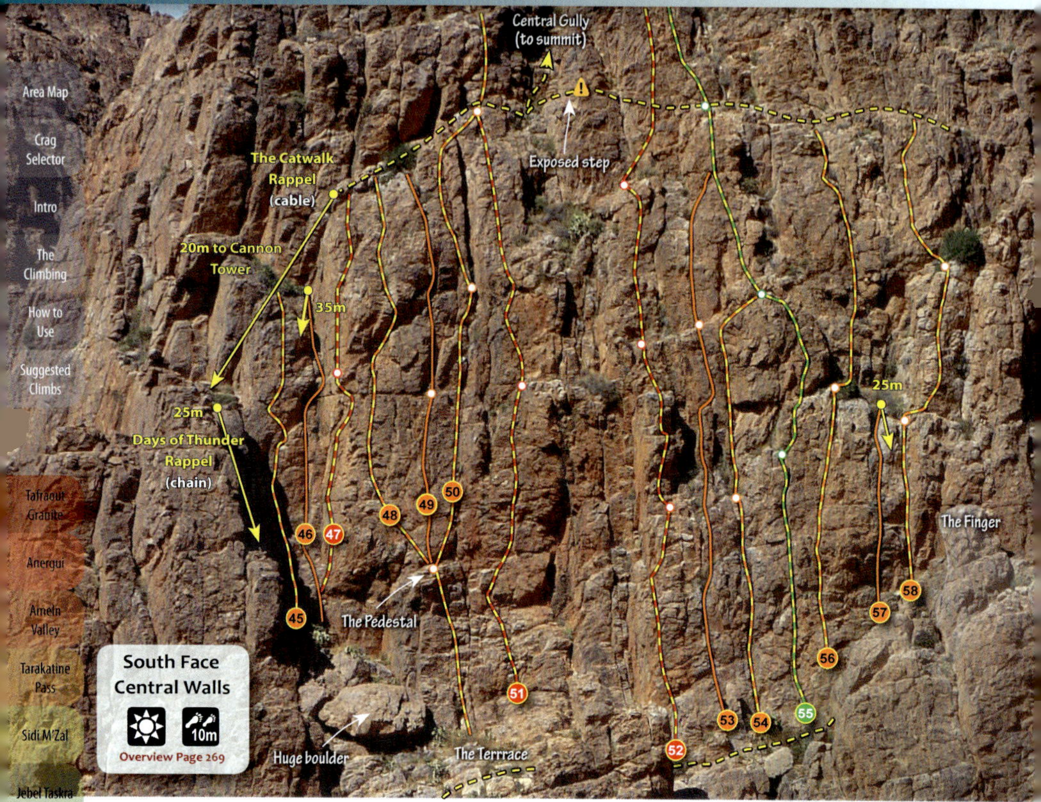

THE CENTRAL WALLS

The walls to the right of the Cannon Tower feature some of the crag's finest climbs, and since the equipping of the Catwalk rappel route, they are no longer the expeditions they used to be. Routes are described from left to right, starting in the bay immediately right of the Cannon Tower, behind an enormous boulder.

45. Civilization HVS 4c ★3 ABSEIL STEEP

30m. Exquisite face-climbing up the back wall above the huge boulder, with well-protected, steep moves on huge holds. Descend by abseil down *Paladin*, or scramble left to gain the Pulpit.

Steve & Katja Broadbent, February 2009.

46. Paladin VS 4b ★3 ABSEIL GEAR

35m. The corner-crack to the right is the quintessential quartzite climb and one of the finest single-pitch routes in the valley, with big holds and perfect protection. Descend by abseil from a variety of thin in-situ tat (care!).

Steve & Katja Broadbent, February 2009. *Photo page 279.*

47. Age of Empires E1 5c ★2 ABSEIL GEAR

30m. A well-protected but tiring excursion up the steep side-wall right of *Paladin*, following the crack-line in the centre of the wall. The climb is safe, low in the grade, and on good rock throughout.

1) 25m (5c) Start as for *Paladin* and step right into the crack on the side-wall. This is followed on good holds to a small ledge from where an easier escape right to the arête is possible. Instead, move back left into the steepening crack, avoiding the final overhang on the right. Above this, move back left around the arête to a poor belay stance beneath a wide crack.

2) 25m (5b) Climb the wide crack until the angle eases, then follow the arête to the vegetation on the Catwalk.

Steve Broadbent & Iza Pstrucha, February 2009.

48. The Colour of Money VS 4c ★3 ABSEIL STEEP

60m. A satisfying climb, taking the left side of the undercut wall above the huge boulder.

1) 15m (-) Scramble up easy ground to a belay on the pedestal.

2) 45m (4c) Pull onto the wall and work leftwards on good holds, heading for a weakness at the left side of the upper overhang. This is furnished with excellent holds and solid protection.

Steve Broadbent, Paul Mainwood & Rachel Mellor, October 2009.

49. Timpani VS 4b ★★

ABSEIL

65m. Even the hollow-sounding flakes from which this climb takes its name do not detract from what is yet another sensational climb at this grade.
1) 15m (-) Scramble up easy ground to the pedestal belay.
2) 20m (4a) Climb straight up above the pedestal, making use of a generous helping of perfect jugs. Belay on a small scree-covered ledge beneath a chimney.
3) 30m (4b) The chimney throws in a few awkward moves and the odd hollow flake to maintain interest before things ease to the top.
Paul Mainwood & Steve Broadbent, October 2009.

50. Radio Sandwich VS 4b ★

85m. A long adventure up the corner system to the right.
1) 15m (-) Scramble up to the pedestal belay as for the previous two routes.
2) 20m (-) Straight up the corner groove past a large bush to a belay in a niche right of a ledge.
3) 30m (4b) Continue straight up past the niche, stepping left below a bulge to avoid a vegetated chimney. Climb a crack to belay on a big ledge below a tree.
4) 20m (-) Go right and up the overhang above (avoidable further right), then continue up easier slabs and walls.
Aeron Buchanan & Caroline Culwick, February 2008.

51. O-Zone E2 5b ★★

STEEP

60m. Exquisite overhanging face-climbing up the wall at the back of the Main Bay. Huge holds and good rests help, but this climb still manages to feel totally 'out there'!
1) 30m (5b) Start from a ledge on the lower slabs and climb straight up to a left-facing flake crack. Climb this with difficulty and continue straight up the wall above via a sequence of overhanging moves to a good ledge.
2) 30m (5a) Head up and left on brilliant steep flakes to a stance, then finish up the pleasant slabby wall above.
Steve & Katja Broadbent, October 2009.

52. Aerobat E1 5b ★★★

STEEP

85m. The narrow pillar at the right side of the bay gives a memorable climb with excellent stances and some steep climbing. Low in the grade, and probably HVS for taller climbers...
1) 25m (5a) Start in the middle of the pillar and make awkward moves to gain a groove up its left side. Follow this to a good rock ledge.
2) 15m (5b) The overhanging pillar above is tackled directly using a combination of brute force, wishful thinking, and a few well-placed heel-hooks.
3) 12m (4b) Easier ground to another good ledge.
4) 33m (4b) The next section of the pillar is steep, but is overcome easily on good holds. Pleasant scrambling then leads to the summit.
Steve Broadbent & Iza Pstrucha, February 2009.

53. Inbetweener MVS 4c ★★

65m. The central crack up the wall between *Aerobat* and *Fallout*.
1) 45m (4c) Climb up to the right of a detached pillar and continue up to a belay on the right.
2) 20m (4b) Move back left to finish up the steep wall on good holds.
Chris Bull & Will Benfold October 2011.

54. Fallout HVS 5a ★★★

WIDE STEEP

80m. An amusing route that tackles the intimidating bomb-bay chimney on the south face. Vegetation detracts only slightly from what is a superb steep climb. Start up the crack left of *Noah's Ark*.
1) 30m (5a) Brilliant steep climbing up the slightly overhanging crack leads to a vegetated belay.
2) 25m (4c) Climb cracks to gain the undercut chimney. A wide crack on the left wall makes things look all too easy, but sooner or later the chimney will suck you in... before spitting you back out again higher up. Finish rightwards with relief.
3) 25m (4a) Go up the excellent wall above on superb holds, finishing directly up steep ground (as for *Noah's Ark*).
Caroline Culwick & Steve Broadbent, March 2011.

55. Noah's Ark HS 4b ★★★

STEEP CRACK

60m. Another superlative climb, with three very varied pitches providing one of the best routes of this grade in the valley. Start from the terrace at the top of the lower tier.
1) 25m (4b) Climb the prominent steep crack past several small bushes to a stance.
2) 20m (4b) Go up the continuation groove, stepping right onto a ledge after 8m. From here make a difficult pull onto the undercut wall above and climb to a large ledge.
3) 15m (4b) The attractive wall above the belay is a gem of a pitch with good holds and spaced protection. This leads to the Catwalk and easy ground right of Central Gully, from where 30m of scrambling gains the top of the crag.
Steve & Katja Broadbent, February 2010.

56. Cornflake VS 4c ★★

CARE! BOLD STEEP

60m. A thought-provoking climb that features some excellent steep moves and a couple of mental hurdles along the way. Start from the terrace, just before the path passes behind a prominent narrow finger of rock.
1) 30m (4b) The smaller crackline right of *Noah's Ark* leads to a precarious balanced flake, which is bypassed with some trepidation on its right side. Belay on a vegetated ledge above.
2) 30m (4c) From the back of the vegetated ledge climb a steep hollow flake (bold) up the back wall... preferably without pulling too hard. This leads to a very pleasant corner which is followed until a step left onto the rib just below the Catwalk. From here it is possible to traverse to the Catwalk Rappel, or scramble to the summit.
Steve Broadbent & Matt Mellor, February 2011.

Area Map
Crag Selector
Intro
The Climbing
How to Use
Suggested Climbs
Tafraout Granite
Anergui
Ameln Valley
Tarakatine Pass
Sidi M'Zal
Jebel Taskra
Idaougnidif
Afantinzar
Samazar
Aouguenz
Tagzene
Tagmout
History
Index

Area Map
Crag Selector
Intro
The Climbing
How to Use
Suggested Climbs
Tafraout Granite
Anergui
Ameln Valley
Tarakatine Pass
Sidi M'Zal
Jebel Taskra
Idaougnidif
Afantinzar
Samazar
Aouguenz
Tagzene
Tagmout
History
Index

57. Hercules HVS 5a ★★

ABSEIL CRACK STEEP

25m. The steep crack to the right of *Cornflake* proves even steeper and more strenuous than it looks, but has good protection throughout. Abseil descent.
Steve Broadbent & Cameron Hall, October 2011.

58. Marimba VS 4c ★★

70m. The wide crack is a very worthwhile climb with superb positions but poor belays.
1) 25m (4c) Scramble up to the start of the wide crack, which provides a couple of concerning situations before things ease. Belay on a poor ledge below vegetation.
2) 25m (4b) Make an airy move right to gain the arête. Climb this, then take a groove on the right which leads to the left side of a tree.
3) 20m (4a) Make a fun step up left on good holds to gain the wall above. Climb more easily up the right side of a prow to reach the Catwalk.
Steve Broadbent & Cameron Hall, October 2011.

For descent details, see crag overview on page 269.

COCKTAIL WALL

This short, steep wall is located at the far right-hand end of the Terrace, and is accessed by scrambling behind a slender pinnacle (the Finger) at the top of the crag's Lower Tier.

The routes finish on a vegetated ledge, from where it is possible either to climb routes on the Penthouse, or scramble up left to reach the top of the crag.

59. Crotchless Scarf HVS 5a ★

STEEP

45m. A steep eliminate, starting about 2m left of the Finger.
1) 20m (5a) Climb directly up to the overhang and pull through this on big holds.
2) 25m (-) Climb up, trending rightwards to join *Euphoria*.
Will Benfold & Chris Bull, October 2011.

60. Euphoria VS 4c ★★

CRACK GEAR

50m. An excellent climb from the narrow gap behind the Finger.
1) 25m The intimidating thin crack directly behind the pinnacle is very well-protected and is made easier with an occasional foot out behind! Belay at a ledge near some vegetation.
2) 25m. Continue up through the wide groove/corner before being forced to traverse right around the blunt rib. Tackle the overhang next to the large bush with surprising ease.
Sally Fitton & Sesh Nadathur, January 2009.

Area Map
Crag Selector
Intro
The Climbing
How to Use
Suggested Climbs
Tafraout Granite
Anergui
Ameln Valley
Tarakatine Pass
Sidi M'Zal
Jebel Taskra
Idaougnidif
Afantinzar
Samazar
Aouguenz
Tagzene
Tagmout
History
Index

61. Champagne Lassitude HS 4a ★2

50m. The blunt rib 5m right of the pinnacle.

Elie Dekoninck & Chris Bull, January 2009.

62. Tequila Sunrise E1 5b ★1 LOOSE STEEP CRACK

30m. The left-hand broken crack-line has some dubious rock, but good steep moves in its upper section. Follow the crack until it is possible to step left into the shallow broken groove that forms the left-branch of the crack (crux). This is climbed on superb holds to the top.

Steve & Katja Broadbent, February 2009.

63. Tomahawk HVS 5a ★2 STEEP CRACK GEAR

25m. An excellent pitch up the cracked wall, taking the third crack from the right, with a small bush low down.

Steve & Katja Broadbent, October 2008.

64. Brandy Alexander E2 5c ★1 CRACK GEAR

30m. The second crack from the right is a strenuous climb with perfect protection throughout.

Steve & Katja Broadbent, February 2009.

THE PENTHOUSE

This small wall at the top right of the south face is best approached by climbing one of the preceding routes.

65. Happy Happy Joy Joy VS 4c PRICKLY LOOSE

30m. The easy-looking broken groove turns out to be surprisingly awkward, and leads to a vegetated gully with a large loose chockstone. Thrutchy chimneying moves then gain better climbing on the face to the right.

Sally Fitton & Sesh Nadathur, January 2009.

66. Pebble Dash E2 5c ★2 STEEP

20m. A steep, strenuous pitch up the centre of the wall below an embedded grey rock. Climb direct to a horizontal break and protection. Pass the overlap at the easiest point then trend slightly left to reach a ledge. From here traverse right into *Bubbles of Hapopy*.

Chris Bull & Elie Dekoninck, January 2009.

67. Bubbles of Hapopy VS 4c ★2 STEEP WIDE

30m. An excellent way up the final wall that is low in the grade. The initial awkward moves are protected by large cams until things ease higher up.

Elie Dekoninck & Chris Bull, January 2009.

68. Penthouse HS 4a ★2 BOLD

25m. The terrifying wall out right is thankfully (much) easier than it looks, and forms the final pitch of the *East Buttress Route*. Nervous leaders may, however, find *Bubbles of Hapopy* less traumatic...

Steve & Katja Broadbent, October 2007.

Area Map
Crag Selector
Intro
The Climbing
How to Use
Suggested Climbs
Tafraout Granite
Anergui
Ameln Valley
Tarakatine Pass
Sidi M'Zal
Jebel Taskra
Idaougnidif
Afantinzar
Samazar
Aouguenz
Tagzene
Tagmout
History
Index

THE EAST BUTTRESS

The right-hand side of the south face gives a couple of fine, long climbs and the easiest continuous route to the summit of Ksar. Although the nature of the rock here does not lend itself to a large number of climbs, the *East Buttress* and *Grand Hotel* are highly recommended.

To reach the foot of these routes continue along the track through the village until a narrow alley leads up left to the broad gully that runs up beneath the steep east face to the East Col. The first climb is accessed by scrambling leftwards onto a large ledge back on the south face.

69. Crazy Days HS 4a

BOLD

30m. A useful approach to the Cocktail Wall, this pleasant pitch is gained by scrambling up and left from *East Buttress* to a large ledge. Climb the rib immediately left of the chimney, with very bold moves to start.

Steve & Katja Broadbent, October 2008.

70. East Buttress Severe ★2

BOLD

130m. An excellent, long and varied low-grade route with large belay stances and some fine positions. The climb is generally well protected, but has a challenging crux right at the top (Hard Severe, avoidable). A variety of possible escape routes (shown opposite) significantly reduce the seriousness of this otherwise adventurous climb, making it a suitable introduction to the multi-pitch routes of Afantinzar. Start beneath a long narrow slab at the lowest point of the rocks above the village.

1) 25m The narrow slab is actually a pleasant stepped buttress with good holds and various belay possibilities.

2) 25m Continue up the buttress to a good rock ledge overlooking the gully.

3) 20m Climb a steep crack above the ledge to reach the crest of the buttress. Go up the crest steeply on its right side to belay below a significant steepening in the ridge.

4) 30m Move left and climb immaculate rock in the bed of the obvious gully. Exit right to a block belay.

5) 10m Climb the steep wall above, trending from right to left. This leads to the Penthouse, from where it is possible to escape left and scramble easily to the summit of the Rock. A much better alternative, however, is to finish straight up *Penthouse* (Hard Severe)...

6) 20m (4a) The final steep wall has some difficult moves but is climbed direct with large holds and lots of exposure.

Steve & Katja Broadbent, October 2007.

71. Grand Hotel VS 5a ★2

BOLD STEEP

95m. A very good climb, brimming with character, following an intricate line up Ksar's East Buttress. The route is superbly varied and features a stunning third pitch up the front of the buttress at the very top of its grade. Start just uphill from *East Buttress Route*, at the left side of the East Face.

1) 25m (4a) Go up a narrow rib, passing a steepening on good holds. Block belay below a wide crack.
2) 15m (4c) A very technical traverse left across a steep slab leads to easier climbing leftwards up the flake crack. Twin cracks then lead to the 3rd belay of East Buttress, on the front of the buttress.
3) 25m (5a) Having summoned every reserve of courage, boulder straight up through the overhang above the ledge to reach a nut runner in the high flake jug. This section is powerful, bold, but mercifully short, and leads to some sublime climbing up the narrow south-facing wall above, just left of the arête.
4) 10m (4b) Walk across to the back of the ledge and climb a short corner crack to another large ledge.
5) 20m (4b) Finish up *Penthouse*.
Will Benfold, Cameron Hall & Steve Broadbent, October 2010.

72. Vertigo E1 5b ★2 BOLD CRACK

100m. A steep, uncompromising climb, tackling the overhanging crack in a south-facing wall at the left side of the east face.
1) 30m (5a) Start up a big crack, then move right and continue up to a tree on a terrace. Go up easier slabs above to a block belay.
2) 40m (5b) Climb the crack nearest to the tree, moving up right at the top to a terrace. Continue easily to the 3rd terrace to belay.
3) 30m (4a) A bold finale. Climb the easy crack to the top of the big boulder, then finish up the right side of the final tower as for *East Buttress / Penthouse*.
Stefan Priem & Mike Bachman, March 2014.

Katja Broadbent pulling through the steep crux of *Desert Storm* (E1), on Ksar's East Face (page 287). ➲
Photo: Steve Broadbent

Area Map
Crag Selector
Intro
The Climbing
How to Use
Suggested Climbs
Tafraout Granite
Anergui
Ameln Valley
Tarakatine Pass
Sidi M'Zal
Jebel Taskra
Idaougnidif
Afantinzar
Samazar
Aouguenz
Tagzene
Tagmout
History
Index

THE EAST FACE

The shady east face of Ksar rock consists of steep corners, soaring arêtes, and huge wide cracks, and is easily visible on the drive up the Afantinzar road. The routes here are secluded, and tend to have a more serious feel to them, with a fair amount of loose rock that requires a careful approach. The face is at its best on hot sunny days, when it provides a superb escape from the heat.

To access the east face park on the roadside close to the track leading to the main village. Walk along this track through the village, until a trail leads between houses and on to terraces up to the East Col. As this approach passes through private property please respect the privacy of the local people.

DESCENT: To regain the East Col from the summit of Ksar rock it is necessary to head west on the north side of the rock and gain the ramp leading down to the West Col. From here, turn right and follow the base of the rocks back east, climbing steadily to regain the East Col. A small trail leads from here back to the village.

73. Voodoo HVS 5a ★1 BOLD

100m. A delicate climb with an excellent and bold first pitch, some rather scrappy climbing to reach the Altar, then a fine finale.

1) 15m (4c) An exquisite pitch on immaculate rock. Start from the left side of the initial wall and climb steeply, trending right to a good runner. From here several bold and fingery 4c moves continue up and right to a comfortable belay ledge.

2) 25m (4b) Continue up the buttress, staying close to the crest to reach a sling belay.

3) 30m (4a) A pleasant short arête, then easy ground leads to a final steep wall up to the Altar. Evidence of local people having gained the Altar is both present, and perplexing.

4) 30m (5a) The stepped arête and exquisite crystal corner above provides a superb finale.

Steve & Katja Broadbent, February 2008 (to the Altar).
Topher Dagg & Henward Nind, February 2010 (final pitch).

74. East Anglia Severe ABSEIL LOOSE

70m. A poor route to the Altar, with some questionable rock.

1) 25m Start above a rose bush and climb right, through a tree, into a groove and upwards to a large ledge.

2) 25m Leave rightwards from the ledge to gain a groove, leading to another ledge.

3) 20m Go up a crack to a ledge, then climb the right wall to the Altar.

Paul Mainwood, Chris Bull & Alison Parker, October 2009.

75. Breaking Strain E4 6a ★3 STEEP

85m. The desperately steep orange groove yields to strenuous jams and inventive footwork, and provides the most difficult route of the crag. The upper pitches are technically much easier.

1) 35m (6a) Follow the groove and crack through bulges to the left of the big downward pointing flake. Finish directly up the left-trending weakness to belay on a ledge.

2) 20m (5b) Airy climbing up the arête, using the crack out right when required. This leads to the Altar, from where a 55m abseil reaches the ground. Alternatively it is possible to finish up the last pitch of *Voodoo*...

3) 30m (5a) Continue up the stepped arête and exquisite crystal corner above as for *Voodoo*.

Topher Dagg & Henward Nind, February 2010.

76. Oestrogen E2 5c A0 ★2 ABSEIL CRACK

55m. This steep, hard route was the first to tackle the intimidating east wall of the Altar, and awaits a full free ascent.

1) 20m (5c A0) Climb the wall to the left of the crack to an overhang. Surmounting this proves awkward, and pulling on gear is a popular option. The wide crack above leads to a belay ledge.

2) 35m Climb jamming cracks on the left, then go up slabs to reach The Altar with some relief. Either abseil from here or continue up the final pitch of *Voodoo*.

Chris Bull & Paul Mainwood, October 2009.

77. If I Sit Still Too Long I Catch Fire E2 5c ★3 STEEP

95m. The front face of The Chandelle provides a memorable and perhaps saltatory challenge that will call upon brute force, technique, and strength of character in equal proportions. Start at the second wide crack to the left (downhill) from the huge corner, to the left of a black-streaked orange face.

1) 30m (5c) Climb, if you can, the corner until twin cracks on the left bypass bushes.

2) 25m (5b) Place a high runner, then step onto the arête, move right under an overlap and continue up and right to twin cracks on the front face. These lead up to blocks and a belay at the base of a monster crack...

3) 20m (5a) The 'thunderbolt' crack requires large cams or big balls. It leads to an airy belay on top of the Chandelle.

4) 20m (5b) Bridge or jump the gap to gain the slabby ramp. This move is hard, bold, and may involve some mild peril. Continue more easily to belay near the summit.

Henward Nind & Euan Strachan, February 2010.

78. Two Day Event VS 5a ★1 MOSSY

85m. The big corner to the right of the Chandelle is a good climb, marred slightly by dirty rock in its upper section. It is also the scene of one of Ksar's many benightments.

1) 25m (5a) Climb the corner, past a steepening at 15m, to a stance on the third of three pale ledges.

2) 20m (4c) The slabby left wall of the continuation corner is rather dirty and features the odd bush. Belay on a stance where the corner opens into a chimney/gully.

3) 40m (4a) Continue more easily up the chimney/gully, passing a number of chockstones to the top.

Ali Walsh, Alan Blackburn & Martin Bennett, March 2010.

79. Desert Storm E1 5b ★2 CRACK STEEP GEAR

65m. A wonderful outing up the wide crack in the wall right of *Great Eastern*, with well-protected strenuous climbing and excellent positions.
1) 20m (4c) Start up the groove just left of *Great Eastern*, with a tricky steepening just below the first belay of that route.
2) 15m (5b) Traverse rightwards across the wall and make a difficult move to gain the good crack. This is followed strenuously to a poor hanging stance below a wider crack.
3) 15m (4c) A brilliant pitch up the wide crack that is easier than it looks. This leads to a good ledge.
4) 15m (5a) Move right around the arête onto the east-facing wall and finish up the tempting overhanging crack above.
Steve & Katja Broadbent, October 2008. Photo page 285.

DESCENT: Continue over the summit, bearing right to descend the northern slopes. Keep trending left to gain a ramp-line that descends to the West Col, then turn right and traverse under the north face to the East Col.

80. Great Eastern VS 5a ★2 CRACK GEAR

75m. A magnificent classic climb up the huge corner. The route has a big, serious feel to it, but the climbing is always very well protected and never as hard as it looks.
1) 20m (5a) Start in a corner behind a rose bush. The corner is difficult to start (understatement!), but succumbs to some brilliant steep bridging. Belay on a poor stance.
2) 10m (4b) Continue up steep ground to a poor belay on the left wall below the huge curving corner. The climb now starts to feel rather sinister...
3) 25m (4c) An excellent pitch, despite the odd prickly bush. Follow the ever-steepening corner to the relief of a large ledge with good belays.
4) 20m (4b) The final wall is a reward for any difficulties below, featuring perfect climbing in a commanding position. Climb the wall, right of the wide crack, trending rightwards on large holds. Scramble down then across a vegetated gully to gain the north slopes of Ksar Rock.
Steve & Katja Broadbent, February 2008.

Area Map
Crag Selector
Intro
The Climbing
How to Use
Suggested Climbs
Tafraout Granite
Anergui
Ameln Valley
Tarakatine Pass
Sidi M'Zal
Jebel Taskra
Idaougnidif
Afantinzar
Samazar
Aouguerz
Tagzene
Tagmout
History
Index

SAMAZAR

For any trad-climber, a drive along the Samazar 'road' is likely to be a memorable experience, and an adventure to these far-flung reaches of Jebel el Kest is one of the many great and varied experiences that await the first-time visitor to Tafraout. Here, beneath the towering, moss-covered and gigantic walls, climbers feel far from home, and the slightly unreliable rental car – your only lifeline to civilisation – feels ominously far from tarmac. Welcome to Samazar!

This tremendous valley is home to some of the biggest rock walls in the Anti-Atlas. The character of most routes here is very different from that further south, and parties should be prepared for a fair amount of loose rock and vegetation on many of the routes. Most climbs are on north-facing walls, which can be out of condition during the winter months. Following a period of drought, however, they will provide memorable adventures that rank amongst the best in this book.

Whilst there are plenty of sustained and clean crag-climbs here, and even the odd south-facing sun-trap, this is *the* place to go for long, adventurous and slightly esoteric routes, many of which involve extensive sections of easy climbing with occasional harder pitches. Despite their moderate technical difficulty, these climbs are usually major undertakings in a relatively remote environment, requiring plenty of big-route experience and a high level of commitment.

The valley is correctly named the *Tamza Valley*, but at some point around 2008 the name was mis-remembered by western climbers as *Samazar*. Not wishing to let truth get in the way of romance, the name *Samazar* has now been adopted. Sometimes referred to as *Shangri-La*, the valley lies immediately north of Afantinzar, and can be accessed from both ends – either via a very poor unsurfaced track turning off the Afantinzar road at Ighir, or more easily from Tanalt via the impressive Samazar Hairpins at the west end of the valley. The drive from Tafraout to Tamdkrt, through Tanalt and down the hairpins takes about 1½ hours, though many parties get hopelessly lost and end up somewhere totally different.

The drive along the full length of the Samazar Road, from Ighir in Afantinzar, past Tamza and Tamdkrt to Tanalt

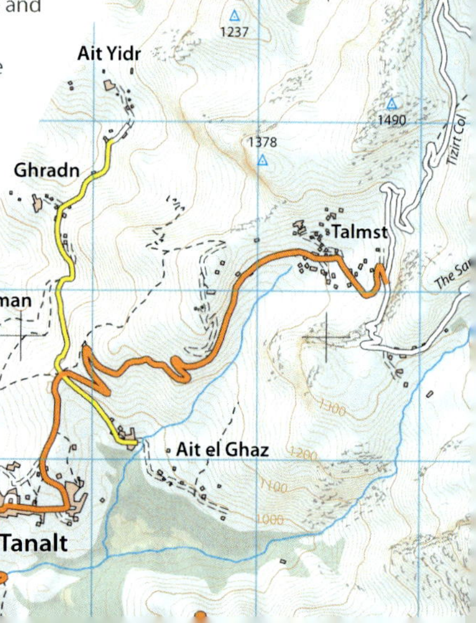

is possible in 2WD vehicles for most of the year, though care is required, particularly at the Ighir end. **This road is something of an adventure for those unaccustomed to taking cars where they're not supposed to go, and is definitely not recommended on wet days.**

There is no accommodation, shops or services in Samazar, though short-term bivouacs are possible close to the schoolhouse junction, midway down the valley. More importantly, there is no assistance when you take the sump off your car...

The crags are described roughly from west to east, according to parking place or turn-off from the Samazar Road, as this is the usual direction of approach via Tanalt. An approach from the eastern end of the valley via Afantinzar and Ighir is actually more spectacular, particular for views of the mighty Great Rock and Waterfall Walls; it is recommended for those not in a hurry to get onto a route!

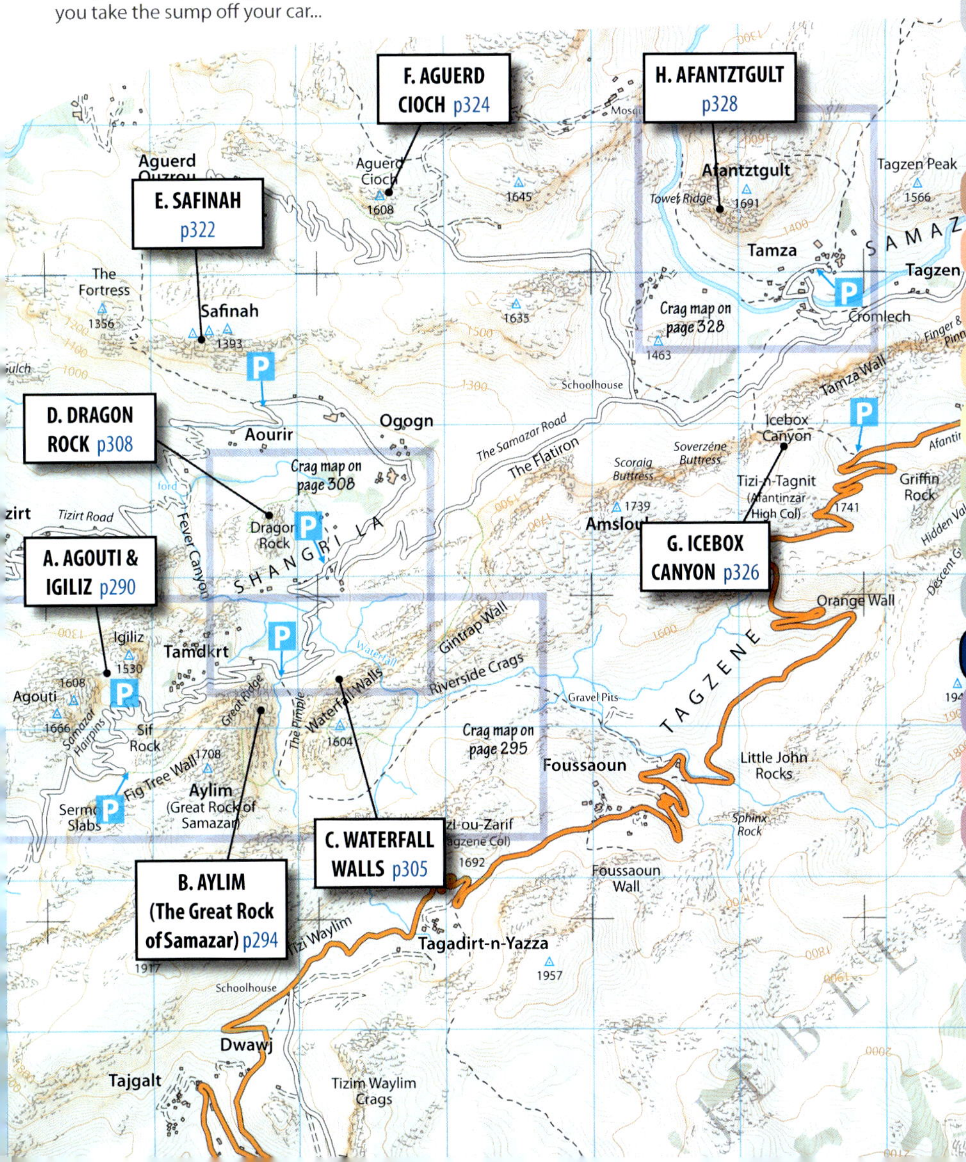

Area Map
Crag Selector
Intro
The Climbing
How to Use
Suggested Climbs
Tafraout Granite
Anergui
Ameln Valley
Tarakatine Pass
Sidi M'Zal
Jebel Taskra
Idaougnidif
Afantinzar
Samazar
Aouguenz
Tagzene
Tagmout
History
Index

Area Map
Crag Selector
Intro
The Climbing
How to Use
Suggested Climbs
Tafraout Granite
Anergui
Ameln Valley
Tarakatine Pass
Sidi M'Zal
Jebel Taskra
Idaougnidif
Afantinzar
Samazar
Aouguenz
Tagzene
Tagmout
History
Index

A IGILIZ & AGOUTI

Shade · Families · Hitch · Roadside

Drive from Tafraout: **1:30**
Walk-in: **2 minutes**

Sitting right at the top of the Samazar hairpins, the attractive twin summits of Agouti provide a magnificent viewpoint over the Samazar Valley and the western Anti-Atlas. To the east, slightly lower down the Samazar hairpins, the shapely little summit of Igiliz also gives a handful of pleasant routes on good rock, but it is the attractive *South Ridge* that sees by far the most ascents.

A traverse of these two peaks – starting right at the roadside on the hairpins and finishing on the highest summit of Agouti – is a very pleasant day out, consisting of extensive and interesting scrambling in a fine mountain setting. Although there are only two or three sections of actual climbing, the full traverse features about 490m of ascent, and will suit parties looking for an easy mountain day out with no walk-in. Allow approximately 5 hours for the full route, car to car.

1. South Ridge of Igiliz Mild Severe ★1

200m. The South Ridge of Igiliz starts on immaculate rock, right at the side of the Samazar Road. The most interesting climbing is on the right-hand side of the initial ridge, though easier options are available to the left. After two pitches of climbing, the angle eases and extensive scrambling leads to the summit.

Mike & Marjorie Mortimer, March 2008.

DESCENT: From the summit, descend in a westerly direction towards the col with Agouti. Some short downclimbs and scrambles are required, but abseiling is not necessary if care is required with route-finding.

2. East Ridge of Agouti Mild Severe ★1

230m. Start by scrambling up to a ledge, about 5m up from the col between Igiliz and Agouti.

1) 45m. Climb an excellent wall, then scramble up to an overhang. Surmount this to a large ledge system.

2) 40m. Easy climbing to a belay on slabs.

3) 55m. Scramble up towards two 'ears' above. Trend left, heading for the left 'ear'.

4) 45m. Climb up past the left side on the left 'ear', moving out with great exposure onto the upper east face. A fine, short, steep wall leads to easy ground.

5) 45m. Scrambling up to the East Summit.

Steve Broadbent & Anna Piotrowski (pitches 1 to 5).
Steve & Katja Broadbent, March 2014 (complete traverse).

From the East Summit, follow the crest of the ridge down towards the higher West Summit. This becomes a magnificent knife-edge, which can be scrambled right along the crest to the foot of the West Summit. About 60m of easy climbing then gains the top.

DESCENT: walk down the west side, then bear left to return to the base of the south face.

Area Map
Crag Selector
Intro
The Climbing
How to Use
Suggested Climbs
Tafraout Granite
Anergui
Ameln Valley
Tarakatine Pass
Sidi M'Zal
Jebel Taskra
Idaougnidif
Afantinzar
Samazar
Aouguenz
Tagzene
Tagmout
History
Index

Caroline Culwick on the first ascent of the Cracked Pillar of Aylim's *Central Buttress* (E1) (page 300).

Photo: Steve Broadbent

Area Map
Crag Selector
Intro
The Climbing
How to Use
Suggested Climbs
Tafraout Granite
Anergui
Ameln Valley
Tarakatine Pass
Sidi M'Zal
Jebel Taskra
Idaougnidif
Afantinzar
Samazar
Aouguenz
Tagzene
Tanmout
History
Index

AGOUTI WEST SUMMIT

This is the higher (left-hand) summit, which sits at the top of the Samazar Hairpins. Its attractive south face holds a handful of good climbs with a short approach, easy descent, and excellent views from the summit.

3. Honeycomb Buttress Severe ★2 STEEP

135m. The steep-looking buttress on the left side of the south face is a remarkable climb, sustained at the grade with lots of exposure and straightforward route-finding. Big holds on steep ground make this route more typical of the Ameln Valley than of Samazar, but the tremendous views make it a worthwhile starting point for those visiting the valley for the first time. Park on the Samazar Hairpins, from where the foot of the buttress is easily reached in about 10 minutes.

1) 30m Easy climbing to a ledge below a steepening.

2) 40m The steeper part of the buttress is taken on its left side to a ledge below an overhang.

3) 30m Pass the overhang on its left side and follow superbly steep rock to a small stance.

4) 30m The ridge remains steep until a large ledge marks the end of the difficulties. Easy scrambling then leads up to the summit plateau.

Steve & Katja Broadbent, April 2008.

4. Central Pillar HVS 4c LOOSE

120m. The obvious steep pillar is easier than it looks, but does have a fair amount of loose rock.

1) 55m (4c) Start by the pedestal on the right side of the pillar and trend up and left along the easiest line. About halfway up the rock quality changes for the worse - at this point shuffle right and continue up some vague cracks to a belay a few metres below the top of the pillar.

2) 20m (-) Scramble up to the top of the pillar, and then along some easy slabs that lead to a belay in a recess at the foot of the steeper wall at the back.

3) 30m (4c) Tackle this wall using the broken section on the left. Move left to a belay at a sudden change in rock type.

4) 15m (4b) Pull over a small bulge directly above the belay and continue easily to the top.

Chris Bull, Sally Fitton & Sesh Nadathur, January 2009.

Steve Robinson, high above Samazar on the Cracked Pillar pitch of Aylim's *Central Buttress* (E1) (page 300).

Photo: Steve Broadbent

5. **Free Fings Dat Fink Feoretically** MVS 4b ★1

150m. This excellent climb is low in the grade and features two fine long pitches followed by easier climbing on the upper buttress. Starts next to a tree at the foot of the gully.

1) 45m (4b) Climb up and right to follow a crack with black streaks then climb straight up the groove / chimney on good holds to a belay at the top of the groove.

2) 40m (4b) Go straight up the face past a small layback flake. Continue below narrow overhangs to a blocky ledge on the right. From here a few tricky moves head up and left onto a fine exposed buttress which is followed to a large ledge.

3) 10m Scramble up the red slab on the right to a stance below the overhang.

4) 50m Start a few metres right of the overhang then move leftwards, following steep faces to ledge. Continue beyond the ledge until the climbing eases to scrambling.

Jayson Orton & Elie Dekoninck, October 2008.

6. **Stairway to Heaven** MVS 4c ★1

195m. An entertaining and varied climb with short technical sections and comfortable belay ledges. Rather more continuous than the previous route, but with more difficult route-finding. The route starts up a series of large steps and finishes up the narrow buttress left of prominent orange overhangs in the upper part of the face.

1) 20m From the top of the initial slab make steep moves up a vague right-trending crack to a second left-slanting slab. Climb this to easier ground and belay below a corner crack.

2) 30m The corner crack gains another shelf leading to a short wall up to three intriguing boulders. Gaining the top of the wall behind them is an entertaining problem, best solved with an unprotected step and difficult mantel from the top of the middle boulder... Block belay out right on a small ledge.

3) 45m Trend up and left on interesting ground to belay on a good ledge below a steepening.

4) 30m (4c) Move left to gain a disappointing flake crack in the steep ground above. This crack is significantly harder than it looks, but is short and well-protected. Belay on a shady ledge opposite the orange overhangs.

5) 35m Continue up the narrow buttress left of the orange overhangs.

6) 35m Progressively easier climbing to the top.

Steve & Katja Broadbent, October 2008.

DESCENT: Walk easily down the left-hand (western) slopes to return to the hillside below. Turn left and follow a good path back beneath the south face to the Samazar Hairpins.

Area Map
Crag Selector
Intro
The Climbing
How to Use
Suggested Climbs
Tafraout Granite
Anergui
Ameln Valley
Tarakatine Pass
Sidi M'Zal
Jebel Taskra
Idaougnidif
Afantinzar
Samazar
Aouguenz
Tagzene
Tagmout
History
Index

B AYLIM (The Great Rock)

Shade · Families · Hitch · Roadside

Drive from Tafraout: **1:40**
Walk-in: **2 to 30 minutes**

The mighty Great Rock of Samazar, or Aylim to give it its correct title, is one of the biggest and most inspiring pieces of rock in the Anti-Atlas, rising over a thousand vertical feet from the Samazar road. This huge and imposing mountain dominates the small settlement of Tamdkrt, yet its summit is surprisingly free from the signs of Berber activity that are present on most of the other prominent peaks in the area. Whilst Aylim does not present such clean sweeps of vertical rock as the nearby Waterfall Walls, it does provide some of the most popular big routes in the range. Indeed the first ascent of the NE front was probably the most prized goal in the early exploration of this valley.

Although usually approached from Tanalt in the west, The Rock is best viewed from the village of Ogogn to the east, from where the long ridges of its north-east flank are seen end-on. The left-hand of these two ridges is the *Great Ridge*, which leads up to a subsidiary summit known as Knight's Peak. This is separated from the main summit by a substantial notch and area of dirty rock, and thus most climbers arriving on Knight's Peak will choose to descend from here rather than continue over the main summit plateau. To the right of the *Great Ridge* is the vegetated Central Gully, with the more gently-angled but complex *Labyrinth Ridge* on its right side. These two ridges separate the slabby east face on the left, and the steep stacked flakes of the North Buttress on the right.

For all routes on the northeast side it is possible to park in a small space (two cars only) at a bend in the road close to the foot of the *Great Ridge*. Walk-ins then vary between two and thirty minutes up the side-valley between Aylim and the Pimple.

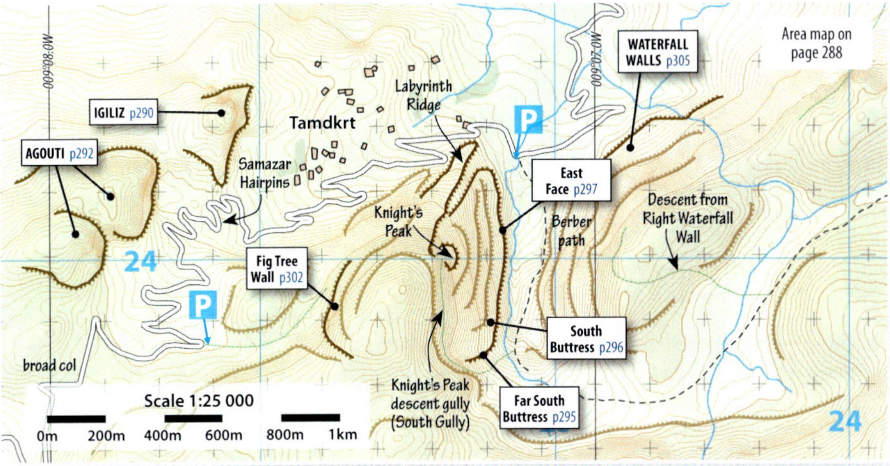

FAR SOUTH BUTTRESS

This smaller crag lies at the extreme left side of the Great Rock's East Face, tucked away on the southern slopes close to the bottom of the standard South Gully descent. Access is difficult due to vegetation - the best route is via the Berber path on the east side of the valley which passes underneath the Pimple. Follow this until close to a small waterfall, beyond the left side of the East Face, from where the southern slopes of the Great Rock are visible. Some bushwhack is then required.

The buttress is more easily reached from the foot of the South Gully descent after climbing a route on Knight's Peak or the South Buttress.

1. Cobra Crack HVS 5b ★3 CRACK GEAR

90m. Sensational, remote, crack perfection, in which connoisseurs will revel in mountain solitude. The route is hard for the grade, but well-protected throughout.

1) 50m (4c) The initial crack soon becomes an entertaining chimney. Above this move right across the wall to gain easy slabs leading to the overhung corner.

2) 20m (5b) The overhanging corner crack is a sumptuously satisfying endeavour, requiring a touch of faith and plenty of flexibility. It is perfectly positioned, perfectly protected... and absolutely desperate.

3) 20m (-) Easy climbing to gain the top of the tower.

Steve Broadbent & Caroline Culwick, April 2011.

DESCENT: Two options are available:

A) Head up left to join the South Gully Descent from Knight's Peak. This is the best option if you have not left anything at the base of the route, as it is the quickest way back to the road.

B) Make an exposed traverse rightwards and descend to a large ledge, from where a 50m abseil regains the foot of the route. This is the quickest way back to the start of the climb, though bushwhack is then required to reach the road.

THE SOUTH BUTTRESS

The South Buttress is the slightly lower, left side of the East Face, below a major notch in the South Ridge. Easy, low-commitment routes are a rare thing in Samazar, so the following climbs are highly recommended for parties looking for some low-grade multi-pitch adventures. The rock is excellent throughout, so it's a good place to head for a 'gentle' introduction to the big Samazar routes. The approach is as for the East Face.

DESCENT: From the top of the routes it is easy to scramble over the South Ridge to the lower part of the South Gully descent (see opposite page).

2. Sunny Side Up Severe 4b ★

180m. The centre of the slabby South Buttress is the first of three superb low-grade routes. The line is rather vague, and although the climbing is mostly easier than on its two counterparts, it requires some route-finding skills and is perhaps slightly less classic.

1) 50m (4b) Climb the gully left of a slab for about 8m, then move right onto the slab. Climb up to an overlap, and traverse right beneath it to gain a slab left of the arête.
2) 50m (-) Continue straight up on good rock to a block belay.
3) 40m (-) Continue straight up to a ledge at 30m, then climb up left of a bush.
4) 40m (-) Easier climbing to the top.

Chris Bull & Will Benfold, October 2011.

3. Serengeti Severe 4b ★

180m. Excellent juggy climbing up the clean rib at the right side of the South Buttress, providing a superb day that is technically the hardest of the trio, but arguably the best.

1) 45m (4b) Start up the back of a vague gully at the left side of The Organ Pipes, heading for a weakness in the small overhang above. Pull through this via a very difficult but well-protected move, then follow easier ground to a good spike belay.
2) 45m (4a) Continue up the excellent black rib at the left side of the slabs to a shady niche, right of the large roof. Move up, then traverse the side wall leftwards to gain the front of the fine rib. Follow this to a small stance.
3) 30m (-) Continue up the excellent rib to belay by a bush beneath steeper ground.
4) 30m (4a) A superb pitch up the steep orange buttress, via a shallow groove on its left side. Continue to a comfortable belay ledge.
5) 30m (-) Easy climbing up the final section of *Thunder Rib*.

Steve Broadbent & Cameron Hall, October 2011.

4. Thunder Rib Severe ★

180m. Very good, clean climbing up the right side of the South Buttress, with good variety and excellent rock throughout. A big outing at this grade.

1) 50m Start from a series of ribs (The Organ Pipes), and take the central rib to a good flat ledge below a prominent black slab.
2) 45m Climb up the rib on the right side of the black slab via some good but bold moves. Belay beneath a pale steep wall.
3) 35m Step left at the initial steepening then make an excellent traverse up left on the second steep wall to gain easy steps up a groove on the left side of the rib. Follow this to an easy step right at a perched block to gain the crest of the rib. Excellent friction climbing then leads to a belay below the right side of a steep orange tower.
4) 50m Climb steep white rock up the right side of the tower to gain a notch on the ridge crest. Follow the crest more easily to easy scrambling.

Steve Broadbent & Caroline Culwick, April 2011.

THE EAST FACE - KNIGHT'S PEAK

The impressive north-eastern aspect of the Great Rock is a tempting objective for climbers and provides long mountaineering routes of great character, giving a fully-blown 'mountain day' just yards from the roadside. All the climbs here are serious undertakings, requiring an early start and long days, and will call upon plenty of big-route experience. The rock is generally sound, but most of the routes require intricate route-finding to avoid the occasional loose or dirty section, adding to the Rock's 'mountain' feel.

Park at the small parking space at a bend in the road right at the foot of the face (just about room for two cars). From here the east face can be accessed by following a vague path along an old water pipeline up the west side of the valley. This approach can be rather vegetated during spring months.

SOUTH GULLY DESCENT: The summit of Knight's Peak is separated from the main summit plateau by a prominent notch, from where most parties will choose to descend by scrambling down into the gully leading south from the notch. This is the infamous South Gully descent, which has been the start of many hideous bushwhack experiences. In order to avoid unpleasant vegetation, care is required, navigating as follows:

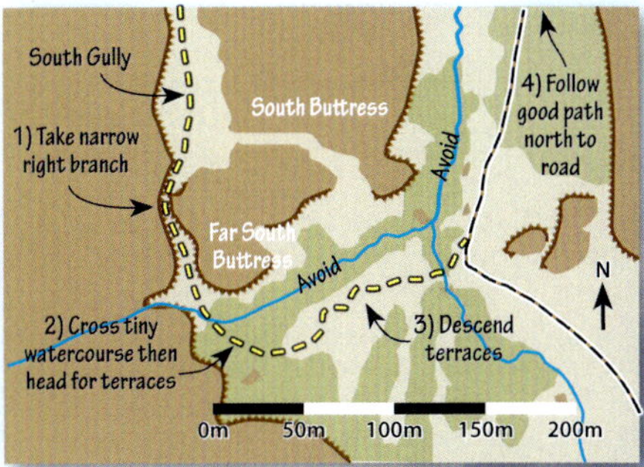

1) Follow the gully easily down until it splits. Take the right-hand branch (looking outwards) to drop into a much narrower section of gully. Descend this (some short sections of scrambling) to the hillside below.

2) Do not be tempted to turn left and descend below the South Buttress. Instead, keep contouring straight on, crossing a small seasonal watercourse and heading for terraces on the opposite side. This section will involve some vegetation.

3) Once on the terraces, turn downhill, heading for a small waterfall at bluffs in the bottom of the valley.

4) Cross the main watercourse and ascend slightly to pick up a Berber path which runs north underneath the rock walls of 'The Pimple' on the right to reach the parking space.

Area Map
Crag Selector
Intro
The Climbing
How to Use
Suggested Climbs
Tafraout Granite
Anergui
Ameln Valley
Tarakatine Pass
Sidi M'Zal
Jebel Taskra
Idaougnidif
Afantinzar
Samazar
Aouguenz
Tagzene
Tagmout
History
Index

5. Delirium E1 5b ★3

325m. Despite large amounts of easy climbing, *Delirium* features two very challenging crux pitches, both in magnificent positions high on the face. The route tackles the sweeping concave wall at the top of the face left of the *Polish Pillar*, and despite a rather vegetated appearance it consists of immaculately clean climbing on good rock throughout. The difficult sections are well-protected and not sustained, but some of the easier pitches involve big runouts. The route starts immediately left of a large patch of black lichen at the base of the wall, just right of The Organ Pipes. From here it is possible to identify both crux pitches - a weakness immediately left of a flat black-streaked square roof at half-height, and the steep wall immediately right of a prominent finger of rock at the top of the cliff. **60m ropes are strongly advised**.

1) 55m (4a) Climb ribs to a belay below a broad shallow gully.
2) 55m (4a) Excellent easy climbing up good rock in the bed of the gully leads to an attractive black wall.
3) 25m (4b) Continue up the excellent black wall to a sling belay underneath the weakness immediately left of the biggest flat roof.
4) 30m (5b) Pull up steeply passing some dubious flakes before swinging right with difficulty to gain easier climbing on the face above the overhangs. Continue to a ledge beneath the enticing sweeping slab above.
5) 40m (4b) Climb up ribs to the base of the sweeping slab, which leads all the way up to the prominent finger at the top of the face.
6) 60m (4c) ***The Concave Wall*** – A long, poorly-protected pitch with good VS climbing in an epic setting. Climbers with short ropes should beware of a lack of gear and stances in the upper section, although a belay at about 40m is possible. Go straight up the clean sweep of rock, heading for the steep wall to the right of the finger. The climbing gets steeper towards the top with a couple of bold moves to gain a very poor stance beneath orange overhangs (high cams in the overhang).
7) 30m (5b) A superb but testing pitch that features some very technical climbing in a fine position. Climb up onto the orange slab then swing left around the arête onto the front face. Some worrying technical moves with blind gear to the right gain a good ledge. Step left from here, back onto the front face, which provides superb steep climbing to an easier groove. Move left to belay on the shoulder behind the Finger.
8) 30m (4b) Easy flakes to gain the rib above, which is followed to the top.

Steve Broadbent & Anna Piotrowski, March 2012.

6. The Free Blast Severe

165m (to Echo Ledge). The slabby, left side of the lower Central Buttress provides the easiest means of accessing the large 'Echo Ledge' from where the next two routes diverge. Start at an obvious right-trending weakness at the left side of black slabs, some 20m left of a large flat-topped pinnacle that abuts the face (East Gully Tower).

1) 30m Work up right to a block belay.
2) 35m Easy rocks trending left to a small stance.
3-5) 100m Continue up the easiest line to a huge ledge (Echo Ledge) at the foot of the vegetated Upper East Gully.

Steve & Katja Broadbent, April 2008.

7. Polish Pillar E1 5b ★2

PRICKLY CRACK STEEP

400m. A superb adventure, despite some vegetation in its middle section. The narrow pillar to the left of Upper East Gully is not quite as long as the neighbouring *East Face Direct*, but what it lacks in length it more than makes up for in steepness, difficulty, and exposure, with a number of overhanging crack-pitches. All difficulties are very well protected, but the route is a serious undertaking, with few escape options.

1-5) 165m (-) Climb to Echo Ledge via *The Free Blast*.
6) 35m (5b) The white pillar off the left side of the ledge gives a challenging pitch. Move left to gain a crack up the front of the pillar, and climb it until a few moves on the right face gain an overhanging crack to a small summit.
7) 33m (4c) Enjoyable climbing up the narrow left-hand flake crack to a vegetated sloping belay.
8) 32m (-) A poor pitch... go straight up cracks then fight through vegetation to gain a notch in the ridge. Cross over to the left side and clamber past a large tree to a ledge on the side of the deep gully.
9) 30m (4c) Climb the chimney and flake in the back of the gully, exiting left to a good ledge and tree.
10) 20m (5a) Go up and right to gain an overhanging crack. There is a poor hanging stance above the steepest section, or it is possible to link this with the next pitch...
11) 25m (4c) Continue up the overhanging crack.
12) 30m (4b) Climb a crack in the front of the narrow brown buttress.
13) 30m (-) Progressively easier climbing to gain the South Ridge, from where 70m of scrambling leads to the summit of Knight's Peak.

Steve Broadbent & Iza Pstrucha, February 2009.

8. East Face Direct HVS 5a ★1

STEEP

450m. Adventurous, committing and sustained, the *East Face Direct* is a classic of its grade and a major undertaking. The route takes a logical line up the face, just right of the Upper East Gully.

1-5) 165m. The *Free Blast*.
6) 20m. Move up to a higher ledge on the right beneath steeper ground.
7) 30m (4c) Climb a steep black groove on questionable rock.
8-9) 60m. Work left up easier ground staying close to the large vegetated gully.
10) 30m. Trend back right into a vegetated niche.
11) 25m. Climb the right wall of the niche to a higher ledge below steeper ground.
12) 30m (5a) The steep crack is the crux of the route, and leads to a good ledge.
13) 20m. Up left to another ledge.
14) 30m. Climb the right wall then continue up excellent rock in a fine position.
15) 40m. Gradually easing ground to Knight's Peak.

Steve & Katja Broadbent, April 2008.

Map Page 288

Area Map
Crag Selector
Intro
The Climbing
How to Use
Suggested Climbs
Tafraout Granite
Anergui
Ameln Valley
Tarakatine Pass
Sidi M'Zal
Jebel Taskra
Idaougnidif
Afantinzar
Samazar
Aougueni
Tagzene
Tagmout
History
Index

Area Map
Crag Selector
Intro
The Climbing
How to Use
Suggested Climbs
Tafraout Granite
Anergui
Ameln Valley
Tarakatine Pass
Sidi M'Zal
Jebel Taskra
Idaougnidif
Afantinzar
Samazar
Aouguenz
Tagzene
Tagmout
History
Index

9. Central Buttress VS 4c / E1 5b ★3

475m. A magnificent and popular classic, giving one of the best mountain days in the Anti-Atlas. A number of alternative direct pitches at E1 provide a good opportunity to push your grade a thousand feet above the valley floor, though the original VS way is just as good! The climb starts at a prominent pinnacle (East Gully Tower) which abuts the East Face just next to Lower East Gully. It is reached in about 10 to 15 minutes from the car.

1) 25m (4a) Tempting cracks up the front of East Gully Tower lead to a small stance on the right.

2) 30m (4b) Climb the excellent narrow rib to a pinnacle belay.

3) (-) 25m Scramble down and move the belay up to a niche beneath a slabby wall.

4) (-) ***The Original Way*** – Avoid the overhang by traversing leftwards onto a white rib, via a perched flake on the left wall. The rib leads to a good belay above and right of a large boulder in a niche.

4-alt) (HVS 4c) ***The Culwick Overhang*** – Climb the wall to gain an obvious crack through the overhang. Climb through this to gain the fine ridge crest above. Follow this to a belay up and right of large niche.

5) 50m (4b) Superb, exposed climbing up the front of the rib to a stance.

6) 40m (4a) Go up slabby ground until it is possible to move right onto the excellent wall above steeper rocks. This features some delightful climbing to a spike belay at the top of Lower East Gully.

7a) 30m (4c) Move right from the belay and climb a steep groove to easier-angled ground. Step right to belay.

7b) 40m (4b) ***The Fresh Air Traverse*** – Move up left from the belay over some questionable rock, and traverse left beneath steep ground to the base of a narrow chimney. Step down left from here, and continue traversing leftwards around the arête, passing another steep crack-line to a small stance on the left face.

7-alt) 30m (HVS 5a) ***The 5a Groove*** – The difficult overhanging twin groove directly above the spike belay at the top of pitch 6 is worth the effort. Exit onto a small oasis, then make an easy but airy traverse left to finish up a short chimney to the Crow's Nest.

8) 20m (4c) Move up, then climb a short steep orange corner on the left. Continue up the rib above to a small white pinnacle.

9) 35m (4b) Some steep moves then easier climbing leads to a ledge. Exit right up a final steep notch (either groove works) to another good ledge.

10) 40m (-) Move up easy ground then a vague gully, exiting rightwards to a stance beneath an impressive cracked pillar.

11) 30m (4c) Climb the groove up left of the pillar, until fine moves up the right wall regain the crest of the buttress. Finish more easily to a sling belay.

11-alt) 35m (E1 5b) ***The Cracked Pillar*** – The steep crack up the front of the pillar gives a superbly positioned finale.

12) 80m (-) Easy climbing to the summit of Knight's Peak.

Steve Broadbent & Matt Mellor (pitches 3,4,5,6,7a,7b,8,9,10,11,12), February 2011.
Steve Broadbent & Caroline Culwick (pitches 1,2,4-alt,7-alt,11-alt), April 2011.

Photos page 291 and 292.

10. The Great Ridge of Samazar VS 5a ★★★ ADVENTURE

650m. The fabulous stepped ridge left of Central Gully gives a great classic climb on magnificent rock, and remains one of the most prized ascents of the Anti-Atlas. Most of it is quite easy, but there are two excellent pitches of 5a on the crest of the first step (avoidable on the left) and an impressive 5a pitch to finish up the third and final tower. Much of the route could be climbed un-roped, but the first ascensionists counted 14 pitches with about 650m of climbing.

Jim Fotheringham & Mike Mortimer (October 2007.

11. Labyrinth Ridge VS 5a ★★★ ADVENTURE

800m. Another tremendous route, and one of the biggest and most sought-after climbs of its grade in the region, providing a full complement of mountain challenges that will test even the most competent of parties. This route's status as one of the longest in the Anti-Atlas makes up for some isolated sections of questionable rock, on which care is required. The initial narrow ridge involves large amounts of easy scrambling over which speed is of the essence, before things take a sinister turn with some fine adventurous climbing on the steep headwall. In total there are about 20 pitches and 800m of climbing, providing a memorable and tiring day out that is comparable in length with Asgaour's *Great Ridge*.

A) The route starts easily, gaining and following a narrow crest of immaculate white quartzite for about 4 pitches to a short steep step. This is climbed at about Severe, before more easy scrambling (now mostly on the left side) leads to the Watch Tower, with a cairn and stone shelter on its summit. Avoid the Watch Tower on its left side to gain a notch. Escape into Central Gully is possible from most parts of this section.

B) A steep pitch from the notch is a sign of increasing difficulties and growing commitment. The Central Ribs offer a variety of options, but feature some bold climbing on suspect rock. Then, after a short walk, the ridge steepens again. Take a chimney on the left side of a narrow grey pillar, stepping left onto an excellent solid face in a fine position. This leads to the start of the headwall, at about 480m.

C) The headwall is tackled trending rightwards initially, to a hidden belay in a vegetated alcove after a couple of pitches. The left wall out of the alcove is the technical crux of the route, with some good 5a climbing in a superb position. This gains an unfortunate tower, forcing a traverse leftwards.

D) Traverse left past vegetation to gain easier looking ground. This eventually leads to an even more unfortunate tower, with apparently no escape (The Priest). The tower is separated from the main face by a gap of about 2m, and ingenuity must be used to gain the wide crack in the wall behind. This can be free-climbed strenuously at about 5b, but some pulling on gear makes the move a little more approachable (A0 & 4c).

E) Sustained scrambling and walking over false summits, with a few short pitches leads to a final tricky chimney right below the main summit.

Steve & Katja Broadbent, February 2008.

DESCENT: Descend over the summit as for Fig Tree Wall (p302).

FIG TREE WALL

The shorter west face of Aylim is the first view of the Great Rock for those travelling into Samazar from Tanalt, presenting a series of impressive pillars and grooves but giving little clue as to the magnitude of the northeastern front. Known as Fig Tree Wall, this west-facing crag, with its tempting pillars and corners, is home to some excellent and very accessible multi-pitch climbs on perfect rock, and also makes for a good reconnaissance day for those attempting *Labyrinth Ridge* as the routes here share the summit descent. Despite its altitude, the crag is very sheltered and catches the best of the afternoon sun whilst providing stunning views to the west over Tanalt. It is easily accessed in about 10 minutes from a small pull-out near the top of the Samazar Hairpins.

DESCENT: From the summit turn right (south) to gain a notch. Turn right again into the narrow gully which is followed with some short down-climbs back to the base, where a tricky rock step alongside the first pitch of *Manzakuneen* provides the final difficulty.

12. One Step Beyond HVS 5a

200m. The rib to the left of *Braveheart*, joining that route near the top. Pitches of 4b, 4c, 5a, 4c, and 5a, followed by easy climbing to the top.

Caty Darlay, Pilou Herin & Simon Destombes, March 2015.

13. Lost Images HVS 5a ★1

ADVENTURE

210m. The line of cracks and grooves to the left of *Braveheart* gives a climb of great character on perfect rock. Most of the climbing is VS, with a difficult pitch traversing rightwards to join *Braveheart*.

Mike & Marjorie Mortimer, October 2008.

14. Braveheart HVS 5a ★3

ADVENTURE BOLD

210m. The superb rib up the centre of the wall is one of the finest routes hereabouts, featuring excellent, bold climbing on immaculate rock. Four long pitches of 55m, 40m, 60m and 50m.

Ben & Marion Wintringham, April 2008.

15. Black Slab MVS 4b ★1

ADVENTURE SLAB

200m. This fine climb tackles the pillar and obvious slab to the right of *Braveheart* and has seen numerous ascents.

1) 55m Follow the rib right of *Braveheart* to a ledge.
2) 40m Go up the centre of the black slab.
3) 20m Continue up and right to a belay.
4) 50m Easier ground to the top.

Mike & Marjorie Mortimer, April 2009.

16. The Arganauts HVS 5a ★1

ADVENTURE BOLD

200m. Another good route, this time taking the broader rib from the lowest point of the face.

Mike Mortimer & Jim Fotheringham, April 2008.

17. Makayen Mushkil MVS 4b

140m. A meandering route up walls and grooves to the left of a prominent diamond slab.

1) 35m Climb a shallow groove before moving right onto a blunt rib to a large vegetated terrace.

2) 35m The easiest line up the wall above, then move left below a large tower.

3) 45m Start up the large corner, then move left onto an easy blunt arête.

4) 25m Follow the right side of the face to the left, moving right to a belay.

5) 45m (4b) Aim for a shallow groove in the tower above, with a bulge near the top.

Sally Fitton & Sesh Nadathur, December 2008.

18. Tifina Very Difficult ★1

120m. The rib to the right of the prominent diamond slab is a pleasant outing with some good varied climbing at this grade.

1) 55m Easy scrambling left of a gully to large ledges (as for *Manzakuneen*).

2) 35m From the left side of the ledge traverse left onto the easy rib, which is followed to a poor belay.

3) 30m Continue up the steep crest of the arête, passing right of a vegetated gully, to a good ledge.

4) 30m Climb a tiny arête in a fine position, and continue easily to a large ledge.

5) 25m Easy climbing up the final buttress.

Steve Broadbent & Elie Dekoninck, December 2008.

19. Manzakuneen Very Difficult ★2

160m. A very agreeable easy climb with large stances and good steep climbing, providing an excellent introduction to Samazar climbing. Protection on the key sections is spaced but adequate, and the route features some very fine situations.

1) 55m Easy scrambling to large ledges and block belay.

2) 30m Move left and climb the buttress easily to a belay on blocks.

3) 20m Step straight up from the belay onto steep ground, following the buttress to another good ledge.

4) 25m A superb pitch with good but well-spaced protection. Move left, then trend up and right on the excellent face to a sling belay.

5) 30m The top is reached by scrambling, with a few difficult steps.

Steve & Katja Broadbent, February 2008.

Area Map
Crag Selector
Intro
The Climbing
How to Use
Suggested Climbs
Tafraout Granite
Anergui
Ameln Valley
Tarakatine Pass
Sidi M'Zal
Jebel Taskra
Idaougnidif
Afantinzar
Samazar
Aougnenz
Tagzene
Tagmout
History
Index

Map Page 288

Area Map
Crag Selector
Intro
The Climbing
How to Use
Suggested Climbs
Anergui
Amelo Valley
Tarakatine Pass
Sidi M'Zal
Jebel Taskra
Samazar
Tagzene
Tagmout
History
Index

C THE WATERFALL WALLS

Shade Families Hitch Roadside
Drive from Tafraout: **1:40**
Walk-in: **15 to 25 minutes**

The massive Waterfall Walls, split by a seasonal 2000ft black waterslide, form the back wall of a vague cirque at the foot of the Samazar hairpins, towering over Tamdkrt. The walls face north, catch little sunlight, and have a sombre and unclimbable feel to them. Not surprisingly all routes here are major undertakings in a serious and committing environment, requiring early starts and confidence at the grade.

THE LEFT WATERFALL WALL

This is the large cliff to the left of the waterslide.

DESCENT: Head up left to descend a broad gully to the left (east) of the cliff.

1. Culmination Corner E2 5c

ADVENTURE

450m. The stunning corner to the left of the huge black waterslide is a long and serious adventure that sees few attempts.

Paul Donnithorne & Steve Findlay, October 2007.

2. Occam's Razor VS 5a ★2

ADVENTURE

400m. The curving arête to the right of *Culmination Corner* is an inspired line and provides the simplest solution to the Left Wall. It is a major undertaking at this grade, featuring almost 400m of sustained VS climbing. Start at the base of the central arête (third rib to the left of the waterfall).

1) 45m (4a) Easy climbing up to the obvious pinnacle ledge on the arête
2) 55m (4c) Follow the arête via an orange corner to a notch by tree.
3) 55m (4c) Continue up the arête to a small ledge below a large ramp (poor belay).
4) 60m (4b) Follow the arête directly, ignoring a large ramp to the left. Belay on a mossy ledge with a 6" crevasse at its back.
5) 30m (4c) Go up left from the ledge on jugs and climb the arête to belay on a pinnacle above a tree-filled notch.
6) 60m (4c) Bypass the tree to the right, regain the arête, and climb it to finish through a short wide crack to a large sloping ledge.
7) 15m (4c) Climb through the bulge to the top of the pinnacle.
8) 10m (-) Walk across left to below an impressive knife-edge arête.
9) 40m (5a) Up the knife-edge arête to finishing blocks.
10) 30m (-) Scramble easily to summit ridge.

Henward Nind & Topher Dagg, February 2010.

3. A Dream of White Butterflies E2 5b ★1

ADVENTURE

450m. Another beautiful climb, particularly when the waterfall is flowing. The climbing is continuously interesting and on good rock with minimal vegetation, reaching the top in about 12 pitches. The key pitch is the slim slab overlooking the waterfall which gives superb sustained climbing in a fabulously exposed position. Details of the exact line are unclear, but the climb roughly follows corners to the right of the *Occam's Razor*, joining that route in the upper pitches.

Jim Fotheringham & Mike Mortimer, April 2009.

4. Above The Water HVS+ 5a ★2

ADVENTURE

400m. The tremendous corner immediately left of the waterfall gives an infamous and adventurous climb. It is only climbable in dry conditions, and even then it lies at the very top of its grade.

1) 80m (4a) Easy climbing up the right side of the waterfall, passing ledges at 25m. Scramble over these to a large ledge by the waterfall.
2) (-) Cross over the waterfall to the base of the main corner. This pitch is slippery when wet, and impossible when the fall is in spate.
3) (4b) Start up the corner to belay at a small stance.
4) (4c) Continue past a loose red section to a belay ledge on the right.
5) (4c) The corner, this time belaying on a ledge on the left.
6) (4c) Climb the short groove above on the right until a step back left regains the main groove to ledges.
7) (5a) Up the groove to a stance.
8) (5a) Go up to bulges, then pull through these and work right to the arête, which leads to a large ledge.
9) (4c) The steep wall above is tackled via the easiest line to ledges beneath a groove.
10) (5a) Climb a steep left-slanting groove over bulges to the left arête, and a good ledge at the top of *Occam's Razor* pitch 6.
11-13) Finish as for that route.

Ben & Marion Wintringham, November 2010.

THE RIGHT WATERFALL WALL

The huge wall to the right of the waterfall has seen much more interest, despite some very mossy and vegetated climbing.

DESCENT: From the top of the routes considerable scrambling leads to the broad and confusing summit plateau. Continue south to descend the short 'back' side of the mountain into a hanging valley. Turn right along this to gain a path which descends beneath the East Face of Aylim. Do not try to descend to this directly down the west face. See map on page 295.

5. Grand Canyon's Edge E1 5b ★2

ADVENTURE

500m. A splendid outing climbing the left edge of the wall, overlooking the waterfall, with a magnificent finale up the great white arête that forms the left edge of the cliff. Start

Area Map
Crag Selector
Intro
The Climbing
How to Use
Suggested Climbs
Tafraout Granite
Anergui
Ameln Valley
Tarakatine Pass
Sidi M'Zal
Jebel Taskra
Idaougnidif
Afantinzar
Samazar
Aouguenz
Tagzene
Tagmout
History
Index

by scrambling to a ledge system 40m above the river bed.
1) 50m (5a) Trend up left under overlaps to a large ledge system.
2) 60m (-) Scramble left along the ledge towards the waterfall.
3) 60m (4b) Trend up left to a belay above the plunge pool.
4) 60m (5a) Traverse left to a pale corner some 30m above the plunge pool. Climb the corner and pull over an overlap to gain a niche.
5) 60m (4c) A slab and groove to a ledge.
6) 60m (4c) Continue up the groove, then climb slabs above to a fine shoulder.
7) 60m (5b) Go rightwards to the foot of the great white arête and climb a steep groove to its right.
8) 50m (5a) Follow the arête to an airy stance on the left.
9) 60m (5a) Climb a crack, then regain the arête and follow it to the top.

Adam Mulholland & Paul Donnithorne, October 2009.

6. La Processionaria da Nert HVS 5a ★1 ADVENTURE

450m. Another good route, which is described for dry conditions. If the river is full the first pitch can be avoided by scrambling in from further right.

1) 50m (4a) Start from the riverbed by the waterfall gorge and climb up slabs to a blunt pointed tower above.
2) 55m (4c) Follow the line of weakness to a spike then go up a ramp.
3) 45m (4a) Step right, then trend left up the slab to a shallow cave.
4) 35m (4b) Traverse 3m right, then follow a shallow groove to the huge ledge system.
5,6) 90m (-) Go up a big ramp above the ledge to the base of an enormous chimney.
7) 55m (5a) Climb the chimney, passing behind the vegetation, to a blocky ledge.
8) 40m (4b) Continue to a red cave.
9) 50m (4c) Follow the corner through a short off-width and up a water crack to the left.
10) 40m (-) An easy crack to the terrace, which then leads rightwards to the summit.

Topher Dagg, Davide Cassol & Luca Vallata, September 2010.

7. To Teo HVS 4c ★2 ADVENTURE MOSSY

450m. A popular adventure that gains and follows the curving arête above the central ledge system. To the right of the previous route it is possible to scramble rightwards up a

ramp to a pale hanging chimney; This may also be accessible from further right if the river is full.
1) 50m (4b) Follow the hanging chimney to a groove and slab. Belay in a small right-facing corner.
2) 50m (4a) The groove leads to a spike belay 10m below a small roof.
3) 60m (4a) Climb up and pass the roof to the left, then continue to the huge ledge system.
4) 50m (-) Easy scrambling rightwards up the ledge.
5) 60m (4b) Climb a clean groove then move left onto the arête. Follow this to a pale pillar.
6) 55m (4c) Continue up the arête until a short overhanging crack and off-width leads to a cave.
7) 55m (4c) A superb pitch. Traverse right up to the spectacular curving arête and follow it to a recess.
8) 20m (4a) Easy climbing leads to the top of the tower.
9) 50m (-) Scramble to the terrace, which then leads rightwards to the summit.
Topher Dagg, Davide Cassol & Luca Vallata, September 2010.

8. Daffodils, Kittens and Pink Bunny Rabbits E5 6a ★1

320m. This epic test-piece takes the hanging groove left of the huge central corner of *From the Deep*. It is a major undertaking, starting immediately behind the bifurcated tower.
1) 55m (5a) Go up the blunt arête to reach slabs with pleasing pocketed cracks. Continue to a belay in the groove system.
2) 25m (4b) Climb up the groove, passing over a flake block and belay soon after.
3) 55m (6a) The groove continues with increasing difficulty, until poor rock forces a step left onto a smooth slab via a tiny hold on the arête. Traverse left into the corner and climb up to a roof. At the roof, step up steeply left onto the face, where easier but unprotected climbing leads up right to a niche.
4) 10m (4a) Finish up a shallow groove to the huge central ledge system
5) 30m (-) Scramble up to a cave and tree.
6) 35m (4c) Pass the roof to the left (alternatively the crack can be taken directly at 5b). Follow the line of weakness left and then right to a slight notch in the roof. Swing through this and belay on the ledge above.
7) 40m (4b) Go up to a small cave.
8) 20m (4b) Step out left and continue up the face to the top of the tower.
9) 50m (-) Scrambling to the summit.
Topher Dagg, Davide Cassol & Luca Vallata, September 2010.

9. From the Deep E2 5b ★2 ADVENTURE

380m. Good, hard climbing up the central groove that bisects the wall. The lower half curves into enormous roofs just before the half-way ledge system. Start behind the pointed tower, at the base of the corners.
1) 55m (4b) Follow the groove to a corner just left of a wide crack.
2) 45m (5b) Continue up the groove pulling through an orange overlap and passing round a flake-block.
3) 55m (5b) The groove steepens ominously under huge overhangs. Follow it until beneath an inverted cave. Traverse right from here across the slab, then step up into the notch and traverse delicately right again to reach the cut in the roof. Ascend this moving left at the top to a ledge.
4) 30m (4b) Move up rightwards on underclings to the arête. Follow this easily to the big ledge, from where a jump leads to a belay at the base of the corner...
5) 55m (4a) Go up the wide crack and corner to a small ledge.
6) 50m (4c) Continue up the corner until a vertical crystal-laden crack provides a pleasant alternative to a vegetated gully. Traverse right at the top to reach a cave (good cam placements here).
7) 40m (4b) Chimney out of the cave and go left up a blocky crack system on jugs to the top of the tower.
8) 50m (-) Scrambling to the summit.
Topher Dagg, Davide Cassol & Luca Vallata, September 2010.

10. The Way of the Pooka E2 5b ★1 ADVENTURE MOSSY

390m. A harder alternative up the right side of the wall, seeking out some challenging ground and providing a big, involved outing with some adventurous climbing on an intimidating face.
1) 30m (4c) Follow twin cracks to a small pine tree.
2) 35m (5b) Traverse diagonally left across the slab and up to a notch in the centre of the curving roof. Pull through this and continue up the groove to a ledge.
3) 60m (4b) Follow the dark water groove to the right of the ledge, then move left to a poor belay.
4) 45m (4a) Continue up the groove and an easy ramp to a grassy ledge.
5) 40m (4c) Traverse left to the base of a corner. Go up this, stepping left at the roof to a spike belay.
6) 55m (5a) Step up and then delicately traverse left to a broken arête. Follow this to a vegetated notch.
7) 50m (4c) Follow another groove and surmount the block via a splitter crack. Belay at the foot of an impressive capped-corner.
8) 35m (5a) Climb the corner (off-width to fingers) and traverse left steeply to a large ledge before reaching huge hanging blocks.
9) 40m (4b) Go up the obvious chimney-crack to belay on summit blocks.
Topher Dagg, Davide Cassol & Luca Vallata, September 2010.

11. Chockstone Climb HVS 5a ADVENTURE

300m. This adventurous route follows the easiest line up slabs and walls on good rock, starting from a giant chockstone. Few details are known.
Jim Fotheringham & Mike Mortimer, April 2009.

Area Map
Crag Selector
Intro
The Climbing
How to Use
Suggested Climbs
Tafraout Granite
Anergui
Ameln Valley
Tarakatine Pass
Sidi M'Zal
Jebel Taskra
Idaougnidif
Afantinzar
Samazar
Aouguenz
Tagzene
Tagmout
History
Index

D DRAGON ROCK

Shade Families Hitch Roadside

Drive from Tafraout: **1:40**
Walk-in: **20 to 25 minutes**

Set amidst the magnificent scenery of the Samazar valley, Dragon Rock is one of the best cragging venues on this side of the range, providing an excellent selection of multi-pitch routes on good quality rock. The climbing is focused around two main buttress – Dragon Rock itself, and the lower (but taller) north-facing wall of Dragon Buttress. The variety of faces mean that it's usually possible to find shade here for at least part of the day, so it's a good choice during periods of warmer weather.

All of the climbing is approached from ample parking next to an electricity pylon on the Samazar road, close to the Ogogn junction.

To access Dragon Buttress, head north across mostly pathless terrain, heading for a notch on the skyline to the right of the crag. Cross through this and descend a vegetated gully to the foot of *Dragon Ridge*.

To access the climbing on the south and west sides, follow small cairns up the hillside, passing a tiny abandoned dwelling and heading for the base of a slanting rake. Ascend this to cross over a col into Corners Gully.

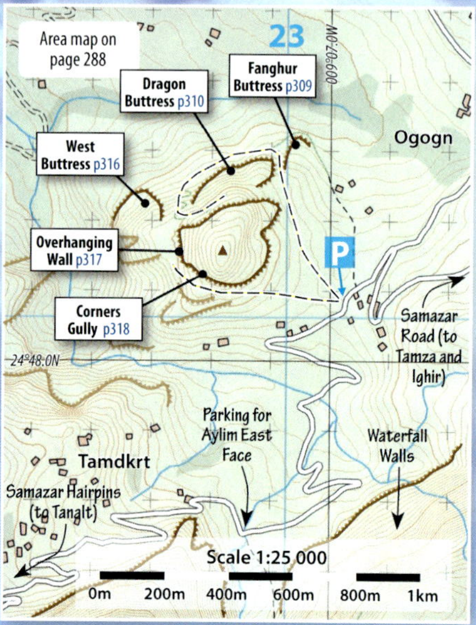

View from the South – for an overview of the north side, see page 316

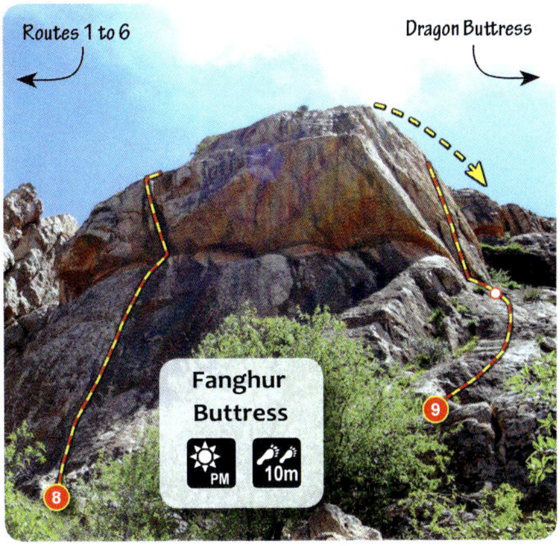

FANGHUR BUTTRESS

This minor buttress is located at the northeastern end of the crag. The first routes lie on the extreme eastern end above a small notch. They can either be approached via the vegetated approach gully or by following a vague path past houses and around the east end of the crag.

1. Dragon Arête HVS 5a ★2 ABSEIL BOLD

35m. The leftmost arête of the buttress gives a good pitch with some bold moves low down. Step off a boulder and climb a flake crack to the bulge, which is surmounted on good holds.
Pete Johnson & Paul Donnithorne, March 2012.

2. Dragonfly VS 4c ★1 ABSEIL

30m. The left-facing corner. Exit right at the top, then move up steeply left through a weakness.
Emma Alsford, Marion Wintringham & Paul Donnithorne, March 2012.

3. Ochre Slab HVS 5a ★1

30m. The crack on the right side of the arête is gained from *Dragonfly*. At the top of the crack, step right and climb the slab to a spike, finishing up another crack above.
Paul Donnithorne & Pete Johnson, March 2012.

4. Ochre Rib E3 5c

30m. The wall between *Ochre Slab* and *Dragnet Crack*.
J.Lines (solo), February 2014.

5. Dragnet Crack HVS 5a ★1 ABSEIL CRACK

30m. The prominent right-facing corner, stepping right at the top and finishing direct up a crack.
Paul Donnithorne & Marion Wintringham, March 2012.

6. Avatar E2 5c ★2 ABSEIL

50m. Excellent, off-balance climbing up the flake crack in the right side of the wall, leading to some nice moves up the upper slab. Swing rightwards through the bulge at the top and finish up the centre of the pinnacle.
Paul Donnithorne & Marion Wintringham, March 2012.

7. Leadbelly HVS 5b ★2 ABSEIL

50m. Starts in a gully 5m right of *Avatar*. Climb the groove then step left and move up to a roof. From the ramp on the right, a lunge leftwards gains the chimney, which is followed to a final steep crack and the top of the pinnacle.
Dan Donovan & Paul Donnithorne, April 2012.

The next buttress to the right is characterised by a slabby lower section and prominent roof above. It holds a couple of good climbs...

8. Chasing the Dream E2 5b ★1

45m. The slab and wide crack are not as dirty as appearances suggest. Start at the lowest point of the slab and climb up to a crack. Trend left up the slab to gain the obvious wide crack above, which provides an altogether 'different' finale.
Dan Moore & Shauna Clarke, March 2013.

9. Waking Dreams E1 5b ★2 CRACK

65m. The striking crack in the west-facing hanging wall is a well-positioned pitch.
1) 40m (4c) Climb a flake and slabby groove up rightwards, then go up the right side of the slab to a ledge.
2) 25m (5b) The superb face-crack in the upper wall.
Paul Donnithorne & Emma Alsford, January 2012.

Area Map
Crag Selector
Intro
The Climbing
How to Use
Suggested Climbs
Tafraout Granite
Anergui
Ameln Valley
Tarakatine Pass
Sidi M'Zal
Jebel Taskra
Idaougnidif
Afantinzar
Samazar
Aouguenz
Tagzene
Tagmout
History
Index

DRAGON BUTTRESS

The main north-facing buttress is accessed down the vegetated gully as shown on the previous page. It holds some of the best and most popular multi-pitch crag routes in the valley.

The first two climbs start on the sidewall at the foot of the vegetated approach gully. See also north face overview on page 316.

DESCENT: From all routes on Dragon Buttress it is necessary to make a very exposed scramble for which care is required. From the summit, head west along a knife-edge ridge, scrambling up a short steep section to reach easier ground. From here a cairned path is followed down to the slopes between Dragon Buttress and West Buttress. See also overview on page 316.

10. Apollo HS 4b ★3

175m. A magnificent route with bold, varied climbing on good rock. It is slightly harder, but just as good as *Dragon Ridge*. Start at the foot of the shallow groove in the sidewall as for that route.
1) 35m (-) Climb the groove then head boldly up the immaculate wall to belay on a comfortable ledge.
2) 30m (-) Step left across a groove and follow a short flake handrail across the black slab. Continue up and climb the right side of a pinnacle below a small overhang. Belay on the pinnacle.
3) 25m (4a) Pull straight up through the overhang in an excellent position, then continue up to a large ledge.
4) 30m (4b) Go up a corner, then move right and climb a second corner with difficult moves near the top. Finish on a large ledge at the top of *Dragon Ridge* pitch 4.
5&6) 55m (-). Easier climbing along the crest of the ridge as for *Dragon Ridge*.
Steve Broadbent & Caroline Culwick, October 2015

11. Dragon Ridge Severe ★3

170m. The left-hand ridge gives a magnificent and continuously interesting climb with good holds and plenty of exposure, providing one of the best routes of its grade in the valley. Start at a very shallow groove in the side-wall, some 10m up the vegetated gully.
1) 45m. From the base of the groove climb up rightwards across the wall on excellent holds (bold) to a stance on the arête. Continue up good rock just left of the arête, then finish up a fine sculpted ridge to a large ledge.
2) 10m. Move the belay to the base of the pillar above.
3) 25m. Climb up to a pinnacle at about 8m, then step right and move up right across the wall towards the chockstone. Steep moves rightwards past this gain the next rib, with a stance a few metres above.
4) 33m. Excellent climbing up the front of the buttress to a large ledge.
5) 30m. Easier climbing to a ledge.
6) 25m. Continue along the crest to the fine summit.
Steve & Katja Broadbent, March 2013.

12. The Almighty E4 6a A0 ★2
CRACK STEEP ABSEIL

65m. The intimidating overhanging crack up the left side of the orange overhangs. Start 2m left of *Inheritance*.
1) 30m (5b) Thin moves up the slab gain a spike at 4m, from where a shallow groove leads boldly to a flake on the left. Move left and follow a vegetated crack to a stance.
2) 35m (6a A0) Desperate moves up the crack lead to a brief respite, before things get sinister again at the top. There are perfect jams throughout, but the route awaits a free ascent.
Emma Alsford & Paul Donnithorne, March 2012.

13. Inheritance E2 5c ★1
ABSEIL

60m. The corner underneath the orange overhangs has some good climbing. Go up the corner to where things get steep, then undercut rightwards to a rest on the arête. Easier climbing above leads to block belays.
Paul Donnithorne & Emma Alsford, January 2012.

14. Shadeslayer HVS 5a ★2
ABSEIL

60m. The entertaining curving chimney involves some comedy manoeuvres with a fig tree at the start...
Emma Alsford & Paul Donnithorne, January 2012.

15. The Clavicle E2 5b ★2
BOLD ABSEIL

60m. The rib up the right side of the *Shadeslayer* chimney. Gain a small ledge on the right at 8m and follow the rib with good wires in disjointed cracks. Finish up the wall to the right of the rib.
Paul Donnithorne & Mike Pycroft, March 2012.

16. Tafod y Ddraig E1 5b ★2

200m. The *Dragon's Tongue* takes the fine pillar midway between *The Clavicle* and *Bad Breath*. Start just right of a groove, directly beneath the red overhang.

1) 35m (5a) Climb up the cracks / groove, then bear left on better rock to the left edge of the roof.

2) 35m (4a) Move up the groove for a few metres until it is possible to step right onto the front face. Continue up to a good stance.

3) 50m (5b) Climb the tongue of clean rock, just left of a groove, to a crevasse. Move up steeply and step left at a spike to gain a niche. Pull over the bulge and continue up to a stance.

4) 50m (-) Continue more easily to the top of the tower.

5) 30m (-) Scrambling to the summit.

P.Johnson & E.Roberts, March 2013.

17. Bad Breath E1 5b ★1

180m. The white rib has an off-putting start but with better climbing above. Start at a prominent off-width crack in an orange corner.

1) 30m (5b) Climb the dirty corner to a difficult exit.

2) 30m (4c) Follow the open groove above to a good stance.

3) 40m (4c) Move left to gain a black groove, which leads to easier ground.

4) 30m (4a) Continue directly to a comfortable ledge.

5) 50m (-) Easier climbing to gain the summit ridge.

S.Brown & M.Mortimer, March 2012.

18. Gorillas in the Mist HVS 5a ★1

200m. A rather dirty start gives way to some good climbing higher up. Start 10m right of *Bad Breath* at a short, thin crack.
1) 45m (5a) Climb the thin crack for 8m, then traverse leftwards past vegetation to gain a groove. Go up this, passing a bulge before stepping right to a black groove. Belay on a stance a few metres below a square-cut corner.
2) 60m (5a) Take the rib to the right of the corner and then follow a wall up and slightly rightwards to a ledge with a huge block (possible belay). A tricky move up left gains a flake crack which leads to a chimney stance.
3) 45m (5a) Pull up into the steep, leaning groove, then undercut right into another groove. Move right again to climb a pleasant slab to a ledge, about 5m left of the tree-filled gully.
4) 50m (4b) Climb a crack to gain the ridge, which is followed easily to the top.
Paul Donnithorne & Emma Alsford, March 2013.

19. The Missing Links E2 5c ★3

200m. A tremendous and varied route, forging a direct line up the golden pillar. Start 20m left of *Brisingr* beneath a shallow groove.
1) 35m (5b) Climb the groove to gain a brown flake, then follow a ramp up leftwards to a spike. Trend right up the slab above to the rake on *Monkey Island*.
2) 50m (4c) Climb the wall to the right of the wide crack, straight up to the pinnacle on *Brisingr*.
3) 55m (5c) Make a committing step off the top of the pinnacle to gain the arête above (the left arête of the big corner on *Brisingr*). Climb this to a stance beneath the overhang.
4) 60m (5a) Climb a flake up left to the roof, then pull around its left side into grooves, leading to a ledge and possible belay. Finish up the arête above.
Paul Donnithorne & Pete Johnson, March 2012.

20. Fantasia E1 5b ★2

185m. Good climbing up the left side of the golden pillar, though with a dirty first pitch. Start 6m right of *The Missing Links* below a thin crack.
1) 30m (5a) Climb the crack using holds on the right, trending left to a chimney. Take the right rib of the chimney to gain the vegetated ledge system, following it leftwards to a belay as for *The Missing Links*.
2) 50m (5a) Climb the big flake, passing the overlap on its right side to gain a flake crack up the centre of the buttress. Belay at the pinnacle.
3) 45m (5b) Climb the slabby left side of the pinnacle and follow a fine hand-crack and chimney above, through an overhang and up left to a good stance.
4) 60m (5b) Step left and climb up a flake groove. A short wall on the right then leads up past the left side of the upper overhangs 2m left of *The Missing Links*. Continue pleasantly above.
Paul Donnithorne & Emma Alsford, March 2013.

21. Monkey Island VS 5a ★1

180m. The central rib up the front face has some good positions and steep climbing, but requires some care to follow the best line. Start at a wild boar den, as for *Brisingr*.
1) 40m (4b) Climb the excellent pale rib up left from the den. At the top, make a tricky step down leftwards past vegetation, then climb the continuation ramp to a ledge above the tree, with a wide crack running up the right wall.
2) 20m (4b) Carry on up the ramp for a few more moves, then step back right into the wide crack. Follow this to a boulder belay.
3) 30m (5a) Boulder up the slabby wall at the back of the ledge to gain a high crack. Climb this and trend up left to a vegetated groove. At the top of this is a platform, from where an exposed stride left gains the pillar left of the chimney. Climb the front of the pillar on huge jugs to a belay beneath an orange crack.
4) 30m (5a) Hard moves up the crack gain a ledge. Cross this and climb a fine wide crack on the right side of the buttress.
5) 40m (4b) Continue up the right side of the pillar to a boulder belay.
6) 20m (-) Easy climbing up rightwards to the summit.
Alt) HVS (5a) An alternative to pitches 2 and 3 continues leftward from the belay on the ramp, to a belay below the upper pillar. Climb straight up from here into a groove on the right side of a small roof, then step left onto the front of the pillar, rejoining the original after the stride left on pitch 3.
Steve Broadbent & Will Benfold, February 2012.

22. Brisingr E1 5b ★3

175m. A superb climb that is full of character, taking the striking golden pillar at the right side of the main face. The route takes a strong line, and is low in the grade, with comfortable stances throughout. Start under trees in a wild boar den at the foot of the pillar, where a pale rib leads up leftwards.
1) 15m (4b) Climb the pale rib up leftwards to a heavily vegetated ledge.
2) 45m (5a) Go around the right side of the bush, then step back left across a chimney to regain the front of the stacked-flake tower. Climb this to a ledge on the left at about 20m, then take tricky cracks close to the right edge of the pillar. These lead to easier ground which is followed to a fine rock ledge on the summit of the lower tower. The slim groove to the right of the stacked-flake tower can also be climbed at a similar grade.
3) 50m (5a) A brilliant pitch up the enticing corner. Squeeze behind an olive tree and make a very bold entry into the corner (the wide crack is hard; the blank wall is hard and bold). Continue more easily above in a superb position to a sloping belay beneath the roof. It is also possible to move out right for the top section of this pitch, following a vague ramp to the right of the arête up to an exposed stance on the arête.
4) 30m (5b) Awkward climbing up the black groove to the right side of the prominent roof. Belay on a fine platform.
5) 35m (4c) Easier climbing up the ramp, finishing with a steep boulder problem on the crest of the rib.
Emma Alsford & Paul Donnithorne, January 2012.

Area Map
Crag Selector
Intro
The Climbing
How to Use
Suggested Climbs
Tafraout Granite
Anergui
Ameln Valley
Tarakatine Pass
Sidi M'Zal
Jebel Taskra
Idaougnidif
Afantinzar
Samazar
Aouguenz
Tagzene
Tagmout
History
Index

Area Map
Crag Selector
Intro
The Climbing
How to Use
Suggested Climbs
Tafraout Granite
Anergui
Ameln Valley
Tarakatine Pass
Sidi M'Zal
Jebel Taskra
Idaougnidif
Afantinzar
Samazar
Aouguenz
Tagzene
Tagmout
History
Index

23. Goldeneye E2/3 5b ★2

BOLD

70m. Although something of an eliminate, this fine wall climb represents the most direct and exposed solution to the magnificent golden pillar. It offers bold, technical climbing in a superb position. Start at the top of pitch 2 of *Firesword*, or by traversing in from *Brisingr* below the roof.

1) 35m (5b) Climb the wide crack of *Firesword*, taking the left branch to the centre of the headwall (This point can also be reached from the groove of *Brisingr*). From here climb straight up on good but small holds to a ledge on the left as for *Brisingr*.

2) 35m (5b) Climb the arête on the right for 2m until it is possible to swing back right onto the face. Make a rising traverse along a line of small flakes, then climb straight up to a ledge. Finish straight up a short overhanging arête to a good ledge at the top.

Steve Broadbent, Dave Arthur & Caroline Culwick, October 2014

24. Firesword E2 5b ★3

170m. The golden face on the right side of the pillar gives an audacious climb with some bold positions, providing one of the best routes in the Anti-Atlas. It is a notch harder than *Brisingr*, and starts at the same point.

1) 60m (5b) Climb up to a small tree in order to gain the slab on the right. Make difficult moves up to cracks on the sidewall of *Brisingr*, and follow these to ledges, belaying a little higher up by a shallow groove right of a block.

2) 40m (5a) Go up the groove, then move right into a wide crack. Trend rightwards above and climb cracks to a ledge and tree belay.

3) 40m (5b) Climb steeply up the big crack, taking the left fork towards the left side of the golden wall. Move right along a break and climb up rightwards to a good ledge below the final corner. A variation to this pitch traverses boldly left to climb the right side of the arête, before a rising traverse up rightwards regains the normal route.

4) 30m (5b) Climb a steep flake crack and continue up a black stain to a short traverse rightwards into the corner chimney. Follow this with interest to the top.

Emma Alsford & Paul Donnithorne, January 2012.

25. Thorn / Tan y Ddraig E1 5b ★2

MOSSY

180m. An excellent route up the centre of the cliff taking the striking overhanging curved corner high up. Start a few metres right of *Brisingr*.

1) 55m (4c) From under the tree climb the straight crack then move right into a second crack following it past a tree. Move slightly left over blocks and ledges to reach the vegetated gully left of *Sisters of Mercy*.

2) 55m (5b) Cross the gully and climb the rib just right of the tree-filled gully to reach a square ledge. Climb an attractive short corner moving left under the overlap before continuing straight up to a step left under an obvious groove. Move left again to reach a golden shield. Climb a crack up the shield and go diagonally up left to its top. Continue steeply above via a thin flake crack to reach a good belay ledge at the base of the big orange corner.

3) 20m (5b) Superb laybacking and jamming up the huge orange corner.

4) 40m (4c) Move up and make an airy traverse left to gain an excellent golden rib. Follow this to the top.

Paul Donnithorne & Emma Alsford, November 2012.

26. Sisters of Mercy VS 4c ★2

180m. The vague rib up the wall to the right of the golden pillar gives a fine outing on good rock. Start on a grassy ledge, just left of a large tree.

1) 50m (4c) Climb directly up, then pull through a steepening via a shallow groove. Step across the small

vegetated gully and climb up to a rib, which leads up to a belay in the large gully.
2) 60m (4b) Move the belay across the gully and climb a flake and rib, slightly rightwards, to a good belay by two large blocks.
3) 40m (4b) Follow the crack above the blocks and climb up leftwards to a small stance, just right of the final corner.
4) 30m (4b) Move up left into the corner and follow it to the fine ridge crest at the top.
Emma Alsford & Don Sargeant, April 2012.

27. Brothers in Arms E1 5b ★2

170m. A good companion to *Sisters of Mercy*, starting at a huge left-facing flake crack.
1) 45m (5b) Awkward moves up the flake crack lead to a step right. Continue up to a good ledge beneath a steep orange corner (possible belay). Either go up the corner (5b) or the easier crack on the left (5a) and continue towards a chimney (some vegetation here). Climb the crack to the left of the chimney to reach the gully above.
2) 10m (-) Move the belay 10m up the gully below a corner and roof.
3) 45m (5b) Climb the corner, moving left under the overhang to gain a steep flake crack. Pull steeply up left and continue up to gain a left-slanting overhung groove. Follow this, then climb up to a comfortable stance by two huge, stacked blocks.
4) 40m (5a) From the right side of the blocks move right and go up the edge of the golden wall, gaining a crack on its right side. Continue up to a stance on a narrow ledge below a large white flake.
5) 30m (4c) Go up rightwards to follow the right side of the flake to the top.
Emma Alsford & Paul Donnithorne, March 2013.

28. Glaedr E1 5b ★3 MOSSY

170m. An elegant climb, starting just left of the leaning buttress of *Shruikan* and finishing up the slabby corner right of *Firesword*.
1) 55m (5b) Start up a short groove to gain a ledge. Step left off this and climb a thin crack to another ledge. Climb an excellent black slab just left of the tree-filled chimney, trending right at the top to finish in a groove. Scramble across the gully and down leftwards to belay at the top of *Thorn* pitch 1.
2) 50m (4c) Bridge up the large block and climb a ramp rightwards to a ledge. Move up and make an airy traverse into the groove, continuing up to the belay on *Firesword*.
3) 35m (5b) Climb the wide crack of *Firesword*, taking the right fork over a roof to gain a groove. Follow this and the crack on the left to a belay in the corner just right of *Firesword*.
4) 30m (5b) Follow the corner to the roof, then swing up right into the superb continuation corner.
Paul Donnithorne & Emma Alsford, November 2012.

29. Shruikan E2 5b ★2

180m. A major undertaking providing very varied climbing up an initial detached pinnacle and dark slab above.
1) 25m (4c) Climb over large blocks, moving left then back right to a belay beneath an overhang-capped corner.
2) 30m (5b) Climb up to the overhang and surmount it to gain a fine crack in the slab above. Move up rightwards to a spike belay.
3) 40m (5b) Follow the rightward-trending ramp for 20m to a bold step off a flat-topped spike. This gains the west-facing headwall above, with a tricky move up right to better holds. Follow a crack and the right arête to a ledge, then continue up to the top of the pinnacle.
4) 55m (5b) Move the belay down across the gully to a good stance by a tree, beneath a small corner. Gain a white flake in the slab above, then step left to follow a line of cracks up the slab. Head up rightwards to belay on a prominent tree in the centre of the face.

5) 30m (4c) Follow a rake leading up left to a corner below overhanging blocks. Avoid these by traversing right, then move back up left to finish up a crack.
Paul Donnithorne & Emma Alsford, November 2012.

30. The Spine E2 5b ★1

90m. The right side of the semi-detached pinnacle gives a couple of challenging pitches, providing an inferior start to *Shruikan*. Start 20m right of that route.
1) 45m (5a) Make technical moves up to a break, then move up this and step right onto the wall to gain another diagonal break. Continue directly past jutting blocks to the spike belay of *Shruikan*.
2) 45m (5b) Climb up left and make an exposed traverse back right underneath a nose to gain a fine crack above. Follow this to the base of an excellent rib, which leads to the top of the buttress. From here it is possible to scramble down to an abseil point or continue up *Shruikan*.
Emma Alsford & Paul Donnithorne, January 2012.

31. Donkey's Lament HVS 5a / A0 ★2

140m. An adventurous route up the right side of the wall, with lots of character. Start at a large chimney to the right of the detached buttress.
1) 30m (5a) Battle up the chimney any way you can.
2) 50m (5a) Follow a foot-rail on the wall behind to gain a groove on the right. Climb this through a tree until forced left to the left side of a flake. From the top of this, step up left and climb the wall to a corner on the left. Follow this, then traverse rightwards to a sloping stance below a tree.
3) 25m (4c A0 or 5b) Head up left under the huge overhung crack towards the chockstone. Either tension left here to gain the rib, or go up the crack at 5b. Belay on a stance below the final golden arête.
4) 35m (4c) Move up the wall and climb leftwards to gain its left edge.
Emma Alsford, Marion Wintringham & Don Sargeant, March 2013.

WEST BUTTRESS

This is the slabby grey buttress to the west of the descent route. It holds a single route up the prominent central arête:

32. Millipede HS 4a

BOLD

85m. This pleasant route climbs an easy-angled arête at the right side of the main black slab. It offers nicely technical climbing that is mild for the grade, but very bold.
1) 30m. Climb the left side of the arête to a ledge.
2) 30m. Climb up to the overhang and pull up rightwards past this to continue up the arête.
3) 25m. Keep following the left-hand arête, staying on its left side throughout for the best climbing.
Steve Broadbent & Caroline Culwick, October 2015.
Named to celebrate Broadbent's one thousandth new pitch in Morocco.

View from the north, looking south. For a south side overview see page 308.

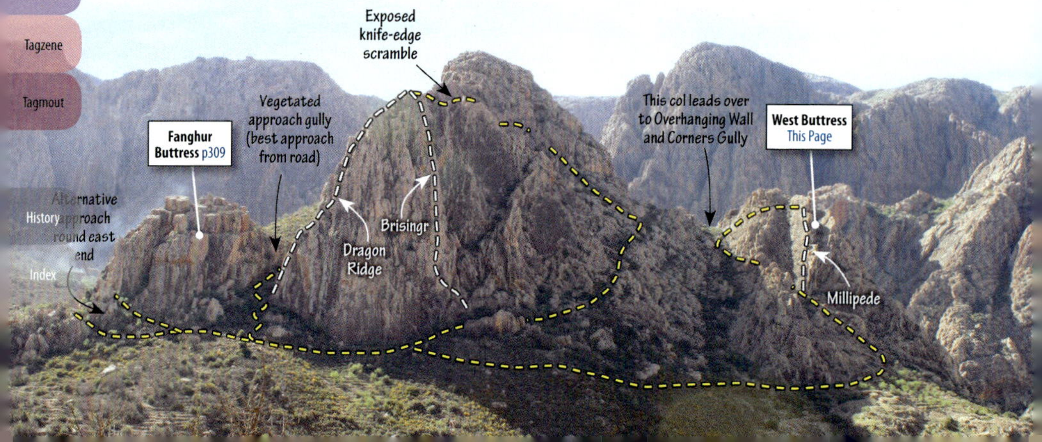

OVERHANGING WALL

This steep west-facing wall is home to a handful of well-protected crack climbs with abseil descents. Approach via Corners Gully (overview on page 318).

33. Rope Dragon VS 4c ★ (ABSEIL)

22m. A bold climb up the left side wall. Start from a boulder and step up into the obvious groove to a break. Move slightly right to the arête, then back left to a small ledge. Regain the arête and follow it to an overhung ledge, avoiding the overhang on its left to reach easier ground.

Lina & Dave Arthur, February 2016.

34. The Cobra HVS 5b ★★★ (ABSEIL)

25m. The excellent chimney requires some big pro to be anything near comfortable. Climb the chimney to a challenging off-width finish, exiting rightwards through vegetation to a final easy slab.

Steve & Katja Broadbent, February 2016.

35. Molotov E1 5b ★ (STEEP, GEAR, ABSEIL)

30m. The left-hand crack in the overhanging wall gives good steep climbing, but requires some care with loose holds. Follow the crack to its top, then make a delicate traverse rightwards across a small slab to a belay.

Steve & Katja Broadbent, February 2016.

36. Kalashnikov E2 5c ★ (STEEP, GEAR, ABSEIL)

30m. The central crackline is steep and unrelenting, with some exposed positions. Care is required with fragile holds.

Steve & Katja Broadbent, February 2016.

37. Falujah E1 5b ★ (STEEP, GEAR, ABSEIL)

30m. Climb the crack to difficult moves through the half-height overhang, finishing up tricky twin cracks above.

Steve & Katja Broadbent, February 2016.

38. Eyrie MVS 4b ★★ (ABSEIL)

30m. Climb the crack to a sloping ledge, then make an airy hand traverse left on good holds. Finish more easily to the left of a vegetated gully.

Lina & Dave Arthur, February 2016.

To the right is a subsidiary buttress, right at the foot of Corners Gully.

39. Of Pavlov E1 5b ★ (LOOSE, GEAR, ABSEIL)

30m. The left-hand crack has some fragile rock. Climb the crack with increasing interest to a ledge, then finish carefully up the broken wall above.

Steve & Katja Broadbent, February 2016.

40. Storm Rider E2 6a ★★★ (STEEP, GEAR, ABSEIL)

65m. A magnificent climb with two varied crack pitches. The first pitch is worthwhile in its own right at HVS 5b; the second is an excellent technical roof crack with perfect protection and superb exposure.

1) 30m (5b) Follow the crack with interest to a belay (cable).

2) 35m (6a) The obvious overhanging crack is steeper, harder, and even better than it looks.

Steve & Katja Broadbent, February 2016.

Area Map
Crag Selector
Intro
The Climbing
How to Use
Suggested Climbs
Tafraout Granite
Anergui
Ameln Valley
Tarakatine Pass
Sidi M'Zal
Jebel Taskra
Idaougnidif
Afantinzar
Samazar
Aouguenz
Tagzene
Tagmout
History
Index

CORNERS GULLY

A remarkable cragging venue, with the best concentration of crack pitches in the valley. For lovers of steep wide cracks and exposed bridging this is a place not to miss, with an easy approach well-equipped abseil descents, and lots of welcome shade in which to sit when you're not climbing.

This south-west facing wall features a number of huge corners, easily seen from the Samazar Hairpins. Corners Gully, the gully which runs beneath these impressive corners, is easily reached in approximately 30 minutes. From the parking by the electricity pylon, head up the hill towards a small col on the left side of Dragon Rock. Pass over this col into the top of Corners Gully (*Flight of the Phoenix* is on the right just after the col). Routes are described from left to right, starting at the bottom of the gully.

41. Pedestal Crack HVS 5b ★3 WIDE ABSEIL

35m. Superb wide crack antics, leading to a wild hanging groove up the left side of the pale-coloured pedestal. From the top of the pedestal continue up easier ground for about 8 metres to an abseil anchor on the right.
Steve & Katja Broadbent, October 2016.

42. Pedestal Layback HVS 5b ★1 CARE! ABSEIL

35m. The tempting looking layback up the right side of the pedestal gives some strenuous and tenuous climbing. Unfortunately it leads to poor rock higher up. Start as for *Pedestal Crack* until it is possible to make a long step right above a lurking death-block (warning: the precarious nature of this block is not evident from below). Continue up the well-protected corner to a scrappy grovel onto the pedestal. Finish up *Pedestal Crack* or *Twister*.

Tom Codrington in the steep corner of *Pedestal Crack*, about to make the step right into *Twister* (HVS 5b) ➲
Photo: Steve Broadbent

Area Map
Crag Selector
Intro
The Climbing
How to Use
Suggested Climbs
Tafraout Granite
Anergui
Ameln Valley
Tarakatine Pass
Sidi M'Zal
Jebel Taskra
Idaougnidif
Afantinzar
Samazar
Aouguenz
Tagzene
Tagmout
History
Index

43. Twister HVS 5b

CARE! ABSEIL

35m. A variation on the previous climb. Start up *Pedestal Crack*, stepping right above the death-block as for *Pedestal Layback*. Move up and go right again into the next corner, which is followed to a very steep finish.

Tom Codrington & Katja Broadbent, February 2016.

44. Icarus E1 5c ★3

GEAR ABSEIL

70m. The obvious wide crack up the side-wall is a tremendous, well-protected climb.

1) 32m (5c) Climb the corner crack to a roof, where interesting moves lead up rightwards to a ledge. Continue to a second ledge and belay.

2) 28m (5c) Continue up the sustained hand-crack past several bulges to a ledge.

3) 20m (-) Scramble up and across to the *Electron* abseil.

Tom Codrington & Sally Fitton, October 2016.

45. Electron HVS 5b ★3

ABSEIL

60m. A delectable and varied climb up the corner, requiring a full rack of large cams.

1) 30m (4c) Start up the narrow wall left of the corner. This gives excellent technical climbing, protected by small cams. Step right at the euphorbia to gain the superb corner, which is followed to a tricky exit onto a good ledge on the right.

2) 30m (5b) Step back left into the corner and follow it to an argan tree. Keep following the crack with increasing difficulty to a rounded exit onto a ledge. Either belay here or climb up to the abseil anchor for the next route.

Steve & Katja Broadbent, February 2016.

46. Proton VS 5a ★3

WIDE ABSEIL

60m. Another superb crack climb, following the left-hand of two cracks in the wall right of *Electron*.

1) 30m (4c) Climb up past euphorbia, then follow the left-hand crack via several steep sections on good holds. Belay on a rock ledge beneath a wide crack.

2) 30m (5a) The upper crack is a bit of a struggle, but is overcome with some superbly exposed bridging. Large cams recommended.

Steve & Katja Broadbent, February 2016.

47. Borrow My Belayer VS 4c

ABSEIL

55m. Pleasant climbing up the long rib.

1) 40m (4c) Start up the broken arête right of *Proton*, moving right to avoid vegetation. Continue generally up the arête, moving onto the left or right faces when necessary. Belay on a small ramp out right.

2) 15m (4a) Make a bold traverse right onto the wall, then climb up trending back left towards the arête. Surmount a block and continue to a large ledge and abseil descent.

Pete Cawley & Lina Arthur, October 2016.

48. Phobos VS 4c ★2

GEAR ABSEIL

60m. A very enjoyable climb, giving one of the easiest routes in the gully.

1) 30m (4c) Climb a short white pillar to gain the corner, following it to a ledge on the left. Continue up the pleasant upper corner to belay at vegetation.

2) 30m (4a) Scramble rightwards onto the belay ledge of *Apogee*, then step up onto the blank wall with difficulty. Traverse right to finish up an enjoyably exposed groove to the abseil point at the top of *Flight of the Phoenix* (as for *Apogee*).

Steve & Katja Broadbent, October 2016.

49. Apogee HVS 5a ★★ GEAR ABSEIL

55m. Superb lay-backing up the corner to the left of the blank wall, with a magnificent first pitch.
1) 30m (5a) Gain the hanging layback flake with some difficulty and follow it to a good ledge.
2) 25m (4a) Move up rightwards with some difficulty to gain a traverse into a fine exposed corner. Follow this to the abseil anchor at the top of *Flight of the Phoenix*.

Steve Broadbent, Caroline Culwick & Aileen Robertson, October 2015.

50. Apogee Direct E2 5c ★★★ GEAR ABSEIL

55m. A more satisfying, but considerably more difficult finish, with steep, fingery climbing and excellent protection.
1) 30m (5a) Climb the layback crack as for the previous route.
2) 35m (5c) Continue straight up and make difficult moves to enter the steep narrow crack. This is followed on good finger locks to an easy traverse rightwards (abseil anchor).

Steve Broadbent, Caroline Culwick & Aileen Robertson, October 2015.

51. Soul and Romance E4 5c ★★★ BOLD ABSEIL

30m. The flawless wall gives some sensational climbing, and one of Tafraout's best E4 routes. Start up *Jungle Book* to reach the first horizontal break. Toe-traverse left along this, then climb straight upwards to a high break and crucial runner. Step left here to a bold crux up to the upper cracks.

Steve & Katja Broadbent, October 2016. Photo page 31.

52. Jungle Book HVS 5b ★★★ GEAR ABSEIL

35m. The brilliant corner gives well-protected climbing to a steep finale. Follow the corner to an exciting hand traverse, then make a difficult pull into the upper layback. Pass the final roof on the left to an easier finish.

Steve & Katja Broadbent, January 2016.

53. Flight of the Phoenix HVS 4c ★★★ ABSEIL

25m. A tremendous pitch up the vague zigzag crack in the slabby wall above the col. Bold climbing leads to the start of the crack, which is followed with interest to a high break. Move up left into a wide crack (bush at its base) which leads to a good ledge and rappel station.

Caroline Culwick, Steve Broadbent & Aileen Robertson, October 2015.

Corners Gully (right)

25m

Overview p308 & p318

E SAFINAH

Shade · Families · Hitch · Roadside

Drive from Tafraout: **1:45**
Walk-in: **25 minutes**

The prominent three-peaked summit of Safinah presents three very distinct buttresses on its southern flank – the lower West Buttress, which rises above a well travelled pass, the curving Central Buttress, and then to the right of a deep gully the steep but vegetated East Buttress, the highest of the three.

Safinah is reached from a poor unsurfaced track that turns off the Samazar road in Ogogn. This track continues west over the Tizirt Col and on to Talmst, but traversing this pass is not recommended in 2WD vehicles. From Ogogn follow the track to roadside parking at a hairpin bend. From here the foot of the peak is easily reached in about 25 minutes.

DESCENT: Go down easy slopes on the mountain's north side, bearing left to gain the col between Safinah and the Fortress. From here a good path leads back to the road.

WEST BUTTRESS

The lower, left-hand buttress gives a less committing climb than its more famous neighbour...

1. West Buttress MVS 4c ★2

165m. The lower west summit of Safinah gives a very fine climb with an easy approach, low commitment, and straightforward descent. Despite some avoidable vegetation in the lower section the upper pitches offer tremendously exposed, clean climbing with superb views over Samazar. The route is a significantly shorter and less serious proposition than *Scimitar Ridge*. Start by scrambling up the gully between the West and Central Buttresses, to where a narrow side-gully joins on the left (true right) side.

1) 25m (-) From the foot of the side gully climb up leftwards to gain the front of the buttress. Walk over broken ground and through some vegetation.
2) 50m (-) Go up a pleasant groove behind the vegetation, then step left onto a clean rib, following the easiest line to a prominent tree-ledge.
3) 30m (4a) Take the easiest line (some loose blocks to the left) to a narrow belay ledge.
4) 30m (4c) An excellent pitch that requires thoughtful protection and a steady leader. Climb up to a left-trending slab, which is followed to a good ledge.
5) 30m (4b) Fine, easy climbing leads to a tempting flake crack through the overhanging summit block. This has perfect holds and protection and leads elegantly to the lofty summit.
Peter Hill & Steve Broadbent, October 2010.

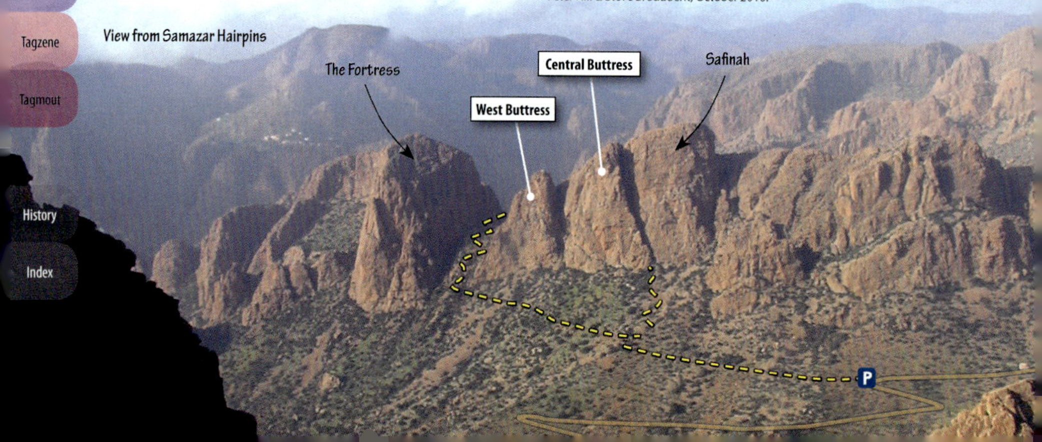

CENTRAL BUTTRESS

The curving central buttress is home to one of Tafraout's most popular mountain VS routes...

2. Goldrush Dihedral E1 5b ★1 PRICKLY

270m. A good line up the massive dihedral up the left side of the buttress, unfortunately marred by vegetation.
1) 55m (4b) The corner starts close to a large flake, and is initially easy, on good rock.
2) 50m (4c) Continue pleasantly up the corner to an unfortunate patch of vegetation. Squeeze past this into a chimney on the right, which leads to a cave.
3) 50m (4c) Climb a ramp on the right, then go up a slab to a grey shoulder.
4) 30m (5a) Drop down to the corner, then climb up to a bulge and move right to another steep corner.
5) 25m (5b) Follow the corner... to a huge corner!
6) 60m (5a) Go up the huge corner, passing vegetation on the left and scrambling up left to gain the ridge.
Paul Donnithorne & Sue Hazel, January 2012.

3. Scimitar Ridge VS 5a ★3

265m. This tremendous climb is one of the most popular routes of its type, and a good introduction to the bigger Samazar routes. It follows the attractive curving Central Buttress of Safinah, providing continually interesting climbing and superb views of the valley.
1) 25m (-) Start steeply from the lowest point of the buttress just left of the steep gully. Follow the crest of the ridge to a block belay.
2) 25m (-) Go up to a chockstone behind a pinnacle and make a high step to regain the ridge crest.
3) 30m (4a) Climb the left side of a steep wall to gain a rightwards hand traverse back to the crest which is followed easily to a belay by a bush.
4) 40m (-) Easy climbing up the ridge to belay by another bush.
5) 20m (4a) The ridge steepens to another good ledge below an impending overhang.
6) 30m (5a) Climb up to the overhang and tackle it direct with excellent holds and protection. The slab above is more technical, but easier than it looks.
7) 20m (4a) A narrow chimney on the right is followed to a steep finish leftwards past blocks.
8) 15m (-) Follow a rightwards trending ramp then move back left to a sloping ledge by a huge perched block.
9) 30m (4c) The compact wall and blunt arête provide a superbly positioned pitch, finishing on a narrow ledge.
10) 30m (-) Move left and climb some loose ground to the summit
Steve & Katja Broadbent. April 2008.

Area Map
Crag Selector
Intro
The Climbing
How to Use
Suggested Climbs
Tafraout Granite
Anergui
Ameln Valley
Tarakatine Pass
Sidi M'Zal
Jebel Taskra
Tagoughidir
Afantinzar
Samazar
Aougdenz
Tagzene
Tagmout
History
Index

Area Map
Crag Selector
Intro
The Climbing
How to Use
Suggested Climbs
Tafraout Granite
Anergui
Ameln Valley
Tarakatine Pass
Sidi M'Zal
Jebel Taskra
Idaougnidif
Afantinzar
Samazar
Aouguenz
Tagzene
Tagmout
History
Index

F THE AGUERD CIOCH

Shade · Families · Hitch · Roadside
Drive from Tafraout: **1:40**
Walk-in: **5 to 15 minutes**

This crag is one of only a handful of south-facing outcrops in Samazar, so tends to be less lichenous than many of the valley's walls, with a character similar to that of neighbouring Afantinzar. The Cioch is situated on a distant hillside to the north of the Schoolhouse junction, reached via an exciting track that makes the Samazar road look like a major highway. For climbers based in Tafraout, therefore, the Aguerd Cioch represents some of the most remote climbing the range has to offer.

To approach, turn north off the Samazar Road at a large ruin about 1.5km west of the Tamza turnoff. Follow the track, passing a school and onwards through a notch to a small junction on a col. The left fork leads down steep hairpins to Aguerd n'Ouzrou and is not recommended in 2WD vehicles. The right fork leads up a hair-raising track to the back of beyond, and is not recommended in anything. Thankfully, parking (and more importantly the chance to turn around) is available at the junction.

THE WEST BUTTRESS

The West Buttress is located to the left of the main crag, and is reached in approximately 15 minutes by traversing the hillside from the base of the Main Buttress.

1. Lavender Very Difficult ★2

85m. Very pleasant climbing up the curved ridge, with good rock and fine positions throughout – a real treat at this grade. Start by scrambling up through a dead tree to a ledge.
1) 45m (-) Good climbing up the ridge to a large ledge.
2) 40m (-) Step left and climb the centre of the excellent wall on good holds. Continue more easily above, via whichever line takes your fancy.
Steve & Katja Broadbent, March 2013.

DESCENT: To descend from these routes it is necessary to head right (east) and walk up behind the Main Buttress, passing over a large col to regain the track above the parking spot. Climbers are, therefore, advised not to leave anything at the base of the routes.

2. Lotus Flower VS 4c ★2

95m. Excellent climbing up the narrow ridge.
1) 30m (4a) Climb pleasant slabs to a ledge.
2) 30m (4c) Pull up left of steep ground, then climb up to another impasse. Move left again via a sequence of difficult and exposed moves until it is possible to traverse back right onto the front of the face.
3) 35m (4a) Easy climbing up the ridge to a final wall.
Steve Broadbent & Anna Piotrowski, October 2013.

MAIN BUTTRESS

The majority of the routes are located on a large, dome-shaped buttress that sits above the junction on the col.

3. Copperhead HVS 5a ★2

90m. A good climb up the west face of the buttress, starting up a pinnacle just right of a recess with a walled-in tree.
1) 30m (4c) Go up the obvious wide crack in the left side of the pinnacle, then climb the cracked face to a ledge with another large crack above.
2) 30m (5a) From the left end of the ledge climb a large corner, trending left to an overlap. Pull through this on good

crimps and finish up a short splitter crack to a large ledge, with excellent horizontal breaks for protection.
3) 30m (5a) Follow the cracked face diagonally rightwards to gain a ramp, which leads left then right to large blocks.
Topher Dagg, Henward Nind & Euan Strachan, February 2010.

4. The Fin E2 5c ★1

95m. The obvious corner below the huge nose at the top of the cliff.
1) 45m (4c) Climb a shallow right-facing corner to belay below a bulge.
2) 25m (5c) Go up the wall and chimney to a bulge, and bridge up to easier climbing past a white fin on the right. Step rightwards onto the fin and follow it to a belay.
3) 25m (4b) Continue up the crack line to finish right of the huge nose.
Niall Adams & Dan Donovan, February 2012.

5. Captain Hornblower HVS 5b ★1

70m. Starts just to the right of the main steep face, directly above the first hairpin bend.
1) 30m (4c) Follow the crack and corner to the 2nd leftward ramp. Go up this onto the face, then move up until a 5m traverse rightwards gains a ledge.
2) 40m (5b) Go directly up from the ledge, through a tricky but well-protected overlap into a crack-line that runs directly to the top, passing the small bush to its right.
Topher Dagg & Euan Strachan, February 2010.

6. Thyme is on our Side HVS 5a ★1

85m. The right fork of the central corner, starting as for the previous route.
1&2) 60m (5a) Climb the corner to belay beneath the large open chimney.
3) 25m (5a) Go up the chimney, pulling around the right-hand side at the top and finishing up a crack above.
Niall Adams & Dan Donovan, February 2012.

7. Scarborough Fair HVS 5a ★1

70m. The most obvious groove on the east face, starting just left of an off-width chimney.
1) 35m (5a) Climb the right-hand flake crack, then move up a groove. Step right at a prickly pear and follow the continuation groove to a stance on the right.
2) 35m (4b) Take the left fork of the groove to finish just left of a small roof. Descend to the right.
Paul Donnithorne & Emma Alsford, November 2011.

Area Map
Crag Selector
Intro
The Climbing
How to Use
Suggested Climbs
Tafraout Granite
Anergui
Ameln Valley
Tarakatine Pass
Sidi M'Zal
Jebel Taskra
Idaougnidif
Afantinzar
Samazar
Aouguenz
Tagzene
Tagmout
History
Index

Map Page 288

Area Map
Crag Selector
Intro
The Climbing
How to Use
Suggested Climbs
Tafraout Granite
Anergui
Ameln Valley
Tarakatine Pass
Sidi M'Zal
Jebel Taskra
Idaougnidif
Afantinzar
Samazar
Aouguenz
Tagzene
Tagmout
History
Index

G ICEBOX CANYON

Shade · Families · Hitch · Roadside

Drive from Tafraout: **1:30**
Walk-in: **15 to 20 minutes**

About half way between the Tamza turn-off and Schoolhouse junction, the Tamza wall is split by a broad diagonal gully. This is Icebox Canyon, home to a selection of steep wall climbs mostly in the upper grades. Although the rock can be rather mossy for much of the winter, the canyon is a good choice during spells of hot weather.

The canyon can be approached from Samazar by parking half way (0.8km) between the Tamza turn-off and the Aguerd (school house) turn-off, from where it is visible as a diagonal gully at the top of the Tamza Wall. A less steep alternative, however, is to approach from Afantinzar, from where the canyon is easily reached in about 15 minutes. Park on the Afantinzar road above Anammer, just before the hairpins leading up to the high col at the top of the valley. From here it is a short walk to a notch on the skyline to the northwest (shown below), where a steep Berber trail leads down into the canyon.

DESCENT: Walk leftwards at the top, then scramble back down to the notch as for the Afantinzar approach.

1. Peanut HVS 5a ★2 MOSSY

80m. A fine and popular wall climb that meanders its way up the pale pillar, giving excellent steep climbing, marred slightly by a mossy finish.
1) 30m (4c) Start from a rake below the wall, climbing rightwards to cross a bulge and gain the white streak. Follow this to a ledge beneath a nose in the overlap
2) 25m (5a) Pull leftwards through the overhang on big holds and climb up right to a mossy exit onto the terrace to the right of the tree.
3) 25m (4b) Finish leftwards up the gully.
Neil Adams & Dan Donovan, April 2010.

2. Polar Bear E1 5b ★1 MOSSY

90m. Starts about 30m left of the orange corner, where a ramp abuts the base of the wall.
1) 55m (5b) From an angular niche above the foot of the ramp move left onto the wall and climb up to a crack. Swing right then go up past numerous spikes to a ledge.
2) 35m (5b) Climb the black wall until it is possible to traverse right into the fine open groove / chimney.
Paul Donnithorne & Emma Alsford, April 2009.

3. North East Passage E4 6a ★3 MOSSY STEEP

100m. The orange and black crack-line provides three superb and demanding pitches (6a, 5c, 5b).
Paul Donnithorne & Mike Mortimer, October 2009.

4. Icebreaker E3 5c ★3 MOSSY

100m. Technical climbing up the steep crack 10m right of the prominent orange corner. Start below flakes just left of the crackline (about 6m right of the orange corner).
1) 55m (5c) Climb up and slightly left to the black crack until after 10m it is possible to traverse right to gain the main crack. Continue up this, and the groove above, then trend up right through a steep bulge to gain ledges.
2) 45m (5b) Go up the wall then traverse beneath the black streak to an open groove. Climb this past a ledge then through a weakness in the upper steepening.
2-Alt) 45m (5b) An alternative finish moves left along the ledge, then climbs a corner to the roof. Step right, then traverse up left to easier ground.
Paul Donnithorne & Emma Alsford, April 2009 (original way).
J. Jones, D.Turnbull & G.McNair, April 2009 (variation finish).

5. Electric Kool Aid Acid Test E2 5b MOSSY BOLD

105m. A bold climb up an incipient crack line, breaking through the overhangs above.
1) 20m (5a) Go up a groove to reach the left end of a flake. Traverse the flake then go straight up to a belay on a sloping ledge.
2) 30m (5b) Climb a steep crack for 10m then more easily rightwards to a corner. Traverse left under the roof before finishing back right up a loose corner through the overhangs.
3) 55m (4a) The easiest line to the top.
J. Jones, D.Turnbull & G.McNair, April 2009.

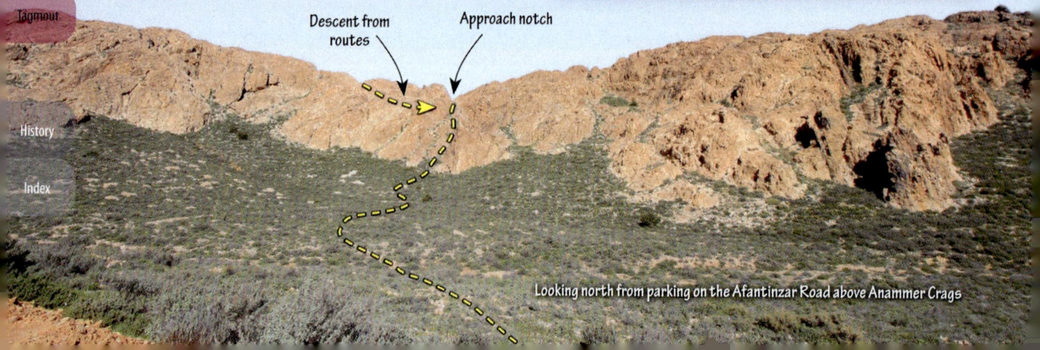

Looking north from parking on the Afantinzar Road above Anammer Crags

6. Arctic Char E2 5b

MOSSY

95m. Start right of *EKAAT* at a boulder step.
1) (5b) Climb to an obvious hollow flake then step up to a vague crackline which leads to a ledge.
2) (5a) Climb up to the overhang and cross it as for *EKAAT*, then follow an easy groove to top.
Mike Pycroft & Pete Johnson, October 2010.

7. And The Nectar E1 5b ★2

MOSSY STEEP

110m. Good climbing on perfect rock. Start at a small pinnacle by a flat boulder. Traverse right along a ledge to step across the crack. Climb steep ground until it is possible to regain the crack, which is followed to a tricky finish up a steep little wall.
Mike & Marojorie Mortimer, April 2009.

8. Pushing 70 E2 5b ★2

MOSSY STEEP

140m. An uncompromising wall climb.
1) 30m (5b) Climb a smooth wall to a ledge.
2) 20m (5b) Move up left then steeply back right to another ledge.
3) 35m (5a) Easier ground leads to another large ledge.
4) 30m (5a) Go left and climb a loose orange corner before stepping back right to finish as for *Black Gold*.
Ben Wintringham, Mike Mortimer & Marion Wintringham, October 2009.

9. Never Never Land E2 5b

MOSSY

130m. A direct eliminate starting up black cracks left of *Bitter Days*, and resisting the easier cracks to the left. 4 pitches direct to the top (5b, 5b, 5b, 5a).
Ben & Marion Wintringham, April 2009.

10. Bitter Days HVS 5a

MOSSY

110m. A direct line up the centre of the wall.
1) 30m (5a) Follow a vague left-slanting groove to a ledge beneath a black groove.
2) 60m (4c) Go up the groove to its top, then step right into an orange groove to another ledge.
3) 30m (4c) Trend left to gain a final groove close to the arête.
Ben & Marion Wintringham, April 2009.

11. Black Gold HVS 5a ★1

MOSSY BOLD

120m. Takes the next black streak, breaking left up the wall at the top.
1) 10m (4c) Climb up to a belay below the left-hand of two black cracks.
2) 35m (5a) Follow the left-hand crack to a ledge (junction with *Bitter Days*).
3) 50m (4c) Continue up *Bitter Days* for 10m until it is possible to climb leftwards, boldly across the black wall.
4) 25m (4c) The wall above to easier ground.
Ben Wintringham, Mike Mortimer & Marion Wintringham, October 2009.

12. Arctic Monkey E3 5c ★2

MOSSY

110m. A direct line between the central and left-hand black streaks, giving one of the best climbs hereabouts. Start by some large boulders below a short groove.
1) 40m (5c) Climb the groove to a ledge with a large detached spike. Wander up the wall above past numerous chicken heads to gain the left-hand crack. Go up to a small overlap at 30m then step right using incut holds to gain the right-hand crack to a good ledge.
2) 40m (5b) Climb the crack and groove then go slightly left to gain a large undercut flake. Follow this rightwards to a stance.
3) 30m (5a) Climb a big flake to a pedestal before moving left to finish up a chimney.
Emma Alsford & Paul Donnithorne, April 2009.

Area Map
Crag Selector
Intro
The Climbing
How to Use
Suggested Climbs
Tafraout Granite
Anergui
Ameln Valley
Tarakatine Pass
Sidi M'Zal
Jebel Taskra
Idaougnidif
Afantinzar
Samazar
Aouguenz
Tagzene
Tagmout
History
Index

H AFANTZTGULT

Shade · Families · Hitch · Roadside

Drive from Tafraout: **1:30**
Walk-in: **15 minutes**

This broad, flat-topped summit lies immediately north of the village of Tamza, mid way along the Samazar Valley. The south face is easily seen from the Samazar road, towering above the village but providing little in the way of good climbing. Round to the left, however, the steeper west face holds a number of worthwhile climbs with a very pleasant approach, good views, and straightforward descent.

The village of Tamza is reached from the eastern end of the Samazar Valley, by taking a signposted turning to Tamza about 4.5km along the Samazar road from Ighir. The track to the village descends slightly, crosses a riverbed, then climbs up into the village, making a sharp turn to the right (east) at the left end of the settlement. After a short way there is parking next to a small mosque on the right-hand side.

From the mosque, walk back along the road to the house on the corner, from where a good path heads west, to eventually swing round beneath the mountain's west face, where the Great Tower, at the foot of *Tower Ridge*, is clearly visible. The routes are reached easily from this path.

DESCENT: The descent from the summit is down a gully on the mountain's east face, where a tiny path becomes ever more distinct as it descends to join a major path in the valley below – turn right along this to return to the village.

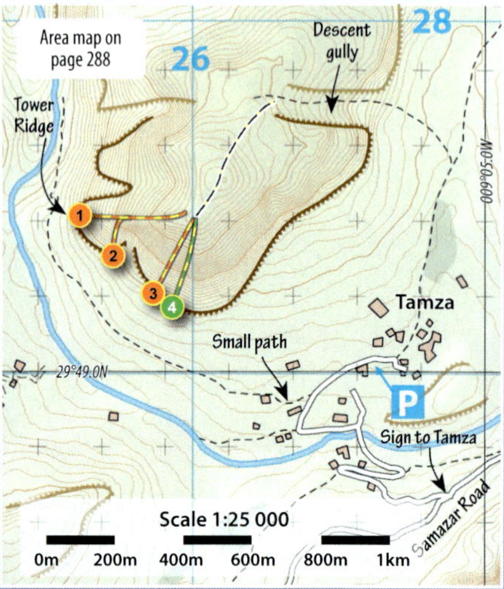

1. Tower Ridge Direct MVS 4b ★2

500m. The long ridge above the obvious tower gives a mountaineering route of great character, and provides an excellent warm-up for some of Tafraout's more infamous big ridges. This direct version starts at the very lowest point of the ridge, and despite some scrappy climbing on pitch 2 it is a very worthwhile climb for those looking for long, mid-grade adventures. The climbing up the initial tower is not quite as good as that on the *Original*, but the line is more consistent.

1) 45m (4a) Start from the toe of the buttress and climb good rock to ledges.

2) 45m (4a) A scrappy pitch. Climb broken ground to a steep band of poorer rock to the right of the ridge crest. This can

be overcome via a steep rotten groove, or broken rocks on the right. Belay on a good ledge out to the right.
3) 45m (4b) Nice climbing up steep slabs on the right side, with some bold sections. Belay on a huge ledge with bushes.
4) 30m (-) Step left and climb easy ribs and grooves to a ledge just above a tree.
5) 45m (4b) Go up the clean rib on the right, then step left into a curving groove above the blank face to the left. This leads to a ledge beneath a final short wall, where the route joins the *Original*.
6) 10m (4a) Climb the steep crack as for pitch 4 of the *Original Route* to gain the summit of the *Great Tower*. Continue as for that route from pitch 5, with an exciting abseil...
Steve Broadbent, Will Benfold & Dave Arthur, October 2014

2. The Tower Ridge Original VS 4b ★2

440m. The original way of gaining the ridge features some excellent steep climbing up the south-western side of the Great Tower. Although the line is less classic than the *Direct*, the excellent climbing on pitch 2 makes this an attractive route with a low crux and sustained easy climbing beyond. Both routes feature some involved ridge traversing requiring competence with ropework. Start by scrambling up to ledges on the southern ridge of the Great Tower.
1) 45m (-) Climb a short wall, then easy ground to ledges beneath a steep orange wall.
2) 45m (4b) Step across left onto the hanging slab and climb excellent cracks to steeper ground. Follow steep flakes with considerable care to a narrow ledge at the top of a huge flake, from where it is possible to move right into the gully and squeeze past a large boulder to a belay.
3) 30m (4a) Climb the stepped wall in the back of the gully to a col, then head up left over easy ground to a ledge beneath a steep crack.
4) 15m (4a) Climb the steep crack to the top of the Great Tower.
5) 50m (-) Abseil down into the notch behind the tower. It is advisable to step across to the other side before reaching the bottom, then climb up to large ledges before pulling the ropes down.
6) 60m (-) Continue up easy ground on the right side of the ridge, passing to the right of a narrow gendarme. Regain the crest after the gendarme and follow it to a short steep wall. Step left here, around the corner, into a niche below a corner crack.
7) 35m (4b) Climb the corner crack, exit right, and follow the front of the ridge to where the angle eases.
8) 55m (-) Go along the crest to an exciting exposed knife-edge. Belay after this at a steepening with right-slanting twin cracks.
9) 40m (4a) Climb up the right side of the ridge, then continue along the crest to the top of a small tower. A 5m downclimb gains the notch beyond.
10) 30m (4b) Go up rightwards and climb steep cracks, moving right onto the right side of the crest above. Continue in an excellent position to ledges.
11) 35m (-) Easy climbing up the final ridge to the summit plateau.
Steve & Katja Broadbent, March 2014

Area Map
Crag Selector
Intro
The Climbing
How to Use
Suggested Climbs
Tafraout Granite
Anergui
Ameln Valley
Tarakatine Pass
Sidi M'Zal
Jebel Taskra
Idaougnidif
Afantinzar
Samazar
Aouguenz
Tagzene
Tagmout
History
Index

3. Viking Buttress HVS 4c ★1

245m. A good mountaineering day out, with some interesting climbing and excellent views. The route takes the broad slabby wall on the southwest front of the mountain. Start by identifying a narrow subsidiary slab, below and left of the main slabby wall. Scramble up towards the base of this slab.

1) 30m (4a) Climb steep blocks on the left side of the buttress to gain a shady belay at the foot of the chimney between the subsidiary slab and the main buttress.

2) 30m (4a) Excellent climbing up the chimney crack to a ledge on the main slabby buttress.

3) 20m (4a) Climb up rightwards on small edges up a vague rib to a block belay on a small ledge, about 5m below steeper ground.

4) 20m (4c) Continue up to the shattered steep wall. Climb up right for a few metres, then make a horizontal traverse left to gain a small broken groove. Follow this leftwards to a poor stance below a small alcove.

5) 20m (-) Climb up through the alcove and continue more easily to ledges.

6) 20m (-) Traverse rightward beneath steep ground to the right side of the buttress. Continue up to a good ledge on the crest.

7) 30m (4a) Easy climbing up the rib leads to interesting moves straight up through steep ground. Belay on a good rock ledge below a short steep crack.

8) 35m (4c) The short steep crack is the technical crux, but is very well protected. Continue up the ridge, then step left into an orange groove. Exit rightwards to easier ground.

9) 40m (4a) Continue easily over blocks, then cross a gully on the right to finish up a fine little corner.

Steve & Katja Broadbent, February 2016

4. Tijuana Buttress HS 4b ★1

245m. The narrow, clean pillar at the right-hand side of the west face gives a pleasant outing.

1) 50m (-) Scramble up until it is possible to access the narrow pale rib from the left side. Follow this to ledges.

2) 50m (-) Continue up the crest of the rib.

3) 30m (-) Climb up easily towards steeper ground. Step left across a small vegetated groove, then move left into a short slot. Exit rightwards and move up to a ledge on the right below a steep wall.

4) 25m (4b) Climb the steep wall, traversing up left to an easier finish. Belay on a good ledge over the lip.

5) 25m (4a) Move round the left side of the roof, then follow a right-slanting gangway up through the overhangs. Belay on the flat shoulder above (***The Picnic Platform***) before re-belaying some 10 metres back in a gully at the base of the next pitch.

6) 30m (4a) Pull steeply onto the wall and climb straight up to a good rock ledge. This pitch is considerably better than it looks from below...

7) 35m (-) Go to the right of the steep ground, then climb up and traverse left to gain clean rock to the top.

Steve & Katja Broadbent, March 2014

Lina and Dave Arthur on the upper section of *Tower Ridge* (VS 4b), one of Samazar's best mid-grade mountain adventures. ➲

Photo: Steve Broadbent

Map Page 332

Area Map
Crag Selector
Intro
The Climbing
How to Use
Suggested Climbs
Tafraout Granite
Anergui
Ameln Valley
Tarakatine Pass
Sidi M'Zal
Jebel Taskra
Idaougnidif
Afantinzar
Samazar
Aouguenz
Tagzene
Tagmout
History
Index

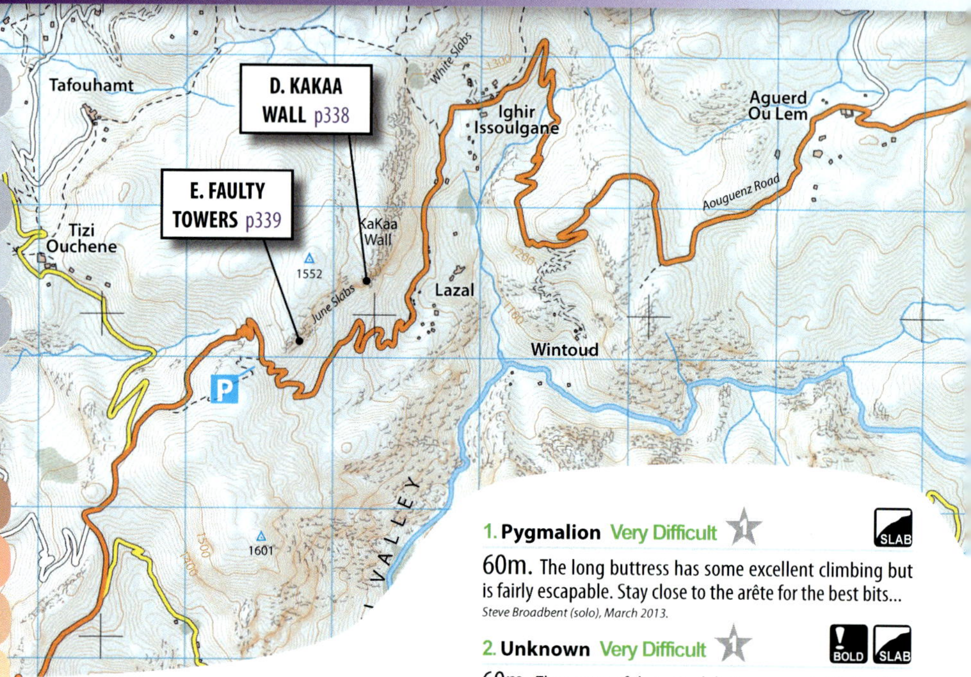

1. Pygmalion Very Difficult ★1 SLAB

60m. The long buttress has some excellent climbing but is fairly escapable. Stay close to the arête for the best bits...
Steve Broadbent (solo), March 2013.

2. Unknown Very Difficult ★1 BOLD SLAB

60m. The centre of the next slab gives good, bold climbing. Even with 60m ropes you'll need to belay above the initial easy boulders to finish in one pitch. Alternatives up the s-shaped crack to the left, or the arête to the right, are easier and better-protected.
Jen Booys, Kerry Mellor & Ben Lister, March 2013.

THE AOUGUENZ ROAD

This mountain road connects the village of Aouguenz in the west with the Afantinzar road on the Tizi-n-Toudma at the top of the Amzkhssan hairpins (often known to climbers as the Aouguenz Junction).

The region is most easily reached via Idaougnidif in the east – take the Afantinzar road up through the Amzkhssan Gorge, ascending the Amzkhssan hairpins to Tizi-n-Toudma and the start of the Afantinzar Valley. Turn right at the junction on the col, just before the houses of Tnine Toudma. Temple Slabs are soon reached on the right-hand side.

A TEMPLE SLABS

Shade | Families | Hitch | Roadside

Drive from Tafraout: **1:10**
Walk-in: **5 minutes**

Shortly after turning right at the Tizi-n-Toudma (Aouguenz Junction) the road swings around to the right, and a series of gently angled slabs appear on the right-hand-side. These are the Temple Slabs, and whilst there is a fair amount of easy broken rock here, the following routes all provide some worthwhile climbing that stays in the shade for much of the day, making it a good venue during warmer periods.

3. Moonshine E1 5a ★3 BOLD SLAB

45m. The steep arête to the right is clearly on the wrong crag, giving a brilliant climb on perfect rock. The crux is bold and technical, but is short-lived and low in the grade. Climb easily up the lower buttress via a groove close to the arête. Fine, technical moves then lead leftwards under the overhang to a ledge on the left face, from where a committing pull gains the slab above. Traverse boldly back rightwards to the arête, then sprint up this easily to the top.
Steve Broadbent & Ben Lister, March 2013.

4. Balto MVS 4b ★1

35m. Climb the centre of the excellent slab to a difficult pull through the overlap at a crack. Continue to a ledge, then step right and climb the gully and rib on its left to the top.
Steve Broadbent & Anna Piotrowski, October 2013.

5. Busnel Severe 4a SLAB

35m. The rather dirty-looking slab set up behind the previous route is better than it looks. Start steeply up the right-hand of two cracks and continue to a crux move through the overlap. Finish more easily to a narrow ledge.
Steve Broadbent & Anna Piotrowski, October 2013.

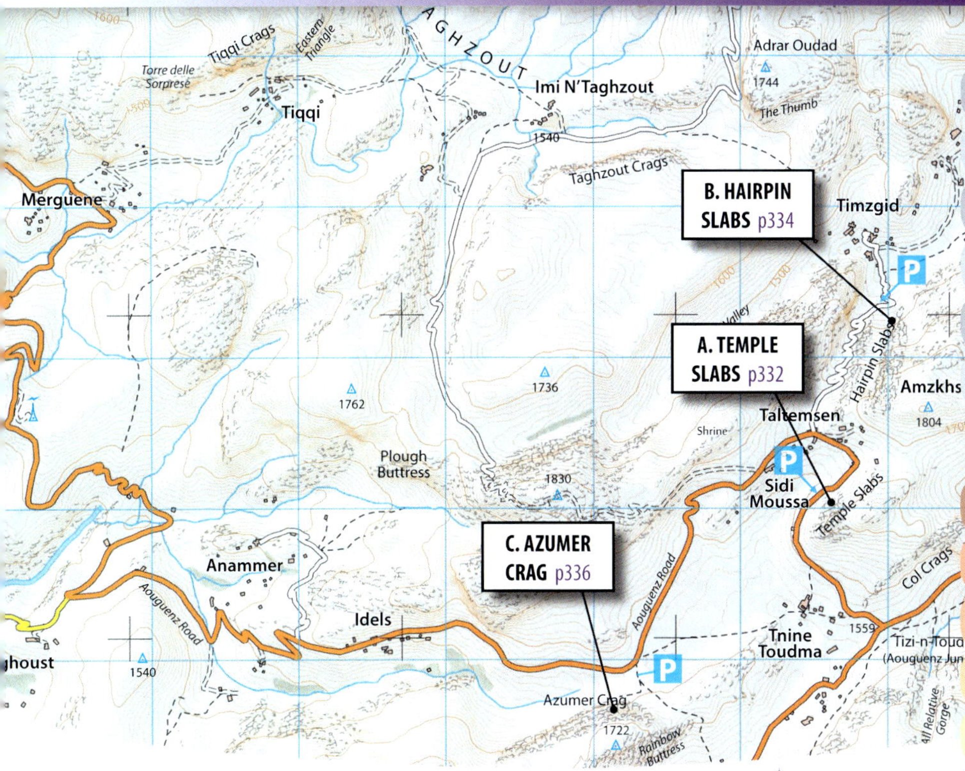

WEST BUTTRESS

This buttress forms the extreme western end of the crag, featuring a slabby northwest face and steeper southwest face. It culminates in a fine, narrow ridge along which the next route finishes...

6. White Slabs Arête Severe ★1

150m. A fine climb, if rather artificial. The route starts immediately left of a small bush. Climb up the right side of the crag, making a number of excellent right-slanting traverses to stay as close to the right edge as possible. Two 45m pitches lead to a superb alpine ridge to easy ground.

Steve Broadbent & Anna Piotrowski, October 2013.

B HAIRPIN SLABS

Shade · Families · Hitch · Roadside

Drive from Tafraout: **1:15**
Walk-in: **10 minutes**

This crag is located at the bottom of steep hairpins descending eastward from Taltemsen – a road that was known for a number of years as the *Fiesta Trap* owing to the challenges of driving back up it! The village of Taltemsen is the first village reached along the Aouguenz road after turning off from the col at the top of the Amzkhssan Hairpins. Turn right in the village and descend very steep hairpins to a small parking spot just beyond a pinnacle on the left side of the road. The slabs themselves are easily visible on the right, some 250m from the roadside.

DESCENT: Descend left (east) down a rocky gully behind the crag. Some small cairns mark the point at which a tiny path then cuts left to descend an easy rake back on the front face towards the road.

1. Beat Poet VS 4c ★1 (LOOSE)

120m. The large corner up the left side of the crag has only one hard move, but features some loose rock throughout.

1) 60m (4a) Follow the corner to a poor stance where it opens out.

2) 60m (4c) Continue up the corner, past a bulge.

Neil Adams, Paul Eastwood & Dan Donovan, November 2013

2. Snakehike HS 4a ★3 (SLAB, BOLD)

155m. An excellent low-grade adventure, snaking its way up the overlap to the right of *Beat Poet* and providing one of the best routes of its type in the range. The climbing is consistently challenging and not overly protected. Start by scrambling up to a ledge, right of the big corner.

1) 45m (4a) Follow slabs immediately right of the overlap, trending generally up right to a stance.

2) 40m (4a) Step right, pull through steeper ground and continue up the corner above to another small stance.

3) 40m (4a) Follow the corner with increasing difficulty to a stance at the bottom of the final chimney.

4) 30m (-) Easier climbing on excellent holds up the entertaining chimney.

Neil Adams, Paul Eastwood & Dan Donovan, November 2013

Katja Broadbent and Dave Arthur on the third pitch of *Snakehike* (HS 4a) at Hairpin Slabs. ➲

Photo: Steve Broadbent

Hairpin Slabs
SHADE · 10m

C AZUMER CRAG

Shade | Families | Hitch | Roadside

Drive from Tafraout: **1:15**
Walk-in: **5 to 10 minutes**

Much of the north-facing rock around Jebel el Kest tends to produce routes that are either in the higher grades, or feature a large amount of moss. Azumer Crag, on the other hand, offers some very friendly climbs that come into their own during periods of warmer weather.

The crag is reached by turning right at the 3-way junction on the col between Idaougnidif and Afantinzar (Tizi-n-Toudma). Follow the road as it swings to the right, then back left, crossing a plateau until the crag comes into view on the left (about 4km from the col). There is a concrete sign (marked Azumer) facing the other way at this point.

The first route climbs a pinnacle to the left of the main section of the crag.

1. Raz's Rocket Severe ★1

20m. The pinnacle gives a fun little climb. Start up the face nearest to the cliff, spiralling to the top via the easiest line.
R. Parmar (solo), November 2012.

2. The Last Resort E1 5b ★2

30m. The buttress below and left of *Malcolm X*, starting below a right-slanting overlap. Gain the overlap and follow it to an exit left. Finish up the left arete.
J.Shiels & C.Shiels, March 2014.

3. Malcolm X E1 5b ★2

30m. Start up a crack to gain an inverted V-overhang, surmounting this to cracks in the upper wall.
M.Phelps, T.Goodwin & R.Parmar, November 2012.

4. Be Prepared VS 4c ★3

30m. Climb the excellent arête, stepping right at the top onto a ramp. Climb the wall above to finish up the left arête.
T.Goodwin, M.Phelps & R.Parmar, November 2012.

5. The Fighting Temeriare E1 5b ★1

45m. The slab to the right of *Be Prepared*. Climb thin cracks for 20 metres, then take the left fork to the top.
M.Glanvill & J.Carter, March 2014.

6. Still Life HS 4b

40m. A right-slanting line up the slabby wall.
C.Woodhead & D.Medcalf, March 2014.

7. Chimney Sweep VS 4c

50m. The undercut arête left of *Razzle Dazzle*, starting in the big chimney. Climb up the slab or bridge up until it is possible to move right onto the arête. Follow this to a chimney, and finish up the wall beyond.
D.Medcalf & C.Woodhead, March 2014.

8. Razzle Dazzle VS 4c ★2

50m. Some fine climbing with a bold top section. Ten metres left of *Moroccan Virgin* is an obvious groove which turns into a right-trending ramp. Climb the groove for 5m then go straight up over the overhang, with the help of a sidepull on the left (crux). Go up rightwards to a square overhang, moving up left here onto the fine buttress above. Pass an overlap at its left side, then move up right onto the excellent upper wall.
R.Parmar, M.Phelps & T.Goodwin, November 2012.

9. Moroccan Virgin HS 4a ★★

45m. Fine climbing up the middle of the clean buttress to the right of the mossy groove. Gain a ledge system, then take the upper wall first on the right, then the left, to finish up a superb crack.
T.Goodwin, M.Phelps & R.Parmar, November 2012.

10. Mist Arête VS 4b

50m. Bold climbing up the arête.
P.Neden & J.Proudfoot, October 2015.

11. Ra Ra Rasputin VS 4b ★★

40m. The superb wall up behind the right side of the lower buttress. Climb the centre of the face passing left of a prominent block at 20m. Finish straight up the centre of the tower above.
R.Parmar, M.Phelps & T.Goodwin, November 2012.

12. Nana's Cracking Corner VS 4c ★★

55m. The corner right of the previous route. Climb sloping ledges on the right, then step left to finish up the corner.
C.Woodhead, D.Medcalf & N.Lyle, March 2014.

The next routes are all on a low buttress that sits in front of the main section of the crag.

13. Azumer Groove VS 4b ★

25m. Good climbing up the shallow groove from the lowest point of the crag, though sometimes mossy in places.
M.Phelps, R.Parmar & T.Goodwin, November 2012.

14. Zoomer Severe ★

20m. The pleasant groove just left of the arch.
M.Phelps, R.Parmar & T.Goodwin, November 2012.

15. Razzamattazz HS 4a ★★

20m. Another fun route, taking the chimney up the left side of the arch and emerging through a hole at the top.
R.Parmar, M.Phelps & T.Goodwin, November 2012.

16. Polo Severe ★

20m. Climb the rib bounding the right side of the arch, then move up left to the obvious hole. Climb up through this to emerge through the right hand hole at the top of the cliff, or traverse left to finish as for the previous route.
T.Goodwin, M.Phelps & R.Parmar, November 2012.

The next route appears to follow similar ground to *Polo*, and has not been confirmed:

17. Playboy Crocodile VS 4c

20m. Follow the obvious fracture up the right-hand side of the buttress. Cross the first overlap, then follow the upper slanting crack in the small roof.
Tim Culwick & Marion Wyllie, September 2013

18. Mining for Scorpions V.Diff LOOSE BOLD

20m. The attractive right-hand arête is climbed on disappointing rock.
Marion Wyllie & Lina Arthur, September 2013

Around to the right of the low buttress containing the previous routes is a short wall with the following climbs:

19. The Nearness of Dinner HS 4a BOLD

15m. Climb the poorly defined crack to the left of the main groove, stepping left at a ledge and finishing up a broken wall.
Dave Arthur & Tim Culwick, September 2013

20. The Certainty of Cake Severe

15m. The prominent left-slanting groove to a good finish up the left side of the flake.
Lina & Dave Arthur, September 2013

21. Yummy Dragons HS 4a BOLD

20m. Climb up the face using the arête. Move left under the overlap for a bold finish to the little summit.
Marion Wyllie & Lina Arthur, September 2013

22. Spectator Sport HS 4a

20m. Climb the obvious corner crack to the break, then finish as for *Yummy Dragons*.
Dave & Lina Arthur, September 2013

23. Hush my Little Baby Dragon Diff

20m. The right-hand arête has good holds.
Dave & Lina Arthur, September 2013

24. Free Nuts for Skinny People VS 4b ABSEIL

80m. A good, long outing, starting at a crack to the left of a black chimney.
1) 45m. Climb the crack to a ledge, then continue to a belay on a large platform.
2) 35m. Climb cracks in the leaning tower behind the ledge to gain the base of the corner crack above. Move up through the overhang and follow a widening crack to the top.
Tim Culwick & Marion Wyllie, September 2013

D KAKAA WALL

Shade · Families · Hitch · Roadside

Drive from Tafraout: **1:45**
Walk-in: **30 minutes**

Some 25km along the Aouguenz road from Tizi-n-Toudma lies the impressive cliff of Kakaa Wall above the village of Lazal. Numerous esoteric routes have been climbed on the front face, but it is on the west-facing side wall that the best climbs are to be found.

Parking is available at a hairpin level with the left-hand toe of the crag, from where the routes are reached in about 30 minutes.

DESCENT: Walk north for approximately 200m, turning left to locate the head of a steep gully. Descend this, then scramble down slabs and a final rocky rib to reach terraces below.

1. King Kong E2 5b ★3

110m. A tremendous climb, tackling the eye-catching chimney line high on the west-facing wall. Start a few hundred metres up the gully up the left side of the crag, beneath a prominent chimney.

1) 30m (5b) Climb a crack in the north-facing right wall of the chimney, then follow a shallow groove up left to a platform.

2) 20m (5a) Climb the groove above the left end of the platform, then go up a slab to a bollard belay.

3) 30m (5b) The excellent chimney.

4) 30m (5b) Continue up the corner crack to an overhang. Make exposed moves up left to finish up an easier slab and corner.

Emma Alsford & Paul Donnithorne, March 2015.

2. The Matriarch E2 5c ★3

160m. Fascinating climbing up a strong natural line. Start below the most obvious left-facing corner.

1) 60m (5b) Start up the clean right-hand groove to gain the chimney. Follow this and the corner above to a small ledge.

2) 40m (5b) Continue up the corner past a tree, then follow a tapering groove up leftwards. Move up right at the top of this, continuing to a ledge and large flake.

3) 60m (5c) Climb the flake to another ledge. Step rightwards off a block and make a steep pull into the upper groove. Follow this to a stony ledge, from where scrambling gains the top.

P.Donnithorne & M.Meaney, January 2015.

E FAULTY TOWERS

Shade · Families · Hitch · Roadside — Drive from Tafraout: **1:45** Walk-in: **10 to 30 minutes**

This is the steep crag some 300 metres left (west) of Kakaa Wall, with a prominent corner running up its right-hand buttress. It provides some excellent and easily accessible routes in a fine setting.

The origin of the crag's name is uncertain, though the misspelling of the popular 1970s TV sitcom is presumed to refer to the prevalence of crack climbs hereabouts – a relatively rare thing on quartzite.

To reach the crag, continue along the road beyond KaKaa wall, all the way to the col at the top of the hairpins where there is ample parking.

SYBIL BUTTRESS

At the left-hand side of the main crags, closest to the road, is an attractive west-facing buttress with the following routes:

1. Juniper Arête E3 5b ★2 ABSEIL

20m. The left-hand arête gives excellent climbing with fiddly protection. Start from a juniper tree on a ledge and make committing moves onto the arête. Move up right to gain a left-slanting crack, then follow this back to the arête which is followed to the top.

Paul Donnithorne & Emma Alsford, March 2015.

2. Pancake Day E2 5c ★2 ABSEIL

30m. Good climbing up the wall right of *Juniper Arête*. Start up a left-trending weakness in a short slab to reach the overhangs. Pull through steep cracks past a block to gain the upper wall.

Paul Donnithorne & Emma Alsford, March 2015.

3. Glowing in the Wind HVS 5a ★2 ABSEIL

30m. A pleasant face climb, starting below a tree 10m left of *Sybil*. Climb a clean rib and deep crack to pass the tree on its right. Pull through a bulge and finish up the quartz face crack above.

Paul Donnithorne & Emma Alsford, March 2015.

4. Snake Flake VS 4c ★1 ABSEIL

30m. Follows flakes to the right of the previous route.

Emma Alsford & Paul Donnithorne, March 2015.

5. Sunset Crack VS 4c ★1 ABSEIL

30m. Climb a finger flake left of *Sybil*, finishing up the groove above.

Paul Donnithorne & Don Sargeant, March 2015.

6. Sybil E3 5c ★1 ABSEIL

30m. The large left-facing flake gives an excellent pitch. Finish more easily up slabby ground above.

P.Donnithorne, B.Watson & D.Sargeant, March 2015.

7. Manuel VS 5a ★1 ABSEIL

30m. Start 10m right of *Sybil* at the right end of the terrace. Pull steeply through an initial bulge to gain an easier groove

Paul Donnithorne & Don Sargeant, March 2015.

Sybil Buttress

PM · 5m

CENTRAL BUTTRESS

Approach in five minutes from the road, following a good cairned path to a dead-end at the base of the buttress. The main buttress has two prominent cracks.

8. Grand Designs E1 5b ★3 ABSEIL

120m. Excellent, varied climbing starting from a terrace 10 metres up and left from the starting clearing of *Nightjar*.

1) 20m (4c) Climb a slab and small square corner to ledges.

2) 30m (5a) Make a technical move leftwards above a small roof to gain a shallow groove. Follow this to a layback flake, which is climbed to a good thread. Traverse right here, under a bulge, to a good ledge.

3) 30m (5b) Regain the groove on the left, and layback the fine flake to a ledge. Step left and follow a thin crack to a terrace. Move right to belay beneath a slim red corner.

4) 20m (5b) Move up right onto the slab, climbing up to gain the slim red corner. Follow this and the rib above to belay behind the tower at the top of *Nightjar* (abseil option here).

5) 20m (4a) Surmount a large block an finish up slabs.

Emma Alsford & Paul Donnithorne, November 2014

DESCENT: Via two abseils (risk of ropes getting stuck on flakes), or one 60m abseil from the end of pitch 2.

9. Nightjar / Crack Addict E2 5b ★3 ABSEIL

100m. The left-hand of the two prominent cracks.

1) 35m (5b) Follow the slab slightly rightwards to a short rightwards traverse beneath the hanging groove. Step up left to gain the groove and climb it steeply to a good ledge on the left. Move up further left to a second ledge below the striking crack.

2) 45m (5b) Go up into the wide crack, then follow the continuation groove up rightwards to a sloping ramp (abseil point).

3) 20m (5b) Finish up the crack / groove on the right-hand side of the arête.

Emma Alsford & Paul Donnithorne, November 2014

10. Bird Song / Crackaholic E2 5b ★3 ABSEIL

100m. The right-hand crack, starting just right of *Nightjar*.

1) 35m (5a) Climb up to the overhang and pull into a niche above. Continue up a steep crack to a ledge (abseil point).

2) 45m (5b) Follow the open groove above a bulge into another steep crack. Follow this with difficulty to a step right into an open groove. Move up this, then back left onto a rib by a bush. Belay on the shoulder above.

3) 20m (5b) Move the belay 3 metres left of the arête to climb a shallow groove. Traverse the slab rightwards to the arête, finishing up this.

Paul Donnithorne & Emma Alsford, October 2014 (pitches 1&2).
Paul Donnithorne & A.Janezko, March 2015 (pitch 3).

11. Stem Ginger E1 5b ★1 ABSEIL

80m. Climbs the orange groove to the right of the previous routes.

1) 35m (5b) Pull steeply into the corner and follow it to a move out left near the top.

2) 45m (5b) A thin crack leads to easier climbing, trending slightly left. After a few metres, swing right on hidden holds to gain the left-trending crack and climb up past the left side of a small roof. Finish up the groove above.

Paul Donnithorne & Don Sargeant, November 2014

SHADY WALL

The next routes are located at the right-hand side of the crag, where a distinctive corner runs up the left side of the right arête.

12. Corner Major VS 4c ★3 ABSEIL

60m. The huge right-facing corner at the right-hand side of the crag is a classic pitch.

1) 45m (4c) Climb the corner to a big ledge on the right.

2) 15m (4c) Continue up a crack, then traverse right to an abseil point.

Paul Donnithorne & Emma Alsford, October 2014

13. On the Beach E4 6a ★3 ABSEIL

45m. The right wall of the huge corner gives another magnificent climb. Start up the corner, then move right and climb through the first overlap (crux). Step left, climb through a second overlap and then up via chicken heads to finish up the right arête.

Paul Donnithorne & Emma Alsford, October 2014

The shady wall to the right of the arête offers three distinctive cracks on perfect rock:

14. Only Fools and Horses E2 5b ★3 ABSEIL

55m. The left arete is the first of several excellent pitches hereabouts. Climb the first 12m of *Zoot Allures* until level with good grey rock. Make a long reach left to gain the arete and climb it the the big break (abseil point on the right).

M.Turner & P.Johnson, November 2014

15. Zoot Allures HVS 5b ★3 ABSEIL

40m. The left-hand chimney is approached from the right via an obvious slanting crack.

P.Johnson & D.Sargeant, November 2014

16. Cheap Thrills E1 5b ★2 ABSEIL

35m. The thinner central crack, finishing up a vegetated groove. Lower off point to the left.

P.Johnson & M.Turner, November 2014

17. Hot Rats HVS 5a ★3 ABSEIL

35m. The right-hand crack, stepping right into an open groove at 2/3 height.

P.Johnson & M.Turner, November 2014

Shady Wall

AM 30m

Area Map
Crag Selector
Intro
The Climbing
How to Use
Suggested Climbs
Tafraout Granite
Anergui
Ameln Valley
Tarakatine Pass
Sidi M'Zal
Jebel Taskra
Idaougnidif
Afantinzar
Samazar
Aouguenz
Tagzene
Tagmout
History
Index

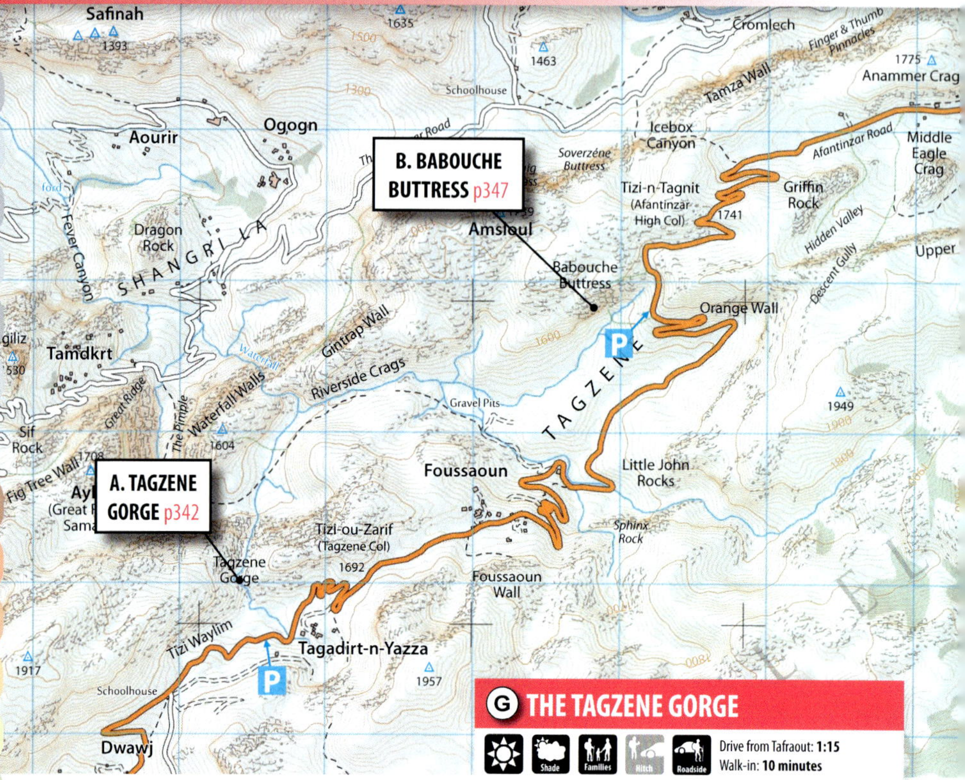

Area Map
Crag Selector
Intro
The Climbing
How to Use
Suggested Climbs
Tafraout Granite
Anergui
Ameln Valley
Tarakatine Pass
Sidi M'Zal
Jebel Taskra
Idaougnidif
Afantinzar
Samazar
Aouguenz
Tagzene
Tagmout
History
Index

TAGZENE

The south-west corner of the Jebel el Kest massif has been under the scrutiny of western climbers for a number of years, and although it does not have the same concentration of 'big' climbs as the other north-side valleys, the two crags described here are of particular merit.

The main road through this area is a continuation of the Afantinzar road, and the high valley of Tagzene can be reached from either end:

1) From Afantinzar, by continuing west over the pass beyond Anammer and Griffin Rock (Tizi-n-Tagnit). This is the obvious route of approach for teams based at the Kasbah Tizourgane.

2) From the west via Tagmout and the Dwawj Hairpins. This is the preferable approach from Tafraout, although it is notoriously easy to get lost by misidentifying the 'northside junction' in the Ameln Valley. This approach passes the impressive slabs at Dwawj – although numerous routes have been climbed here they tend to remain mossy for much of the year and are not described in this volume.

G THE TAGZENE GORGE

Shade · Families · Hitch · Roadside

Drive from Tafraout: **1:15**
Walk-in: **10 minutes**

Whilst the surface rock in this area is generally not up to the same standard as elsewhere, there is some excellent climbing to be had in the narrow Tagzene Gorge, which cuts its way down into a band of immaculate quartzite, draining the fertile Upper Tagzene valley into Samazar. Here there is a high concentration of good quality low-grade pitches in an attractive and friendly setting. This, combined with a short approach from the car, straightforward descents and plenty of opportunity to escape from the midday sun provide for a very pleasant cragging experience... despite the unnerving presence of occasional eldritch artefacts.

The gorge is located on the north side of the road, about 3km east of Dwawj, and is best approached from Tafraout via Tagmout and the Dwawj hairpins. There is room to park on the roadside next to an electricity pylon above a cultivated area, just beyond the pass above Dwawj. A small path heads down from the road and through the fields, heading for the prominent gorge entrance. The climbing is located in several sectors that offer varying amounts of sunshine and shade to suit most days. They are described in order of approach from the southern entrance of the gorge.

SHADOW WALL

There is a short section of very easy scrambling on the left side of the stream to enter the gorge. This leads almost immediately to a small bay with a tall, shady wall on the left - the first good climbing in the ravine.

DESCENT: Either head left down easy rocks back to the entrance of the gorge, or go right and down-climb the gully (moderate).

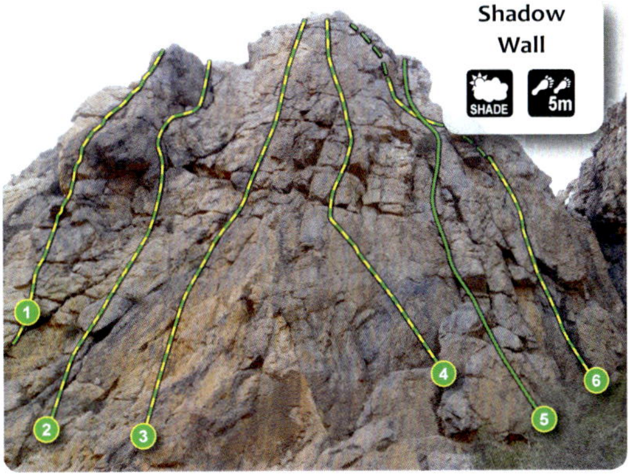

1. Calypso Severe ★1

20m. The little overhanging nose.
Steve Broadbent & Kerry Mellor, March 2013.

2. Caiman Corner HVD ★1

20m. The left side of the wall, passing a perched block to reach the upper corner. This provides a surprisingly challenging layback move.
Steve Broadbent (solo), December 2009.

3. Blue Sky Severe ★2

20m. A very fine climb up the centre of the face, requiring a delicate touch. Start in the centre of the wall and climb easily up to finish up a shallow left-facing groove.
Steve Broadbent (solo), December 2009.

4. Shadow Wall Severe ★1

20m. The front face of the pillar.
Lindsay Griffin, October 2015.

5. Azegzaw HVD ★1

20m. Pleasant climbing up blocks and cracks at the right side of the face, with a challenging move to gain the small bush.
Steve Broadbent (solo), December 2009.

6. Slilou Chimney Very Difficult ★1

20m. Climbs the wide crack / chimney in the left wall of the deep gully, crossing the previous route above the bush.
Steve Broadbent (solo), December 2009.

SECTOR SHARCH

This short clean wall forms the back of the first bay on the left side of the gorge, just right of the deep gully next to Shadow Wall.

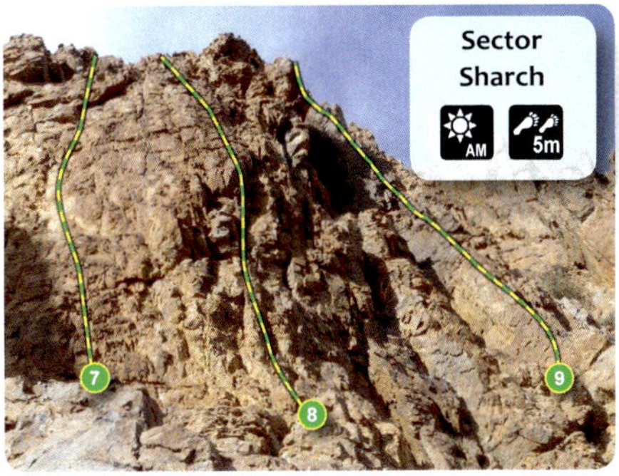

7. Sharch Severe ★1

10m. A nice wall climb, though rather bold in its lower half.
Steve Broadbent (solo), December 2009.

8. Algumad Very Difficult

10m. The vague rib that forms the right side of the clean wall is easiest for those with no knowledge of Berber.
Steve Broadbent (solo), December 2009.

9. Desert Ground Rib Difficult

12m. The long slender rib to the right is easily escapable.
Steve Broadbent (solo), December 2009.

DESCENT: Descend leftward, either down the deep gully or back to the entrance of the gorge.

Area Map
Crag Selector
Intro
The Climbing
How to Use
Suggested Climbs
Tafraout Granite
Anergui
Ameln Valley
Tarakatine Pass
Sidi M'Zal
Jebel Taskra
Idaougnidif
Afantinzar
Samazar
Aouguenz
Tagzene
Tagmout
History
Index

SECTOR DU SOLEIL

Beyond the first bay the stream becomes hemmed in by steep rocks and a short scramble traverse is required to access further climbing areas. Sector du Soleil is the attractive wall right above the stream bed on the east side of the gorge just beyond this step. A great spot for beginners, soloists, and sun-worshippers...

10. Slab & Groove Difficult ★

20m. The left-hand groove leads to a delightful easy slab.
Steve Broadbent (solo), December 2009.

11. Mouzi Hard Difficult ★

20m. Climb the groove immediately left of the small tower to easier ground, before finishing straight up steep cracks in the rib above.
Steve Broadbent (solo), December 2009.

12. Asgen Groove Very Difficult ★

20m. A very good pitch with a tricky start up the steep shallow groove just right of the small tower. Finish more easily up the centre of the buttress above.
Steve Broadbent (solo), December 2009.

13. Ladybird Very Difficult ★

15m. Good climbing up the vague groove. Step right at the top for a difficult steep finish up the smooth final wall.
Steve Broadbent (solo), December 2009.

14. What Are Birds? Very Difficult ★

15m. The twin cracks have a tricky exit.
Steve Broadbent (solo), December 2009.

15. Ambre Solaire Mild Severe ★ GEAR

15m. The left-hand of two cracks is a fine climb, giving a short well-protected layback.
Steve Broadbent (solo), December 2009.

16. Piz Buin Mild Severe ★ GEAR

10m. The right-hand crack also has a couple of nice layback moves before an easier finish.
Steve Broadbent (solo), December 2009.

The next route is located on the wall just to the right of sector du Soleil.

17. Maybelline Mild Severe

20m. Start 3m from the right side of the wall at a clean groove. Go up the groove, then follow a slab, moving left at the overlap. Finish over a smaller overlap above.
Martin Bennett (solo), November 2014.

SECTOR DJINN

The showpiece of the Tagzene Gorge is located on the left (west) side of the stream just before it cascades down an unclimbable drop.

DESCENT: To descend, either walk left back to the entrance of the gorge, or descend by abseil from a terrace in the centre of the sector.

18. Ne T'inquiêtes Pas Hard Difficult — ABSEIL

35m. The left-hand arête is relatively straightforward, moving right to avoid a steep section at 15m.
Jamie & Clare Wakeham, February 2010.

19. Waiting... Very Difficult — ABSEIL

35m. Climb the vague groove just right of a low arête to gain the more obvious upper groove. Follow this then step right at the top to finish up the face.
Steve & Katja Broadbent, February 2010.

20. Dyoudo Voodoo Severe — ABSEIL

35m. Easy climbing up cracked ground leads to a short steep crack high on the face. This is overcome with some fine layback moves, or avoided on the right at Very Difficult standard.
Steve & Katja Broadbent, February 2010.

Map Page 342

Area Map
Crag Selector
Intro
The Climbing
How to Use
Suggested Climbs
Tafraout Granite
Anergui
Ameln Valley
Tarakatine Pass
Sidi M'Zal
Jebel Taskra
Idaougnidif
Afantinzar
Samazar
Aouguenz
Tagzene
Tagmout
History
Index

23. Tag Crack HVS 5b ★3

ABSEIL

33m. The tempting layback crack on the north side of the buttress is another fine and varied climb, that could almost be at home in the Lake District. Climb a short but technical slab to a difficult pull into the crack. This section is mercifully very well-protected. Follow the crack to a small ledge and then step right to gain a very bold wall that provides a challenging climax to this test-piece route. Easy blocks remain to the top.

Steve & Katja Broadbent, February 2010.

24. Grey Crack HVS 5a ★1

ABSEIL

35m. The left-hand of two face cracks to the right of *Tag Crack*.

Paul Donnithorne & Pete Johnson, March 2012.

25. Black Crack VS 4c ★2

ABSEIL GEAR

35m. The right-hand crack is a fine pitch, that pretty much defines the VS grade. Protection is good throughout, but a hard move through the overlap will certainly give you something to think about.

Pete Johnson & Paul Donnithorne, March 2012.

21. The Wizard's Sleeve VS 4c ★2

ABSEIL

33m. A magical outing up the steep brown corner that is not as loose as its name suggests... or is it? Climb the lower corner with care, then continue via some superb bridging to an exposed step left and wild finish in the upper groove. Good stuff.

Steve & Katja Broadbent, February 2010.

22. Djinn HVS 5a ★2

ABSEIL

33m. This superlative arête is one of the best routes in the gorge, featuring very spirited climbing and some superb positions. It is accessed from the right and followed with some difficulty to an easier upper groove.

Steve & Katja Broadbent, February 2010.

B BABOUCHE BUTTRESS

Drive from Tafraout: **1:15**
Walk-in: **15 minutes**

This imposing, south-facing buttress was one of the first crags to be climbed in the valley, and despite a fair amount of vegetation on some of the lines it has become popular in recent years thanks to the superb *Crazy Mushrooms Ridge*, which takes a dominating line up the steep left-hand arête.

The crag gets all the sunshine there is going, and at almost 200m in height gives good length climbs that benefit from a very easy approach and descent – both are downhill from the car!

Parking is available at a bend in the road, on a vague shoulder between the pass from Afantinzar and the Orange Wall, though in fact the approach is fairly obvious from any parking hereabouts.

DESCENT: From the top of the route there is some scrambling to reach the summit, from where vague trails lead easily down rightwards to regain the road just below the Afantinzar col.

1. Crazy Mushrooms Ridge HVS 5b ★3 STEEP

190m. The left side of the daunting pillar gives a scintillating climb on perfect rock. An easy approach, simple descent, and enjoyable climbing, have helped this route to achieve classic status, despite constant debate about the grade. The crux pitch is hard, but the route is not as sustained or committing as it looks.

1) 28m (-) Climb a small slab leading up right to the ridge, which is followed to a good terrace with a big block.

2) 25m (5b) The magnificent overhanging orange arête is no place to hang around, but not obvious enough to power through. Climb cracks up leftwards, then pull up right onto a short wall. This leads to a spike below steeper ground. Move right here, making awkward moves (5a) to enter a slim groove, with easier climbing above to a stance out left on the arête. A variation (5b) continues straight up from the spike and probably warrants E1.

3) 35m (4c) Climb up the left side of the arête, then continue up the superb ridge to the summit of a tower.

4) 35m (4c) Step down 3m, then climb the yellow wall straight up to a curving crack. Follow this, and some more cracks above to an easier finish to a large terrace.

5) 47m (-) Scrambling to the top.

Alberto Rampini & Silvia Mazzani, October 2011.

Area Map
Crag Selector
Intro
The Climbing
How to Use
Suggested Climbs
Tafraout Granite
Anergui
Ameln Valley
Tarakatine Pass
Sidi M'Zal
Jebel Taskra
Idaougnidif
Afantinzar
Samazar
Aouguenz
Tagzene
Tagmout
History
Index

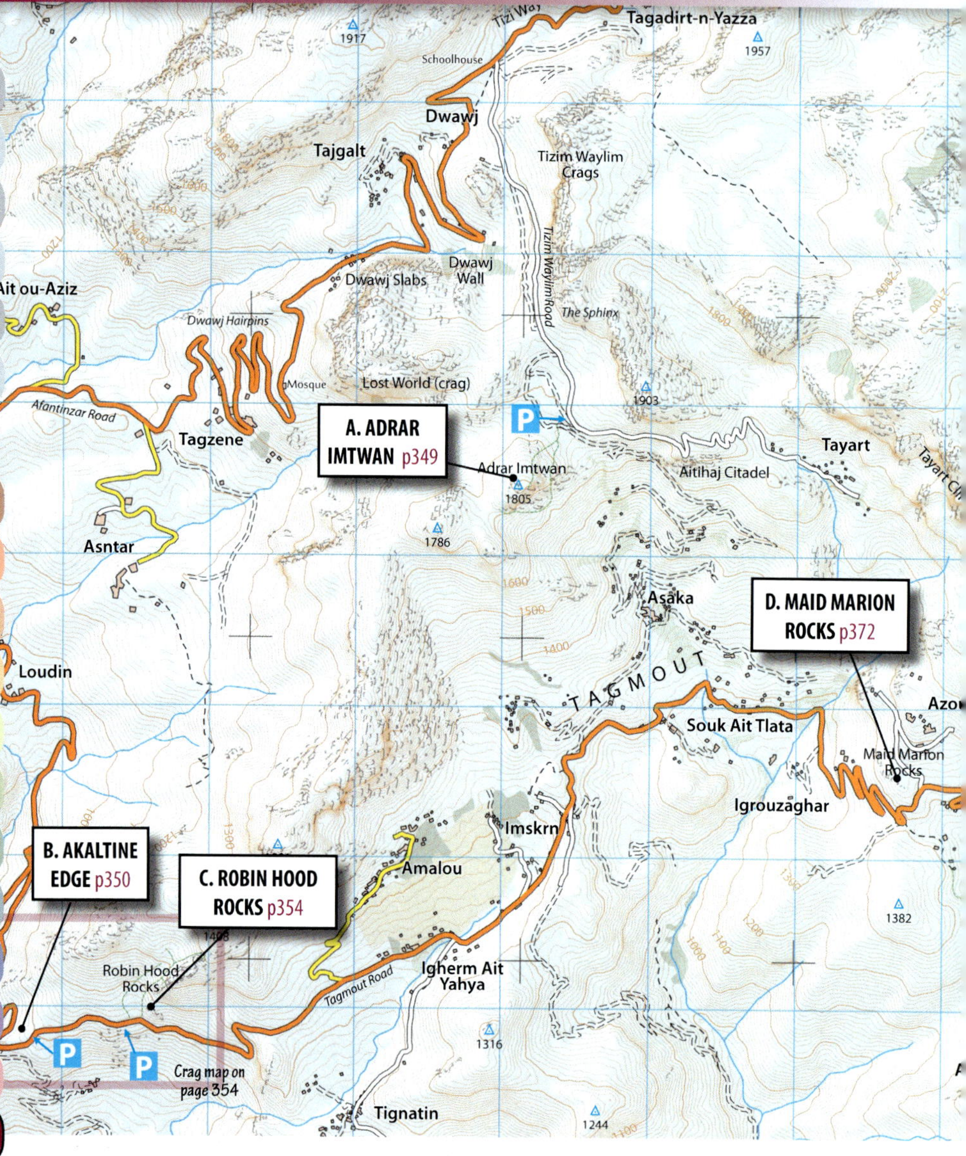

TAGMOUT

The impressive high cliffs at the western end of the Jebel el Kest escarpment have seen little interest from climbers; long walk-ins and poor quality rock make the big multi-pitch crags here generally unappealing. However, a number of excellent single-pitch venues can be found along the Ameln - Tanalt road, making this a very popular area for roadside cragging.

The region is approached from Tafraout by taking the main road west out of Ameln. Turn right at a junction by a compound, 7.9km from the Ameln junction, signposted to Anezi. This is also the turn-off for Anergui, and is shown on the map on page 59. The road passes through a small gorge, then bends left and climbs up to traverse a narrow ridge, then on into Tagmout.

The area is dominated by the picturesque summit of Adrar Imtwan, which holds the first routes...

A ADRAR IMTWAN

Shade Families Hitch Roadside
Drive from Tafraout: **1 hour**
Walk-in: **30 to 40 minutes**

Adrar Imtwan (The Twins) dominates the northern skyline above Tagmout, guarding the pass to Dwawj over which the very poor Tizim Waylim road winds its way. The summit is an excellent viewpoint with relatively easy access and simple descent. Approach from the south side is possible only in a 4WD vehicle, or via a very unpleasant slog on foot up the steep hillside, but a better alternative is available from the north. Take the small track that leaves the Afantinzar road above Dwawj, and follow it south from Tizim Waylim until it starts dropping down into an attractive hanging valley. A parking and turning area exists just before the road deteriorates and descends towards Tagmout.

EAST SUMMIT

From this parking area the attractive *East Ridge* is visible right above the road, with an easy descent path on the right side. To the left is a notch on the skyline that indicates the start of the approach gully for routes on the south face.

1. East Ridge Easy / Moderate

100m. The attractive-looking ridge above the track provides a pleasant scramble to the summit. Difficulties can usually be avoided on the right.

The south face of the mountain is best accessed via a steep approach gully, the top of which is visible from the parking area. At the bottom of the gully stay on the true left and scramble down beneath chockstones through a tunnel to gain easier ground (this section can also be abseiled from the rock spur in the centre of the gully). Turn right and traverse beneath the south face to gain the following route...

DESCENT: Descent from the east summit is a straightforward walk down the northern slopes of the mountain, bearing right at the bottom to regain the Tizim Waylim Road.

2. Falcon Ridge HS 4c

190m. A pleasant outing up the left arête of the East Twin, with some excellent steep climbing on good holds and fine views over Tagmout. Start right of the ridge and climb straight up for 3 pitches, aiming for the top of the second step in the ridge at 90m. The 3rd pitch features some challenging steep ground. Above this follow the fine ridge more easily to the summit (3 further pitches).

Steve Broadbent & Iza Pstrucha, February 2009.

WEST SUMMIT

The next route is on the western summit, and can be accessed either via the gully as for the previous two climbs, or by walking around the north side of the peak to its west col (slightly easier).

3. Old Eagle Ridge VS 5a

180m. A pleasant mountaineering route with a difficult start and easier climbing higher up. The route begins below the west ridge of an obvious detached pinnacle just below the west col.

1) 30m (4b) Steep climbing up the pinnacle to a belay on a flake.
2) 20m (5a) Climb straight up above, passing a roof on its right side via an overhanging crack (crux). Belay on a ridge over the top of the pinnacle.
3) 40m (4b) Pleasant climbing up the good ridge.
4) 45m (-) Easy climbing up the ridge to a belay in a vegetated gully.
5) 60m (-) Easy rocks on the left of the gully to reach the lower west summit. Go over a saddle to the summit cairn on the main west summit.

Alberto Rampini & Silvia Mazzani.

DESCENT: To descend from the west summit, scramble down to the col between the west and east summits. Do not go down the gully here, but instead traverse left to reach an ancient Berber trail and easy gully. This leads back to the hillside and the Tizim Waylim track in about 20 minutes.

Area Map
Crag Selector
Intro
The Climbing
How to Use
Suggested Climbs
Tafraout Granite
Anergui
Ameln Valley
Tarakatine Pass
Sidi M'Zal
Jebel Taskra
Idaougnidif
Afantinzar
Samazar
Aouguenz
Tagzene
Tagmout
History
Index

B AKALTINE EDGE

Shade · Families · Hitch · Roadside

Drive from Tafraout: **0:40**
Walk-in: **2 minutes**

This small family-friendly outcrop is located just beyond Robin Hood Rocks, close to the Akaltine turn-off. It faces northwest and stays in the shade until early afternoon, making it a good choice when things get too hot at Robin Hood Rocks.

Park on the roadside at the second left-hand bend after Robin Hood Rocks, from where the top of the crag is reached in 2 minutes across open ground.

See map on page 354.

LEFT END

1. Shambaholic Moderate

8m. A teenie mico-route up the short wall

Steve Broadbent (solo), January 2017.

2. Flavour Chat Difficult

8m. The short broken rib behind the tree.

Steve Broadbent (solo), January 2017.

3. Kalia HS 4a ★1 SLAB

15m. An excellent, varied problem. Start up the steep corner to gain the left side of the slab, which is climbed via a thin crack.

Steve & Katja Broadbent, October 2016.

4. Major Oak Difficult ★1

20m. Good climbing on large holds. Pull steeply onto the slab and follow the break rightwards to finish up the corner.

Steve Broadbent (solo), January 2017.

5. The Scoop VS 4c ★3 SLAB BOLD

20m. Brilliant climbing up the immaculate slab, best enjoyed in the sunshine at the end of the day. Pull onto the wall, then zigzag up to the tempting scoop. Make an awkward move into this and continue to the blank upper slab. Climb the centre of this boldly to the top.

Steve & Katja Broadbent, February 2016.

6. Six Inch Snails HS 4b ★1 GEAR

20m. Fun steep climbing over the nose, which is overcome athletically on good holds. Finish more easily up the groove above, taking the left-hand crack at the top.

Steve Broadbent, Katja Broadbent, Cecilie Mueenuddin & Zoe Bouras, January 2017.

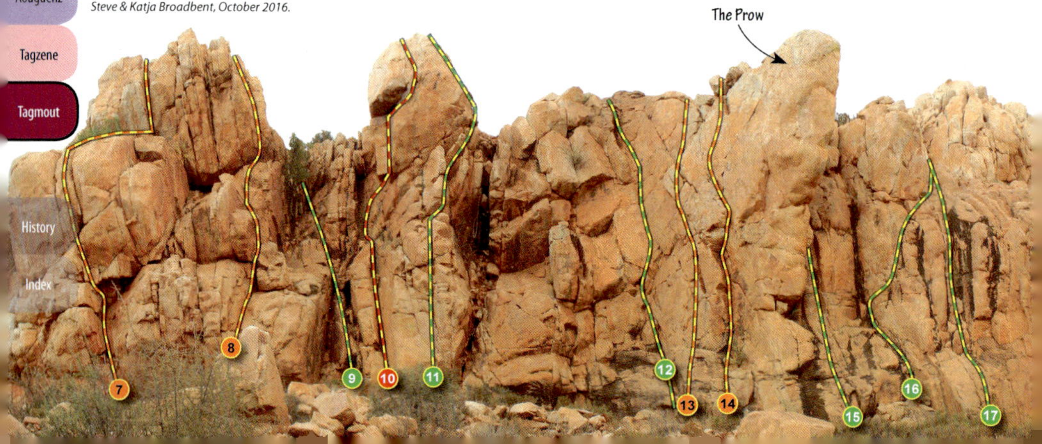

CENTRAL AREA

Bounded by slabs to the left and right, the central walls feature numerous excellent climbs, including the brilliant and obvious prow taken by *Don Turqouise*.

7. Mister Creosote HVS 5a

STEEP

20m. A steep climb up the buttress right of the slabs. Climb up to gear in the niche, then pull up left into twin cracks to a ledge. Move right and finish up a wide crack.

Will Benfold & Tom Codrington, October 2016.

8. Diplomat in a Bag VS 4c

STEEP

20m. Climb a thin layback crack 2 metres left of the arête, then follow easier ground to finish up the right side of a vague arête.

Will Benfold & Tom Codrington, October 2016.

9. Incompetent Gully Moderate

15m. The gully can also be used as a descent by the competent.

Dave Arthur (solo), October 2016.

10. Orange Lovers E1 5b

BOLD

15m. The slim groove in the sidewall of the gully gives some difficult and bold moves, usually protected by naughty side-runners.

Steve Broadbent & Dave Arthur, October 2016.

11. Korean Error Exchange HS 4b

20m. Climb directly to the bulge, where awkward moves lead around the right side.

Pete Cawley & Sally Fitton, October 2016.

12. Korma HS 4b ★1

15m. The attractive corner gives a fine climb, despite some questionable rock at the top.

Steve & Katja Broadbent, October 2016.

13. Cute Fuzzy Alien Creature VS 4c ★1

15m. Blocky cracks up the left-hand side of the prow.

Lina Arthur, Dave Arthur & Aileen Robertson, October 2016.

14. Don Turquoise HVS 4c ★2

15m. Brilliant climbing up the sidewall of the prow. Start steeply up the wide right-hand crack to a rest, then make technical moves up rightwards to blocks at the top. Small wires protect.

Lina Arthur, Aileen Robertson & Steve Broadbent, October 2016.

15. One Move Blunder HS 4b

20m. The gully crack up the right side of the prow.

Tom Codrington & Will Benfold, October 2016.

16. Airdrop Very Difficult ★1

15m. Good climbing, traversing up rightwards from the gully. Climb the right corner of the gully for a few metres to gain a line of holds traversing up right.

Steve Broadbent (solo), October 2016.

17. Nosebag Severe ★1

15m. The vague crackline has some nice moves.

Steve Broadbent (solo), October 2016.

18. Quarx HVS 5b ★1

GEAR STEEP

10m. The slippery, high v-groove has difficult moves to enter it, but is a well-protected struggle.

Steve & Katja Broadbent, February 2016.

19. Rumpelstiltskin HS 4a ★1

GEAR

10m. The stepped crack is a pleasant and well protected little pitch.

Katja & Steve Broadbent, February 2016.

20. Spanky VS 4b ★1

GEAR STEEP

10m. Climbs the centre of the little buttress, just left of slabs. The steep finish is best tackled on the left side.

Steve & Katja Broadbent, February 2016.

21. Bolero Difficult

20m. Meander up the slabs, curving right beneath the overlap to cross *Embele*. Keep going straight up over blocks towards the summit, where optional fun can be head with a 'tunnel' type exit.

Katja & Steve Broadbent, February 2016.

Map Page 348

RIGHT-HAND BUTTRESS

At the right-hand end of the crag is an overhanging buttress split by numerous cracks. These provide some strenuous but very well protected climbs:

22. Embele VS 4b

12m. Start up a shallow v-groove, then follow slabs up leftwards.
Steve & Katja Broadbent, February 2016.

23. Pisa HVS 5b 1 star. STEEP

12m. Pull up from very high holds to gain the scoop, then follow the flake more easily. Move left to finish up a final bold slab.
Steve & Katja Broadbent, February 2016.

24. Walewska VS 5a 1 star. GEAR, STEEP

12m. Good steep climbing up the twin cracks. Make a very steep move to gain a prominent jug out left, from where things ease a little.
Steve & Katja Broadbent, February 2016.

25. Occorom VS 5b 1 star. GEAR, STEEP

12m. The crack up the centre of the buttress, with a perched chockstone at half-height. A steep start (hard for the grade!) leads to excellent climbing in the upper groove.
Steve & Katja Broadbent, February 2016.

26. Chomahom E1 5b 2 stars. GEAR, STEEP

15m. Excellent steep climbing. Gain the chockstone of *Occorom*, then move right up the hanging slab to creative moves up the overhanging arête.
Steve & Katja Broadbent, January 2017.

27. Tiwenya VS 5a GEAR, STEEP

12m. The steep flake groove on the right-hand sidewall of the buttress has very difficult moves to start.
Steve & Katja Broadbent, February 2016.

Lina Arthur on *Don Turquoise* (HVS 4c) at Akaltine. This excellent outcrop is a good choice for families and picnics, providing some challenging mid-grade climbs just yards from the road. ➲

Photo: Steve Broadbent

Area Map
Crag Selector
Intro
The Climbing
How to Use
Suggested Climbs
Tafraout Granite
Anergui
Ameln Valley
Tarakatine Pass
Sidi M'Zal
Jebel Taskra
Idaougnidif
Afantinzar
Samazar
Aouguenz
Tagzene
Tagmout
History
Index

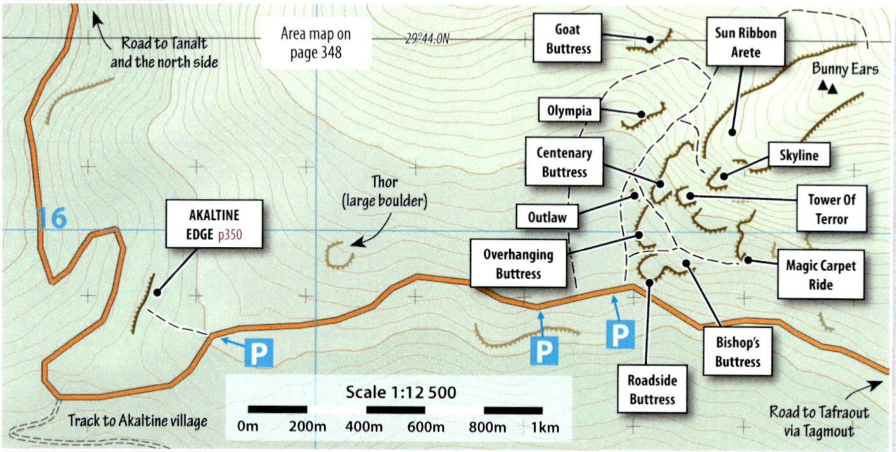

C ROBIN HOOD ROCKS

Shade · Families · Hitch · Roadside

Drive from Tafraout: **40 minutes**
Walk-in: **2 to 30 minutes**

Located on the west end of the massif, Robin Hood Rocks lies on the boundary between the north and south sides of the range, and consequently has a character rather different to much of the climbing in the Ameln Valley. The rock here is an unusually granitic, compact quartzite which forms arêtes, cracks and walls that are a joy to climb, and whilst the crag once had a reputation for being the domain of the extreme climber, it now boasts dozens of excellent short routes across the grade range, along with one superb long outing up the ridge to the prominent 'Bunny Ears'.

The numerous buttresses are scattered across the open hillside, in some cases just yards from the roadside, giving the crag a very relaxed feel and making it a popular destination throughout the winter. Despite the low-commitment atmosphere, however, steep slopes, drop-offs and prickly vegetation make this an unsuitable venue for families.

The routes here come into their own during the late afternoon, when the setting sun often creates spectacular colours on the rock – it's hard to imagine a better place to watch the sun setting on the Maghreb than from the well-positioned *Centenary Balcony* at the top of *Centenary Buttress*.

Robin Hood has long had a reputation for being something of a sun trap, so whilst the crag is a perfect choice when low cloud obscures the higher crags, it is best avoided during periods of extreme heat.

GOAT BUTTRESS

This excellent buttress lies high on the left side of the rocks above Olympia. It can be approached from the broad gully running between Olympia and Centenary Buttress, but a better approach from the road is to head up the open hillside and traverse in above the level of Olympia.

1. Under the Nose E2 5c ★2

35m. Start up the wall to gain the wide crack, which leads up to the roof. Traverse out left to gain a crack on the front face, and follow this to a ledge. Step right into the magnificent hanging crack to finish.

Ian Wilson & Bruce Kerry, March 2014

2. The Italian Job HVS 5c ★1 WIDE

50m. This route climbs a series of chimneys up the left side of the right-hand buttress.

1) 20m (4b) Start up the arête and corner on the left side of the buttress, with a tricky move to gain a ledge. Continue up the chimney above.

2) 30m (5c) A good pitch. Step up right and climb a white flake, then move left around the arête to enter a tempting wide crack. This has a very hard thrutch to enter, followed by fine bridging above.

Steve Broadbent & Sarah Pemberton, November 2012.

3. Webster's Dictionary HVS 5a ★3

40m. An engrossing climb, featuring delicate, thuggish and slightly ridiculous climbing. Start from trees and climb up left to gain the front of the buttress. An excellent layback flake leads insecurely to a steep crack, which provides reassurance before things turn pear-shaped. Climb a wide crack to gain a cave beneath the roof, where the remains of previous leaders probably rest deep within the crag. Without further ado (or perhaps with it?) exit left into a short off-width crack. This leads to a tiny stance, from where the antics of the second can be viewed. Easy climbing then gains the top.

Steve Broadbent & Anna Piotrowski, March 2012.

4. Goat Evaporator VS 4c ★2 CRACK

30m. The enticing corner-crack has some predictably excellent climbing, though crumbly rock requires caution.

Steve Broadbent & Anna Piotrowski, March 2012.

5. Quartzite Delight E2 5b ★3 BOLD

30m. More excellent climbing up the centre of the wall to the right.

Egg & Ruth Everitt, March 2014.

6. Cristal E3 5b ★3 BOLD

30m. The majestic arête gives one of the most enjoyable pitches on the crag. A bold approach probably works best, despite the protection being perfectly spaced to keep you off the deck for most of the moves...

Steve Broadbent & Anna Piotrowski, March 2012. Photo page 393.

7. Gravity's Rainbow E2 5c ★3 GEAR STEEP CRACK

20m. The fine arch up the right-hand wall of *Cristal* is an unrelenting delight, requiring an intriguing mix of powerful arms and delicate footwork. Hard for the grade, and almost as hard to second as it is to lead...

Steve Broadbent & Sarah Pemberton, November 2012.

DESCENT: Descent is via a short scramble off the back, then an easy walk down the right hand side.

OLYMPIA

This buttress on the left side of the broad scree gully is not visible from the road, but sits opposite Centenary Buttress and Outlaw Wall. It is accessed in about 15 minutes by following the scree up to Outlaw Wall, then striking leftward across the broad gully. A huge boulder (*Zeus*) sits on the top of the undercut right side of the buttress, aiding identification.

8. Strange Glue VS 4b ☆1

25m. A good, varied route with a technical start on the left wall, some taxing laybacking up the crack, then a fine exposed finish on the upper wall.

Steve Broadbent (solo), October 2009.

9. Persephone's Bush HS 4a

15m. Start from a large ledge and climb a thin crack to another ledge. Finish up the corner crack, capped by a small block.

Sesh Nadathur & Chris Bull, January 2009.

10. Hercules Has a Rest Day HVS 5a ☆2 STEEP

20m. Start in a little recess between two boulders, and follow a steep crack to a powerful hand traverse left which gains a shallow groove just to the right of the arête. Follow this to the top.

Chris Bull & Sesh Nadathur, January 2009.

11. Odysseus Mild Severe

20m. Starts 5m right of the previous route in a chimney recess. Climb the left wall of the chimney to finish up a crack above.

Bob Larkin & David Platt, March 2013.

12. The Song of Achilles VS 5a STEEP

25m. Five metres right of *Odysseus* is a buttress with an overhang and tree at half-height. Start up a crack 1m left of the corner to gain the top of a block. Go up to the roof, then make strenuous moves up left to finish in the hanging chimney.

Bob Larkin & David Platt, March 2013.

13. Nemo and the Sheep Severe CRACK

20m. Start in the corner, then climb a crack in the slabby left wall.

Sally Fitton & Chris Bull, January 2009.

14. Aphrodite's Crack Severe CRACK

20m. The curving corner-crack is relatively straightforward.

Sally Fitton & Chris Bull, January 2009.

15. Wish You Were Hera HS 4b ☆1 PRICKLY

20m. A pleasant route, starting in the prominent corner that appears rather vegetated. Move straight up to a prickly pear, then step out right (crux) and follow the wide diagonal crack to a little ledge and easier climbing above.

Sesh Nadathur & Elie Dekoninck, January 2009.

16. On the Wings of Pegasus VS 4b ☆1

25m. Pleasant climbing up the wall to the left of the huge overhang. Start up a corner and pass a small overhang on its left, continuing straight up the wall above.

Chris Bull & Sally Fitton, January 2009.

17. The Face That Launched a Thousand Ships VS 4c ☆3

20m. A great pitch. Start at the left end of the large overhang beneath a slight bulge which is passed on the left. Follow the curving crack system above to the tree and the belay above it.

Sally Fitton & Chris Bull, January 2009.

18. Pandora's Box HVS 5a ☆3 STEEP

25m. An excellent climb with much variety. Start as for the previous route, tackling the bulge strenuously on its

right side. From the top of this, follow the line of good holds traversing rightwards to the large cave halfway up the face. Pull out of the cave on the right and follow a crack-line diagonally up and right before moving back left to easier ground.
Chris Bull & Sesh Nadathur, January 2009.

19. By the Beard of Zeus HVS 5a ★★★ CRACK

25m. Another superb outing. The tempting crack line above the massive roof on the right side of the wall is accessed via a delicate traverse from around the corner. At the top, continue straight up over the 'beard' of the head-shaped block, from where a short abseil or down-climb is required.
Chris Bull & Sally Fitton, January 2009.

20. Grzegorz Brzeczyszczykiewicz E3 5b ★

12m. The very shallow groove up the left side of the short wall. Good holds in the lower section soon fade into scary smears, before a very high runner protects a tricky exit.
Steve Broadbent, Anna Piotrowski & Leanne Common, April 2014.

21. Orgasmogizmo E2 5a ★

10m. The centre of the wall has no runners, so you'd better not fall off...
Steve Broadbent (solo), April 2014.

Steve Broadbent enjoying the sun-kissed quartzite of *Orgasmogizmo* (E2 5a), Olympia Buttress. ➲
Photo: Anna Piotrowski

Area Map
Crag Selector
Intro
The Climbing
How to Use
Suggested Climbs
Tafraout Granite
Anergui
Ameln Valley
Tarakatine Pass
Sidi M'Zal
Jebel Taskra
Idaougnidif
Afantinzar
Samazar
Aouguenz
Tagzene
Tagmout
History
Index

Area Map
Crag Selector
Intro
The Climbing
How to Use
Suggested Climbs
Tafraout Granite
Anergui
Ameln Valley
Tarakatine Pass
Sidi M'Zal
Jebel Taskra
Idaougnidif
Afantinzar
Samazar
Aouguenz
Tagzene
Tagmout
History
Index

OUTLAW BUTTRESS

This is the short clean wall that stands on its own in the broad scree gully, just underneath Centenary Buttress and level with Olympia.

22. Outlaw VS 4c ★2

15m. The left-hand curving crack-line in the wall has some interestingly technical moves, and an awkward hollow flake.
Steve Broadbent & Elie Dekoninck, December 2008.

23. Will Scarlet VS 4c ★3 STEEP

15m. The right-hand crack has a handful of technical moves to a small overlap which is overcome on big jugs.
Steve Broadbent & Elie Dekoninck, December 2008.

CENTENARY BUTTRESS

The finest collection of low-grade routes on the crag more than justifies the 10 minute approach. These routes are reached by walking left behind Outlaw Buttress to where a small path cuts right back to the top of the main crag. The buttress tops-out on a superb rock ledge known as the Centenary Balcony, which can also be accessed by a short scramble from the right.

DESCENT: From either belay of Centenary Buttress it is possible to walk rightwards and regain the small path.

24. Jungle Life VS 4b BOLD SLAB PRICKLY

45m. A long and very varied climb up the left wall to the Balcony. Start up a difficult groove and continue up the slab above with a couple of tricky friction-moves to gain a vegetated crack at about 25m. Follow this to a peculiar niche and steep finish in a wide crack.
Steve & Katja Broadbent, February 2009.

The next three routes lead to the mid-height belay. From here it is possible to walk off rightwards, or continue up the second pitch of Centenary Buttress.

25. Varsity Games HS 4b ★2

30m. Vegetation in the twin cracks in the slabby left wall does not detract from a good way to the midway belay ledge.
Sally Fitton & Sesh Nadathur, December 2008.

26. Senior Members' Variation ? UNCHECKED

50m. Climbed in one long pitch, no grade has been given to this line. Start as for *Varsity Games*, but trend left to finish up the left side of the upper slab.
Andre Ike & John Wilkinson, October 2010.

27. Britannia Crack HS 4b ★2 CRACK

30m. The obvious wide crack is much easier than it looks, being furnished with good holds throughout.
Steve Broadbent & Elie Dekoninck, December 2008.

28. Oxford Crack VS 5a ★2 GEAR CRACK

30m. The corner to the right gives excellent easy jamming, with a well-protected but challenging move rightwards at the overhang.
Steve & Katja Broadbent, December 2008.

29. Sundial E1 5a ★2 BOLD

30m. The short arête is a lot more independent than it looks, giving technical climbing with marginal runners. A tricky rock-over onto the upper slab marks the end of the difficulties.
Steve Broadbent, Leanne Common & Anna Piotrowski, March 2014.

30. Centenary Buttress HS 4b ★3 BOLD

60m. The front of the buttress is a deservedly popular climb, and one of the best routes at this grade in the area. Although many people walk off after the first pitch, it is the fine upper section that gives the best climbing. This route is also the first two pitches of *Sun Ribbon Arête* (see page 362).

1) 35m (4a) Scramble up easy blocks to a pedestal, from where a good crack leads up through steeper ground. Follow this to an excellent slab, and a fine bold finish up the crest of the arête (those who move left here will miss all the fun). Block belay.

2) 25m (4b) Move left over blocks then go back up right into a blank-looking groove, which is gained with difficulty (crux). Follow the groove with increasing trepidation to an easy finish along the alpine-style ridge.
Steve Broadbent & Elie Dekoninck, December 2008.

31. Encore Une Fois HVS 5a ★1 BOLD

15m. A one-move wonder up the front of the buttress to the right of the second pitch of *C.B.* Step off the large block on the belay ledge and move rightwards up a small hanging slab to a difficult and bold rock-up right onto the wall above. If it all seems too difficult then an escape leftwards up the arête is a bold VS...
Steve Broadbent & Iza Pstrucha, February 2009.

The following two routes climb the south-facing wall on the right, above the middle belay.

32. The Bedlam Cube E2 6a ★★

20m. The tempting right-slanting crack up the front of the buttress is both sustained and fingery. Fortunately it is as safe as they come, as it sees more than its fair share of air-time.
Steve Broadbent & Iza Pstrucha, February 2009.

33. Freefalling E1 5b ★★

20m. An excellent and varied test-piece up the leaning groove in the south-facing wall. Gain the groove with difficulty and follow it until the crack closes up. From here several very technical moves (or a long reach) are required to reach a good hold out right. The subsequent steep finish is at the top end of the grade.
Steve Broadbent & Elie Dekoninck, December 2008.

Area Map
Crag Selector
Intro
The Climbing
How to Use
Suggested Climbs
Tafraout Granite
Anergui
Ameln Valley
Tarakatine Pass
Sidi M'Zal
Jebel Taskra
Idaougnidif
Afantinzar
Samazar
Aouguenz
Tagzene
Tagmout
History
Index

THE TOWER OF TERROR

The steep tower that overlooks the descent route from *Centenary Balcony* has a single route up the leaning northwest face...

34. Tower of Terror VS 4c ★ BOLD LOOSE

30m. A sustained and serious pitch with some rickety flakes, providing a fun adventure for those willing to relish the challenging rock, rather than fear it. Start at the right side, stepping left as soon as possible into the central groove. This is followed to good rock and easier climbing above.
Steve Broadbent & Iza Pstrucha, February 2009.

SKYLINE BUTTRESS

Tucked away at the top of the crag, above and behind the Tower of Terror, lies one of Robin Hood's unexpected gems. There's not much here, but what there is is of superb quality in a delightful setting, and an ascent of *Skyline* at sunset is a genuine treat.

The approach is certainly the longest at the crag, but is not unpleasant and only takes about thirty minutes. Follow the broad gully up towards Centenary Buttress and Olympia. Opposite Olympia there is a prominent vegetated gully leading up to the ridge that runs up to the Bunny Ears. Scramble up this gully to cross through a notch in the ridge, from where Skyline Buttress is clearly visible.

Ben Lister catching the last of the day's sunshine on *Skyline* (E1 5b) at Robin Hood Rocks.
Photo: Steve Broadbent

DESCENT: From the left side of the buttress it is an easy scramble down leftwards into the vegetated gully. For routes up the right-hand buttress the easiest descent is a 20m abseil from a small block on the summit.

35. Champagne HVS 5c ★2 GEAR WIDE

25m. A superb climb, with two contrasting pitches.
1) 15m (5c) Climb the wide corner crack with difficulty, pulling past the overlap and into the chimney above. Belay on a large chockstone.
2) 10m (4c) A magnificent, airy pitch up the arête to the left, with good but spaced protection.
Steve & Katja Broadbent, January 2013.

36. Borax HVS 5c WIDE

25m. This route shares the first pitch with the previous route, but continues more easily up the obvious corner above.
Steve & Katja Broadbent, January 2013.

37. Skyline Corner MVS 4a ★2 ABSEIL WIDE

20m. The obvious wide corner crack gives a very pleasant climb that eases with height.
Steve Broadbent & Sarah Pemberton, November 2012.

38. Flutter E2 5b ★1 BOLD

20m. The attractive arête right of *Skyline Corner* gives some exciting climbing on good rock. Start from *Skyline Corner*, moving right to follow the arête to an escapable finish. Small gear protects.
Andy Moles, March 2015

39. Skyline E1 5b ★3 ABSEIL GEAR

20m. A sustained and highly photogenic climb in a fine setting. Start up a difficult layback in the corner (crux), then swing right onto the front face. Shake out, then launch up the superb pumpy face above, with good protection in the right-slanting cracks. Previously given HVS, the route is technically tricky, but not serious for E1.
Steve Broadbent & Sarah Pemberton, November 2012. Photo opposite & page 26.

40. Icarus E4 6a ★3

25m. The cracks in the buttress right of *Skyline*, moving right at the big undercut.
Jim Slater & Chris Hindley, March 2015.

Skyline Buttress
PM 30m
Overview page 354

Area Map
Crag Selector
Intro
The Climbing
How to Use
Suggested Climbs
Tafraout Granite
Anergui
Ameln Valley
Tarakatine Pass
Sidi M'Zal
Jebel Taskra
Idaougnidif
Afantinzar
Samazar
Aouguenz
Tagzene
Tagmout
History
Index

Map Page 348

THE BUNNY EARS

The distinctive 'Bunny Ears' dominate the skyline of Robin Hood Rocks and provide a mountaineering route of great character. Early attempts to link up the various buttresses and sections of ridge were surprisingly unsuccessful, but the following route manages to find a very enjoyable combination of easy climbing and scrambling, with the added bonus of topping out on a superb little summit.

The easiest approach is from roadside parking at a right-hand bend just beyond the lower roadside buttresses. Traverse across the hillside, heading for the left side of Outlaw Buttress. Immediately above Outlaw Buttress a path cuts right underneath the start of the route (*Centenary Buttress*).

DESCENT: From the notch at the end of the route, turn left and follow vague trails back down between the Bunny Ears and Olympia.

41. Sun Ribbon Arête HS 4b ★3

510m. The southwest ridge up to the Bunny Ears is the only long route at the crag, and is an excellent climb with a distinctly alpine character. Although the route is long, large sections of easy scrambling and walking make it a non-serious outing on which many parties will move together. Start up *Centenary Buttress*.

1) 35m (4a) Scramble up easy blocks to a pedestal, from where a good crack leads up through steeper ground. Follow this to an excellent slab, and a fine bold finish up the crest of the arête. Block belay.

2) 25m (4b) Move left over blocks then go back up right into a blank-looking groove, which is gained with difficulty (crux). Follow the groove with increasing trepidation to an easy alpine-style ridge to the Centenary Balcony.

3) 15m (-) Walk left along a shady ledge below the steep buttress above.

4) 40m (4b) From the end of the ledge, climb up, moving left onto a small nose. Continue up some stepped slabs, passing

the first overhang to reach the larger second overhang. Climb through this via a weakness on the left side, making a difficult pull up right onto the slab above. (This overhang can also be overcome via a difficult crack through its widest part). Continue up pleasant slabs, trending right to a belay in a niche on the arête.
5) 15m (4a) Go up the knife-edge arête to easy ground.
6) 40m (-) Walk along the ridge crest to belay in a major notch with large chockstones. The approach to Skyline Buttress crosses the route at this point.

7) 35m (4a) Climb the wall beyond the chockstone, trending up left to blocks on a ledge. Step up onto a smooth ledge on the left, then move up right of the small overlaps to belay on easier ground.
8) 140m (-) Scrambling and walking along the ridge to where it begins to steepen.
9) 40m (-) Continue up to a small rib which leads up to First Slab. Enjoyable climbing up this leads to a belay on the right.
10) 25m (4a) Step left into a short groove, and make an unlikely-looking exit rightwards onto the front of the Second Slab. Go up this to a belay on the right of the highest ear.
11) 20m (-) Pleasant climbing on good holds up the right side of the ear, finishing up a shallow groove to the summit.
12) 80m (-) From the summit, continue along the ridge, dropping down onto the right (south) side initially to bypass a steep section. About 80m of very enjoyable ridge scrambling gains the notch with the hillside.
Steve Broadbent & Elie Dekoninck, December 2008 (pitches 1&2).
Steve Broadbent & Sarah Pemberton, November 2012 (from the Chockstone Notch).
Steve & Katja Broadbent, October 2016 (pitches 3 to 6).

Pete Cawley on the Second Slab of *Sun Ribbon Arête* (HS). ➲
Photo: Steve Broadbent

Area Map
Crag Selector
Intro
The Climbing
How to Use
Suggested Climbs
Tafraout Granite
Anergui
Ameln Valley
Tarakatine Pass
Sidi M'Zal
Jebel Taskra
Idaougnidif
Afantinzar
Samazar
Aouguenz
Tagzene
Tagmout
History
Index

Map Page 348

OVERHANGING BUTTRESS

The intimidating overhanging buttress at the left side of the main crag forms the northern wall of the main descent gully.

42. Tree Hugger HVS 5a ★1 PRICKLY CRACK

20m. The corner crack to the left of the big overhangs is a good climb, despite the trees! Start with a rightwards traverse across a big slab to gain the elegant corner crack, which is followed past the tree to a difficult pull over a chockstone.
Arnaud Viel & Emmanuel Freudenthal, October 2009.

43. Processing E4 6a ★1 STEEP

25m. The much looked-at roof gives an impressive climb. Start as for the previous route, but traverse right along the break under the first overlap. Go straight up to the big roof to an exposed finish.
Liam Halsey & Esther Bott, January 2017.

44. Dogs' Day Out E2 5c ★2 WIDE

30m. A big, varied climb up the front of the fin-like buttress. The initial off-width crack provides a very hard start, for which large cams are useful, before things eventually ease and the route is forced rightwards through an unusual niche in the overhang.
Jayson Orton & Elie Dekoninck, October 2008.

45. Call to Prayer E1 5b ★1

30m. A very technical outing up the vague groove on the wall of the descent gully.
Jayson Orton & Elie Dekoninck, October 2008.

46. Owl Crack E1 5b ★3 WIDE

20m. The wide crack rising from the depths of the descent gully provides a memorable pitch... Gain the cave with difficulty (occasional resident) then launch up the tremendous layback crack above. Large cams and marginal small gear protects.
Steve Broadbent & Jayson Orton, October 2008.

DESCENT: Descend from routes 46-48 by scrambling up to the top of the buttress, past a huge boulder, then turning left into the middle of the descent gully beneath *The Helvetica Solution*.

A handful of routes have been climbed on the short wall above the rocky ledge at the top of Roadside Buttress:

47. Little John HVS 4c ★1 BOLD

12m. A bold amusement above the ominous crevasse! The wall is gained with a brave step from close to a large boulder, and is climbed steeply on big holds with no worthwhile protection.
Steve & Katja Broadbent, April 2008.

48. Friar Tuck HS 4b

10m. Begin at the right-hand end of the crevasse, 2m to the right of a flared crack. Gain the leftwards-trending ramp via a short crack on the right side. Step to the highest point of the ledge and a rounded finish.
Will Benfold & Henry Northern, February 2011.

49. Above and Beyond E2 5c ★3 GEAR

12m. The thin crack at the right side of the upper wall is a technical pitch with good nut runners. Low in the grade.
Steve & Katja Broadbent, April 2008.

50. The Helvetica Solution E1 5a BOLD

12m. A worrying lead up the wall at the top of the descent gully. Start up a crack at the right side, place an assortment of inadequate protection, then make an increasingly bold traverse up the wall to welcome runners and an easier finish.
Steve Broadbent & Elie Dekoninck, December 2008.

Ben Lister on *Above and Beyond* (E2 5c). Photo: Steve Broadbent

Area Map
Crag Selector
Intro
The Climbing
How to Use
Suggested Climbs
Tafraout Granite
Anergui
Ameln Valley
Tarakatine Pass
Sidi M'Zal
Jebel Taskra
Idaougnidif
Afantinzar
Samazar
Aouguenz
Tagzene
Tagmout
History
Index

ROADSIDE BUTTRESS

This is the attractive clean buttress right by the bend in the road. Most of the routes finish on a large rock ledge, separated from the upper tier by a narrow but deep crevasse (not visible from below).

51. The Sword of Damocles HS 4b ★2

20m. The clean wide crack is followed on its left side to a large finger of rock. Move left and finish up a short wall.
Steve & Katja Broadbent, April 2008.

52. The Good, The Bad, and The Ugly VS 4c ★1

25m. Pleasant easy slabs lead to a difficult steep crack.
Steve & Katja Broadbent, April 2008.

53. Green Agenda HVS 4c ★1 BOLD

15m. The tempting short arête at the top of the buttress can be gained with interest up a slabby rib, or more easily from the right. The arête itself is a bit of a one-move-wonder, totally unprotected, and rather difficult for shorter climbers.
Steve & Katja Broadbent, April 2008.

54. The Blue Lizard Layback VS 4c ★2

15m. Another route that is difficult to grade. Easy climbing past hollow flakes leads to the intimidating upper crack. This provides a short, strenuous layback.
Steve & Katja Broadbent, April 2008.

55. Sheriff's Wall Severe ★2 CARE!

35m. A good way up the buttress, and a big lead at this grade, combining a technical initial pitch with a bold finale.
1) 20m (4a) Go up blocks past an interesting mantel to a large ledge (Junction with *Down and Out*). Continue up easy ground to a higher ledge.
2) 15m (4a) The wall to the left of the chimney is easy but very serious for the grade, giving an excellent exposed pitch on good holds.
Steve & Katja Broadbent, April 2008.

DESCENT: From the ledge at the top of the routes it is possible to traverse leftward into the central descent gully.

56. Jam Boys HS 4b

20m. The twin cracks in the left side of *Sheriff's Wall* provide a safer but less satisfying alternative.
Jayson Orton & Elie Dekoninck, October 2008.

57. Robin Hood Chimney VS 4b 1

15m. A unique and intriguing climb requiring a variety of techniques and a fair amount of imagination. The chimney is best climbed right at the front, where at least some protection exists. The back of the chimney is harder, bolder, and altogether less pleasant.
Steve & Katja Broadbent, April 2008.

58. Down and Out E1 5a 2 BOLD

20m. An excellent technical pitch in a fine position up the front of the buttress. Follow *Sheriff's Wall* to the first large ledge at 15m. Step right onto the compact slab, which is climbed on thin flakes. After a sloping ledge the upper slab culminates in a difficult and bold move onto the right arête. Low in the grade, particularly for taller climbers who will almost certainly consider the route to be HVS. A benchmark E0, perhaps?
Steve & Katja Broadbent, April 2008.

The next routes lie on the right-hand wall of the buttress, and can be approached from the road via some prickly vegetation or by abseil from the large rock ledge.

59. Queen of the Chimney VS 4b 2

25m. An excellent adventure, providing a much better way of accessing *Robin Hood Chimney*. A route not to be missed by chimneying aficionados! Start in a corner down and left of *Hello Picasso*, and climb an interesting corner crack to a notch. Pull through this to enter the wonderful chimney, which gets more traditional the deeper in to it you get (staying close to the outside is strangely easier and better protected.)
Katja Broadbent, Steve Broadbent, Dave Arthur & Lina Arthur, February 2016

60. Hello Picasso E4 6a 3

20m. A tremendous classic, and one of Tafraout's big E4 ticks. Start up the diagonal break of *Pasha* to reach sublime technical climbing up the vague groove, which is adequately protected and never desperate. Awaits a direct start.
Steve & Katja Broadbent, April 2008.

61. Pasha E3 5c 2

20m. An eliminate up the centre of the wall to the right of *Hello Picasso*. Start up that route, making difficult moves to gain the first niche. From here, make a tricky step right onto the wall and sprint up sidepulls to an easier finish.
Steve Broadbent, Katja Broadbent & Lina Arthur, February 2016. Photo page 382.

62. Dead Arm on the Panic Button E4 5c 2 CARE!

20m. An action-packed classic heart-stopper that's as bold as they come (some pre-placed gear makes it more amenable). The optimistic line of holds up the wall right of *Pasha* gives an exacting and utterly committing climb, requiring a cool head. From an initial rock-up off the large boulder the only sensible way is up... And may God help you from here... Another desperately bold rock-over above a hideous landing gains an assortment of small wires which *may* protect a stylish finale.
Steve Broadbent, October 2009.

Area Map
Crag Selector
Intro
The Climbing
How to Use
Suggested Climbs
Tafraout Granite
Anergui
Ameln Valley
Tarakatine Pass
Sidi M'Zal
Jebel Taskra
Idaougnidif
Afantinzar
Samazar
Aouguenz
Tagzene
Tagmout
History
Index

BISHOP'S BUTTRESS

Further right is a more broken buttress with a high overhung corner above a tempting lower wall. There is a good rock ledge at the top of the lower buttress (The Balcony) which can only be accessed by climbing one of the initial routes.

The following climbs lead up to the Balcony...

63. Take it Easy HS 4b ★2 [GEAR]

15m. The narrow recessed rib is an excellent way up to the Balcony and is well protected with medium cams.

Steve & Katja Broadbent, October 2008.

64. Lyin' Eyes VS 4c ★2 [CRACK] [GEAR]

15m. The obvious crack-line up the front of the buttress was once vegetated but now provides the most aesthetic and popular way up to the Balcony. Gaining the crack is by far the hardest part, particularly for the short.

Jayson Orton & Elie Dekoninck, October 2008.

65. Orbital E3 5c ★2

20m. A deliciously technical outing up the blank face, with well-spaced gear just about protecting the bold finishing moves.

Steve & Katja Broadbent, October 2008.

Steve Broadbent on *Bishop's Balcony* (HVS 5a).
Photo: Elie Dekoninck

66. Battle of the Bulge E3 6b [STEEP] [GEAR]

35m. A very varied climb starting up the front rib of the lower tier, and finishing through the overhangs above.
1) 20m (5c) Follow a cracked groove past the spike onto the nose of the arête and climb to the Balcony.
2) 15m (6b) Step right from the Balcony and follow a thin crack up the hanging slab to reach the overhang with some trepidation. The obvious crux is sharp and strenuous but well-protected and mercifully short.

Topher Dagg & Henward Nind, February 2010.

67. There Goes Everything HVS 5a [LOOSE]

15m. The tempting off-width. Start up the crack until a huge tottering flake encourages bold moves out right on small holds, although a direct finish using the flake is probably easier.

Steve & Katja Broadbent, October 2008.

The following routes start from the Balcony...

68. Bishop's Bypass VS 4b [CRACK] [GEAR]

20m. An easier alternate pitch to *Bishop's Balcony*. Start from the left side of the balcony, step down and traverse left to a pock-marked hollow flake. From here climb straight up the wide crack on good holds with plenty of protection.

Ian Dugdale & Lee Healy, February 2011.

69. Into you Like a Train E2 5c ★2 [CRACK] [GEAR]

15m. Desperate jamming up the overhanging crack will stop most folk in their tracks.

Jayson Orton & Elie Dekoninck, October 2008.

70. Bishop's Balcony HVS 5a ★3 [CRACK] [GEAR]

20m. An audacious classic that takes the obvious roof-crack through some seriously steep ground. From the Balcony, climb sandy rock up the large corner to the huge roof. Place good high cams, then swing left on perfect jams to an escape up jugs.

Steve & Katja Broadbent, October 2008.

71. Hotel California HVS 5a ★1

15m. The upper rib on the right side of the buttress is a superb pitch that requires careful protection. It can also be approached from the ground via...

Steve & Katja Broadbent, October 2008.

72. Marmite on Toast VS 4c

15m. A bold and balancy direct start up the rib leads to some worryingly weathered holds...

Sesh Nadathur & Chris Bull, January 2009.

DESCENT: Go left and scramble up to the very top of Roadside Buttress, from where it is possible to drop down behind a large boulder into the main descent gully. Descent from the Balcony requires down-climbing or abseil.

Area Map
Crag Selector
Intro
The Climbing
How to Use
Suggested Climbs
Tafraout Granite
Anergui
Ameln Valley
Tarakatine Pass
Sidi M'Zal
Jebel Taskra
Idaougnidif
Afantinzar
Samazar
Aouguenz
Tagzene
Tagmout
History
Index

THE BOND WALL

Hidden beyond the top of Bishop's Buttress is an inaccessible south-facing bay with a slightly impending back wall. This is the magnificent Bond Wall, home to a pair of desperate test-pieces that see their fair share of attempts.

The bay faces south and can turn into a bit of an oven on hot days. It is unfortunately awkward to approach from below, so the wall is best approached either by climbing a route on Bishop's Buttress, or by scrambling up the main descent gully to gain the top of Bishop's. From here it is possible to scramble down broken rocks to gain the large ledge at the base of the Bond Wall.

DESCENT: scramble up and left from the top of the routes to gain the top of Roadside Buttress, then descend the main descent gully.

73. Live and Let Die E3 6a ★2 (STEEP, CRACK, GEAR)

20m. The crack up the left side of the wall is significantly steeper and more difficult than it looks, providing a popular test of grit, determination, and jamming technique. It probably lies somewhere between 5c and 6a. After a straightforward start up the wide corner crack, swing out from the cave and launch up the surprisingly overhanging jam-crack that proves unrelentingly difficult, albeit exceptionally well protected. A loose flake adds interest along the way...

Jayson Orton, October 2008.

74. Die Another Day E3 5b / E4 5c ★2 (BOLD)

20m. The centre of the wall is a traumatic lead, and continues to provide endless grade debate. Climb to a low ledge, place good gear then sprint easily up the paper-thin flakes to a good diagonal break and protection. Most folk escape left from here at E3 5b, but the original way steps up right onto the blank wall. The moves above are theoretically safe, but somehow still manage to feel utterly desperate as strength evaporates and the holds get smaller. Finish on tiny crimps to a deceptive top-out (crux).

Steve & Katja Broadbent, October 2008.

Photo page 399.

SARACEN BUTTRESS

Yet another buttress dominated by overhangs, and this time guarded by featureless smooth walls. *Saracen* sits high at the right side of the crag, but can be approached relatively easily from the road up steep terraces to the right (south) of the crag.

DESCENT: Head left from the top to gain the central descent gully as for the other buttresses.

75. Saracen E1 5c, 5b ★2

CRACK GEAR

35m. An excellent route. The climbing is never serious, but is sustained and very technical throughout.

1) 15m (5c) Make difficult moves in from the left, protected by multiple tiny cams, to gain the narrow crack. Follow this with interest to the large ledge. A superb pitch.

2) 20m (5b) Climb a crack from the left side of the ledge past some dubious rock to the corner beneath the roof. A technical traverse left then leads to an easy finish up the arête.

Steve & Katja Broadbent, October 2008.

76. Vertigo E1 5c, 5a ★3

CRACK

35m. A worthwhile alternative to the second pitch of *Saracen*, and arguably the better option. The E1 grade applies to the first pitch only, with the upper groove providing some good HVS climbing. From the right side of the mid-height ledge, make an exciting step right to gain the wide crack. Enter this with difficulty and climb it with some fine bridging moves.

Steve & Katja Broadbent, October 2008.

MAGIC CARPET RIDE

This small buttress is well worth seeking out. It can be accessed either by following the path easily eastward from Centenary Buttress, or by gaining the same path from the top of the main crag (this point can be reached by ascending the central descent gully). Approach takes about 15 minutes from the road.

77. Trivial Pursuit Severe ★2

WIDE

15m. The wide crack / chimney is bit of a battle for most, but amusingly trivial for aficionados.

Steve & Katja Broadbent, December 2008.

78. Westway HVS 5a ★2

15m. An excellent pitch up the wall to the right. Start easily up the good crack until the angle steepens and tricky moves lead up and right to a tempting flat hold. Mantel onto this if you can, then reach up for the top.

Steve & Katja Broadbent, December 2008.

79. Magic Carpet Ride E5 6a ★3

20m. A memorable excursion that tackles the beautiful arête on its right side. There are some good rests and questionable gear just about where you need it, but a confident approach is certainly called upon. Gain the arête from the right with increasing difficulty to a good rest and runner at 10m. Easy moves then lead to a spectacular finale (hard for the short) that may or may not be protected by tiny wires behind the hollow flakes. One of the crag's finest, and most technical challenges.

Steve Broadbent & Elie Dekoninck, December 2008.

Area Map
Crag Selector
Intro
The Climbing
How to Use
Suggested Climbs
Tafraout Granite
Anergui
Ameln Valley
Tarakatine Pass
Sidi M'Zal
Jebel Taskra
Idaougnidif
Afantinzar
Samazar
Aouguenz
Tagzene
Tagmout
History
Index

D MAID MARION ROCKS

Shade · Families · Hitch · Roadside

Drive from Tafraout: **20 minutes**
Walk-in: **2 to 5 minutes**

This small crag holds a handful of pleasant climbs that dry quickly and are worth stopping off for on the way home from other areas. The approach is short, the rock is excellent, and the crag is ideal for families, picnics, or a quick evening climb.

The rocks are somewhat difficult to spot when travelling west, but are located 11km from the Anergui turnoff from the main Ameln Valley road, at a set of hairpins that drop down into the dispersed settlements west of Tagmout. Just before the hairpins are reached a small track turns off up the hillside to the right to the village of Azouran. Just after reaching the top of the short hill the track levels out onto an attractive plateau, from where the tiny east face of the crag is visible some 50 yards across fields on the left. The larger west face of the crag is easily reached around either end.

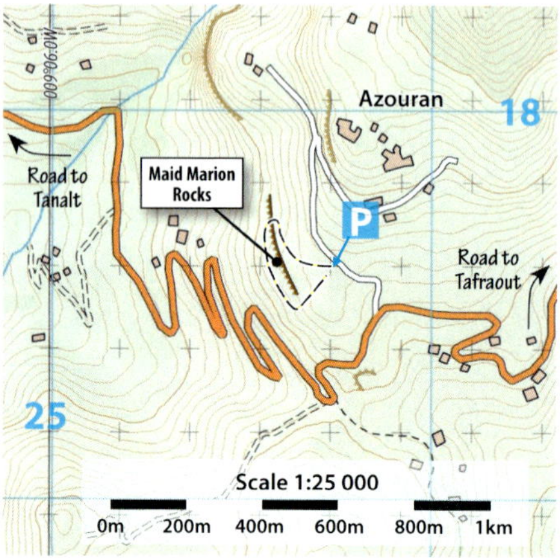

THE BACK FACE

The east face holds a handful of tiny micro-routes above the pleasant flat plateau, and is a useful spot for families, kids, and picnics.

1. Mini Jedi VS 4b ★2

7m. The wall on the left end.

2. Porda Severe 4a ★1 CRACK

7m. The wide crack is a very pleasant route.

3. Bowie's Bulge HS 4b CRACK

7m. The small crack 3m to the right has a tricky steep exit.

4. Pointless Difficult

7m. The chimney.

5. Keercat Difficult

7m. Start next to the previous route and climb up rightwards via the obvious weakness.

6. Quartz Break VS 4c ★1

7m. The diagonal quartz break has runners just before the crux, but is bold nevertheless.

7. Conga Very Difficult

7m. Pleasant climbing up flakes at the right side of the wall.

8. Tinga Severe

7m. The rib just right of the descent.

9. Dude, Where's my Nut? Severe

7m. This route climbs the sidewall on the left side of *Rock Goblin*. Climb the wall and crack to a jug, then swing left to finish up the arête.

10. Rock Goblin Difficult

7m. The corner to the right. Using the left arête is 'out' if you want to be pure about such things...

11. Toddy Teapot Moderate

7m. The corner / gully.

12. Lightning Beer Severe ★1

7m. A nice mantelshelf up the right-hand wall.

13. Stolen Bread Very Difficult ★1

7m. The quartz crack line running diagonally up the wall.

The next route is located on an undercut slab, some 20m to the right of *Stolen Bread*.

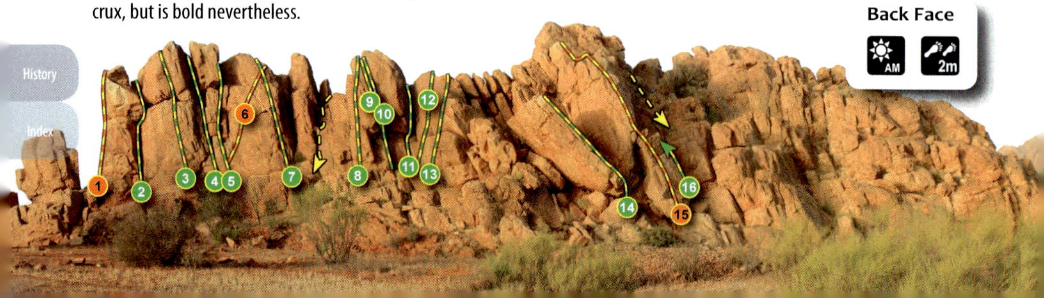

14. Edgy Severe ★1

7m. Make a difficult move out of the corner to gain a pocket on the left edge of the slab. Continue up the edge of the slab to an easier finish.

15. Popty Ping'd Wibbly Wobbly VS 4b ★1

7m. Start easily up blocks right of *Edgy* to reach the cracked rib, and climb this to a block. Move slightly left and continue up a thin crack in the rib above to a blocky ledge.

16. Plastic Tax Very Difficult

7m. The short wall immediately right of *Popty Ping'd*.

The next routes are located at a short steep wall at the right-hand end of the crag, about 20 metres beyond the previous route.

17. Monkey Brains VS 4a

7m. Straight up the steepest part of the overhang.

18. Twin Cracks Severe ★1

7m. The twin cracks just right of *Monkey Brains*.

19. 5 Kilos of Tangerines Hard Difficult

7m. The face right of *Twin Cracks*.

THE WEST FACE

The west face is not visible from the parking, but is accessed round either end of the Back Face.

20. Sweaty Edam Hard Severe ★1

15m. This route climbs the largest crack on the slab at the left end of the face.

Laurence King & Grace Aldridge, February 2011.

21. Sulphagne HS 4a ★1

35m. Some nice climbing linking ledges and chimneys up the left side of the buttress. The climb starts with an excellent technical traverse up the lower wall to gain the first ledge. From here, exit with ease up a chimney, then escape left up broken ground. *The Direct Finish* (VS 4c) continues up the curving slab to a difficult finish.

Steve & Katja Broadbent, Elie Dekoninck, December 2008.

22. Imhotep Severe ★3

35m. A tremendous climb on immaculate rock, that more than justifies a visit to the crag for climbers operating in the lower grades. Start with difficulty to gain the wide corner crack, then exit right on superb holds to more cracks to a ledge (possible belay). Head straight up a diagonal crack in the slab above to a steep direct finish... no skulking off rightward!

Steve & Katja Broadbent, Elie Dekoninck, December 2008.

23. c'Donalds Theorem E1 5c ★2 GEAR STEEP

30m. A strenuous test-piece that consumes gear and energy in equal amounts. Climb the wildly overhanging crack to gain easier ground and a finish up the pleasant upper arête.

Steve Broadbent & Peter Hill, October 2010.

24. Iron DeHavilland HVS 5b ★1 WIDE LOOSE

40m. The bold-looking blunt arête in the bay to the right of *Imhotep* is accessed with difficulty from the right.

1) 20m (5b) Step up from a cactus to gain a large niche and follow the wide horizontal break out left to the arête (some loose rock). Excellent, delicate climbing then leads up the left side of the arête to a good ledge.

2) 20m (4c) A short overhanging layback crack followed by an easy finish up a cracked slab.

Steve Broadbent & Elie Dekoninck, December 2008.

25. Berber Man Watches Kissy Wissy Difficult ★1

35m. The kinked crack on the far right of the crag. From the crack head up left to a large ledge, then climb a groove onto easy-angled slabs above.

Laurence King & Grace Aldridge, February 2011.

Area Map
Crag Selector
Intro
The Climbing
How to Use
Suggested Climbs
Tafraout Granite
Anergui
Ameln Valley
Tarakatine Pass
Sidi M'Zal
Jebel Taskra
Idaougnidif
Afantinzar
Samazar
Aouguenz
Tagzene
Tagmout
History
Index

Area Map
Crag Selector
Intro
The Climbing
How to Use
Suggested Climbs
Tafraout Granite
Anergui
Ameln Valley
Tarakatine Pass
Sidi M'Zal
Jebel Taskra
Idaougnidif
Afantinzar
Samazar
Aouguenz
Tagzene
Tagmout
History
Index

HISTORY

Climbing in Morocco seems to have been on the brink of taking off for as long as anyone can remember, but despite all of the articles and features in the climbing magazines, the Maghreb still retains its unique charm and tantalising mystery. Wherever you look in the history of Moroccan rock, the story is the same – exciting tales of new-found climbing paradises to which the authors eagerly await return visits: the fascinating reports of Hamish Brown and his early explorations in the High Atlas mountains; the famous *Grimper* magazine article that somehow remains a definitive source to Todra, despite this now being a household name in the sport-climbing world; and the handful of modern big-wall reports from the world-class Taghia Gorge, which promises something between Yosemite and the Himalaya in terms of style and scale. These places burst into public awareness with promise, only to simmer away in the background, providing a slow trickle of climbers with the magic of exploration, year after year. Tafraout, and its Anti-Atlas mountains, was no different.

The first climbers left very little written evidence of their visits to the oasis. Tony Howard and friends climbed on the area's granite boulders in 1962, and in the late seventies French climber Jacques Desautels climbed numerous long routes around the Samazar valley, including the Waterfall Walls. Written record of these ascents does not exist, and their routes have not, therefore, been included in this guide. American climber Paul Bowles was the first to document the climbing potential, commenting that, "The area around the Tafraout Oasis is like the badlands of Dakota, with fingers of granite and high peaks all around", words which inspired Dennis Gray to travel overland to Tafraout over Christmas 1987. On his arrival in Tafraout, Gray described "cliff after cliff, some several dozen metres in height, in front of a backdrop of Jebel el Kest." Each day he would run into the desert alone to boulder and solo on the granite, convinced that he had found an area equal in significance to Joshua Tree or Hampi, though no record now exists of his specific climbs.

On his return to the UK, Gray spoke of his discovery to Ron Fawcett and photographer John Beatty, and the three returned to the oasis in March 1988. They climbed exclusively on the granite, and in the years that followed a number of European and American magazines carried striking pictures of climbers doing their stuff on the painted rocks – images which seemed set to open up Tafraout as a granite paradise. Today, however, only a scattering of isolated pegs serves to record those early routes. The exotic mystery of Morocco was, once again, not to be quashed by such innocent forays as these.

The original Ameln pioneers. From left to right: Pete Turnbull, Joe Brown, Trevor Jones, Les Brown, and Claude Davies.
Photo: Claude Davies collection

In 1991, the first Gulf War provided an unexpectedly significant turning point for Tafraout climbing, diverting Les Brown and Trevor Jones from their planned Jordan trip and landing them instead in the Anti-Atlas where they intended to go walking with their wives. Their visit, whilst not the first by western climbers, was perhaps the most significant: for the first time interest was cast beyond the pink granite to the quartzite of Jebel el Kest, where Brown and Jones discovered something very special. Crossing the Tarakatine Pass, they marvelled at a breathtaking view, and with mounting excitement they soloed some small outcrops. On seeing this, Margaret and Anna realized that the plan to go walking with their husbands would need to be altered. "Don't worry – we'll enjoy the walking by ourselves. Let's go down to Tafraout and you can sort your gear." The rest, as they say, is history.

Original Route (HVS 5a) at Tifghalt was the first recorded quartzite climb, and impressed Brown and Jones so much that they passed on news of their discovery to Claude Davies and Joe Brown, who visited the area the following spring, putting up a handful of climbs including *Opening Bid* (HVS 5a) and *Central Route* (E1 5b) at Tifghalt, and discovering the enormous potential of the Tizgut Gorge. The pair returned the following year with an extended team to pick off the magic line of the gorge – *Tizgut Crack* (E2 5b) which remains an essential tick some twenty years down the line.

Back on the granite, Spanish and French climbers equipped a number of bolted routes throughout the late 1990s, and Dennis Gray returned with Nigel Scarth to set many 'outstanding' boulder problems,

The master in action. Joe Brown scrambles up to the base of the unclimbed *Tizgut Corner* (E1) in 1992, Tafraout's answer to his own Cenotaph Corner. This was one year before he returned to make the first ascent.

Photo: Claude Davies collection

although details of much of this development have not survived. The pair also made the first ascent of the elusive *Supercrack* in 1997, reporting that there may be thousands of pitches of similar quality around the Tafraout Oasis.

By this time, the 'quartzite team' had expanded to include Pete Turnbull, Paul Ross, and Derek Walker, who all made repeated visits throughout the late 1990s and first half of the next decade. Following the initial developments of the high crags at the eastern end of the Ameln Valley, explorations were extended to crags further west along the southern flank of Jebel el Kest, reaching as far as Anergui at the extreme west end of the range. Ameln's famous *Lion's Face* was conquered in 1995 by Paul Ross and Les Brown, and three years later Brown returned with Pete Turnbull to finally climb the magnificent *Great Ridge* (HVS 5a), which remains the longest route climbed in the Ameln Valley. 1998 also saw Joe Brown, Les Brown and Derek Walker pick off one of the region's best routes with their ascent of the reclusive *White Tower Original* (HVS 5a) at Tifghalt.

Although the original team concentrated their efforts on the vast swathes of quartzite that were visible from the very agreeable terrace of the Amandiers, the huge crags of the north side did not totally escape their attention. As early as 1993, Brown and the gang had put up the first route on Sidi M'Zal's tremendous Arch Wall, and over the coming years several teams attempted the obvious curving corner itself – arguably Tafraout's most striking line. Walker and Brown had the first go, but were forced left onto the slabs, leaving Sidi M'Zal with the classic wide-crack frightener of *Bowline* (E2 5b). The feature was not climbed in its entirety until 2006, as *Saif Din* by Fotheringham, Walker and Ben Wintringham.

In February 2000, Joe Brown, Pete Turnbull and Roy Warner decided to avoid the usual flights and instead drive to Tafraout in motor homes. An epic journey followed, accompanied early on by a strong "never again", particularly from Joe Brown. Alone in his unnecessarily large vehicle, Brown was attempting to follow the others as they made their way overland to the Anti-Atlas: an endeavour in which he encountered mixed success. Memories of going the wrong way down one-way streets, getting lost in chaotic cities, and the prospect of it all happening over again on the return journey prompted Brown

Joe Brown pointing out a line on The White Tower to Chris Bonington, during the early days at Tifghalt.

Photo: Claude Davies collection

Area Map
Crag Selector
Intro
The Climbing
How to Use
Suggested Climbs
Tafraout Granite
Anergui
Ameln Valley
Tarakatine Pass
Sidi M'Zal
Jebel Taskra
Idaougnidif
Afantinzar
Samazar
Aouguenz
Tagzene
Tagmout
History
Index

Can anyone spot Les Brown? Blending in with the locals during an early exploration of the crags at Asseldrar on the Takoucht escarpment of Jebel Taskra. *Photo: Claude Davies collection*

to cut short his planned long-stay, opting instead to set off early for his solo mission back to the UK.

In 2001 the team of pioneers were joined by Sir Chris Bonington, on the first of his many visits to the region. He had the unenviable privilege of being the first leader to take a fall on the quartzite, and was badly bruised in the process. On the way back to Tafraout the group stopped for refreshment at a small café. The local people were extremely interested in the activities of these scruffy-looking westerners, though it took some considerable time to explain the principle of climbing cliffs purely for fun. An English-speaking Berber stared intently at Bonington, who was sporting not only an increasing array of technicolor bruises, but a fine beard as well. With an expression of disbelief, he asked "Ali Baba doesn't climb, does he?"

Throughout its early development, and to some extent even up to the present day, rock climbing on Jebel el Kest has been very much focussed on adventure, rather than technical difficulty, and only a handful of routes have been pushed above mid-extreme grades. This is probably due to a number of factors, not least of which is the group of activists that Tafraout's four-star hotels and clement weather tends to attract; of course the remoteness of some of the crags, and the sheer volume of unclimbed rock will play a part as well.

In the early part of the last decade word about Tafraout's excellent winter sun-rock started to spread, and as an increasing number of climbers visited the area, grades were gradually pushed. *Waiting for the Babarians* (E3 6a), from Chris King, Ron Kenyon and Shaun Brown was briefly the hardest quartzite climb on the massif back in 2003, just in time for inclusion in the new Cicerone guidebook. It was, however, soon eclipsed by Trevor Woods and Guy Robertson's epic ascent of *The Flying Scotsmen* (E6 6b) later that year. Following one retreat already from this stunning blank face on the north wall of the Asgaour Gorge, a small flake broke off on the second attempt, launching Woods into a character-building 30ft fall that resulted in an open head wound to his belayer. Undeterred, the pair returned the following day, repeated the 6b first pitch and set out once more up the bold wall above. This time Woods found a way through the poorly protected, technical moves to complete one of Tafraout's boldest ascents to date.

By 2004 the original team of Anti-Atlas pioneers had opened up some 150 routes on 25 crags along the Ameln Valley, and their exploits were published in 'Climbing in the Moroccan Anti-Atlas' by Claude

Sir Chris Bonington, Joe Brown and Paul Ross at the Hotel Les Amandiers in Tafraout. *Photo: Claude Davies collection*

The extended team of Ameln pioneers, two years after Claude Davies and Cicerone published the area's first guidebook. Development of the 'northside' crags was just about to begin...
Photo: Claude Davies collection

Davies. This book, more than any other work in Moroccan climbing, went some way to putting Tafraout on the map of mainstream destinations, although there was still a long way to go. Davies and the original team of pioneers had not only raised awareness of Tafraout climbing, but paved the way for others to follow – notably a new generation of pioneers who began to explore new routes and new crags throughout the range. The focus of this 'second wave' of exploration was the north side of Jebel el Kest, along the newly constructed Tanalt to Idaougnidif road.

In 2005, just one year after the publication of 'Climbing in the Moroccan Anti-Atlas', Geoff Hornby and Susie Sammut turned their attention to the unchartered hillside above Tanalt: an area not even mentioned in the Cicerone guidebook. Camped on a terrace below the Dwawj Slabs, they spent day after day picking off the main lines on the crag and enjoying the curious interest of local villagers. Hornby returned later that year with Brian Davison, and between them they completed at least 15 climbs on this one crag alone – the first of the northside crags to be developed. The same crag was 'discovered' independently that year by the original Ameln team, now supplemented by Ben and Marion Wintringham who put up the first routes above the schoolhouse at Tizim Waylim. Then, the following spring, OUMC climbers Sven Letourneau and Jude Waller visited Dwawj, somehow squeezing in an independent line without any knowledge of the existing routes – it just goes to show how a different pair of eyes sees different 'obvious' lines!

Letourneau and Waller did not limit their exploration to Dwawj, however, and brought back word of vast unclimbed crags along the new Idaougnidif road, which was still under construction at the time. The pair returned the following year (seemingly a tradition in Tafraout new-routing) with Steve and Katja Broadbent, who were immediately enchanted by what they saw. After a long drive on unsurfaced roads through Tagmout, Dwawj, Tagzene and on into Afantinzar, the pair set eyes upon the unnamed and unclimbed Amelu Wall. It was midday by the time they set off up the first recorded climb in the Afantinzar Valley – *Oxford Route* (VS 5a) – a 350m mossy adventure that resulted in yet another unplanned bivouac on the summit.

2007 also saw early development of the roadside crags at Anammer, and on the other side of the valley the superb Grand Wall of Lower Eagle Crag saw ascents by multiple teams including Chris Bonington, Dave Absolom, Paul Donnithorne, Emma Alsford, Mike and Marjorie Mortimer, as well as the Broadbents and Wintringhams. *Pink Lady* (VS 4c), now one of the valley's most popular outings, was

Steve Broadbent, back in Afantinzar having spent a very cold night on Amelu Wall, the valley's first recorded climb in 2007.
Photo by Katja Broadbent

Area Map
Crag Selector
Intro
The Climbing
How to Use
Suggested Climbs
Tafraout Granite
Anergui
Ameln Valley
Tarakatine Pass
Sidi M'Zal
Jebel Taskra
Idaougnidif
Afantinzar
Samazar
Aouguenz
Tagzene
Tagmout
History
Index

Katja Broadbent, high on Aylim's infamous *Labyrinth Ridge* (VS) during the first ascent in 2008.
Photo: Steve Broadbent

climbed the following year by Johnson and Roberts, with Donnithorne and Alsford making the first ascent of the classic *Infinity* (E4 5c) during the same week. By the end of 2008 Lower Eagle was established as one of the most important crags on Jebel el Kest, accessed easily via the newly-surfaced Afantinzar road.

Over the next 3 years, two main teams were involved in extensive new-route activity across the north side of the range. A strong group from the Climbers' Club, 'led' by Ben Wintringham, was responsible for many of the difficult, long climbs that litter the range today – most notable were their ascents on Upper Eagle Crag during 2008, and the development of Griffin rock between 2007 and 2010. In neighbouring Samazar, where big multi-pitch routes abound, the Climbers' Club picked off significant ascents including *First Up* (E1 5a) by Fotheringham and Mortimer, which was the first climb recorded in the valley. On the way down from their successful ascent they came across an OUMC team of Niall Hedderley and the Broadbents, making their first reconnaissance of the valley. There was surprise in both teams to find other western climbers in Samazar at that time, and a spate of adventurous new routes would inevitably follow.

Samazar's biggest walls then became the focus of attention, and it was Donnithorne and Findlay who got things rolling in October 2007 with their impressive ascent of *Culmination Corner* (E2 5c). At the same time, Fotheringham and Mortimer were repulsed by the Right Waterfall Wall, opting instead for Aylim's 600m *Great Ridge* (VS 5a), and completing it in a single afternoon. Access routes to Samazar were unmapped and unfamiliar, and with no details of how to descend from the summit this was a typically bold and confident ascent. For Fotheringham and Mortimer, however, the real goal was still the Right Waterfall Wall, to which they returned the following spring to create *Terminator Wall* (E2 5b), believing it to be the easiest and only feasible line of ascent on the Right Wall. Further up the valley, the mind-boggling Tamza wall received its first complete ascent in March 2008 at the hands of the Mortimers; their *Walk to the Paradise Garden* (VS 5a) epitomising the adventurous spirit of Samazar climbing and providing a memorable day out on 'perfect' rock. During the descent, Mortimer stumbled across Icebox Canyon, which would see a blitz of new routes by the Climbers' Club teams in coming years. Similarly, the Pimple came under close scrutiny by Fotheringham, Mortimer, Alsford, Donnithorne and the Wintringhams in 2008 after a fire had cleared large areas of vegetation that had previously restricted the descent route.

Throughout this early development of Afantinzar and Samazar there was concurrent exploration by numerous teams from the OUMC, generally focussing on the sunnier south-facing crags. Ksar Rock at Anammer saw extensive activity mostly from the Broadbents who opened up a large number of classic shorter routes including *Solar Event* (E1 5c) and *Cannon Buttress Direct* (E1 5b) as well as the hugely popular *Sahara* (MVS 4b) and *Jedi Groove* (HVS 4c). Their initial attempt at the prominent wide chimney-crack above the Cannon Tower led to an escape rightwards up the superb overhanging flake of *Castles in the Sky* (E2 5c) and a vow to return once they'd got a bit more offwidth experience under their belts… 2008 saw the first ascent of the shady East Face via the infamous *Great Eastern* (VS 5a), and by 2009 rumours about the superb quality of climbing on Ksar led to increased interest from extended teams. Ksar's hardest route came in 2010 thanks to Topher Dagg and Henward Nind – *Breaking Strain* (E4 6a) on the East Face providing a long and tiring climb up some desperately steep ground.

Oxford teams were also active on the bigger routes across the north side of the range throughout this

Sally Fitton, making the first ascent of Adrar Umlil 2 via *The Lion King* (HVS) in 2009. This tremendous mountain crag has seen extensive development in the intervening years, and is now one of the most popular mountain crags in the Anti-Atlas.
Photo: Steve Broadbent

period, with Steve and Katja Broadbent putting up *Manzakuneen* (V.Diff) on Fig Tree Wall whilst seeking the descent route from Aylim, prior to their ascent of the 800m epic *Labyrinth Ridge* (VS 5a) in 2008. Whilst in the valley, they also opened up the first climbs on Safinah, in the shape of *Scimitar Ridge* (VS 5a) and Agouti, via *Honeycomb Buttress* (Severe).

After this the pair went on to record the first climbs on three major new crags above Amzkhssan. *Goldrush* (HVS 5a) on Adrar Iffran, *Wild Country* (VDiff) on Adrar Asmit, and *Rock the Kasbah* (E1 5c) on Adrar Umlil paved the way for a new wave of development in the Idaougnidif area, creating some of the best multi-pitch cragging on the massif. Climbers' Club teams were quick to respond, and in October that year the main tower of Umlil was blitzed with routes, including the tremendous *Jaws* (E1 5b) and *The Beckoning* (E3 5c) from Donnithorne and Johnson, *Snow White* (E3 5c) by Donnithorne and Mortimer, and the intimidating *Comes the Berber* (E4 6a) by Ed Bulman and Steve Pack.

Within just one year, most of the big lines on Umlil 1 had been climbed, whilst the other four independent towers remained untouched. These all saw first ascents by OUMC teams between 2009-2010 in the shape of *The Lion King* (HVS 5b), *Carousel* (MVS 4a), *Auld Lang Syne* (MVS 4b, and *The South Ridge Direct* (HVS 5a). Meanwhile, a similar level of new-route activity was recorded on Adrar Iffran, where several attempts at the stunning north face resulted in retreat. This face had become something of a 'last great problem' of the north-side, but was remarkably overcome on the same day in October 2009 by at least four different teams in what must have been one of the crag's busiest days to date. *The Nibbler* (E4 5c) from Adam Mulholland and Laura Jones can probably claim to be the first route up the true north face, and it is believed that this audacious climb remains unrepeated. *Light My Fire* (E3 5c) from Freudenthal and Viel, *Rainy Day Dream Away* (HVS) from Johnson and Pycroft, as well as *Learning on the Job* (HVS) by Tasha Smith and Amy Colson were other notable successes that day.

Elsewhere in the range OUMC made repeated visits to the ever-sunny Robin Hood Rocks, particularly during a number of very wet winters between 2008-2010. Searching, as ever, for low-effort roadside routes the Broadbents put up a number of popular extremes here, including *Hello Picasso* (E4 6a) and *Die Another Day* (E4 6a), and culminating with an ascent of the striking *Magic Carpet Ride* (E5 6b), further enhancing Robin Hood's appeal as a venue for short, sun-drenched extremes.

February 2010 saw torrential rain in the Anti-Atlas, flooding Tafraout, destroying roads and buildings, but replenishing vital water supplies and transforming the previously brown landscape into the much greener scene that climbers are now familiar with. During this period the Samazar road was closed, forcing climbers to look elsewhere for adventure. The short crags at Tizi Gzaouine provided some wet-weather discoveries for the Broadbents, whilst Fotheringham and Mortimer concentrated on the left side of the rather neglected Amelu Wall, solving the tremendous *Wall of the Djinns* (E2 5b) and developing the Golden Wall to its left.

Back in Samazar, Freudenthal and Viel made a bold ascent of the very blank-looking wall to the right of Terminator Wall to create the staggering *L'Echo Vaporeux* (HVS 4c) – a feat which surprised almost everyone at the time, specially given a suggested grade of Very Severe. This ascent did, however, hint that the Right Waterfall Wall was not as formidable as previously thought, and in 2010 whilst the finishing touches were being put to the new north-side guidebook a joint Scottish-Italian team of Topher

Area Map
Crag Selector
Intro
The Climbing
How to Use
Suggested Climbs
Tafraout Granite
Anergui
Ameln Valley
Tarakatine Pass
Sidi M'Zal
Jebel Taskra
Idaougnidif
Afantinzar
Samazar
Aouguenz
Tagzene
Tagmout
History
Index

Dagg, Davide Cassol and Luca Vallata turned a previously blank wall with 'no lines' into a fully-developed crag, criss-crossed by many excellent long climbs. Camped by the schoolhouse in Samazar, the team enjoyed first ascents of the brilliant *To Teo* (HVS 4c), and the modern-classic *The Way of the Pooka* (E2 5b) among others. They also recorded Samazar's hardest climb – the stunning *Daffodils, Kittens and Pink Bunny Rabbits* (E5 6a) up the super hanging groove in the centre of the face.

Moroccan Anti-Atlas North, a guide to the climbs on the north side of Jebel el Kest, was published by the Oxford Alpine Club in December 2010, and a number of articles in the British climbing press once again re-invigorated interest in Tafraout as a winter sun destination. With continued expansion of low-cost air travel, Tafraout had finally found its niche – accessible, warm winter trad-climbing. The adventurous nature of both the travel and the climbing, combined with the exotic charm of its Berber culture was enough to ensure a steadily increasing flow of climbers from the UK, Europe and beyond. Across the range, the major lines started to see numerous repeat ascents, whilst the number of people putting up new routes also continued to grow.

Within six months of publication of the new guidebook, some one hundred and fifty new climbs were recorded on the north side alone, whilst development of the south side ticked along at a steady pace. As gaps continued to be filled across the range, perhaps the most significant ascents were those on Adrar Aiyur by Donovan, Adams, Donnithorne & Dave Noddings. Adrar Aiyur had been attempted twice by Broadbent, who became so disillusioned with the lack of climbable-looking lines that he jokingly posted a declaration that the peak was 'un-climbable' on the Climb-Tafraout website – a fact that guaranteed an immediate response in the form of four routes to the summit that spring. Meanwhile, Broadbent spent two separate days on the east face of Aylim with Caroline Culwick and Matt Mellor, creating the superb *Central Buttress* (E1 5b). Over in Afantinzar these three also put up a dozen or so routes on the surprisingly unclimbed Akida.

First ascent of *Daffodils, Kittens and Pink Bunny Rabbits* (E5) in 2010 – one of the hardest big routes in the range.
Photo: Topher Dagg

Ben Wintringham, one of the driving forces behind Anti-Atlas exploration between 2006 and 2011. His tragic death in an abseil accident was a huge blow to the development of Tafraout climbing.
Photo: Claude Davies collection

October 2011 saw the darkest day in the history of Tafraout climbing, when activist Ben Wintringham was killed in an abseiling accident in the Aouguenz valley. Ben had been one of the key players in the development of this region and the documentation of the ever-growing number of routes on the north side of the massif. His death was the first of a climber in the Anti-Atlas.

Development, of course, continued at an unfaltering pace, the biggest discovery of 2012 being the superb Dragon Buttress in Samazar. It was Donnithorne and Alsford who picked off the big lines here, with the first ascent of the stunning *Brisingr* (E1 5b) and *Firesword* (E2 5b), not to mention a host of other magnificent climbs over the coming months.

Throughout all of this north-side development there had been a steady trickle of new routes in the Ameln Valley, recorded by a loyal group of Tafraout climbers who must have been enjoying the fact that everyone else was driving north to Afantinzar and Samazar. Graham 'Egg' Everitt was at the forefront of this development, and along with his wife Ruth Everitt, James Strongman, Tom Leppert and Ian Wilson, he opened many hard extremes in the valley and developed a number of excellent new crags including Mosque Valley Slabs.

By now, an increasing number of teams were making repeated visits to Tafraout, and it was not surprising that new crags were 'springing up' every season in the bulging *Livre d'Escalade* in the Amandiers Hotel. Fylde MC members including Dave Wood, Alan Blackburn, Ali Welsh and Martin Bennett repeated many classic routes in the area, and opened up their eponymous Fylde crag and nearby Octet crag in 2011.

In March 2012 Johnny Dawes pushed standards of trad in Tafraout to new levels with his ascent of *Shine* (E7 6b) on Marmalade Wall at Dimlalen – a line that had repulsed a number of reconnaissances in the past. Dawes had arrived in Tafraout with very little in the way of climbing gear, but a home-made harness, borrowed rack and a good deal of 'Dawes magic' saw him through what was by all accounts a rather traumatic ascent, completed partially on-sight with very poor protection.

Later that year yet another new guidebook, *Morocco Rock* (Crack Addicts), added once more to the growing momentum of Tafraout trad climbing, further securing the town's future as a major winter-sun destination, and arguably pushing it ahead of Todra in terms of popularity. Although this guide covered little new ground it was the first to describe the excellent Tizi N'Takoucht Escarpment on Jebel Taskra, which had been extensively developed during 2009-2012.

Once again a new guidebook led to yet another increase in visitor numbers, and although the flow of new routes continued, 2012 saw a huge increase in the number of repeat ascents, with a number of lines starting to gain 'classic' status. This change in emphasis from new routes to repeat ascents, driven by the increase in climber numbers, is an indication that Tafraout and the Anti-Atlas are finally starting to find maturity as a climbing destination.

Around the same time, members of the Oxford Alpine Club had immersed themselves in a mission to decipher the chaotic *Livre d'Escalade* and unearth exactly what had and hadn't been climbed on the south side of the range in the years since the original Cicerone guidebook had been published.

Cameron Hall on the first ascent of *White Tower Direct (HVS)* in 2011, during research for the OAC south-side guidebook.
Photo: Steve Broadbent

This process took some three years, but along with lots of baking-hot cragging days, it rewarded Steve Broadbent and Cameron Hall with the first ascent of *White Tower Direct* (HVS) in 2011, alongside Joe Brown's original masterpiece. The research also led to the first ascents of the popular *Angel's Crest* on Jebel el Kest, and the magnificent *Pinnacle Ridge* (Severe) by Steve and Katja Broadbent.

The definitive south-side guidebook was published as part of a two-volume edition in 2013, followed by a smaller, three-volume selective series in 2014.

Today there are more than 2000 recorded routes, across Jebel Taskra, Jebel el Kest and the Ameln Valley, many of them seeing multiple ascents each season. Climbers now come here with wide ranging levels of experience, and at many of the crags the most prominent lines have all been climbed. Climbers are well catered for by numerous businesses in the local area, and Tafraout is starting to recognise itself as a significant centre for rock climbing.

So what of the future? Well, after twenty-five years of relentless new-route activity we have, perhaps, merely scratched the surface. Isolated pockets of well-developed climbing now litter the range, but looking beyond these there still seems to be an endless expanse of unclimbed rock. Amongst it, no doubt, are hundreds of first-class rock climbs waiting to see a first ascent, and Tafraout seems set to have plenty to offer the adventurous climber for many years to come.

INDEX OF ROUTES

Steve Broadbent on *Pasha (E3 5c)* at Robin Hood Rocks (page 367). ➲

Photo: Lina Arthur

Area Map
Crag Selector
Intro
The Climbing
How to Use
Suggested Climbs
Tafraout Granite
Anergui
Ameln Valley
Tarakatine Pass
Sidi M'Zal
Jebel Taskra
Idaougnidif
Afantinzar
Samazar
Aouguenz
Tagzene
Tagmout
History
Index

Will Benfold making the most of a rest day in Palm Tree Gorge. This excellent, sheltered crag is a good choice when long walk-ins seem too much, or bad weather threatens the high crags. ➲
Photo: Steve Broadbent

Area Map
Crag Selector
Intro
The Climbing
How to Use
Suggested Climbs
Tafraout Granite
Anergui
Ameln Valley
Tarakatine Pass
Sidi M'Zal
Jebel Taskra
Idaougnidif
Afantinzar
Samazar
Aouguenz
Tagzene
Tagmout
History
Index

Area Map
Crag Selector
Intro
The Climbing
How to Use
Suggested Climbs
Tafraout Granite
Anergui
Ameln Valley
Tarakatine Pass
Sidi M'Zal
Jebel Taskra
Idaougnidif
Afantinzar
Samazar
Aouguenz
Tagzene
Tagmout
History
Index

Steve Broadbent on *Cristal (E3 5b)* at Robin Hood Rocks – one of Tafraout's classic bold arêtes (page 355). ➲
Photo: Ben Lister

Area Map
Crag Selector
Intro
The Climbing
How to Use
Suggested Climbs
Tafraout Granite
Anergui
Ameln Valley
Tarakatine Pass
Sidi M'Zal
Jebel Taskra
Idaougnidif
Afantinzar
Samazar
Aouguenz
Tagzene
Tagmout
History
Index

Katja Broadbent making the hilarious move off the Priest, 18 pitches up *Labyrinth Ridge (VS)* on Aylim (page 301). ➲
Photo: Steve Broadbent

Jayson Orton about to start the long run-out on *Die Another Day (E4 5c)* on the Bond Wall at Robin Hood Rocks (page 370). ➲
Photo: Steve Broadbent

Area Map
Crag Selector
Intro
The Climbing
How to Use
Suggested Climbs
Tafraout Granite
Anergui
Ameln Valley
Tarakatine Pass
Sidi M'Zal
Jebel Taskra
Idaougnidif
Afantinzar
Samazar
Aouguenz
Tagzene
Tagmout
History
Index

Rachel Mellor starting out on the *Great Ridge (VS)* in the Ameln Valley. This 800m adventure is still one of Tafraout's most infamous climbs, and scene of more benightments than any other route.
Photo: Steve Broadbent

Area Map
Crag Selector
Intro
The Climbing
How to Use
Suggested Climbs
Tafraout Granite
Anergui
Ameln Valley
Tarakatine Pass
Sidi M'Zal
Jebel Taskra
Idaougnidif
Afantinzar
Samazar
Aouguenz
Tagzene
Tagmout
History

Shuffling along the fun arête pitch of *Central Buttress (VS)* on Aylim's east face (page 300). ➲

Photo: Caroline Culwick

OAC

Dave Arthur and Katja Broadbent on the top pitch of *High Sierra (5.7)* on the granite near Aguerd Oudad.
Photo: Steve Broadbent